OVER
HER
DEAD
BODY

Yet, sister woman, though I cannot consent to find a Mozart or a Michael Angelo in your sex, cheerfully, and with the love that burns in depths of admiration, I acknowledge that you can do one thing as well as the best of us men – a greater thing than even Milton is known to have done, or Michael Angelo: you can die grandly, and as goddesses would die, were goddesses mortal.

Thomas de Quincey

OVER HER DEAD BODY

*Death, femininity
and the aesthetic*

Elisabeth Bronfen

ROUTLEDGE
New York

Published in 1992 by

Routledge
An imprint of Routledge, Chapman and Hall, Inc.
29 West 35 Street
New York, NY 10001

Published in Great Britain by
Manchester University Press
Oxford Road
Manchester
M13 9PL

Copyright © Elisabeth Bronfen 1992

Printed in Great Britain

Library of Congress Cataloging in Publication Data
available on request

ISBN 0–415–90660–1 *cloth*
ISBN 0–415–90661–X *paperback*

Contents

Contents

Contents

Illustrations

Every effort has been made to trace the copyright owner of all illustrations, and any person claiming copyright should contact the publishers.

Paperback cover illustration: *The Nightmare*, by the Swiss artist Henry Fuseli, 1741–1825. © The Detroit Institute of Arts, gift of Mr and Mrs Bert L. Smokler and Mr and Mrs Lawrence A. Fleischman.

Preface

How can a verbal or visual artistic representation be both aesthetically pleasing and morbid, as the conjunction of beautiful woman and death seems to imply? How can we delight at, be fascinated, morally educated, emotionally elevated and psychologically reassured in our sense of self by virtue of the depiction of a horrible event in the life of another, which we would not have inflicted on ourselves? Representations of death in art are so pleasing, it seems, because they occur in a realm clearly delineated as not life, or not real, even as they refer to the basic fact of life we know but choose not to acknowledge too overtly. They delight because we are confronted with death, yet it is the death of the other. We experience death by proxy. In the aesthetic enactment, we have a situation impossible in life, namely that we die with another and return to the living. Even as we are forced to acknowledge the ubiquitous presence of death in life, our belief in our own immortality is confirmed. There is death, but it is not my own. The aesthetic representation of death lets us repress our knowledge of the reality of death precisely because here death occurs *at* someone else's body and *as* an image.

Given, then, that representations of death both articulate an anxiety about and a desire for death, they function like a symptom, which psychoanalytic discourse defines as a repression that fails. In the same displaced manner in which art enacts the reality of death we wish to disavow, any symptom articulates something that is so dangerous to the health of the psyche that it must be repressed and yet so strong in its desire for articulation that it can't be. In a gesture of compromise, the psychic apparatus represents this dangerous and fascinating thing by virtue of a substitution, just as the aesthetic enactment represents death, but at the body of another person and at another site; in the realm of art. A symptom hides the dangerous thing even as it points precisely to that material for the failed repression of which recourse to an indirect articulation, to psychic representation, was taken in the first place. Fundamentally duplicitous by nature, a symptom tries to maintain a balance of sorts, but does so by obliquely pointing to that which threatens to disturb the order. In respect of death, one could say, it names one thing ('I am the spectator/survivor of someone else's death, therefore I can tell myself there is no death for me') and means something else ('someone else is dead, therefore I know there is death'). In short, representations *as* symptoms articulate unconscious knowledge and unconscious desires in a displaced, recoded and translated manner.

The seminal presupposition underlying this book can be formulated in the following way. Narrative and visual representations of death, drawing their material from a common cultural image repertoire, can be read as symptoms of our culture. Furthermore, because the feminine body is culturally constructed as the superlative site of alterity, culture uses art to dream the deaths of beautiful women. Over representations of the dead feminine body, culture can repress and articulate its unconscious knowledge of death which it fails to foreclose even as it cannot express it directly. If symptoms are failed repressions, representations are symptoms that visualise even as they conceal what is too dangerous to articulate openly but too fascinating to repress successfully. They repress by localising death away from the self, at the body of a beautiful woman, at the same time that this representation lets the repressed return, albeit in a disguised manner.

As my title indicates, the interstice between death, femininity and aesthetics is negotiated over the representation of a dead feminine body clearly marked as being other, as being not mine. To represent *over her dead body* signals that the represented feminine body also stands in for concepts other than death, femininity and body – most notably the masculine artist and the community of the survivors. These find an allegorical articulation even though they are not the literal meaning of the image. In other words, what is plainly visible – the beautiful feminine corpse – also stands in for something else. In so doing it fades from our sight and what we see, whenever an aesthetic representation asks us to read tropically, is what is in fact not visibly there. As we focus on the hidden, the figurative meaning, what is plainly seen may not be seen at all. Not only, then, does western culture dream of beautiful dead woman to repress its knowledge of death; not only does it, by dint of such representations, fail to repress these two threatening concepts successfully, even as the disguised articulation is a form of self-protection. Rather, the gesture of an aesthetic substitution is such that what is literally represented – femininity and death – often entirely escapes observation.

To speak about the interrelation between femininity and death in representations, however, is to acknowledge that these are always misrepresentations. They repress what they purport to reveal and they articulate what they hope to conceal. To speak of misrepresentation refers to the fact that both death and femininity are necessarily constructed by culture and as such always in some sense tropic. At the same time culture connects femininity and death with the non-semiotic materiality and facticity. That is to say, on the one hand death and femininity serve as ciphers for other values, as privileged tropes. Each term grounds the way a culture stabilises and represents itself, yet does so as a signifier with an incessantly receding, ungraspable signified which invariably always points self-reflexively to other signifiers. On the other hand, precisely because death and femininity are excessively tropic, they point to a reality beyond and indeed disruptive of all systems of language; they evoke the referent that texts may point to but not touch. Death and femininity both involve the uncanny return of the repressed, the excess beyond the text, which the latter aims at stabilising by having signs and images represent. The word representation is here self-consciously used in its double meaning – as a metaphorical figure in the psychoanalytic and aesthetic sense of a symptom, a dream or an artistic image that stands for, by making present again, another concept, and as a metonymic figure in the political sense of standing in for, in lieu of, someone or something else. However, as representations of feminine death oscillate between the excessively tropic and a non-semiotic materiality, this real referent always eludes the effort at recuperation which representation seeks to afford. It disrupts the system at its very centre, and it is precisely this gesture of naming only to miss the mark – misrepresentation – which I seek to trace.

The following is a central trajectory for the narrative texts to be discussed. Femininity and death cause a disorder to stability, mark moments of ambivalence, disruption or duplicity and their eradication produces a recuperation of order, a return to stability. The threat that death and femininity pose is recuperated by representation, staging absence as a form of re-presence, or return, even if or rather precisely because this means appeasing the threat of real mortality, of sexual insufficiency, of lack of plenitude and wholeness. And yet the 're' of return, repetition or recuperation suggests that the end point is not the same as the point of departure, although it harbours the illusion that something lost has been perfectly regained. Instead, the regained order encompasses a shift; that is to say it is never again/no longer entirely devoid of traces of difference. The recuperation is imperfect, the regained stability not safe, the urge for order inhabited by a fascination with disruption and split, and certainty emerging over and out of uncertainty.

The shape my argument takes is informed by the question: wherein does the power, the necessity, the fascination and the danger inherent in the conjunction between femininity and death lie? Issues of sight, of alterity, of the unknown and of a feminine subject position emerging out of and against the cultural construction of Woman, let my material fall into a five-part structure. Part I serves as a theoretical frame and in my first chapter all the thematic and rhetorical points that will be explored at length are touched on as I analyse a painting of an anatomist preparing for a post mortem. By beginning with this image, I self-consciously imply the analogy between his preparation for an autopsy on a beautiful feminine corpse and my own position, preparing to cut into, dissect, label, categorise and describe in writing a corpus of texts about women dying, dead, resurrected, dead in life, living beyond their deaths or returning as revenants.

In the next two chapters I unfold much of the psychoanalytic and semiotic terminology and raise issues concerning representation, the interstice between the dead body and the image, the sacrifice of the body for the production of art and the re-establishment of order. In these two chapters I also theorise my own critical position, especially the desire to preserve an ambivalence between the way our culture constructs a link between femininity and death, and the real effect this convention may have on historical women's lives. Even as I point to the disturbing implication this topos has on historical reality, I emphasise our inability to discard the dominant cultural image repertoire, convinced that we can deny neither the powerful fascination emanating from, nor the psychic necessity for these images, even as we seek to disclose them.

In Part II, the prevailing analogy is that both death and femininity are treated as images. Beginning with a discussion of myths of femininity and beauty (chapter 4), I move on to present a socio-historical discussion of death since the mid eighteenth century and in its relation to the new value ascribed to femininity during this period (chapter 5). The next three chapters deal with specific facets of the feminine body as death turns the woman into an object of sight – the dead feminine body comparable to an exhibited art object displayed in a glass coffin (chapter 6); exchanged for and engendering portraits (chapter 7); suicide as a form of feminine authorship (chapter 8).

In Part III the ruling analogy is that both femininity and death are ascribed the position of alterity, and I begin with a psychoanalytic discussion of the opposition of self and Other, only to enlarge my presentation of the psychic usage of the stereotype by moving to an anthropological and semiotic discussion of sacrifice (chapter 9). Using Lacan's typology of gender constructions, I present *Jane Eyre* as the typical Victorian example for a tripartite feminine death figure (chapter 10). To complete this discussion of the exchange between bodies and signs, I focus on the way that the death of the bride constitutes social bonds much as the more obvious bartering of daughters for purposes of marriage does (chapter 11).

The issue of dead brides turns into the central theme of Part IV, where the prevailing analogy now is that both femininity and death serve as western culture's privileged topoi and tropes for what is superlatively enigmatic. Introducing the issue that a bridal plot may serve to conceal imperfectly a death plot on the basis of an analysis of a Courbet painting (chapter 12), I move on to explore the Janus-faced bridal/death plot. In all the texts discussed, a woman's death engenders the desire for detection, mourning and representation – the premarital daughter's choice of death over marriage (chapter 13), the dead bride as revenant (chapter 14), a first dead beloved returned at the body of a second woman (chapter 15), the position of the bride between life and death as the site of storytelling (chapter 16) and the dead beloved serving her mourning lover as muse (chapter 17). I conclude by discussing how women writers install, comply with, critique and rewrite the cultural image repertoire that links the feminine subject position to a speaking through and out of death.

Owing to the prevalence of representations of beautiful dead women during this particular historical moment, my textual corpus begins with the mid eighteenth century, the so-called modern period, and ends with contemporary texts, though most of my examples are drawn from the nineteenth century. I indicate some explanations for the blossoming of this cultural topos during this historical period when I sketch the social history of death. The examples I chose represent the most striking of a much larger corpus, and my concern is to present an exemplary pattern. Rather than emphasising the Romantic or Symbolist period, where the conjunction of femininity with death has already had extensive critical visibility, I focus on texts, or moments in texts, not usually read in relation to issues of feminine death. Within the historic period I have isolated, my presentation is, however, not chronological. My material is structured around the enmeshment of rhetorical and thematic patterns, not around questions of period or genre so that certain authors like Poe reappear fugue-like in several chapters, while a seminal text like *Clarissa* is discussed more than once.

Though I offer a social-historical discussion of death in Part III and an anthropological discussion of death rituals in Part II, these serve to frame what is first and foremost an attempt to work out the hidden or ambivalent semantic encodings harboured by these images; the psychic material they serve to articulate and the rhetorical strategies by which they function. My book is neither a social nor a literary historical presentation of the development of the feminine death figure. Nevertheless, my debt to psychoanalytic–semiotic–deconstructionist discourses at various moments draws added power from taking recourse to historically based anecdotal narratives. These excursions into the interrelation between historical reality and cultural representations are further underlined by my two case studies on Elizabeth Siddall and Alice James. The other excursions – the two picture essays – point in the exact opposite direction, by invoking, as the context for my textual interpretations, not historical reality but rather a further plethora of culturally formed images.

In the course of the book I move from narratives representing dead women, in the sense that these texts are about, or stand for examples of a beautiful woman's death to texts that stand in for dying women in the sense that these historical women served as the muses whose deaths were not just object but also catalyst for their aesthetic representation. I conclude with the problem of how women, inscribed within this cultural convention, can successfully carve out a space for their own authorship. In a sense, two currents underwrite the flow of my argument. On the one hand, an elaborate presentation and analysis of the many facets of the feminine-death-figure is necessary for the pattern as a whole to resonate with its multifarious, at times even ambivalent or contradictory, meanings. On the other hand each individual textual reading only gains its full import in conjunction with the many others.

This method is most obvious, perhaps, in respect to Gabriel von Max's *Der Anatom*, and the status of this painting within my presentation in a sense epitomises the aporia on which the structure of my argument is based. The full resonance of the image, which serves as ground and vanishing point for my own installation and critique of cultural texts, can only really be appreciated once the entire corpus has been displayed. At the same time my entire critical presentation of narrative and theoretical representations of feminine death requires an introductory image so as to tease out and focus on implications before they can be developed. For this effect to be achieved, the image, for which the entire book could be seen as a long embellishment, must resonate long after it has been discussed. In that my own critical display of cultural representations of feminine death requires even as it defies this quintessential image as its point of origin, it self-consciously enacts its own inevitable circularity.

Acknowledgements

Much of the preliminary research for this book was done during a nine-month period spent as a Mellon Faculty Fellow at Harvard University. I want to thank the Mellon Foundation for awarding me this grant. In the process of writing *Over Her Dead Body* many other people helped me with their critical advice and their suggestions about materials to use. I want to thank Ina Schabert and Birgit Erdle who, each in her own way, posed as the ideal reader and implied critic to whom the book could be addressed. For extended discussions on issues of death and representation early on in the writing stage I want to thank Mieke Bal, Margaret Higonnet, Sarah Goodwin and Regina Barreca, fellow travelers in the field of thanatopoetics. For spirited conversations held pertaining to this morbid subject and for critical comments that helped shape my manuscript my thanks also extends to Maria Tatar, Eric S. Downing, Jane Bellamy, Ellen Martin, Leigh DeNeef, Sander Gilman, Ellie Ragland-Sullivan, Roger Sales, Elizabeth Wright, Klaus Poenicke and Renate Hof. For their general encouragement as well as for specific turns of phrase, images and relevant critical texts given to me at the right moment I wish also to thank Alexandra Felts, Mandy Jackson, Annette Keck, Erika Zeiss, Susanne Hermannski, Franziska Lamott, Anke Heimann, Brigitte Bruns, Hans Walter Gabler and Werner v. Koppenfels. For her critical eye cast over my prose style and her encouragement about long sentences I want to thank Steffi Habermeier. Gratitude is due also to my students at Munich University and at Harvard University, who not only patiently listened while so many lectures seemed to end in a discussion of death, but who also supported my enthusiasm when they did so. Finally I want to thank Anita Roy at Manchester University Press who ultimately made this book possible.

Premliminary versions of chapters of this book first appeared in the following publications: 'The Lady Vanishes: Sophie Freud and Beyond the Pleasure Principle', *South Atlantic Quarterly 88.4* (Fall 1989); 'Violence of Representation – Representation of violence', *Literature Interpretation Theory 1.4* (1990); 'Dialogue with the Dead: The Deceased Beloved as Muse', *Sex and Death in Victorian England* ed. Regina Barreca. London: Macmillan, 1990.

Acknowledgements

Throughout this book, all translations from French and German, unless otherwise attributed, are my own, and reference is given to the original text. Further,
references to a cited text will appear with page reference after quotations and
unless otherwise stated, refer to the same text; passages without page references
are from the last-cited page. Unless otherwise stated, all italics are the author's
and all ellipses mine.

PART I

Death – the epitome of tropes

If we cannot see things clearly we will at least see clearly what the obscurities are.
Sigmund Freud

1

Preparation for an autopsy

The woman is perfected.
Her dead
Body wears the smile of accomplishment
Sylvia Plath

The pictorial representation of dead women became so prevalent in eighteenth and nineteenth century European culture that by the middle of the latter century this topos was already dangerously hovering on the periphery of cliché. I have chosen, in lieu of preliminary remarks, to concentrate on Gabriel von Max's painting *Der Anatom* for the simple reason that at first glance it is exemplary of nineteenth century salon painting: commonplace, spectacular, kitsch. Yet a closer analysis allows an intricate network of signification to emerge, so that the painting begins to take on exemplary status of another kind. Not only because it leads to a more general display of the modes of figuration of death and its linkage to femininity, but also because it does so in a way that forces us to take the explicit, literal and referential dimension seriously even as we seek to decode the multiple hermeneutic layers configured and debated over this dead body. In so doing it demonstrates perfectly one of the leitmotifs of this book. Like the purloined letter in Poe's story, representations of feminine death work on the principle of being so excessively obvious that they escape observation. Because they are so familiar, so evident, we are culturally blind to the ubiquity of representations of feminine death. Though in a plethora of representations feminine death is perfectly visible we only see it with some difficulty.

Gabriel von Max's painting, shown for the first time in 1869 at the international art exhibition in Munich, encompasses the dual interest of this German artist: his concern with positivistic anthropology and the study of material nature on the one hand, and his fascination with spiritualistic speculation and the study of an existence beyond material life on the other. An avid student of Darwin's theories of evolution as well as Carl Du Prel's work in parapsychology, he was intrigued both with the anatomical constitution of the human body and its connection to other animal organisms and with that part of the human organism

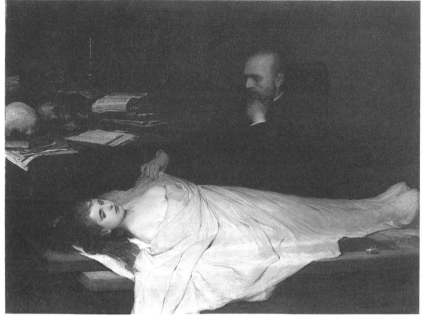

Fig 1   Gabriel von Max. *Der Anatom* (1869)

which could not be discovered after dissection: the immaterial kernel, the psyche.[1]

Concerned with the question of the soul's life independent of the body's, that is its survival after material death, Gabriel von Max repeatedly chose to depict scenes of humans on the threshold between life and death or in contact with the dead. In this concern he was clearly influenced by spritualist practices of his time. It was commonly believed that the hypnotised, often feminine medium, in its corpse-like state, could gain access to the realm of the dead and enter into a dialogue with the deceased. While Jean-Martin Charcot was experimenting with the use of hypnosis to treat patients for hysteria, spiritualists maintained that at the site of a figuratively deadened feminine body the immaterial realm of the beyond could become visible, a contact between the living and the dead be established or secured, and the boundary between the here and the beyond blurred. At the same time anatomists believed that opening a corpse during dissection allowed the unseen realm of the human body's interior to become visible, so that at the site of a literally dead female body theories about sexuality could be verified.[2] Since von Max conceived of spiritualism as the final conse-quence of human evolution, the corpse could serve as the nodal point for his studies both in natural history and in the invisible, parapsychic aspects of human existence.

It is precisely such an accumulation of seemingly contradictory or ambivalent gestures that informs this painting. The depicted objects, the setting and the figures themselves allow for a plurality of potential meanings to be attributed to this representation. Only when the painting is seen in connection with its title can the semantic coding of the male figure and his enterprise be fixed as that of an anatomist preparing for a dissection or a post mortem. In the posture of one meditating or musing upon an enigmatic and desirable object, he seems to be gazing at the upper part of a young woman's corpse. Owing to its excessive whiteness, as well as the stark contrast between body and background produced through the direction of the lighting, the corpse seems to be the centre of the painting. However, while the corpse is positioned as the thematic subject, the anatomist is the subject of the action, because he functions as the internal focalisor of the picture, who guides the spectator's view of the depicted object. Along with that of the anatomist, our attention is immediately drawn to the one exposed breast, artificially raised and figuring as the one moment where natural perspective is not maintained. Yet strictly speaking it is the anatomist's hand which is placed midway along the painting's vertical axis, and as such it serves as the defining nexus for all other relations.

The moment von Max has chosen to arrest in his painting is one where beauty is defined in its contrast to destruction. On the one hand, the soul has departed from the woman's body, but her beauty has not yet begun to disappear, as it will in the natural process of decomposition. On the other hand, the anatomist has not yet begun his dissection, in the process of which he will cut into and destroy the lines of her perfectly shaped body. The painting enacts a crucial moment of hesitation: the draping of the shroud underscores the aesthetisation by suggesting the materialisation of a statue. The feminine body appears as a perfect, immaculate aesthetic form because it is a dead body, solidified into an object of art. The aesthetically pleasing unity this corpse seems to afford draws added power from the fact that implicitly we know it is about to be cut into. This image of a feminine corpse presents a concept of beauty which places the work of death into the service of the aesthetic process, for this form of beauty is contingent on the translation of an animate body into a deanimated one. Beauty fascinates not only because it is unnatural, but also because it is precarious.[3] Even as the painting articulates stillness, wholeness, perfection, it presages the dissolution of precisely these attributes of beauty. It is not just the translation into the inanimate that defines the relation between beauty and death, but also the fact that this form of beauty, even as it signifies an immaculate, immobile form, potentially contains its own destruction, its division into parts.

My elaboration of this moment of hesitation focuses on three questions. How can we interpret the anatomist's highly ambivalent hand gestures? What is the relation between the corpse, the dead objects to the left of her head and the living moth at her feet? Finally, does the image of the corpse simply represent, or signify, a material female body, or does it rather invite the viewer to look over the body to a knowledge about sexuality, death, and spiritual survival? The painting is structured by a series of triangular relations about two central axes. The first axis is the one between the anatomist's and the dead woman's heads, interrupted by the anatomist's hand. The line between skulls and manuscripts forms part of the second central axis, connecting these dead objects to the moth. In so doing this second diagonal axis cuts through the dead woman's body, including in its trajectory two important points – again the anatomist's hand and the veiled genitals of the corpse, articulated under erasure.[4] These occulted genitals are, in fact, emphasised by virtue of the fact that their position lies midway between the hand and the moth. At the same time the visual mark of this corpse's gender is displaced upwards to the one exposed breast just beneath the anatomist's hand.

The painting is divided into two sets of parallel triangular relations. The first is a relation connecting the anatomist's and the corpse's head, with either the living moth or the dead objects as its apex. These dead objects are themselves arranged in a triad of skulls, books, manuscripts, whereby the line connecting skulls to books continues on to the anatomist's eyes. The second is a relation connecting the moth and the skull, with either the anatomist's or the corpse's head as its apex. The anatomist's hand functions as the central point in the painting since it is here that the two diagonal axes cross.

How then are these structural triangular relations semantically coded? Iconographically, the conjunction of corpse and dead objects refers back to baroque *vanitas*. In this version, however, the woman's body is used as substitute for both the feminine torso or feminine figure common in allegorical depictions of *vanitas* and *melancholia* imagery as well as the traditional fruit or animal objects in the *nature morte*. In funerary sculpture, death engenders a stable relation between subjects and objects,[5] and indeed this corpse is endowed with statuary qualities.

In addition its treatment as an object is both aesthetic and textual. As an object of the anatomist's gaze it belongs to the paradigm of writing, so that the analogy presented is not only one between corpse and art object but also one between deanimated human body and text as a body of dead letters. If a corpse poses a 'hermeneutic task',[6] the conjunction, in this particular case, between the dead body and the anatomist's paraphernalia suggests the promise of an answer to the enigma of mortality, sexuality and the origin of human existence. As object of his analytic gaze the corpse is positioned between three sets of signifiers – his books, other fully decomposed heads and his manuscripts. The corpse will be read as a body of signs in relation to and in comparison with these other texts; with the readable skulls. More significantly, the production of signs the corpse will in turn engender are his own writings. Because signification works on the basis of replacing an object with a sign, one can see it as supplementing and substituting its material objects of reference. Therefore signification can be understood as implying an absent body or causing the signified body's absence. The dead body as text serves as a metaphor of the correlation between designation, as well as interpretation, and absence.

Yet the moment of hesitation staged in this painting is that of invoking the indeterminacy inherent in every attempt at clearly distinguishing between original model and secondary copy. Indeed, the Greek verb *mimesthai* is fraught with ambiguity, given that it refers both to the creation of a new object and the

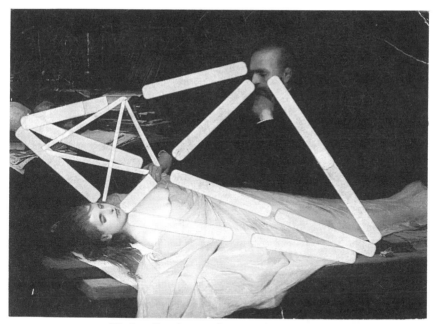

Fig 1a *Der Anatom*, showing relational axes

copy, or imitation of a pre-existing one.[7] Although the corpse supplements and reanimates the anatomist's books, it will also facilitate if not inspire his own writings, which in turn will substitute the corpse. Though supplementing previous texts, the corpse also authenticates and verifies these same texts, because the positivist discourse uses the opposition between text and body to ascribe authority to materiality. As point of mediation between reception and reproduction, the corpse functions as the site through which a particular realm of knowledge can be translated into another version, which carries the signature of the anatomist; signifing his gaze, his analysis, his authorial inscription. The corpse signifies mimesis in a complex sense.

The word *translation* points to another conjunction between corpse and textuality, since one meaning of translation involves the notion of conveying to heaven or to a non-temporal condition without death. In its intermediary position the corpse is destabilised and split in the sense that the soul has departed while the body has not yet fully decomposed. The end of the death process is marked by a successful division of soul from body, and a translation of the decomposing body into two new forms. The ephemeral body, and with it the destabilising process of change, disappears completely. Instead what is secured and eternally preserved are the immaterial soul and the skeletal remains, perfectly severed from each other. The corpse mediates between the survivor's animate body, the skulls as stabilised traces of death and the text as a product of reanimation, which will substitute and re-present this dead woman, once her natural body has been dissected and decomposed into absence. The end of the death process means an effacement of the split between body and soul, and a translation into both the immaterial eternal realm of the spiritual and the material realm of textuality. Metaphor, in turn, can be seen as the rhetorical correlation of the completed death process, given that it involves the transfer of a schema between two realms. For as its root word *metapherein* implies, metaphor transfers a word into a semantically different, though similar realm, so that the ensuing figurative expression articulates both semantic realms simultaneously. I will, therefore, call the diagonal between the anatomist's body and the body of the dead woman the metaphorical axis. However, both metaphor and its pictorial analogy, the text the anatomist anticipates writing, have a moment of hesitation inscribed in their act of representation. They double the absent body through a comparison based on similarity in appearance, but they double without producing a perfect identity with the first signifier, with the lost or transferred object, namely the corpse itself. By implication the difference brought about by this doubling is such that the anticipated manuscript will both represent the dead woman in her absence and refer to its own status as representation. For, the addition of the second signifier, which makes up the metaphoric turn, causes self-reflexivity to become part of the utterance.

This triangular relation contains, however, another disquieting aspect, for it implies that the anatomist constitutes himself as surviving, analysing and writing subject only in relation to the other dead objects. His subject position is also in between and contingent on two sets of signifiers – the texts and the corpse/skull. This triad, securing the metaphoric analogy between corpse and text, signifies the survivor's ability to translate an ephemeral object of sight into stable signs, which, in addition to the translated signifier, will carry his own signature. At the site of the corpse his sense of self is stabilised not only by virtue of the power any survivor experiences but also because a transcription of his experience of this death serves in part as a form of self-articulation. This self-stability is undermined, however, in the sense that his authorship is seen as secondary – his authority is always inscribed by previous signifiers (text, skull) and contingent on external validation (corpse). Even as we are given an image of death engendering a stabilising self-presentation, we are asked to acknowledge that the ensuing self-construction is neither original, unique nor authentic.

Turning to the second triangular relation brings the figure of the moth into play, and with it an entirely different kind of indeterminacy. While the first triangle explores the proximity of writing and effacement, this part of the painting addresses the interrelation between mortality and sexuality. In contrast to the passive horizontality of the corpse, which places the dead body completely at the disposal of the anatomist's gaze and touch, his upright posture signals a form of control and domination culturally ascribed not only to the survivor but also to the masculine position of the lover.[8] Yet with the moth another rhetorical mode is introduced, namely the allegorical. Traditionally defined as an extended metaphor, allegory informs this painting in the sense that it produces a juxtaposition and tension between all figured relations. What distinguishes the allegorical mode is that it reveals at the same time that it hides, and so explicitly points to the incommensurability or disjunction between signifier and signified. Based on the Greek *allos*, Other, allegory indicates a figurative speaking, a speaking in other terms, of other things. Its rhetorical turn is such that it articulates the difficulty of determining a conclusive or binding referential relation between signifier, signified and a nonsemiotic reality.[9]

In European folklore, the moth, also called 'death bird' because the traces on its body suggest the patterns of a skull, is iconographically read as a figure of death and immortality. Because it is a nocturnal butterfly, often found hovering above graves, classical Greek tradition saw the moth as a figure for the soul (*psyche*) departing from a dead body, if death occurred in the hours of the night. The moth is also used as a figure for souls in purgatory or for the good or bad spirits of the deceased, wandering restlessly on earth, which may include demons and witches. Finally the moth is understood as a messenger carrying oracles or omens, and again due to its colouring and its nocturnal appearance, its presence is thought to presage illness or death.[10]

Which signified concept should the viewer attribute to this figure, that in its relation to the skull forms what I will call the allegorical axis? Is it meant to signify the dead woman's soul, and so articulate the destabilized and disquieting aspect of the corpse, posed in the liminal zone between the body's total decomposition (skull) and the spirit's secure position in the beyond? Or is it meant to signify the spirit of some other deceased person, in which case the anatomist uses the dead woman's body as his medium for a dialogue with the dead? Indeed, in line with von Max's own interest in spiritualism, the body resembles a hypnotised medium about to speak in trance. Her face is not yet/no longer as pale as the rest of her body, as though reanimated by his gaze. Or is the moth a messenger of death? In that case, since the woman is already dead, it can only forbode the anatomist's own death? This possible reading is supported by the similarity in colouring of the skull and the moth, and the similarity in shape of the skull and the anatomist's head.

If in the first 'positivist' triangle the central transformation is that of her body into his writing, this transformation remains within the realm of physical materiality. The translation represented in this second, 'spiritualist' triangle, however, involves a transgression into immaterial spirituality, and as such the conjunction of two totally separate realms. What is signified is the translation into the beyond of either her soul, or more intriguingly, of his – that is the event of a dialogue with the dead or the event of his own death.

Above all, the moth implements the sense that at the site of the corpse the anatomist too is placed on the threshold between life and death, between material physicality and spiritual immateriality. Max Raphael analyses how the colour black in portrait painting signifies the indeterminate, the unbounded, the immaterial, while white is determined, bounded, constant. The contrast between the whiteness of the corpse and the blackness of the anatomist and his surroundings can be read as signifying the position of indeterminacy from which a surviving subject gazes at death.[11] He is seated in a private study, at a distance from the public world. Though there are books, there are no anatomical instruments. His position, a citation of St Jerome and of baroque *melancholia* figures, is that of the man of contemplation and analysis rather than of action. The lighting is such that in this pose he seems almost without body, reduced to hands and gaze. This is a space free from social laws for, as the ring on his hand suggests, though married he is able to touch this feminine body with impunity. In public this ring would signify his sexual knowledge as well as his 'impotence', in the sense of a culturally imposed constraint of his desire to touch a woman unbetrothed to him. At stake is the aporic gesture of both overcoming and maintaining this duplicitous restraint. In this liminal position he is allowed to have sexual knowledge of this woman's body (touch her) because she is dead, but because she is dead, this form of sexual knowledge is ultimately analytic. The result of his knowledge of her will be scripture rather than progeny, will be a celibate, self-produced and self-referring form of reproduction.

Regardless of whether the inspiration comes to him from the moth (as figure of a dead spirit) or from her body (as figure of deanimated life), reading her places him in a position closer to the dead than to the living world. The study of death both requires and implies some form of identification with the dead object; pictorially signified in the similarity between their semi-closed eyes. He can see the Other, death, by not seeing, because of the 'blindness' de Man ascribes to all allegorical reading. Even if his analysis is from the position of the survivor, with the intention of displacing the knowledge of mortality on to the dead woman or of analysing death by proxy, he, in so doing, is placed into a death-like position himself. The corpse is not only the passive medium through which he will gain knowledge and writing, he too is dependent as object and receiver of this alterior knowledge of death or of sexuality, which the dead woman has.

He hovers between two desires, expressed in the discrepancy between the two hand gestures – the left hand supports the chin, and with it an impersonal, distanced, safe gaze, while the right hand moves toward a more immediate, personally dangerous touch. The conflict is that of preserving her as an intact object of sight, cleanly severed from him, and uncovering, breaking into this other body. The latter means destroying the wholeness of the body and its ability to signify perfection and unity, as well as undoing the safe boundary between himself and her. Exposing himself to the dangers of infection means recognising death and femininity as extensions of himself. Yet Freud has argued that the touch is both derived from and a natural extension of the gaze, so that the relation between hand and eyes is contiguous, not oppositional. The tension between the cupped hand touching the viewer's chin and the hand grabbing the shroud is such that it implies a conflation of touching and looking in two ways. Gazing at the body of the dead, feminine Other serves a form of self-touch or auto-eroticism, while the gaze of the anatomist is also already a form of touching the dead woman. It is as dangerous to her integrity as the physical contact that will lead to exposure and dissection.[12]

The disjunction between the two hand gestures could also be read as an anxiety that breaking up the moment of liminality through action may cause the expected fulfilment of the hermeneutic potential posed by the corpse to ricochet back in the form of a total inaccessibility of the Other, be it femininity or death. Cutting into the body, entering the labyrinth of this Otherness may in fact only lead back to an encounter with oneself as survivor; to the recognition of being irrevocably marked by a knowledge of death that always again recedes, to remain just beyond reach. But again the security that a preservation of this object of sight might afford is subverted by the opposite realisation that suspending temporality and with it narrative also leads to death in the form of stasis.

If in the first triangulation the metaphorical analogy is between corpse and art object/text, the allegorical figuration depicted in this second one is that of the use of the feminine body as trope for castration and mortality. Freud has termed 'death' and 'femininity' as the two most consistent enigmas and tropes in western culture. Within psychoanalytic discourse itself the anatomy of the feminine body serves two diametrically opposed moments – extreme confirmation and extreme destabilisation of the self. The maternal body is experienced by the child as a site of wholeness and stability, with the breast as one of several partial objects that engender the feeling of unity and intactness. Even though this sense of wholeness is illusory, precariously constructed over a post-natal lacuna, with one of its occulted signifiers precisely the loss it tries to assuage, the 'phallic mother' can be seen as a model for culture's privileging of the feminine body as a figure for unity and timelessness; for the triumph over disseverment and facticity.

The female genitals have, however, also served as a privileged trope for lack, castration and split and by metonymic association, as a trope for decay, disease and fatality. The exposure of the breast (signifier for a comforting wholeness) and the veiling of the female genitals (signifier for dangerous facticity) suggest the representation of a double 'arrestation of death'. The woman's animated body has been arrested in death, while traces of death, like decomposition and decay, have likewise been arrested. A feminisation of death occurs even as the body is desexualised. It is an aesthetically pleasing corpse, suggesting harmony, wholeness, immortality, because it is a 'secured dead body' (much like the skulls). Above all its beauty marks the purification and distance from two moments of insecurity – female sexuality and decay.

But, much like the figure of the moth, which pierces the 'metaphoric' triangulation of corpse–author–text, the hand punctures any stabilising allegorical image of narcissistic purity to be figured over the feminine body, by introducing the moment of real temporality. As the only point of tension in the painting, as the moment of juncture between the metaphorical and the allegorical axes, the hand introduces the excluded reality of death by pointing to the future; as the destruction of the illusion of aesthetic wholeness; as the end of this interval of the unified, secured corpse. It introduces narrative, the sequentiality of events, and with it facticity, even as it disrupts the equally fatal stasis, metaphorically figured over the eternal, immobile image. The hand will expose the disquieting female genitals, will cut the body into fragments, will translate it into written characters. As the instrument for change it serves above all to expose rhetorically any safety a semantically fixed figuration is meant to afford.[13] As signifier for process it disrupts the image's illusory stability and unity. It points to that 'excess' of meaning, the moment of difference, that the metaphoric translation generates and to the 'Other' part of an allegorical figuration, its occulted signifier, always present though under erasure. The hand functions as a detail that disrupts any totalising or totalised meaning. By referring to a realm excluded from imaginary and symbolic signification – to real death as process – the hand points to the fact that the exclusion and occultation undertaken in this representation are gestures of negation and denial that must always also affirm and acknowledge the repressed. The position of the hand emphasises that the two visual metonymies for death – decaying body, castrated genitals – are articulated under erasure. The hand marks the point in this painting where any attempt at representing a body preserved from fragmentation, seems necessarily to contain its own failure. The allegorical mode supports this form of double articulation because it can say something different from and even contrary to what seems to be intended through it. Because allegory speaks of the Other and speaks of itself while speaking of something else it precludes semantic totalisation.[14]

Two forms of death are, then, being represented: Firstly, death in the form of deanimated objects, endowed with the trait of eternal survival in the material realm, interpretable and engendering the production of more signs and hermeneutic quests and secondly, death as the real process of division to be expressed through a figure of liminality that speaks the non-signifiable 'Other' through negation or displacement. The first centres on and signifies the positivist, metaphorically informed relation of the anatomist to his texts. This relation secures the surviving author's signature but only as a supplementary one, dependent on death's objects. The second is expressed in the spiritualist, allegorically informed relation between anatomist and moth, which destabilises the author's position by connecting him directly to the possibility of death, yet doing so indirectly – the corpse is intact, gendered but without genitals. The inclusion of the moth and the hand as moments of indeterminacy mark a displacement of time, a shift in signification from 'what is' to 'what will be'. Because both signify in a way that forbids semantic fixage – the hand as signifier for death as process, the moth as allegory of death whose object cannot be determined – what is ultimately expressed is that any representation of death necessarily works over a constantly receding, ungraspable signified.

The reading I propose for this painting is that it represents a conjunction of two contradictory forms of self-articulation. The left triad states 'I will have represented myself', for the texts the anatomist will produce as a result of this experience of death signify both the corpse and his inscription of it. They will be about her dead body but also about his signature, his gaze, his masculinity, and his survival. Over the dead woman's corpse, his status as subject will have been secured. But equally in the future perfect the painting states in the right triad 'I will have died', for even as he signs his description of this dead woman's body, in a gesture of triumphant power over femininity and over mortality, he is signed by death. His contact with the dead body of another turns into a sign of his own inevitable disempowered submission to death. He desires the feminine corpse as signifier for wholeness even as he desires this dead body as signifier for his own fragmentary and mortal nature.

But – the medium for this articulation is the dead woman. The feminine corpse inspires the surviving man to write, to deny or to acknowledge death, while at the same time the corpse is the site at which he can articulate this knowledge. In this representation of a feminine corpse we may privilege the metaphoric or the allegoric axis, we may choose a thematic meaning (the painting as a dialectic between positivist and spiritualist approaches to death) or a rhetorical reading (the painting as the dialectic between a metaphorical and allegorical figuration of death). We may choose as signifier for the moth the woman, the mother, an ancestor or the anatomist. We may even choose to say that the crux of the painting is precisely the articulation of contradictory hermeneutic positions, which signify a hesitation between oppositions and a disruption of the image's unity. In the midst of all these moments of indeterminacy, however, what remains persistently constant is that signification in all possible cases occurs over her dead body.

Notes to Chapter 1

1 J. Muggenthaler, 1988.
2 S. Gilman, 1989; L. Jordanova, 1989 and R. Richardson, 1989.
3 Without the title a very different kind of precariousness could be read into this image. If we don't know that the masculine figure is an anatomist, we could read the grabbing hand as a preparatory gesture for rape. It is also interesting to note that while the title identifies the male figure as an anatomist, the female figure remains anonymous. A determination of her previous position in life remains totally up to the viewer. The usual reading that this is the body of a prostitute who commited suicide in fact reflects the interests and projections of the commentators.
4 I use this term in J. Derrida's sense of a written word, crossed out and printed on the page along with its bar, that is to say as word and deletion, 1976. Erasure marks the absence of a presence, the lack inscribed in any notion of origin.
5 M. Serres, 1987.
6 M. Higonnet, 1986.
7 M. Bal, 1982, 'The accusative that accompanies (the word mimesis) can indicate the model as well as the "copy", the preexisting object and the resulting creation', p. 172.
8 See Plato's 'The Symposium', 1961.
9 P. de Man, 1983; also J. H. Miller, 1981.
10 See H. Bächtold-Stäubli, vol. 7, 1987, pp. 1238–54.
11 M. Raphael, 1983.
12 See S. Freud's discussion of voyeurism, 1905. One could develop the discussion of the anatomist's analytic gaze in the direction of psychoanalysis. Taking the title figuratively, this anatomist could easily be read as a metaphor for the psychoanalyst,

listening to the unconscious speech of his hypnotised patient. Though totally incidental, the similarity between the anatomist's and Freud's own physiognomy is
striking.

13 Strictly speaking, of course, the hand distinguishes decomposition as a cutting into
parts from decay, for what dissecting the body in fact does is prevent decay. As such,
one could argue that the hand marks a self-reflexive moment in the painting, referring
associatively to the artist's own hand. Both eliminate the dangerously destabilising
mobility of the decomposing body, arrest decomposition through the recomposition of
the painting and the discomposition of the post mortem. M. Foucault, 1973, describes
how eighteenth-century clinical anatomy virtually suppressed the effects of organic
decomposition. Opening up corpses allowed the last stage of pathological time and the
first stage of cadaveric time almost to coincide.

14 J. Derrida, 1986, p. 11.

2

The lady vanishes

Distance – woman – averts truth – the philosopher. She bestows the idea.
And the idea withdraws, becomes transcendant, inaccessible, seductive. It
beckons from afar. Its veils flout in the distance. The dream of death begins.
It is woman.
Jacques Derrida

On 25 January 1920 Sophie Freud-Halberstadt, aged twenty-six, died of
influenzal pneumonia, 'snatched away' in Sigmund Freud's words 'from glowing
health, from her busy life as capable mother and loving wife, in four or five days,
as if she had never been'.[1] The language Freud uses to describe his reaction to
the unexpected death of his Sunday-child is significantly poised between a
deference to the irrevocable reality of death and a defiance of what an unconditional acknowledgement of death would imply: namely the ego's relinquishing
of its narcissistic libidinal cathexis.[2] To Sophie's husband Max Halberstadt
Freud describes her death as a 'meaningless, brutal act of fate', a 'joke played on
helpless, poor humans by higher forces'.[3] To Max Eitingon he comments that it
is 'such a paralyzing event, which can stir no afterthoughts when one is not a
believer . . . blunt necessity, mute submission'[4] and to Ernest Jones, whose father
had also recently died, he admits that 'we all must [die] and I wonder when my
turn will come. Yesterday I lived through an experience which makes me wish it
should not last a long time.'[5]

Freud's rhetorical move from the Other to the self, which reads the death of
the daughter as a sign for his own vulnerability and mortality is repeated in a
second letter to Jones, dated 8 February 1920: 'You know of the misfortune that
has befallen me. It is depressing indeed, a loss to be forgotten . . . Now I may be
declining in power of thought and expression, why not? Everyone is liable to
decay in the course of time.'[6] Even if death, as dissolution of the subject, is the
object of these utterances, it can be articulated only in relation to the self, so that
these utterances simultaneously confirm what they mean to abrogate. Any articulation of another's death, it seems, invariably returns to the surviving speaker. It

returns to support the ego's narcissistic cathexis because it is coupled with a realisation of one's own mortality.

Yet the necessary recuperation of a sense of ego stability when faced with the blunt reality of death is even more markedly traced in those passages where Freud directly comments on his own position in this fatal episode. While he assures his mother that 'mourning for the splendid, vital girl . . . is permissible'[7] he writes about himself to Oscar Pfister, 'I do as much work as I can, and am grateful for the distraction . . . as for mourning, that will no doubt come later.'[8] In a similar vein he writes to Sandor Ferenczi, 'As for us? My wife is quite overwhelmed. I think: La séance continue . . . Apart from feeling rather more tired I am the same. The death, painful as it is, does not affect my attitude toward life . . . "the unvaried, still returning hour of duty" and "the dear lovely habit of living" will do their bit toward letting everything go on as before.'[9] Striking, however, is that while he claims that as a confirmed unbeliever he has no one to accuse and no place to lodge a complaint, Freud nevertheless turns to a trope that implies both injustice and opposition. In the letters to Pfister and Ferenczi he describes Sophie's death as a deep, bitter, insurmountable narcissistic wound ('ganz tief unten wittere ich das Gefühl einer tiefen, nicht verwindbaren narzißtischen Kränkung').[10] His stance, then, is one of ambivalence. Freud uses his work to deny the grave cut into his narcissistically fashioned self which 'deep down' he is forced to acknowledge.

Since what I want to focus on is the choice of trope, or semantic encoding enacted in Freud's description of this fatal event, it seems worth recalling the responses occasioned by the other significant loss in his life – the death of his father on 23 October, 1896. In his letter to Wilhelm Fliess, Freud comments: 'All of it happened in my critical period, and I am really quite down because of it' (26 October), 'I find it so difficult to write just now . . . By one of those dark pathways behind the official consciousness the old man's death has affected me deeply . . . I now feel quite uprooted' (2 November). The most illuminating response, however, is that in the second edition of the *Interpretation of Dreams* (1908): 'For this book has a further subjective significance for me personally – a significance which I only grasped after I had completed it. It was, I found, a portion of my own self-analysis, my reaction to my father's death – that is to say, to the most important [significant, *bedeutsam*] event, the most poignant [cutting, *einschneidendsten*] loss, of a man's life.'[11]

Sophie's death elicits a gratitude for the distraction of work, an effort to continue an established routine, but his father's death is seen as bringing forth a break in established patterns – it is difficult for him to write, he feels uprooted. Furthermore, the significant influence this death has on the formulation of a new theoretical position is acknowledged, though only after a belated recognition. At the same time, an interesting exchange between the impersonal and the personal, between the general and the specific manifests itself in the two responses. In the case of Jacob Freud the nominal designation is always specifically 'my father,' 'the old man'; Sophie Freud's name, on the other hand, is at times elided ('a loss to be forgotten') or glides into the impersonal ('the loss of a child').

Yet the death of his father is depicted, in reference to Freud's own position, in far more general terms; it is stylised as the most important event in 'a man's life'. The superlative 'most', furthermore, modifies the abstract, impersonal concepts of 'significant event' and 'incising loss.' In contradistinction, Sophie's death, though not acknowledged as a break in his stance toward life, affects his specificity; it wounds, injures, offends his narcissism. What is modified as superlative in the second occurrence of death is not its significance nor its incision, but rather the fact that it is an offence with which he can never reconcile himself ('nicht verwindbar'). That is to say, his father's death, though relegated to the realm of the impersonal, the general, is explicitly acknowledged as having led to his theory on dreams, by way of the detour through self-analysis. The death of his daughter is, on the other hand, explicitly acknowledged as belonging to the realm of the personal and specific. Yet this event's possible influence on theory-building remains hidden. His reaction to his daughter's death is not seen in terms of a decisive break but rather as continuation – work continues. The generic significant event in a man's life, the incision of a loss, becomes an irreparable narcissistic wound.

The gesture of 'doing as much work as one can' as an antidote to a 'deep narcissistic wound' becomes even more significant when one recalls that, at the time of Sophie's death, Freud was not only in the process of formulating his theory of the 'death drive', but that *Beyond the Pleasure Principle* was meant as an alternative to his work on narcissism. Freud's concern with the concept of a death drive was meant to restore balance to a system of thought in danger of being captivated by the notion of narcissism. The situation, then, is one of Freud doing as much work as he can in an effort to restore his wounded narcissism, while the work he is engaged in is meant to wound his theoretical notion of narcissism.[12] Writing about death seems to become a way of regaining control after the disrupting experience of death, of reassuring continuity in the face of dis-continuity, of mastering the absence of the Sunday-child ('snatched away as if she had never been'). Yet the resulting text is one that articulates precisely this ambivalent interplay between disruption and control, between loss and the reassurance of substitutional 're-presencing/re-presenting', between the fear of death and a narcissistic libidinal cathexis. By May of that year, Freud writes to Eitingon, 'I am now correcting and completing "Beyond" that is, of the pleasure principle, and am once again in a productive phase. Fractus si illabatur orbis impavidum, ferient ruinae.'[13] The theme of the piece of writing, which is meant to assure Freud's equilibrium, by definition, however, undermines this recuperative gesture. Ambivalence and duplicitous encoding mark both the setting and the discursive strategy of this text.

Several commentators have speculated that Sophie Freud in some sense functions as muse for her father's theory of the death drive, though Freud himself acknowledged this influence (in contrast to that of his father's death) only in the form of negation. To Wittels he writes that 'I certainly would have stressed the connection between the death of the daughter and the concepts of Beyond [the Pleasure Principle] in an analytic study on someone else. Yet still it is wrong. Beyond was written in 1919, when my daughter was young and blooming, she died in 1920. In September of 1919 I left the manuscript of the little book with some friends in Berlin for their perusal, it lacked then only the part on mortality or immortality of the protozoa.'[14] When Freud informs Eitingon that the 'Beyond is finally finished', he begs his friend 'to certify that it was half finished when Sophie was alive and flourishing'.[15] Both the vehemence of the refutation and the semi-contradiction that underlies his assertion of the autonomy of his theory from biographical events indeed seem to demand further speculations on what could have been at stake for Freud in refusing to acknowledge an inter-dependence between the theoretical formulation of a death drive and the experience of his daughter's death.[16] Was it only the fear that any reference to personal experience, rather than lending authority, would seem to invalidate a theory that was based so heavily on speculation? Or was it because an acceptance of the intersection between a real event of death and a theoretical speculation would counteract the reassurance this piece of writing was to afford?

Though Max Schur's suggestion that uncovering a death instinct permitted Freud literally to live with the reality of death is compelling, I will shift my discussion away from speculations about how much and what kind of significance can be attributed to the influence the daughter's death had on Freud's theoretical considerations. I will focus instead on the one specific moment in *Beyond the Pleasure Principle* where Sophie Freud plays a direct part.[17] This is the episode in chapter two, where Freud describes his observation of a child playing with a cotton reel (*Holzspule*) in response to its mother's absence. Though neither character is directly identified, the child is his grandson Ernst, and the mother, whose absence in a highly intricate way is both literally and figuratively at stake, is his Sunday-child Sophie, dead several months after the writing of the chapter.

Having described in great detail Freud's response to his daughter's death and then the completion and reception of *Beyond the Pleasure Principle*, Ernest Jones adds as an afterthought, 'Incidentally, the child whose behavior played such a significant part in stimulating Freud's theory of the repetition-compulsion was his eldest grandson, Ernst.'[18] The extraordinary omission in this comment, the displacement from a daughter's significant part to that of a grandson's (a shift assumed by most commentators on this chapter), is precisely the blind spot into which I will insert my discussion. While many critics have elaborated on the notion of fading or absence and its necessary precondition for symbolisation, as this is enacted in the child's game, the discussion in general has doubled Freud's own gesture of severing theory from historical event, at least in respect to an occultation of Sophie Freud's role. What I will do instead is privilege the fourth piece in this game of disappearance and re-presencing, which binds a child, a spool, and a chain of signifiers (*fort, da*) – the absent mother.

Samuel Weber suggests that the silent pathos of the death drive has depended upon a certain 'non-reading' of the text in which it is first formulated.[19] Sophie

Freud, and the significance of the disappearance of the maternal body, marks the site of precisely such a non-reading. Yet by unwittingly demonstrating the interplay between symbolization and maternal absence, the second chapter of *Beyond the Pleasure Principle* contains another narrative about the relationship between culturation and death to the one involving the dead father in *Totem and Taboo* (1912–13). That this narrative is articulated as a moment of non-reading may have to do with the fact that behind the narrative figure of a mother's absence stood the real event of a daughter's death.

Freud's metapsychological writings distinguish themselves through the addition of an 'economic' point of view to the 'topological' and 'dynamic' factors informing psychic processes. Freud begins his article on the death drive with a discussion of the merits of this economic model, in order to support his argument that the exchange psychoanalysis has 'no hesitation in assuming' is one that replaces an unpleasurable tension with a lowering of that tension, replacing or supplementing this 'unpleasurable tension' with 'an avoidance of unpleasure or a production of pleasure'.[20] The economic strategy is one of sidestepping detour (*Vermeidung*) or/and of creation (*Erzeugung*); its motive a consideration (*Rücksicht*) of the 'yield of pleasure' (*Lustgewinn*). In order to study the workings of the psychic apparatus as it is regulated by the economically oriented interest of the pleasure principle, Freud turns, in the second chapter, to the first, self-invented game played by a one-and-a-half year old boy. He justifies his choice of illustration by explaining that though his finding is the result of a 'chance opportunity', it is nevertheless more than 'a mere fleeting observation, for I lived under the same roof as the child and his parents for some weeks, and it was some time before I discovered the meaning of the puzzling activity which he constantly repeated' (14).

From the outset, the narration of this game is doubly inscribed. An interest in an uncanny mode of representation (in a mode of signifying that hides even as it articulates), is crossed with an interest in economic relations.[21] The possibility of familiarity between the observer Freud and his object of observation, the playing child, is indicated obliquely, which suggests that something beyond a scientific interest in this game might be at stake. The text delineates the process of constructing and releasing tensions, binding and unbinding libidinal energies. It serves to illustrate Freud's argument that pleasure and ego preservation are contingent on replacing an unpleasurable experience with a repetition of this event, which in some way reduces the tension. A reproduction of new tensions is, however, also required to avoid the zero point of tension – what Freud characterises as the anorganic state of life that precedes and is the goal of human existence.

Yet the strategy of the text at times contradicts its narrative intent, for it is one of tensions produced through unbound, potential, floating meanings. Freud emphasises the speculative nature of his investigation, offers interpretations only to retract them in exchange for other possible interpretations. At stake on the discursive level of Freud's observation and narration of a child's game is not only an argument for a death instinct beyond pleasure, but also the validity of an economic model concerned with notions of interest, gain, loss, exchange and investment. This economic concern informs the semantic register of the offered interpretation even as it forms the object of Freud's demonstration.

Let us turn to the way Freud sets up the narrative situation for his observation. Of the playing child Freud says that it was intellectually not precocious, could say only 'a few comprehensible words', though also in command (*verfügen*) of several meaningful sounds, comprehensible to those around him. In linguistic terms this means that some of the boy's utterances are semantically bound, their meaning based on common consent, others semantically unbound, i.e. requiring an externally imposed semantic fixture if they are to be meaningful to 'those around him'. What makes this point worth noticing is that the crux of Freud's interpretation of his observation of the child's vocal sounds 'o – da' is based precisely on the exchange of arbitrary sounds for comprehensible words in a claim which presupposes that the semantically non-determined sounds (o – da) are nevertheless comprehensible to the two observers (though the child, as yet an unskilled speaker, can not confirm this claim). The reading Freud offers is an arbitrary semantic coding of sounds, though one informed by his vested interest in finding a validation of his theory.

There are, then, two subject positions in the narration of this game: that of the subject of the action, the playing child and that of the subject of focalisation, the gazing and analyzing relative, who turns the playing child into the object of his viewing. The image we receive of the focalised object is not only determined *by* the focalisor but also says something *about* him.[22] The narrative reflects the position of the focalising Freud, in addition to that of the playing child, so that the attributed meaning in fact distorts the game. The ensuing incommensurability between narrative and signified game is such that the child's intended meaning remains obscured, since Ernst never serves as focalisor of his own narrative. Instead, the narrative reflects its focalisor and becomes a form of self-articulation for Freud. This game marks a moment of potential semantic plurality, and the choice in semantic encoding made sets up the narration it is meant to support. The chosen reading enacts the double binding of non-semanticised sounds through alterior supplementation in that it first claims comprehensibility for the sounds in their non-semanticised form and then translates them, through the addition of three consonants (frt), into meaningful words.

Freud establishes a significant (though in its meaning not identified) relation between the boy's 'limited' language ability and his 'generally good' interaction with external reality, by using the contrasting modifier 'however' to introduce the list of examples that demonstrate the boy's advanced stage of culturation – his relations with his parents are of good rapport, he is praised for his correct behaviour, he conscientiously accepts his parents' prohibitions (*Verbote*) (15). Freud highlights the fact that the child never cries when the mother leaves him for several hours, even though he was fondly attached to her. The situation, then, within which this significant game emerges, is one marked by ambivalence. The mother is the exclusive object towards which the child can direct its demand for gratification of its needs, but it never cries at her disappearance; the child accepts the prohibition of its parents (that is, already accepts culture's demand for a restraint of impulses) but as yet commands only a few words and sounds. Freud presents the child as one that has learned to obey laws before it has learned the language of these laws. Furthermore, the laws forbidding certain libidinal impulses are imposed by and refer to both parents (implicitly to a sexual relation – 'he did not disturb his parents at night').

This child has accepted culture's interdiction, the 'no', but of both parents. It knows the negative before it is initiated into language and into play. For we must recall, the game the child plays is the '*first*' self-invented game.[23] What Freud sets up in this preliminary description, then, is a different scene in the developmental stages of a child from the one governed by the Oedipal complex, another ✓ narrative for the way in which language acquisition and subjectivity is grounded on an acknowledged experience of loss. The negation that serves both as catalyst for the game and as object or reference of its articulation marks a site independent of the father's castrative 'no'. The anxiety engendering symbolisation and self-consciousness in this narrative is of another kind. Initially there is no father in this game at all, not even an absent one. Though the child plays in an intermediary zone connecting the imaginary register of the mother/infant dyad (governed exclusively by unrestrained drives) and the symbolic register (governed by prohibitions), the anxiety at stake does not involve the father as the disrupting third element. Freud implies that what also disrupts and decentres human existence, producing both nostalgia for a previous state (the complete unity of the child with the maternal body) and a directedness toward detour and creation in the form of symbolic play, are the many inscriptions of death that mark the human body from birth on.

Freud's observation of the child's game moves through several stages. At first he notices the child throwing away any small objects available, and accompanying this gesture with a loud, long-drawn out 'o-o-o-o'; a signifier for interest and expression. The observer and the mother agree ('nach dem übereinstimmenden Urteil') to bind this utterance of a mere interjection to the semantically fixed signifier *fort* (gone). One could argue that this translation, which stabilises the polysemantic potentiality of the child's sound, precisely repeats the 'murder of the soma', the renunciation of the body, enacted by the playing child, and understood by the commentators of this episode as the precondition for an entrance into the symbolic exchange with language. Therefore this translation is a form of violence. Kristeva describes this process as a form of sacrifice, which sets up the symbol and the symbolic order at the same time. In her description, the ' "first" symbol, the victim of a murder, merely represents the structural violence of language's irruption as the murder of soma, the transformation of the body, the captation of drives'.[24]

Only through this translation can Freud come to realise that the child's gestures are those of play, more exactly playing 'gone' with his objects. He becomes more confirmed in this interpretation (that is the binding of a child's gesture and sounds to the semantically stable concept of 'playing gone') only through repeated observation, or to be more exact, only when he can supplement his first observation with that of a slightly different version of the child's game. Meaning emerges not only through the encoding of sounds and gestures, based on the interests of the focalisor, but also through difference in repetition. In the altered version of the game he observes the child throwing a reel with a piece of string around it, with great skill, over the edge of his curtained cot, 'so that it disappeared into it, at the same time uttering his expressive "o-o-o-o". He then pulled the reel out of the cot again by the string and hailed its reappearance with a joyful "da" . . . This, then, was the complete game – disappearance and return. As a rule one only witnessed its first act, which was repeated untiringly as a game in itself, though there is no doubt that the greater pleasure was attached to the second act.'

Freud adds a footnote which repeats and completes his own game with the child's enactment of disappearance and re-appearance. In this footnote he explains that a further observation of yet another version of this game 'fully confirms' (*gesichert*) this interpretation.[25] In this new version, the child greets its returning mother with the communication (*Mitteilung*) 'Bebi o-o-o-o!', an utterance incomprehensible until it is supplemented with another activity. In his long solitude the child had 'found a method of making himself disappear. He had discovered his reflection in a full-length mirror which did not quite reach to the ground, so that by crouching down he could make his mirror-image "gone" '. The contradiction involved in these games is that the signifier *da*, complementing the reel's presence, in fact continues to articulate the mother's absence, just as the conjunction of 'o-o-o' with 'Bebi' establishes the presence of the child as speaker in the same moment that it allows the child to conceptualise its absence to others.[26]

Freud's interpretation of the game is informed by his interest in an economic interpretive model. Asking himself what kind of investment does the child make with this game, what kind of interest is earned, he chooses to read these actions as related to 'the child's great cultural achievement – the instinctual renunciation (that is, the renunciation of instinctual satisfaction) which he had made in allowing his mother to go away [*Fortgehen*] without protestation'. This is, though Freud does not make the point, a different kind of cultural renunciation from the one mentioned before, which was directed towards the parents' nocturnal activities (where the mother's absence from the child was occasioned by the father's presence). If we recall that Freud demonstrates in great detail in *Interpretation of Dreams* how any words or images connected with the notion 'fort' can be deciphered as symbols of death, then this narrative of the game can also be read as his figuration of the narcissistically wounding notion of human mortality – offending and disillusioning any desire for a permanent and stable union with the maternal body, as well as any ego stabilising notions of omnipotence, self-permanence and intactness. It is a renunciation of the demand to have the mother permanently present and involves the narcissistically wounding recognition of her necessary absence. But the play of absence and presence involves, in the first place, the child's conceptualisation of death, and only secondarily that of paternal competition.

If we reframe this narrative within Freud's economic terminology we can reformulate the child's strategy in the following way: he withholds instinctual energies (renounces a total investment in the mother), which, now in excess (unbound), can be invested in a game that is marked by sidestepping substitution and creation. Freud suggests that 'he compensated himself for this, as it were, by himself staging the disappearance and return of the objects within his reach'. Again implied, though not explicitly stated, is the reference Freud makes to his notion of mourning.[27] The child's game enacts willingly what the experience of death forcibly imposes on the survivor. A freeing of libidinal energies that must be reinvested, on the axis of substitution and creation, in an image of the deceased, marks the healthy trajectory from mourning to remembrance or commemoration. Though it is clear that the interest gained through this game is pleasure, the 'other point' to which Freud directs his interest is to ask about the form pleasure takes in a gesture that continually repeats an unpleasurable experience. For he remarks that 'the child cannot possibly have felt his mother's departure as something agreeable or even indifferent'.

The ambivalence within Freud's discursive strategy in turn repeats itself in his attempt to explain the gain of pleasure. While an interpretation of the game as one repeating and substituting the mother's absence is secure, 'no certain decision' can be reached from the analysis of this one single case. What is 'confirmed' is a semantic encoding of the child's action (an encoding that brings the mother and her fading into play, makes her into what is at stake), which is informed by the projections of the focalisor. A semantic securing of the motive for and the gain resulting from the game with the mother's body is avoided. Freud offers two readings. An 'unprejudiced view' he tentatively suggests, gives the impression that the pleasure involves the exchange of 'the passivity of the experience' for 'the activity of the game,' a passage from a 'passive situation' to an 'active part'. The interest gained is a 'sense of mastery' even as the mastery always points duplicitously to the remembered unpleasurable event.[28]

Freud's second interpretation is presumably meant to be less 'unprejudiced'. Freud suggests that 'throwing away the object so that it was "gone" might satisfy an impulse of the child's, which was suppressed in his actual life, to revenge himself on his mother for going away from him. In that case it would have a defiant meaning: "All right, then, go away! I don't need you. I'm sending you away myself" ' (16). Both motivations offered see repetition as a form of control, as a return to self-assertion in response to an endangering moment of absence – one directed toward re-creation, symbolising absence and presence as a confirmation of the child's omnipotence of thought, the other directed toward destruction, aggressively abusing the supplement object as a confirmation of the child's autonomy from its mother. But in both cases the pleasure produced through repetition is doubly broken. It is the result of a trajectory of both detour and disunity, and exists only in correlation to its counterpart displeasure. Though the repetitive act of mastery puts under erasure the loss/absence upon which it is founded, the pleasurable self-equilibrium gained always articulates its negative.

At this point I will insert into my reading of Freud's narration of the 'fort–da' game a presentation of the way psychoanalytic theory has used and commented on this episode. Acquiring the ability to symbolize is the crucial way for a child to establish its relation to the world. Though she doesn't directly comment on the 'fort–da' episode, Melanie Klein places fantasies of destructive impulses at the centre of her theory on symbol formation and ego development.[29] The maternal body, both real and internalized, functions as the first site for the child's aggressions because it calls forth anxiety in the child, in respect to both potential loss and potential injury. Since the outside world is experienced as an extension of the mother's body, these aggressive fantasies in turn perpetually engender a chain of new symbol formations, and ever new affective relations to the world.

Klein isolates two dimensions in symbol formation. First a moment of aggression initiates the ego's cathectic gliding from one supplementary object to another that marks its introduction into the world of symbols (and signifiers substituting for symbols) and binds the developing ego into the cultured external world. Then the partial renunciation of the soma (enacted by a renunciation of the maternal body, its exchange for figures of the mother and the acknowledgment of a distinction between material body and external world) is contingent upon a stabilised 'good' internal body. But this image of the good internal body, stabilised and unproblematic, is in turn contingent on the fact that the material maternal body is already fading before the child's ego. A stable relation to the external cultured world not only doubles an internal stability, but in both instances stability is gained through a moment of destruction and loss. The self is constructed and preserved by virtue of a detour relation over other, externalised body-objects, but this 'love' relation ambivalently crosses love and hatred and works on a ceaseless interplay between stability and instability. Klein significantly sees this emotional trajectory – from destructive impulse, through idealisation and denial to the ambivalent sense of guilty yet triumphant omnipotence in respect to a potentially wounding other – as the central position in the child's development; as a part in the 'process of organization and integration that is *parallel to* but *different from* and *other than* sexual development'.[30] In fact she argues that the 'fear of death enters into and reinforces castration fear' rather than figuring as analogon, for the 'loss of the genital would mean the end of the creative power which preserves and continues life'.[31]

Using Klein's work as his point of orientation, D. W. Winnicott reads the complete game of 'disappearance and return' as the last part of a full sequence of 'incorporation, retention and riddance'. The loss of the real mother is 'a test of the child's relation to his *inside* mother'. Owing to the correspondence between internal and external mother, the child's mastery of its internal relation (including an aggressive riddance) also means the mastery of the disappearance of the external mother. The child's gesture of throwing away is more than just the rejection of an internal and external mother, who has provoked the child's aggression. In this game the child 'also externalizes an internal mother whose loss is feared, so as to demonstrate to himself that this internal mother, now represented through the toy on the floor, has not vanished from his inner world, has not been destroyed by the act of incorporation, is still friendly and willing to be played with'.[32] A relationship between an external body and an internal representation is negotiated over an external symbol (binding both oppositions 'internal/external' and 'body/figure' on to one object). For Winnicott the 'meaning' of this game is that 'the child gains reassurance about the fate of his internal mother', i.e., that this internal representation will not fade, will not become meaningless. Though Winnicott connects this sense of the reliability of an image with notions of reparation to and revivification of the loved object whose loss is feared (or experienced), this reassurance can also be connected to the child's ability to 'image'. For, in respect to the question of preservation, Winnicott significantly shifts his interest from body to image – it is not the maternal body that is to be secured from fading, but rather the child's internal image. I would add that, if what is secured as 'reliable' in the process of this game is the internal image created of the mother, then what is also secured is the child's ability to create. The substitution of a real, external maternal body for an internal representation and external symbol is one that includes the move from disappearing/reappearing mother to revenging/re-presenting child.

If we now return to Freud's footnote about the child's second version of the 'fort–da' game, in which the child plays with its own mirror-image, what emerges is another dimension of the disturbance built into this duplicitous game of narcissistic self-confirmation. This first self-invented game shifts absence of the Other to absence of the self. Not just a revenge for and a triumph over the mother's absence is what is being played (as Freud would have it), but a game that simultaneously confirms and denies the child's own mortality in response to the vulnerability exposed by the mother's wounding absence. This game with self-reflections is analogous to the destability Lacan has worked out in his emphasis on misrecognition and belatedness as central moments of the narcissistically informed imaginary self-fashioning enacted during the mirror stage. But what is also contained in this second version of the game, not usually noted by critics, is the notion of imaging as a moment of erasure of the Other when this Other is substituted for an image of the self.

Lacan emphasises that for a subject to imagine itself as having a stable identity is always an act of mis-recognition (*méconnaissance*), a fiction, an illusion of autonomy.[33] Though language allows for a differentiation between self and Other (so that the entrance into the symbolic register functions as a disruption of narcissistically informed imaginary unity and points to the truth of human existence as that of lacking, of being split), this differentiation is never complete and the imaginary register never disappears. The jubilation experienced in seeing oneself as coherent and whole in an exterior image – a regaining of the sense of completeness lost with birth – is carried on into adult life. It remains as a trace in the chain of projections on to others that structures the libidinal economy of each individual subject, whereby the Other is cast into the role of an object of desire. The function of this imaginary other is to repeat and re-enact the sense of safety experienced by the subject in the first narcissistic mirror stage, when the reflected image brought about a sense of coherent unity. For the subject, the function of the other is to reaffirm and guarantee the stability of its position in the world, a sense of self-identity and self-centredness.[34]

The ego uses the 'other' as a means for self-definition, first its 'other image' to constitute, and then the 'images of others' to protect its own image of a unified self. In this process of identification it produces for itself an image of wholeness, autonomy and integrity, encoded culturally as the desire to regain in life a repetition of prenatal unity. The desired 'other' is part of a chain replacing a primary lost object that is endlessly repeatable because the satisfaction longed for is never found in any surrogate. Because the genesis of the ego in the imaginary indissolubly links the self with the other, in later life this detour over the other to the self is so fascinating and necessary.

Lacan, focusing on the linguistic aspect of the 'fort-da' game, reads it as a trope for the fading (*aphanisis*) of the subject before and within the process of signification. If in one sense the 'fort-da' game marks the child's aggressive/creative response to its frustration with its dependency on the mother for gratification of its needs, the price for the autonomy gained is that of another dependency. For Lacan the reel does not represent the absent mother, but rather 'a small part of the subject that detaches itself from him while still remaining his'. The repetition symbolised is that 'of the mother's departure as cause of a *Spaltung* in the subject', which in two ways articulates self-reflexively the child's own absence. Covering the split of the self through the alternating game of absence and re-presence has two aims. Firstly, the 'fort–da' enacts how the production of meaning is contingent on the difference between two opposites, between disappearance and return, between the phonemes *o* and *a*. It serves as figure for the way the subject is determined only by its position between two signifiers; i.e. within the process of signification. Secondly, in the doubling of the reel by the phonemes *o* and *a*, the symbol is replaced by a signifier, analogous to the ego's substitution by the subject of the unconscious. For Lacan, this shift to a secondary form of representation is an illustration of the fact that once subject to the laws of signification, the subject will identify itself only imperfectly – faded from any sense of self-presence – in relation to signifiers, whose identity is determined by their difference to other signifiers. The game is aimed at 'what essentially is not there, *qua* represented'. Since for Lacan the signified of this game is 'absence' not 'absent mother,' what the child enacts through this play of repetition is an identification with the notion of disappearance, aphanisis, referred to *as* representation.[35] Significantly, however, Lacan repeats Freud's focalisation, repeats the fading of the maternal body, in order to make the game 'mean'. In his reading he merely exchanges her fading for the fading of the subject.

In a sense any image is the death because the negation of the thing, for it signifies that something was thought or recognised, not as real but as an image. This is most clear when an image is formed in the absence of an object. Negation, which for Freud is one representation of the death drive, engenders the peace which allows for thought and reflection.[36] Where processes of abstraction and generalisation presuppose negation, diverse forms of creativity make it possible to master that which is absent. One could argue that the revenge of Freud's playing child is articulated not only in the throwing away of the spool but already prior to that, in the designation of the spool as substitute of the mother – an act which replaces the mother with an image and in so doing negates her. The progressive interplay of negation and creation traces the following pattern. The child negates the maternal body by substituting it with a symbol (the reel) and an internal image. The mother and the observer (Sophie and Sigmund Freud) negate the symbol by translating it into a semantically coded signifier 'fort'. The second substitution undertaken by the observer (now without the mother's consenting interpretation), designates the 'fort' as figure for her absence, which opens the space for several explanations. Finally, the child substitutes the spool for its own self-image, negating the mother a second time, in this case as referent of the game.[37] What the child acquires is the representation of representation and an ability for infinite rendition of her image, severed for ever from her body – an autonomous and disposable representation.

In the mirror version of the child's game, the act of negation through substitution is taken one step further, for, by shifting from a symbolisation of the mother's absence to a staging of its own 'fort', the child doubles the disappearance of the mother, gliding from her to his own effacement.[38] Where the 'complete' game initially included the return ('da'), which always confirmed the absent body, this shift from reel (internal image of the mother) to self-image transfers the moment of reassuring return from the mother to the self. She, whose disappearance had initiated the game and who was its initial signified, now disappears, first (as signified) from the game (and from Freud's narration), and then, as the next footnote indicates, as point of reference in the material world: 'When this child was five and three-quarters, his mother died. Now that she was really "gone" (o-o-o) the little boy showed no signs of grief.' In an uncanny and disturbing manner the disappearence of the mother in the real world acts as return for a progressive substitution of disappearances of the figured maternal body in a child's game.

Symbolic play (representation) is both mastery over negation and grounded on negation. As Lacan puts it, the symbol 'manifests itself first of all as the murder of the thing'.[39] But what needs to be emphasised is that, regardless whether the final aim is abstraction and generalisation, reality-testing or the reliability of an internal representation, the site over which the grounding and mastering negation is negotiated is the maternal body, both figured and real.

Jacques Derrida has worked out a dimension usually neglected by other commentators – namely the investment and interest at stake for the triple personae, the speculator-narrator, the observer and the grandfather. Suggesting that this text may not only be about a child's game but rather also about a father's speculation (combining scientific observation, theoretical meditation, self-reflection and financial risk-taking) that hopes to turn loss into gain, Derrida focuses on the intersection between two moments – the autobiographical and the rhetorical strategy of self-reflexivity. For him the central concern of the text is the the self-presentation of re-presentation, the necessary return of and to the self. He suggests that Freud identifies structurally with the grandson Ernst's jealousy, using repetition as a means of repossessing. On the second footnote Derrida comments: 'This falling off would suggest that a dead woman is easier to keep for oneself: one's jealousy is relaxed and idealization interiorizes the object out of the rival's grasp. Thus Sophie, daughter and mother, is dead, preserved from *and* surrendered to each "sole possession." '[40] The analogy suggested is one between the child Ernst's game and Freud's work – in both instances the mother's disappearance is experienced as a narcissistic wound (the one primary, the other paternal) and engenders a play of signification (a spool and the chain of signifiers 'fort-da', a narrative and its footnotes). This is a play, furthermore, that both negates and returns the absent mother.

Returning again to Freud's text, one notices that the position of the second footnote, telling obliquely of Sophie Freud's death, is indeed a curious one. In order to support his second interpretation, that the child's game is an expression of revenge, Freud returns to another repetition of it – played a year later and now involving the father's absence. By suggesting that the child equates the pleasure gained from throwing a toy with that of the father's absence due to war, Freud attempts rhetorically to move away from a theory about symbolisation and its relation to the disruption of the mother/infant dyad caused by loss, toward one that links symbolization with anxiety about the father's intervention. This suggests that the mother's death can be acknowledged in Freud's text only at the exact moment when her structural position as ground of the child's ego construction is being effaced by that of the father. As yet another moment where this text structurally repeats the fading it narrates, the normative cultural narrative is here 'certified' by the disappearance of its alternative. Freud shifts from maternal loss to paternal castration, from the position of mourning to that of rivalry and possession. But, although he interprets this game as an expression of the child's desire not to be disturbed in his possession of the mother, he contradicts this interpretation with the claim in the footnote, that at the real 'loss' of the mother, the boy showed no signs of grief (*Trauer*).

What are the implications of the second footnote? What is the meaningful relationship between the comment on the boy's lack of mourning, his earlier lack of tears, his various games and Freud's various interpretations? Is it that the child's game was so successful, the symbols so valid, that the real event only confirmed them? Is this an instance of successful mourning by virtue of anterior decathexis? If this footnote is to support the idea of the child's revenge, what is the connection between revenge and desire for sole possession? If the analogical progression implied is that between a symbolic game of 'disappearance and return', substituting and repeating a mother's absence on the one hand, and no mourning, substituting and repeating a mother's real disappearance on the other hand, what exchange between figural and literal is being implied? For if we reconstruct the chronology of the events, a series of symbolic/linguistic repetitions is repeated by a real event, which in turn is subsumed back into a series of signification. A child plays with a symbol that displaces the mother, not only repeating her action of disappearing and returning, but already repeating her absence by exchanging her body with a symbol. This initiates a chain of substitutions which moves from symbol to signifiers, until it shifts to a second symbol, the child's own self-reflection, in turn occulting the signified 'mother' completely. Freud uses the narration of this game of disappearance and return, retracing in his interpretation the child's displacement of the signified mother through self-image and father until the mother's figural absence turns into her literal death and she reappears once more in the text, in a footnote.

What Freud significantly omits to say directly in this footnote is that the mother whose absence is repeatedly staged long before any real absence occurs is his daughter, and that the real loss ('wirklich "fort" (o-o-o)') to which the child Ernst responds by showing 'keine Trauer', is a loss Freud experienced as an insurmountable wound/offence to his narcissism, so that he had to postpone mourning ('that will come later') by replacing it with work. The work is that of completing (the last two chapters) and correcting the text in which the figural absence of the daughter/mother serves as inspiration for the grandson/son's first self-invented game and the father's conceptual coupling of the narcissistically wounding experience of the disappearance of the maternal body with a form of symbolic repetition that uncannily articulates both the notion of re-presencing return ('da') and self-absence ('bebi o-o-o'). The corrections following Sophie Freud's death must have included, if nothing else, precisely this *cryptic note* pertaining to her death, and this doubly absent referent (she is dead, she is not named) suggests that on some level Freud's speculations on the death drive form a narration in which his own compulsion to repeat, as an attempt at healing an injured narcissism, is itself implicated. The real loss is not just caught up in symbolisation but can also catch up with symbolisation. Though the manner in which it chooses to do so may be indeterminate, life reciprocates narratives. This is an uncanny moment – a term Freud after all uses to designate moments where the dead return, where something is repeated unintentionally, where castration anxiety but also a belief in the omnipotence of one's thoughts arise. For the rhetorical move that traces a trajectory of the symbol 'murdering' the object can ricochet back in the occurrence of material death.

Like a cryptic tombstone for his Sunday-child, the footnote brings the disappearing mother back into the interpretive game, even if in reference to her irrevocable absence. It repeats an absence rather than a presence: both the mother's absence and the repression of this absence which 'absents' the experience from the child's and Freud's consciousness.[41] With the 'da' of the footnote Freud in some sense returns to his initial model, which proposed symbolisation as contingent on and articulating maternal loss; the model which had been displaced by the game of the absent father. The footnote suggests that symbolic repetition and substitution can assuage the gap created by loss, and with it the anxiety about one's own mortality as well as the yearning for a state anterior to loss, while simultaneously re-presenting the absent lost body, if only as a trace marking its absence. The notion of return duplicitously articulates both a triumph over loss (death, narcissistic injury, castration) and its incompassability.

The work of writing as repetition in some sense always coexists with a negation of the real world for representation renders present what is absent, fashions itself out of an absence, which at the same time it specifically confirms. 'The work of writing', Green suggests, 'presupposes a wound and a loss, a work of mourning, of which the text is the transformation into a fictive positivity.' But this mastery of the pleasure principle, once introduced into the play of disappearance and return, is always ambivalent and incomplete. Representation affords pleasure in that it stands in for a lost satisfaction which is to be regained in an indirect manner. Yet if representation in one sense serves to negate loss, in another it emerges as the work of mourning.[42]

The rhetorical strategy of *Beyond the Pleasure Principle* is such that it self-reflexively repeats its thematic concerns. Repetition is doubly inscribed, for one by the death drive; directed toward a reduction of tensions; toward an original position of complete identity; toward the inanimate state anterior and posterior to life. It is also inscribed by the pleasure principle, directed toward the production of tension through division of unity; separation leading through the detour of substitution to the production of new unities. In this interstice repetition serves to acknowledge the death drive beyond the pleasure principle in the sense that the mother/infant dyad must be renounced and translated into supplementation because the division death threatens is always inherent in this pleasurable unity. Repetition serves a return to the pleasure principle in that its substitutions afford the means for a denial of the workings of death in life. The figure of division, however, not only breaks but also constructs. For the aporia inherent in all these narratives about ego development and the work of symbolisation is that the self can be constructed only over a narcissistic wound, division, difference and substitution serving as safeguard against the short-circuit (*Kurzschluß*) of premature death, of the prenatal static and inanimate position of identity with the surrounding body.

The dialectic within which repetition, grounded on or inspired by death, engages the survivor is one where the interplay of absence and presence of the maternal body (undoing even as it states the irrevocability of her 'fort') is embedded within a second matrix of presence/absence, the latter in respect to a return to equilibrium and control. If this game of 'fort–da' is about mastery over loss and absence, it also enacts the absence of mastery. The substitution made possible through acts of repetition like narration or symbolisation affords assurance in that either the lost loved object always returns in the form of some duplicate or the loss is replaced by some other loved object. But any form of substitution also fails to reassure precisely because it introduces a moment of difference. Freud writes to Binswanger on the birthday of Sophie, ten years after her death: 'Although we know that after such a loss the acute state of mourning will subside, we also know we shall remain inconsolable and will never find a substitute. No matter what may fill the gap, even if it be filled completely, it nevertheless remains something else. And actually this is how it should be. It is the only way of perpetuating that love which we do not want to relinquish.'[43] Repetition acts to cover up a narcissistic wound, but this wound ('unverwindbar') never heals without leaving its mark. The second footnote figures as just such a scar.

In the narratives that use the 'fort–da' game as privileged example for the child's acquisition of language, it functions as an allegory for the symbolic or linguistic mastery of sensations and drives. Commentators of this narrative posit that the origin of language and subjectivity is based on loss, on the figurative 'murder' of the body, the soma, the thing, the real; representation is grounded on absence of the object of reference. Culturation is understood as a deferral of pleasure, as a renunciation of instincts, as an entrance into the economy of substitution and the interplay of absence and re-presence, disappearance and return.

My argument is that the third value, which prevents a closed circuit, which prevents the stasis of the dyadic trap, need not be connected only to the sexually inscribed figure of the father (his name, law, phallus). The identity and unity of the mother/infant dyad is already constructed over a postnatal lacuna, figuring as substitute repetition of the first uteral unity, and the division threatening this unity is also that of death grounding life, of the mother's potential *Fortgehen*. Death, with repetition as its privileged figure, writes itself into life in two directions – towards an anterior position of inanimate unity and towards division and supplementation. While the reality principle injures narcissism, it is also through repetition that narcissism reasserts itself, tries to antidote the incision of the real by substituting it with images, with narratives, with objects. The protection of the ego works in two directions as well. It asserts itself against the castrative laws of social culture (which require the renunciation of primal aggressions and desires) and against the mortal laws of the real (which force a recognition of the limitation and finitude of human existence, its inherent trajectory toward decomposition). In Freud's words, the death instinct articulates itself in the fact that 'everything living dies for internal reasons . . . death is the aim of life' (38).

Freud locates the mortal threat to self-preservation in two different registers – society's prohibitions (the primordial dead father) and biological destiny (return to the inorganic state before birth, the maternal body of death). In *Ego and Id* (1923) he maintains this gender division, when he categorises castration anxiety in respect both to the threat and to the loss of a loved object (the maternal body) and to the threat of injury through or loss of the superego (the intervening father figure). The experience of a situation of danger is in some sense, he argues, the repetition of and thus the same as 'that which underlay the first great anxiety – state of birth and the infantile anxiety of longing – the anxiety due to separation from the protecting mother. These considerations make it possible to regard the fear of death, like the fear of conscience [*Gewissensangst*] as a development [processing, assimilation, *Verarbeitung*] of the fear of castration.'[44] Yet the notion of castration that is privileged in psychoanalytic theory is the one in reference to the Oedipal father (catalyst for an anxiety about sexual castration and about conscience) so that other 'castrative' anxieties, notably in respect to loss and death, are effaced.[45] My argument is that the former model (sexual castration, conscience) is negotiated over the figure of the dead father (a metonymy for culture), the latter over the figure of the disappearing/lost maternal body (metonymy for the real/reel of death), which is always already the repetition of an ambivalent play – indeterminate and unencompassable.

It is striking that this maternal body is caught in a series of absences, dis-appears, so to speak, far more than once. Its loss marks the initiation both into life and into culture, but, disappearing as significant paradigm from psychoanalytic discussion, the loss of the maternal body also grounds the privileging of the paradigm of the 'dead' Oedipal father. The maternal body can be conceived as an interstice for various moments of prohibition. Culture's law against incest literally forbids the maternal body as an object for sexual desire in order to assure a social bonding among families. But the maternal body is also forbidden in a figural sense, as a trope for the 'soma' which must be restrained or renounced by the child as it moves from the position of primary narcissism to that of the speaking subject bound by symbols and laws of the community. This maternal body must concretely disappear as an object of libidinal investment and be replaced with substitute love objects, while it is simultaneously 'sacrificed' as metonymy for the pre-symbolic state of pleasure, of unstructured and unrestrained instinctual gratification, outside the negating economy of society and the reality principle.

But, one can also conceive of the maternal body as 'forbidden' because originally site of and then privileged trope for the real loss or death which must be denied by the imaginary and symbolic registers. The mother assumes the status of trope for death because she recalls the position anterior to life so immediately connected with her body.[46] Renouncing the mother as first object of bonding is also occasioned by the physical necessity of her absence (potentially turning into concrete death), her disappearing from the child's presence. My discussion of the 'fort–da' episode showed how the maternal body is the site of death because of the way her disappearance brings notions of human mortality into play. Renouncing the unity with the maternal body means acknowledging our lack of wholeness and continuity. We fade before the play of signifiers and representations, externally impressed on our psychic apparatus, questioning our sense of uniqueness, originality and authenticity. But we also fade in the real sense that growing means degeneration. It is this non-gendered other 'no', death's ubiquitous castrative threat to the subject, which is connected to the maternal body and which is at stake in its disappearance.

The maternal body functions as a duplicitously pivotal site, since it combines the phallic with the castrated.[47] At first a symbiotic organiser, the mother offers the fantasy of a fusion or intact union. She seems to double the primordial mother by collapsing all distinctions between self and Other. She 'heals' the fragmented body, 'heals' the first loss marked by the navel and as such is the source of hope for ego stability and wholeness. As midwife of individuation, however, she is the source of disillusionment, forces upon the child a recognition of differentiation, loss, lack and so reaffirms the split she initially meant to deny. She wounds anew any sense of perfect and constant identity.[48] Owing to this ambivalence inherent in her function, she serves cultural discourses as privileged trope for the hesitation between confirmation and denial, between desire for a constant intact union, for perfection and identity and the acknowledgement of difference, of imperfection, misrecognition and insufficiency.

Furthermore, the renunciation of the maternal body grounds language acquisition and moral development in the sense that the erasure of the mother allows for a recognition of difference, of the split between self and the unconscious, of social laws and symbols; in short it engenders a recognition of Otherness.[49] While a discussion of what is specifically eliminated when the mother is put under erasure must wait for my later textual analyses, a general pattern can be determined. The 'erased' maternal body (already an imaginary refinding of the original lost object) is maintained in its substitute forms, in the many objects of desire that preserve the mature ego's narcissistically informed libidinal economy.

I have already indicated how Freud narrates the 'fort–da' game in such a way that the sacrifice of the daughter ultimately represents the renunciation of the mother. This collapsing of two feminine bodies will figure centrally in my discussion of narrative depictions of sacrificed daughters and lovers in later chapters. The erasure of the maternal, the symbolic exchange as 'murder of the soma', evolves into a repetition of this sacrificed unencompassable body of 'mother–materiality–death,' in the form of regained desired objects that are not only overdetermined but also insufficient. For these substitute or 'refound' objects of desire articulate what always recedes – the impossible union in life with the lost primordial – that is the impossibility of grasping death in images or symbols as well as the impossibility of receding from death's traces in life.

Given the fact that the theme of death is as basic to Freud's theory as the theme of sexuality, Pontalis suggests that the latter has been widely put forward so as to cover up the former. Freud's privileging of the Oedipal paradigm of castration anxiety based on sexual difference reveals 'his wish: if only the whole affair could be taken care of by Oedipus, and by a conquering of Oedipus'.[50] The non-reading of this other paradigm, which centres on the maternal body and on the anxiety of death, may be part of a strategy of denial necessary for a sense of self-preservation, correlative with Freud's often reiterated assertion that our unconscious cannot imagine our own mortality.

What would happen if we focused on this other narrative, on a notion of anxiety not based on sexual difference? In an effort to degender the castration concept and to propose a counter paradigm to Freud's dead father, Luce Irigaray describes the passage from intra-uterine life to birth, to the cutting of the umbilical cord, as an inevitable and irreparable wound, as the original scar, preceding all other threats of injury to the ego and all bonds between separate bodies. In her model, phallic erection is seen as a repetition of the earlier umbilical bond, in a manner similar to Green, who sees the 'reference to castration as castrising other forms of anxiety'.[51] She suggests that castration anxiety is an unconscious rememoration of the sacrifice which consecrates phallic erection as the unique sexuel value. For the shift away from privileging castration in reference to the phallus would allow us to avoid rekilling the mother who was sacrified at the origin of culture.[52] Privileging sexual difference in narratives about the interdependence between loss/separation and culturation/symbolisation, psychoanalytic discussions not only work to cover up the other theme, death, but also work by virtue of a strategy of double disappearance.

The narrations both of the dead father and of the dead maternal body serve as tropes for the passage from a state of undifferentiated heterogeneity to one structured on the principle of difference, substitution, deferral and renunciation. Both models suggest that the passage is enacted over murder, and because the reaction to the murdered family member hovers between veneration and denigration, the response to this act of violence couples self-affirming triumph with guilt. The central difference is that the repeated staging of the murder of the father explicitly and directly asserts his presence and power, even if as the figure of a 'murder of the thing'. As metonymy for society's codes and laws he is always securely positioned in the symbolic register, is conceived unambiguously as a signifier.

The story of the disappearing maternal body in the 'fort–da' episode, however, is one in which repetition evolves as an ambivalent play between absence and presence, for the repeated versions of the child's game hesitate between articulating and effacing the maternal body. Whereas in the repetition of the father's murder, the paternal body as signified always remains within the field of vision, the games with the maternal body are such that they engender a play between visibility and invisibility. The paradox lies in the fact that we don't see the maternal body even though and/or because it is so ostensibly and so insistently visually present in our culture's symbols and images. As I have already argued for von Max's painting the crux is that the 'maternal body,' and its surrogate, the 'feminine corpse,' fade over the display of this dead body.

At stake in the representations of the maternal body is the ambivalent and indeterminant shift between real body and image/symbol, as well as between real body of the mother and maternal body as figure for one's own soma. It is precisely this dialectic that 'returns' so uncannily when the narration about a daughter's *Fortgehen* turns into her real 'Fort'. While the forbidding father (and the notions of gender transmitted through his word) may castrate, this intervention is directed at securely positioning the subject within cultural codes and pro-hibitions. A mastery of the father figure ultimately means usurping his lot, or one in relation to him. Mastering the maternal body, on the other hand, means mastering the forbidden and the impossible, for the maternal body serves as a figure doubly inscribed by the death drive – as trope for the unity lost with the beginning of life and also as trope for loss and division always already written into life, pleasure and imaging.

What is put under erasure by the gendered concept of castration is the other, so often non-read theme of death, forbidden maybe because far less conducive to efforts of stable self-fashioning than notions of sexual difference. To see the phallus as secondary to the scar of the navel means acknowledging that notions of domination and inferiority based on gender difference are also secondary to a more global and non-individuated disempowerment before death. In the midst of all this aporia, it is no coincidence that this other theme, the theme of death, would be tied to the forbidden maternal body.

By tracing the theme of the dead feminine body in a variety of narrative and visual texts, I will use the following chapters to elaborate the implications for aesthetic and social symbolisation that have emerged from this theoretical dis-cussion. At the same time I hope to offer an apotropaic gesture against the feminine body's insistent and incessant fading within cultural representations, by making visible the excessively obvious but often non-read figure that crosses femininity with death.

Notes to Chapter 2

1 Letter to Oscar Pfister, 27 January 1920, quoted in M. Schur, 1972, p. 330.
2 S. Freud, 1923, writes: 'It would seem that the mechanism of the fear of death can only be that the ego relinquishes its narcissistic libidinal cathexis in a very large measure – that is, that it gives up itself, just as it gives up some external object in other cases in which it feels anxiety', pp. 58f.
3 The letter is dated 25 January 1920; see S. Freud, 1960, p. 343, my translation.
4 Quoted in E. Jones, 1953–7, vol. 3, p. 19.
5 Quoted in E. Jones, 1953–7, p. 19, letter dated 26 January 1920.
6 Quoted in M. Schur, 1972, p. 330. Both to his mother Amalie and to his friend Ludwig Binswanger he explains that what is at stake in this death is 'the monstrous fact of children dying before their parents', see M. Schur, 1972, p. 329.
7 S. Freud, 1960, p. 344, my translation.
8 Quoted in M. Schur, 1972, p. 330.
9 Quoted in E. Jones, 1953–7, pp. 19f.
10 For the original German letters see S. Freud, 1960, pp. 345f.
11 Quoted in S. Freud, 1985, pp. 201–2.

12 See S. Weber, 1982; and Jean Laplanche, 1976.

13 Quoted in M. Schur, 1972, p. 331. The quotation is from an Ode by Horace: 'If the sky should fall in pieces, the ruins will not daunt it.'

14 Quoted in E. Jones, 1953–7, p. 41, translation slightly modified.

15 Quoted in M. Schur, 1972, p. 329.

16 P. Gay, 1988, comments, 'Was it an accident that the term "death drive" – Todestrieb – entered his correspondence a week after Sophie Halberstadt's death? It stands as a touching reminder of how deeply the loss of his daughter had distressed him. The loss can claim a subsidiary role, if not in the making of his analytic preoccupation with destructiveness, then in determining its weight', p. 395. J. Derrida, 1979, disacknowledging an empiricobiographical explanation, nevertheless counters Freud's own denial: 'Still, we must begin by recognizing that Freud himself admits that the hypothesis of such a connection between the death drive and Sophie's death is not senseless, by the very fact that he anticipates it in order to defend against it', p. 140.

17 M. Schur, 1972.

18 E. Jones, 1953–7, p. 41.

19 S. Weber, 1982.

20 S. Freud, 1920, p. 7. My discussion focuses on chapter two, pp. 14–17. It is interesting to note that Freud begins his discussion, which ultimately leads towards thoughts on death, with a discussion of the validity of an economic model.

21 See S. Freud's discussion, 1919, of the 'uncanny'. He defines *das Unheimliche* as a mode of expression that articulates two opposite sentiments, for example the familiar and the strange, anxiety and desire. Since the concept is germane to my own discussion, I will offer a longer analysis of it in later chapters, and, though the English translation 'uncanny' does not fully correspond to the connotations inherent to the German *das Unheimliche*, I will be using the two terms interchangeably, but always in relation to Freud's definition.

22 M. Bal, 1985.

23 The emphasis is mine. Later in the text Freud will mitigate this statement by adding, 'It is of course a matter of indifference from the point of view of judging the effective nature of the game whether the child invented it himself or took it over on some outside suggestion', p. 15.

24 See J. Kristeva, 1984, p. 75.

25 It is worth bearing in mind that Freud's attention was initially drawn to this 'child's habit' of throwing objects (before he knew it was a game) because it was disturbing, imposing on the caretakers the 'often not easy task' of recollecting the toys. If it was the mother who was chiefly responsible for caretaking, the game forced her attention away from the observer, her father, and focused it on the child.

26 See P. Widmer, 1984.

27 See S. Freud, 1917.

28 This is a similar duplicity to the one developed in by S. Freud, 1912–13, where the repetition of the death of the father marks a triumph over the father even as it articulates guilt, and thus the triumph of the father over the murdering sons.

29 M. Klein, 1975a, pp. 219–232. It is interesting, as an aside, to note that Dick also plays with trains, and trains, in Freud's interpretation of dreams, are common symbols for death, like the word *fort*.

30 M. Klein, 1975a, p. 347, my italics.

31 M. Klein, 1970, p. 278.

32 D. W. Winnicott, 1975, p. 68.

33 J. Lacan, 1977, pp. 1–7.

34 The seminal duplicity in the concept of the Other/other resides in the fact that this 'Other' can either mark the moment of complete alterity or, as imaginary 'other', reflect the self. This division is never straightforward, and I will add to it the notion of uncanny Other, canny Otherness in later chapters.

35 J. Lacan, 1981, pp. 62f.

36 E. Rechardt, in A. Green, 1986b.

37 M. Safouan, 1983, explains that the staged absence opens a field where ' "to be" is dissociated from "to be perceived" and becomes synonymous with "to be thought" ', p. 57. See also the discussion of the 'fort–da' game in J. Laplanche and S. Leclaire, 1975.

38 This move parallels the one Freud undertakes in his letters to Jones after Sophie Freud-Halberstadt's death, shifting from her death to statements on his own mortality.

39 J. Lacan, 1968, p. 84.

40 J. Derrida, 1978 p. 140.

41 I take the formulation from S. Rimmon-Kenan, 1980, who applies it, however, only to the child's game.

42 A. Green, 1978.

43 Quoted in L. Freeman and Dr H. S. Strean, 1987, p. 72.

44 S. Freud, 1923, p. 59.

45 Although he does not refer to the scenario of the 'fort–da' game, A. Green, in an article entitled 'The Dead Mother', 1986a, proposes that one should also discuss the dead mother from a structural point of view. See also J. Choron, 1964 who cites psychoanalytic studies that demonstrate that 'children are traumatized by the experience of death just as they are by the primal scene . . . an interesting conclusion by the authors is that Freud's assertion that the unconscious does not seem to contain anything that would lend substance to the concept of annihilation of life has put a taboo on the subject of death in psychoanalytic literature', p. 143.

46 S. Freud, 1913, writes 'One might say that the three inevitable relations man has with woman are . . . the three forms taken on by the figure of the mother as life proceeds: the mother herself, the beloved who is chosen after her pattern, and finally the mother Earth who receives him again', p. 301.

47 See J. Kristeva, 1980, pp. 237–70 and J. Gallop's discussion of the phallic mother, 1982, pp. 113–31.

48 See J. R. Greenberg and S. A. Mitchell, 1983, pp. 270–303, for a discussion of Margaret Mahler's work on motherhood.

49 See M. Homans's discussion of the mother's body as first absent referent, as grounding laws and language, 1985. In a similar vein J. Kristeva, 1987b, speaks of the sadness of children prior to language acquisition, for they must renounce the maternal paradise in which every demand was immediately gratified. Language begins in a mourning inherent in the evolution of subjectivity.

50 J. B. Pontalis, 1978, p. 90. See also E. Becker, 1973, who argues that 'culture was built upon repression – not because man was a seeker only of sexuality, of pleasure, of life and expansiveness, as Freud thought, but because man was also primarily an avoider of death. Consciousness of death is the primary repression, not sexuality', p. 96.

51 A. Green, 1986a, p. 145. In this connection it is interesting to recall Aristophanes' tale

of the origin of sexuality in Plato's Symposium, to which Freud has recourse at the end of his discussion. After Zeus cut all human beings in half, he asked Apollo to turn each face, 'with the half neck that was left, toward the side that was cut away – thinking that the sight of such a gash might frighten it into keeping quiet – and then to heal the whole thing up . . . but he left a few puckers round about the belly and the navel, to remind us of what we suffered long ago', Plato, 1961, p. 543.

52 L. Irigaray, 1981, pp. 11–33.

3

Violence of representation – representation of violence

Everything moral is bound to life in its drastic meaning, namely where it fulfills itself in death as the absolute site of danger. And this life, which concerns us morally, and that means concerning us in our individuality, appears from the position of all art production as negative, or should at least appear thus. Because art in turn can in no sense allow that to its works be attributed the function of an advisory conscience hence letting the represented thing be seen rather than the representation.
Walter Benjamin

Between February 1914 and January 1915 the Swiss painter Ferdinand Hodler made over seventy sketches, gouaches and oil paintings of his mistress Valentine Godé-Darel, as she was dying of cancer. She was buried on 27 January 1915 in Vevey, near Geneva. During her illness Hodler wrote to his friend Mühlestein, 'This beautiful head, this whole body, like a Byzantine empress on the mosaics of Ravenna – and this nose, this mouth – and the eyes, they too, those wonderful eyes – all these the worms will eat. And nothing will remain, absolutely nothing!'[1] Hodler's sketches and paintings meticulously document the progess of her illness – her loss in body weight, the alteration in her skin colouring, her change from an upright posture, implicitly responding to her viewer, to the horizontal position of the body caught in the pain of dying, drawn within itself, the eyes averted. In several cases he made more than one sketch a day, depicting the same posture from different angles, or duplicating the same angle while changing the drawing technique; moving from sketch to oil painting, from oil on wax cloth or paper, to oil on canvas. On 26 January, the day after her death, Hodler made one sketch and five oil paintings of the corpse on paper and canvas. A final frontal portrait of Godé-Darel, painted six months after her death, depicts her cleansed from all traces of illness and dying, as if resurrected as an immaculate image in Hodler's memory.[2] In comparison to earlier portraits the style of this last painting is almost two-dimensional, reminiscent of Byzantine mosaics. The first exhibition of individual paintings from this series was in Zürich in 1917, and since then most of the paintings and some of the sketches have been on display, though they were shown together for the first time in an exhibition in 1976 which commemorated the Swiss artist precisely in his relation to Valentine Godé-Darel.

I will use this sequence of images as a third example of how a representational corpus is called forth by and recalls a feminine corpse. I will not, however, undertake an analysis of Hodler's representation of death, depicting the process of the fading within which Godé-Darel's cancer-ridden body is caught. Rather I will turn to a third aspect of our culture's need to ground theoretical and aesthetic representation on the displayed 'erasure' of the feminine. By addressing the issue of how different discourses, depending on their epistemological and political interest, in turn represent the interrelation between death, femininity and aesthetisation, my aim in this final introductory chapter is to ask, how can we look at, how can we speak about representations of feminine death? How can we make this event speakable? Does articulating death always mean turning it into a meaningful event, into a narrative moment? How is the meaning of the represented death process as a sequence of events contingent on the discursive position of its spectators? How is it inscribed by each focalisor's interest? Although I will develop these questions in response to visual representations, my discussion of the positionality of meaning already anticipates the analysis of literary representations that will follow. And it does so not least of all because the serial quality of these images is such that it provokes a narrative reading. Meaning is produced on the basis of a semantic encoding of the sequentiality of these

 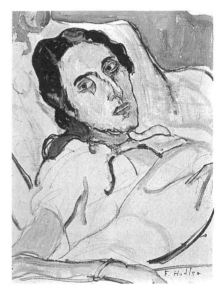

Fig 2 Ferdinand Hodler. *Bildnis Valentine Godé-Darel* (1914)

Fig 3 Ferdinand Hodler. *Die kranke Valentine Godé-Darel* (1914)

Fig 4 Ferdinand Hodler. *Studie zur sterbenden Valentine Godé-Darel, Halbfigur, Rechtsprofil* (1915)

Fig 5 Ferdinand Hodler. *Die sterbende Valentine Godé-Darel, Rechtsprofil* (1915)

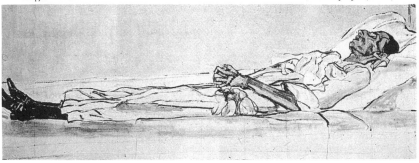

Fig 6 Ferdinand Hodler. *Die tote Valentine Godé-Darel* (26 January 1915)

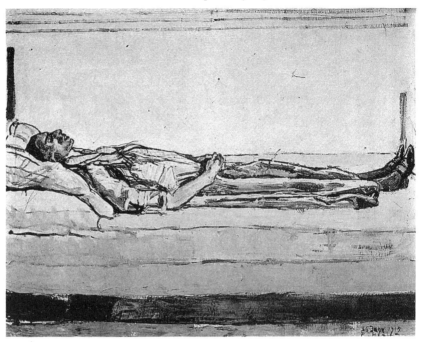

Fig 7 Ferdinand Hodler. *Die tote Valentine Godé-Darel* (26 January 1915)

Fig 8 Ferdinand Hodler. *Sonnenuntergang am Genfersee, von Vevey aus* (1915)

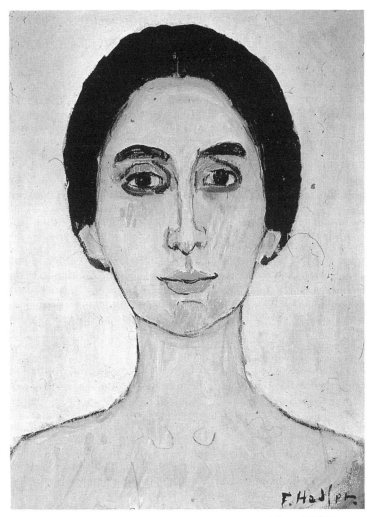

Fig 9   Ferdinand Hodler. *Bildnis Valentine Godé-Darel, frontal* (1915, post-humous)

images as events and on each external focalisor's (the critic's) identification with the internal focalisor (the present though non-figured artist), the focalised object (the dying model), both or neither.

As I was doing my preliminary research on Hodler's representation of the death of Valentine Godé-Darel, I encountered two contradictory positions that probably make up the extreme poles of reaction to and critical reception of this sequence of images. On the one hand a young male art historian repudiated my intention to discuss the violence inherent in any aesthetic transformation of the experience of death as a mistaken and depreciative approach. For him these sketches and paintings were 'beautiful', 'skillfully made'. Because he insisted that there was nothing violent about these paintings, he also rejected the validitiy of analysing them from this theoretical perspective. Clearly there was nothing real for him about the way death was represented or figured in this cycle, as though the formal construction of an image could ever be completely severed from its subject matter. Even though death is understood by our culture, in René Girard's words 'as the worst violence that the human being is subjected to' – or maybe because of this fact – the art historian denied that death in its threatening aspect was represented in Hodler's images.[3] In this way he could foreclose and also resist my questions, namely whether every representation of dying is not violent precisely because it implies the safe position of a spectator ('voyeur') and because a fragmentation and idolisation of the body – i.e. a severing of the body from its real materiality and its historical context ('fetishism') – is always built into such images. The body – always already the site of exterior and alterior inscriptions – is explicitly exposed as such an inscribed site when it is in the process of dying, so that in representations of the dying body this 'alterior' inscription is doubled through aesthetisation. For the art historian, the exclusively aesthetic perspective had the function of confirming a stability in his viewing of these images. This allowed him to exclude any reference to a potentially destabilising non-symbolic real, and allowed him to establish a secure and stable relation between himself and these representations.

On the other hand a woman photographer, who, against her will so to speak, had to reproduce these images from the exhibition catalogues, thereby repeating Hodler's act as producer of copies of these images, argued from a diametrically opposed position. She had found the job 'horrible' and pitied the 'poor woman'. It wasn't clear from her statement whether she meant the historical Valentine Godé-Darel, and if so, whether she found the way in which she had to die, or that she had to die horrible, or whether it was the fact that she was sketched and painted while dying that offended her. Or whether she simply meant the images, that is simply found 'horrible' (inadequate, unskilful) the way Godé-Darel was represented, or whether she meant me, as the woman who has to study and describe these 'horrible' images. This position is in turn informed by a diffuse identification with the pain of the model, a response that comes about through the exclusion of an aesthetic spectatorship.

I will leave aside the question whether the gender of the speakers was significant in determining the position from which they responded to these images. Both are partially blind. Does the photographer let herself see something which the art historian, for whatever reasons, is blind to? Does she, in turn, miss something, when she sees and speaks about the 'horrible' which he does not see?

This sequence of representations of a dying woman places us as spectators in the interstice between an aesthetic and an empathetic response. The choice we are faced with seems to be as follows. Should one assume the position of a morally involved spectator, treating the represented body as though it were the same as the material body it refers to, focusing, that is, on the question of reference and in so doing denying the representational aspect? From this position, these images appear monstrous because, in some way inadequate to the demands of the real, losing the real so to speak to the needs of a representational unity. Or should one assume the position of the aesthetically involved specator, distanced, disinterested, treating the representation of a dying body only as a signifier pointing to many other signifiers; judged on the basis of comparison with other signifiers (previous images in the painter's oeuvre, in the image repertoire of his culture); foreclosing the question of the real? The question then becomes: need these two positions – the one producing the meaning of a representation in relation to its point of reference in the material world, the other producing meaning in relation to other signifiers – be mutually exclusive? Can we formulate a position of spectatorship that could encompass both moments? One would then neither occlude the real of the represented body, in the sense of the real as marking a moment where unity and individuality is punctured but which is also univocal in its meaning because beyond semiotic categories. Nor would one hide the inability to represent the real of a dying body, in the sense of representation as always being whole, unified and at the same time grounded on a slippage and multiplicity of meaning. What the two contradictory reactions point out is the polysemy of possible readings. Interpretations, as a form of semantic encoding, bind these images, because meaning can emerge only from such binding of freely floating signifiers. But any one semantic fixage, though elicited, is not intrinsically offered by the images themselves.

On the contrary, the 'instability' of these images, their withdrawal from any semantically fixed encoding, such as the labelling 'beautiful' or 'horrible' would imply, entails not only their fascination. It is precisely this 'instability' which also allows for a conceptual entrance into the interstice of violence and the production of images. Do these images unsettle us because they confront the spectator relentlessly with the process of dying or because the ultimately private process of mourning was made public through the act of representation? Do they unsettle us because, as traditional aesthetics claims, art can create and enlarge sympathy with the pain of the other? Or do they scandalise us because they force us to engage with the obscenity of death? Can we even localise the unsettling quality emitted by these images? The loss and the gain of each interpretation must be delineated in order for us to make the interests and the limits of each approach visible.

As Elaine Scarry has argued, 'the inherent instability of the verbal (and visual) sign is that a representation can work in two ways; it can coax real pain into visibility or push it into further invisibility'.[4] Furthermore, what is intensely real to the dying body is intensely unreal to the spectator of this dying body (be this Hodler or us). I will focus on two moves undertaken by discussions of these paintings as they 'double' the moves undertaken by the paintings themselves: namely an attempt to re-stabilise one's position in the world when faced with an event as destabilising as that of death *and* the failure inherent in such an undertaking.

The 'closure' that occurs at the end of the image sequence can be read as a triumph, a resurrection of the dead woman by the mourning painter. This substitution can be seen as part of what cultural anthropology calls the 'second burial', which marks the end of the liminal period of bodily decomposition. The fully decomposed body is buried a second time, or the decomposing body is laid to rest, clearly severed from the living and firmly replaced by a stable image/sign of that body, in the form of funerary sculptures, portraits or gravestones.[5] But the end of this sequence can also be read as a failure on the part of the artist to re-present the real of Godé-Darel's death, without resorting to a figuration that on some level always denies or eliminates this real.

For one of the central questions seems to be – what do we see when we see these images? Does Godé-Darel become visible? Is her experience of dying transmitted? The paradox is the following. In order to be 'sharable', her experience of the death process has to be translated beyond the boundaries of her real body – the private into a public world of signs – but this act of figuration or representation also forecloses the real. The 'unsharability' of pain results from its resistance to language. Transforming the real body experience of death into an objectified form mitigates the violence posed by the real. Hence such a trans-formation can be seen as a personal or cultural strategy of self-preservation. The threat that real death poses to any sense of stability, wholeness, individual uniqueness or immortality is antidoted through representations that 'exteriorise' this real by transferring it on to an image/signifier. The paradox is heightened by virtue of the fact that the 'fixing' which occurs in the act of representation is a captation, in Lacan's sense of the *point de capiton*, by which, at certain privileged points, the mobility of the chain of signifiers comes to be arrested or fixed on to a signified.[6] At the same time it is also a puncturing, in Barthes's sense of the *punctum* or obtuse meaning, as a moment or detail of an image that wounds any obvious meaning, that points beyond semantic fixture, because it is discontin-uous, indifferent to the narrative, and has 'at least a distancing effect with regard to the referent, to "reality" as nature'.[7] As such the *punctum* disturbs because it opens up a plurality of meaning and reference. One instability, that of the forces of the real, is exchanged for another, semantic instability (or rather polysemy). The translation into representation is one that permits a break with the material referent of the signifier – and in the gap that is opened it can refer either to the real body, to a gliding chain of culturally coded signifiers or to the producer of the representation.

Whose experience is being shared in these images – the dying woman's, the viewing lover's, the painter's? All three? Because there are two axes of reference involved in representation, the real experience of dying remains invisible to others or rather, the visual images makes the experience 'visible' even as they exclude the real aspect of it. On the one hand there is the axis between the signifier of the representation and other signifiers – the image repertoire of the artist, the spectators, their culture, which includes a concept of reality as constructed in the act of experience. On the other hand there is the axis of reference between the signifier and a non-symbolic real, the material world as it falls outside semiotic categories. The choice the spectator is faced with seems to be that of either focusing on the real, and thus momentarily disrupting language (*punctum*) or focusing on language, and that means momentarily erasing the real (*point de capiton*). On the one hand, focusing on the violence engendered by the move from a real body to a sign makes one blind to the aesthetic issue of representation, which involves only the relation between various clusters of signifiers. On the other hand, focusing exclusively on representations of violence engendered by the relation between signifiers, on the aesthetic rendition of violence severed from any real body, makes one blind to the concrete physicality of someone else's dying.

The question 'is Godé-Darel and her death made visible or invisible through these images?' prompts me to ask further, does seeing one dimension preclude, exclude or include another? Do we decide which dimension (s) we see based on something inherent in these images, or based on a non-representational demand – be this general cultural education, theoretical concerns, ethical or political interests? It is not just a question of what the image refers to but why some real process, in this case death, is visible or not, and what this process of seeing or not seeing entails.

I will first briefly sketch the 'standard' critical discussion of this so-called cycle, concentrating on Jura Brüschweiler's introductory essay to his exhibition catalogue; not least because it includes the commentary by other art historians preceding his work. I will then offer a feminist critique of this approach only to finish by criticising my own critique, in order to suggest that the problem of representations of violence or death is one that demands a shifting between positions; a suspension of the 'either/or' spectatorial stance suggested above.

The title of Jura Brüschweiler's exhibition catalogue is significantly: 'A painter between love and death. Ferdinand Hodler and Valentine Godé-Darel. A cycle of works 1908–1915.'[8] We can sketch two trajectories in this undertaking. On the one hand Brüschweiler claims to want to redress a mishap in the history of art, namely collect all the paintings of Godé-Darel and to present the facts of her life and her relationship with Hodler as objectively and thoroughly as possible. He uncovers what had to remain hidden for years, since Godé-Darel had been the mistress of Hodler and mother of his illegitimate daughter. Owing to this circumstance, these pictures were initially private and the exhibition in 1976 presented many of them to the public for the first time. This means that we see these images always detached from their original context, their 'private' quality for us as belated viewers is not reconstructable. One could speak about a certain violence on the part of the exhibition organisers in their translocation of private paintings into a public space. More important, however, is that this points to the fact that in our spectatorship we are always already dealing with a cultural construction of a painter and his paintings. This cultural construction, including the obliteration of the differences between private and public works, as well as the individualistic notion of the 'author', transforms the images into a narrative. Speaking about these paintings means not only speaking belatedly, but also from another site; means treating them textually.

This leads to the second trajectory of Brüschweiler's undertaking; the fictionalisation of the real of death. The title of the catalogue already indicates that the acting subject is 'the painter', the objects, in relation to which his action, and he as actor are established, are 'love and death'. From the very beginning the allegorical figuration of this event in Hodler's life is privileged over the historically real personages (named second in the title). A reference to the body's materiality, the facticity of the two people involved in this exchange is immediately subordinated to a significatory process concerned with the cultural construction of an artist figure. Brüschweiler's intention – to document objectively and thoroughly – subverts into the allegorical portrait of a painter faced with death. He in fact admits that he reads these images like 'a sequence of episodes in a Stendhal novel' (13). He reconstructs historical events on the basis of representations and not the other way around. In that he moves from a literary text to the historical events, these events always already take on the position of being supplementary to any historical event.

As he describes both Godé-Darel and Hodler it becomes clear that while there is little material on her marriage, living conditions, work, experiences during her illness, there is a plethora of material on him. More important, the historical occultation of Godé-Darel is doubled by the discussion of her, in the course of which, by virtue of a reduction to her first name 'Valentine', she is already deindividualised into the 'beloved' in the classical tradition of the muse; comparable to Dante's 'Beatrice' or Petrarch's 'Laura'.[9] Furthermore, the signifier 'Valentine Godé-Darel' (referring to a historical individual) is progressively replaced by the non-personal signifiers 'femininity', 'vulnerability', 'mortality'. On top of this a second form of occultation of the real Valentine Godé-Darel occurs. Brüschweiler postulates that Hodler begins to draw self-portraits after a twelve- year break when faced with her illness and dying, because he can paint himself only from the recognition of the 'ephemerality of life, the foolishness of fame and glory'.[10] If the self-portraits must necessarily be seen in relation to Godé-Darel's dying (as Brüschweiler argues), it seems to follow that the representations of her dying must also be seen in relation to his self-representation. The images of the dying Valentine Godé-Darel become in a sense 'self-portraits', because over her dying body the artist can recognise and give figure to his own mortality. The duplicitous nature of such self-representation is interesting – for by depicting the dying body of another as, in a displaced sense, a signifier for the survival of the gazing and painting artist, Hodler also gives articulation to his own mortality. As in von Max's painting, self-representation occurs over an identification with the decomposing, fading body of another, even as it defies the notion of mortality.

The aim of Brüschweiler's discussion is to see this cycle of paintings as an example of the artist's heroic confrontation with death, as an experience of liminality, which initiated a new period of creative genius in Hodler. In his discussion he, therefore, does not privilege the real dying of the represented body, but rather the skill with which these images render this body. The analogy on which he focuses his attention is the one between the way in which the cancer inscribes its traces on the body of Godé-Darel and the way the painter inscribes his lines on the canvas – the body of the dying woman becoming a cipher for the mutually constitutive relation between decomposition (through cancer) and representational composition (as re-composition of the ultimately absent, decomposed body). In Brüschweiler's discussion death on the one hand, art on the other, figure as the displaced signifiers for these images – and in both cases they are to be seen in relation to the painter's reactions – his despair when faced with death, his ability to translate death into adequate brushstrokes, his courage when triumphing over death in the act of painting.

This discussion decomposes Godé-Darel a second time by denying her signification. It is not her dying, her courage, her despair which are read as the signifieds of these representations. Rather at stake is the artist's emotional response, the artist's prowess when faced with death. Furthermore, Brüschweiler does not see the particular death of Valentine figured in these images but rather death in general, effacing her ever more. The artist does not look into Godé-Darel's face, but rather, over her body, looks death in the face. The dying woman functions as mediatrix between the painter and the absolute. The signified of the signifier 'dying/dead' Godé-Darel is neither just the histori-cal woman, nor femininity, but also death as it constitutes the artist.

Yet another occultation of Godé-Darel occurs in Brüschweiler's discussion, when he constructs the relationship with the landscapes Hodler supposedly drew on the day of her death, for the sequence is then seen as signifying the dissolution of the human body into nature. The parallelism reassuringly suggests that there is ultimately no distinction to be drawn between death, the corpse, woman, land-scapes. The trajectory of his discussion is aimed at de-individualising the real body referred to in these representations, at diminishing the material physicality of the model in favour of an allegorical reading that re-establishes the image of the artist and the concept of the human process as a stable one. The reading he offers of this cycle is one that ultimately re-establishes a stable order. The threat and disruption caused by death is conceptually foreclosed by translating this bodily event into the allegorical story of the decomposed body reunited with nature, and the disrupting experience of death on the part of the artist is one that initiates a new artistic phase. In the words of another art historian: 'with this cycle, Hodler has set a monument to his empathetic, not sympathetic ability, so unique that no rival can be found'.[11] The signifieds that are attributed to these representations of a woman dying include death, as a global or abstract figure; the artist's unique empathetic and creative ability; the liberation of the artist's creative talent; the staging of a perfect unity between artistic means and artistic expression. Yet effaced in each case is the subjectivity of the dying woman, her position within the death process, her body and her pain.

The 'standard' discussion of this sequence of images, then, interprets them as signifying the artist's self-portrait, his confrontation with death, but grounds this reading on an occultation of the feminine body. The second position or discursive space I now want to sketch is one that would in turn revolve around the following question. Why does this account appear to be so violent? Is it because this construction of the artist as hero, this movement from the literal into the figural, suppresses another dimension of violence, namely that which can be attributed to the material, non-symbolic real?

Teresa de Lauretis argues that representations of violence cannot be separated from notions of gender, because the meaning that a certain representation of violence assumes is dependent on the gender of the violated object being depicted. To demonstrate to what degree violence is 'en-gendered' by discourses, she discusses Jurij Lotman's theory of plot typology, according to which a text contains two characters, one a mobile hero whose movement through plot/space establishes differences and norms and the other an immobile obstacle or boundary, representing a function of this space. This second, closed space can, according to Lotman, be interpreted as grave, cave, house, woman, with the corresponding features of darkness, warmth, dampness. Entry into this space can be interpreted as death, conception, return home, and 'all these acts are thought of as mutually identical'.[12]

De Lauretis points to the fact that in this typology the hero must be masculine because the obstacle must be feminine. Furthermore the feminine is always identified with the inanimate, immobile space which, functioning as a boundary, cannot constitute itself as hero/subject. As such it does not have its own meaning but rather produces meaning for another. It is this equation of feminine and object which de Lauretis sees as the locus of a 'rhetoric of violence'.

If we apply her discussion to the cycle of paintings we can arrive at a different reading from the one suggested by Brüschweiler. As in Lotman's typology we have a hero, the artist, who gains his meaning based on an entry into and re-emergence from an enclosed space – the feminine space of Godé-Darel's death. What Brüschweiler simply states – namely the rhetorical transformation of Godé-Darel's body into an inanimate figure, with a semantic coding that is exterior to any personally chosen meaning – is, from the position de Lauretis occupies, an example of rhetorical violence.

From this discursive position, the heroic attempt of the painter to recognise death over the body of his dying beloved, to fulfil his mourning through painting this body, looks like an expropriation of the feminine body, a reduction of this body to an object externally coded; an act, furthermore, marking the site of his prowess, his imagination, his creativity. What is violent about this rhetoric is that it displaces the point of view on to a formal level; that the pain, the courage of the dying woman is subordinated to notions of artistic ability and aesthetic effect. This is a form of violence which stages the absence of violence, a move that allows the painter and spectator to ignore the painful battle of a dying woman. It allows a blindness toward the real by privileging the beautiful play of forms, lines, colours. From this position it seems as though Hodler were denying Godé-Darel her pain, her individual meaning, a possibility of signifying other than in relation to him. The death of the woman appears as condition and pretext for a meaning that lies elsewhere and allows the painter and spectator a stable position before the death of the other and thereby implicitly his or her own death.

However, Lacan emphasises that the subject is not constituted in the stabilising imaginary order but rather based on a break or gap in the imaginary relation with the Other, in the repetition of the lost primordial object, the 'objet a'. The self-reflexivity inherent in these images is potentially of a different nature from that argued by Brüschweiler. It is a self-reflexivity that articulates how the triumph or jubilation inherent in any imaginary relation – the stabilising and securing of the 'I' – is always connected to a self-conscious realisation of the subject as split. For the imaginary relation to work over it as detour, the 'objet a' (which is re-enacted in any form of image-making), must always be split off from the subject and it both confirms the viewing and image-making subject in his wholeness *and* indicates his own split – his being signed by death, by that exteriorised Other space. Godé-Darel's fading before death in the form of cancer, her fading before a signifying chain that transforms her lines into the lines of a landscape can then also be read as an allegory for the way the subject is constituted as he enters language, for in so doing he fades (*aphanisis*) before the gliding chain of signification.[13] Such a reading continues to obscure the reality of her death, though the image of self gained through the process of identification with the Other is not that of a stable and whole self or a stable position before death but rather the instability of one's position in life, because always already carrying traces of death.

Depending on the position from which we view, we are dealing either with a violent decomposition of a female body through cancer or with a violent rhetoric which effaces the real pain through an allegorising gaze. For do we ask ourselves, are these paintings skilfully done? Or do we ask ourselves, does the woman suffer? Do we see the woman's pain? Can we really see this pain? Do we see the real, while denying the representation or do we see the representation, thus putting the real under erasure? This is, furthermore, a form of figuration which, using the feminine body as a displaced signifier for masculinity, in this case in its confrontation with death, effaces the femininity of the depicted body. This leads to the seminal question underlying my own inquiry – what is being sacrificed in this act of aesthetisation – the *real* violence of dying, the woman or femininity?

But – to introduce my own self-criticism – if we highlight this blindness which seems so common to discussions of images of women; if we highlight this partisan view towards the literal quality of images, towards the reference to a body external to signs, or rather, if we emphasise the rhetorical violence inherent in discussions of representations of women that use these images as displaced signifiers for something semantically external and other to femininity – if we do this in our critique, do we not ourselves glide into a form of blindness? Because even if it is valid and urgent to speak about the feminine body as cipher for the artist–hero, what remains, if we shift our position, is the dying body of a woman. To point out the violence inherent in constructions of masculinity, making violence the privileged signified of these representations, ultimately also, in its turn, hides the real violence of the process of dying.

A way out of this impasse may be not only to emphasise the relation between various sets of signifiers (and as such the displacement of femininity through masculinity) but rather to explore also the relation between signifiers and body. I will, therefore, not only analyse the cultural, political and aesthetic norms negotiated over the dead body of a woman, for which this feminine corpse serves as displaced signifier, but also include examples where the rhetoric of representation is such that figuration collapses into the literal and the material. My discussion of the 'fort–da' game has shown that symbolisation is based on an ambivalent and indeterminant shift between real body and substituting image or symbol. The body serves as a duplicitous intermediary in the relation between language and the material world. The real body is positioned before or beyond semiosis. As that which is replaced by signs and images, it can serve as the medium through which language hooks back into the world, through which it returns to the referential. But because the body marks a site of real insertion into the world, it also serves to establish social laws and allows culture to materialise ideas. The word turning flesh can serve to establish and authenticate a political, theoretical or aesthetic discourse. Focusing on this conflation of the real with the semiotic, Valie Export argues that the language of the body as present is merged with the language of the body as absent, in the triumph of culturation *as* body, which is also a triumph *over* the body.[14] The body, even as it encompasses the pre- or nonsemiotic real, is always also positioned within the symbolic register of the reality principle: as a cultural construction inscribed by alterior or exterior meanings; as a culturated body; as a figurative extension and transformation of the real.

Hodler's representations of dying sketch the following dynamic. The non-semiotic real breaks into, disrupts a stable presentation of self and is immediately translated or transferred back into the demands of representation. Its heterogeneity must be sacrificed to the representational demands for unity. That this dynamic is given figure at a dying body is no coincidence. Blanchot points out that the corpse initially marks a moment of total destabilisation of categories like position, site and reference; that death suspends relations with the place; that the cadaver is not in its place, not here and yet it is not elsewhere.[15] A stability of categories must again be recuperated, namely in the act of representation, so that we move from the experience of decomposition to composition, from the dying body/corpse to a representation and narration of the dying body/corpse.

The corpse can be understood as a representative of the order of the real, which Lacan defines as beyond semiotic, imaginary or symbolic categories: as 'that which is – minus its representation, description or interpretation'.[16] It belongs to what Kristeva has called the 'semiotiké', a violent force disrupting the symbolic order, which must be repeatedly transferred into culture through a sacrifice. This 'semiotiké' is nevertheless preserved, though regulated in the forms of exteriorisation, erasure, repression. The 'semiotiké' is not so much pre-symbolic as enmeshed with and never detachable from the symbolic it breaks into, so that language is understood as a self-protective structural violence, as 'murder of the soma', while the somatic, the 'semiotiké', in turn perpetually endangers the stability of the symbolic categories, laws, norms, images that sustain and support culture.[17]

Within such a theoretical frame Hodler's representations of a dying and dead feminine body can be seen as a dynamic interplay with violence. While one image could conceivably have a stabilising, securing effect, the sequence exemplifies how the violence of the real is translated only precariously into representations. As a *point de capiton*, representation attempts to attach the dying, decomposing body, destabilising in its mobility, to a fixed semantic position. The 'arrêt de mort' enacted in this sequence not only encompasses the final arrestation of the living body into a corpse, but also includes a form of captation which arrests death as process or drive into a semantically stable image of death.[18] But along with the fact that any image is stable only to a certain degree and as the result of its focalisor's efforts or projections, it is the sequentiality or narrative, the obsessive repetition enacted by this sequence, which disrupts its own gesture of representational unity. This cycle of paintings stages the necessary translation (captation) of the violent real (the death of the Other) into a fixing signifier, i.e. the necessary sublation of the literal into the figural. It points out the protection that an allegorising gaze affords, when it renders real violence as *figure* of death, of mortality, of unity between self and world. At the same time the sequentiality inherent in Hodler's images enacts the failure of this representational process, because it self-reflexively articulates the exteriorisation and occultation that is inherent in it. The aporia of representation seems to be that part of putting the real under erasure means articulating it, enacting that is not only how representations falter and stumble before the real but how the real must also fail before representation.

Our position as spectator should shift away from focusing only on the semantic coding of rhetorical figures (death, self-portrait, violence) to the figural dynamic staged in these images. This brings two movements simultaneously into our field of vision – firstly the representational need to shift our gaze away from the violent act of dying, within which Godé-Darel's body is caught, and secondly the violent failure inherent in the attempt of these representations to counteract the spectator's sense of destruction of a safe position in the world, by turning real soma into images, to counteract the destruction of a stable construction of self, which is called forth by an experience of the violence of death. Even as this sequence stages the self-protection inherent in the aesthetisation of death, it points to the limits of this process. Not only because real death, by definition, recedes from these images, but because death disrupts the shielding narcissistic allegoric, as well as the symbolic encoding. Provoking the spectator or reader to hover between denial and acknowledgement, narrative representations of death (whether visual or textual) serve to show that any 'voyeur' is always also implicated in the field of vision and that the act of fragmenting and objectifying the body of another ricochets back by destabilising the spectator's position as well.

My previous argument has been that the privileging of the 'phallus' as trope for the loss and division inscribing human existence serves to recuperate such a 'safe' position in the world, by focusing on sexual castration as an issue of gender and in so doing occluding the more global theme of death. A focus on the 'navel,' as site of a universal, non-gendered 'castrative' moment of facticity, may be a way to retrieve the multifariously obscured subjectivity of the deaths of the anonymous corpse in von Max's painting, of Sophie Freud, and of Valentine Godé-Darel. It may also be the way to understand the position and function of death in art.

The paradox inherent in representations of death is that 'death' is always culturally constructed, since outside any speaking subject's personal experience, outside and beyond the imaginary and symbolic registers. Since no one writes from an immediate experience of death, Kenneth Burke points out, it can only be an idea, not something known as a bodily sensation and the imagining of death necessarily involves images not directly belonging to it.[19] Placed beyond the register of images that the living body can know, 'Death' can only be read as a trope, as a signifier with an incessantly receding, ungraspable signified, invariably always pointing back self-reflexively to other signifiers. Death remains outside clear categories. It is nowhere, because it is only a gap, a cut, a transition between the living body and the corpse, a before (the painful fear, the serene joy of the dying person) and an after (the mourning of the survivor), an ungraspable point, lacking any empiric object. At the same time it is everywhere, because death begins with birth and remains present on all levels of daily existence. It is the one privileged moment of the absolutely real, of true, non-semiotic materiality as de-materialising or de-materialised body; it is a failure of the tropic. Non-negotiable and non-alterable, death is the limit of language, disrupting our sign system and image repertoire. Signifying nothing, it silently points to the indetermination of meaning so that one can speak of death only by speaking other. As the point where all language fails it is also the source of all allegorical speaking.[20]

Given that language hooks into the world at the most extreme locus of materialisation, the body, the privileged site of such a connection occurs when the body loses its materiality in death. It is part of the positivist assumptions grounding western culture that a crisis in belief is antidoted by a turn to the material. As Scarry argues, 'when some central idea or ideology or cultural construct has ceased to elicit a population's belief either because it is manifestly fictitious or because it has for some reason been divested of ordinary forms of substantiation – the sheer material factualness of the human body will be borrowed to lend that cultural construct the aura of "realness" and "certainty".'[21]

In the course of this book I will juggle three contradictory positions. The body caught in the process of dematerialisation is a privileged moment of connection between the world and language (be it theoretical or aesthetic representation), given the fact that language is always in danger of losing its referential capacity. Death, however, is both most referential and most self-referential or tropic, a reality for the experiencing subject, but non-verifiable for the viewing/surviving subject. Finally, to resort to the body as validation for a crisis in belief turns the body again into a cultural construct, hides precisely the aspect of real materiality on the basis of which it was chosen as privileged trope in the first place.

The ensuing chapters will explore how gender factors into this problematic. The cultural construction of femininity is such that it, too, has no fixed signified in the symbolic register. Although the position assigned to the feminine is often on the side of materiality, of the real, it is always also tropic, that is to say, most self-referential. In the rhetoric of representation the feminine functions analogous to the body – a recourse to the feminine serves to validate beliefs in crisis, to authenticate discourses, but does so by occulting 'femininity' in the process. It is the tragedy of this aporia, however, that the obliteration is never relegated entirely to the realm of figuration, but finds its thematic reflected in instances of real, materialised death, as the case histories and anecdotes I will have recourse to demonstrate so disquietingly.

Notes to Chapter 3

1 Quoted in J. Brüschweiler's introductory essay to his exhibition catalogue, 1976, p. 23; my translation. All further citations will be marked with page references in the text.

2 J. Brüschweiler, 1983, p. 17, dates this portrait as posthumous, though in the earlier 1976 exhibition he thought it should be ascribed to the year 1909. In his discussion of it, he nevertheless points out that the style is different from Hodler's portraits of this period. Lacking the naturalistic perspective, it seems to him more 'modern', reminds him of 'primitive art', 'Romantic frescos', 'Modigliani'. He sees a dreamlike quality in this portrait, as if Hodler had painted it from memory; also S. Guerzoni, 1959.

3 R. Girard, 1972, p. 380.

4 E. Scarry, 1985, p. 3.

5 R. Hertz's 1960 discussion of 'second burial' will be developed more precisely in later chapters.

6 See J. Laplanche and S. Leclaire, 1975. The term '*point de capiton* refers to the attachments that hold upholstery down.

7 See R. Barthes, 1985, p. 55.

8 J. Brüschweiler, 1976; original title 'Ein Maler vor Liebe und Tod. Ferdinand Hodler und Valentine Godé-Darel. Ein Werkzyklus 1908–1915.'

9 I will return to the issue of how the loss of the patronymic turns a historical woman into a signifier, usually signifying her artist–lover and his creative power in my discussion of Elizabeth Siddall.

10 It is interesting to note that not all paintings and scetches are signed. One of J. Brüschweiler's concerns in his narrative reconstruction is to determine the sequence of these images.

11 F. Bauman, in Brüschweiler et. al. 1983, p. 370.

12 T. de Lauretis, 1987, p. 42.
13 See J. Lacan, 1981, pp. 203–28.
14 V. Export, 1987.
15 M. Blanchot, 1981.
16 E. Ragland-Sullivan, 1987, p. 188. S. Leclaire, 1971, explicitly ties the rupture that the real causes to any symbolic relationship of signifiers with a moment such as death.
17 J. Kristeva, 1984.
18 J. Derrida, 1979, discusses the double meaning of 'arrêt de mort', pp. 75–176.
19 K. Burke, 1952.
20 L.-V. Thomas, 1979.
21. E. Scarry, 1985, p. 14.

PART II

From animate body to inanimate text

Writing was in its origin the voice of an absent person; and the dwelling-house was a substitute for the mother's womb, the first lodging, for which in all likelihood man still longs, and in which he was safe and felt at ease.
Sigmund Freud

4

The 'most' poetic topic

Though the objects themselves may be painful to see, we delight to view the most realistic representations of them in art, the forms for example of the lowest animals and of dead bodies.

Aristotle

Edgar Allan Poe's famous proposition, 'the death of a beautiful woman is, unquestionably, the most poetical topic in the world', has made his essay 'The Philosophy of Composition' an infamous text.[1] Some critics, who assume a compatibility between lived reality and aesthetic depiction, have accused Poe of misogyny.[2] Beth Ann Bassein claims that by connecting women with 'the most passive state occurring, that of death', Poe has done damage to the 'self-image and aspirations of generations of vulnerable readers', and advocates that Poe's imagery be 'exorcised' from contemporary culture. From a similar, though less programmatic, theoretical position Bram Dijkstra has explored the way that the 'dangerous fantasies' of nineteenth-century culture – of which 'woman in a state of sickness unto death' became an 'icon of virtuous femininity' – permitted the implementation of a suppression of women, and concludes that such images 'constituted a further step in the marginalization of woman'.[3]

In so far as I will repeatedly return to examples of how a woman, by virtue of dying, materialises earlier aesthetic renditions, the unsettling exchange between figural and literal meanings that seems to occur when representations of 'femininity' and 'death' are at issue also informs this book. Yet any theoretical insistence on a direct, unambiguous and stable analogy between cultural images and experienced reality defuses both the real violence of political domination and the power of representations. For it seems as necessary to stress the fundamental difference between real violence done to a physical body and any 'imagined' one (which represents this 'dangerous fantasy' on paper or canvas without any concretely violated body as its ultimate signified), as it is necessary to explore the way in which these two registers come to be conflated and confused. Not because the latter can then be absolved from any responsibility towards the material of its depiction but because to collapse the two levels on which signification works might also mean not doing justice to the uniquely horrible violence that occurs when a body is used quite literally as the site for an inscription by another.

Furthermore, to attribute only a sadomasochistic vogue, a necrophilic misogyny to the 'feminine life-in-death figure,' as Mario Praz does, is a semantic reduction which ignores the multiplicity of themes that are condensed and displaced in this image. Nina Auerbach correctly argues against such a restrictive reading when she designates images belonging to this cultural paradigm as a contradictory 'amalgam of imprisonment and power'.[4] I would add that to locate art's influence in the modes of identification it offers to its readers also means ignoring the instability and indeterminacy so fundamentally inscribed into the narrative and representational process; the slippage between signifier, signified and a non-semiotic real, the incommensurability between intention and reception due to the inclusion of points of focalisation, the duplicity of the image's enmeshment of a conservative and a subversive drive.

Rather than exorcise Poe's conjunction of femininity, death and aesthetics, I will instead take his poetics seriously and begin by questioning the presuppositions underlying his claim. What does it mean to maintain that the death of a beautiful woman is unquestionably the most poetical topic? Why a dead woman, why a beautiful woman? Does the choice of the feminine gender as object of celebration imply erotic desire? What is the reciprocity between femininity and aesthetisation, between beauty and death? And above all why the unconditional 'unquestionably', why the superlative '*most* poetical'?

These questions point to a strange and trenchant contradiction, which is further enhanced by the popularity of an aesthetic coupling of Woman and death. For this motif is not limited to the works of the eccentric outsider Poe; rather it appears as a popular though diversely utilised thematic constant in literature and painting from the age of sensibility to the modern period. The contradiction can be formulated in the following way. The colloquial understanding of femininity is such that Woman is primarily connected with the domain of life, with life-bringing and nourishing nature. If she dies, commits suicide or is killed, this is not beautiful because it endangers the survival and procreation of her race. Equally a contradiction in terms is the combination of 'beautiful', 'poetical' and 'death', since death is a decomposition of forms, the breaking of aesthetic unity. Furthermore, the fear of death is so strong that European culture has made the corpse into a taboo. It sees decomposition as the body's most polluted condition, so that touching and seeing a corpse can be dangerous, and requires subsequent purification.[5] Why, then, the reversal of this colloquial understanding in art, where it is precisely the death of a Woman that guarantees the survival of a family, a clan, a community, or brings about the production of an artwork? Why, then, the many narratives about experiences of the sublime at the sight of a corpse?

Poe himself justifies his choice of the superlative only as the logical consequence of foregoing premises. He intends, in this poetological essay, to describe the process of artistic composition, using his poem 'The Raven' as his example.

His first premise is that all works of art should begin at the end, that the inanimate state of resolved narrative tensions is the initial point for the composition of a story: 'only with the *dénouement* constantly in view [can we] give a plot its indispensable air of consequence, or causation'.[6] Death is, then, from the start integral to his notion of poetics, since the incidents described, the tone used to describe them, each draw their poetic power and their legitimacy from a predetermined, inevitable return to the inanimate. Indeed, as Peter Brooks suggests, all narrative may well be obituary in that it seeks a retrospective knowledge that comes after the end, which in human terms places it on the far side of death.[7] After determining the proper length for his poem based on the 'limit of a single sitting', Poe proceeds by considering the general intended effect and, in so doing, maintains that Beauty is the supreme atmosphere and essence, the 'sole legitimate province' of the poem. For 'that pleasure which is at once the most intense, the most elevating, and the most pure, is, I believe, found in the contemplation of the beautiful'.[8] By 'Beauty' Poe means an effect rather than a quality: to be exact, 'that intense and pure elevation of *soul* – *not* of intellect, or of heart', so that truth and passion must be 'toned into proper subservience' to this predominant aim.

Poe adds that sadness and melancholy are the 'most legitimate of all poetic tones' since here Beauty finds its 'highest manifestation'. Because he is concerned with the supreme expression of the lyrical, with 'supremeness, or perfection, at all points', he concludes that 'obviously' death is the universally acknowledged superlative of all melancholy topics, and that his melancholy topic is most poetical when it 'most closely allies itself with Beauty'. The coupling of 'death' and 'beautiful Woman' offers him the unconditional, universally acknowledged highest degree, the superlative of his basic principles 'Melancholy' and 'Beauty'. He adds another seminal point: 'equally is it beyond doubt that the lips best suited for such a topic are those of a bereaved lover'. Poe concludes that the 'richness' of a poem depends on some amount of complexity and of suggestiveness of meaning, while an excess of suggested meaning engenders a turn into the prosaic. His use of the superlative must, then, refer to another kind of excess – the indeterminacy, hesitation or contradiction in respect to meaning inscribed into any representation.[9]

To contemplate death is to introduce into thought the epitome of doubt, Geoffrey Ward suggests, because there are 'two certainties in life. One is that death will come. The other is that no one can be sure of this.'[10] What emerges from Poe's repeated insistence on the superlative *most* (as a moment of supreme suggestiveness) in conjunction with expressions of determination – 'universal', 'obvious', 'unquestionable', and 'equally beyond doubt' – is precisely a poetics of such a death-induced doubt. While the sequentiality of his narrative, because it is predetermined and inevitable, evokes a sense of unambiguous stability, the excess of the superlative in his poetics, the heaping of one superlative on to another, provokes the absurd impossibility of a 'superlative of the superlative' and could be seen as marking the breaking point or limit of this poetic system. By implication, then, to speak about representing 'feminine death as the most poetical topic' means speaking of an aesthetic moment of excess. It is a superlative theme because it marks the moment where a text turns back on to itself, where it undoes its own premise, where it discloses what it sets out to obscure – a hypertropic moment.

By allowing that the point or topic of Poe's poetics may in fact be the articulation of a culturally prevalent aporic attitude to death, to feminine beauty and to art, his decision to conflate these three terms is less contradictory than initially supposed. Rather it points to another, equally conventional set of cultural norms. For if any discussion of death involves masking the inevitability of human decomposition, it does so by having recourse to beauty. We invest in images of wholeness, purity and the immaculate owing to our fear of dissolution and decay. The function of beauty, Lacan suggests, is to point to the relation man has with his own death, but to indicate this only as a dazzling sight.[11] The idea of beauty's perfection is so compelling because it disproves the idea of disintegration, fragmentation and insufficiency, even though it actually only serves as substitution for the facticity of human existence one fears yet must accept. Paradoxically, in Barbara Johnson's words, beauty is nothing other than 'the very image of death, castration and repression which it is designed to block out and to occult'.[12]

That beauty is only superficially death's antithesis is in fact an extremely common notion in western culture. In his discussion of the theme of the three caskets, Freud shows how in many myths the choice of the last of three women, surpassing the other two because she is 'the fairest, best, most desirable, most loveable', coincides with the choice of death, so that this third woman is either dead, death itself or a goddess of death. Choosing her serves to express a superlative – the most complete contradiction ('unwahrscheinlichste Steigerung').[13] Freud argues that to substitute death with its contrary, beauty, serves a highly ambivalent form of wish-fulfilment: 'Choice stands in the place of necessity, of destiny. In this way man overcomes death, which he has recognized intellectually. No greater triumph of wish-fulfillment is conceivable. A choice is made where in reality there is obedience to compulsion; and what is chosen is not a figure of terror, but the fairest and most desirable of women.'[14] By locating a two-fold substitution – that of beauty for death, that of choice for submission to fate – Freud argues for an ambivalence inherent in the opposition between beauty and death, allowing for a hidden identity between the two, and embedded in this the aporic co-existence of a resistance to and an acknowledgement of death.[15] The allegorical reading Freud finally attributes to this theme is the eternal wisdom of primitive myth; to renounce love, choose and befriend oneself with the inexorable and inevitable necessity of dying.

Two moments can, then, be isolated as relevant for my discussion of Poe's poetics – the superlative in conjunction with beauty and femininity serves as a figure for an uncanny contradictory relation to death, the translation of anxiety into desire. The structural ambivalence is such that the object of this hybrid anxiety/desire cannot be determined. Is it the desire for the death of the other, or for a dead other? Is the death of the beloved, or the dead beloved, a substitute figure for one's own death? Or/and is the stake in fact the universal truth of death as it surpasses love, gender, sexuality? The structure of ambivalence is such that in it two opposite meanings are simultaneously affirmed. The duplicity of the play of imagination that allows for the substitution of death through love is such that it encompasses an idea, which allows one to guess at the figure of death beneath that of love, and a desire, which allows one to misrecognise death because what is visibly figured is not death itself but its double, love. Pleasure at the beauty of Woman resides in the uncanny *simultaneity* of recognising and misrecognising it as a veil for death.[16]

If we recall that for Poe death is hidden not only by beauty but by superlative *feminine* beauty, another dimension of this problematic emerges. The sublation of gender can be figured only over a gendered body. Freud splits his triad of desired objects into the mother, the beloved chosen on the pattern of the mother, and mother earth, who will receive him again. The equation of death with a third woman, mother earth, leads Paul Ricoeur to ask whether the acceptance of death necessarily coincides with a regression to the mother figure or whether Freud's point is that 'the woman figure must become the figure of death for man, so as to cease being fantasy and regression?'[17] Part of the equation between femininity and death resides precisely in the fact that Woman as man's object of desire (*objet a*) is on the side of death not only because she repeats the always already lost primordial mother but because she so often serves as a non-reciprocal 'dead' figure of imaginary projection, given that, in Lacan's terms, 'the whole of [man's] realization in the sexual relation comes down to fantasy'.[18]

How then are we to understand Freud? Is death the first and only moment of an Otherness beyond a narcissistically informed economy of fantasy and regression? Is the feminine inextricably bound to cultural fantasies, so that only in death can Woman be real, autonomous, alterior? But if the renunciation of the feminine is what is required for the figure of death to emerge, then conversely, culturally constructed femininity protects man (and androcentric culture) from death. To hold on to the 'fantasy' of gender allows one to occult death, which, once disclosed, requires the obliteration of gender. In Freud's superlative – 'fairest and most desirable thing' – death once again emerges as the antithesis of femininity, because the 'death of a beautiful woman' comes precisely to serve as a figure for the turn beyond gender difference. The paradox of this superlative is such that it marks the moment where the oxymoron 'dead woman' subverts into a pleonasm. Because the semantically opposed terms 'feminine beauty' and 'death' prove also to be identical their conjunction marks a moment of rhetorical redundancy. Again, the 'most' is positioned as a limit element, in this case as the breaking point in a rhetoric of distinctions.

The replacement of Woman by death reveals another contradiction inscribed into cultural representations of feminine death. Though in the process of death anatomical sexual differences remain, a colloquial understanding of the corpse is that it is not gendered, that it is an anonymous, inanimate body, pure materiality without soul or personality. In fact Sally Humphreys points out that while the living body is associated with individuality, 'death threatens to put an end to differentiation'.[19] Because the corpse is a figure without any distinguishing facial traits of its own, one could say that semiotically it serves as an arbitrary, empty, interchangeable sign, an interminable surface for projections.[20] Paradoxically (to conflate Poe's and Freud's propositions), this obliteration of gender, along with all other socially constructed features, is represented in western culture through a gendered body, the superlatively beautiful, desirable *feminine* corpse.[21]

The fashioning of beauty is intimately connected not only with the protection that fantasies of gender afford, but also with the apotropaic power ascribed to the imaginary faculty in the face of death. Kristeva argues that so as not to die of the other's death, the mourner imagines for himself an artifact, an ideal, a beyond, in order to take up a place outside himself. The immutable beautiful body replaces perishable psychic values.[22] The imaginary capacity is such that it functions as a self-illusion, by affirming the omnipotence of temporary subjectivity. It is crucial, however, that the production of beautiful images (aesthetics) and the construction of femininity are culturally equated because they are analogously positioned in relation to death. The beauty of Woman and the beauty of the image both give the illusion of intactness and unity, cover the insupportable signs of lack, deficiency, transiency and promise their spectators the impossible – an obliteration of death's ubiquitous 'castrative' threat to the subject.[23] Beauty, however, always also includes death's inscription, because it requires the translation (be it in fantasy or in reality) of an imperfect, animate body, into a perfect, inanimate image, a dead 'figure'. Lemoine-Luccioni suggests that beauty places man's object of desire at a distance, but preserves this object in its status as object. Beauty arouses sexual desire at the same time that it forbids it, because it is intangible.[24] The beauty of woman and of the image is evasive, receding because this shield against real death is itself not real, a fantasy, an illusion.

It is then only logical that for Poe beauty should find its supreme manifestation in the melancholic tone, and that the speaker best suited for the 'most poetical topic' should be 'a lover lamenting his deceased mistress'.[25] For melancholia is, according to Freud, failed mourning, an inability to accept the death of a desired object. Melancholia involves a denial of loss, which emerges from an initial acknowledgement of this loss and provokes its perpetual articulation. Sarah Kofman, in turn, argues that all effective art is the work of melancholy precisely because it involves such a duplicitous attitude towards loss.[26] The creation of beauty allows us to escape from the elusiveness of the material world into an illusion of eternity (a denial of loss), even as it imposes on us the realisation that beauty is itself elusive, intangible, receding. Because it is created on the basis of the same elusiveness it tries to obliterate, what art in fact does is mourn beauty, and in so doing it mourns itself. The self-reflexive moment, which makes art effective, is heightened by virtue of the fact that, in its contingency on loss, art exemplifies a surplus meaning. Substituting for or doubling an absent object, it represents something which it both is and is not, while at the same time the beautiful form both is and isn't eternal. I would add that when this structural analogy between mourning and art is doubled thematically, as is the case in Poe's proposed scene, the self-reflexivity exemplifies an excessive surplus of meaning – the superlative.

But why is the mourner masculine? Is Poe's reference to a masculine speaker and spectator of 'the death of a beautiful woman' arbitrary, or can one conclude that a culture which ascribes death to the feminine position necessarily sees survival as masculine? Elias Canetti invokes such gendering when he describes the moment of survival as a moment of power and triumph. Horror at the sight of death turns into satisfaction, since the survivor is not himself dead. The dead body is in the passive, horizontal position, cut down, fallen, while the survivor stands erect, imbued with a feeling of superiority.[27] By implication the corpse is feminine, the survivor masculine. However, such gender designations occur in the image repertoire of a culture, not in biological reality, and can in fact lead to a contradiction between the two registers. Depending on the values attributed to positions of the feminine (vulnerability, inferiority) and of the masculine (domination, superiority), an anatomically 'male' corpse may be gendered 'feminine' in a given cultural construction. In the same way an anatomically 'female' spectator or narrator may, because she has accepted a fixed position in masculine culture and supports its norms and semantic encodings, embody a 'masculine' spectator or focalisor position. One cannot speak of an 'essential' self preceding the social and cultural construction of the self through the agency of representations. Cultural practices are defined as signifying systems, as sites for the production of representations which are not to be equated with beautiful things evoking beautiful feelings. The word *representation*, Griselda Pollock notes, 'stresses that images and texts are no mirrors of the world, merely reflecting their source. Representation stresses something refashioned, coded in rhetorical, textual or pictorial terms, quite distinct from its social existence.'[28]

At this point I will recall cultural myths of femininity which associate woman with death by referring back to the plot typology of Jurij Lotman, already discussed in chapter 3. 'The elementary sequence of events in myth', he argues, 'can be reduced to a chain: entry into closed space – emergence from it . . . In as much as closed space can be interpreted as "a cave," "the grave," "a house," "woman," (and correspondingly, be allotted the features of darkness, warmth, dampness), entry into it is interpreted on various levels as "death," "conception," "return home" and so on; moreover all these acts are thought of as mutually identical.'[29] The lack of boundaries between concepts such as womb, tomb, home is traditionally linked to the analogy between earth and mother, and with it, that of death and birth, or death–conception and birth–resurrection. Death is here conceptualised as the return to a symbiotic unity, to the peace before the difference and tension of life, to the protective enclosure before individuation and culturation.

If the death drive in one sense corresponds to the alienation or wounding of the subject's narcissism due to its insertion into the repetitions, desires and constraints of the Other (be this culture's laws, the unconscious drives or the imposition of a non-semiotic real), the death drive in another sense corresponds to the tensionless, undifferentiated stasis of the Other as beyond, grounding and prefiguring biological and social human existence. As Freud suggests in his discussion of the mythic motif of the choice between three caskets, this second site of Otherness as point of return to a fusion beyond any split, a reconciliation with a 'lost' harmony, is implicitly understood as feminine because equated with the primordial mother. Yet this feminine Other as 'womb–tomb–home' is the site of death in an ambivalent way. It is the site from which life as death's antithesis emerges even as it is the site that generates the mortal inscription of the body at birth, the navel's mark.

One aspect of popular mythology implicitly present in Lotman's typology is that of casting objectivity, reason, distinctions, mind, scientific thought as masculine and feeling, fluidity, nature, the domain of scientific inquiry as feminine.[30] Using the feminine form as allegory of nature, European culture could express nature as the mother and bride, whose primary life-giving functions were to comfort, nurture and provide. Yet nature also embodied unruly disorder, uncivilised wilderness, famines and tempests that threatened generation by destroying crops and killing infants. In the equation with nature, earth, body, Woman was construed as Other to culture, as object of intense curiosity to be explored, dissected, conquered, domesticated and, if necessary, eliminated.[31]

In her pioneering analysis of cultural myths of femininity, Simone de Beauvoir argues that if in the construction of myths of gender man is the subject, the absolute and Woman the Other, posed by the One to define itself, then Woman 'seems to be the inessential who never goes back to being the essential, to be the absolute Other, without reciprocity'.[32] Because the concept of alterity is based on ambiguity, Woman incarnates no stable concept. Because she is semantically encoded as good and evil, as the possibility of wholeness and a frustration of this dream, the connection to the infinite beyond and the measure of human finity, the one stability to be found in myths of femininity is in fact ambivalence. Woman so often not only embodies values associated with death but enacts death's work rhetorically by virtue of functioning as an inessential figure (a disembodied sign without a referent) and as the site of uncanny ambivalence ('Unheimlichkeit'); both rhetorical figures for death's presence in life.

One of the most poignant examples for such ambivalence is the conjunction of Woman as nature, for as body Woman also comes to allegorise the danger of sexual lust, uncontrollable passion and spontaneity. There are indeed two 'mothers of culture,' from whom a diversity of feminine types is derived – the temptress Eve and the healing Virgin Mary. These are not only posited as diametrically opposed. More importantly, both are the source of culture even as they are equated with aspects of death and as such also mark the limit and vanishing point of the culture they give birth to. Derived from Eve, Woman can serve as allegory of evil, sin, deception, destruction and negation that finds one of its superlative embodiments in the dangerous sexuality of the witch. Because for the inquisition 'Woman's name is equal to death', her body had to be constrained, punished, exorcised. Rather than signifying the source of fertility and healing, Woman's body is seen as polluted, as fatal to the masculine touch, an agent and carrier of death. Because Woman is used as an allegory for that deterioration of flesh which the surviving subject wishes to deny yet knows is his destiny, the beauty of Woman is conceived as a mask for decay, and the sexual relation with her as a form of death rather than of conception.

This paradigmatic coupling of Woman and body serves to allegorise the aspect of corruption, vulnerability and disembodiment inherent in human existence. The conjunction of woman–death–womb–tomb reduces to the ambivalence that the mother's gift of birth is also the gift of death, that the embrace of the beloved also signifies a loss or dissolution of the self. The maternal body and its substitute love objects are fundamentally deceptive, the source of life clothed in beauty but infested by the ferments of death, the site of the promise of unity and memento of the wound grounding life. The maternal figure (womb) not only equals death in the sense of a return to an inanimate stasis (tomb). Rather, both mother and beloved function as allegories of man's mortal state, as the fixed image of human destiny. Woman, de Beauvoir finds, 'is the life that is necessary to his existence but that condemns him to the finite and to death.'[33] Eve, as privileged figure for the primordial mother, embodies and evokes this uncanniness of unity and loss, of independent identity and self-dissolution, of the beauty and pleasure of the body and its decay.

While figures of Eve incarnate the woundedness of humanity, types of femininity emerging from the figure of the Virgin Mary, the Mater Dolorosa lamenting over the dead body of Christ, come to allegorise the nourishing and healing mother, the redemption from flesh, sin and guilt. The Virgin Mary often shares the pomegranate as attribute with Persephone, in order to associate the fertility of the latter with its Christian corollary of renewal and immortality, the Resurrection. In her function as Virgin of Mercy, Mary is a figure for the triumph over the 'bad' death of sin and decay, introduced by Eve; a mediator for the living, sheltering the penitent under her cloak, an intercessor before God for the souls of the dead at the Last Judgement. Because she is the source of healing, consolation and reprieve she functions as a figure of promised wholeness, so that paradoxically her special sphere of influence is Purgatory's ambivalent, liminal realm. From her derives the notion of the disembodied, ethereal, non-essential muse, mediatrix and angel as bridge to the beyond, supplying knowledge of the Unknowable, of Divinity, or serving as assistance in the transport of the living to the realm of the dead.[34]

The stories of the miracle of her death significantly involve the notion of an absence of body to signify a triumph over death. Marina Warner notes that the perplexing aspect of this event was the lack of any contemporary records: 'there was no knowledge of her grave – no body to venerate, no relics to touch . . . the disappearance of Mary's body . . . inspired the most fertile imaginings . . . For the symbol of purity itself could not rot in the grave.'[35] In her mythic Assumption Mary is reanimated immediately after her death and transferred to heaven in the company of angels. Conceptually a collapsing of first and second burial occurs, which completely circumvents a dissolution and corruption of the body, and by implication places her from the start outside the 'feminine' realm of material time and bodily decay and into the 'masculine' symbolic realm of eternal unchanged forms. Equating sexual impurity with the presence of death in the living body as well as with bodily decay after death, Christian dogma confirms, after the event, the purity of the Virgin Mary's body as, significantly, a purity from death. Against the dissolution of the boundaries of the body fusing with alterity in sexuality and death, the myth of the Virgin Mary serves as a repository for fantasies about the preservation of body wholeness and integrity, about the union of body and soul.

Her figure serves as the antidote for the ambivalent wound of the navel each child is given with birth. It also serves as the dissolution of the ambivalent liminal period between death and resurrection. During this period, the body dissolves in the grave, where the soul separates from the body to enact the uncanniness of the double. The assumed Virgin becomes the sublime example of a Christian longing for the immutable and unchanging perfection of each resurrected individual.[36] Just as a feminization of demonised flesh is the material representation of alterity, of Woman as an animal creature, so too the feminisation of the ideal, the glorified substance, is a representation of alterity, of Woman as an ethereal being, to be venerated in her intact splendour. The Virgin Mary functions as an epitome of timeless, of undifferentiated, immortal beauty and bliss, as an allegory for the defeat of death and the promise of eternal life, precisely because in her mythic construction the materiality or body is missing from the start.

The 'bodiless' Virgin Mary signifies a conquest over death by virtue of being a figure of wholeness and mercy, and as such she seems to be constructed in diametric opposition to Eve, the deceiver and temptress, whose association with death and decay is based on her equation with the human (or animal) body and sexuality. Nevertheless a significant parallel between these two 'mothers of culture' resides in the fact that Eve in another sense is also associated with 'bodilessness', though in the pejorative sense of the unnaturalness of artifice and rhetoric. Not only does the mother's gift of birth deceive the underlying fermentation of death, not only does feminine beauty and decoration mask decay. R. Howard Bloch notes that the creation of woman as supplement to man and the creation of language as supplement to things is coterminous in Genesis. Though Eve, in her position of secondariness to Adam's unity, is associated with temporality, difference, body and matter, her coming into being is also seen as synonymous with the loss of the literal, with the creation of metaphor, of the figural as derivation, as deflection, as denaturing, as a tropological turning away. Eve is 'side-issue'.[37]

By virtue of her secondary nature, her alterity, Woman is conceived as ornament, artifice or decoration, so that death as corruption, division or duplication presides in two opposed realms which are both associated with the feminine; firstly in the weakness, vulnerability and corruptibility of the flesh, and secondly in the artificial clothes and signs that supplement the naked body of nature. Paradoxically Woman is linked to nature and the material body as it endangers stable, eternal, cultural forms because it lies outside semiosis. She serves as signifier for an originary, paradisical wholeness of the body and for the unity of signifier and signified before a disruptive fall to earth, birth (womb), body (soma) and language (sema). At the same time she is also linked, by virtue of her derivative nature, to figural representation and artifice, to the break between signifer and signified (sema/tomb). Bloch's point is that the pejorative conjunction of the feminine body with the artifice of words or verbal signs serves a misogynist encoding of feminity as 'perverse', as 'excess', given that words are 'in excess to and a perversion of' images in the mind, just as the corporeal or sensitive is 'in excess to and a perversion of' the spirit or soul. In its conjunction with the figurative and the rhetorical, however, femininity is not only also idealised. Woman emerges in this model once again as the site of an allegorical speaking 'in other terms', within a rhetorical strategy that is precisely one where the body is missing. Woman is positioned either as truth or in opposition to truth; in the position of a rhetoric that articulates the nonarticulable Beyond or Divine by virtue of speaking 'in other terms', or in the position of a rhetoric that seduces with false arguments, that is deceptive because fundamentally instable in its articulation. As man's copy and supplement, Woman doubles and distorts even as she represents his truth.

This ambivalent positioning of Woman as the agency that heals the wound of death's presence in life even as she is also seen as its source, finds yet another expression in the notion of the beloved as site for self-fulfilment. 'In woman is incarnated in positive form the lack that the existent carries in his heart', de Beauvoir suggests, 'and it is in seeking to be made whole through her that man hopes to attain self-realization.'[38] Yet even as the woman as desired sexual object undoes the work of death by promising wholeness, her body is also seen as the site of a wound, its sight a source of death for man.[39] Next to the image of the Virgin Mary without a tomb, and Eve as the womb from which death enters the world, the myth of Medusa offers a third variation on the conjunction woman–death–womb–tomb.

If we understand the feminine diabolic as arising from the Greek *diaballo* – meaning to translate as well as to split, cause strife and difference, reject, defame, deceive – a further cultural association between femininity and the agency of death emerges. Not only does the powerful sexuality of the femme fatale cause her lover to lose his head, and with it his social identity and his sense of safe ego boundaries. Female genitalia represent, in Freud's discussion, another aspect of the feminine as site of a dangerous, deceptive split: 'the terror of Medusa is thus a terror of castration that is linked to the sight of something', namely the absence of the penis. The split genitalia are here replaced by or translated into a multitude of snakes as a 'multiplication of penis symbols'.[40] Freud points to one ambivalence when he suggests that the sight of Medusa's head makes the spectator stiff with horror (which he reads as a trope for erection) even as its spectacle translates into a scene of consolation: 'he is stiff in possession of a penis and the stiffening reassures him of the fact'. Like the fetish, this mythic figure is 'uncanny' in that she frightens and reassures, in that she functions as both a site of lack and what covers the lack. Analogous to the way the sight of the corpse imbues the survivor with a sense of mastery over death, this spectacle of 'sexual' lack allows the viewer to isolate his own Otherness (the vulnerability of and split in the self), by translating it on to a sexually different body, and in so doing it works once again on the principle of an interchangeability between dead and feminine body.

Given that for Freud 'to decapitate = to castrate', the threat of castration emerging from Medusa not only threatens to kill the viewer, but conversely the decapitation of Medusa also means a castration of castration. It enacts a killing of the metonymy for Other sexuality, for feminine genitalia, which have been culturally construed as a signifier for castration. More important, this double castration equally involves a staging and then violent disseverment of the head as metaphor for the feminine genitals which are also culturally constructed as trope *par excellence* for the conjunction of birth and death, for the absence and split upon which existence is based and an acknowledgement of which is to be denied in the consolatory illusion of wholeness for which, in turn, 'erection' is the privileged western trope. What is also always implied in the conjunction womb–tomb is a position of the feminine in proximity to a non-semiotic real, in the sense of death's ineffability as a void grounding life and yet beyond narcissistic desires and cultural laws, against which these are constructed but before which these also falter. The lack of wholeness or absence, the 'not all', 'not one' of the feminine body causes a terrifying realisation of one's true condition, which is overcome by isolating this facticity in the other and thus not in the self and then, a second time, by dissevering the sign of facticity from the body, isolating it even more. At the same time, the horror of lack is also articulated and mitigated through a rhetorical replacement by excess, the multiplication of penis as snake symbols, no longer dangerous but reassuring, once the head has been dissevered from the body. In precisely this conjunction of monstrous 'less than whole' and tropic replacement as 'excess', woman serves to demarcate a cultural system as well as marking its vanishing point, its moment of failure.

De Beauvoir concludes that Woman is invented, yet also exists apart from this construction: 'she is not only the incarnation of [man's and culture's] dream, but also its frustration. There is no figurative image of woman which does not call up at once its opposite . . . under whatever aspect we consider her, we always find the same shifting back and forth, for the nonessential returns necessarily to the essential.'[41] Woman is culturally constructed as Other to man and as the uncanny site where two opposing values collapse into one, including the ambivalent fact that she serves to articulate that which is exterior to a culture as well as that interiority which is repressed, rejected or foreclosed. Furthermore, Woman functions duplicitly not only owing to her contradictory semantic encoding but also because, like death, she is at once assigned to the realm of culture's mythic image repertoire, to rhetorics and textuality and to the non-semiotic real, to natural materiality. She is the site of mediation between having recourse to the sheer facticity of the body and a translation of this body into a sign from which it is missing.

To return to the 'Philosophy of Composition': if beauty, femininity and melancholy are culturally related to death, we can understand Poe's final term, the 'most poetical', in the following way. By dying, a beautiful Woman serves as the motive for the creation of an art work and as its object of representation. As a deanimated body, she can also become an art object or be compared with one. Not without reason does the word *corpus* refer both to the body of a dead human or animal and to a collection of writings.[42] Because her dying figures as an analogy to the creation of an art work, and the depicted death serves as a double of its formal condition, the 'death of a beautiful woman' marks the *mise en abyme* of a text, the moment of self-reflexivity, where the text seems to comment on itself and its own process of composition, and so decomposes itself.[43] Poe's choice of the superlative indicates that the literary depiction of feminine death is not limited to the thematic dimension of a representation. Rather it includes a reference to a text's poetic effectiveness, as this is contingent on self-referentiality. Roman Jakobson defines the poetic function of language as a 'focus on the message for its own sake' and argues that it is the dominant and deter-mining though not sole function of verbal art. The poetic function privileges the self-referential dimension of a sign and stresses least a referentiality to a non-semiotic world: 'by promoting the palpability of signs, (it) deepens the funda-mental dichotomy of signs and objects'.[44]

The 'poetic', 'self-reflexive' dichotomy between signs and objects or bodies engendered by the image of feminine death is, then, such that it articulates a reciprocity of the deanimated 'soma' and its seeming opposite 'sema'. The poem commemorating a dead beautiful woman functions – like the inscribed slab, relief sculpture or statue which stands, since classical antiquity, over tombs – as a 'sema' or sign to indicate the burial place of a 'heroine' by substituting the body of the deceased. Equally, because mortal existence is a form of decay, life may be equated with death and death with life, so that for Plato the body is a tomb, 'soma' equals 'sema'.[45]

Poe's poetics seem to endorse a spectatorship that ignores the referent, the non-semiotic body and focuses its reading exclusively on the image as a self-reflexive, materialised sign. Analogous to the recourse beauty affords culture, this turn away from referentiality can serve to protect culture's privileged modes of self-presentation, namely representation and language. 'If the perfect fulfillment of the constative, referential function of language would consist in the total obliteration of the object of that function,' Johnson suggests, 'then language can retain its "innocence" only by giving up its referential validity.'[46] Because it is a 'poetical' topic, Poe's fantasy of feminine death remains 'innocent' of real violence. What some of my examples will show, however, is that the conjunction of 'poetical,' as self-reflexive, with the superlative 'most' may involve an excess of self-referentiality that turns to conflate the articulating self with its object of articulation. The 'most poetical' can then refer to an aesthetic event where self-reflexivity rebounds in a return to referentiality in the form of an annihilation of enunciator and enuncee, where 'soma' comes again to equal 'sema'.

What Poe's '*most* poetical' emphasises then, is an extreme disjunction between signification or representation and referentiality. Rhetorically raising the poetical, in its expressive and protective self-referentiality, to the highest degree also points to the limits of representation. Death, because it is beyond any speaking subject's experiential realm, is always culturally constructed, always metaphorical; a signifier of lack which itself lacks a fixed signified in the symbolic register; a signifier of certainty against which all other cultural values are measured and confirmed, but which is itself unmeasurable, certain only in its negativity. It comes, in Michel Deguy's words, to function as a 'metaphor *par excellence*', as the superlative trope, as an *a priori*, unknown event that inscribes itself into human existence in the form of a 'prefiguration' ('pré-figuré') and thus invokes the figural quality of all things.[47]

Poe's conjunction of the most poetical with death, however, points to this aspect of representational impossibility as it ironically reverts into an excessive production of figurations. For the 'most poetical' also refers to the cultural plethora and ubiquity of images of 'the death of a beautiful woman'. Owing to this question of unrepresentability, death comes to be associated on yet another level with the other unrepresentable aspect of human existence, the multiply coded feminine body, in its triple function as site of an original, prenatal dwelling place, as site of fantasies of desire and otherness, and as site of an anticipated final resting place. Once again Poe's seemingly antithetical coupling of death and femininity emerges as significantly logical for western cultural mythology.

In the following chapters of Part II, I will analyse various aspects of this poetical self-reflexivity as it revolves around the conjunction of femininity, death and aesthetisation, and as it involves the translation of the corpse into a feminine body, and into an artefact. I will show how the aesthetic staging of the death of a woman can serve an epistemological discussion about how one can appropriate the world through the act of seeing and how the spectacle of another's death may impart knowledge about one's own death, or about the hereafter. At the same time I will demonstrate how the objectification and depersonalisation of Woman in/through death can also serve an aesthetic discussion about the conditions of artistic creation, or more precisely the sacrifices representation requires; the ambiguous fascination involved in translating a body that is perceived or culturally constructed as an animate natural material into the inanimate aesthetic form; the dangerously fluid boundary between these two registers. The equation between femininity and death is such that while in cultural narratives the feminine corpse is treated like an artwork, or the beautiful woman is killed to produce an artwork, conversely, artworks emerge only at the expense of a beautiful woman's death and are treated like feminine corpses.

Notes to Chapter 4

1 E. A. Poe, 1846, p. 19.
2 B. Bassein, 1984.
3 B. Dijkstra, 1986, p. 24
4 See M. Praz, 1973; N. Auerbach, 1982.
5 H. Bächthold-Stäubli, 1987, vol 5, p. 1035. Laws involving restrictions in respect to the touching of corpses can also be found in the Old Testament, Numbers 19. 11 following: 'He that toucheth the dead body of any man shall be unclean seven days . . . but the man that shall be unclean and shall not purify himself, that soul shall be cut off from among the congregation, because he hath defiled the sanctuary of the LORD': The Holy Bible. King James Version, 1974, pp. 143f. See also M. Douglas, 1966.
6 E. A. Poe, 1846, p. 13. James Nohrnberg sees literature as marked by 'a deep posteriority', for the reader's response is necessarily retrospective, and all literature from his standpoint preterite. Quoted in W. J. Ong, 1977, p. 241.
7 P. Brooks, 1984. See also F. Kermode's discussion, 1966, of the need for narrative closure as that which will confer significance on experience.
8 E. A. Poe, 1846, p. 16.
9 E. A. Poe, 1846, p. 24.
10 G. Ward, 1986, p. 673.
11 J. Lacan, 1986. See also S. Gilman's discussion, 1989, of representations of sexual diseases like syphilis using images of female beauty as masks of decay.
12 B. Johnson, 1980, p. 48.
13 S. Freud, 1913, p. 298. It is interesting to note that Freud begins his discussion with another substitution, that of casket for woman. The inability to decide whether the choice of the third casket/woman means the choice of a dead woman, of one's own death, or of an acceptance of a divinely ordained mortality (though Freud chooses to privilege the third) reminds me of the ambivalence of meaning inscribed in the moth as 'figure of death' in the painting by Gabriel von Max.
14 S. Freud, 1913, p. 299.
15 B. G. Walker, 1983, describes a similar conflation of beauty and death in matriarchal societies, where beauty and death, decay, corruption, ugliness were conceived as different forms of the same Goddess: 'on the one hand she was the beautiful nubile virgin or the tender nurturing Mother; on the other hand she was a hideous ghoul, herself corpse-like and a devourer of corpses – and these two forms of her were to be adored equally', p. 216.
16 S. Kofman, 1987.
17 P. Ricoeur, 1970, p. 332.
18 J. Lacan, 1985, p. 157.
19 S. Humphreys, 'Introduction: comparative perspectives on death', 1981, p. 6.
20 L.-V. Thomas, 1980, suggests that the corpse remains as an empty signifier and functions without a phenomenal subject; which is why its presence refers to an absence.

21 In Shakespearean English, 'nothing' was the bawdy word for female genitalia, implying a correlation between feminine sexuality and death, since the latter is also a
semantic value of the word 'nothing,' and this semantic conjunction may well have
continued to resonate in eighteenth and nineteenth-century culture. See E. A. M.
Colman, 1974. E. Showalter, 1985c, suggests, 'in the male visual system of representation and desire, women's sexual organs represent the horror of having nothing to
see', p. 70.

22 J. Kristeva, 1989.

23 Unless I specify it otherwise I use the word 'castrative' in a global, 'non-gendered'
sense to indicate an act of depriving of vitality, of cutting up a unity, of severment that
curtails power, of loss. I will be concerned with 'castration' understood in terms of a
sense of cut or lack induced by death, as this merges with an awareness of a lack
induced by an acknowledgement of sexual difference. In the representations of the
beautiful feminine body, as my discussion of von Max has shown, what is presented is
not *any* lack, nor *the* lack, neither the dead woman's sexual lack nor her mortality.
Rather, what is presented is 'nothing'; the fully intact body, the body smooth without
break. This non-gendered notion of castration involves the encroachment of real
death in life and on representation.

24 E. Lemoine-Luccioni, 1976.

25 E. A. Poe, 1846, p. 19.

26 See S. Kofman, 1985b, and M. Bal's discussion of this book, 1987, pp. 317–44. It is
one of the central aspects of recent scholarship that deals theoretically and not just
thematically with the issue of representations or figurations of death to emphasise the
binding interrelation between writing and loss. As a typical representative of this
theoretical position, M. de Certeau, 1975, argues that at the beginning of writing is
loss and that writing repeats this lack with each of its graphemes. It spells out an
absence which is its prerequisite and its destination.

27 E. Canetti, 1980. E. Vermeule, 1979, speaks of the dead warrior as lying on the earth
'horizontal, feminine, white and helpless', exposed to the violation by vultures in the
way his wife and children will be exposed to the violation by the surviving warriors, p.
105.

28 G. Pollock, 1988, p. 6. See also Victor Burgin's essay 'The Absence of Presence',
1986, p. 41.

29 J. Lotman, 1970, p. 168. E. Morin, 1970, also explains that the analogy of death – birth
excludes boundaries. Mother, grotta, earth, uterus, cavern, house, tomb, night, sleep
are concepts that mutually recall and refer to each other.

30 See E. F. Keller, 1985.

31 C. Merchant, 1980. As Ludmilla Jordanova, 1989, notes, the woman/nature and
men/culture associations were far from consistent. The notion that women are closer
to nature than men could support the claim that women are more emotional, credu-
lous, superstitious and less analytical even as it could be used to posit woman as carrier
of a new morality through which the artificiality of civiliation, the corruption and
exploitation of masculine reason and society could be transcended. As my discussion
will show, however, the contradiction goes further, in so far as woman is often also
associated with the corruption as well as the salvation found in artiface and culture.

32 S. de Beauvoir, 1974, p. 159.

33 S. de Beauvoir, 1974, p. 187.

34 J. Hall, 1974.

35 M. Warner, 1983, p. 82.

36 M. Warner, 1983.

37 R. Howard Bloch, 1987, refers to Philo Judaeus' reading of Genesis 2. 21: 'These words in their literal sense are of the nature of a myth. For how could anyone admit that a woman, or a human being at all, came into existence out of a man's side', p. 11.

38 S. de Beauvoir, 1974, p. 160.

39 S. de Beauvoir, 1974, quotes Michel Leiris: 'At present I tend to regard the feminine organ as something unclean or as a wound, not less attractive on that account, but dangerous in itself, like everything bloody, mucous, infected', p. 190.

40 S. Freud, 1940, p. 273.

41 S. de Beauvoir, 1974, p. 210.

42 A. D. Hutter, 1983, argues that a comparison of a *corpus* of literature with the display of bodies in a real morgue is not outrageous, 'given the history of the morgue itself and of the publics' relationship to the morgue as theater, where the bodies were displayed as they might have been at a waxwork . . . spectators . . . came there not just to identify bodies but to *view* them as spectacle', p. 11.

43 In a similar way W. Ong, 1977, argues that because 'writing carries within it always an element of death . . . a work about death often modulates readily, if eerily, into a work about literature', p. 239. He locates the reason for this connection between writing and death in several characteristics of writing: (1) that all writing is preterite, pointing posthumously to a past, (2) that the immortality of texts is comparable to that of dead bodies or monuments, paradoxically continuing the existence of its creator after his or her death, although it is itself dead, a non-living surrogate for a dead person, (3) that texts are apotropaic in that by exemplifying a kind of life after death they also intimate a life without death, (4) that in the act of writing the person addressed is absent, in the act of reading the writer is absent, so that the text can be seen as functioning beyond the death of sender and receiver.

44 R. Jakobson, 1960, p. 365.

45 S. Humphreys, 'Death and Time', 1981.

46 B. Johnson, 1980, p. 92

47 M. Deguy, 1969. G. Stewart, 1984, makes a similar case for the tropic and thus self-reflexive nature of all narrative representations of death, arguing that 'Death stands as a pivotal moment for language on the edge of silence, for evocation on the verge of the invisible, for narratability on the brink of closure', p. 51.

5

Deathbed scenes

The word soma, translated as body, originally designated a corpse, that is to say, what remains of an individual after his incarnated life and physical vitality have left him, reducing him to a pure inert figure, an effigy. He becomes an object of exhibition and lamentation for others, before he disappears, burned or buried, into invisibility.
J.-P. Vernant

Michel Foucault argues that an epistemic shift occurred at the end of the eighteenth century, and sees as one of its traits the rediscovery of the baroque conviction that knowledge is possible on the basis of death. 'Death as the absolute point of view over life and opening on its truth', he argues, 'is also that against which life, in daily practice comes up against.'[1] What re-emerges is an epistemological focus on the perception of death in life; on the presence of immobility in change; on the awareness that beauty and pleasure veil a skeletal fixity. Similarly to the late Renaissance, the perceived kinship between knowledge and eroticism lets death open up to the 'infinitely repeated attempts of language'.[2] The image Foucault uses to describe this re-discovered relation between language and death – as the limit and centre toward and against which we write – is that of a mirror to infinity erected vertically against death. He explains, 'headed toward death, language turns back upon itself . . . to stop this death which would stop it, it possesses but a single power: that of giving birth to its own image in a play of mirrors that has no limit'.[3] Given that writing always involves absence and reduplication, the transformation Foucault locates in cultural practice at the end of the eighteenth century must be seen as a self-conscious implementation of the affinity between death, indefinite repetition or striving and the endless self-representation and reduplication of language. As such it calls forth a literature where language is explicitly and self-consciously 'made into an image of itself and transgresses the limit of death through its reduplication in a mirror'. It calls forth a 'double of this already doubled writing' – the 'most poetical' of Poe's poetics.[4]

The difference Foucault locates in the baroque and the modern perception of death in life is contingent on the emergence of a focus on the self. The baroque 'macabre' implies a sense of homogeneity, since differences of fate, fortune and condition are effaced by death's universal, irrevocable and egalitarian gesture. In the late eighteenth century, with its 'morbid' version, death is in turn constitutive of singularity and offers an escape from a dull, average life. Death emerges as that moment in a person's life where individuality and absolute rarity could finally be attained, in a singular and unique severment from common or collective affiliation. Death began to be conceived as the moment where an inherent though invisible truth could apotheotically be fulfilled, where an otherwise incommunicable secret could be made visible.[5] Modern attitudes toward death are intrinsically connected with notions of individuality and consciousness of self. Witnessing death affirms a sense of personal individuality in the survivors, while society resorts to rituals that imply the refusal to accept mortality.[6]

Striking about this late eighteenth-century encoding of death is that it reverses the conventional understanding of death as a state of indifferentiation from which the deceased person's individuality can be rescued only by virtue of a commemorative effort of her or his survivors. This new conception of death's presence in life ascribes a certain autonomous power to the dying person, since not only the preservation in the memory of others but also the form of death, which can be shaped by the dying person, comes to determine her or his individuality. One of the most poignant paradoxes of the modern period is that death, as that which most threatens individuality, should also be its supreme confirmation. The elaboration of strategies to occult death call forth an equally elaborate staging of it.

Death is not just the end of organic existence, but also the removal of a social being from society. Because death emphasises the impermanence of social experience and elicits attempts to preserve some aspects of it in permanent form, the ambivalence between the transient and the permanent it invokes is as much a social as an epistemological focus for reflections.[7] The ritualisation of the deathbed scene, for example, serves to close the gap in social relations produced by death. As such it becomes the site where a transformation and reorganisation in kinship succession is negotiated, whose aim is to preserve or re-establish the social stability. This reassuring closure, however, occurs in relation to anteriority as well as posteriority. It is a literary convention of the nineteenth century that in their last moments the dying have a vision of the after-life, of dead kin waiting for them on the other side. At the same time a central part of the deathbed ritual includes the farewell greetings from kin and friends and the redistribution of social roles and property rights.[8] The continuity that is assured is one that involves the dying person in her or his relation to ancestors as well as to survivors.

Equally significant is the way the deathbed scene regulates the mourners' psychological adjustment to their loss, again in respect to the past and the future. Notions of 'good death' were introduced into Christian culture to suggest that the moment of death be seen as the correct fulfilment of and so a judgement on a person's life. One of the most crucial aspects of the mourning process includes the transformation of what was a living person and then an inanimate but destabilised decaying corpse into a permanent and stable inanimate representation: in Humphrey's words, into 'mummy, monument or memory, ash, ancestor or angel'.[9] The reduplication Foucault ascribes to language's relation to death can be seen as part of this return to stability. In two ways gender figures in the social rituals of death. On the one hand many societies, because they construct femininity as most markedly detached from the rhythms of everyday life, assign roles to women that involve the closest contact with the corpse.[10] On the other hand, 'the good death', is that of a virtuous and preferably innocent person: of children or virgins.[11] Given that the eighteenth century is also the crucial period for the discovery of femininity, the death of a beautiful woman can be seen either as the supreme recognition of this new discovery or as the recognition that notions of civilisation attached to it had no place in the world.[12]

The literary convention of the deathbed scene of a virtuous young woman has its most distinguished source in Samuel Richardson's sentimental epistolary novel, *Clarissa, or the History of a Young Lady* (1748).[13] Its heroine, Clarissa Harlowe, setting an example for the triumph of virtue by giving up her life willingly, as a glorious example, after several attempts at eluding her rapist Lovelace and asserting her independent will against the tyranny of her family, is the most striking model for all subsequent narrative representations of a 'good death'. Surrounded by her loyal friends, she dies forgiving and blessing her survivors and expecting Christ's embrace: 'Bless – bless – bless-you-all – and-now – and now . . . come – O come – blessed Lord – Jesus!' (IV.347). A 'charming serenity overspreading her sweet face', her corpse is a manifestation that her 'eternal happiness' had begun (IV.347). In a manner that is typical for this topos, her viewers claim they 'never saw death so lovely before', that death had not altered her features (IV.357). The lid of the coffin is kept unscrewed, so that her relatives, not present at her deathbed scene, can have one last sight of the corpse of this 'most admirable young creature', can kiss her lips and forehead once more, can address her with a tenderness and admiration before denied to the living body. The sight of her corpse confirms their image of her as 'injured saint', while they had cursed her as strong willed and too independent during her life-time. They stress her benign countenance, her sweet smile and composure, her natural dignity. The 'questionless happiness' they read in this composure is meant to assure them of the legitimacy of their pain in mourning her. It endows them with a sense of righteousness that allows them to place all the blame for her demise on Lovelace, as 'cursed author of all this distress', in order to absolve their own guilt (IV.399). Ringlets of her hair set in crystal, along with various portraits of her, are distributed among her closest friends, her letters are circulated among her survivors – all in an effort to stage her death as the meaningful closure to her life, though its meaning is open to each survivor's interpretation. As her friend Anne Howe exclaims in frustration at the finality posed by Clarissa's corpse –

'And is this all – is it all of my Clarissa's story?' (IV.402). Because I will treat this novel at length in a later chapter I will turn for my analysis of deathbed scenes first to Jean-Jacques Rousseau's *Julie, ou la Nouvelle Héloïse* (1761), and then to two Victorian examples: the deaths of Charles Dickens's Little Nell and Harriet Beecher Stowe's Little Eva.

In an effort to save her son from drowning, Rousseau's Julie de Wolmar throws herself into the water after him and dies of a fever resulting from the fear and excitement this accident induced. Although her survivors' reactions are an ambivalent mixture of rationalism and superstition, Julie's death exemplifies an ultimate expression of individuality and of her power to shape her life in death. As her husband explains, that she had to die is part of the common lot of mortals, but the way in which she died can be seen as unique to her.[14] His rendition of her death in a letter to Saint-Preux, the illicit lover of her youth, serves to delineate the peculiarities of this 'beautiful death'. That his narration is inscribed by a personal interest is made explicit from the start: 'what remains of her are only memories, my heart is pleased to recollect them' (536). Recollecting her death in writing is the only way to assure a tangible possession of the otherwise receding deceased.

The main purpose of Julie's deathbed scene is to name successors to her social role and assure the preservation of family unity. Gathering her family about her, she presents the plan for her children's future education, designating that Clare d'Orbe be their new mother and that Saint-Preux be integrated into her family, by entrusting him with her children and proposing a marriage to Clare as his 'other' Julie. Over her dying body the integrity of the family bond is restored, and this restitution is assured by virtue of an artful staging of death that aims at producing an indefinite relay of sentimental sympathy among the dying woman and her friends. By decorating her death chamber with flowers, dressing herself up in fine clothes, entertaining her children, debating with her pastor, conversing with her friends as she shares her meals, her sleeping and her waking hours with those who will survive her, Julie produces a situation of collective sentimental love that binds her family, friends and servants in their mutual participation in her death. The composure and joy she commands on her deathbed provokes an empathetic mixture of pain and awe, which is reduplicated in that everyone sees her or his response reflected both in the dying woman and in the other mourners.

The living share Julie's pain, which she, unlike a stoic, does not hide, while simultaneously admiring the inner nobility she demonstrates through her serenity, her love and her submission to death. She in turn suffers their pain, their despair, their inconsolability while admiring their endless love.[15] The beauty of her death consists in the self-possessed composure and honesty with which she accepts her end and enjoys her last moments. Her last hours are perceived as an apotheosis of her life: 'Never before was she more tender, more true, more caressing, more loveable, in a word more herself . . . she was more pleasing, more amiable than in health, and the last day of her life was also her most charming one' (556).

Her serene and happy acceptance of death is in part contingent on a conviction that, by leaving behind her family united, her spirit and her heart will remain with them. This continuity in affective ties serves to assuage any notion of death as an irrevocable or insurmountable gap. Indeed the family bond she so meticulously arranges on her deathbed includes her as well. As long as she can remember her earthly existence, she will be connected to them in love and their collective commemorative effort will serve to make her imaginatively present though bodily absent. In fact the integration of Saint-Preux into her family is seen as the creation of a commemorative community that will reanimate her and as the creation of a monument to herself: 'That all whom she loved may reassemble so as to give her a new being. Your cares, your pleasures, your friendship, all will be her work' (565). A final aspect of the continuity of their affective bond, as a sublation of death, is the popular notion of a reunification in heaven.[16]

Focusing on the deathbed scene as a moment of summing-up, or re-collecting and transmission, as a moment of truth, Walter Benjamin draws a connection between the publicly anchored ubiquity and metaphoric power of death and literature's power to communicate experience. His claim is that, along with wisdom, it is a man or woman's lived experience which, making up the material of narratives, first assumes transmissible form at the moment of his or her death.[17] The proximity of death provokes in the dying person a succession of images from that life which is about to end, along with one's interpretations of past occurrences, one's convictions, one's advice to posterity. In this final confrontation with the past events of one's life, the dying person not only reduplicates herself or himself but also senses the unforgettable or eternal quality of these 'remembered' events. All s/he has to tell is imbued with authority and it is this 'authority', arising from the aporia of speaking or writing in the shadow of death and against it, that lies at the origin of all narratives. Death is the sanction for all that a storyteller might relate. She or he borrows authority from death.

Benjamin locates our fascination for narratives in the sure knowledge of the death of the protagonist, not only because death legitimises any tale but because it is also the one experience that always recedes from our knowledge. Representations of dying are significant because the flame of destiny which consumes the protagonist radiates a warmth to us as readers which we can never receive in our own lives. What draws the reader to the novel, he claims, is the hope that he may warm his life at this representation of death.[18] This fascinating warmth is so 'authoritative' because it feeds off its own impossibility. Used as a strategy to legitimate convictions, decisions or advice, the death of another nevertheless remains untransmissible to any surviving spectator. The particular power that a narration of one's past life has for someone about to die is sharable only on an imaginative level for those whose period of listening is not limited by an approaching death. What lends authority to the narrative of a dying person is not a self-present, immediate truth of experience or knowledge of death that seemingly becomes transmissible at the deathbed of another. Rather, it is the reduplication that occurs in the narrative between a narrator whose past events will survive eternally by virtue of her or his tale and a narrator about to cease speaking. Combining the limit with the indefinite, the tale of a dying woman or man marks the site where the opposition of here and there; other and self collapse in such a way as to point simultaneously toward that beyond signification, towards the act of signification and towards the imaginative expectations and desires of the readers.

Julie's deathbed scene exemplifies the authentication that death lends to narratives in precisely Benjamin's sense of endless reduplication. Her survivors, and implicitly the novel's readers, 'interpret' her two narratives – one oral and one written – to find the epitome or key to her life and to discover how better to live their own lives. The absolute form of aposiopesis, silence, that is a necessary performative condition of all last words[19] legitimises the advice she has to give. Yet one must bear in mind that her narrative is already duplicated by her husband's 'recollection', and that as dying narrator she 'writes' a beautiful death with her body in two separate registers. She 'authors' a united familiy and she creates that death, which draws her friends and the readers to her narrative. In so doing she mirrors the text's composition – her 'recollecting' of characters into a family unity and thoughts into a narrative unity reflect the text's act of re-collecting, in the double sense of bringing separate events into a unified form and of re-presencing (in the double sense of representing and making present again) absent bodies. As its dying centre, Julie is also the text's self-reflexive moment, by commenting on the end or decomposition that always also informs textual production: by literally embodying the illusory warmth as it recedes from the reader's grasp.

The main advice Julie transmits to her family – that the best preparation for a death is a good life – is then in part written materially, with her own body. Not only does the proximity of death lend authority to her narrative, but the calm and happy composure she shows on her deathbed legitimises her Protestant convictions. Her claim is that, since her life has been a continual belief in and love for God, since it has been a dutiful existence based on dignity, good intentions and virtue, the thought of death was never terrifying. By implication the peaceful end she has fashioned for herself is understood by her friends as an admonishing text to follow in their own lives. Her final recapitulation of her life shows this as a long succession of sweet and fortunate circumstances. Her friendship to her cousin Clare, her illicit love for Saint-Preux, her marriage and motherhood, even her sorrows and sufferings are presented in a favourable light, as advantageous to her general design of a 'good life'. The interruption of this mounting degree of joy due to the unexpected accident leaves her at the height of her happiness. It is a superlatively poetical death, because it fulfills the 'text' of her good life before it can move into a decline.

In the letter she writes to Saint-Preux, however, she gives this moment of death a somewhat different meaning. Her fatal fever emerges not as an accidental result of her attempt to save her son but rather as a suicidal desire.[20] Here, too, death is seen as a form of rescue, not from decline, however, but from temptation

– from the danger to her honour that a reunion with Saint-Preux may have brought about. While the oral narrative emphasises her ability to control her life, to live in good conscience and virtuous happiness, the second narrative focuses on her inability to control her amorous sentiments, on the involuntary resurgence of her desire for her illicit lover. Since her self-fashioned life of virtue, duty and happiness cannot include her heart (that part of herself which she can not trust), death serves as her only sanction against future culpability and sin. In this second, written narrative she also presents her death as occurring at a perfect moment, as 'the happiest hour', but the implication is that of a more ambivalent sentiment. She is happiest because on her deathbed she can allow her love for Saint-Preux to 'be born again', since she need no longer fear it. She can allow her love for him to support her body at exactly that moment that all other powers leave her, to 'reanimate her as she dies' (564). Death sanctions not just the authority of her final unconditional declaration of love but also its 'innocence'. She need not have shame at expressing all she feels, at expressing her desire for their reunion in heaven that virtue deferred on earth, because hers is a 'dead letter', self-referential, its sender in death's arms, the face and heart eaten by worms. Where the reduplication inscribed in the oral narrative was that of an embodied beautiful deathbed scene as legitimising the Protestant norm of a good life, this second letter is presented as a legitimising signature to her self-composed fatal letter – death warrant and obituary in one. The emphasis in this narrative is not on the escalation of fortunate circumstances but on the sacrifices this fashioned 'happiness' required. Julie concludes that this final separation cannot be cruel after so many other sacrifices: 'it only means dying one more time' (565).

In describing her life as a series of deaths Julie connects her own death implicitly with that of her mother, which initiated the detour of her 'happy life' – her separation from Saint-Preux, her marriage to M. de Wolmar, her fatal jump. Two moments are crucial in this otherwise inconspicuous deathbed scene. Firstly, disregarding the fact that the cause of her mother's death is a physical illness, Julie believes that her illicit affair with Saint-Preux has made her guilty of matricide. Secondly, the loss of her mother is perceived as death's entrance into her own life in the form of loss, disgrace, sorrow and pain; 'deprived forever of your care, your advice, your sweet caresses, I have become dead to happiness, to peace, to innocence . . . I am more dead than you' (231). This death discloses the illusion, because sinfulness, of her romantic attachment: 'the veil is torn; this long illusion has faded' (232). Ironically this romantic fantasy is reinstated in her own death.

Saint-Preux repeats the substitution or conflation of dead mother and dead daughter in a dream he has shortly before Julie's actual death. In it Julie, desiring death from her mother, because she feels guilty of having robbed the life of her to whom she owes her life, is suddenly in her mother's position, dying, with her face hidden by a veil that cannot be removed. Antithetical to Julie's description of her mother's death, which was associated with the tearing of a veil, this image shows death as linked to an irrevocable occultation. If the mother's death scene articulates the belief that death serves as an anti-illusory moment, this second dream version subverts any belief in death's transparency, renders it again as an ambiguous moment where separate figures can be condensed into one, where the object of desire turns into an object of death, where desire and anxiety, guilt and triumph merge, where over the body of the beloved the tangibility and visibility of death is precisely put into question.[21] The hermeneutic ambiguity that emerges when Julie's two 'final narratives' are seen in conjunction with these other deathbed scenes is duplicated on a formal level. The paradox informing both the oral and the written 'final words' is that this superlative aposiopesis combines the figure of an incomplete thought or sudden interruption with that of a figure of conclusiveness and closure. As such it places an indeterminacy into the centre of the unified image or narrative that the authority of death seemingly provokes.

While the moment of death is eclipsed in the text, Julie's corpse provokes a succession of reduplications that stage various ways in which the gap death produces can be denied or mitigated, in which the absent body can be 're-pre-senced'. Clare d'Orbe's first response is to try to reanimate Julie's body by throwing herself on to the corpse, warming it and pressing it with her own body, and passionately calling to it. The servants, more susceptible to superstition, choose to believe in her resurrection. Death triggers the imaginative faculties of the servants and at the sight of her corpse they begin to reinvent her: 'soon the deceased had not only made a sign, she had moved, she had spoken, and there were twenty eye witnesses to detailed events that had never happened' (561). They dress her lavishly and display her on her bed by leaving the curtains open, so that the exposed corpse turns into a 'mortal spectacle'. As a corpse Julie resembles her former self, even as death has changed her body into something else.

The covering of death that is attained by dressing Julie's corpse and transform-ing her into a sign for an imagined resurrection is but the pagan or 'morbid' side (in Foucault's sense) to Julie's own 'Protestant' spectacle of a 'serene end', which also served to 'veil' the reality of death. In the superstitious attitude of the servants we have the replacement of the departed individual Julie by her deanimated body, where the cadaverous double uncannily serves to articulate both an undoing of mortality and the death it attempts to overcome. It is a materialised version of the mental image Julie's family will preserve against death's finality; a self-reflexive moment that illuminates the equatability of corpse with representation. Again the superlative self-reflexivity, the fact that here death lets the body become its own image, also marks the limit of this apotropaic gesture against death. Since the 'material' of this representation of Julie is the body itself, it cannot elude material decay. Spurred on by the summer's heat, Julie's corpse begins to decompose. In a chiasmic move, Clare repeats the covering of death initiated by the servants (when they displayed Julie's ornamented body as a reanimated version of itself), by throwing a veil over the dead woman's face and accompanying this with an interdiction against lifting it again. Literally covering all signs of material death, she completes the translation of Julie's body into a sign. Veiled, the corpse is no longer a double of the deceased individual but transformed into a totem which commands awe and fear, and can safely be buried.

In a less literal manner Julie's family uses the strategy of doubling to deny her death; they reduplicate her in their memories and their letters. This is Wolmar's intention when he 'gathers together' his memories of his deceased wife, as it is Clare's aim when she invites Saint-Preux 'let us collect all that was dear to her. Let her spirit animate us' (567). Yet the relation between living and dead proves to be one of reciprocity. Even as they reanimate her by preserving her living image in their mental and sentimental lives, she reanimates them. Even as they keep a part of her on earth (Clare hears and feels her presence), she serves as the site for reflections on their own death. She reflects back to them the Beyond. Their commemorative gathering is but in anticipation that Julie, as death's medium, will ultimately collect them. Clare's imagined resurrection of Julie serves to express her own desire for death; 'I feel myself carried away ... I hear the murmer of a plaintive voice ... her coffin does not hold her enirely' (567). For each of the survivors, Julie's corpse does not stand for itself but rather is used as an additional, surplus sign, 'outre-signifiant'.[22]

Discourses and representations dealing with a corpse turn back to other matters, to the living, desperately trying to endow their lives with meaning. Even though death is the measure and limit of all human knowledge and lends authority to life's meaning, the living can have access to death only through the death of another. Death transforms the body into a sign in the sense that the living can interpret the spectacle of the corpse as the repositiory of knowledge about the nature of our postlapsarian existence that is in fact inaccessible.[23] By making death representable in the dramatisation of the deathbed scene, that state which is outside human knowledge becomes accessible to the experience of the surviving spectators. But the paradox inherent in any representation of death in art is that it is tied to narrative, and that means to the focalisors' hermeneutic interests and needs. The represented corpse marks a threshold in so far as it points to the Beyond, but it does so by irrevocably reflecting the speculating spectators, whose view ultimately always ricochets back to the Here. The survivors read the death of the deceased as a moment of a truth in meaning, as a transparency between signifier and signified, as a sublation of the division between illusion and reality. Reading the corpse is meant to guarantee the possibility of true signification.[24]

Yet the problem is that the corpse, much like the image in general, is always a body-double, so that whatever the survivors see is only a reference to some absent and more meaningful concept or image that is always already lost, always again receding from our perceptual grasp. The corpse as signifier for true signification is the product of a hermeneutic desire, its condition, pretextual need and its failure. The futility of an attempt to attain a true expression of death is, further-more, doubly inscribed. In the same way that death always recedes from the epistemological grasp of the living, the process of representation is such that the reference of signifiers to other signifiers is indefinite, that representations are always in some sense figural, speaking 'other', referring to a meaning that is located 'elsewhere'. To return once more to Poe's poetics, the self-reflexivity of representations of death is such that they point not to any one fixed object (since death, and with it the possibility of a transparent truth, is always absent), but rather to the process of hermeneutics and signification. Much like the corpse, empty of its soul, representations of death refer to the absence of full meaning by signalling the presence of meaning elsewhere. The analogy between image and corpse – so supremely exposed when the image is that of a corpse – resides in the fact that both conceal and reveal at the same time; both are doubled in that they point to what is absent and to their own act of representing. For Blanchot the image and the corpse stage a 'strangeness' because they are compiled of a doubledness and a lack of material reference: 'where there is nothing, that is where the image finds its condition, but disappears into it.'[25]

Because the transitory nature of human existence and the possibility of an afterlife have always preoccupied the living, the deathbed has always been ritualised. All earthly life is directed toward death and one's conduct is fashioned in view of death and the possibility of salvation. Burial rites are used to reinforce social or political ideals; tombs and funerary sculptures endorse concepts of continuity, legitimacy and status.[26] Recently historians have been eager to demonstrate that different periods are characterised by different cultural images of death and attitudes to it. Philippe Ariès distinguishes five different periods based on the change in 'man's' relationship with nature.[27] The early European attitude is that of a natural expectation and acceptance of death as an inevitable facet of life. Death was perceived not as a frightening event but as an organic and integral part of a harmonious reciprocity between living and dead. With the emergence of individualism two conceptual changes occur. The destiny of each individual or family takes precedence over that of the community, hence a new emphasis on the funeral as a sign for social status and material wealth. At the same time the focus on the self provokes a passionate attachment to an existence in the material world and a lust for life, hence the emergence of a serious resentment of death. For the epistemic shift in attitudes toward death, which Ariès, like Foucault, locates in the eighteenth century, he isolates four psychological elements: a consciousness of the self, society's defence against a construction of nature as 'savage', a belief in survival and in the existence of evil.[28]

By the eighteenth century the double threat of loss of autonomy and of a separation from the world that death poses to the individual brought forth an attitude of denial that found its expression in a duplicitous mixture of fear and fascination. The dead body became increasingly an object of scientific research while at the same time health reformers, in order to protect the living from the dangers of the decaying body, demanded that cemeteries be removed from churches and city centres to the outskirts. Yet this symbolic expulsion of the dead from the community of the living, this social severment of death from life, was interlinked with an imaginative blurring of the distinction between living and dead.[29] The distanced death remained at hand if only in the displaced form of the 'dead body'; as object of anatomical research and of embalmment; as erotic object of desire.[30] The eighteenth century marks an increase in necrophilia, in an anxiety about premature burial and a fear of the living or reanimated corpse, the vampire. At this historical moment, previous cultural familiarity with death, its integration into life, turns into a retreat from death in a double gesture of denial and mystification. The secular nature of modern existence, the partial loss of an exclusively religious regulation of death, along with the so-called triumph of reason in the Enlightenment, produced this spirit of alienation. Even as the scientific and philosophic emphasis on rationality tried to combat death by exploration and explanation, a new uncertainty about the status of the dead body and a return to superstition was equally prevalent.

In folklore the ambivalence in attitude connected with the corpse is such that the corpse is endowed with magical powers that are both dangerous and beneficial. To see or to preserve a corpse could be harmful since the spirit of the dead could draw other living beings into death. At the same time the corpse was thought to have magical healing powers and the ability to presage the future.[31] 'If the soul left the body at death and migrated to its heavenly resting place,' Ruth Richardson explains, 'there would exist the danger that, disembodied, it could remain hovering around the haunts of the living. If on the other hand, it slept in the grave, then it would somehow be present in or near the body after death.'[32] Equally contradictory is the fact that death was often eroticised. Even as the death of a virtuous woman served to establish and confirm social morality, an analogy between the aggressivity of death and the violence of love was used to convey both as part of that dark nature which fundamentally disturbs the autonomy and rationality of the self and which provokes a transgression of morality. Because nature, conceived as an all-powerful force of destruction, was exteriorised into an object of control and domination, it also became dangerously foreign, untamed and savage.[33] By the nineteenth century, 'love' and 'death' were culturally constructed as the two realms where savage nature could break into 'man's' city, at the same historical moment that society believed that its achievements in technology and rationalism had served to colonise nature completely. Since it combines these two disruptive elements, the dead body of a woman served as a particularly effective figure for this triumph over 'violent nature' and its failure to expulse the Other completely; a superlative figure for the inevitable return of the repressed.

By 1750, an attitude to death which Ariès calls 'the death of the Other' is securely in place. The emergence of the modern family, of a new spiritualisation of human experience, of the new emphasis on personal affections, sentiments and the imagination brought about a new welcoming of death, but with the attention on the surviving family not on the dying individual. Ariès also calls this period 'the age of beautiful death' because beautification was used to hide the physical signs of mortality and decay and to overcome any sense of separation or loss of individuation. Death became a private event, assuring continuity in the form of a family unity and an androcentric domestication of heaven that saw it as a continuation or repetition of earthly existence, not as a completely other sphere.[34] The literary theme of a blissful reunion of domestic life in heaven, supported by consolatory literature, grave inscriptions, monuments and the keeping of mementos of the dead, implies that death was no longer ugly or frightening, because the separation it caused was temporary.[35] Finality could be denied because continuity was excessively staged.

This period is known for its taste in elaborate public funerals, extravagant tombstone sculptures and pompous cemetery monuments.[36] The tomb, as last resting place, was revered in perpetuity, visits to the cemetery not only served to display family piety but were also conducive to meditation. This cult of tombs is a fetishisation of death, for the tomb is both a representative sign of the beloved family members that the living have lost and a preservation of the deceased by virtue of the worship of an object reminding of them.[37] The souls of the deceased were thought not to be irrevocably severed from the living but to continue to dwell nearby, inviting a dialogue with the living and inducing the hope of a future reunion.

One form of masking death was a cultivation of the world of memory, supporting the notion that the precious dead are not really dead, in fact continue to live. At stake in this aesthetisation of death is the memory image, and the survivors' ability to imagine. As death became unfamiliar and as such connected with fear, it was not only put under cover but also relegated to the site previously occupied by love – the imaginary.[38] In conjunction with this cultural construction of the fantasy of death, memory as a preservation of the dead could also be dangerous. Sentimental longing for a reunion in heaven turned into the horror of vampirism. The contradictory attitude toward death became such that society was as anxious to secure itself against the dead, and to use commemoration as the irrevocable severing of any possible dialogue between the living and the dead, as it was eager to believe in continuity.

A belief that death was not the end of a beloved person turned the presence at the deathbed into a comforting and exalting spectacle. Visiting a house of mourning became comparable to visiting a picture gallery. Yet the apotheosis of death that its merging with beauty produced contained a crucial contradiction. As Ariès puts it, this death was no longer death but rather an illusion of art; death hiding beneath beauty.[39] The conceptual equation of death with the beautiful and the scene of dying with a museum took on other shapes in the eighteenth and nineteenth centuries. In this period morgues were visited like picture galleries while the wax museum conflated the fascination for the preserved dead body with aesthetic pleasure. This period also perfected the technique of embalming and mummification. What characterises this 'cult of the beautiful dead' is a subjective fascination with idealised images of the deceased in such a way that permanently embalmed bodies and stable images displace and replace impermanent materiality.

Carol Christ argues that this cultural period's intense anxiety about bodily dissolution after death is integrally related to the aesthetisation of mourning in funerary monument and rituals. The fetishism peculiar to nineteenth century funerary practices was one that identifies the dead body with iconisation by displaying the dead body as symbol and as material substance of the deceased. The best example for this was the public display of Jeremy Bentham's mummified corpse, an 'auto-icon', because in this effigy the ideal funerary monument is the body itself.[40] As part of the Victorian fascination for concealment, this bodiliness of the embalmed corpse is precisely what covers death, in the superlative manner of a self-reflexive double substitution. An 'image' replaces a destabilised body, but this 'image' is also the body. By effacing the death of the Other in this act of preservation, death is effaced in proxy. What becomes clear, however, is that this is also part of a fascination for the intermediary, the double, the uncanny. Vovelle suggests that the historical shift Ariès identifies as 'the death of the self' transforming into 'the death of the Other' presupposes the association between woman and death.[41] Along with sentimental mourning, superstitious horror and aesthetisation, the feminine gendering of the corpse serves as a strategy for veiling death.

Two contradictions emerge from this historical discussion – firstly the ambivalent location and status of the dead body, neither entirely in the Beyond, nor entirely Here, along with its conjunction of malign and healing powers, and secondly the interconnection between a conceptual exclusion of death and its representational ubiquity, as though the more a culture refuses death the more it imagines and speaks of it. Aesthetisation, meant to hide death, always also articulates mortality; the memorial icon or the artistic image are dead letters, inanimate bodies; the act of denial, as Freud repeatedly demonstrates, in part affirms what it tries to occult. Death not only marks a self-reflexive turn from any non-semiotic material reference, but the ubiquity of images of death in the eighteenth and nineteenth centuries occurs over the social displacement of death to the city's periphery. Because death's presence is not culturally affirmed, representations of death also turn from any reference to social reality. Self-reflexivity is inscribed in images of death in that, because their objects of reference are indeterminate, they signify 'as well', 'besides', 'other'. The signifieds that can be attached to the signifier 'corpse' are legion. Given that dying is a solitary, highly individual and incommunicable event, McManners concludes that the historian writing about death is really writing about cultural attitudes toward survival; about society affirming itself; about the family expressing its coherence, the Church exemplifying its beliefs. I will add, as a poetic motif, death is also about the mourning lover-poet demonstrating his aesthetic skills and his ability to create beautiful images.

In order to illustrate these contradictions I will now present two typical Victorian deathbed scenes. In *The Old Curiosity Shop* (1841), Little Nell's moment of death is eclipsed from the narrative, recountable only after the event, as its temporal reduplication. The narrator focuses on her corpse, which is 'so fair to look upon' because it is an unnatural perfection of serenity and beauty: 'the solemn stillness was no marvel now she was dead' (653). Death recreates the body into a perfect version of its former self. Nell's corpse *seems* a beautiful, calm and 'fresh creature' because it hovers between two moments of animation, no longer and not yet a living body, marked by God's 'breath of life', that is by the traces of suffering, pain, care and fatigue. In fact, seemingly located outside facticity, it seems to efface not only the general category of temporality but also all evidence of past events specific to Nell's life. Her corpse allegorically signifies the possibility of the human body overcoming sin and all other signs of difference; it aesthetically stages the death of sorrow and the 'birth of peace and perfect happiness . . . imaged in her tranquil beauty and profound repose' (654). This figuration is meant to confirm the survivors' and readers' belief that death is the liberation from earthly care. Like all representations, even when they speak an 'other' meaning, the corpse in its function as image works on the principle of similarity. It is not only strange, no longer itself, but also familiar: 'and still her former self lay there, unaltered in this change . . . that same sweet face . . . the same mild lively look' (654). The triumph over death figured over her dead body includes three moments. Her perfect corpse effaces all traces of death's inscription in life, it resembles its living counterpart and it generates commemorative stories, the latter two assuring continuity.

The retrospective description of Nell's death follows the conventional pattern. In her transition between material and spiritual existence she relives and recounts scenes from her past in a final, thoroughly positive version ('no painful scenes'), she fantasises the heavenly state to come ('beautiful music . . . in the air') and kissing those friends present at her deathbed farewell, she dies in the arms of her grandfather. Leslie Fiedler suggests that this Victorian version of Shakespeare's Cordelia can also be seen as a Protestant *Pietà*.[42] Indeed this secular replacement of Christ's body with that of a virginal, innocent woman serves the same double meaning that the scene of the cross has in Christian iconography – the great triumph over sin and death as it is linked with the tragic spectacle of suffering. Dickens emphasises this notion of a 'triumph over death' based on the sacrifice of innocence by using Nell's corpse to turn her into the allegorical figure of an angel: 'so shall be known the angels in their majesty, after death' (654). Yet the paradox inherent in this Victorian narrative is that it can give body to knowledge of the Beyond, to knowledge accessible 'after death' in the representational garments of the Here. Nell's dead body serves in Benjamin's sense as the authority on which Dickens can claim a 'mighty, universal Truth . . . When Death strikes down the innocent and young, for every fragile form from which he lets the panting spirit free, a hundred virtues rise, in shapes of mercy, charity, and love, to walk the world, and bless it' (659). The pathos of Dickens's deathbed scenes have both a social and a religious purpose. The heart senti-mentally warmed by pity for the dead may not only more readily feel compassion for the living, but it may also more readily dissolve religious doubt.[43] Like the ubiquity of images of death in the absence of a social acceptance of death, their Christian encoding was connected with another kind of absence: with a religious crisis.

But the triumph over death is also implicitly staged by Nell's mourners as they translate her, in their memories, into the allegorical figure of an angel and replace her body with 'the story of good Miss Nell', a perpetual remembrance in the form of a narrative monument that can be passed on to posterity even as the place where Nell lived is so altered that the narrators of the story can no longer be certain of the spot (672). This form of commemoration triumphs over death by generating an indefinitely transmissible text that preserves Nell's continuity in an anterior and a posterior form; in the events of her past life and in her figure as a celestial body. This text ultimately is useful to the living, for it serves as the 'last preserve of truth, (it) conveys the basic importance of the moral scheme';[44] it serves, as Kit's rendition to his children shows, to educate and entertain (671).

Yet an ambivalence is fundamentally inherent in the status of the corpse. Preserving a dead body functions analogously to the concept of the 'pharmakon', invoked by Derrida in his discussion of writing – a 'drug' hovering between magic charm, healing potion and poison, the effect determined by the dose taken. In the old man's form of commemoration, which also preserves Nell's body by replacing it with images, the pernicious aspect of imaging as tropic embalmment of a corpse becomes evident. While the other mourners can turn away from Nell's tomb once the vault is covered and the stone fixed down, the old man, sitting at her grave, uses his imaginative capabilities to recreate her and invent new episodes of their shared life: 'How many pictures of new journeys over pleasant country . . . how many visions of what had been, and what he hoped was yet to be' (661). While the others' perpetual remembrance serves to confirm the continuity of their earthly existence in the gesture of a 'healing' fetishistic denial, the old man's disacknowledgement is a celebration of death that is precisely not fetishistic because it culminates in the desire to be fetched by Nell, as angel of death, and to embark with her on a last mutual flight. What determines the effect of the corpse–image as pharmakon seems to depend on whether the translation of the corpse into heaven and into narrative is acknowledged as a tropic turn or whether the reduplication produced by the imaginary 'represencing' is endowed with the literal, i.e. not severed from material referentiality. The stability that an image, doubling the corpse, affords can point in two directions. It can lead to the stabilising closure of the gap opened by death and the generation of moral values or art, or it can lead to the stability of death itself.

In *Uncle Tom's Cabin* (1852), Eva's passage from the Here to the Beyond explicitly illustrates the way the deathbed scene serves to pass on a moral responsiblity to others. Like Nell, Eva stages the death of innocence, and her Christ-like sacrifice is meant to convert its spectators to Christianity and to correct the evils of American slavery. Of course, the question remains open whether her death is too fundamentally decorative to be morally effective, whether it is morally effective as a citation of its culture's central myth – the story of the crucifixion – or whether it fails to lead to concrete political action because the fact of death can never fully be denied and so a general helplessness underlies any call for action induced by death.[45]

Eva's deathbed scene focuses on the moment of translation from this world to the next. Though she understands heaven as the place of a future reunion with her family and friends, and secures a continuity in affectional bonds by distributing curls of her hair, heaven is above all the place of a union with Christ, her 'bridegroom'. In this version of the deathbed scene the horror of death, its 'ghastly imprint', is also veiled under an expression of sublime serenity and the corpse turned into the allegorical figure of the angel – a high celestial expression on its face, a mingling of rapture and repose in her body.[46] The rhetoric of the Victorian deathbed scene seems to promise its spectators a fleeting glance of what might lie beyond death.[47] Yet the clarity staged by Eva's death is implicitly connected with bodily purity. Death is encoded as the 'overshadowing presence of spiritual natures, the dawning of immortal life in that childish soul' (426), as a translation of the body into a dematerialised form that eternally preserves the virgin girl.

As part of the convention of a good Christian death, Eva is transported to heaven before she has become too contaminated by the world. But by implication, the death of Eva, bride of Christ, prevents her sexual contamination. So that her sexual purity can be assured the narrative requires her death.[48] Leslie Fiedler points out that the bridal bed conjoins the site of defloration and death, because the virgin dies to be replaced by the woman.[49] However, if the bridal bed can be the deathbed and the loss of virginity a form of death, the deathbed can also be a bridal bed. The superlative quality of Eva's defloration is that it leaves her body perfectly intact; it is signified without any material reference and occurs so to speak in the Beyond.

Stowe's narrative also exemplifies the way a fascination with death is concerned with the representationability of the Beyond. As Tom explains 'When that ar' blessed child goes into the kingdom, they'll open the door so wide, we'll all get a look in at the glory' (425). Dying, Eva can look at God with impunity, and she serves as a medium for those for whom an unmediated knowledge of what lies beyond earthly existence is unattainable or dangerous. While facing God directly blinds the mortal, watching the other facing God serves an imaginative figuration of the forbidden knowledge. It is in part this hermeneutic desire which makes for the breathless tension of Eva's deathbed scene: 'The child lay panting on her pillow . . . the large clear eyes rolled up and fixed. Ah, what said those eyes, that spoke so much of heaven . . . but so solemn, so mysterious, was the triumphant brightness of that face, that it checked even the sobs of sorrow' (427f.). As they 'pressed around her, in breathless stillness', what her survivors do is press her for an answer to their most urgent and impossible question. Yet the failure contained in any attempt at representing the Beyond for the living is made explicit in Eva's response to their desire to tell them what she sees. She must resort to a rhetorical move into the allegorical and into cliché: 'O! love, – joy, – peace!' (428). Witnessing the death of the other means witnessing one's own limit (the 'bright eternal doors of heaven' irrevocably close behind the child) and one's necessary return to the here and the self. There can be no experience of the death of the other, for the living see it only externally, as spectators, projecting on to the dying their own fantasies. The promise of absolute knowledge, raised to the highest degree is also supremely disappointed; speaking of death means speaking from a heightened 'sphere of illusions', for one grasps death only through others and only as a living being.[50]

Edgar Morin argues that the two fundamental apotropaic myths invoked to defend against death are those of the resurrection or immortality of the soul and those of the double. In both cases individuality is preserved and secured through reduplication or images of a 'double life'. This affirmation of immortality, which always implies a conscience of death is, furthermore, connected to a person's image of the self. Death returns when the self looks at death or looks at him or herself.[51] The image in its function as double, eternalises the self even as it splits it, even as it confirms or signifies the self's death. And because, as the *vanitas* convention exemplifies, a supreme form of self-reflection, a narcissistic love of one's own image, often carries death's signature, representations of mirrors signify the conjunction of love and death with the image as a double of the self.

It is precisely this irrevocable return to the imaginary in the face of death that I have wanted to highlight in my discussion of deathbed scenes. By the mid eighteenth century it takes a particular turn, given that that particular period's fascination with death is contingent on death no longer being familiar. Death, conceived as an external, alterior and potentially malign force, is recuperated into the cultural symbolic order by virtue of a narcissistically 'healing' imaginary process. Because this culture conceived of itself as alienated from death, any representation of it always included the question of a self-conscious, mitigated and imperfect relation to its object of depiction. What emerges as culturally specific to representations of death after the mid eighteenth century is this moment of self-reflexivity that allows the depiction to serve an aesthetic discussion of the representational process itself; of the image's double function as producer of ambiguous division and of a stable, continuous whole. The conflation of death with unfamiliarity lends a particular salient power to the image of feminine death. For what makes the death of a woman so impressive is not just her embodiment of innocence and virtue but also her position in culture as the unfamiliar Other, like death recuperable in the form of an image.

Notes to Chapter 5

1 M. Foucault, 1973, p. 155. See also 1970, where he sets the parameters of this break between 1775 and 1825.
2 M. Foucault, 1973, p. 171.

3 M. Foucault, 'Language to Infinity', 1977, p. 54.
4 M. Foucault, 'Language to Infinity', 1977, p. 56.
5 See M. Foucault, 1973, pp. 170–2.
6 E. Morin, 1970.
7 S. Humphreys, 'Introduction', 1981.
8 See J. McManners, 1985, who calls the last farewell 'a supreme reward of family solidarity', p. 256.
9 S. Humphreys, 'Death and Time,' 1981, p. 268.
10 A particularly resonant example for this proximity between femininity and death in Christian culture is the relationship between Christ's dead body and women. Though his dead body is taken down from the cross by Joseph of Arimathae, there are mainly women under the cross during Christ's last hours. And it is the women, going to anoint Christ's corpse, who find his sepulchre empty and believe in his resurrection without material proof.
11 S. Humphreys, 'Death and Time', 1981. As an aside it is interesting to note that from the Middle Ages to the eighteenth century the most common depiction of the deathbed scene is that of Mary's *dormitio*; see P. Ariès, 1983, chapter three on the passage from the deathbed to the grave.
12 See J. McManners, 1985; T. Laqueur, 1990.
13 M. Vovelle, 1983, argues that one must not underestimate the importance *Clarissa* had in fashioning the new collective sensibility.
14 J.-J. Rousseau, 1761: 'the employment of her last moments, her discourse, her sentiments, her soul, all that belonged only to Julie. She did not live like another; no other person I know died like her', p. 536.
15 R. Meyer-Kalkus, 1977, pp. 106–10.
16 See C. McDannell and B. Lang, 1988.
17 Of course W. Benjamin, 1977, argues from a nostalgic position, associating the modern decline in narrative plausibility with a repression of death in late nineteenth-century culture.
18 W. Benjamin, 1977.
19 R. Macksey, 1983.
20 J. McManners, 1985, argues that Julie allows herself to die because she has done her duty to her husband and now looks forward to heaven as the place of reunion with the only man she passionately loved.
21 J.-J. Rousseau presents this ambiguity in the two different responses to Saint-Preux's dreams. While Claire d'Orbe sees it as a dangerous premonition, and follows Saint-Preux in her fantasies, imagining Julie as dying, M. de Wolmar interprets the dream as an unconscious desire for the Julie legally forbidden to him. This difference is repeated in the letter announcing Julie's death. While Clare connects her death with Saint-Preux's fantasies – 'imprudent man . . . unhappy visionary! Never will you see her again . . . the veil' – Wolmar emphasises the authority of her last wish, referring to her desire that Clare marry Saint-Preux and be integrated into her family – 'honor her last wishes', p. 535.
22 L.-V. Thomas, 1980, p. 58
23 J. Koerner, 1985.
24 In a similar vein, J. Rose, 1989, argues that the ambiguity of the concept of the death drive in Freud is the concept itself, that since death can not be located in a specific object, the 'object becomes the very structure of representation through which it fails

to be thought, the impasse of conceptual thinking itself', p. 34.

25 M. Blanchot, 1981, p. 79
26 J. Whaley, 1982.
27 P. Ariès, 1977. I place the word 'man' in quotations to emphasise the cultural construction of masculinity underlying Ariès work. Because, unlike Vovelle, he deals neither with a difference in men and women's social experience of death, nor with the cultural gendering of death, it remains unclear what the generic term 'man' is meant to encompass.
28 P. Ariès, 1977, sees this shift as one of several, noting an earlier break in the twelfth century.
29 J. Whaley, 1982.
30 P. Ariès, 1977.
31 See H. Bächtold-Stäubli, 1987, vol. 5, pp. 1024–60.
32 R. Richardson, 1989, p. 16.
33 P. Ariès, 1977.
34 See A. Douglas, 1977, 'The Domestication of Heaven', pp. 240–72.
35 T. Castle, 1987.
36 See J. Morley, 1971; T. Laqueur, 1983, pp. 109–31 and N. Llewelyn, 1991.
37 P. Ariès, 1977.
38 P. Ariès, 1977.
39 Ariès, 1977. He also argues that the lying in state of the corpse in her or his dying chamber is a ritual originating in the eighteenth century.
40 C. Christ, unpublished manuscript, forthcoming a.
41 M. Vovelle, 1983.
42 L. Fiedler, 1966. N. Auerbach, 1982, speaks of the iconic force of Nell's corpse, which becomes 'a magic and magnetic object, a totem not of peace, but of personal and divine power', and sees her death as serving a 'collective ceremony . . . a public, communally resonant activity', p. 87.
43 W. Houghton, 1957.
44 J. Reed, 1975, p. 163.
45 A. Douglas, 1977; J. Tompkins, 1985; P. Fisher, 1985.
46 H. B. Stowe, 1852, p. 424: 'The child felt no pain, – only a tranquil, soft weakness, daily and almost insensibly increasing; and she was so beautiful, so loving, so trustful, so happy.'
47 G. Stewart, 1984.
48 This is another aspect of the interrelation between death and virtue exemplified by Julie, dying in order to prevent herself from becoming morally contaminated again.
49 L. Fiedler, 1966, suggests 'The only safe woman is a dead woman; but even she, if young and beautiful, is only half safe . . . the only safe, safe female is a pre-adolescent girl dying or dead', p. 267.
50 L.-V. Thomas, 1979.
51 E. Morin, 1970.

6

Bodies on display

Does death stabilise the relation of the subject to the object? Does the object, in turn, stabilise the relation the subject has to death? Individually and collectively, does the subject stabilise the relation between death and the object, to the degree that it can no longer decide?
Michel Serres

Unlike Clarissa's relatives and friends, content with seeing and embracing her corpse one last time, Richardson's rake Lovelace, upon hearing of Clarissa Harlowe's death, devises a monstrous scheme. In an effort to 'preserve the charmer from decay' as long as possible, he wants to steal the corpse and have a surgeon open the body and embalm it. When the body can no longer be kept from its 'original dust' he plans at least to keep Clarissa's heart 'in spirits . . . It shall never be out of my sight' (IV.376). Lovelace's fantasies about preserving Clarissa's corpse suggest both an anxiety about her bodily dissolution and a desire to demonstrate his unlimited right to possess her. He justifies himself by explaining, 'whose was she living? – whose is she dead but mine?' Embalming her corpse would be an exquisite form of control over the mobility that enabled Clarissa to continually elude his grasp. For if the process of decomposition can be prevented, then death is the perfect moment when Clarissa's body can be completely and indefinitely at his disposal.

His first attempt to claim her body, the rape that occurred while she was in a drugged state similar to death, necessarily failed because once reawakened, she again receded from his possession, fleeing from him and preventing any further meeting. As a dead body she can no longer elude him and yet her preserved corpse, especially once it has been reduced to an embalmed heart, forbids direct bodily contact. Lovelace imagines his claim to Clarissa fulfilled when he can possess her by observing her, when he has transformed her into an eternal object of his usurping gaze. By implication, the perfect stability of Clarissa as an object of desire, confirming Lovelace's control, requires two changes in their relationship; a shift from physical touch to sight and the replacement of Clarissa's animate body by her preserved corpse or parts of it, which function as a kind of 'auto-icon', signifying a representation that consists of the thing itself.

Yet the satisfaction that this act of embalming an object of desire can afford is ambivalent. Clarissa's preserved corpse would be a body situated outside temporality while functioning as a supreme sign of facticity, and meant to afford erotic pleasure even though or maybe because death has made her completely inaccessible. Lacan defines the concept of desire as being inherently unsatisfied and unsatisfiable because it does not primarily relate to a real object, independent of the subject, but rather to an imaginary object, a fantasy. With this definition in mind, the embalmed corpse demonstrates how superlative satisfaction is connected with the imaginary, with the death of the other and with impossibility. If desire is a state whose fulfilment is necessarily always deferred, then the simultaneous death and preservation of the object of desire indefinitely stabilises the relation between desiring subject and its object by producing a situation of eternally controlled deferral. Clarissa's auto-icon, as it is the product of Lovelace's fantasy, would stage the death of desire, which in her inaccessibility to desire she represents while at the same time inducing the fulfilment of desire in its own impossibility. In my discussion of the 'fort–da' game cultural language and imagery emerged as the 'murder of the thing', and language acquisition as a 'scene' which is enacted over the renunciation of the maternal body. Lacan adds to this definition, that 'this death constitutes in the subject the eternalization of his desire. The first symbol in which we recognize humanity in its vestigial traces is the sepulture.'[1] As part of the psychic interchangeability of mother and daughter, the death of a beloved can serve as repetition of this first symbolic death. Since it is her heart which Lovelace intends to keep perpetually in his sight, his scheme to assure his possession over Clarissa's bodily remains. His amorous fantasies show how fetishism can serve as a strategy to occult death and female sexuality simultaneously, pointing once more to the proximity between these two signifiers. This double substitution of the decomposing body of his dead beloved for a part, the embalmed heart, prevents both the anxiety of a threat of castration as it is induced by the sight of the female genitals and, in the more global sense, by the sight of the corpse.

To clarify the term 'fetish' I will turn to Freud's discussion of this phenomenon, in which he focuses on the duplicitous blindness that allows the fetishist to hesitate between acknowledging that a body is 'inadequate' and denying, disavowing or negating this 'inadequacy' in order to experience pleasure. Though Freud is eager to fix the semantic encoding for the substituted object – namely as the boy's fantasy of a phallic mother – the purpose of the fetish is to preserve something which the fetishist should have given up or knows is lost. This attitude can also be seen in relation to more global forms of loss or separation. Indeed the crucial aspect of the phallic mother (though this is not Freud's point) is that she is an image in her child's fantasy and either always already dead (because a desired image), or, in her concrete reference to the maternal body, figuratively dead because renounced. The lost object preserved by virtue of the fetish substitute is not just the 'impossible' feminine phallus but an 'imagined' maternal body, so that the loss the fetishist denies is not just the 'castrated' female body, its lack of a penis, but much more generally the fact that this perfect body is and always was absent from any real experience.

By implication the strategy used to endow the 'castrated' feminine body with its lacking part is equally prevalent in attitudes of mourning, where the corpse, the body 'castrated by death', is endowed with a substitute form of animation, because the fetishist refuses to acknowledge death.[2] Yet the fetishist's attitude toward feminine sexuality and toward death is a duplicitous compromise that not only replaces or augments an 'object of desire' in an effort to restabilise a conception of self dependent on the image of an 'adequate' other, put into question by the unwelcome perception that the feminine body is neither phallic nor immortal. Denying a loss by virtue of a substitute turns into acknowledging the loss and the inadequacy of the substitute. The fetish allows its creator/ spectator to retain a belief that antidotes an unwelcome perception, threatening to his narcissistic sense of self as whole and immortal, for if the feminine body can be 'castrated', thus the logic, his own penis is in danger; if the other body can die, his own survival is at stake. At the same time the fetish object lets the fetishist give up the unwelcome perception by transferring the values of this 'inadequate' body on to another site, on to that 'something else' which has taken the place of the 'lacking part' (the penis, the re-animated body) – in my examples the doubly 'castrated' body of a dead woman embalmed as a self-reflexive reduplication, as its own auto-icon.

The indetermination of the fetish is such that it can signify that the woman is castrated/dead, or that she is not castrated/dead, or even allow the proposition that the viewing man is castrated/inscribed by death. In Freud's terms, the fetish as a token of triumph over the threat of castration, as the safeguard against it, contains a superlative moment ('außerordentliche Steigerung') since what occurs is that 'the horror of castration has set up a memorial to itself in the creation of this substitute'.[3] The result is a 'double attitude' combining denial and asseveration with a recognition of the fact of 'castration'/death; merging a debasement of with a reverence for the fetish. Above all the fetish is connected with sight, more precisely with the desire to deny that something is absent from sight. The trope central to androcentric culture for the threat of castration is the absence at the centre of feminine genitalia, its 'nothing', just as blindness, the fear of losing one's sight, and castration are conceptually associated with each other. Triumphing over this anxiety is always connected with making things present to sight.

As though she had a presentiment that as a dead body she would become a fetish, in particular for Lovelace's gaze, Clarissa explicitly states in her will that she desires not to be unnecessarily exposed to the view of anybody, that her dead body should not be touched by members of the other sex, and above all that Lovelace not be permitted to see her corpse unconditionally: 'but if . . . as I am nobody's, he insist upon viewing *her dead* whom he ONCE before saw in a manner dead, let his gay curiosity be gratified.' (IV.416) By pointing to the analogy between her displayed dead body and its earlier drugged condition, Clarissa implies that to be gazed at in a state when she can no longer determine how she is seen nor reciprocate the gaze is in itself a form of rape. She minutely plans every moment of her cadaverous presence between death and interment, owing to her contempt for this supremely vulnerable status of being 'nobody's', during which her body is open to an indefinite array of incursions, be they of a bodily or hermeneutic kind. She also decrees how her dead body is to be seen because of her anxiety that as a corpse she will be completely at the disposal of others and completely beyond the self-determination that has been the aim of her life.

As part of this last will to self-protection she insists that the 'ghastly spectacle' of her displayed dead body be exposed to Lovelace's view only in conjunction with a text she has prepared: 'Gay, cruel heart! behold here the remains of the once ruined, yet now happy Clarissa Harlowe! See what thou thyself must quickly be; – and REPENT' (IV.417). By using her text to dictate how she wants her dead body to be read, namely as a Christian *memento mori*, her intention is that of turning her body into a trope for his guilt and her triumph; into a trope with the didactic value of eliciting repentance and atonement. Clarissa's text, comparable to the title and signature on a painting, and implicitly commenting on the analogy between representation and corpse, functions as the last resource available to her, in her anxious desire to divert Lovelace's interpretation of this object of his gaze and his act of gazing away from erotic pleasure and usurpation. In so doing she inserts herself into the *vanitas* tradition of Christian iconography. The motif of 'death and the maiden' combines the eroticism and beauty of the feminine body in full bloom with bodily decay, ephemerality and the abrupt termination of a life of pleasure. As death's opposite, as an attempt to deny the transience of the human body, vanity nevertheless serves as a measure for mortality. The more vain and self-admiring a person, the more extreme a loss of beauty and erotic charm will be felt.

In a duplicitous manner that could in itself be termed fetishistic, the conjunction of a beautiful feminine body with death in the *vanitas* depicts the transience of human existence in order to warn against any vain belief in the immortality and in the importance of the human body. Yet it does so by highlighting precisely the bodiliness of human existence. As an image of ephemerality it subverts what it is meant to signify by aesthetically presenting the beauty of the body against its natural decay, which is meant to be the message of the image. To celebrate the feminine corpse can serve as a double fetish, for insensible and impenetrable, the body becomes 'phallic'. As a corpse, the feminine beloved loses her quality of being Other (another sex), and becomes the site where the gazed-at object and the object desired by the gazing subject merge perfectly into indistinction. In a superlative manner, she confirms the imaginative power and desire of the mourning lover. This absolutely untouchable dead woman signifies, in Kristeva's words, jouissance as nostalgia, within reach but lost for ever. By turning the feminine into a dead body, phallic idealisation places itself on a pedestal. Yet this fusion of gaze and gazed-at object is also fetishistic in the sense that its object of reference remains indeterminite What remains undecided is who has been turned into a dead body – the feminine beloved or the 'feminine' in the masculine lover?[4]

That Lovelace's fetishistic fantasy of embalming a dead body so as to counteract anxieties about the decomposition of the corpse and feminine sexuality are but an extreme version of eighteenth and nineteenth-century sentiment is suggested for example by the popularity of wax anatomical models, of which the collection in La Specola (Royal and Imperial Museum of Physics and Natural History), set up between 1776 and 1780 in Florence, was one of the largest. These wax models were initially created to give medical students access to the human body without having to be present in the anatomical theatre, so repellent because of its horrible putrefaction and its ghastly forms of dismemberment. The wax specimens were modelled directly from cadavers in a technique also used to recreate relics of saints and martyrs. Producing a substitute of the corrupt and putrified dead body that would mask death, these models are endemic to a general cultural effort to eliminate the impure state of mutibility and decay by replacing it with a pure and immutable wax body double. Sander Gilman argues that this shift from the realm of religious art to the world of anatomical study is typical for a general secularisation of the eighteenth century, as is the privileging of the rational sense of sight.[5]

Much like the deathbed scene, the wax cast of the cadaver was meant to afford access to a truth of human existence, in this case the centre and origin of human life as signified by the interior of the feminine body. The fascination engendered when the wax cast depicts a feminine body has to do with the fact that the two enigmas of western culture, death and female sexuality, are here 'contained' in a way that exposes these two conditions to a sustained and indefinite view, but does so in such a way that the real threat of both, their disruptive and indeterminite quality, has been put under erasure. Gilman points out that these scientific specimens of anatomical casts served to cover, distance and control both sexuality and death by rendering the mutable, dangerously fluid, destabilised feminine body in a cleansed, purified, immobile form that signified less its object of material reference than the survivor and in part the implied gaze of its spectator. By virtue of this transforming embalmment in wax, the cadaver turned into an art object. The anatomical museums were visited like the great art museums of the eighteenth century.

That Lovelace's desire to preserve the body of his dead beloved in such a way as to make it indefinitely available to his sustained gaze is not all that unusual for eighteenth and nineteenth-century cultural imagery is further corroborated by one of the most popular folktale images – Snow White. Seventy years after Richardson condemns his 'misguided libertine', the Brothers Grimm offer, in their written narrative 'Sneewittchen' (1819), an image of a beautiful dead woman exhibited for the gratification of her viewers that suggests one way how Lovelace's fantasy could be realised; 'the dwarves let a transparent coffin of glass be made, so that it [*sic*] could be seen from all sides. They placed it into the coffin and wrote its name in golden letters on the glass, and that it was the daughter of a king. Then they placed the coffin on the top of a hill.'[6] The contents of the coffin can not only be viewed from all sides, but owing to the prominence of its position, the body virtually offers itself to the gaze of others, draws this gaze on to itself. In much the same way that Ariès compares the body lying in state with a museum exhibition piece, Snow White in her coffin elicits an aesthetic viewing. Since the dwarfs have written her name and her heritage in gold letters on to the coffin, Snow White resembles an art object displayed in a labelled frame. Like Lovelace, the prince privileges the gaze over all other senses, desires an object that shall never be out of his sight. In fact he demands of the dwarfs not Snow White but rather the coffin; not the displayed body but rather the entire display. His claim is that his life depends on being able to see her dead body exhibited under glass, on being able to honour and worship her as though she were his beloved. Erotic desire for the beloved shifts to the level of viewing. By implication the act of seeing means possession and pleasure while the act of idealising annuls both the femininity of the adored dead object and its insertion in temporality. By embalming a beautiful woman she is idealised in a way that obscures the possibility of decay and with it the possibility of the survivor's death.

Striking in the example of Snow White is that she becomes the prince's desired object only after she has become a 'seemingly' dead body. Unlike Lovelace, the prince's desire for this embalmed body is not a form of mourning for a lost beloved. Rather his desire is from the start connected to a dead woman; as the dead object of his gaze she is *like* his beloved. Snow White's auto-icon elicits a self-reflexive turn on three scores. If mourning is involved, then it is such that the prince uses this displayed dead body to mourn himself. More importantly his

Figs 10, 11, 12 & 13   Clemente Susine and Guiseppe Ferrini, *The wax Venuses* (1782)

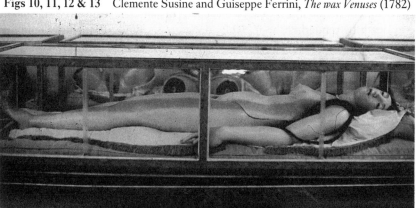

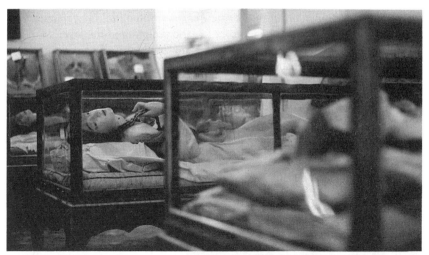

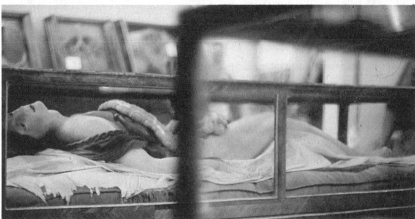

desire for an unknown beautiful feminine corpse exemplifies to perfection how the object of desire is never real but rather the symptom of the lover's fantasy. Finally, as auto-icon, Snow White performs the apotheosis of one of the central positions ascribed to Woman in western culture; namely that the 'surveyed' feminine body is meant to confirm the power of the masculine gaze. In Lemoine-Luccioni's words, Woman doesn't look; she gives herself to be looked at; she is beauty and being beauty, she is also an object of love.[7]

Snow White's preserved corpse also suggests that the relation between seeing a beautiful body and conceiving of this beautiful body as a loved object can be ambivalent. Freud's argument about scopophilia (Schaulust) is that seeing leads to physical appropriation; that it should be preparatory to the sexual activity of touching the other body.[8] In this case 'seeing' makes the desire to touch obsolete, or rather functions as a form of touching. It collapses the opposition between the two categories. The 'embalmed corpse' satisfies as an object of sight and alleviates the viewer of any need to progress to the 'normal sexual aim'. Death sanctions what would otherwise, for Freud, be a perversion – the exclusive privilege of the gaze as it becomes, supplants, and excludes the sexual activity connected with touching the other. The aesthetic staging masks the prince's 'perversity', for art too remains in the register of the gaze, forecloses touch, displaces touch on to the gaze, transforms the gaze into a form of touch. At the same time the 'gendering' of the dead displayed body, which occurs when it is semantically encoded as a figure of 'feminine beauty,' not only veils death but also induces a blindness toward the subjectivity of the corpse as this includes its sexual alterity. Owing to this 'gendering', death as state or process is focalised externally, signifies the 'death of the other', both totally appropriated by the viewer's fantasies and totally inaccessible, while the agent of death, the woman, has no subject, because no internal focalisor position.

Snow White's displayed body auto-iconically gives figure to death in order to assure that, though death is undecidable and uncertain, it is not inconceivable. It is part of representation's fetishistic quality that by offering a stable image it confirms the producer or viewer's position even as its semantic encoding is that of the instability of the feminine or of death. Irwin notes that man's images of death substitute the undecidable for the inconceivable, the uncertain for the unknowable. To witness a death not only always implies that the observer's consciousness persists beyond the spectacle of death but that he survives as an observer of an image of death.[9] Likewise any image of death contains as one of its signifiers the observer's survival, much like the signature the dwarfs have placed on Snow White's coffin. The emphasis on the visibility of a 'preserved' body, as signifier for an arrested and eternalised moment countering all notions of mutability, suggests that the eternal stasis of the displayed body is used by the narrative as a moment where narrative, in its conjunction with temporality and change, can be cut off.

This representation of an arrestation of/by death illustrates how the aesthetisation of a woman's dead body serves to repress the so-called 'destructive' force of nature. It elicits and allows a kind of spectatorship which Norman Bryson has defined as the activity of the gaze: a prolonged, aloof, disengaged form of contemplation across a tranquil interval. In counterdistinction to the glance, a subversive and disorderly furtive look, the gaze seeks to confine what is elusively slipping out of bounds and tries to extract the permanent form from a fleeting process.[10] At stake in this image of the embalmed feminine body is not just the power of the survivor and/or the masculine gaze but also a form of vision that places the viewed object and its viewer outside temporality and that allows a triumph over any vacillating energies. If the central function of the fetish is to make an object present to sight which stands in for the absent phallus (as the privileged signifier for the security of wholeness), then Snow White's auto-icon fulfills this desire on two levels. The absence produced by bodily decay is filled with the embalmed body, and the 'nothing' of the female genitals is supplanted by an untouchable idealised feminine body.

Yet the duplicity inscribed into the way this narrative employs the 'unnatural' arrestation of Snow White's bodily decomposition is such that temporality must ultimately again be recuperated. At the embalmed feminine corpse, death is given a figure in a manner less explicitly tropic than the more conventional funerary statues, gravestones and commemorative texts. The monstrosity of the auto-icon is its desire to materialise that 'point of death' which according to Ariès is real but ungraspable by human consciousness; which is always supplanted by the 'imaginary'. The monstrosity is the auto-icon's gesture of subverting death as process by fetishising death into an idealised figure. The ambivalent logic inscribed into cultural representations of dead feminine bodies presents the desire for immutability only to undo it again, because, in the end, the corpse is reanimated or allowed to decompose and be replaced by its tropic reversion, by a commemorative sign. Iconicity is ultimately always recuperated into allegory because the materiality invoked by the icon is associated with the maternal, as the 'natural' which must be renounced.

In his model of double burial rites, Robert Hertz distinguishes between primary and secondary burial in order to demonstrate that death is not completed in one instantaneous act of destruction, but rather implies a procedure, a transition or passage, that progresses to a form of rebirth.[11] In the intermediary state between death and resurrection, the body decomposes, the bereaved mourn and the spirit of the deceased hovers about the corpse. It is a period of instability because, though the dead individual has been excluded from society, s/he has not yet completed her/his translation from the visible society of the living into the invisible society of the dead. The corpse occupies a position of doubleness, in that it is neither in its social existence nor in its new, spiritual existence. The doubleness comes to an end with the second burial, a repetition of the first, which signifies the completion of decay and of mourning, to indicate that the spirit is definitely established in the beyond and replaced with a commemorative monument.

The duplicity of the ambiguous position of the mortal remains has repeatedly

suggested a resemblance between corpse and artwork. For Aristotle, both lack
the traits of a living organism because the statue, like the corpse, both is and is not
the deceased.[12] Blanchot in turn suggests that the corpse and the image share the
quality of 'strangeness'. The corpse is 'neither the same as the one who was alive,
nor another, nor another thing'. The cadaverous presence simultaneously
occupies two places, the here and the nowhere. Neither of this world nor entirely
absent from it, the corpse stages a relation between these two incompatible
positions. Strangeness emerges because the corpse, resembling the deceased
person, is in a sense doubled. It has no relation to the world in which it appears
except that of an image, of a shadow, constantly present behind the living form
even as this living form is about to transform into a shadow. The corpse
pre-eminently marks an instance of resemblance; a moment of reduplication that
turns back on itself to sever all links to any exterior world. What makes the 'pure
and simple' resemblance of the cadaver to itself so haunting is that its point of
reference is ultimately nothing. Behind its resemblance is the inaccessible,
ungraspable notion of death, the fixity of the corpse and the image, unstable
because it does not pose, does not establish any relation to the world. The
resemblance signified by the corpse 'is the position of that which remains because
it lacks a place'. Though the embalmed corpse is used as a fetish to supplant the
condition of Nothingness (be it in respect to sexuality or death), the fact that as a
double resembling itself it ultimately signifies this Nothingness, makes this
attempt at triumphing over the destructive, fragmenting nature of death as
castration precarious. This dangerous though fascinating interzone must cease.
In Blanchot's words 'one does not live with dead people under penalty of seeing
here sink into an unfathomable *nowhere*'.[13] Second burial replaces the dangerous
fetish with a safer memorial image that works on the principle of a resemblance to
the deceased but nevertheless also emphasises its difference, its allegoric relation
to the object it serves to resurrect commemoratively.

In the narrative of Snow White the second burial takes on the form of rebirth.
A conventional reading could see this as a trope for the cyclic rhythm of nature or
for the reincarnation of souls. This reanimation of Snow White can, however,
also be seen as a sacrifice of the haunting fetish, the double. The cultural rhetoric
at stake in the narrative is that of staging the dangerous double only in order once
more to replace it, and again the fascinating and threatening ambivalence is
intimately connected with the trope of the maternal body.

Snow White, whose birth is the cause of her mother's death, functions
throughout the tale as the threatening double to the second queen, who will not
tolerate another woman's surpassing her superlative beauty, and who uses her
mirrored image to reassure herself of her supremacy. The mirrored
reduplication of the self both confirms the ego's narcissistic desire for integrity
and immortality and exemplifies its division and mortality. Yet in the example of
the queen's mirrored image, the convention that beauty, even as it masks death,
also articulates it is given an additional twist. For the mirror's description of Snow
White's rivalry points to the problem of the doubled superlative. Its message after

all reads 'Queen, you are the most beautiful here, but Snow White is a thousand times more beautiful than you.' Within the limit of a spatial frame of 'here,' the queen's superlative beauty, and with it her immortality, can be affirmed. Extending the frame to include more than one position reduplicates superlative feminine beauty to excess, presents a moment of division that threatens the supremacy of the one, unique perfect body and makes a blindness towards the presence of death, which the queen seeks to forget, impossible.

While the mirrored image is the queen's 'good' confirming double, Snow White's presence serves as a 'bad', destructive double that causes the mirror to speak its ambivalent, contradictory message – 'you are most beautiful' and 'you are mortal'. The ambivalence staged is connected with the 'oddity,' inherent to what Lacan calls the 'imaginary duality'. A specular illusion of symmetry – initially experienced in the mother–infant dyad, and repeatedly sought in adult life to confirm a sense of stability and integrity – the image of the other can either narcissistically reinforce or absolutely devastate identity. The illusion works by denying any dependence on accident or contingency which might subvert its proposition of unity, and offers only two possible states of existence – absolute oneness or absolute non-existence. Lacan, however, stresses, that in counterdistinction to the 'imaginary duality', identity is always also inscribed by difference, Otherness and temporality – by the symbolic order. As rival to the position of superlative beauty, Snow White figures as the third element disrupting the queen's 'imaginary duality.' She is an agent of symbolic tension, signifying that at the heart of the superlative lies difference; that all narcissistically induced images of perfection and unity are constructed over and include Otherness and division; that they are inhabited by the death drive.

The implication is that only one reduplication of the 'most beautiful' may exist in this cultural logic if death is to be successfully occulted. An excess or double of the superlative seems to undo its apotropaic charm. By eliminating her bad double, by letting Snow White figure death explicitly, the queen hopes to eliminate what has disrupted her perfect self-image, and in so doing triumph over mortality. By deflecting her own death anxiety on to another, the queen's aim is to preserve her supreme and unique position of beauty and metaphorically also eliminate the figure presaging her own death. Her logic seems to be – if the supremacy of my position as 'most beautiful' can be questioned, then too the eternity of my superlative beauty is threatened. If I can lose my superlative beauty I can die. For the queen to eliminate Snow White means reassuring herself that she as a unity exists independent of difference, Otherness and temporality: in the 'imaginary duality' with her doubled image.

Yet the death the queen gives to her 'fatal' double turns Snow White's body into another kind of double, which itself serves to occult death. This move will ultimately be fatal to the queen because, in Derrida's terminology, she believes the supplement to be simple exteriority, pure addition, which can be annulled into pure absence, rather than accepting an 'originary differance', an 'irreducible complexity that is neither absence nor presence', within which she is implicated from the beginning of her existence. Accepting the latter would imply acknowledging that death from the start cuts into life, is irreducible from it.[14] Within the representational logic of western culture, the stasis of the 'imaginary duality' is that form of the death drive which, because it insists on absoluteness, cannot be preserved. Once the mirrored Other does not reinforce identity completely, the gazing queen can only be cancelled out.

In the narrative, the queen's jealousy initiates a sequence of killings of the double that only serves to augment reduplication. Because the hunter is overwhelmed by Snow White's beauty, he does not commit the murder and she enters into a phase of liminality. Nominally dead, or rather metaphorically effaced because bodily absent from the court, she continues to live in the marginal realm of the forest. While the queen's first two attempts at murder fail because the dwarfs reanimate Snow White, the successful third attempt with the poisoned apple points out further aspects of the double. The apple is itself a double of the beautiful feminine corpse it will produce: 'on the outside it looked beautiful, white with red cheeks'. Its beauty arouses desire even as it hides death: 'whoever *saw* it desired to have it, but whoever ate even one piece of it had to die'.[15] As though she were imitating her instrument of death, Snow White as a corpse, and then in her glass coffin, has the same beautiful red cheeks that veil the presence of death beneath the surface.

The third gift transforms Snow White into an auto-icon, raises the earlier 'nominal death' to the higher degree of physical inanimation. As Snow White returns to the state Freud calls the preorganic state, the death drive as agent of difference that she seems to figure for the queen subsides and the tensions in the queen's envious heart also move to the zero-degree: 'her envious heart found peace'. Snow White, transformed into a cadaverous presence that resembles itself, into an image, allows the queen successfully to occult all aspects of difference and division that signify her own mortality, by exteriorising them on to Snow White's dead body. The mirror once again confirms her unique position, confirms the 'imaginary duality'. For its spectator, however, the displayed corpse signifies an artificial preservation of the body against natural decomposition. In her coffin Snow White does not decay, but rather looks as though she were sleeping.

Because the queen's imaginary duality with her specular image, and the doubleness of the preserved corpse engender a threatening ambivalence, all moments of reduplication – Snow White and her corpse, the mirror's double reflection of Snow White's and the queen's superlative beauty – must be eliminated. Chiasmically the narrative undoes the surplus of doubles in order to return rhetorically to a position of one unique, singular superlative. As the poisoned apple piece falls out of her throat, Snow White awakens to undo the duplicitous status of her cadaverous presence. Returning to court she closes the gap between her nominal absence and her bodily preservation. At her wedding her double, the queen, who comes because she must *see* Snow White, is tortured to death and buried. The irony of the text is such that, though the queen ultimately disappears from sight, the process at stake, which will allow only one superlative, which is fascinated by and yet seeks to annihilate the contradiction and ambivalence inscribed in the double, is not. At the end of the narrative the reanimated Snow White has replaced both doubles, the queen and her displayed embalmed corpse, both of which served to figure a desire to escape from temporality. Though the ambivalent fragmentation invoked with the double is undone, she returns to a state of mutability. Implicitly her resurrected beauty does not deny its dependence on temporality, difference and Otherness.

The cultural economy at stake is the replacement of the dead body (signifier for an 'imaginary duality') by a text (signifier for semiosis that acknowledges absence and difference at its centre). The 'auto-icon', requiring a duplicitous form of viewing, is an aberration; Lovelace's desire to preserve Clarissa is a perversion; Snow White's unburied 'auto-icon' haunts in a way that can not be sustained.

That this aberrant fascination for the preserved body could be seen in conjunction with pagan forms of idolatry, as they re-emerged in nineteenth century's cultural image repertoire to subvert and/or reconfirm Christianity caught in a 'crisis in belief', is suggested by Oscar Wilde's interpretation of a Renaissance anecdote: 'In 1485 some workmen digging on the Appian Way came across an old Roman sarcophagus inscribed with the name "Julia, daughter of Claudius." On opening the coffin they found within its marble womb the body of a beautiful girl of about fifteen years of age, preserved by the embalmer's skill from corruption and decay of time . . . Borne back to the Capitol, she became at once the centre of a new cult, and from all parts of the city crowded pilgrims to worship at the wonderful shrine till the Pope fearing lest those who had found the secret of beauty in a Pagan tomb might forget what secrets Judaea's rough and rock-hewn sepulchre contained, had the body conveyed away by night and in secret buried.'[16]

At stake in the disposal of the auto-icon, Wilde suggests, is a certain religious belief, a specific cultural logic. Because Christianity sees the proof of Christ's resurrection in the absence of his body and its supplementary re-presentation and dissemination in the gospels, and because Christian burial traditions are based on the translation of impermanent flesh into the permanency of the gravestone, a cultural veneration of the embalmed corpse threatens, for here the presence of the body suggests a triumph over death. Christian notions of resurrection include the re-establishment of clear distinctions between living and dead and point to the culturally prevalent analogy between resurrection and art as an explicitly allegorical relation, because the aesthetic rendition, though similar to the object it re-animates, always also emphasises its difference. The preservation of the inanimate, however, connects fetishistic idolatry to art in those instances where clear distinctions between body and sign, living and dead are denied or merged, and tries to oppose tropic translation and textuality. Given this opposition two aspects need to be emphasised within the cultural iconography I am concerned with. Firstly, the fascination for the icon or fetish occurs within and is conditioned by Christian culture and cannot be seen as severed from or external to it. Indeed, a crucial exception to the translation of flesh into sign would be found in the Christian veneration of the embalmed corpses of martyrs. Secondly, thematically representations may be concerned with undoing the opposition between body and sign by turning the body into an auto-icon; with opposing a semiotics that dictates an absence of the body; with avoiding the dictate of substitution and repetition. However, they present this desire for transparency within the structure of narrative and that means within a system structured by a play of repetitions and replacements.

Freud's discussion of the death drive suggests two aspects of repetition, one a triumph over temporality by returning to and repeating the preorganic inanimate stasis beyond division, the other the long sequence of repetitions that fragment, alter and reformulate a body into new versions. This sequence functions as life's detour toward death in an effort to avoid a short-circuit. For a narrative analysis Freud's terminology can be applied to two separate dimensions of a text. The representation of a dead body may serve thematically to figure loss and disinvestment ('fort'). It may serve as signifier for a desire for an end; for a transparency, for the pre-animate state of zero-tension; for an obliteration of division, strife, ambivalence. At the same time the tension produced on a structural level by sequentiality, by the opacity between signifier and signified, is always preserved. The text always returns ('da') to the reader, preserves repetition and transformation, can never escape the economy of substitution, replacement, supplementarity. In this double gesture of giving figure to an idea of transparency, of stasis or of immutability in an opaque mode – figuring the imaginary duality in the symbolic register that is always inscribed with difference – in this contradictory attempt at figuring death which lies outside the economy of narrative, representations of death are always a fetishistic cross between both aspects of repetition.

Notes to Chapter 6

1 J. Lacan, 1977, p. 104.
2 S. Freud, 1927, explicitly draws this analogy in his discussion of two young men who had both refused to acknowledge the deaths of their fathers, while at the same time being fully aware of the fact: 'a piece of reality which was undoubtedly important had been disavowed by the ego, just as the unwelcome fact of the woman's castration is disavowed in fetishists', p. 156.
3 S. Freud, 1927, p. 154.
4 J. Kristeva, 1987a.
5 S. Gilman, 1989.
6 J. and W. Grimm, 1819, p. 306.
7 E. Lemoine-Luccioni, 1976. See also J. Berger, 1972.
8 S. Freud, 1905.
9 J. T. Irwin, 1980.

10 N. Bryson, 1983.
11 R. Hertz, 'A Contribution to the Study of the Collective Representation of Death', 1960, pp. 27–154. A detailed presentation of second burial will follow in Part III.
12 S. Humphreys, 1981.
13 M. Blanchot, 1981, pp. 81–85. In a sense Snow White presents a counter model to the example of the vampire, also a body preserved in the interzone between death and total decomposition/resurrection, to be discussed in chapter 16.
14 J. Derrida, 1976.
15 J. and W. Grimm, 1819, p. 304, my emphasis.
16 Oscar Wilde, 1891, pp. 1066f.

7

The lady is a portrait

Woman is man's art work; the art work is man's wife [la femme de l'homme];
in fact these two enounciations mutually implicate and explicate each other.
Nancy Huston

In an effort to theorise the conceptual association of femininity with imagery in western cultural practices, Teresa de Lauretis argues that 'the representation of woman as image (spectacle, object to be looked at, vision of beauty – and the concurrent representation of the female body as the *locus* of sexuality, site of visual pleasure, or lure of the gaze) is so pervasive in our culture that it necessarily constitutes a starting point for any understanding of sexual difference and its ideological effects in the construction of social subjects, its presence in all forms of subjectivity'.[1] The cultural convention of reproducing women as images becomes particularly poignant, however, when the process of image-making is shown to be the cause/result of a woman's death, with 'cause' and 'result' forming an ambivalently reciprocal relation. Explicitly thematising a conjunction of image, femininity and death, the narrative representations I will discuss equally address the relation between identification, pleasure and subjectivity, as this too is unseverable from death.

If my previous examples were each representations of a beautiful woman's dead body treated like a materialized image or auto-icon, I will now turn to narratives where the equation of corpse with artwork means a translation or exchange that erases rather than preserves the body; to narratives of portraits which substitute for dead bodies, and which, as representations of representations, are twice removed from their object of reference. While the semiotic form of the reduplication staged by the embalmed corpse could be termed iconic, in that it doubles itself and works as a sign whose meaning is based on an analogy or resemblance with the object for which it is a likeness, the replacement of the body by its portrait forms a symbolic relation, emphasising the necessarily arbitrary but conventionally accepted relation for signification between signifier and signified, the *allos* of allegory.[2]

Mieke Bal suggests that cultural anti-iconism coincides with the semiotic preference for symbolicity, to support a paternal/patriarchal ideology, which considers both index and icon to be dangerous grounds of signification, since they dispense with convention.[3] A rhetorical privileging of symbolicity over iconicity can serve to articulate a 'tendency to prefer arbitrary, pure but unmotivated, ungrounded signs that represent fatherhood' as opposed to a form of semiosis that is analogous to the bodily contact of maternity, because it works on the basis of motivated signs. The following narratives about dead women's portraits serve to express themes like the rivalry between a material presence of the body and its immaterial represence/representation in art; the rivalry between genius and *gynein*;[4] between a form of creation, coded as 'natural', indexical, maternal, and one coded as 'artificial', arbitrary, paternal.

The 'maternal' is itself of course an ambivalent position, signifying both a lost maternal body, which in its real material absence is disruptive of any sense of self-stability and the imaginary maternal body of plenitude, a safe and satisfying image for narcissism. The 'maternal' must not be reduced to a positive value, set against an arbitrary symbolicity of paternal semiotics. It is a split concept, embodying and engendering, like the image itself, the ambivalently inscribed tendency toward stability and disruption. The move from icon to symbol thematises the desire informing certain forms of semiosis to suppress the unencompassable body of 'matter–materiality–maternity', which indexically figures death. A paradox, however, remains: both the 'iconic' embalmed corpse and the 'symbolic' portrait function on the representational level (and in counterdistinction to their thematic desire) as fetish doubles, similar to but also different from the body they resemble. They hover between an absence/presence of their object of reference, an identity/castration of their implied spectator. In this duplicity they continue to be aligned with the feminine position, even if or maybe because on the thematic level the suppression of the maternal is at stake. Again, gendering arrives in the fading of the body.

The coupling of a beautiful dead woman and her image is taken up by Poe in his metapoetic story about creation and image-making, 'The Oval Portrait' (1842), in order to problematise the conventional idea of art as transformation of living matter into inanimate form. The tale's narrator is so 'vehemently moved', so deeply agitated by an 'absolute *lifelikeliness* of expression' in the portrait of a young woman, that he eagerly seeks the 'volume which discussed the paintings and their histories' (482).[5] Reading about the situation within which this image was produced is meant to counteract the 'spell' of the picture, which, at first 'startling, finally confounded, subdued and appalled him' (482). The text is meant to stabilise by answering the enigma the painting poses. The story the narrator reads reveals that the model, 'a maiden of rarest beauty', had an unhappy marriage with a painter because of his 'passionate, studious, austere' devotion to his first 'bride, his Art' and her jealousy of this rival. The conflict between his two brides provokes in the painter a desire to merge the two, to transfer his living wife into the wife he already had, to exchange the disturbing odd couple with a transparent unity – the perfect resemblance. The painter, so fervidly engaged in producing this marvel, is blind to the fact that his bride visibly pines away, weakens, grows dispirited. So wild is the ardour for his work that as the painting draws closer to completion his gaze is almost exclusively fixed on his art and he no longer even looks at his model. The portrait sittings become the scene of a transfusion, the 'tints which he spread upon the canvas were drawn from the cheeks of her who sat beside him' (483). When the last stroke has been completed, the portrait is 'indeed *Life* itself!' but his wife lies dead beside the canvas (484).

Ariès points out that in the sixteenth century a new theme entered portrait painting which found its acme in the art and photography of nineteenth century culture – the realistic depiction of a man or woman just after death, as an expression of an attempt to preserve not only the features of a living face but to preserve these features in death.[6] Yet the final moment in 'The Oval Portrait' – a perfect portrait standing next to/in for its dead model – presents a significant reversal of such representations as Claude Monet's *Camille sur son lit de mort* (1879). The latter shows a painter, faced with death, exchanging an emotional response for the impulse to isolate and objectively notate sense impressions and to record these on canvas.[7] Poe's artist, however, does not try to record the last image of a woman who has departed for ever; rather his fervid obsession to re-present her is the condition of her death. Poe's story of the reciprocal relation of creation and destruction cites another cultural convention, namely the confusion of woman and art. Marina Warner suggests the mutual implication of these two concepts is a paradigmatic metaphor for the act of artistic creation as analogous if not superior to natural birth where, in a mythic reversal of biology, man is a maker and woman made.[8] Poe's inversion of Pygmalion's animation of a deanimated art form significantly presents the dangerous consequences of masculine creation. The incompatability and rivalry between art's created image and nature's created bodies implies that, by substituting for life, mimesis works on a principle of division and negation which can prove fatal to the model.

Poe's story comes to express the tragic paradox that the resulting portrait alternates between destruction and preservation. The woman, representative of natural materiality, simultaneously figures as an aesthetic risk, as a presence endangering the artwork, so that as the portrait's double she must be removed. She is after all his second, not his first bride. At the same time it is the woman's material body upon which the effect of the aesthetic risk is carried through. A form of creation which seeks to recede from the ephemerality and death of bodily materiality can achieve this only by deanimating the organic body. For the masculine artist, incorporating the feminine power of creation engenders and requires the decorporalisation of the woman who had inspired the artist as model and whose capacities to give birth are what the painting sessions imitate. Because the power of representation is that of vision and division, the artist's attempt at overcoming facticity by turning away from life, which is always inscribed by decay, and toward the immortality of art, itself stands under the auspices of the death drive.

In his discussion of the concept *das Unheimliche*, Freud turns the lack of a clear definition into the crux of this concept's rhetorical strategy – namely a semantic subversion based on the blurring of stable concepts. In order to explain the fundamental instability at the core of the uncanny, Freud focuses on two central features. Because the word *unheimlich* refers both to the familiar and agreeable and to something concealed, kept out of sight, it comes to signify any moment where meaning develops in the direction of ambivalence until it coincides with its opposite. Semantic oppositions collapse and a moment of ambivalence emerges that induces intellectual hesitation (*Unsicherheit*).[9] As a situation of undecidability, where fixed frames or margins are set in motion, the uncanny also refers to moments where the question whether something is animate (alive) or inanimate (dead), whether something is real or imagined, unique, original or a repetition, a copy, can not be decided. One could extend Freud's definition to include instances that involve the ambivalent distinction between a material animate, immediate and literally self-present body and its representation, as immaterial, inanimate, belated 'figural' body signifying through the interplay of absence and presence. Because the uncanny in some sense always involves the question of visibility/invisibility, presence to/absence from sight, and the fear of losing one's sight serves as a substitute in western cultural myth and image repertoire for castration anxiety, the uncanny always entails anxieties about fragmentation, about the disruption or destruction of any narcissistically informed sense of personal stability, body integrity, immortal individuality.

Freud locates the main source for an experience of the uncanny in the compulsion to repeat, to re-present, double, supplement; in the recurrence or re-establishment of similarity; in a return to the familiar that has been repressed. This doubling, dividing and exchanging can, furthermore, involve the subject in his relation to others as he either identifies with another, as he substitutes the alterior self for his own, or as he finds himself incapable of deciding which of the two his self is. Since the most important boundary blurring inhabited by the uncanny is that between the real and fantasy, Freud sees analogies to the animistic belief in an omnipotence of thought in primitive cultures and to the developing infant's unrestricted narcissistic valorisation of psychic processes over material reality, as this gesture is repeated in adult neurosis in a defence against the manifest constraints and prohibitions of the symbolic and of the real. This effacement of the boundary distinction between fantasy and reality occurs when something is experienced as real which up to that point was conceived as imagined; when a symbol takes over the full functions and meanings of the object it symbolises; when a symbol enacts a sublation of signifier into signified or an effacement of the distinction between literal and figural.[10]

One could also extend Freud's definition to say the uncanny marks a moment where desire for something, along with an unbroken belief in the omnipotence of one's ideas, sublates into anxiety about something, into a disbelief in one's own self-construction. When Freud says that the most common images of the uncanny are the 'Doppelgänger' and 'the returned dead', he points to another fundamental instability in our attitude toward death. In the figure of the double death returns as something known but defamiliarised by virtue of repression. Like the fetish, where something repressed also returns, defamiliarised by virtue of a substitution, instances of the uncanny mark psychic moments where that which returns points to the 'castration' of human existence, more globally understood as its fragmentary, imperfect and mortal aspect. The double is an ambivalent figure of death since it signifies an insurance that one will continue to live, that the soul is eternal even as the body decomposes and as such signifies a defense against death. The composition of representation serves as a triumph over and against material decomposition in the realm or system of the real. However, the double is by definition also a figure for a split or gap, a figure signifying that something that was whole and unique has been split into more than one part, and as such a figure for castration or fragmentation. The double, simultaneously denying and affirming mortality, is the metaphor of the uncanniness of the death drive, of '*Unheimlichkeit par excellence*', grounding all other versions of the uncanny because it points to what is most resistantly and universally repressed, namely the presence of death in life and at the origin of life.[11]

The first title of Poe's story, 'Life in Death,' indicates that one of the narrative's rhetorical strategies along with its theme is precisely the staging of an uncanny subversion of life by death.[12] As the painter tries to immortalise his bride he moves into a position of liminality himself. The painting sessions take place in a 'dark high turret-chamber', his ability to create is contingent on a blindness toward the material world; he sees only the image he has represented on his canvas, not his model. In an effort to deny death by denying the living mortal body, he moves into a position of 'death in life', which in turn engenders both his wife's literal death and her 'life in death' in the form of the portrait resurrecting her likeness. If her translation into a corpse also marks his ambivalent hesitation between life and death, the replacement of her corpse by her portrait provokes this same hesitation in the spectator of the portrait, the narrator and implicitly in the reader. The ambivalence is enhanced by virtue of the fact that the signified to be attributed to the portrait that is exchanged for a woman's body remains indeterminate, for over her body death is given a form of figuration. Yet the duplicity of the allegory is such that it leaves undecided whether flesh becomes word, or whether the word is embodied. By definition, portraits cannot be seen independently of their artist's signature, and in some sense also represent him. The portrait refers simultaneously to the replaced woman and her aesthetic resurrection; to the fact of her substitution, her 'murder'; to death thus given representational form; to 'the power of the painter' and 'his deep love for her whom he depicted so surpassingly well'; and self-reflexively to its own device of substituting and representing, as well as the duplicity inherent in the conjunction 'and' that connects destruction with preservation.

If in addition to this set of indeterminate moments one seeks to define the exact cause of the woman's death, yet another unsettling of stable meanings is shown to inhabit the picture. Does the narrative's formulation, 'the painter . . . turned his eyes from the canvas rarely, even to regard the countenance of his wife' imply that her death is caused by the averting of his gaze? Or his preference for the likeness he has created over the model? In either case his denial of her literal body stands in direct correlation to his affirmation of her figural body, to his rendition. Because neither the painter nor his wife can draw a clear distinction between the presence of the model's body and its representation, the completion of the inanimate copy which makes it as good as the original indeed erases the difference between the two, and with it the life of the model independent from the image.[13] Two uncanny moments end the narrative, conflating model and image, the living and the dead – a literal deanimation of the woman and a figural animation of the portrait.

This story illustrates an anxiety as prevalent in nineteenth-century culture as that about bodily decomposition – namely an anxiety about pictorial composition when this is seen as a confusion between the literal and the figural. A sense of the uncanny is provoked when depth, the one dimension that differentiates model from copy, seems to have been added to the imitation. Anxiety about portraits expresses the fear that the transformation of matter from one form to another can engender the literal sacrifice of the 'depth' of the model. As Poe's contemporary Hawthorne writes of pictorial skill, 'some deemed it an offense against the Mosaic Law, and even a presumptuous mockery of the Creator . . . others, frightened at the art which could raise phantoms at will, and keep the form of the dead among the living, were inclined to consider the painter a magician'.[14] Anxiety is based on a confusion between the imaginary register with the real; a misunderstanding of the portrait as an iconic rather than an arbitrary symbolic sign; a misunderstanding that the production of an image can cause an incursion into the materiality of its object of reference. Even though the creation of the portrait can be seen as an effort to privilege a symbolic form of semiosis that clearly distinguishes signifier from signified (because it always contains the artist's signature and a self-referential moment), its perfect execution denies the self-referential dimension and evokes a scandalous return to the literal; reintroduces an uncertainty about the distinction between a body and its image.

In the frame of the story we find that the narrative as a whole is provoked by an experience of ambivalent hesitation and a desire to recuperate semantic stability even as this desire to decide the disturbing question posed by the uncanniness of the image is thwarted. The turn to the figural is a way for language to retain its 'innocence', for by giving up its referential validity it forecloses the possibility that a perfect fulfilment of the referential, constative function of language would obliterate the object of that function. Yet the uncanniness of the image is such that it reintroduces the literal as that to which we always return. The narrator, having entered forcibly into an abandoned chalet, because his illness would not permit him to pass the night outdoors, does not initially see the 'uncanny' portrait. Only after he has gazed at and read the descriptions of many other paintings does a chance move of the candelabrum reveal 'in vivid light' a picture all unnoticed before, and along the lines of Bryson's distinction between two forms of vision, the first abrupt and spontaneous glance perturbs: 'I glanced at the painting hurriedly, and then closed my eyes' (482). By implication, the first glance presented the uncanny mixture of 'life into death'/'death into life' in such a way as to make a distance between viewer and viewed object impossible. The glance subverted the security and superiority of the spectator's stance, destabilised him in such a way as to reveal the literality of his own mortality.

Sarah Kofman has compared the good portrait to the uncanny double – to the ghost hovering in a liminal zone, neither living nor dead, neither absent nor present, staging a duplicitous presence, at once sign of an absence and of an inaccessible other scene, of a beyond. Similarity, she argues, topples all categories of oppositions that distinguish model from copy, the animate from the inanimate and makes signs semantically indeterminate, meaning undecidable. Yet the anxiety that an experience of perfect similarity incites in the viewer can successfully be masked by a move to the figural, a posture of scrutiny and judgement of the portrait, which binds the mobility of meaning to a fixed signified. However, the issue of fetishism remains. To admire the fact that life, that flesh has been perfectly rendered, means concealing from oneself that there is no life, no flesh, that has not already been struck by death.[15]

By averting his gaze, the narrator unwittingly doubles the artist's gesture of privileging a mental over a sense impression. The second, sustained gaze moves the object of sight outside the realm of temporality and facticity. The narrator uses the thought he has formulated in the interstice between the two forms of vision to mediate between himself and the viewed object, to filter, distance and protect himself from the implication of his own mortality. By taking on the stable position of viewer, he can scrutinise the painting for a satisfactory explanation of its uncanny effect. Judging and admiring the portrait engenders a semantic binding of its previously so disturbing unbound, ambivalent and indeterminate quality. He decides to explain 'the true secret of its effect,' by the designation 'an absolute lifelikeness of expression'; by fixing the uncanny gliding of signifiers on to this chosen signified. In a second, once again sustained form of vision, he seeks to shed further light on the portrait by reading its narrative description, by supplementing his judgement with that of the authorised text. Significantly, he can do so only by replacing the candelabrum to its former position, and the portrait falls back into its initial 'deep shade'. He repeats his first gesture of making the object of disturbance disappear by closing his eyes, exchanging it, as before, with mental images. Analogously to the story he reads about, uncanniness is produced on the basis of a lack of clear distinctions between representation and model, between deanimated and animated object, and this lack of distinction metaphorically figures the experience of one's own mortality. A second, sustained, objectifying gaze, accompanied by a semantic designation undoes the initial startle and replaces it by subdued appallment, by a safe boundary drawn once again between self and Other.

The irony of Poe's tale is that the narrative meant to afford a final explanation for the deeply agitating phenomenon only repeats the uncanny gesture. It thematises the narrator's experience of a diffusion or exchange between life and art, yet offers no distinct answer. Much as the frame of the portrait fails clearly to mark the 'absence of life, and the presence of artifice,' the story's frame stabilises an impression only to destabilise it again.[16] The moral one is left with addresses the dangerous consequences of the rivalry between natural and artistic creation as well as the fear that a translation of body into image may kill. Blanchot ascribes a quintessential ambiguity to the image. On the one hand an image denies the material body, and as vitalising negation of the thing requires the effacement of the world so that it can recapture the thing in an ideal way; can continue to affirm a thing in and after its disappearance. On the other hand the image refers not only to the absent thing but also to an endless dialectic of absence as presence. The image as substitute of a body implies that the body must disappear so that it can again be grasped and yet the distancing and exchange this involves implicates the viewer as well.[17]

Poe's story addresses the issue of the vitalising negation as well as that of the irrevocable instability of any image. The latter involves the notion that, although an objective gaze engenders a semantic fixture that decides a question, it does so by making the image disappear again and ultimately fails at explaining univocally. The paradox the story leaves us with is that both painter (in respect to his portrait) and narrator (in respect to the portrait and its supplementary narrative) use the double to hide the fact that life is always already struck by death and yet their choice of the perfect portrait, superlatively *unheimlich*, necessarily again evokes what they seek vainly and in vain to efface.

In D. G. Rossetti's poem 'The Portrait' (1870), the painted double of a beautiful dead woman is used as a displaced representation of the viewer's own mortality, so that a blurring of portrait and self-portrait emerges as yet another semantic instability inherent in the uncanny image. The poem begins, 'This is her picture as she was: / It seems a thing to wonder on, / As though mine image in the glass / Should tarry when myself am gone / I gaze until she seems to stir. – / . . . And yet the earth is over her.'[18] By claiming of the portrait 'Yet this, of all love's perfect prize, / Remains", the speaker not only draws an analogy between image and skeletal remains but also sets the image up as the limit or boundary to the "secret and unknown'. Along the lines of Foucault's metaphor, the portrait turns self-reflexively back on itself and on to its viewer. The experience of uncanniness ('wonder') evokes several moments of hesitation – the knowledge that the woman is dead, out of sight ('the earth is over her', 'nought left to see or hear') and her presence to the viewer's sight in the form of an image, which is and isn't identical to its model; the knowledge that the image is inanimate and a belief that his gaze can animate the portrait and resurrect her absent body; but above all the possible substitution of the dead woman's image for his own.

Again the question arises which signified to attribute to the equation of death with image in this portrait of a deceased beautiful woman. Does the portrait immortalise her against death or express her death as material absence? Is it a portrait in which death in general is given figuration over the body of a woman or in which the painter sees his own mortality but also his ability to image and to remember articulated? The latter possibility – where the woman is doubly absent, because dead and because no longer signified of the image – refers back to an aspect of symbolisation discussed in relation to the 'fort–da' game. The child's substitution of the spool for its mirror-image (Bebi-o-o-o) performs the notion of imaging as a moment of erasure of the Other, when this Other is substituted for an image of the self. Representing the absent body of a beloved can turn into a representation of absence *per se*, i.e. of one's own absence by proxy. Representation in some sense always implies negation or absence of its object of reference, since some material body is recognised not as real but as an image. Representation, however also arises out of the narcissistic wound it is meant to heal, and as such sets a permanent memorial to precisely the knowledge of loss, separation and the presence of death that grounds life, as it attempts to sublate or replace these experiences.

Because the first significant experience of the dialectic between absence and symbolisation (the fort–da game) is connected with the maternal body, the relation of death to image-making is culturally associated with the feminine position. The lost object, be it the maternal body or its repetition in the objects of adult desire, is imaginatively made present again, as mental image or portrait, on canvas. Yet this body-double confirms and denies real absence on several scores – the absence of the desired object because it has been renounced or lost; the absence of the other's body because it is always mediated by the desiring subject's image-repertoire, by the inanimate signs through which he understands the world; the absence of the original primordial object, always already lost. Lacan suggests that 'the interest the subject takes in his own split is bound up with that which determines it – namely a privileged object, which has emerged from some primal separation, from some self-mutilation induced by the very approach of the real, whose name . . . is the *objet a*'.[19] The fascinatory element introduced by the gaze is connected with this separation (constituting the subject), in that it attempts to arrest another living body into an image, in an illusory recuperation of the lost object, and articulates the very separating it attempts to occult. Rossetti's painter addresses precisely this duplicity of the image. For if his beloved by virtue of the portrait will tarry after bodily absence, so might he remain, recuperated from death. Yet the double, the tarrying remains, articulates death because it is an inanimate presence, 'less than her shadow on the grass or than her image in the stream'.

In one of Freud's interpretations of the 'fort–da' game symbolisation controls absence, places the absent body at one's disposal. This kind of mastery is at stake in the painter's act of representation which he conceives as an act of enshrinement – 'In painting her I shrined her face.' The formulation points to the way any act of idealisation is necessarily inscribed by death. Shrining her face means holding her sacred as a relic and since shrine means either a tomb for a sacred body-icon or an alcove for the representation of a sacred body, the portrait is in fact a painting within a painting, with the embedded image implicitly signifying either a sacred relic or a saint. Though, unlike Poe's story, the cause of the woman's death is a textual ellipsis, the portrait is presented as a metaphorical 'killing' of the woman on two scores – the image, by replacing body with sign negates her presence, while in a more specific way it addresses her death semantically by representing her as a saint or relic, invoking her death before its actual occurrence. Her premature deanimation is further enhanced by the fact that in his portrait the painter situates her face within a liminal realm; within a mystic, covert place hardly lit, a site of uncanny contradictions (a wandering flame, shapes incognisant of their names, footsteps separated from and meeting their owners). Though in this case the painting precedes the woman's death she is painted as though already in death's realm.

A causal relation between representational idealisation, immortalisation and deanimation of the model is left undecided, yet the explicit conjunction is such that what was initially only the function of the embedded image turns, by virtue of its model's death, into the function of the entire portrait. The painter's final interpretation of his portrait is that it signifies the site of memory and resurrection – 'with her face doth memory sit . . . till other eyes shall look from it' – comparable to his personal 'Holy Sepulchre'. It serves as a sign of hope specifically for the reunion with his lost love object and more generally for a recuperation of that wholeness lost with birth. Like all fetish objects, it simultaneously articulates the 'hope and aims long lost with her', i.e. the fact that all image-production occurs over loss, separation and renunciation. As site for memory, the portrait as a whole is situated in a liminal position, between an original wholeness in some sense always already lost and a desire for this state. It self-reflexively doubles the uncanny position of its object of depiction – a woman made relic before her decease; the desired body always already lost before and beyond any material absence.

The portrait also addresses the issue that the image is the site of death's presence not only because it refers to the absence of its object of depiction but because our access to the real is always barred by signs and images. Safouan notes 'what is properly "inanimate" are the name and image, from which the subject could never strip "reality" and outside which reality is simply inconceivable'.[20] The portrait exemplifies how the subject's relation to the world always includes death in that it is a relation to inanimate images as these mediate and construct reality. It also exemplifies how a recognition of an experience is always necessarily belated and shifted to a supplementary site. The portrait after all is an attempt to capture the privileged moment of a perfect understanding between the painter and his beloved that significantly occurred outside language. The confession of his love, interrupted by rain, occurs at a later time and at a different, now interior scene, and the portrait, in another uncanny turn, merges both scenes – the external forest decor of the first staged in the domestic interior of his room. This performance turns the natural into an artifical mystic realm. Articulating the temporal and spatial difference inscribed in this representational repetition it points to the inadequacy between the first experience of bliss and its expression, be the latter verbal or visual. Paradoxically, the repetition of an experience in a textual or visual mode becomes its very first performance.[21] The moment of bliss can be understood only after the subsequent scene of confession and only in relation to inanimate supplementary signs, of which the portrait assumes a privileged place. In a destabilisation of temporal sequentiality analogous to the fact that the image of the woman as relic precedes her death, the perfect union can be articulated and commented on only after its disappearance, from the position of belatedness and loss induced first by rain and then by the woman's real absence. Any representation includes death because it implies the absence of its lost object but also because it sets up the relation between survivor and his lost object as a relation with inanimate images.

The portrait of a deceased woman serves to illustrate how the pleasure representation affords, as this supports imaginary identification, is never severed from some form of death. In a global sense creation or transformation can be understood as a transposition of sign systems, whose genesis is the destruction of the old body and the formation of a new one.[22] The question remains, however, as to why the exchanged position, the aesthetic victims and blood donors, whose destruction and substitution is the starting point and the condition for the creation of the new, should be gendered feminine. If an eroticised narcissistic self-contemplation in some sense always involves an absent body – because as *objet a* it refers to the primordial body lost with birth or because it substitutes the real body of another with images – then it finds its most superlative form when the body used for self-projection is a body absent due to death. The portrait of a dead beloved, serving simultaneously as the painter's self-portrait, functions like a screen memory and what it simultaneously represses and represents is the 'castrative threat of death'. It achieves this duplicitous figure by virtue of a transposition from self to Other that involves a turn to the feminine gender. However, it is not the woman's death that is at stake in the portrait and the narrative surrounding it, but rather the way she serves as cypher for the painter's ability to image and to remember. The poem displaces commemoration on to the other, feminine body in order ultimately to immortalise the painter himself. Strictly speaking what tarries in the poem is an image of him, in relation to the inanimate images of her he possesses. Absence is also written into the narrative about the portrait in that the woman disappears as signified of the image. The process that separates and absents the model from her portrait is articualted by the 'mystical' non-referential quality of the portrait's depicted scene as well as its narrative presentation as a product of memory images: 'the memories . . . still vibrated . . . till I must make them all my own.'

If my previous discussions have shown that the corpse does not only stand for itself (nor allegorically for death) but rather is used in L. V. Thomas's term as an additional, surplus, excess sign – 'outre-signifiant' – Rossetti's poem demonstrates that Woman, because she so often functions as sign for masculine desire and self-construction, takes on a similar status of the 'over and above' in cultural representations. Though Woman is the visual sign, she is not a straightforward signifier. She serves to signify something more and other than simply a materially referent female body or the allegory Woman. There is, of course, nothing empirically feminine about the corpse, nor anything objectively feminine about the image. Yet the opposite position, namely that of survivor and of the viewer, is culturally constructed as a masculine one. John Berger writes, 'men act and women appear. Men look at women. Women watch themselves being looked at . . . The surveyor of woman in herself is male: the surveyed female. Thus she turns herself into an object – and most particularly an object of vision: a sight . . . the "ideal" spectator is always assumed to be male and the image of woman is designed to flatter him.'[23]

Recent feminist critics have used psychoanalysis to theorise the necessity for the condensation and displacement occurring at the signifier Woman and the masculine gendering of the gaze. As Pollock argues, cultural representations use the figure of Woman to negotiate masculine sexuality. In these representations Woman is a sign, 'not of woman but of the Other in whose mirror masculinity must define itself. That Other is not, however, simple, constant or fixed. It oscillates between signification of love/loss, and desire/death. The terrors can be negotiated by the cult of beauty imposed upon the sign of woman and the cult of art as a compensatory, self-sufficient, formalized realm of aesthetic beauty in which the beauty of the woman-object and the beauty of the painting-object become conflated, fetishized.'[24] This twofold double coding of the signifier Woman – signifying feminine and masculine sexuality, desire and death – refers to two aspects of woman's position in culture.

Firstly, the point of the cultural construction of femininity is woman's difference to man, as the non-male, the lacking, supplementary body. Sexual difference is constructed upon the threat of a loss which is known by virtue of sight: the 'castrated' feminine body. Woman takes on the position of the 'lost object' (*objet a*) which, as loss and difference, underpins symbolisation in that it is simultaneously 'cause of' and 'stand in' for desire. As the place on to which lack is projected and simultaneously disavowed, Woman is a 'symptom' for man, his constitutive object of fantasy. The image of Woman as difference, lack, loss troubles and endangers, while the image of Woman as displaced self-portrait of man, as crystallisation of his fantasies, satisfies and reassures.

The image is both a source of anxiety (when it is alienated from and a rival to its model), and a source of pleasure (when it serves as a salutary or confirming fiction based on the notion of a fundamental mis-recognition at the basis of subjectivity). In this duplicitous function of threat and assurance femininity takes on a similar position to the one culturally ascribed to the image. Because of the detour, the mitigation, the non-identity between image and model, art images can give the viewer a threatening sight and protect him from its danger. Beautification and aesthetisation mitigate a direct threat by severing image from its context or reference, as in the myth of Medusa, where a direct glance at the woman's head turns the viewer into stone while the head reflected in a mirror can be gazed at with impunity.

At stake in representations which explicitly signify the image of a 'lost' woman and as such self-reflexively point to their own device of deflection is the chiasm 'Woman as image'/'image as Woman'. The portrait of a beautiful dead woman allows one to see not just the woman in the representation but also an Other, which she momentarily stands in for. To posit Woman as the difference to man and align her with loss or death turns man rhetorically into the non-woman, lacking lack, lacking death. The artistic image retrieves what is lost, so that the conjunction Woman and image articulates and alleviates a posterior and an anterior anxiety of death – anterior in the sense of the 'castrated' Woman signifying the threat of man's future death, posterior in the sense of the 'lost' Woman signifying the man's position as severed from a preceding unity (even if imagined).

This leads to the second aspect of Woman's position in culture, her repetition in representations of the 'phallic/castrated' maternal body in its double coding of plenitude and lack. As figure for imaginary wholeness, her sight heals the fragmented body marked by the navel, the presence of death with birth, articulated in absence and separation. As midwife of individuation, on the other hand, she engenders renunciation, separation, an acknowledgement of the human existence as split, of the secondary figuration of death as sexual castration. The maternal body is coded as a site of threat on three scores; as the cut produced by birth and marked with the navel; as the cut on social terms that requires her renunciation; and as the cut on sexual terms that brings the concept of castration into play. Paradoxically, even as the maternal body articulates loss and split, it mitigates this anxiety and is used to cover and contradict lack.

Since the pleasure and satisfaction of primary narcissism is dependent on image-formation in connection with the maternal body, femininity is here too aligned with sight. Identifying the other with the self allows the as yet unstructured subject to return self-consciously to an image of the self, allows a construction of the self as whole in the Otherness of the image.[25] Yet this provokes the realisation of a double displacement, for as image of Otherness the narcissistic reflection in the other, maternal body, causes the realisation of sexual difference and potential absence. The reflection, because it must be understood as an Otherness of image, a mis-recognition, causes the realisation of difference between image and object of reference and presents an image of the self as a non-referential, self-reflexive image, as this image refers to the negation and potential absence of its object of reference: the death of the self.

Along with the desired object (the bride), the portrait functions as an *objet a*, repeating the maternal body in adult life. For the artist's narcissism is supported by his creation, with which he strives to attain another kind of imaginary unity, more perfect, maybe, given that the 'lost' maternal body was from the start an image itself. If security and empowerment is connected with the gaze in that something is made present to sight, then what remains absent from sight perturbs and questions power – notably woman's sexuality ('nothing') and the body absent in death. In the case of the feminine corpse and the portrait of a deceased woman, the non-visible is given figure, visual presence. In a contradictory manner, the act of seeing works on eliding and articulating difference (be this sexuality or death as difference to presence). From the sight of the maternal body during the mirror stage arises both a sense of unity, stability, security ('da') as well as the realisation of death through absence to sight ('fort') and sexual castration. The sight of another as locus for identification and fantasy evokes both a sense of unity and of separation, and the culturally privileged 'site' for this interplay is the maternal body and its repetition in the desired objects (*objet a*) of adult life. The unity provoked by the beauty of the image serves as an apotropaic charm against the threat of death and sexual castration at the same time that the uncanniness provoked by the double of the image undermines the unity of beauty and articulates the 'castrating' threat of disruption it seeks to cover.

The conjunction of femininity and image reduces to the fact that both assume the rhetoric of the fetish. The feminine body always recalls the initial fetish of the maternal body, and along with the aesthetic image functions as guarantor of completeness, and as memory of lack. In her seminal article on narrative and visual pleasure, Laura Mulvey formulates the contradictory responses to femininity as image in the following way. The image affords pleasure to the scopophilic urge because it allows another body to be used as an object of sexual stimulation through sight and affords pleasure to the narcissistic urge in that the constitution of the ego comes from identification with a seen image. Because sight always also refers to the trauma of sexual castration and the displeasure of the death drive, she concludes 'the look, pleasurable in form, can be threatening in content, and it is woman as representation/image that crystallizes this paradox'.[26] In order to undo the threat posed by femininity on the content level of a representation, culture undertakes two semantic recodings. The feminine body is either used as a scapegoat, to exteriorise threatening values rhetorically, to expel these values by sacrificing Woman, or turned into a fetish so that Woman becomes reassuring rather than dangerous. Where the former will result in her complete disappearance, the latter preserves her presence in part, as auto-icon or doubled portrait, but does so outside linear time, occulting both feminine sexuality and facticity.

Given the fact that the sight of Woman is doubly coded – as object of desire and object of fear – it becomes clear why portraits satisfy. Constructed rhetorically like the fetish, the art object works by denying the existence of the very thing it refers to, by masquerading as entirely self-sufficent, as a non-referential sign, severed from materiality. Because it is the double, not the thing itself, it can give the viewer a forbidden sight and shield from its dangers.[27] Yet the image is less stable than required so that one can augment Mulvey's thesis by adding – in respect to images of Woman, along with the content *even* the form of the image is threatening.

In a duplicitous dialectic of assurance and destability similar to that of the image in general Woman is culturally positioned both as the safeguard and the sanction of the image and somewhere else, outside the system of representations that repeatedly constitutes her as image. Even as the notion of Woman as image serves to appease the threat culturally ascribed to the feminine body, the image as Woman serves to stabilise the otherwise disruptive moment posed by the portrait as it introduces difference into its relation of similarity. In their reciprocal stabilisation of the other, the two terms 'femininity' and 'image' come ultimately to enounce the point of impossibility; the blind spot the representational system seeks to refuse even as it constantly addresses it; the vanishing point of its attempt to construct itself as a system. As the mark of the limit that rebounds back on to the system, it demarcates – like Foucault's self-reduplicating mirror to infinity – how the cultural constructions of 'femininity' and 'image' collide with the position also ascribed to 'death'. 'In so far as the system closes over that moment of difference or impossibility,' Rose argues, 'what gets set up in its place is essentially an image of the woman.' The same is true for an image of death, which, when combined with the signifier Woman, raises both to their superlative degree. Rose continues, 'the system is constituted as a system or whole only as a function of what it is attempting to evade and it is within this process that the woman finds herself symbolically placed. Set up as the guarantee of the system she comes to represent two things – what the man is not, that is difference, and what he has to give up, that is, excess.'[28]

Both difference and excess are that which the image, as a stable form of representation, seeks to exclude and it can do so paradoxically over the signifier Woman. But because the semantic encoding of Woman as displaced signifier for difference and excess metonymically includes death, it is the intention to exclude death that is equally at stake in the dispensation of the maternal, material, feminine from semiotic space. Yet this 'exclusion' (of femininity, death, the image) occurs over a rendition of the feminine body, and most perfectly when it is an absent, a dead body. That is to say, it is not simply rhetorically but literally displaced. To repeat one of my central paradoxes – the erased or occulted is also what is most visible. Femininity (like the image, like death) is a fundamentally uncanny position. As site of assurance and disruption it stages control and its impossibility. It endorses an intellecutal hesitation between fear and desire, between self and other, between a surmounting of loss and its irrevocable fulfilment.

In the last section of *Denkbilder*, entitled 'Nach der Vollendung,' Walter Benjamin presents the scenario of artistic creation in such a way as to connect it explicitly with feminine death.

> One has often thought of the creation of great works of art in the image of birth. This image is dialectic; it circumscribes the process in two directions. One has to do with creative conception [*Empfängnis*] and its genius concerns femininity. This femininity exhausts itself after the fulfilment [*Vollendung*]. It

gives life to the art work and then dies. What dies in the master artist once creation has been fulfilled is that part in him, in which the creation was conceived. Now, the fulfilment of the art work – and that leads to the other side of this process – is nothing dead . . . here, too, one can speak of birth. For in the process of being fulfilled the creation gives birth once again to the creator. Not in his feminine mode, in which his creation was conceived, but rather in his masculine element. Reanimated, he exceeds nature . . . he is the masculine first-born of the art work, which he once conceived."[29]

Benjamin's argument works by virtue of gendering the two positions involved in the artistic process which he sees as a dialectic between creation and destruction. The feminine is that part of the creative act that conceives and gives birth to the artwork. It fulfills itself in the course of creative birthgiving and is eliminated once the act has been completed. The 'thing' murdered by the symbol, the artist's work, refers to the maternal function in semiotic space, conceiving and bearing, in an indexical or iconic mode. Yet the effacement and deanimation of the feminine is coupled with another form of animation, resulting from the production of an art work. Not only is a text created over a dead feminine body, but this sacrifice also gives a second birth to the artist.

This second birth signifies the elimination of threatening natural materiality, implicitly associated with decay. It signifies a triumph over death figured as the triumph over natural maternal birth, genius over *gynein*. The artist, born a second time, assumes the site of self-sufficient, self-created masculinity, superseding the 'dark realms of nature' by supplanting them with the 'lighter realms' of autonomous symbolicity; with an arbitrary though conventional form of semiosis, safely distanced from any contact with maternity, materiality, facticity and decay. While the feminine as source and executor of inspiration dies, the masculine artist is born. In this scenario femininity disappears twice – substituted for the 'fulfilled', perfected text and for the artist as the text's (not a woman's) first progeny. The male artist receives, creates and is created. Because he translates into himself the feminine principle, the latter can be 'killed'. The double elimination of the feminine is such that it 'dies' having been exhausted in the process of creation, and also 'dies,' because the feminine has been integrated into the masculine artist.

The subversion of a clear distinction between producer and product is such that the artist not only creates an art work but is also its creation. He not only controls and forms art but is in turn controlled and formed by it. In one and the same gesture he produces signifiers and fades as these signifiers produce him. He is the work's medium through which it gains birth and it is the medium through which he articulates himself. The dialectic of decentration/centration of the subject, of self-effacement and self-construction, sketched in this scenario must, however, be understood as one constructed over an irretrievably lost feminine body, deprived of all presence, marked as initial source of the creative process only in absence, under erasure. My last two textual examples are meant to demonstrate the monstrosity underlying the notion that artistic creation requires the elimination of the feminine, natural, maternal.

In his story 'The Birth-mark' (1843), Nathaniel Hawthorne presents a man driven by a desire to 'lay his hand on the secret of creative force', and, like Poe's painter, this philosopher acts out the rivalry between his 'love of science' and his 'love of woman' (764). Though his beautiful young wife is the object of a 'spiritual affinity more attractive than any chemical one', Aylmer is too devoted a scientist to be 'weaned from his studies,' so that his second passion must be intertwined with his first. The union of the two brides engenders, as in Poe's story, the production of a masterpiece and the destruction of the woman, though what is created is not the woman's double in the form of a portrait. Rather this creation entails the removal of a part of her body that seems uncannily to mark a moment of excess in the woman's physique – namely the singular pigmy-sized handlike mark deeply interwoven with the texture and substance of Georgiana's cheek, her third 'mimic hand'.

The tragic paradox of the 'truly remarkable consequences' and the 'deeply impressive moral' resulting from the double marriage to his science and his wife is that perfecting Georgiana, whose natural materiality figures as an aesthetic threat to his philosophic system, by removing the one flaw, the 'stain' and 'stigma' from her otherwise immaculate body is equivalent to destruction. The effect of the aesthetic risk is carried out on the woman's material body. The feminine corpse serves as a sign for her complete submission to his fantasies of perfection and proves to perfection that repeatedly 'his most splendid successes were almost invariably failures, if compared with the ideal at which he aimed' (774).

As Aylmer uses his scientific knowledge to eliminate 'this birth-mark of mortality', this 'visible mark of earthly imperfection' he discovers, as Georgiana had presaged, that its removal means 'relinquishing mortality itself,' because the mark clutches its grasp into her heart so as to be inextricable from her being. As in Poe's story a transfusion takes place. To the same degree that the red stain of the birthmark on the marble paleness of Georgiana's cheek loses its former distinctness, her breath also parts from her body, until both marks of human imperfection fade completely. Her soul 'took its heaven ward flight' and beside Aylmer lies the 'now perfect woman', an empty form (780). Any reference to death's indirect presence in life can only be removed by replacing it with the presence of death itself. Perfection is so compelling because it contradicts the idea of disintegration. In this case the effort to undo the state of disintegration by making the loved object beautiful and perfect incites another kind of loss. The crucial question grounding this scenario of creation and destruction is, however, 'why Aylmer should have felt so compulsively threatened by this mark to turn the need for its effacement into such an obsession'.

On the most obvious level Aylmer is fascinated by the crimson hand as a mark by which to prove both his ultimate control over and his ability to surpass nature: 'I even rejoice in this single imperfection' he explains, 'since it will be such a rapture to remove it' (771). The crimson hand marks the impossibility of a 'living specimen of ideal loveliness', and its removal will prove that the artificial creation of ideal beauty necessarily involves a translation from the animate into the inanimate. Because the birth-mark designates the transience of human existence, Aylmer, who seeks artificially to construct the immortal, immaculate and infinite in competition with natural feminine creation, sees it as the fatal flaw used by nature to subjugate man. He fetishistically isolates it as the one point of interest in his wife, 'as the symbol of his wife's liability to sin, sorrow, decay, and death' (766). This act of translating a body part into a trope marks the beginning of Georgiana's deanimation, the privileging of her symbolic over her material, indexical meaning – the mark, as symbol for human flaws, causes him more trouble and horror than her beauty had given him delight. Because Georgiana was meant to be the sign for his own immaculate, infinite and immortal existence, this 'symbol of imperfection' takes a fatal hold on his fancy. For it mars the perfect self-reflection he wishes to assure himself of as he gazes at his wife, his good double; it introduces a disturbing difference into this relay of gazes. Where he wants to idealise the other as displaced self-idealisation, he is confronted with a 'spectral Hand that wrote mortality' so that his double, rather than satisfying his desire for an image of wholeness and integrity, in fact signifies the antithesis of his desire, namely death's signature of life, its inextricable grasp on human existence.

He obsessively gazes at her to seek what he knows he will not find, the absence of the mark which, in a brilliant reversal of cultural coding of anatomy, marks through its presence the absence normally ascribed to feminine sexuality, along with the absence that is the threat of death. Like any fetishist, he seeks what he knows is impossible, the phallic woman, as a sign for wholeness and stability safely severed from facticity. Yet what he repeatedly returns to is the red mark, taunting him with an ever stronger visibility as his gaze provokes a deathlike paleness in Georgiana's cheek.

His obsession with the hand is a desire to replace his image of the feminine body 'castrated' by the mark with the fancied image of the 'phallic mother', the figure of wholeness *par excellence*. Yet this image of unity and stability is a response to the first 'cut' that simultaneously initiates birth and death, whose manifest scar is the navel. Laid upon Georgiana 'before she came into the world' (768), the birth-mark is the signature of the maternal function within semiotic space as this coincides with the child's entrance into facticity, its being marked outside and beyond its entrance into paternal symbols and sexual difference. In a sense, the birthmark is a repetition of the navel displaced upwards. The removal of the mark means controlling and surpassing nature on two scores – as the natural body always indicates maternal creation and as it always indicates the work of death. The second birth Aylmer wants to give his wife is meant to produce a flawless feminine body no longer marked by a liability to sin (sexual difference) and decay (the navel). With this masterpiece he hopes not only to surpass nature's masterpiece – man – but to contradict nature's interdiction that while man can 'mar', he can 'on no account make'. As inspirational muse, leading him ever deeper into the heart of science and nature's secrets, Georgiana's fatally marked body is also the site at which this scientist's fatal jealousy of feminine generative powers is carried out. It is set up by Aylmer to guarantee his ability to transform earthly nature into its perfect double, to create 'man's masterpiece', the immaculate Woman. This monstrous act, in which a scientist sacrifices his bride for an idea, is meant to signify the elimination of the mark of materiality, maternity and mortality and exchange it for a paternal, artificial recreation. That it fails, in so far as man's 'recreation' is a dead body, is an indication of Hawthorne's acknowledgement of the dangerous consequences of masculine creation. Nature's jealous patent has the last word – man is permitted only to mar. Even if the woman's body serves to secure a Christian world order that ascribes human creation to maternity and designates human existence as finite, limited by mortality, it is nevertheless the woman who pays with her life. The proof rests, so to speak, with her dead body.

There are, however, other dimensions to the question of why the mark must be removed at all costs. Because it is a sign for Georgiana's liability to decay and sin, it merges the mark of mortality with that of her sexual difference and her erotic charm. Her lovers see the mark as a token of her magic ability to 'sway over all hearts' and even Aylmer finds himself erotically drawn to it: 'once, by a strange and unaccountable impulse, he pressed it with his lips' (779). In part the hand signals the disgust he feels at being possessed by her erotic charm. To designate it as the signifier for her liability to sin, sorrow and death allows him to displace the sinfulness he feels for desiring the woman on to her body. She must have sorrow, she must be sinful, she must be punished for *his* desire. Removing this charming mark means terminating the erotic fascination Georgiana may have for himself and for others, assuring himself that she is his sole and exclusive possession, while he is no longer possessed by her.

Furthermore, one of the fascinating aspects of the birth-mark is that it marks a point of semantic indeterminacy. Not only does Aylmer hesitate between terming it 'a defect or a beauty', but different viewers interpret it differently. Where masculine observers may find that the mark heightens their admiration, feminine observers see in it the destruction of Georgiana's beauty. It is the point in her countenance where different gazes intersect, marking the fact that she is beyond one exclusive interpretative version and that means autonomous from Aylmer's narcissistically informed desire to use her as his identificatory other. Owing to the mark she is more than his gaze, the focus of a plurality of meanings, and as such threatens his stability.

Above all else the uncanny mark is the target of Aylmer's obsession owing to the fact that it is fundamentally incalculable, perpetually hesitating between being 'imperfectly defined' in its shape and assuming 'an almost fearful distinctness'. At times visibly present, at times completely absent, it is a sign for the movement that constitutes life; for inconstancy, for the never entirely ascertainable: 'when she blushed, it gradually became more indistinct, and finally vanished amid the triumphant rush of blood ... but, if any shifting emotion caused her to turn pale, there was the mark again, a crimson stain upon the snow

... now vaguely portrayed, now lost, now stealing forth again, and glimmering to-and-fro' (765f.). As a result of its constant alternation between visibility and invisibility, this unstable mark signifies human *aphanisis*, defined by Lacan as a constant interplay between appearance and disappearance, presence and absence. The subject's entrance into the symbolic order, resulting in an exchange with language and a murder of the soma, is contingent upon acknowledging the split within. Not only does the acquisition of language and cultural laws produce the division between conscious and unconscious self, it also forces the subject to fade before the chain of culturally inscribed signifiers in the sense that the subject is never self-present: 'Hence the division of the subject – when the subject appears somewhere as meaning, he is manifested elsewhere as "fading," as disappearance.'[30] However, we fade not only before the symbolic law that dictates our subjection to language and cultural codes but also before the real law that death inscribes all human existence.

Aylmer's fateful logic suggests that if a mark, which explicitly stages this process of 'aphanisis', can be effaced, then by extension, his own split, his own fading may be overcome. Yet an ego stability gained by procuring, as object of its gaze, a body whose vacillation has been arrested in a mortified figure, is precarious. Though it successfully denies that aspect of death's drive, articulated in the unstable play of absence and presence, it acknowledges the other aspect of death – the inevitable return to an inanimate immobility – which in turn comes to reflect the psychic stasis of the survivor and his gaze.

As the narrator in fact critically comments, while the birth-mark's 'presence had been awful; its departure was more awful still' (779). Removing death's signature from the human body only means a totalisation of the death drive. It is, then, less a question of the feminine body being 'castrated', in Lacan's terms 'not all', than of her indicating to the masculine viewer that he too is not all; that he too is not omnipotent; that he is vulnerable before nature and God's laws. The feminine corpse becomes a trope for that immaculate wholeness impossible in life. The paradox this perfect dead feminine body poses is that if Georgiana, once her soul has departed, is in a double sense 'not all' – not alive (as body split from its soul) and sexually lacking – man, in distinction to her, is 'all'. The masculine survivor knows he is alive and potentially immortal because death is with the Other. But if the dead woman is also 'perfect', she simultaneously comes to signify the surviving man's imperfection. The removal of the mark returns its surveyor to the hesitation between possession and elusiveness, between control and impotence, that its prior presence had provoked in Aylmer.

The hand functions rhetorically as the antithesis, as that mark of semantic limit and difference from which binary oppositions emerge so that meaning can function. The hand is that in opposition to which perfect beauty draws its meaning: the one moment of failure, the 'almost', where beauty comments on itself because it comments on its limit and its Otherness. Along with signifying difference (in respect to femininity as opposed to masculinity, and death as opposed to life), it signifies the rhetorical function of difference itself.

129

Aylmer's mistake then, is to believe that the mark is merely a supplement, simply exterior and can be annulled into pure absence, while it is in fact a mark of 'originary difference', an irreducible and integral figure that is neither absence nor presence: 'the stain goes as deep as life itself'. He is blind to the natural interwovenness of opposites, and he wishes to collapse distinctions into a transparent relation, so that the woman's sensible frame shall correspond perfectly to her spirit which has 'no taint of imperfection'. The mark is what keeps meanings apart even as its indeterminate nature demonstrates the interwovenness of opposite meanings. It stages ambivalence as a cross of meaning and non-meaning. It is a sign that Georgiana is alive and not dead, even as it marks that she is inextricably signed by death.

To remove the mark that divides and connects, to collapse oppositions into a relation of perfect correspondence is fatal. As Barthes says of perfection, 'it exalts (or euphorizes) in so far as it puts a stop to the leak of replications, wipes out the distance between code and performance, between origin and result, between model and copy; and since this distance is part of the human condition, perfection, which annuls it, lies outside of anthropological limits'. Perfection exalts until, because it is excess, because it is that which lies beyond the human, coincides with what is short of this code's limit, what is outside the human, the monster.[31] In Aylmer's story, perfection involves two aspects: the fixture of the indeterminate (be it of life or sexuality), in an effort to deny that *aphanisis* within which all human existence is implicated *and* the erasure of difference in an effort to produce the woman's body as a trope for wholeness and integrity. Rhetorically Aylmer's operation involves a relief from intellectual hesitation and from ambivalence. But an uncanny antithesis is preserved in the end, for the success of Aylmer's 'noble and lofty aim' is also his superlative failure. In its scandalous return to the literal, Georgiana's corpse demonstrates that the desire for transparency, for an erasure of divergence, opacity, ambivalence and vacillation in meaning is an expression of the death wish – it is the moment where the ideal, the 'more than human' turns into the monster 'the less than human'. An obsession with the immaculately pure, with a denial that life is always inextricably interwoven with death, lets death emerge as pure presence.

Mary Shelley's *Frankenstein* (1818) is also a narrative about the monstrous and fatal consequences of masculine creation emerging from a rivalry between a man's affinities to his family and to science. As in 'The Birth-mark' the scientist seeks to 'penetrate into the recesses of nature', into the hiding-place of her 'deepest mysteries of creation', in order to 'banish' what he sees as the greatest evil of existence, namely the human degradation and waste beheld in 'the corruption of death' (92ff.).

Recently critics have begun to read the novel in relation to Shelley's own ambivalence about motherhood and about artistic creation linking the two in so far as both can engender destruction and in so far as the desire for the created object is often mingled with feelings of rejection. Ellen Moers was the first to emphasise that Shelley's personal experiences of birth were, by the time she wrote *Frankenstein*, so hideously and inextricably intermixed with death to explain her fear, guilt, depression and anxiety in relation to maternity.[32] She had lost her first illegitimate child within one month of its birth and had to bear the physical and mental strain of two more children in the next two years.[33] She saw her half sister Fanny Imlay commit suicide upon discovering her illegitimacy and Harriet Shelley drown herself because she was pregnant by someone other than her husband. In an uncanny repetition of events, the fact that another woman's death makes her marriage, her social birth as Mrs Shelley, possible points back to the fact that the complications of her 'first' natural birth were the cause of her mother's death. Mary Shelly must have fashioned her self-image as reader, writer and wife under the auspices of her adoration for her dead mother, given her habit of taking her books to Mary Wollstonecraft's grave in St Pancras Churchyard to study there and clandestinely meet Shelley.[34]

The personal anxieties Shelley translates into her story of the 'workshop of filthy creation' address not only the guilt a creator may feel about wanting to reject her or his creation and the narcissistically wounding acknowledgement that the event of death cannot be revoked, but also the death and obviation of the mother as necessary prerequisite for the formation of the speaking and creating subject. In Benjamin's scenario, the birth of the writer means a usurpation of the maternal role that leads to its elimination, as the writer gives birth to her or himself through her or his text. Particularly striking in Mary Shelley's case is the blurring of the figural and the literal since her birth as a writer was a repetition of the matricide that her physical birth entailed.[35]

Although the ambivalent interconnection of creation and destruction is figured most prominently in the scientist Victor Frankenstein and his brother in ambition Robert Walton, Shelley's text also explores how the animation of dead material as contingent on the deanimation of animate material involves the feminine position. This process seems to entail the elimination of the maternal on two scores; firstly, Frankenstein's masterpiece involves a motherless birth, and secondly, this artificial creation competes with and repeals nature in an attempt to eliminate maternity entirely, because maternity gives birth to death along with life. At stake is not only the notion of the mother as an entity which must be lost for the constitution of the subject to take place and which must be absent from the creative process, although she is the model. The text also argues that within this economy of motherless creation there may be no brides. Reanimated out of a conglomeration of corpse material is a masculine body; deanimated and preserved as an image is the feminine body – the portraits of the mother, the mental image of the bride. Shelley deconstructs the premises upon which artificial creation is based to reveal that in the need to sever her or himself from context and reference, the artist must renounce materiality for the symbolic; must be severed from the maternal to create her and himself as an autonomous entity. But taken to its logical conclusion, this process can mean the complete obviation of the unencompassible body of 'maternity–materiality–mortality', a totalised autonomy of the simulated over the natural world, which even as it tries to deny or surmount the absent presence of death as a force of life turns into death's full presence in life. The logic of Shelley's narrative is that total autonomy from materiality leads not only to the destruction of all that are born of woman but also to the destruction of the self.[36] To exclude the feminine as natural difference results in a relationship where the creator is exclusively constituted by his creation such that it ultimately implodes and destroys itself. Having severed Victor from all social bonds the monster chases his creator until he finds his death on Walton's ship, caught in the frozen waters of the North Pole.

What Frankenstein cannot accept is the duplicity of the double – as it embodies the fact that any substitute figures of the 'lost' mother both recuperate lost wholeness and confirm that it has vanished. Victor wants a dual relationship with an other that reinforces his identity and assures his sense of autonomy completely, by eliminating any disturbing elements of Otherness like the natural, the material, the feminine. Privileging the 'creation of a being like myself' (97) that would bless him as 'its creator and source' over his bride Elizabeth is meant to afford a perfect form of self assurance. 'No father,' he fantasises, 'could claim the gratitude of his child so completely as I should deserve theirs' (98); implicitly because he would be the only parent, explicitly, however, because he would have broken through and overcome the 'bond' of that element most threatening to any self-constituting duality – namely death. Where the mother and her surrogate objects disappoint because their potential difference and absence signifies the subject's own mortality, the 'new species' of 'excellent natures' would reflect his hopes of immortality. The logical consequences of his success at bestowing 'animation upon lifeless matter' would be 'to renew life where death had apparently devoted the body to corruption'. If he can create a new race out of lifeless matter, the success of his experiment will engender his own renewal as an immortal being. The maternal creation is superceded on two scores – the maternal body is no longer necessary as site for creation and the 'flaw' inscribed in each human of woman born, the mother's given mark of mortality, the navel, would be overcome. Yet the flip side of this conception of a perfect duality is that if the other doesn't reassure completely it turns into the total cancellation of the self. As Victor works among the 'unhallowed damps of the grave', finds his materials for the perfect other in the vaults, charnel houses, dissecting-rooms and slaughter houses, he experiences a preview of his own deanimation as it will be fulfilled in his arctic death: 'I seemed to have lost all soul or sensation but for this one pursuit' (98).

While Frankenstein's real mother's death defers his entrance into university at Ingolstadt, this death in a sense initiates his symbolic activity since the studies are meant not only to replace her but also to revoke what her decease confirmed – the 'irrevocable reality of the evil of death'. As site for the sense of imaginary wholeness, the maternal body is replaced by two 'objects of desire', two brides; firstly the orphan Elizabeth, whose scarlet fever was the immediate cause of Victor's mother's death and whose union to him the mother requests on her deathbed, and secondly the bones, the decaying flesh Victor begins to study in Ingolstadt, from which the monster will emerge.

Elizabeth is etherealised from the start, placed into the paradigm of the angelic: 'the saintly soul of Elizabeth shone like a shrine-dedicated lamp . . . the sweet glance of her celestial eyes . . . ever there to bless and animate us' (82). He can accept Elizabeth as loved object only upon turning away from his scientific studies after the creation of the monster and he must defer the marriage to return once more to his 'workshop of filthy creation', to animate the monster's feminine counterpart. Only when Victor turns away from the bits and pieces of reanimated corpses, when he denies that his subjectivity is constituted in relation to inanimate objects – the dead matter and the texts that inspired him – does real death occurs. By rejecting the first monster he engenders the child William and the maid Justine's death, destroying the second monster provokes the death of his friend Clavel, his bride and his father.

Because Elizabeth, as one potential self-confirming Other, is marked by mutability in the sense that she causes the death of the mother and already seems ethereally part of the Beyond, she embodies a notion of human existence that works along a metonymic axis; one feminine body destroying and replacing a prior body. The dead matter Victor relates to as an alternative Other to his self involves an attempt to foreclose difference inherent to replacement because it is geared towards renewing the already present rather than exchanging it for a substitute object. The bride reflects that part of Victor that is 'victim' to the natural laws of decay and mutability, while the monster reflects the other part resisting this 'evil' subjugation. That both Elizabeth and the monster, however, function as two interdependent aspects of death's presence in the world becomes most clear in the dream Victor has after giving life to the monster, a representation of Elizabeth that will be uncannily repeated on his wedding night, as the monster executes its creator's unconscious fantasy.

Recalling Lacan's formulation that 'femininity becomes the place in which man reads his destiny, just as the woman becomes a symptom for the man', we can ask whether the dream representation of her death is a symptom of his repression of death, as it connects with his repression of femininity.[37] If the dream is a form of wish-fulfilment, does he desire the death of his bride so as to be able to embrace death by embracing her corpse? Is her death, induced by his kiss, a sign that he wants to die or a sign that, owing to his studies, he has been in death's embrace so exclusively that he is now the creator of death in others? Is this in turn a sign of his guilt or of the fact that his scientific research into an autonomy from nature was from the start inscribed by a murderous intent? Victor repeatedly refers to the creature as his 'own vampire', his spirit 'let loose from the grave and forced to destroy' all that was dear to him (120). For Victor, Elizabeth's introduction into his family was interpreted as a gift, a 'pretty present' promised by his mother. Later she is the 'one reward I promised myself' after the detestable toil of the second creation (194). If Elizabeth is the symptom of Frankenstein's living towards death, as this, in turn, is his mother's gift to him, is the monster the symptom of his unconscious desire not to marry, not to enter into family bonds and the process of natural procreation, not to accept the gift of the bride?

Victor narrates his dream in the following way:

> I thought I saw Elizabeth in the bloom of health, walking in the streets of Ingolstadt. Delighted and surprized, I embraced her, but as I imprinted the first kiss on her lips, they became livid with the hue of death; her features appeared to change, and I thought that I held the corpse of my dead mother in my arms; a shroud enveloped her form, and I saw the grave-worms crawling in the folds of the flannel. I started from my sleep with horror . . . I beheld the wretch – the miserable monster whom I had created. He held up the curtain of the bed; and his eyes, if eyes they may be called, were fixed on me (102).

The juxtapositions that occur in this dream scenario are complex. On one level the dream serves as trope for the idea of artificial creation as producing the death of maternity: infusing life into an inanimate body is seen as directly related to drawing life from the animate body of his bride. In his fantasy the sexual embrace turns into a deathly embrace, foreshadowing the translation of the bridal into the death chamber. This transfusion connects the bridal/death scene with the birth scene in so far as Elizabeth as potential mother is 'killed' after his successful motherhood. To recall Benjamin, after the act of creation, the feminine part of the creator dies and he becomes the monster's 'creation', drawn out of his social bonds and into its trajectory of pure destruction of others and of himself. As his autonomous creation succeeds, the body of the bride as site for natural creation turns into a dead body and recedes from his grasp, transforming into the corpse of his mother.

The dream image cites the tripartite figure of Woman Freud calls 'the mother herself, the beloved who is chosen after her pattern, and finally the Mother Earth, who receives [man] again'.[38] As in Saint-Preux's equally presaging dream of Julie's death, a conflation of dead beloved into dead mother occurs, though in this scene Elizabeth repeats the death of his mother not her own, in the same way that she dies as the result of his not her own birthgiving. Significantly the image of the bride disintegrates and the image it is replaced with is one of disintegration – it is not the maternal image of beauty, wholeness and integrity but rather that of the maternal body punctured by grave worms.

The juxtaposition of the dream of the doubly castrated decaying feminine body and the image of the animated daemonical corpse he awakens to demonstrates that Victor's subject position is irrevocably one between two forms of death and is based on a confusion between the two. The beloved and the mother transform into a decaying body comparable to those he has been working with for two years. His turn to 'mother earth,' to the vaults and charnel houses, is an attempt to reverse his own birth, a return to nature's 'womb' to get the material for a 'creation' that will outdo his own birth by his mother because his reanimated corpse will deny the mark of death cointroduced with birth. By possessing the dead material of mother earth he hopes to possess not only his mother's creative power but also to possess death.

Yet the dream already indicates that what is monstrous about his creation is its superlative failure. Even as the monster is meant to signify how Victor has reversed the process of decomposition in his recomposition, it serves as a memorial to precisely that decay he deems man's 'evil'. The monster is a gruesome 'arrestation' of death, an animated 'daemonical corpse', recalling the worst threat to Victor's sense of self – namely the loss and disintegration of the mother's body. If his intention was to recreate his immortality out of the production of revitalised matter, the dream articulates his unconscious fear that what he has created is his own death and indeed the monster will be a carrier of death that, unlike natural bodies which engender a sequence of substitutions, totalises death by excluding the process of substitutions. In a perfectly uncanny manner, his dream reveals that his desire to overcome death, to eliminate the maternal creation which contains mortality subverts into the desire for an all-encompassing presence of death. The two signifers/figures in between which he finds himself positioned are the natural feminine body marked by decay and the artificial masculine body, a resurrected patchwork of corpses.

For Kristeva the loss of the mother is a biological and psychic necessity; matricide a vital necessity for individuation.[39] If the mother is not metaphorically 'killed', then aggression turns toward the self or, if an identity with the mother is unbroken, the self will be 'killed' in the process of the elimination of the maternal. By turning the mother into an image of death the necessary aggression can be preserved while the culpability of matricide is effaced. However, if an autonomy from the maternal is not achieved, if the maternal is not renounced, madness ensues. What Shelley's text argues is that even as the image of the dead mother is the safeguard of culture and connects family members, when it comes to be confused with an exclusion of maternity, madness and self-annihilation ensue just the same.

A 'beautiful' image of the dead mother comes significantly to connect almost all the victims of Victor's 'unhallowed arts'. Initially given to the maid Justine, the miniature is worn by the child William, on his breast, on the day he is killed by the monster, who takes it only to replace it securely in the folds of Justine's dress, so that it comes to serve as the circumstantial evidence that leads to Justine's execution. For the monster this 'portrait of a most lovely woman' reflects his own 'castration', his exclusion from the 'delights that such beautiful creatures could bestow' and it is in response/relation to her image that he demands of Victor a feminine counterpart, even though the feminine monster is to be as 'deformed and horrible' as he, a monstrous parody of the 'beautiful dead mother,' an animated arrestation of his nightmare image of the decaying punctured maternal corpse.

The final sequence of deaths is precipitated by the destruction of this feminine body, of this 'horrible' double of his mother's portrait meant to reassure the monster's narcissism. Nominally afraid that the feminine monster would propagate 'a race of devils', Victor 'tears to pieces the half-finished creature', and drops these body fragments into the sea. At the sight of his destruction, confusing the deanimate with the animate, he says 'I almost felt as if I had mangled the living flesh of a human being', and this experience will be literally carried out by the monster on Victor's wedding night, so that Elizabeth's death in her bridal bed reduplicates the feminine monster's death and Victor's dream image (211). As sign for the elimination of the paradigm connecting maternity with the iconic and the natural in semiotic space, Elizabeth's destruction by the monster chiasmically completes Victor's destruction of the feminine monster as potential mother.

Elizabeth's is the pivotal murder scene because for the monster it marks the entrance into pure evil, an almost mechanical completion of his 'daemonical design for destruction' – 'when she died . . . I was not miserable. I had cast off all feeling, subdued all anguish.' For Victor it marks a final turn from the world of society in an equally mechanical mission to destroy his creation and seek his own death (258). At the same time its representation is the most pronounced. As though Elizabeth's death was shown to be the acme of a sequence of deaths by being presented as a sequence in itself, her corpse is the only one repeatedly and explicitly described at several stages; in the pose the murderer leaves her ('helpless and inanimate . . . her head hanging down and her pale and distorted features half-covered by her hair . . . her bloodless arms and relaxed form flung on her bridal bier'); in the posture of veiled serenity that the innkeepers have placed her for her public display ('her head upon her arm and a handkerchief thrown across her face and neck . . . the deadly languor and coldness of the limbs . . . the murderous mark of the fiend's grasp . . . on her neck'); and finally, as object of public grief ('there were women weeping around; I hung over it and joined my sad tears to theirs') (235f.).

The second pose is the one constructed as a repetition of his dream for as he raises himself from his embrace of the deadly langour and coldness of Elizabeth's limbs he sees the 'grinning' face of the monster again, though in this literal experience of death the horror of decay is significantly replaced by the despair at having lost the loved and cherished Elizabeth. As image of a beautiful feminine body she is now exactly like the mother, 'whose countenance expressed affection even in death' (88), her perfect repetition and a recuperation of this stabilising image of the dead mother/bride as antidote against the nightmare image. Her veiled face covers over the threatening image of the fragmented dead mother/bride of his dream, as it replaces the monster, whose revivification he refused. The literal death of the bride brings Victor's creation to completion. The rivalry between bride and science has found its stable manifestation in this two-headed masterpiece, where Elizabeth, to evoke Barthes's definition of perfection, embodies excess as the ideal essence, the beyond and the more than human, a literalisation of her angelic traits, a repetition of the idealised mother, while the monster embodies excess as that which is less, short of and outside the human limit. Where the former is the living image of a dead body (and Victor can, after her death, endlessly recall her 'soothing voice' in memory), the latter is a living corpse producing death. Both come to image the condition of being a corpse for the surviving Victor, and in this fulfilment Elizabeth's bridal bier does become the site of maternity; her death gives birth to Victor's explicit desire for his own demise.

A most extreme example of the interrelation of femininity, death and the image, Shelley's text takes this topos almost to its limit. If my previous examples addressed the issue of how the image double of a woman was in some way either the condition or the result of her death, what is at stake in *Frankenstein* is the aspect of failure inherent in the project of masculine creation. As another aspect of the 'anti-pygmalion' topos of nineteenth-century culture, Victor fails not only to create the 'excellent natures', surpassing humanity because without the 'flaw' of mortality, he also fails to create and resists creating the feminine. In his attempt to reverse man's creation by woman he succeeds only in creating by displacement the inanimate feminine body and preserving the dead mother. His monster, a conglomeration of different corpse parts, forbidden to reproduce, produces instead a series of feminine corpses, returns the animate to its primordial inanimate form and as such is a representative of the pure death drive as counterproductive as Frankenstein's desire to obviate death's presence in life. The radicality of Shelley's narrative lies in the fact that while the maternal can not or will not be created by Victor it can be destroyed by his monster.

The question remains, what does Victor, what does the narrative gain by this failure to recreate a feminine monster, a deformed version of the maternal image? What convention is supported, or put into question? For one, femininity, and its prime trope, the maternal image/body must remain pure, kept distinct from monstrosity; neither a feminine monster nor a feminine monstrous production may exist. The two doubles, the more than human ideal and the less than human fiend must remain cleanly severed as in the constellation of the wedding night. The future production of monstrosity must remain the prerogative of masculine creation, maybe to reconfirm by negation the ethic value of maternal creation. The completely tropic status ascribed to the maternal image/body is, however, also at stake. Because the 'mother' grounds and confirms subjectivity and culture given that she is always already dead, renounced from birth on (as the navel indicates), and present as an endlessly receding entity, her death can not be reversed or repeated. It is not a question of killing maternity but of avoiding the resurrection of the maternal into a fully present body. The function ascribed to femininity over the maternal position is that of difference leading to a constantly mobile dialectic of destruction and new creation, loss and recathexis, an indication of a split in any dual relation between self and other which leads to unity over difference and loss. As that which is always receding, the 'mother' brings ambivalence into the libidinal play, introduces the notion of an inadequate third, the substitute bride, who recalls but never entirely duplicates the lost mother, figuring as a mitigated form of death's presence.

Shelley's bleak argument is that to eliminate this duplicitous 'third' in the relationship of son to mother and privilege an other created in his own image turns into a self-imploding duality, the pure presence of the death drive. Her text questions the premise on which the successful displacement of desire from mother to bride occurs and deconstructs a logic of love where in Freud's formulation the finding of an object is in fact a refinding of it. She suggests that repetition as refinding may involve fantasies of the bride as inanimate image or dead body. In the same way that Victor cannot allow the death of the mother to be reversed, he cannot allow himself to refind or repeat her in another embodied love object. Elizabeth fulfills the role of replacement ascribed to her by Victor's mother through her own death, which translates her into the position of memory image. The dead mother is shown to be unique, a fundamentally ambivalent figure, absolutely tropic, constantly receding, neither resurrected as reanimated corpse nor replaced, but prominently present as a 'miniature' passing from breast to hand to dress fold. She is not just always already lost but also irreplaceable, her absence irreversible yet as such a fading element massively present in the individual and cultural image repertoire. For though she recedes and remains present only as an image, the fatal consequences of Victor's creation implies she can neither be eliminated completely from the creative process nor be fully re-embodied but must be retained as an absence at the point of origin.

The central misunderstanding informing this text is to insist on making literal what should remain a figural fantasy as this involves a blurring of the boundary between the living and the dead. The monstrosity of Shelley's tale is that it shows how an attempt to deny death by reanimating matter only ricochets back in the form of a death-producing creature. Victor's inability or unwillingness to accept the irrevocability of death lets him be blind to the difference between corpse and human body, which results in a reanimated corpse but also in the 'mortification' of his and his loved objects' living bodies.[40] The final consequence of culture's dictate to preserve the irreversibility of the mother's death, which Shelley's narrative supports, is the need to preserve the difference between living and dead, to draw a non-transgressible boundary between the animate and the inanimate.

These representations of dead feminine bodies treated like portraits articulate the desire for a return to a stable image after a moment of disturbance; for the preservation of distinctions after these have been uncannily blurrred by death. Their contradictory narratives construct a doubled opposition – the feminine against the masculine, overlapping with the dead against the living – to defend against the knowledge of an incommensurable difference at the origin and centre of life. By representing the narrative of 'double castration', the subjet stages his identity as as unified entity. For the dividing force, be this sexuality or death, is seen in opposition to the self, outside rather than inextricably interwoven with it. As trope of castration *par excellence*, the dead feminine body is both rejected and preserved in these narratives about creation. Yet what is also represented is the irrevocability of this originary difference and the failure inherent in any strategy that, in an effort to save the self, constructs oppositions rather than accepting originary difference. As the subject articulates its identity on the basis of a narrative of 'double castration' it is forced to incorporate precisely that split of which and against which it narrates. As the subject defends itself by constructing its position in opposition to femininity and to death, the visual and narrative image it uses engenders instead a differential, reciprocal relation with femininity and with death.

Notes to Chapter 7

1 T. de Lauretis, 1984, pp. 37f.
2 I use Peirce's distinction between icon, index and symbol, 1955, pp. 98–119.
3 M. Bal, 1988, p. 103.
4 I want to thank Klaus Poenicke for pointing out this distinction to me.
5 For a longer thematic presentation of the motif of the haunted portrait see T. Ziolkowski, 1977, pp. 78–147.
6 P. Ariès, 1983.
7 See L. Nochlin, 'Death in the Mid-Nineteenth Century', 1971a. She quotes Monet's conversation with his friend Clemenceau about the last painting of Camille: 'One day, when I was at the death-bed of a woman who had been and still was very dear to me, I caught myself, my eyes fixed on her tragic forehead, in the act of mechanically analysing the succession of appropriate colour gradations which death was imposing on her immobile face. Tones of blue, of yellow, of grey, what have you? This is the point I had reached. Certainly it was natural to wish to record the last image of a woman who was departing forever. But even before I had the idea of setting down the features to which I was so deeply attached, my organism automatically reacted to the colour stimuli, and my reflexes caught me up inspite of myself, in an unconscious operation which was the daily course of my life – just like an animal turning his mill', p. 63.
8 M. Warner, 1985.
9 S. Freud, 1919, pp. 248–50.
10 S. Freud, 1919.
11 S. Kofman, 1973.
12 E. A. Poe, 1978, p. 662.
13 F. Meltzer, 1987.
14 N. Hawthorne, 1837, p. 459.
15 S. Kofman, 1985a.
16 F. Meltzer, 1987, p. 107.
17 M. Blanchot, 1981, p. 81.
18 D. G. Rossetti, 1870, pp. 73–5.
19 J. Lacan, 1981, p. 83.
20 M. Safouan, 1983, p. 93.
21 S. Rimmon-Kenan, 1980.
22 J. Kristeva, 1984.
23 J. Berger, 1972, pp. 47 and 64.
24 G. Pollock, 1988, p. 153.
25 See M. Bal, 1987, pp. 317–44.
26 L. Mulvey, 1975, p. 11.
27 See V. Burgin, 1986.

28 J. Rose, 1986, p. 219.

29 W. Benjamin, 1972, p. 438.

30 J. Lacan, 1981, p. 218.

31 R. Barthes, 1974.

32 See E. Moers, 1977, pp. 139–51.

33 On 19 March 1815 she wrote in her journal, 'Dream that my little baby came to life again, that it had only been cold, and that we rubbed it before the fire, and it lived. Awake and find no baby. I think about the little thing all day. Not in good spirits', quoted in E. Moers, 1977, p. 147.

34 See S. Gilbert and S. Gubar, 1979; M. Poovey, 1980, who discusses the monster as a trope for Shelley's anxieties about the artistic enterprise in general and the price paid for her ambition to be an artist in particular.

35 B. Johnson, 1987. In *The Confessions*, a book Shelley would certainly have read, Jean-Jacques Rousseau, 1781–8, suggests how the position of the writing subject implies a dead, absent mother, whom he recalls in her person and surpasses as he recreates himself autonomous from materiality through his text. His birth 'cost' his mother her life, and for his father he serves as a fetish monument to loss: 'he thought he saw her again in me, without being able to forget that I took her from him'. From his mother he inherits his first reading material, some 'novels' left behind, which initiates his uninterrupted self-consciousness, that leads ultimately to the confessions, the text of his life, that recreates him as its first masculine progeny, 'myself, alone', pp. 33–6 passim.

36 M. Homans, 1986, points out that each mother dies shortly after being introduced into the narrative; Victor's mother is herself an orphan and dies after she has taken care of the orphan Elizabeth. The maid Justine, who is said to have caused the death of her mother, serves as substitute mother to William and is executed for his murder. See also U. Knoepflmacher, 1979.

37 J. Lacan, 1985, pp. 162–71

38 See my previous discussion of S. Freud, 1913, as well as L.-V. Thomas's discussion of the 'terre-mere', 1980, pp. 53–77. M. Jacobus, 1986, notes in a similar vein that 'the most striking absence in *Frankenstein*, afterall, is Eve's', p. 101. She draws the analogy, however, between the monster, as hideous travesty of a woman and her ideal, Elizabeth, and not, as I suggest, between the monster and Victor's own decomposing mother.

39 J. Kristeva, 1989.

40 Because I will repeatedly use the word 'mortification' in an unorthodox way, I refer at this point to W. Ong's discussion, 1977, of mortification as 'a putting to death', a 'killing off', a fixing of something once and for all, 'so that it is no longer subject to change', p. 235.

8

Noli me videre

To write means to disappear in a certain sense.
Michel Deguy

It seems fitting to end this discussion of the translation of animate bodies into inanimate texts by returning to that novel which historically stands at the beginning of my textual corpus. 'Upon the whole,' Lovelace explains in self-justification after Clarissa's prolonged staging of her courtship with death, 'had not the lady died, would there have been half so much said of it, as there is? . . . And have there not been, in a million cases like this, nine hundred and ninety-nine thousand that have not ended as this has ended' (IV.454). While I have, up to now, treated representations of women as passive objects and privileged tropes of masculine imagination and desire I will now address the question of how an aesthetically staged performance of death may not also signify a moment of control and power, given that the woman's self-disintegration also becomes an act of self-construction. Each of the three texts to be discussed – Richardson's *Clarissa*, Tennyson's 'Lancelot and Elaine' (1859) and Flaubert's *Madame Bovary* (1857) – depicts a woman using death as a conscious act of setting a mark, as a form of writing with her body, a materialisation of the sign, where the sheer material factualness of the dying and dead body lends certainty, authority and realness to this attempt at self-textualisation.

If I have up to now emphasised the notion of the feminine body as site for an exterior form of inscription and emphasised the existence of two subject positions, the subject of the action (the dying woman) and the subject of focalisation (the masculine survivor/spectator), wherein the former is seemingly more passive because object of identification and desire of the latter, these examples can be read as instances where the two positions collapse into one. Dying is a move beyond communication yet also functions as these women's one effective communicative act, in a cultural or kinship situation otherwise disinclined towards feminine authorship. It involves self-reflexivity in so far as death is chosen and performed by the woman herself, in an act that makes her both object and subject of dying and of representation. The two points Lovelace indicates are crucial. Only the death of the heroine, in response to loss, in this case the loss of her virtuous self-image, engenders such an abundance of texts, 'so much said of it'. This death is exemplary, different from the conventionally expected outcome of rape, because it involves the conscious and explicit choice of death as a strategy for lending authority to the woman's version of her story.

Two thematic concerns subtend my discussion. Firstly, the representation of a woman killing herself in order to produce an autobiographical text can serve as a trope for the relation of the writing process to death in general. Such an interpretation presupposes a concept of writing as disembodiment or absence of the writing subject, based on the notion that the image or symbol functions as the negation of the thing, be it the speaker, the addressee or the object of speech. It also presupposes a notion of death as offering, in Michael Ryan's formulation, 'the possibility of an absolute alterity', 'the passage into otherness'. In death's movement toward alterity Ryan sees an obvious analogy to autobiographical desire. In autobiography the self desires a 'literary' alterity, 'one which repeats the self within a text at once parallel to and radically different from the conscious-ness'. While the literal attainment of alterity implies death, autobiography figurally attains alterity because it marks the self's 'attempt to know itself as other', so that by implication 'the self undertakes a relationship with death whenever it performs autobiography'.[1] Suicide, in turn, is both the literal attain-ment of alterity through death and the performance of an autobiographical desire. For suicide implies an authorship with one's own life, a form of writing the self and writing death that is ambivalently poised between self-construction and self-destruction; a confirmation that is also an annihilation of the self, and as such another kind of attempt to know the self as radically different and other from the consciously known self during life.

The second concern is that of the position culture grants femininity. The choice of death emerges as a feminine strategy within which writing with the body is a way of getting rid of the oppression connected with the feminine body. Staging disembodiment as a form of escaping personal and social constraints serves to criticize those cultural attitudes that reduce the feminine body to the position of dependency and passivity, to the vulnerable object of sexual incursions. Feminine suicide can serve as trope, self-defeating as this seems, for a feminine writing strategy within the constraints of patriarchal culture.

Both concerns, however, involve a central contradiction, for the aesthetical staging of suicide always implies a turn to the sheer materiality of the dying and dead body to legitimate textualisation. A conjunction of the aesthetic with the superlative involves an excess of self-referentiality that collapses the articulating self with its object of articulation. The 'excess' of these representations of feminine death is such that they stage a conjunction of the arbitrariness and conventionality of the symbolic with the contingency and analogy of iconicity, so that death's scandalous return to the literal also involves an extreme form of figurality. Writing death at/with the body means using the body as sign and embodying a sign; a re-introduction of materiality into the symbolic by literally giving birth to the death of the soma. The 'most poetical' death of these beautiful women emerges as a perfect form of self-authorship, as supreme fulfilment of the referential function of language that obliterates both the enouncer and the enouncee of that function, in a conjunction of death and the beauty of representation, where soma comes again to equal sema.

If in my previous examples masculine rivalry with nature gave birth to the symbolic portrait by killing the woman's body, these suicides stage how, by virtue of killing her own soma, the woman destroys the cultural construction of the feminine as 'dead' image ruled and violated by others in order to construct an autonomous self-image. Because culture so inextricably connects femininity with the body, and with objectification, because culture makes the feminine body such a privileged trope or stake in aesthetic and social normative debates, a woman can gain a subject position only by denying her body. Though a renunciation of the soma is part of all cultural development, the bind a woman is placed into in cultural representations is that her position in the symbolic or cultural order is that of feminine *body*, so that undoing her body, because it is the site of paralysis, because desires connected with it can not be realised, also means subverting the position cultural laws have ascribed to her. By undoing her body, she undoes the gender construction which places her in an inferior position, even as cancelling the 'illusion' of gender lets death emerge.

Paradoxically she can do so only by re-emphasising the body in an act of disembodiment, only to confirm once again the cultural attribute from which her fatal authorship tries to dissever her. These suicides as self-textualizations position the woman ambivalently between subjectivity, self-assertion and autonomy on the one hand and a repetition of alterior signs on the other; between the construction of a personal, original and authentic autobiography and a falling prey to already existing cultural conventions, to literary precursors. They position her between self-inscription and inscription by Otherness. Though the feminine is so inextricably bound to cultural fantasies that death may be the only moment where a real, autonomous and alterior self comes into being, the authorship implied in these acts of suicide allow the 'fantasy' of gender to re-emerge and occult death. The same gesture of recuperation occurs on the level of textuality, for even as these representations of suicide as authorship break with the system of representation by posing the dead body beyond and outside semiosis, the aesthetisation translates the corpse back into semiotic, textual categories. As long as one deals with representations and discourses, the natural materiality of the dying/dead body used as a last resort in validification is always also and already inextricably inscribed by signifiers.

Because the word absents what it names, there is a long tradition in western thought that speaks of the 'letter that killeth,' and sees the text becoming the body it thereby kills.[2] The writing subject is always caught in a figural 'suicidal self-alienation,' in *aphanisis* – a fading before signification. Francis Barker argues that the logic of bourgeois representation is inscribed by a proclivity toward death, in respect to both its object and its subject. Any representational discourse implies the absence, non-being or death of the object it seeks to designate, because the text is substituted for the body, the material object of its reference. The lacuna that in this sense grounds language is repeated in discourses about texts, so that commentary and interpretation, like the survivors' narratives about each heroine's death, 'kill' the body-text by replacing it with their respective texts, and as such reduplicate and mirror this scenario of representational absenting.

This 'fatal distancing', involves not only a multiple death of the textualised object, abolished and called into being in one and the same representational gesture. Rather, equally at stake is a 'suicidal denaturing of the subject which the decorporalized discourse defines'. The ambivalence of power is such that while the author creates a text in order to mean through it, possess and control it, it in turn equally possesses the writer, means and controls her or him. Representation splits into a form of self-possession and into a form of self-alienation, so that, as with the ambivalently absent/re-presented object, the text 'inaugurates the presence of the subject in order immediately to effect an erasure of that presence'.[3] In representations that are both explicitly autobiographical and the result of a literal suicidal alienation of the self into a text, this twofold death – of the object, killed by the text and an ensuing series of commentaries, and of the subject, poised between the presence of self-articulation and the absence of self-alienation – finds its superlative expression.[4]

From this conventional notion of writing as a carrier of death which exhausts life Derrida deduces the opposition between 'a good and a bad writing'. While the latter, as it betrays and paralyses life, and cuts life short in the endless repetition or series of signifiers, is 'the principle of death and of difference in the becoming of being',[5] the former expresses the desire for a natural or living writing, for a regaining of full and truthful self-presence, for an obliteration of difference, opacity, division and loss of self, as this is inaugurated with birth and given the physical mark of the navel. Language, abiding fundamentally by an economy of death, engenders a dispossession of the subject that institutes even as it deconstitutes: 'All graphemes', Derrida argues, 'are of a testamentary essence. And the original absence of the subject of writing is also the absence of the thing or the referent.'[6]

Writing, however, is not only a becoming-absent, or becoming-unconscious, of the subject. As it produces the economy of derivation, deferral and supplementation it inspires the desire to return to 'good writing,' the desire for full and true presence, even if this, like the wholeness of the imaginary unity, is constructed after and on the basis of an experience of lack or loss. At the same time that 'bad' writing (the dead letter) operates as 'a power of death in the heart of living speech', making any living, natural writing impossible, it opens as much as it threatens the possibility of the transparent relation between signifier and signified, which 'good writing' implies. One could extend Derrida's analysis to say that the desire for the 'good' natural, living writing marks an attempt to triumph over the economy of death, as it inscribes living existence with division, loss, difference and opacity and that this desire articulates itself in a move away from symbolic signs and in a return to the body as medium of self-expression. For writing death with the body not only confirms to excess the notion of textuality as obliteration of the natural subject and object of the representation. It also seems to be used as a strategy to regain a transparent form of signification, to obliterate the difference between signifier and signified, between enouncer and enouncee, object and subject, even if this full, truthful, non-alienated self-presence and self-expression means the reduction of all living tensions and all semantic indetermination, even if it means the stasis of real death.

The autobiographical texts of the heroines I will discuss are of a testamentary essence. Each of the body-texts embedded in their respective narratives is literally a 'dead letter', each carries the death, exhausts the life of its object and its subject. But the insignie of the conjunction of femininity, death and the aesthetic, consists in a significant conflation – the subject is also her own object, her disembodied text is also her textualized body. The 'letter killeth' and represents the body textually as well as physically making it present once more, albeit as a dead letter. Again, though the disappearance of the author is at stake, visibility and the aesthetically displayed presence of the 'dead' author is the crucial strategy of these representations.

In this ambivalent hovering between being and not being, presence and absence, materiality and textuality, being in the world and inaccessible to the world, these heroines mark once again the self-referential moment of the narratives in which they are embedded, signify, as *mise en abyme*, the status of literature and of the writer. Blanchot attributes to the writer a strangeness of existence in which, in the grasp of an impersonal power, she or he is neither alive, nor dead, simultaneously eliminating her or himself as s/he writes that text which also affirms the writing subject: 'But as one realizes the void, one creates a work, and the work, born of fidelity to death, is in the end no longer capable of dying.'[7] All three heroines write in response to an experience of loss, exchange the fidelity to their family or their lover with a fidelity to death. They write in response to the realisation of a void, an experience one could interpret as a wound to narcissism that forces upon each an acknowledgement of death, because what has been disrupted is the illusion of wholeness constructed in relation either to familial law (Clarissa), to love (Elaine), or to literature (Emma). Writing, as instrument of division and loss, is, because it occurs over the body, also the means to gap or assuage loss, in search of 'regaining' totality and wholeness.

For Clarissa, rape, experienced as a kind of death, means the complete destruc-tion of any sense of self-esteem, of any self-supporting narcissistic sense of wholeness and value, so that in support of the disintegration of body, mind and social personality she feels, her letters, following the event of rape, are fragments articulating, in various modes, her sense of being 'nothing'.[8] Because virtue is the primary value for both her position in the symbolic order of her family and society, and her imaginary self-construction, for the privileged role she has chosen to assume, its loss means a radical break from both stabilising registers. Her loss of virtue points to the illusory, even if necessary, quality of any sense of wholeness, immaculate perfection and invincibility, and lets death emerge.

Realising the vanity of her previous proud self-assurance that she would be the object of her world's admiration, adulation and applause, Clarissa writes 'I am no longer what I was in any one thing' (loss of imaginary unity), 'I don't know what my name is' (loss of a position in the symbolic system of kinship). She feels her body torn in pieces (like the letter fragments she tears in two), her body a 'broken chain', made the site of all possible vileness by her ravisher's act, until in her last fragment she explicitly courts death. Recognising that a return to her body means 'to mourn' her now irrevocable sense of being cut, of her loss of honour, she imagines death not only as the source of 'relief', but as a vindication of her primary innocence.[9]

Where before her rape Clarissa wrote letters to supplement her public construction of herself as a figure of 'conscious merit' and 'applauded purity', who, as 'paragon of virtue' could affect the reformation of sinners (notably Lovelace), after her rape she repeats this double form of authorship, which involves the writing of letters and the turning of her body into a sign. She disseminates the story of her loss of honour and of her failure to remain pure and perfect with as equal a verve as her previous epistolary activities; 'glad if I may be a warning, since I can not be an example' (III.336). At the same time her body is befallen by an unnamed illness and stages the woundedness, the marring she writes. This writing finds its fulfilment when she writes texts about her death supplemented by and supplementing her body writing her death literally, whereby both processes serve to turn her, as a conglomeration of letters about death and a dead body, into her own doubled auto-icon, her auto-biography, which finds another reduplication in the strategy of Richardson's novel.

Clarissa's writing death with the body serves to signify both the relation of writing and a political strategy to subvert her society's suppression of the feminine body. Eagleton argues that Clarissa's 'elaborate dying is a ritual of deliberate disengagement from patriarchal and class society', and as such signifies the political gesture of 'an absolute refusal of political society; sexual oppression, bourgeois patriarchy and libertine aristocracy together'.[10] Because a resistance to power is not clearly distinguishable from collusion with power, because Clarissa realises that a proclivity to impurity was not supplementary to her virtue and innocence but rather formed part of an originary difference grounding her being, she must acknowledge that she both courted the illicit and supported the social structures that deny her an independence of will. Repeatedly she blames herself for 'preferring a libertine to a man of true honour' (IV.275) and desires the forgiveness of those parents who have disempowered and disacknowledged her. Because she finds herself inextricably implicated in power structures that castrate her and make a separate innocent and autonomous existence impossible, her only expression of an independent choice is the tragic option for an obliteration of the body, over which to preserve or resurrect that image of the self she cannot live in her body. Yet Clarissa's death, as a form of writing her body out of existence to undo its impurity and to release herself from the confinement that binds her into a subordinate position in her society, gains its authority from precisely her turn to the materiality of the impure, disintegrating body.

The doubled form of writing Clarissa practises is from the start connected with deanimation. While before her rape Clarissa writes letters to establish repeatedly her sense of independence, will and merit, she also turns herself into a figure of virtue, alienating her self even as she constructs her public self, and it is precisely this act of self-allegorisation that makes her such a challenge to Lovelace. Because she has, from the start, turned her body and herself into a text, his pursuit and rape becomes an allegorical matter: 'my principal design is but to bring virtue to a trial' (II.325). Letter writing is seen from the start as a form of transgression, potentially wounding to the stability and integrity of the self as well as the stability of the familial order and integrity. Clarissa sees her letters as the result of her one vice and her one passion for scribbling (II.128), while her letters are condemned and sought by her family and her violator. They are a sign of her independent will, and continue to be so when she uses them to record her version of her rape and direct the outcome of her dying. But they are also token of her vulnerability. By writing letters, Clarissa illicitly courts Lovelace and in so doing courts her own dissolution. Not only does Clarissa repeatedly suggest that she is to blame for her loss in so far as she allowed a 'prohibited correspondence' and as such a transgression of her family's dictates. She implies that writing also invokes eroticism as a potential form of self-dissolution, in Bataille's sense of the word.[11] This second notion is supported by her recording of a dream shortly before she escapes from her imprisonment in her father's house, in which Lovelace is represented as a displaced signifer for death. Lovelace, believing her to have a hand in a plot formed to destroy him, carries her into a churchyard and there 'notwithstanding all my . . . protestations of innocence, stabbed me to the heart, and then tumbled me into a deep grave ready dug, among two or three half-dissolved carcasses; throwing in the dirt and earth upon me with his hands, and trampling it down with his feet' (I.433).

In a perfect reversal, after her rape, Clarissa's courtship of death that culminates in her celebration of her coffin, is also seen as a forbidden, even 'perverse' correspondence, where death is now a signifer consciously chosen to replace Lovelace. But by staging her death as a gradual weaning from the world (IV.258) she is bent on transmitting an image of death as the peaceful experience of intactness and unifying closure meant as an antidote to this other image of her corpse as 'castrated' body, cut and violently placed among disintegrating carcasses. It is probably with this threatening image of dissolution in mind that she imagines her appearance among her ancestors in the coffin she has meticulously designed for this occassion (IV.258).[12]

After her rape she exchanges the agent of her rape, Lovelace, with death, seeks death's violation of her body as a repetition, finalisation and sublation of the first, sexual incursion. The destruction of her sexual integrity is to be perfected by full bodily disintegration. Lovelace, in his jealousy, points to this equation between object of sexual desire and object of death when he says that Clarissa shuns him but woos death, prefers this 'more a skeleton than a man' to him (III.495). If she postulated earlier that she would 'sooner undergo' the death of immolation in the 'awful vault' of her ancestors than marry the wrong suitor Solmes, she now repeats the preference for death over marriage to a dishonourable man. Because any duality with Lovelace would be marred by the implicit presence of death in the form of the narcissistic wound he has inflicted on her body and her self-image, she privileges the unmarred duality with death itself as a triumph over this cut, an obliteration of all tensions, of difference and division. Exchanging her white bridal garments, now for ever tainted, for the 'all-quieting garb' of the shroud, she writes, they are 'the happiest suit, that ever bridal maiden wore for they are such as carry with them a security against all those anxieties, pains, and perturbations which sometimes succeed to the most promising outsettings' (IV.303). The suit of death's clothes replaces her rapist's inadequate suit.

Her existence after her rape is then dictated by her two obsessions, writing and death.[13] She wishes to speed up her illness so that she will be released from the confinement of her now impure body, while at the same time her rapidly growing weakness endows her writing with a sense of urgency. What she writes are letters 'which will set my whole story in a true light' (IV.186), her will that gives minute descriptions of how she wishes her possessions to be divided and her body to be disposed of, and a set of twelve 'posthumous letters', so that, though a dead body, she can assert her power and her will. Ironically, she, whose death in part is the result of total dispossession by her family, in death regains her possession and her judicial right to bequeath these on to others.

As she enfolds her final meaning, or rather the image with which she wants to remain in the world, and her last wishes pertaining to her body, inside the covers of these sealed texts, she also designs the container that will envelop her dead body. Though her friends consider it an 'unusual', 'extraordinary' object to display one's fancy upon, Clarissa's coffin is the product of as much skilful and planned design as her letters. Ornamented with the device of a crowned serpent, with its tail in its mouth as an emblem of eternity, a winged hour glass, an urn, the head of a white lily snapped short off, three biblical citations, and an inscription with her name, the date she left her father's house in lieu of her closing day, and her age, the coffin is another version of 'setting her whole story in true light' (IV.256ff.). As she chooses to have these objects of death (her burial garments and her coffin), always within her sight, reading and writing upon this self-designed 'house' or second body giving her pleasure and spirits (IV.271), she increasingly merges her two forms of self-textualisation. Both forms of 'writing' occur under the auspices of death – the translation of her living self, her story, her convictions, her last advice into written and sealed texts ('dead letters'), designed for the posthumous sight of her survivors, as well as the translation of her living body into a dead body, to be enveloped in a coffin that tells her story to her ancestors, out of sight from her survivors (though they, intrigued by the writing on the coffin desire to see the corpse inside).

The latter, materialised form of writing, which stages her bodily dematerialisation, is meant to give authority to the privilege death has as the most meaningful and powerful instance in human existence. It is meant to exemplify human subjection to death. To justify her death preparations to her friends Clarissa explains, 'Believe me . . . there is such a vast superiority of weight and importance in the thought of death . . . that it in a manner annihilates all other considerations and concerns . . . teaches me to forgive the injuries I have received' (IV.258). Before death the wounds to narcissism and to her social position lose in significance. In fact the coffin is seen as the restoration of an intact frame lost through rape; it simulates the re-closing of her body, incised by rape and death, as the nails of the coffin obliterate all gaps; it signifies a rigid and composed outer body that occults the decomposition of the corpse inside; it stands for a whole, univocal text that effaces the semantic indeterminacies her story may contain.[14]

Her other form of writing, her textual dematerialisation, lends, in Benjamin's sense, authority both to the text written on the coffin and to her last words. Because she supplements her writing about death with bodily death she can triumph and supersede death in so far as she continues to have effect and influence after her demise precisely because of her demise. Like the coffin, these posthumous letters are in Belford's words 'so many beautiful works' caused by death 'to spring from her fingers' (IV.356), embracing death, even as an existence beyond death is designed that will occult it again. The tone of these letters celebrates Clarissa's status as dead writer, and from the authority this absence lends her, she humbles herself before her survivors, disseminating in writing the words of forgiveness and comfort she will utter in actuality on her deathbed, admonishing against sinful behaviour, calling for reformation in the style of the *memento mori*, and praising the virtuous. In so doing she not only ensures that her story is documented, compiled and circulated by her friends among her society, to resurrect her fame out of and after death, to assure that her corpse, the 'nothing' (IV.429) violated by a rake and by death, will not be, in Anne's fearful terms, 'all of her story' (IV.402). She also uses these letters to accuse indirectly her family and her culture for allowing the destruction of virtue. Even as she embraces death as the source and inspiration of her writing, she supersedes death with her texts; even as her behaviour supports the Puritan ideology of her patriarchal bourgeois class, she exposes it to critique.

In response to the violence of rape, Clarissa turns to death, the most radical form of disruption of the integrity and unity of human existence, to reassert her control. In order to counter the figural 'death' of rape, she takes this disruption of her body to its full consequence and writes toward and against literal death. She turns writing on itself to give birth to two aspects of her self-image that are always also reduplications of writing itself. By falling ill, by nourishing her wound consciously and explicitly, she transforms, in Freud's terms, the necessity or destiny of 'castration' (in the mortal and sexual sense) into choice, and continues to exert and affirm her control by dictating the exact proceedings of her death ritual and assuring the resurrection of her will, beyond bodily death. She undoes the loss of subjectivity during rape, since dying in conjunction with writing becomes her superlative form of subjectivity. She reverses her deprivation of speech during rape, because the suicide as spectacle becomes in excess the expression of that experience previously felt as being 'inexpressible'. Though she claims that after her rape, her story can be meaningful only as warning, what the turn to the sheer materiality of death rhetorically effects is a relegitimation of her virtuous position, a proof of her chastity, the reconstitution of her reputation – by dying, as dead, she becomes a 'glorious example'.

The ambivalence inherent to this writing project is that death, the most supreme form of self-destruction, serves as form of re-composition after the experience of 'discomposure' in rape *and* that turning to writing as a form of obliteration of the body in fact emphasises the 'vile body' when it replaces this body with letters that are written from the certainty of physical absence about to occur, and gain their legitimacy from the dying body used to supplement them. Repeatedly Clarissa points to the discrepancy between the desires of the body and those of the mind. Fainting away as she writes, in the end supported by others as she traces her last letter 'on her knees' (IV.330), her gestures emphasise how the weakness of her body, forcing upon her an 'unsteadiness of her pen', interrupts her writing and her strength of mind. Though the image of Clarissa, fading before her epistolary activity, recalls Lacan's notion of human aphanisis before culture's signifiers, Clarissa uses this discrepancy to devaluate the body as mere 'rags of mortality' (IV.305) from which death will be a delivery and allow for a superior form of pure, transparent meaning, without the taint of difference between signifier (author's utterances) and signfied (figure of virtue). Death makes her body vanish from sight; 'her faded cheek . . . as if iced over by death . . . her hands, white as the lily, with her meandering veins more transparently blue than ever . . . hanging lifelessly' (IV.332). It articulates her belief that her meaning will be semantically more determined, more univocal when articulated only through a series of disembodied letters, while the body of the author, which allowed for interpretations different from those she had desired, is hidden away in its textualised coffin envelope.

Yet the privileging of her will (the written pages and the dictates they contain) and of her function as allegorical figure for virtue and glorious merit, which is effected by the death of her body, collapses into a resurgence of the privilege of her body. Its process of dying minutely transcribed by the spectators of Clarissa's death, and once transformed into a corpse, displayed to the view of her family, it is precisely the body, as the auto-iconic materialisation of the sign, which makes Clarissa's death so effective, which assures an interest in her 'symbolic' texts, the letters. As Clarissa gives birth to her self as text, in an act conforming with Benjamin's description of self-authorship, she does so by letting the iconic as maternal form of semiosis cross the paternal symbolic epistolary activity, and this gives back to death – as primary wound of human existence and as it finds its mark in the navel, which is maternity's gift to the new-born child – the privilege over the father's and culture's law of gender. The text Clarissa leaves, once her body has been interred, points to the navel of this 'second birth/burial', which, if we take her coffin inscription seriously, marks a closure to the liminal period that began when she left her father's house. In its duplicitous function as absence and re-presence her death marks the closure of an ambivalent, uncanny period between two fixed positions in society, between life and death, a period of liminality in which the 'death of rape', and the 'writing of death' in all its complexity could take place.

If in the deanimation of feminine models into perfect portraits, the artist's bond proves to be quintessential, in these representations conjoining suicide with autobiography the question of signature is also stake. What if there is a mediating signature, but it is that of the replaced model? What if the space between model and representation is abolished, but by the subject herself, and over her dead body?

Perfection implies that the sign can not retain its 'innocence' precisely because it does not give up its referential value. In fact these suicidal autobiographies stage a self-reflexivity that entails the perfect fulfilment of the referential function, with its contingent obliteration of the object of that function and the space between representation and its model. However, because this form of auto-biography also involves the author's suicide, the perfect fulfilment of the referential function subverts into an obliteration of the referential value of the sign, turning these representations of death, whose signified remains ungraspable, into supreme instances of Jakobson's 'poetic' function of language as well. The excess of the superlative, i.e. the most poetic of these representations, abides in the conjunction of these two contradictory semiotic values in one image.

Harry Berger distinguishes between messages transmitted through the channel of the body as an extension of it (detextualisation) and those messages abstracted from the body and reconstructed in a graphic mode (textualisation); the former an aspect of iconicity, the latter of symbolic textuality, arbitrary though conventionally bound. Textualisation is a form of signification that emphasises the difference between model and representation. Detextualisation is a way to preserve authority by defending against a plurality of interpretations called forth by the fundamental semantic instability of verbal and visual signs.[15] The effect of this detextualising procedure is that, by virtue of its referential primacy, it imposes a limit on interpretation, on unbound meaning. It conceals the arbitrariness of signs and controls semiotic richness as well as the slippage between signifier and signified. The turn to the sheer materiality of the body as a strategy for legitimating an argument is a form of detextualising whose erasure of the signature of art is motivated by an anxiety of a plurality of interpetations. When detextualisation involves bodily death, however, the turn to the tropic or textualisation is again inevitable. The corpse is the example *par excellence* for a transmission of meaning through a medium that is an extension of the body, at first sight most univocal in its message. Yet because it poses a hermeneutic task, forcing the survivors to read this death, the corpse is immediately reinscribed in textuality, replaced by messages abstracted from the body, by narratives and gravestones. These representations leave the dead woman uncannily hovering between the order of the body, the sheer materiality of the corpse, and the order of the text, between the Otherness that death implies (Lacan's real, disrupting the stability of the symbolic order) and the construction of self implied by autobiography, as this reconfirms the narcissistically informed imaginary register of the dead woman and finds a recipient in the imagination of her survivors.

The episode 'Lancelot and Elaine' in Tennyson's *Idylls of the King* narrates the lily maid Elaine's fatal love for Sir Lancelot. He wears her token, a red sleeve embroidered with pearls, as he jousts incognito at a tournament whose prize is the last of nine diamonds, all others previously won by him as well. Once his identity is revealed, the rumour of their mutual love spreads through Arthur's court. Yet Lancelot has pledged his love irrevocably to Queen Guinevere. As Elaine heals his bodily wounds from the joust, he in turn, inflicts a deadly wound to her narcissism by not responding to or reciprocating her love. Though Elaine's loss is the exact reverse of bodily rape, she, like Clarissa, exchanges the lover she can not have for an embrace of death: 'and "Him or death," she muttered' (381).

Her 'imagined' lover's refusal to respond to her love cuts her narcissistic self-assurance, which a union with him would have assured. In this narrative the body, as source of her pain, is again to be cancelled and again the manner of dying emphasises the body. To Elaine death expresses a longing for the other, whom she continues to hear in his absence, whose picture still 'form'd / And grew between her and the pictured wall' (383), at the same time that it expresses a longing for her own alterity. In 'The Song of Love and Death', which she writes after Lancelot's departure, death emerges as the sweet Other to the bitterness of love, the experience of loss her earthly existence is marked with and, while Lancelot, the object of her love, rebukes her offer 'I care . . . but . . . to follow you thro' the world' (382), death takes up the suit: 'I needs must follow death, who calls for me' (383). The mode of death she chooses will allow her to merge both calls, will let her follow Lancelot and follow death. As a bride of death she immortalises herself as the bride of Lancelot as well, constructs in death a union with the lost beloved impossible in life, as much a part of the imaginary as the image she retains of him. Turning herself into the perfect image of her desire to be the object of Lancelot's desire, she fills the gap left by his absence, even as she immortalises this *as* desire, never to be fulfilled. She accentuates the loss and impossibility of wholeness her suicidal autobiograpahy is meant to efface.

On her deathbed she asks her brother to write a letter 'for Lancelot and the Queen and all the world', yet adds 'but I myself must bear it' (384). The last of her 'strange fancies' is that the letter be placed in her hand just before she dies, so that her hand can be closed upon the written text, guarding it 'even in death'. Then her bed, 'on which I died', as site of her embrace with death, and by implication site for the absence of her embrace with her lover, is to be decked richly like the Queen's and placed on a barge clothed in black, so that she can go to court 'in state' to meet her rival. Since she is convinced that in this state 'surely I shall speak for mine own self, and none of you can speak for me as well', she wishes only a dumb old man to steer, row and guide her to the palace. She floats down the river as she had expressed in her last will, lying on her black decked 'bridal/burial' bed, in one hand a lily, in the other her letter, 'all her bright hair streaming down – and all the cover lid was cloth of gold drawn to her waist, and she herself in white', a dead body/dead letter and its mute pilot.[16]

In her letter she expresses in the order of the text what her corpse already signifies in the order of the body – that she comes to take a last farewell from him who would not take farewell of her, that her love for Lancelot had no return; was self-reflexive, like a message refused by its addressee and turned back to the sender. This closed circuit of her love, denied the deferral on to an other, turns the imaginary energy of narcissistic self-protection into an expression of a self-annihilating death drive: 'And therefore my true love has been my death.' The effect of this double form of signification, by letter and by body, is to impress her name, her image and her story on to the memory of her survivors She finishes her letter by asking her survivors to 'pray for my soul, and yield me burial' (387).

Because she cannot speak to Lancelot, because he would not return her call, she reverses the non-reciprocity of their relation through her autobiographical suicide, a form of self-textualisation that forces Lancelot into her prior position – facing a respondee, present as image but absent as a living person. Suicide helps Elaine articulate the limitlessness of her love for Lancelot and stage herself as a spectacular and beautiful object of sight. By transforming suicide into an act of self-textualisation, Elaine at last controls her own life and insists on the public recognition of her love denied to her during her lifetime. The paradox inherent in suicide is that it can either disintegrate identity or reaffirm a woman's autonomy after defilement or abandonment. Higonnet suggests that the choice of death is one of the nineteenth century's privileged tropes for a denial of woman's ability to choose freely during her life and for the constraints and incisions imposed on her due to the cultural construction of femininity over her body. Since the feminine body is the cause for constraints, the only freedom of choice open to her is to eradicate the body.[17]

Like that of the fetish, the rhetoric of suicide is an ambivalent simultaneity of acknowledgement and denial of lack, a corrective remaking of the self, a narcissistically informed design of self-construction, which gives a particular life the shape of a whole at the same time that it is a radical unmaking and disintegration of the self. Suicide emerges as the radical confirmation and extension of the narcissistic wound, of the split or lack informing life, in response to which each of the heroines I am concerned with turns to voluntary death, as a form of assuagement, in the first place. Suicide is a revitalising self-assertion in death against the lethal self-alienation in life. In Tennyson's narrative, Elaine, once she has given the detailed directions for her death ritual, 'grew so cheerful that they deemed her death was rather in the fantasy than the blood'.

The fact that this narrative presents a woman, whose body is not only transformed into an aesthetic object and destroyed in favour of it, but who is also the author of this translation, is crucial. The question of authenticity and intention inherent to this transformation of the quintessentially nonsemiotic categories of 'death' and 'body' into signs that are highly tropic takes on a different dimension from earlier examples not involving voluntary death. Though bodies in culture are always inscribed by exterior signifiers, it matters whether these external inscriptions are chosen and accepted or simply imposed; whether the woman does the translation into semiotic category or has it done to her. Authenticity and autonomy enter at precisely the moment she 'realises herself' by taking on the position of agent of the action that turns the body into a sign, choosing the interpretation intended, rather than being 'derealised' because placed as a sign by someone else, having an alien or foreign meaning merely imposed on her.

Though in the case of these suicidal autobiographies the woman literally undoes herself into a sign, radically fades before the symbolic, it is her language, in so far as it is chosen. Though the choice is from a foreign code, she exerts the freedom to decide which cultural conventions are most adequate to her self-expression. In the 'arrêt de mort' staged by Elaine, she becomes an image yet also produces this image as a way to transcend death; arrested by death as an extreme form of her loss of self and arresting death as a supreme form of her regained autonomy. Though this does not make the dead body less semiotised, the implication is that the interpretation it will elicit corresponds more closely to the meaning intended.

Significantly in Elaine's death scene, by having the letter slipped into her hand just before death sets in, all aspects of a real, non-semiotised death are eclipsed and the rupture this event of dissolution usually causes is recuperated literally *avant la lettre*. With her letter she not only chooses the signifiers that make up her self-construction as sign, that will present her story of a loss as the regaining of wholeness. She also stages Derrida's definition of textuality: 'what opens meaning and language is writing as the disappearance of natural presence.'[18]

This turning of her body into a sign is legitimised only by virtue of the fact that it is also the embodiment of a sign and its superlative effect is one of disrupture, produced because the non-semiotic category of real death comes into play. Elaine supplements her text with her body to assure the meaning she intends. Conveying her message both through a channel that is the extension of body (her corpse) and one that is abstracted from it (her letter), she seems to signify also through detextualisation, to authenticate the truth of the statement she wants to make about her love for Lancelot; to stabilise semantic plurality and call for a univocal interpretation. For she claims that this double mode of signifying, this cross between iconicity and textuality, is the only way for her to speak 'for mine own self'.

At first sight the beauty of Elaine as floating corpse and floating signifier ascribes to what de Man has called the specifically romantic delusion that believes in a harmonious expression of the transparency and unity between the body or outward appearance (signifier) and inner idea or soul (signified meaning), in the opaque medium of language.[19] Though Elaine, by staging her death in such a way that her body becomes the medium for her message, exemplifies the birth of meaning as the absence of natural presence, the presence of this, now wholly semioticised, body changes the conventional function of the sign. Normally the sign takes the place of an absent object (be the relation one of arbitrariness or contingency), while here the absent body not only takes the place of the sign but becomes its realisation at the same time that it is supplemented by/supplementing a pure text, the letter. Elaine's inner idea seems to coincide perfectly with her appearance, because her body as a 'dead letter' suggests a perfect congruence between signifier or material form of expression and signified, or content of the expression. Her body-sign functions as the tautology that in the absence of a natural body stages the natural presence of an idea, an unbroken identity between substance and message. The transparent relation between signifier and signified she stages invokes a form of 'good writing' without any deferral or shift in meaning, without the difference inherent in language. She stages a literal realisation of the sign, a re-materialisation of the symbolic, made possible through her death and the beauty of its performance. Death is conceived as a moment where the normally distinct realms of soma and sema are allowed to collapse.

But Elaine, attempting to get out of the contradictory relationship of textual representation and body, as well as the semantic plurality inherent in any interpretation, only reconfirms this double contradiction through her fatal staging. Because she uses this materialisation of the symbolic through death as the most appropriate medium to express an intended meaning and so as to reach the superlative degree of intended effect on her audience, she remains inscribed within the economy of representation. Any signification is always such that the body functions as a signifier whose signified and whose referent is inevitably gliding and whose materialization is never complete. The body, especially the dead body, belongs to the real outside representation, and can only be re-presented and figured, but never presented in its material presence.

Because the signified that Elaine means to express with her suicidal autobiography is death, she in fact articulates exactly that facticity and split of human existence which a turn to the beautiful, as moment of harmonious balance, and a turn to suicide, as moment of rendering her life as whole, was meant to sublimate. Her survivors seek to recuperate Elaine's corpse into the stability of symbolic representation, to retextualise her 'meaning'. Because her form of signifying through the medium of her body is not only exchanged with a form of articulation that is abstracted from this body, the repetition of her 'story' on a gravestone, but this exchange is also repeated on the more global level of the text, in the 'refictionalisation' of her message undertaken by the narrator, this woman's aesthetically staged death serves as a *mise en abyme* of the grave and of the narrative in which she is embedded.

Significantly Elaine's barge floats past the Queen's window at exactly the same moment that Guinevere, in anger at Lancelot, flings down the diamonds he has presented to her as proof of his faithful love. For the sheer materiality of her corpse, exchanged for the sinking diamonds, not only works to persuade her survivors of the truthfulness of her love for Lancelot but also serves to confirm his fidelity to the Queen. It literalises his claim that he will stay faithful to the Queen, even as Elaine's performance of love unto death lets Lancelot realise, by virtue of contrast, that the Queen's jealousy is in fact 'dead love's harsh heir' (388). Elaine's self-textualisation is successful both as a legitimation of Lancelot's love (the Queen asks his forgiveness) and as a disruption of stability (Elaine accuses the members of the court of insincerity in love).

Its effect is drawn from the structural conjoining of signifier, signified and referent into an excess of the tropic subverting into the non-semiotic real, and the thematic conjoining of a narcissistically informed self-construction that also unremittingly celebrates the break of its subject's narcissism. This is an uncanny moment, neither just text nor just non-semiotic body, neither total self-annihilation (because narcissistic construction of the self into an image) nor complete self-protection (because dead); a destruction of the self before death and a resurrection of the self out of death. The court's response is to undo the uncanniness of this intermediary arrestation of death by replacing Elaine's iconic recoding with complete retextualisation; by severing once again the three parts of the sign. In the manner of a second burial, putting closure on the liminality Elaine entered as she floated from her father's house to her lost lover's dwelling place (and recalling Clarissa's liminality between her father's house and her ancestor's vault), she is laid 'low in the dust of half-forgotten kings'. The message of her body-text is translated to a gravestone that replaces her body, now vanished from sight, with her image, including the 'lily in her hand'. This textualised gravestone articulates the desired but impossible union with Lancelot that she staged detextually, by having 'the shield of Lancelot at her feet be carven'. The text of her letter is in turn repeated, as the 'story of her dolorous voyage' is 'blazon'd on her tomb in letters gold and azure' (387).

Though the re-establishment of order out of tension and turmoil accedes in the end, Elaine's suicidal autobiography contains one last disturbing effect. For one could ask, is the central notion expressed by her body-text not less her romantic love for Lancelot and the wound he inflicts on her narcissism and rather the more global statement 'I am dead'? To describe the problem of a self, articulating radical Otherness, not-self/death, Roland Barthes elaborates on the notion of a scandalous return to the literal. He discusses the encroachment of death on life that occurs on the level of language when the metaphorical is turned into the literal in the moment that a subject expresses its own death. For any utterance that articulates the notion 'I am dead' is a radically impossible metaphor, an enunciation literally foreclosed and therefore it turns the utterance self-reflexively on to itself, says nothing but itself, designates itself tautologically.

The scandal refers not only to the thematic dimension of a narrative, to the

dead body or death as primordially repressed social taboo. Rather the scandal
'irrupts directly into language' by posing a representational impossibility. By
virtue of the attribute dead, the story or utterance which the speaking self tells
comes to occupy an 'empty point', a 'blind spot' of language, and, along with the
scandal of the dead body what is at stake is a 'scandal of language'.[20] The self that
is articulated in these suicidal autobiographies is itself not clearly in its place,
analogous to Blanchot's definition of the corpse, disrupting stable categories of
place, identity and reference. The self whose simultaneous disintegration and
wholeness is at stake refers as much to the dead person/author as to the
language/medium and strategy of the authorship, the text. The *mise en abyme*
produced by this beautiful woman's death is not just located on the thematic or
semantic level of the narrative (indicating a body-text, replaced by a gravestone
text embedded within a narrative about both). Rather this figure/topic is *most*
poetic because the self-reflexivity is located on the level of language as well,
simultaneously designating that death is only transmissible as a metaphoric
process, receding from a repetition of signifiers and represented as an image of
an image while at the same time designating that language cannot speak death at
all.

My discussion of Flaubert's *Madame Bovary* will again focus on the relation
between imagination, its materialization in writing, and death, for here a woman's
authorship is shown as the act of voluntary fading before the text she writes, and
serves self-reflexively to comment on the function and status of novel reading and
writing in general. As Emma writes herself out of existence to become the
romantic heroines she has been so possessed by in her reading, she does so
almost exclusively in the order of the body, supplemented by very few pieces of
writing in the order of the text.[21] Her self-textualisation engenders a form of
self-obliteration while at the same time suicide generates texts and constructs the
dead self as author.

Emma Bovary's suicidal autobiography is the most complex of my three
examples because Flaubert presents his heroine's life as that of a lengthy process
of dying, which begins with her entrance into the imaginary world of romantic
and religious fiction.[22] Reading is shown to be the source of a figural suicide,
because it places the reader into the liminality between living reality and the dead
figures of the imaginary; because it consumes the life of the reader, who reads
instead of living, and whose living is killed by these books.[23] Reading is also a
form of suicide in the sense that it offers images of plenitude and unbroken
identification, a repetition of the jubilation the child experiences in relation to the
phallic mother, but which life disillusions. Reading initiates a process of desire
that points to a lack in the reality of social existence, to the split from wholeness
inherent to this existence, and to the presence of death's ubiquitous 'castrative'
threat to life. The conjunction of death with the image resides in the fact not only
that death is the radical opposite of the stability and wholeness an image evokes
but that the image itself produces an ambiguous division in its spectator and is

itself also the location of death. The texts Emma uses to construct herself and her world mark the double presence of death. They serve as the 'inanimate' words and images outside of which reality remains inconceivable, the inanimate shield on the basis of which reality is constructed. Yet they are also clichés, commonplace conventions, a 'corpse of a metaphor', killed through overuse.[24]

For all three heroines death expresses the longing for alterity and perfection as a response to loss, to a narcissistic wound, to a disruption of the illusion of wholeness. While in Clarissa's case rape meant an incursion into the body's integrity as well as her self-construction of immaculate virtue, Elaine's loss was that of her privileged object of romantic desire, through which she would have gained completion. In Emma's case, marriage as an experience of wounded narcissism and the ensuing desire for romantic fulfilment in adultery only supplements the much earlier loss of the imaginary sense of wholeness produced through fiction. For all three, a longing for death comes to assuage the gap between their ideal self-image and the existence in social reality, a courtship with death serving as substitution for an inadequate lover or death as the first realisation of love. They court death, turning necessity into choice, and turning the narcissistic castration of romantic desire experienced in life into a self-completion through death. Death emerges as that entity only imperfectly veiled by beauty and love, as that which was in fact always the aim and object displaced in the search for the beauty and love transmitted by the imagination.

Emma, who slips and changes, and has difficulty locating herself in one name and one role, can be diagnosed as a hysteric, owing to her histrionic simulation and her *belle indifférence* for each one of her roles. Her narrative exemplifies what was only implied in the other two – the proximity between writing with the body and hysteria. In Emma's story the issue is once more the notion that a fatal perfection occurs when a copy resembles the model to such an extent that the space between the two has been obliterated. Flaubert, however, gives his narrative two crucial alterations, so as to set himself up as an iconoclastic commentator on the convention I have been tracing. Firstly, in his narrative the model is the corpus of novels Emma reads while the copy is her body-corpse. Not only does Emma partake of a confusion between the figural and the literal, not only is her hysteria such that she can't distinguish between the reality of the body and a fictionality of the sign. She subverts the conventional relation between the two, making the body a supplement to the sign. The notion that an imaginary wholeness is always constructed in response to a cut induced by the presence of language and of death is repeated in her autobiographical suicide. For in this act the imaginary wholeness constructed with her body against the double wound of language and death collapses with these two when she conjoins death and textuality at her deanimated body. Secondly, though his heroine's detextualisation seeks to fulfil a self-disintegration as re-integration of the self into narratives she has read, Flaubert depicts the failure of this process, as death emerges not only as the fulfilment but also as the destruction of the beauty and integrity of the image.

From the very beginning Emma's imagination connects unfulfilled romantic desires with death. She is dissatisfied early on in her marriage, because it does not fulfil expectations and desires raised by literature, does not seem to materialise 'the words of *felicity*, of *passion* and *drunkenness*, which had appeared to be so beautiful in the books she read' (61). The token of this marriage lets thoughts about death arise. As she sees the marriage bouquet of Charles's first, now dead, wife, she thinks of her own bouquet 'and asked herself, dreaming, what they would do with it, if by chance she were to die' (58).[25]

At stake is less an identification with the dead first wife than a fascination for the dead heroines in the novels she read while she was being educated at a convent, and this fascination for beautiful images of death serves as a way to eclipse the reality of death, to cap its unremitting wound. This is shown in her response to her mother's death, which is one of aesthetisation, the first instance of her self-authorship against death and under its auspices. She has a sombre painting made of the hair of the deceased, writes a letter to her father in which she designs her own death in the same tomb as her mother's. She finds narcissistic satisfaction in imagining for herself 'that rare ideal of pale creatures . . . she let herself glide along Lamartinien meanders . . . pure virgins who ascended to heaven' (67). Her hysteria is characterised by volatility ('ungraspable illness, which changed its manner like clouds' (69)) and lets her endlessly seek new roles to express her dissatisfaction with life. Yet the death of the mother serves as a quintessential cornerstone in a dialectic of death and imagination which Emma will endlessly repeat. It provokes satisfying images that triumph over her absence, yet the paradigm Emma chooses for her texts is one connected with absence.

In Emma's imaginary register there is a rivalry between nature (or domestic love) and art. On the one hand she places the 'bad' natural dyad of marriage with her husband Charles, which leads to states of death-like boredom and melancholy and functions as the Other whose existence can cancel her own, while on the other she places the 'good' artifical dyad with the objects of her fantasy, interchangeably money and material objects of luxury, lovers as romances she lives, romances she reads and images of the self. All of these are metonymies for the Otherness she lacks and as such aspects of the Other that reassure and reinforce her identity. She constructs the image of the other man long before any concrete lover enters her life and preserves it beyond each lover's exit. Only when she can no longer hold on to these good images of the other (whether of romance or of luxury), when she can not sustain her hysterical *belle indifférence*, does real death, kept at bay though always also the source of the imaginary images, break into her existence.

Yet her ambivalent gesture of desiring fiction as a simultaneous disavowal and acknowledegment of death surfaces in the semantic encoding of her self-image. In the first of several mirror scenes it becomes clear that reading, writing and death merge as the three faces which an escape from her limitations can assume: 'She bought herself a blotter, stationery, a penholder and envelopes, although she had no one to write to; she looked at herself in the mirror, taking a book, then, dreaming between the lines, she let the book fall to her knees. She wanted to voyage or to return to the convent. In one and the same moment she wanted to die and to live in Paris' (93). The purchase of writing implements is meant to satisfy the lack her desire expresses, yet to do so in a self-reflexive way, since she has no addressee. The message remains within a closed circuit. Equally self-reflexive is her reading activity, since it returns her to herself – she watches her self in the mirror, she reads herself 'between the lines,' foreclosing the book's alterity. Finally two of the sites she desires are connected with mortality, the liminality of the convent, the site of her first seduction by literature and death itself. In the same manner, imagining catastrophes and dangers that would let her first imagined lover suspect her desire for him while at the same time celebrating her position of loss, Emma tells herself with pride and joy, ' "I am vituous," and she looked at herself in the mirror, assuming poses of resignation' (152). Staging her wound becomes part of the self-construction.

The crucial mirror scene occurs after her first embrace with Rudolfe: 'noticing herself in the mirror, she was astounded to see her face . . . She would enter into a marvellous state where all would be passion, ecstasy, delirium . . . she remembered the heroines in novels . . . these adulterous women . . . she would herself become like a veritable part of these imaginations and realise the long dream of her youth, by conceiving herself as that type of lover which she had so strongly desires . . . now she triumphed' (219). For the first time she can successfully merge her bodily sensations with the desires aroused by her imagination as she finds in her illicit love the passion so long expected. Her triumph consists in two gestures. She experiences with her body the passion she has up to that point known only imaginatively, as she realises her youthful imaginations at her body. She embodies the texts she has read, becomes a sister to the adulterous heroines, by textualising her body into 'a veritable part of these imaginations'. She finds a sense of wholeness in Rudolphe because he fills her romantic lack, but also because he allows her to construct herself as part of the texts she has read, filling a lack in her desire to write herself into these texts.

The important omission in this mirror-reverie is that the fate of her sister adulteresses is usually death, and it is this occulted event that she will need to write with her body to perfect her triumph and be like them completely. Death is implicitly present in this self-reflection on two scores. Emma identifies herself with fictional heroines whose adulterous love, in the cultural conventions they support, is inextricably connected with suicide or execution. At the same time she identifies herself with inanimate figures or dead letters in texts, metaphorically killing herself into an inanimate art work. Again the duplicity of the mirror as device supports Emma's ambivalent position between integration and disintegration. For even as the mirror allows Emma to triumph over the experience of lack by eternalising and unifying her image as one with other, textual images, this is a form of seeing oneself that confirms the split between self and unified image of self, that shows wholeness as being a misrecognition.

Two forms of death are invoked in the imaginary gaze into the mirror – a good dying, which supports Emma's narcissistic illusion of entering into a self-stability by virtue of writing herself into a text, and a bad dying, where the non-semiotic real of death disrupts the self-affirming images of a beautiful death. That the good death is inextricably connected with writing shows itself by virtue of the fact that Emma begins to write the letters she had up to that point only intended. Rudolphe embodies her privileged addressee, even though on some level the closed circuit of her epistolary activity is kept upright, since his status is that of imaginary other.

Emma's psychic changes are registered in her somatic changes, so that she not only collides her body with deanimated textual feminine bodies but writes with her body so it can be read as a text of her emotions. Three times a psychic wound to her imaginary wholeness occurs after the loss of a lover, and each episode induces in her the wish to write this woundedness in the order of her body. After the first loss of Léon she poses as an old maid with facial folds that signify 'disappointed ambitions', she grows 'completely pale, white like linen'; she stares 'in a vague manner', speaks of 'her old age', and has a spasm of spitting blood (174). She materialises with her body the last of the four sites of escape she had imagined before her mirror – the escape 'or die'.

Far more elaborate is her body's staging of the wound to her imaginary wholeness after the loss of Rudolphe. In this second instance an important dimension is added to her displaced courtship of death, namely the question of reciprocity between Emma and her lover. For both Rudolphe and Emma the other as object of desire has been killed before a consummation of their passion ever occurs. In Emma's case Rudolphe is one of a series of metonymies in the chain of desired objects meant to fill the lack she experiences, along with the waltzing vicomte at whose ball her vainglory had found its first realisation, as well as with Léon. In the same manner that she loses her particularity before the other adulteresses of fiction, merging with them, Rudolphe is also deanimated into a cipher for that Otherness which will complete her. In Rudolphe's case, his fascination for Emma was from the start coupled with a disposal of her, 'but how to get rid of her after the affair' (180). Flaubert highlights the reciprocity in their gestures, so as to emphasize that because these objects of love were always also imaginary, their relationship was always grounded on deanimation.

When Rudolphe decides to abandon Emma after she has proposed a mutual flight, she becomes for him a sign of death, a phantom, fading into the shadows and then a dead letter, no longer of any real practical consequence; the story of a beautiful romance, 'she had been a pretty mistress . . . and soon Emma's beauty reappeared in his mind' (264). While he can not endure her constant presence, a designation of her absence, 'she had been' allows him to re-invoke her in her beauty, as one re-invokes a dead person. This gesture implies both that she is now a dead person for him, an object of memory, and that her fascination in part resided in her imaginary, non-real quality – he recalls her beauty as that of an absent body.

The conjunction of imagination and deanimation which Emma stages with her image before the mirror is analogous to Rudolphe's form of disposing of her. He merges first her body with her image and then Emma as an image with the images of other past lovers until in this process of integration all distinctions are effaced: 'he had close by . . . the miniature given by Emma and in an effort to study this image and evoke a memory of the model, Emma's traits became confused in his memory, as though the living face and the painted face rubbed one against the other; and fusing, reciprocally effaced each other' (267). Rummaging in the box containing her other letters he finds strands of the hair of other lovers, their letters – dead body parts that converge into the monster of his romantic memory: 'In fact, these women, all rushing into his thoughts at the same time, disturbed each other, reduced each other in size, as though the same level of love made them all equal.' To demonstrate the levelling of individual identity, and the killing into sameness his memory undertakes, he merges all the letters into one pile, before he writes Emma his farewell. This series of lovers correlates with Emma's serialisation of adultresses and of her own lovers, though here again the question of who is the agent of semantic encoding is crucial. While Emma fades out of existence in Rudolphe's series of letters, she intends to fade into existence when she perfectly enters her series of adultresses and dead heroines through her literal death. Though it is the repetition of earlier texts, her deanimation is the way she intends to leave a distinctive mark.

Yet before she chooses death directly, Emma reciprocates Rudolphe's killing in a lengthy detextualising procedure that emphasises precisely the sheer materiality of the body and its presence, even as its message is the threat of bodily disintegration. Flaubert disrupts the possibility of a conventional beautiful suicide by defenestration to let his heroine descend not to death but rather to the domestic banality of soup already served. Emma, responding to Rudolphe's wounding rejection in the form of a brain fever, becomes the dead letter to which he has reduced her, by living a despondency in which no tension exists, 'as though her body and her soul had come together, taking leave of all their agitations' (277). This staging of death as stasis is followed by another version of death, the deathbed ecstasy. As she awaits her last sacrament she experiences a self-annihilation before the love of God, the 'splendid vision' of seraphic harps, azure sky, God the father on a golden throne amidst saints holding green palms and angels with flaming wings descending to fetch her. This vision is a copy of the texts she has read in the convent as well as an alteration of her privileged image of adulteress, exchanging the social transgression of illicit love for the etherealisation of the earthly body as it transcends into an ecstatic enjoyment of divinity.

In the final part of the novel, Emma's writing activity continues to be directed at the three paradigms of desired objects – romance, luxury and self-textualisation – while the connection to death is made ever more explicit. Having refound in her adulterous relation with Léon all the 'platitudes of marirage', Emma nevertheless holds on to the idea that a woman must always write to her lover. Yet her writing becomes a way of dematerialising her lover, turning the addressee and object of her desire once again into a dead letter, a figure of her imagination: 'as she wrote, she perceived another man, a phantom made up of her most ardent memories, of her most beautiful reading experiences . . . and in the end he seemed to become true and accessible' (376). Existing as long as she is able to imagine him, this phantom lover becomes the proof of the textual superseding bodily existence. Once again the self-reflexivity, as obliteration of the referential validity and emphasis on sheer textuality is shown in conjunction with death. To avoid the gap reopening once again, Emma resorts to a form of writing that obliterates her addressee, returns to the semiotic situation of a closed circuit. While her last romance ends in a superfluity of texts without a recipient or a reference point in reality, her desire for luxury commodities results in another form of textual production, a surplus of bills of debt, carrying her signature. Here too, the response, in this case by her creditors, is to read materiality as dematerialised signs. As they examine her possessions, her clothes, her linens, 'her existence, down to the innermost intimate recesss was like a corpse at an autopsy, spread out before the gaze of these three men' (383).

With her object of romantic desire and addressee of her epistolary activity a phantom, her possessions the dead body parts of a corpse-existence, Emma can have recourse only to her body as the last tie at which to preserve the wholeness she has longed to construct. Yet this means writing herself out of existence, turning herself into a phantom as well. Though Flaubert leaves the exact reason for Emma's suicide unspecified, one could speculate that Rudolphe's refusal to lend her money is the final shattering of her narcissistically informed self-fashioning, leaving not a wound but a real and irrevocable abyss. All reminiscences, all assuring images diminish, leaving her with the feeling that her existence is disappearing from her. As she displaces the nominal reason for her distress, money, on to the more ambivalent term, 'she suffered only from love' (403), Rudolphe's refusal forces her to face the lack she has tried to cover with the various versions of her imaginary fictions. Her debt is the last of many signs for the failure of her ambitions, and Rudolphe's refusal to support the fiction of their romance enables death to emerge as that which she has ambivalently tried to conceal and to court with her multifarious shades of self-fashioning by dint of romance or luxury. Death was the signifier displaced by her series of fictions, yet once these images of desire fail, she is forced to recognise that the effacement or patching of an originary gap was always based on the illusion of misrecognition, so that the signifier or image of death translates into a real state.

Admittedly ambivalence remains till the end, since Emma preserves an image of death even as she enters death as the shattering of her imaginary register. Death is both the fulfilment of her desire to transform her life, modelled on literary principles into a text; a last effort to live romance by dying a romantic death. It is the radical disruption of the imaginary, effecting the recognition that all romances are illusory. Her final death scene is significantly doubled, recalling medieval tombstone sculpture, where the intact body of the deceased, the *gisant*, is doubled with a figuration of the decayed body, the *transi*.[26] The first death performs the beautiful, good death induced by romantic fiction. It comes as a painless death that allows her to write one last letter for posthumous reading (the complete fulfilment of writing as death staged earlier before her mirror) and glide out of life. She thinks, 'Oh, it is very little, death..I will fall asleep, and all will be finished!' (406).

Along the lines of Benjamin's definition of the death of the maternal force giving birth to the author as the first progeny of his (or her) text, the death of Emma's mother initiated a trajectory that culminates in a suicidal autobiography. This body-text is informed by a wish to completely possess oneself by becoming author of one's existence as dead body/letter, which will generate com-memorative texts and render the body analogous to heroines in texts. Emma intends her self to emerge after death as a work of art, an image of the romantic notion of a *belle morte*, and presenting a hermeneutic task to her survivors, so that her corpse poses as part of and repetition of the romantic corpus.

Yet the second ugly phase of her death subverts this first beautiful image. Equally functioning as representation (because always implying the spectatorship of her husband and friends), what it signifies is the realistic detail of the dying process. It is a horrible spectacle of pain, agony and physical decomposition. Though both phases are representations, their contradictory conjunction implies that the real of death recedes from both depictions. Ironically Emma's death, as the moment that radically shatters all images and puts the assurance which images lend to the narcissistically informed process of self-fashioning into question, engenders only another phase of images on the part of her survivors, who use her dying and her dead body as image of re-stabilisation. Homais brings his two sons to her deathbed so that her dying can serve as 'a lesson, an example, a solemn picture which will remain in their mind' (415).

In her dying moments Emma returns to aspects of the death imaginarily staged before. She experiences again the visions of external beatitude, the voluptu-ousness of her first mystic thrust. With an expression of serenity she seems to awake as from a dream and desires, as last object of her gaze, a mirror, 'and she remained leaning over it for some time, until the moment when large tears rolled from her eyes' (417). Though Flaubert denies his readers a semantic encoding of this last pose, Emma dies confirming the control over her self, in the detour of her reflected image.

After her death she becomes an object of sight for her survivors, and though this hovers between the romantic image of the beautiful corpse, serene and intact, as if in slumber, and the realistic image of the ugly corpse, with black liquid coming out of its nose and putrefaction beneath its veil, the crucial point is that Emma's suicide spurs on her husband's imagination, so that, over her dead body, she passes on to him the dialectic of imagination as response to and resulting in death. He adopts her predilections, her ideas, preserves her room, designs an elaborate grave. While the living Emma found no sympathetic response to her fancies in her husband, the dead Emma corrupts his imagination 'from beyond the tomb'. Once again the insecurity of the image is stressed, for the more

Charles seeks to retain Emma's image, the more it escapes his memory, and the beauty of the absent woman he preserves by dint of commemorative objects is counteracted by his nightmare vision, where as he approaches Emma 'she decomposes in his arms' (441).

Charles repeats her desire to transform herself into a text, though in his case it is the text his wife has written with her body, until he too dies, holding a braid of her black hair in his hand. The equation between Emma's suicide and her writing falls into two parts. It is a moment of supreme authorship because it offers her her first authentic reader in Charles, who empathises with and imitates her text to perfection, while her love letters never produced a real response. Her corpse is the result of a series of previously read texts, subverting the opposition between model and copy, authenticity and secondary appropriation. The corpse is shown both as a unified body, assuring the stability of the author's self-conception, and as an image of decay, and both representations have the function of reassuring her surviving spectators in their process of self-construction. As an uncanny movement, death hovers between stability and castration, thematically and, on the level of language itself, articulating a disruption of the process of imaging, a falling out of an economy of representation, even as it returns to confirm it.

The paradox that repeatedly emerges in all these representations of feminine death is the visibility and presence of the dead body. Though representation is used to repress or deny both femininity and death, it does so by virtue of fetishism – by acknowledging precisely those values to be negated – so that the veiling of death comes also to be its articulation. If one considers Freud's definition of the symptom as failed repression, the ubiquity of images of death in the nineteenth century as cultural symptom indicates that death was neither successfully repressed nor worked through.

Woman, constructed by culture as man's symptom, marks the site where repressed material resurfaces, materialises, returns. The feminine body is used to figure death as the repressed *par excellence* and the displacement of death on to the feminine allows a mitigated articulation of that value otherwise threatening to the stability of the system. Because it is bound to a signifier encoded as radically Other, non-masculine, the material inadequately repressed finds a conscious articulation, but in a way that allows it to be exteriorised, and in the form of a representation as symptom, the subject/community compulsively repeats what it tries to repress in the displacement on to another. This strategy is a way of removing any immediate threat but does so by constructing a permanent memorial to precisely the threat it wishes to occlude. Like a symptom, these representations deny death in the sense of suspending it – an arrestation of/by death. By finding a signifier for that which threatens, they can provisionally discharge it, yet the partiality of a repression that articulates denial and acknowledgement suggests that any representational symptom effecting the closure of a disruption, as it is posed by death, is less stable than meets the eye.

Notes to Chapter 8

1 M. Ryan, 1976, p. 204f.
2 I follow W. Ong, 1977, who adds to the judicial reading of 2 Corinthians 3.6, 'The letter kills but the spirit gives life', a reading that suggests this biblical passage can also refer to the 'presence of death in the text,' in that the mortifying letter is opposed to the spirit, which gives life. The ' "spirit," *pneuma*, is of course breath which gives being to sounded words, spoken words, the only real words there were or are or ever will be', p. 237.
3 F. Barker, 1984, pp. 106f.
4 See also M. Foucault, 'What is an Author?', 1977, pp. 113–38, who argues that the writing subject endlessly disappears. The heroines writing their autobiographical texts over their own dead bodies are, however, both absent and excessively present as a result of this representational effort.
5 J. Derrida, 1976, p. 25.
6 J. Derrida, 1976, p. 69.
7 M. Blanchot, 1981, p. 58.
8 See M. Bal's, 1991, discussion of the semiotics of rape.
9 Clarissa writes 'Death only can be dreadful to the Bad: / To Innocence 'tis like a bugbear dress'd / To frighten children' (III. 209). The implication is that if her death, far from frightening, is on the contrary a beautiful experience, then she belongs to the innocent.
10 T. Eagleton, 1982, pp. 73ff.
11 G. Bataille, 1957, speaks of eroticism in conjunction with experiences of the sacred, in terms of a transcendence of the discontinuity of individual existence into a continuity that is death. Clarissa privileges the unmitigated transparency of a continuous, non-differentiated being of death, over the ultimately limited experience of such a transparency in eroticism.
12 One could see an analogy here to Frankenstein's desire to replace his nightmare vision of the 'castrated,' decaying maternal body with that of wholeness and purity preserved, despite the absence of the mother, in the form of the miniature.
13 Criticism has emphasised Clarissa's enjoyment in staging her own death. M. Doody, 1974, shows how her meditation upon and desire for death can be seen as part of the Puritan death ritual. Other critics, notably Ian Watt, 1957, sees Clarissa's death as an expression of Puritan new individualism and a spiritual inwardness, coupled with a perverse fear of the flesh, that desires the obliteration of the body, since this is never without originary impurity. As N. K. Miller, 1980, augments, Clarissa's, like Julie's death, is a protection against the disruption of sexuality.
14 According to L. Kauffman, 1986, the coffin signifies both the relation of death to writing and of writing to the feminine body. In a manner similar to my own, T. Castle, 1982 and W. Warner, 1979, argue that death is a form of self-expulsion from signification, with death as a breakdown of language. A rejection of art and of the instability of the signifying code, of textuality and of indeterminate interpretation means an entrance into death. The inscribed coffin, encasing, literally, its dead author is, in Castle's words a 'concretized metaphor for textuality itself', p. 144.
15 See H. Berger, Jr, 1987, pp. 144–66 as well as my discussion of E. Scarry in chapter 3.
16 Tennyson treats a similar theme in his poem 'The Lady of Shalott', where another woman, falling in love with the sight of Sir Lancelot turns from the mirror, through

which she has experienced the world in mediated manner and reproduced in yet another step of mediation in her weaving, to look at him directly. Signifying a break in her narcissistic shield, or self-assurance the 'mirror crack'd from side to side' and the Lady of Shalott moves to the other spectrum of dyadic relations, the absolute cancellation of her existence. Writing 'round about the prow' of a boat her name, she places herself, like Snow White, into this floating coffin, and dies, singing a mournful carol, just as she enters Camelot. See also E. Showalter, 1985a, pp. 77–94, for a discussion of woman and drowning in nineteenth-century representation.

17 M. Higonnet, 1986. See also B. T. Gates, 1988, who shows how suicide is constructed as a feminine form of death in nineteenth-century culture.

18 J. Derrida, 1976, p. 159.

19 P. de Man, 1983.

20 R. Barthes, 1981b, pp. 153f.

21 See also N. Shor, 1985, pp. 3–28, who argues that Emma's ambitions to be a writer focus on her desire to transform the texts she has read into lived experience as well as in her choice of a lover as initiator and receiver of those letters that will make her the author of an epistolary novel. She argues that Emma's suicide is a form of authorship because writing comes to be equated with becoming the inanimate shadow of the text itself, writing as absence of the self even as suicide generates texts. Like Clarissa, Emma's fatal passion is for reading and scribbling letters, forbidden by her mother-in-law as the source of all misfortune.

22 See T. Tanner, 1979, who argues that Emma's story can be read as a long process of disintegration based on the loss of an ability to distinguish image and model, a confusion of the literal and the figural, of reality and literature.

23 M. Robert, 1977.

24 See H. Michie's discussion of cliché as dead metaphor, following the language philosopher Donald Davidson, 1986.

25 Having pricked her finger on one of the wires, she burns this bouquet just before leaving Tostes for Rouen, a gesture in which she destroys the object at which her first conjunction of death and marriage took place, as a triumph over the mortification this marriage has come to mean.

26 See M. Vovelle, 1983.

CASE STUDY

Wife to Mr Rossetti – Elizabeth Siddall (1829–62)

One face looks out from all his canvases,
   One selfsame figure sits or walks or leans:
   We found her hidden just behind those screens,
That mirror gave back all her loveliness.
A queen in opal or in ruby dress,
   A nameless girl in freshest summer-greens,
   A saint, an angel – every canvas means
That same one meaning, neither more nor less.
He feeds upon her face by day and night,
   And she with true kind eyes looks back on him,
Fair as the moon and joyful as the light:
   Not wan with waiting, not with sorrow dim;
Not as she is, but was when hope shone bright;
   Not as she is, but as she fills his dream.
Christina Rossetti

This historical digression about Dante Gabriel Rossetti and Elizabeth Siddall serves as an example of how the cultural representations discussed up to now could literally inform the lives of a painter–poet couple. Siddall, immortalised in the paintings of the Pre-Raphaelites as an embodiment of the Victorian saintly, angelic woman as she fades into death, seems, in Barbara Gates's words, to have become so obsessed with the representations for which she sat as model, 'to have decided to live – and die – a fiction'.[1]

The daughter of Elizabeth Eleanor Evans and Charles Siddall, a cutler, was 'discovered' in 1849, working in a milliner's shop off Leicester Square (as the myth surrounding Elizabeth Siddall has it), by the painter Walter Deverell, and introduced into the Pre-Raphaelite circle. She was discovered as an 'image', a tall, slender, perfectly modelled figure with a delicate, ethereally haunting face, semi-closed grey eyes and long, sumptuous red gold hair, to serve these artists as the cult image of the 'stunner' and known almost exclusively through the images and descriptions others made of her.[2] She became one of the most popular models, sitting to Deverell, to Holman Hunt, to John Millais, notably for his rendition of Ophelia. As the myth continues, though of a sickly nature, she was cramped into a magnificent brocade dress with silk embroidery and asked to lie for hours in a bath tub filled with warm water, with small candles beneath the tub to preserve the temperature. Apocrypha has it that Millais was so absorbed by his work that during one session he allowed the candles to go out, and when some friends saved the model from the chilly water she was close to pneumonia.[3]

By 1852 she was serving solely as Dante Gabriel Rossetti's model, and soon became his mistress as well as his student. She wrote poetry, dealing primarily

Fig 14 Dante Gabriel Rossetti. *Elizabeth Siddall in a green dress* (1850–65)

Fig 15   Dante Gabriel Rossetti. *Miss Siddall reclining in a long chair reading*
(1854)

with sorrow, death and the passing of love and left over one hundred drawings, sketches, watercolours and a self-portrait in oil. Though she had the friendship and support of Ruskin, from whom she received an annuity in exchange for her drawings, and though her work was exhibited twice during her life-time, she is remembered today above all as Rossetti's muse.[4] Her deanimation occurred on two levels. In his numerous portraits Rossetti painted her sitting, sewing, reading, resting at her easel, but always as an enigmatic woman, her gaze withdrawn into herself, the eyes semi-closed, averting the spectator's gaze. Her continual illness seems to have predestined her for these portraits that render her as a languid, aloof, withdrawn woman, with almost translucent pallor, in the weakness and flickering febrile flightiness of the consumptive ill woman, supportive of the conventional notions of the transitory nature of feminine beauty, femininity as virginal and vulnerable, ideal and tainted.

Though Rossetti supported her creative work, she is rendered by him as a beautiful figure of *melancholia*, of feminine beauty signed by death, in the liminality between life and death. As Ford Madox Brown records in his diary on 6 October 1854, Elizabeth Siddall appears to him thinner, more death-like, more beautiful and more pale than ever before while Gabriel Rossetti produces portraits, each of which is redolent of fresh, invigorating aesthetic fascination, stamped with immortality.[5] It seems that from the start she was to be his Beatrice – a romantic ideal, inspiring his artistic production as model and muse, but as the embodiment of unattainable, adored beauty, for ever receding from his reach. The young Rossetti not only translated Dante but also took from the *Vita Nuova* the idealisation of love, the fascination for a poet's continuing relation to a dead beloved and rewrote them in *The House of Life* (1881). It is remarkable that Rossetti was possessed by the notion of a dead beloved while his chosen muse was still alive, indeed even before he had met her. It seems as if Elizabeth Siddall had to die so that she could fulfil the role he had designed for her in his imagination.[6] By contrast, her own self-portrait in oil represents a far more astute and critical woman than the one in Rossetti's glamorous renditions. Her eyes are open and respond directly to, rather than fading from, the implied spectator's gaze.[7]

During her life with Rossetti, Siddall staged several instances of disappearance, returning again unexpectedly, sometimes in ill health, sometimes filled with creative energy. She lived a literalisation of the volatile, etherealised creature of purity and taintedness she was figured as in the artist's rendition. It remains open to speculation whether she was ill, flighty and melancholic from the start or

Fig 16   Dante Gabriel Rossetti. *Mrs D. G. Rossetti* (1860)

Fig 17 Dante Gabriel Rossetti. *How they met themselves* (1860)

learned to live the icon into which the artist had transformed her. She may have
staged her life as a prolonged illness, always short of impending death, to gain
Rossetti's attention, otherwise diverted by his own amorous fickleness.[8] The
myth-making about this couple suggests that Rossetti wanted to keep his muse at
bay, that he repeatedly refused to marry her until, after one of her longer
disappearances, she returned extremely ill and he thought she was literally on the
verge of death.[9]

One can speak of deanimation in the sense also that during her life she was
translated into the artist's cipher, the instrument and medium for his self-
presentation as the creator of a glamorous and enigmatic feminine figure.
Griselda Pollock persuasively argues that the fact that Siddall's name was

changed to 'Siddal' as she entered the Pre-Raphaelite circle (to become Lizzie, Liz, Guggums, Gug, The Sid, Miss Sid, Miss Siddal, Ida) suggests the transformation of a historical personage into a construct of Pre-Raphaelite literature, over the loss of her family name and with it of her fixed position within her kinship system. The absence of a fixed name, repeated in most documentation of her life, lets 'Siddal' function as a sign that does not simply refer to a historical woman or even Woman, but rather whose signified is masculine creativity. The image of Elizabeth Siddall is overdetermined in a specific way. 'Siddal' 'is constructed as a creature relative to Rossetti: she is said to appear transparently on the surface of his drawings. In effect "Siddal" becomes a cipher for masculine creativity inspired by and fulfilled in love for a beautiful feminine face.'[10] The alternation

Fig 18   Dante Gabriel Rossetti. *Beata Beatrix* (*c.* 1860–70)

Fig 19   Elizabeth Siddall. *Self-Portrait* (1853–54)

of the name constructs femininity as a position of 'the negative, the foil to the masculine usurpation of activity, productivity, creativity, health',[11] just as Rossetti's images of the fading Elizabeth Siddall, beautiful in her dying, signify the virility and immortality of his art and by implication of himself as artist. The construction of masculinity and of the masculine artist is made not only in opposition and in precedence to a feminine body caught in the process of fading, but also in opposition and in precedence to absent femininity, because the feminine figure functions as a sign whose signified is masculine creativity.[12]

The marriage Rossetti had designed to save Siddall's life took place in 1860 and produced two signatures that can be interpreted as commentaries on the relation between these two artists: on Elizabeth Siddall's deanimation into an image invoking Dante Gabriel Rossetti's reanimation, and his desire for a fully absent idealised, adored beloved as fulfilment of his fantasised image. Elizabeth Siddall signed her wedding certificate, though weakened by illness, with her proper family name, as if in defiance of the mortifying cipher she had been turned into and literalised herself with her own body. As Violet Hunt describes the document, her signature 'like a cockroach scrawling over the tiny oblong indicated for signature, suggests her weakness, while the second "l" in the letters of her name is hardly made out at all'.[13] Rossetti, in turn, used the honeymoon to

Paris to reproduce an ominous nuptial drawing, *How They Met Themselves*, a copy of an older picture he had drawn in his youth. In the shadows of a forest, a pair of lovers, modelled on himself and Siddall, meet their doubles, framed by a white glow. The *Doppelgänger* encounter, conventionally used as a sure sign of impending death, affects the feminine figure, who is arrested in this image as she is about to sink to the floor. Of course it remains open to speculation whether the drawing represents the husband's well-founded concern for his wife's health, a foreboding of death or in fact serves as a form of dream wish-fulfilment.

Fig 20 Dante Gabriel Rossetti. *Elizabeth Rossetti* (*c.* 1861)

Regardless, it preserves the theme of this couple's artistic relationship – his survival and surveyal of her fading.

The marriage turned into a catastrophe. Siddall's melancholia and illness prevailed, though were never forceful enough to let natural death occur, and instead kept her, as had been the case all her life, as well as in Rossetti's art, suspended in a position of liminality between life and death. She was anxious, restless, in part because of Rossetti's infidelities, heavily addicted to laudanum, to release her from the pain of both disease and distress. As if to find an acme to her courtship with death, she gave birth to a stillborn daughter. In February 1862 she died of an overdose of laudanum. Though the coroner proclaimed the verdict of an accidental death, Rossetti and his friends feared it was suicide. In this death by an overdose of laudanum, whether voluntarily taken to end her life or taken out of a careless disregard for the danger of the drug, two characteristic traits mark her figure to the end – an absent-minded flightiness, a moody volatility on the one hand, and on the other hand a torpid, languid sleepiness, coalescing with an image of fading, of lived dissolution into the nothingness of death and of the image.

Rossetti's response to his wife's death, however, significantly suggests a complex mixture of grief, self-sacrifice and guilt. He decided to bury a little green book, into which he had copied his last poems, with his wife's dead body. The corpus of his last creative effort was now literally a 'dead letter', placed on the left side of her corpse, between her hair and her cheek. He explained 'I had often been working at these poems while she was ill and suffering and I might have been attending to her, and now they shall go!'[14] With her dead body he seems to have wanted to renounce his writing to exist only as a painter, to bury his last testimony of his poetic gift.

Yet the second tribute to his deceased wife, the painting *Beata Beatrix*, begun around 1863 and completed 1870 as a last obsessive attempt to recall the deceased in an image, suggests duplicity at work in these mourning and commemorative gestures.[15] Inspired by Dante's *Vita Nuova*, the painting depicts the beloved woman in the liminal transition from earth to heaven. Recalling the semi-closed eyes of the enigmatic and ethereal quality in the expression of the previous portraits of Siddall, the picture perfects the series. Elizabeth Siddall's eyes are here completely closed in an ecstatic expectation of the Beyond. In Rossetti's words, this last portrait of his wife was meant as an ideal image of a trance of death, and one could add, the perfect closure to the preliminary exercises Siddall traced on her body and Rossetti, using her body as model, traced on his canvas during her lifetime. It symbolises, in Rossetti's words, a 'sudden spiritual transformation. Beatrice is rapt visibly into heaven seeing as it were through her shut lids', the suddenness a clear contrast to Siddall's actual pining away.[16]

Yet the replica of this painting, commissioned by William Graham and augmented by a second image, showing Dante's meeting with Beatrice in heaven, signifies more than the payment of a debt to his wife, for whose death Rossetti felt responsible. It can be read as the sign of remorse for a second form of betrayal of the dead woman. Two years before he had published a volume of poems which also contained those buried with Siddall's coffin. Seven years after her death he had authorised an exhumation of her corpse to retrieve these texts. Rather than depending on Beatrice to inspire him spiritually from the Beyond, Rossetti literally went to another site of death, mother earth's grave. More like Frankenstein, delving among the charnel houses and vaults, than Dante, he sought among the dead body parts of his wife to find those 'dead letters' he wanted to resurrect and form into a volume of poems.

It is significant that romantic hearsay has transmitted this disinterment as a sensational scene, yet another example for the way Siddall so readily transformed into legend. In his absence, his friends gathered together at Highgate Cemetery on 4 October 1869, a bonfire was lit to dispel unpleasant smells and in the light of the flames the coffin was lifted once again out of the grave, opened and the little green book removed. Supposedly, because the body was so well preserved, or because the spectators of this macabre resurrection of a dead body and 'dead letters' were mesmerised by the effect, Siddall, in the belated cultural construction, is said to have appeared radiantly beautiful, a figure of fine pallor among an abundance of red golden hair.[17] Robbed (or one could say raped) of her possession, the corpse was buried a second time, putting, in the tradition of second burial, a closure on to an intermediary period I call the uncanny position between the animate and the inanimate out of which, in this case too, artistic production emerges. The cultural conventions and representation of their times seem to have entered literally into the lives of Siddall and Rossetti as they repeatedly enacted a deanimation of the feminine body as engendering an animation of the artist, a production of images and poems, resurrecting the deanimated body as source and theme of these representations.

One last episode confirms the literalisation of cultural conventions in the life of this painter-poet couple, as the deanimated 'Siddal' is irrevocably turned into her husband's cipher. To the midwife who had attended Elizabeth Siddall's tragic confinement, namely the birth of a stillborn baby, Rossetti gave, as a memento, a coloured photograph, showing his wife in the typical pose of semi-closed eyes and hands clasped beneath her breast, the hallmark of her existence as his ethereal muse. Though it was later sold by Rossetti as a genuine miniature to the collector J. Pierpont Morgan, to purchase an annuity for the old woman, it was in fact a portrait painted on to and covering one of few surviving photographic images of Siddall. The artist's marks and signature bar any relation of verisimilitude, any indication of a referential value, as this could more readily be transmitted in photography. In the pose of one between life and death, between mutability and vanishing, disappearance and reappearance, the many traces of effacement she literally embodied are confirmed by the superimposition of one artistic medium on to another, as Siddall's photographic image disappears into and is resurrected in the paint of Rossetti.

177

Notes to Case Study

1 B. Gates, 1988, p. 149.
2 G. Daly, 1989, quotes Deverell's first description of her to his artist friends: 'You fellows can't tell what a stupendously beautiful creature I have found. By Jove! she's like a queen, magnificently tall, with a lovely figure, a stately neck, and a face of the most delicate and finished modelling; the flow of surface from the temples over the cheek is exactly like the carving of a Pheidean goddess', p. 35.
3 G. Daly, 1989.
4 See J. Marsh, 1989, for a discussion of her poetry and painting, as well as for the first detailed analysis of the ideological uses to which the image of Elizabeth Siddall was put in the course of the past century. For general biographical information see A. Sutherland Harris and L. Nochlin, 1979.
5 Cited in the exhibition catalogue ed. by K. Gallwitz and G. Methen, 1973, p. 184.
6 G. Hough, 1949.
7 J. Marsh, 1987.
8 B. Gates, 1988.
9 V. Hunt, 1932, quotes from a letter Dante Gabriel Rossetti wrote to his mother after Siddall's return: 'She is dying daily and more than once a day', p. 237.
10 G. Pollock, 1988, p. 94.
11 G. Pollock, 1988, p. 96.
12 G. Pollock, 1988.
13 V. Hunt, 1932, p. 317.
14 Cited in G. Daly, 1989, p. 93.
15 See *The Pre-Raphaelites*, Tate Gallery 1984, p. 209. The pose of Siddall resembles that in the earliest drawings Rossetti made of her in 1851 for *The Return of Tibullus to Delia*.
16 Cited in J. Marsh, 1987, p. 141.
17 See P. Jullian, 1971, p. 96 for a particularly lurid legendary construction of this event.

PART III

Strategies of translation, mitigation and exchange

In all societies . . . the issue of death throws into relief the most important cultural values by which people live their lives and evaluate their experiences. Life becomes transparent against the background of death, and fundamental social and cultural issues are revealed.

Richard Huntington and *Peter Metcalf*

9

Sacrificing extremity

Everything longs for what it lacks, and nothing longs for what it doesn't lack. Desiring to secure something to oneself forever may be described as loving something which is not yet to hand. I love you, but, because inexplicably I love in you something more than you – the object petit a – I mutilate you.
Jacques Lacan

While my focus in the last part was on the mutual interdependence between feminine death and aesthetic innovation or renewal, I will now turn to representations involving a social sacrifice of the feminine body where the death of a beautiful woman emerges as the requirement for a preservation of existing cultural norms and values or their regenerative modification.[1] Here feminine death serves as the site at which cultural norms can be debated.

While western cultural discourses construct the self as masculine, they ascribe to femininity a position of Otherness. As Other, Woman serves to define the self, and the lack or excess that is located in the Other functions as an exteriorisation of the self, in respect to both gender and death. Woman comes to represent the margins or extremes of the norm – the extremely good, pure and helpless, or the extremely dangerous, chaotic and seductive.[2] The saint or the prostitute; the Virgin Mary or Eve. As the outsider *per se*, Woman can also come to stand for a complete negation of the ruling norm, for the element which disrupts the bonds of normal conventions and the passage through which that threat to the norm is articulated. The consturction of Woman-as-Other serves rhetorically to dynamise a social order, while her death marks the end of this period of change. Over her dead body, cultural norms are reconfirmed or secured, whether because the sacrifice of the virtuous, innocent woman serves a social critique and transformation or because a sacrifice of the dangerous woman reestablishes an order that was momentarily suspended due to her presence.

Sander Gilman points out that stereotypes are crude representations of difference, which structure the world and localise anxiety at the body of another, at the site of alterity, as proof that what one fears or what one glorifies does not lie

181

within.[3] To produce stereotypes is concomitant with individualisation, allowing the developing self to distinguish itself from the world and to separate the good from the bad within, as well as undertaking a division of the outside world, by translating it into objects of love and hate. These objects function as reflections or distortions of the self. Signifying that which eludes the order of the self, because it is lacking or excessive, the stereotype of the Other is used to control the ambivalent and to create boundaries. Stereotypes are a way of dealing with the instabilities arising from the division between self and non-self by preserving an illusion of control and order.

However, even as stereotypes of the Other appear as absolutes and confirm a yearning for rigidity in response to an anxiety about boundary disintegration, they are inherently protean, the site on to which difference, as a tension between the security of control and a fear of its loss has been projected – be this in respect to the difference of self and other, of the masculine and the feminine, of the living and the dead. Even as it is constructed to exteriorise anxiety outside the self or the community, the Other functions as the body at which the anxiety produced out of this tension between control and loss of power or distinction takes shape and continues to be preserved: the site of *Unheimlichkeit*. The power of stereotypes of Otherness is enhanced by duplication and often embodies an interrelationship of images of difference, as is the case when femininity and death coalesce in representations of feminine sacrifice. In this third part I will explore how western culture uses narratives to establish not only myths and stereotypes about the essence of Woman, but also about the relation between femininity and social order as this involves death. Both femininity and death inspire the fear of an ultimate loss of control, of a disruption of boundaries between self and Other, of a dissolution of an ordered and hierarchical world.

Roland Barthes has argued that myth serves as the foundation of collective morality in that it assists culture in transforming history into essential types, and in so doing legitimises cultural norms by designating them as facts of nature. The aim of myth is to obscure the ceaseless making of the world, by fixating it into an object, to embalm the world so that it can be possessed for ever, to inject into reality some purifying essence which will stop its transformation.[4] The duplicity I will be concerned with involves the attempt to overcome historical facticity by turning to an aesthetic form that seems immune to death's inscription, even as the stasis of the 'essential type' serves only to articulate a different kind of death. The fixing of ambivalences and a discussion of the costs such a fixture entails will continue to emerge as the crux of representations of death. Yet my emphasis will shift to questions about what discourses the cultural construction of the feminine body serves. What values are negotiated over the feminine body, and then her dead body, among the characters within a narrative? What ideological use does the rhetorical duplicity of effacement as presentation of femininity through death take on for each text as a whole?

If up to now the equation of femininity with death has been shown to involve their mutual status as image – what I will highlight in this part is that they are also both culturally constructed as aspects of 'Otherness'. The rhetorical strategy of emphasis, doubling and excess contained in the topos of 'feminine death', as Poe's term 'most poetic' suggests, will now be explored under the auspices of pleonasm. Because 'death' and 'femininity' belong to the same paradigm, namely that of alterity, their rhetorical conjunction points to moments of excess as redundancy; i.e. to emphasis or precision in definition through the admission of superfluity.

In my discussion of von Max's painting of the anatomist, I suggested that although allegory is traditionally defined as an extended metaphor, these two figures of speech can be understood as emphasising different aspects of the rhetorical turn. Metaphor exemplifies a semantic translation or transfer, as this generates an excess of meaning based on a moment of difference. The allegorical mode, though partaking of a similar gesture, functions as a rhetorical device that reveals even as it hides. Because it is based on the notion of *allos*, it explicitly indicates a figurative speaking, a speaking in other terms, of other things. It always also articulates the occulted signifier, present though under erasure. While my previous textual discussion illuminated the metaphoric aspect of a conjunction of femininity and death, by focusing on instances which involved the translation of animate bodies into inanimate texts, this section will illuminate the allegorical quality of this topos; instances which elaborate how stability and ordering engenders an effacement of dynamic process by turning it into a stereotype, a figure, an 'essential type' of process, so as to re-establish a closed social order. If in one sense the pleonasm 'dead woman' will serve to explicate the cultural myth that death is woman's apotheosis, in another sense I will want to connect the alterity so quintessential to the cultural construction of 'femininity' and 'death' with the *allos* of allegory. Because women continue to occupy the space of the Other, Marina Warner notes, they lend themselves to allegorical use so well.[5] The pleonasm I will elaborate on is not simply that of redundancy produced through two semantically equal terms but rather redundancy 'in excess', because tripled by virtue of self-reflexively involving the rhetorical mode itself.

Prosper Mérimée's novella *Carmen* (1845) is one of the most persistent myths responding to archaic desires and fears about woman marked as 'Other' because she embodies a fascinating sensuality and passion which is disruptive of masculine order, reason and control. Significantly Mérimée prefaces his narrative with a Greek motto from Palladas, of which it seems but an elaborate gloss. 'Every woman is as bitter as gall; but she has two good moments, one in bed, the other at her death' (181). Not only are sexuality and death linked since both mark instances of feminine excellence. A comparison of woman with the gall introduces values like venom, peevishness and bitterness, making woman into the source of vexation, irritation and exasperation. Since 'gall' can also designate an abnormal outgrowth in plant tissue caused by certain parasites, the comparison implies that Woman is not only living at the expense of others but in her status as excess also a danger to the healthy, normal order of the community as body. Finally, the archaic synonymity between gall and bile refers to either of two bodily humours, one of which was thought to cause melancholy, the other anger.

With this preface Mérimée equates Woman with death on two scores. The moment of eroticism is in some sense synonymous and interchangeable with that of death, and by implication, the feminine object of desire corresponds in her lover's fantasies to a corpse. And, the feminine body produces an irritation in her lover that can move either in the direction of masochistic self-destruction or of sadistic violence directed outward. Both forms, as Freud has argued, can be understood as traces of the death drive on the psychic apparatus.[6] The ambiguity Mérimée sets up from the start is that Woman is a figure of death both in the sense of being a trope for a dead body and for an experience of self-dissolution, as well as in the sense of being a source or carrier of disruption to the surveying lover and the normative order he represents. The former can be seen as expressing the desire for a return to the static pre-natal condition of a non-differentiated unity, the latter to a breaking of existing unities in the service of dynamic generation of new entitites. The feminine body promises narcissistic gratification even as it also poses as the source of annoyance to this illusion. Death eliminates the irritation by effacing its object or cause and re-affirming the fantasy of self-stability and security.

The frame-narrator of *Carmen*, to whom Don José tells the story while in prison, and who collects and transmits narratives from Spain out of an archaeological interest in this region, is used by Mérimée to endow the 'sad adventures' of a man who murdered his faithless lover a social relevance beyond that of individual tragedy. The fact that he meets the 'dangerous creature', the 'sorceress' Carmencita several months before her murder, under circumstances that suggest his own erotic fascination for this 'strange and savage beauty one can't forget' (197) implies a collusion between his point of view and that of the murderer that becomes most explicit in their final evaluation of her. What is at stake for José when he murders his desired object and what more general norms are being debated as the narrator condones this act of violence? Why must Carmen be killed, and what is eliminated, what is gained with her death?

Throughout his narrative, José presents Carmen as the embodiment of all that is opposite to himself, of a life style that fascinates him because of its Otherness, but that also threatens to absorb him and in so doing to destroy his self and the normative order he belongs to. Being a gypsy she is neither of pure race nor of a fixed region, travels everywhere and speaks all languages, while he is defensively Basque and Christian, with a 'geneology written on parchment' in his home town (203a).[7] As a soldier José represents the law and believes in following orders, while the gypsy woman Carmen is typified by José as being a paragon of what is not controllable, 'following the custom of women . . . who don't come when one calls them and who come when one doesn't call them' (205). While Carmen's constant mobility, exemplified in an inexhaustable ability to change place, costume and roles not only signifies the freedom so quintessential to gypsy self-conception but also assures her ability to flee constraints, this volatility is understood by José as 'always lying', as never saying a word of truth.

The scene of their encounter introduces in essence the difference underlying José and Carmen's being; namely that between a masculine order, where self-identity depends on accepting a set of codes, whose laws must be clearly defined and preserved, and a feminine disruption and transgression of such an order. José is sent into the tobacco factory to re-establish peace among three hundred barely dressed women, 'all crying, screaming, gesticulating' (205) by arresting Carmen, who instigated this disturbance when she used a knife to draw a cross on another woman's face. Carmen is able to escape because she can transgress her gypsy role and convince José of her impersonation of a Basque woman. In so doing, she stages the power feminine disruption has to dismantle the clear distinctions and laws of the male order. In her presence José experiences a dissolution of the self and of the law he represents that will ultimately lead to a complete transgression: 'I was like a drunken man; I began to say foolish things; I was ready to be foolhardy' (208). This first scene also affirms that the security of self-definition provided by the law must be sustained. In opposition to Carmen's dictum 'freedom is all', José accepts the punishment of imprisonment and the humiliation of being degraded in rank to preserve his 'soldier's honour' (211).

In their incompatible conception of love, the general opposition between Carmen's desire for mobility and volatility on the one hand, and Jose's desire for permanence and univocal identity on the other, takes on a fatal aspect, revealing a multiple conjunction between death and the erotic. José's sure knowledge that he loves Carmen is based on his jealous desire to be her sole possessor. Not until he has returned from prison and sees Carmen as the object of other men's seductive flattery does he recognise his love for her. While he will ultimately abide by her scorn for the restraints of social laws, he maintains his desire for security and duration in love. Out of jealousy that he is not her only lover, he kills an officer, is forced to desert his regiment and becomes a smuggler.

For Carmen, any form of bondage to a lover – be this the requirement that she love only him, that she be unvaried in her love or that she love him for ever – is as unacceptable as any physical imprisonment because incompatible with her gypsy proclivity to a constant change of roles and regions. Yet José wants her love to be exclusive, stable and lasting; he wants to be 'sure of you' (221). Like the mother/daughter in Freud's 'fort–da' narrative, Carmen stages the disturbing dialectic of disappearance/appearance. Not only does she make herself unavailable to José's erotic claims without a warning, only to reappear just as unexpectedly as his object of desire. She also physically disappears to reappear in different roles, disguised as a well-established lady or as the wealthy lover of a British officer in Gibraltar. As in Freud's scenario, an experience of the incessant play of fading/returning of his loved object provokes in José fantasies of destruction, of mastery and revenge. Against the 'castrative' wound to his narcissism that Carmen's changes inflict, he posits an image of her dead body. In so doing, the 'fort–da' translates into a synonymity between 'fort' and 'da'. Whenever she mocks his jealousy, he confesses to a desire for murder 'I had the desire to strangle her' (221). Carmen disturbs because her desire is never arrested on one man but glides from one masculine signifier to another, and possibly beyond the male reference altogether.

Ironically, while José desires to be 'sure' of the living Carmen, her dead body is the only form of security he can attain. Not only because his notion of 'faithfulness' figuratively means her death, because analogous to a cancellation of her need for freedom, but also because only a dead body is not caught in the dialectic of fading; only death is a triumph over dying. If the function of the loved object is to reflect the lover in a stable, secure manner, translating the Woman into a signifier for masculine wholeness or completion, then for a woman to have more than one lover, to be faithless, turns her into a deceptive mirror, more disruptive than supportive of his illusion of wholeness.[8] She no longer reflects one lover's unified self-image but rather his division, since as lover of many she is explicitly more than and other than his sole possessed object. She functions not as a signifier for his possession but instead for the fact that he is dispossessed of a secure and eternal being. In this sense she becomes the signifier of ambiguity, because she is positioned between several signified masculine self-images and, in this inbetweenness, she also articulates her autonomous desire.

Tired, in the end, of killing her lovers in an effort to eliminate them as the symptom of an ambiguity Carmen's inconstancy stages, José decides to kill her instead, as the source of his irritation.[9] Though this murder will be fatal to him as well, it contains several aspects of a triumph over death. By killing his object of desire, José is able in fact to kill his desire as this manifests itself as a force that overpowers him, that lies beyond his control. Repeatedly José describes Carmen as a being that absorbs him to the point of a figural self-dissolution. Because of his desire he can no longer think of other things and is powerless before her: 'I was so helpless before this creature that I obeyed all her caprices' (222). He expresses his disgust at being possessed by her erotic charm while never sure that he possesses her and significantly describes this relationship as a form of decapitation: 'a beautiful girl lets you lose your head' (225). Carmen's presence is felt as a figural 'castration' of his sense of omnipotence because she arouses a desire that makes him dependent on another, promises the bliss of an eternal union, yet only serves, once the erotic moment is over, to point to a double loss or deprivation – the loss of self in the erotic act and the acknowledgement that such absorption is not sustainable.

George Bataille has analysed the cultural convention that describes the erotic act as a 'small death'. The fascination of eroticism, he suggests, lies in its promise of suspending the discontinuity of each individual existence in an experience of profound continuity, which in fact foreshadows death. The latter he defines as precipitating a discontinuous being into the continuity of being. While humans suffer from their individual isolation, eroticism promises the illusion of a continuity of discontinuous beings. Eroticism evolves into death; death evolves into a negation of individual duration.[10] Mérimée's narrative exemplifies that the erotic union of self-dissolution is not only the source of fascination, because a liberation from the separating boundary between self and other, but also a source of anxiety. Once forced to become conscious again of the state of discontinuity, both the loss of self in the erotic act and the loss or non-durance of the experience of continuity is intolerable to any definition of self.

Murdering the object and source of this 'uncanny' experience of continuity in discontinuity paradoxically helps to redraw boundaries that allow a unified self, distinct from the Other, to emerge; a self which is again endowed with a sense of power. Murder produces something which has endurance – the beloved as a dead body turned into an image of memory. While eroticism manifests death as the dissolution of self-boundaries, the death of eroticism (which is figured over the corpse of the woman who would otherwise repeatedly arouse this experience of continuity as a 'death' of the individual, only to again disillusion it), produces a return to duration in the form of the law and to continuation in the form of narratives. While eroticism was an experience of dispossession (a loss of power over himself and over his beloved), murder allows José the experience of repossessing Carmen, having power over her by surviving her.

This murder ends José's experience not only of libidinal liminality, but also of social outsiderdom. Over Carmen's corpse he returns to the symbolic order of his culture, to die not outside but rather on the side of the law. He delivers himself up to the police. He also returns to his original religion, making sure that a priest will pray for Carmen and say a mass for her soul, so as to assure that his erotic and murderous relation with her is ultimately framed within the Christian order. Finally he bridges the gap between himself and his family by giving to the narrator a medallion to be returned to his mother. In the same manner that he confesses Carmen's murder without disclosing the whereabouts of her corpse, he wants the narrator to transmit the message of his death without disclosing its circumstances. This double statement of death is meant to hide all transgressive elements, to exclude all moments of difference within the self. It is the defined and terminal figure of death effacing death as indeterminate and interminable process.

At stake in the murder of Carmen is not only a triumph over death, manifesting itself as a dissolution of the discontinuous self as it merges with Otherness, and the ambiguous presence of difference within the self. The semantic encoding which attributes to her such values as heterogeneity, volatility, fickleness, duplicity against such normative values as fidelity, security and univocal identity suggest that Carmen is also the site of death's presence in life due to her fundamentally incalculable nature. Her constant alternation in attitude, her hesitation between availability and denial, appearance and disappearance fundamentally questions the security of notions of possession. She stages the process of *aphanisis* as a fading before cultural symbols like laws, social roles, and language as well as before death, and radically subverts notions of continual, secure presence.[11] She, who is semantically encoded as having no fixed position – because she is a gypsy, because she is volatile in her desire – is not just signifier for her respective lovers' unified self-image. She equally functions as a signifier for the process of fading that disrupts any sense of stable self-presence. Because she explicitly practises the disintegration and imperfection of love, she signifies the process of ambivalence that subverts all categories of security, wholeness, integrity. Her attitude is summarised in her declaration of love to José: 'I think I love you a little? But that can't last' (216).

Carmen's fascination as a character emanates in part from her radical refusal to assume the position of the victim, be it before love or violence. Diametrically opposed to José, who repeatedly attempts to deny death, Carmen in fact emphatically acknowledges death as her only master. While her desire to be 'free and to do what pleases me' (233) is directed against the arbitrary symbolic laws of culture, it is based on the acceptance of the one non-arbitrary constraint which inextricably inhabits life – namely death's advent. Not only does she warn José repeatedly that she will bring him misfortune and death, but she accepts the fate that has designed him as her instrument of death.

One could in fact argue that the incompatibility between José and Carmen's values can be reduced to their opposed attitude toward death. Carmen's volatility, her disruption of all narcissistic self-constructions, be this in respect to love, to work or to national identity, can be read as the acceptance of the ubiquity of death's castrative presence in life. Because it draws its power from such an acknowledgement, hers is also a freedom from death and her way of living discloses how notions of self-unity, wholeness and stability are illusions emanating from an anxiety about and a denial of death. José, instead, uses his conception of love as the last resort against a knowledge of being 'cut' by mortality. His desire to be 'sure' of Carmen is part of an effort to stop her from being a signifier not only for the fact that he is dispossessed of her and in that sense not whole, but also for the fact of his own fading reflected in her unstable presence. Until the end he wants her pledge of fidelity, not her death: 'let me save you and save myself with you' (239), as sign of his own intactness.

Her final 'castrative' no, accompanied with the gesture of throwing away his ring, can then be read in more than one way. It leads to her murder, after which José is able to construct an intact image of the beloved, to serve as ultimate defiance of death and supportive of his narcissistic self-construction even if this is the image of Carmen as unfaithful and dangerous Other: 'that woman was a demon' (239). The tale he presents to the frame-narrator is that of his survival of the disruption Carmen's presence evoked. Yet it can also be read as the acme of Carmen's freedom, based on an acknowledgement of death as the only law she will follow and working against the illusion of love. Though José has the right to kill her according to gypsy marital customs, she will not cede to his wish that she remain with him, since this means supporting his narcissistic desire for an image of security. That she will follow him only when this leads to death remains the final proof that Carmen 'will always be free', never in bondage to a lover, but always and only to death.

By virtue of murder the indeterminate, the fading that Carmen signifies, can be overcome. As corpse and as transmitted narrative she has a fixed position; the body now exclusively hidden, present only in José's version of the story, in which Carmen is clearly defined as Other, because feminine, because raised by the gypsies, because dead. Murder makes her constant – she is now a secure image of José in the sense that she can no longer reflect other lovers. Once a dead body grown stiff, the beloved can be translated into the immobile and petrified realm of eternity. The dead beloved does not grow older, does not alter or become different, is no longer unfaithful. As an eternal being the dead beloved is the survivor's sole possession.[12] The feminine Other, promising to sustain images of self even as she endangered these due to her difference, which manifested itself in a constant process of negation or disruption of categories rather than as a static figure of difference, is translated, through her death, into precisely such a figure of Otherness, which, though signifying difference, does so in a stable manner. The dead Carmen, the 'demon woman', is always the same, does not alter, is for once faithful, at least to the stereotype ascribed to her.

What is controlled with Carmen's murder is Otherness as constant volatility, as sexual difference, and as death's presence in life in the form of fading. What is controlled is Otherness, when this functions as a force disruptive of the security of sameness, of clear oppositions and stable identities. Femininity and death as dynamic difference, as integral parts of masculinity and survival are values repressed as Carmen turns into a static, allegorical figure for difference. Her murder not only stabilises the drifting desire she arouses in her lover, but also serves to stabilise her function as subversive sign, as she turns into a sign of the subversive so that a univocality of culture and hierarchical coherence based on binary oppositions can again be re-established.

Shoshana Felman suggests that femininity should not be conceived as the canny opposite of masculinity, the lack and negative reflection safely positioned outside. Femininity should be conceived as masculinity's uncanny difference from itself. It inhabits masculinity as Otherness, as its own disruption.[13] In order to translate femininity, articulating an uncanny (*unheimlich*) difference within the self, into a canny (*heimlich*) trope for otherness, Carmen must be killed. The last section of the novella demonstrates that she comes to be merely representative for a type of social group, the gypsies and their 'wandering life'. While she serves the narrator José to reaffirm his sense of self as a sinful but repentant Christian, she serves the frame-narrator as a means of transmitting an 'attractive idea of my study of the gypsies' (247).

Analogously to the image, femininity also serves a duplicitous function within cultural representations. It can take on the position of uncontrollable real sexual difference as Otherness, not in opposition to masculinity but as that which subverts the construction of oppositions. Or, in an effort to counteract such disruption, femininity can serve as the second term in the controllable opposition of the masculine norm to the other. Killing (be it implicit or explicit sacrifice) a feminine body is a way of distancing femininity as real sexual difference and as a signifier for death, and stabilising it into a figure of Otherness, clearly secured from the masculine as norm, rather than inhabiting it. The category of Otherness, as it finds its signifier *par excellence* in femininity, can be used to subvert oppositions and/or fix them; to articulate and/or cover human fading or 'castration;' to express difference and/or to express its repression in representations.

My analysis of *Carmen* has tacitly operated with such notions as 'dangerous liminality', 'boundary construction', and 'sacrifice', which call for a more precise theoretical definition. I will provide this by returning once more to the psychoanalytic model of the child's imaginary relation to the maternal body and its acquisition of symbolic laws and language through the sacrifice of primary narcissism, in order to find an analogous model in anthropological theories about social preservation. Two aspects of this model will gain particular emphasis in the evolving discussion.

Firstly, the maternal body is 'unheimlich' not only in its contradictory articulation of the 'phallic' and the 'castrated' but also in that it embodies a contradictory merging of the self with the other. This first imaginary relation (structuring all of the subject's later libidinal relations) is such that in it the self gains a sense of unity by virtue of a reflection in and through another body, even as the maternal body is also perceived as radically Other. Functioning as *objet a*, the desired other compensates for the incomprehensible sense of loss grounding birth at the same time that it points to this real void at the centre of being.[14] Against an experience of destability arising from the acknowledgement of real difference between the self and another being, a recuperation of the self involves two steps; firstly, reassuring oneself that the Other functions as the lost object, that it gives the illusion of complementing the self, and secondly clarifying any ambivalence by drawing a stable boundary between self and Other, that eliminates real Otherness from conceptions of the conscious self. The Other serves as the limit against which the self can be defined and as the realm on to which it can project what lies within. Its function is fundamentally contradictory, in so far as it is both mirror, confirming or rejecting aspects of the self and limit to the self, embodying a form of radical Otherness beyond the self's narcissistic reflection. Even as the Other is semantically encoded as the site on to which anxieties about loss of control and boundary dissolution are projected, it marks precisely such a loss of boundary distinction and locates the issue of alterity at an interstice between the thematic and the rhetorical aspect of a representation.

Secondly, the culturation of the subject as well as the preservation of a given social system involves sacrifice, as a violent elimination of a norm-disruptive violence, and this is given a privileged figure in the first 'sacrifice' culture requires – the renunciation of the mother as desired object, as this is also a figure for the sacrifice of the unstructured soma. At the core of both sacrifice rituals lies a personal or collective response to death. Freud argues that our personal demand for immortality lets death be acknowledged as unavoidable yet also eliminated from life.[15] We can represent death to ourselves only as the death of the Other and we can intuit our own mortality only by identifying with the dying of another person whose death we simultaneously fear and desire.[16] Freud emphasises that our attitude towards death as the death of the Other is inscribed by an 'ambivalence of feeling', emerging from a dangerously fluid distinction between self and Other. The dead Other may be perceived as part of the self, with death evoking anxiety and pain as proof of one's own mortality. But the dead Other may also be perceived as different from the self, and can then evoke satisfaction, because if the alterity is perceived as potentially dangerous to the self it is successfully eliminated by virtue of death. The death of the Other provokes an uncanny hesitation between an experience of one's own mortality (momentarily suspending the Otherness of the dead person) and that of one's survival (in turn occluding any sense of identity with the Other). Freud implicitly works with a distinction between recognising the other as a component of the self, and as such a familiar, safe body, as opposed to designating the Other as representative of alterity, and as such a strange, potentially hostile body. This distinction points once again to the nodal point between melancholic and sadistic impulses, where the threat of the other, when perceived as part of the self, leads to self-dissolution while if it is perceived as alterior, it can produce aggressive destruction of the Other as an expression of self-protection. If death is always conceptualised as the death of the Other, the Other is always connected with death – the Other is dead because not the surviving self, or the Other is a metonymy of death since it potentially poses as the source of danger.

The attitude of the self to death as invariably connected to another's body is based on yet a further complication in so far as one's relation to alterity merges a stance of idealising veneration with that of degradation and revenge. In *Totem and Taboo*, drawing an analogy between the attitudes of primitive cultures and the workings of the unconscious, Freud describes rituals commemorating ancestors as an ambivalent veneration of the dead as lost love objects [*Ahnenehrung*] and a fear of the dead as demons [*Dämonenfurcht*]; as a contradictory awe of the sacred and fear of the dangerously unclean. The ambivalence of feeling that these rituals enact is that on the one hand they draw a boundary between the living and the dead to protect the surviving subjects. On the other hand they recall the unpleasant presence of death in life and imply a disruption of the boundary between living self and dead Other, for the sake of which the ritual was enacted in the first place. Identifying with the dead, the survivors feel their own vulnerability (melancholy), while identifying with the process of destruction, which is possible due to a denial of any identity with the other, they feel their own triumph and power (sadism).

Analogous to the totem, signifying lost ancestors, the maternal body refers back to the primordial mother lost with birth, and in response to her, the developing child also needs to distinguish itself from its stimulating and/or dangerous internal objects by deflecting them outside the self in order then to draw distinctions between good and bad versions of the Other. The enmeshment of destruction with desire, of aggressive revenge with veneration, is such that one and the same object is perceived as a hated source of perturbation and as the desired object capable of annulling this perturbation. Annihilating this experience of ambiguity requires an annihilation of the perturbing object itself. Annihilation can be an indication of the presence of the death drive in desire as well as a defence against an experience of desire by annihilating the desired object and that part of the self desiring the object. There are two sources of danger involved – the subject's own sadism (death drives) and the seemingly threatening object which is attacked.[17]

While for the developing child annihilation may refer to a figurative 'destruction' as separation of the fantasised internal object from the self, my analysis of *Carmen* has suggested that in narrative representations this scenario is translated into fantasies of a murder of the beloved. The Woman is killed as a substitute, in that she functions as the site at which a perturbing ambivalence as well as the sadistic death drives are projected outside on to an external object of desire, so that these can be given a body. She comes to stand simultaneously as signifier for the subject's own sadism and for the Other, the strange and potentially hostile body.

In cultural representations, the elimination of a feminine body serves to stabilise a perturbing ambivalence in the various aspects raised so far. Over her dead body a clear boundary between self and Other, as this implies the primary distinction between living and dead, can be reaffirmed. At the same time the enmeshment of desire and destructive aggression within and potentially endangering to the self is exclusively directed away from the self as it splits into two, in turn separated figures – the ideal, pure Woman and the dirty, demon Woman. Woman (like the ancestors and the maternal body) becomes a privileged metonymy for death so that her sacrifice serves to stage an imaginary triumph over mortality and over the ambivalence of feeling inherent in our attitude toward the lost, the dead.[18]

Yet psychoanalytic discussion of ritualised aggression has pointed out that symbol formation and stereotyping is a way to destroy what one fears, by setting boundaries to alterity, so that a symbolic re-enactment of death may serve to antidote primal fears of death. At the same time symbolisation, as one of the main ways of establishing a relation to the outside world and to reality, is grounded on violence, initially on the sadistic relation to the maternal body. These violent, sadistic impulses produce fantasies of appropriation and destruction that become externalised in the process of symbol formation and set a process of object exchange, destruction and creation in motion which constitues the subject's link to reality.[19]

There is, however, another dimension at issue in the sacrifice of threatening, violent or destructive elements, be they located within or outside of the subject. Freud not only locates the death drive at the heart of desire, and as such in the imaginary activity of the subject, but also at the heart of guilt, and as such in the subject's relation to cultural norms and laws. The subject discharges its internal destructive impulses by deflecting them on to a chosen external object, at whose body they can be sacrificed with impunity, even as it covers the knowledge of a loss initiating life through fantasies of wholeness and security gained by an appropriation of the beloved other as self. The symbolic order of culture equally uses the sacrifice of disruptive, mortifying elements within its system to occult death. Culture requires not only a renunciation of full instinctual gratification and pleasure (for which the 'sacrifice' of the maternal body is a privileged trope) but also a renunciation of the subject's aggressiveness as the 'first, maybe the most difficult sacrifice, that society demands of the individual'.[20] The super-ego is introduced into the psychic apparatus as the agency that sanctions and provokes the individual's sacrifice to the demands of society. It assures that the individual self subjects itself to the destructive tendencies of the community rather than exerting its own aggression; i.e. that it sacrifice its internal death instincts.

Because of the harshness with which the superego, and its cultural counterpart, the normative law, may impose on the subject, Freud has defined the ensuing production of guilt as another aspect of the workings of the death drive. When the destructive component has entrenched the superego to such a degree that it turns against the ego, it can be said to have become the site of a 'pure culture of the death drive'.[21] Self-preservation (and by implication the preservation of a community) against the presence of death is aimed in two directions – against the murderous demands of the unconscious, and against the equally fatal requirements of subjugation that the punishing superego imposes on the subject's narcissistically informed desire for pleasure. In my discussion the term *sacrifice* refers to the notion that symbol formation and stereotyping depend on acts of violence. It also refers to the notion that an explicit symbolisation of sacrificial violence may be used to produce guilt as a cultural form of self-protection. Culture allows life to prevail against death by employing internalised violence against externalised violence In Paul Ricoeur's terms 'its supreme ruse is to make death work against death'.[22]

Regardless of whether letting death work against death involves the exteriorisation of internal violence to protect the self or the production of internal violence to annihilate violence from outside, the 'sacrificed' feminine body serves as the site at which this struggle is negotiated; the feminine corpse serves as the figure at which personal fantasies and collective symbols revolving around a submission to the norm can be enacted. Because the establishment of guilt may be too severe, cultural representations enact a focus of the violence of the law on to one body, which is killed to work metonymically against death, so to speak by proxy. Representations of sacrifice involve two forms of violence as expressions of death's work in society; firstly a violence that produces strife, conflict, perturbation but also dynamisation (the feminine body); secondly, a violence that puts a forceful closure on to such disruption, that recuperates instances of destability into stability (the sacrifice of the feminine body).

Julia Kristeva has formulated this notion of a double violence in relation to culturation by combining psychoanalytic discourse with that of social anthropology, as she describes the signifying process and its relation to social and psychic processes. Distinguishing between a 'semiotic chora' and a 'symbolic' modality of signification, she locates the former on the side of the primary processes of the unconscious and of somatic utterances.[23] The chora, though part of and dependent on fully symbolic personal and social systems of representation, is understood as a non-expressive, essentially mobile, extremely provisional, uncertain and indeterminate articulation of rhythms, ruptures and movements. These pulsions are gestures responding to the constraints of the social, symbolic order imposed on the body and, like the primary processes of displacement and condensation, produce meaning. However, the chora can never be given a definitive position; it is generated in order for the subject to attain a signifying position, so that all representation depends upon this heterogeneous, interminably non-symbolic force. It must also be refused and repressed in the process of socialisation or culturation of the subject, and marks its presence in representation through the disturbances these pulsions create in the orders of rational discourse, in the form of contradictions, ambivalences, insignificance, silence, breaks, evasions and ellipses.

The semiotic chora is non-symbolic in the sense that Kristeva connects it to a form of signifying in which 'the linguistic sign is not yet articulated as the absence of an object and as the distinction between real and symbolic'. As such it is a psychosomatic modality of the signifying process, for which the maternal body is seen as the site, the ordering principle of the semiotic chora.[24] In its full presence the chora (like the maternal body) is necessarily imaginary, since only conceivable from a position within symbolic signification and in that sense experienced as an absence.It can be understood as designating the moment of disruption of fixed positions, of radical ambivalence, the site where the subject as well as the social order is both generated and negated. At this site the unity of the subject succumbs before the process of charges and stases that produce it. This non-defined position is also the site of femininity and death when these function as 'real difference'.

Though she is not explicitly concerned with femininity, Kristeva formulates an important connection between signification and the death drive which I will extend to include a discussion of sexual difference. The chora disturbs the social censorship that is also culture's protection, by disrupting its laws – such as the signifier/signified break, the constraints imposed on the soma, the detour on to surrogate libidinal objects to prevent the short circuit of a premature death. Though the precondition of representation (the symbolic order's main legitimising edifice), it is also that which destroys the symbolic, and as such it marks an influx of the death drive. The social order confines the death drive through a 'sacrifice' that also occurs at the level of representation, namely in the regulation of the semiotic in the symbolic modality of signification. Culture protects itself against the indeterminate, ambivalent and uncertain position of the chora as it diverts and confines the death drive by translating it into the symbolic and in so doing gives this violence a fixed position.

Recalling Lacan's designation that the symbol is the murder of the thing, Kristeva analyses the cultural (and psychic) ritual of sacrifice as a linguistic moment in which the social order violently 'puts an end to previous (semiotic, presymbolic) violence, and, by focussing violence on a victim, displaces it onto the symbolic order *at the very moment* this order is being founded. Sacrifice sets up the symbol and the symbolic order at the same time, and this "first" symbol, the victim of a murder, merely represents the structural violence of language's irruption as the murder of soma, the transformation of the body, the captation of drives.'[25] By implication, the rejection of primary processes that allow the unconscious, speaking and cultured subject to develop entails a process that is similar to the sacrifice of a body necessary for the founding of a social community. In Kristeva's discussion this sacrifice emerges as an ambivalent act, simultaneously violent and regulatory.[26] At the corpse of the sacrificed victim, the violence of the semiotic chora is confined to a single place, receives a signifier, a fixed position, and by virtue of this representation, it can be detained and admitted into the symbolic, social order.

Sacrifice enacts the power that representation has to stop violence by focusing it on to a signifier thereby preserving a safeguard of univocal hierarchy against the violence posed by the non-semiotic real. Furthermore, the social order is based on an act of murder and on representation, for the irruption of the symbol is a form of violence, given that it kills substance to make it signify. In the representations I am concerned with this interconnection of violence, representation and order is enacted on the thematic as well as the structural level to indicate that the social norm re-established at the end of each narrative is procured over the rhetoric of turning bodies into signs.

The contradiction around which these narratives circle is that the stability of social and aesthetic order depends on being ruptured by alterity – the semiotic chora – yet also obliterates and rejects this disruptive force. Representations of sacrificed femininity can be interpreted as depictions in which Woman, metonymically representing the semiotic chora of unpositioned, uncertain mobility, of death drives, is secured into a fixed position as a dead body. Her ambivalent meaning is averted by virtue of being translated into a signifier, and conforms to the semantic opposition of fixed meanings supportive of a normative social order. The sacrificed feminine body marks a dual position of power – the semiotic chora, having momentarily penetrated the symbolic order, is forcibly transferred into a signifier (an allegorical figure of Otherness).[27] The sacrificed feminine body stages a triumph over the violence of the death drive as dynamising force which needs to be contained and rejected and serves as a confirming mirror which guarantees the stability of the social construction of the world. It is a representation of excess that dispels the disruptive quality even as it renders it, for the combination of beauty, death and femininity covers the 'castrative' aspect of sexual difference and fatality in a seemingly unified figure, so that the spectator can, confronting this signifier of sexual difference and death, have the illusion of avoiding an apprehension of lack, of real difference, because it is momentarily frozen in place.

Sacrifice works as a metonymic strategy, with one body killed as representative of an entire semantic realm. The body literally incorporates the values of the 'hostile' paradigm, so that by virtue of such a somatic concretisation these non-concrete values can be expelled. The transformation of semiotic chora into a symbolic signifier is not just the transformation of soma into sign but also a somatisation of the idea. Because the sacrifice entails a literal murder of the body, not only is substance killed so that it can signify, but immaterial signifiers are given concrete substance, in the form of the 'real' signifier of the corpse. The corpse itself is *unheimlich* because semiotised body (marking the break between the semiotic and symbolic modalities of signification) and non-semiotised body (marking that which lies beyond language, its Other, the real). Here too it is the sheer factualness of this somatic-signifier that endows with authority the values established through this sacrifice.

Finally, though rejection and exteriorisation, represented as sacrifice, is culture's work of death, it is also a form of reactivation. Though its aim is an equalisation of tension, a state of inertia and death, it perpetuates tension and life.[28] Social anthropology works on the assumption that death is generally seen as a regeneration of life, and that mortuary rituals are a rejection that also reconstitute and create new entities, displace boundaries, introduce heterogeneity into the norm, lead to a second birth. In the specific case of sacrifice, one member of the community draws all the evil or pollution on to its body and purifies the city metonymically through her or his destruction. Sacrifice is ritual violence that keeps communal violence, agitation and disorder at bay, or ends a sequence of violent events to re-found a social order.[29] Because fertility is called forth by death, sacrifice, beyond its purifying function, also partakes of mythic laws involving death-rebirth, death-fecundity, death-new life.[30] An ambivalence is inherent in sacrifice, not only because the *pharmakos* or scapegoat is both a lamentable and a venerated person but also because the notion of *pharmakos* can be connected to that of the *pharmakon*, signifying poison and its antidote; a perturbing, polluted substance and its beneficial remedy; any substance capable of inducing a very favourable or a very unfavourable event, depending on the doses taken – in short a fundamentally ambivalent, *unheimlich* drug.[31]

The central trajectory of sacrifice is that the process of rupture is stabilised and its tendency towards death deferred by virtue of a symbolic reinscription of rejection or rupture, which represents it in its absence, as a sign. The gain involved in 'the representation of sacrifice' can be divided into three aspects: firstly, contradiction as non-positioned ambivalence is translated into the construction of semantic opposites; secondly, the mobility of the libidinal investment is bound on to an object/signifier; thirdly, the uncanny enmeshment between psychic and external reality is sublated into a clear boundary distinction between the two. Representations of feminine sacrifice reject and control the chora as a modality of existence that has no fixed position and no clear distinctions, and as it encompasses the unconscious process, the destructive drives, and femininity. While death is the translation of an animated subject into an inert object, ritual sacrifice involves a slaying of death, where the physical body is actively offered up so that it can be reborn symbolically, as an image.[32]

At this point I will turn once more to the anthropological discussion of liminality and second birth/burial in order to discuss the special position femininity takes on in relation to death. Whaley extricates a gendered binary opposition under-lying and articulating death rituals characteristic of ancient Greek mentality. The feminine paradigm includes values like disorder, pollution, nature, separation and death, while its masculine counterpart includes order, purity, society/culture, integration and life. The central pair to which all others can be reduced is that, while mourning is feminine, burial is masculine. Supporting this distinction Humphreys argues that 'many societies assign to women the roles which involve the closest contact with the corpse and the most marked detachment from the rhythms of everyday life, while leaving men to deal with the more public aspects of funeral'.[33]

Whaley himself points to two seminal Greek myths supporting this gendering of death. In contrast to the masculine figure of Thanatos, the feminine figure of doom, Ker, as well as the dangerous part-human evil-bringing female monsters who seduce to death, the Sirens, 'fuse two fundamental male anxieties, the fear and abhorrence of death and the fear of the alien female nature'.[34] The myth of Persephone, daughter of the goddess of agriculture who was raped and then married by Hades, ruler of the Land of the Dead, connects, at her body, death with the fertility of the earth. Burkert interprets the maiden's tragedy of figures like Persephone as a sacrifice, where an encounter with death, an act of killing, simultaneously guarantees the perpetuation of life and food. He also connects this myth with that of the ritual slaughter of the virgin, for the most part a prelude to war, and suggests that this is the most graphic demonstration in ancient Greek culture that men decline to love in order to kill, that hunting and war take precedence over courtship and marriage.[35]

The most far-reaching and consistent effort to conceptualise the proximity of femininity with death from an anthropological perspective emerges, however, through an application of van Gennep's discussion of the tripartite structure of all 'rites of passage' or transitions, be this initiation, marriage or death.[36] The first phase involves the separation of an individual from an earlier fixed position in the social structure or from a cultural or biological state of being. The second phase marks a margin or threshold, a liminal period, characterised by ambivalence and is followed by a third phase of reaggregation or reincorporation into a second, clearly defined social status. In death rituals this development involves the body first dying then dead, decaying but not interred and finally dead, interred and symbolically replaced by a tombstone.

Victor Turner has expanded the discussion of the liminal phase by pointing out that it always involves death. Designating it as betwixt-and-between, as an inbetween state of life-in-death, as the site of the double, the ghost, he argues that individuals in the liminal phase are dying from what was and passing into a state which is dead to the inhabited world of those living in social systems.[37] The period of liminality, which separates ritual dying from ritual rebirth, often carries feminine encodings and suggests an equation between Woman, the threshold and death and an occultation of this paradigm. This model, furthermore, applies both to social and to biological transitions, so that liminality may also involve a body socially dead but not bodily interred, as well as the decaying corpse.

Turner discusses liminality as a crossing of boundaries, as a suspension or violation of norms, which helps a social group in re-evaluating these norms, and serves either to re-establish, modify or reject them. Like the *pharmakos–pharmakon*, the person in liminality is dangerous, inauspicious or polluting precisely due to the fact that this person can not be clearly classified or falls between classificatory boundaries and unambiguous concepts. Yet this position also fructifies in the sense that liminality generates myths, symbols, rituals, philosophical systems and works of art.[38] It is crucial, however, that regeneration solicited by death also requires the termination of the phase of liminality, the redrawing of boundaries and a recreation of unambiguous concepts. Death is not considered real, Eliade notes, 'until the funerary ceremonies are duly completed'.[39] A second set of ritual operations must be undertaken to create a new identity for the deceased and reintegrate her or him in this new symbolically inscribed status, into the community. The second birth after the liminality of death, unlike biological birth, is not natural. Rather than being given it is ritually created, with death an initiation into a new mode of being and any initiation consists of a symbolic death followed by rebirth or resurrection.[40]

Regeneration occurs on two separate levels, both supportive of the symbolic order of a social system and of the symbolic modality of signification. The deceased finds a symbolic rebirth or resurrection and the community regenerates itself over an experience and rejection of death.[41] Eliade uses this dual formulation to point to the paradox inherent in a conception of dying as a paradigmatic model of any significant transition. While all acts of change or transition are seen in terms of death (marriage as death, birth as death), death leads to a state of spiritualisation that is expressed through metaphors and symbols of birth or resurrection. The notion that rebirth marks the end of the death process denies the irreversible and terminable nature of death.

Given that notions of fertility and sexuality often have considerable prominence in funeral practices, Bloch and Parry try to illuminate the specific combination of female sexuality, human reproduction, natural fertility and death. They base their discussion on Hertz's argument that the deceased is both a biological individual and a social being, whose death endangers the social order. Society counteracts this threat by recuperating from the deceased what it has given of itself, so that two phases mark mortuary rituals: a phase of disaggregation (the dangerous period of temporal disposal of the corpse and the mourners' separation from everyday life) and a phase of reinstallation (second burial), which reasserts society because it emerges triumphant over death. Two strategies help the social order expel those aspects of death that threaten continuity. Death as process is socially identified with pollution and, based on this equation, a tangible designation is given to that form of death which society seeks to reject. And continuity is reasserted by equating death with birth. Bloch and Parry argue that in double obsequies 'the first disposal is associated with the time-bound individual and the polluting aspects of death, and the second with the regenerative aspects which re-create the permanent order on which traditional authority is based'.[42]

These two phases come to represent a 'good' and a 'bad' death, where the former suggests some degree of mastery over the arbitrariness of the biological occurrence, precisely in the form of symbolic reburial, through which an eternal continuity by virtue of rebirth, for the individual and her or his social group, is assured. The latter, 'bad' death, in contrast, implies an absence of control, with death recognised as truly terminal, and as a loss of regenerative potential.[43] Within this duality gender enters by virtue of the fact that 'female sexuality is often associated with death only to be opposed to the "real" fount of human and natural creativity ... it is the temptation of Eve which brings death into the world'.[44] Human fertility, associated with feminine sexuality, is seen as intrinsically flawed and accompanied by death and as such antithetical to cultural procreation. Given this opposition between 'sexuality' and 'fertility', the former paradigm includes values such as biological birth and death, flesh and decomposition, all of which are constructed as 'an intrusion of the wild, the natural sphere of women' while the latter, the 'true ancestral fertility', is symbolised by the tomb and the (male) bones.

At stake in rituals of second burial is the necessary defeat of this combination death–feminine sexuality, and its severment from masculine bones/symbols as signifiers for the infinite re-creation of life: 'Victory over death – its conversion into rebirth – is symbolically achieved by a victory over female sexuality and the world of women, who are made to bear the ultimate responsibility for the negative aspects of death.'[45] The feminine is associated with the polluting world of biology, with the time-bound individual, with corrupting flesh, with the putrescence of the corpse, with 'bad' death, i.e. those aspects with which first burial is concerned. Second burial enacts a sublation of the 'feminine' body/ death, as this involves the fully decomposed body and its replacement by the eternal forms of a tomb or burial mound, which serve as a signifier for a place of permanence, stability and non-differentiation and assure the continuity of the social world of the fathers. Because women are often culturally associated with sorrow, mourning, decomposition, with first burial (they are the prime mourners, they wash and guard the corpse), an assault on the feminine body serves to transcend these negative values, serves as triumph over the 'bad' death as pollution and division. By vanquishing Woman, death is vanquished and vice versa.

While the rituals Bloch and Parry describe enact such an assault on Woman during mortuary ceremonies as a metonymic assault on the aspect of death they represent, the narratives I will discuss employ this exchange in a modified manner. Though here, too, an antithesis is constructed, it is not the world of women connected to the corpse but rather one feminine body turned into a corpse that is symbolically eliminated. Woman is socially constructed as representing pollution, sorrow, an agent of death and division, while a triumph over these values is debated over her vanquishment. The crucial difference here is that the dead body collapses with the body of the symbolic assault to become literally the feminine body.

The final paradox Bloch and Parry raise is that denial is always also an articulation of acknowledgement. If masculine 'fertility', as eternal stable, life-giving element can be constructed only in antithesis to such notions as feminine sexuality, biology, individuality, flesh, the body, this construction recognises what it devalues. In order to construct an eternal source of fertility where life and death are merged beyond real sexual difference, one must first revel in the dangerous liminality of decomposition, division, pollution, so that the trope that emerges once again is that of the *Unheimlichkeit* of the *pharmakon*. Women as agents of death and division assume both the negative and the creative role, given that the creation of symbolic order is dependent on negation.[46]

The regenerative power of death can be recoverd by virtue of canalising away its polluting side, and this occurs by virtue of gendering. While the texts to be discussed in this part exemplify the re-construction of a social order over the double rejection of the feminine body that occurs when it is firstly designated as liminal, polluted or excessively pure and secondly symbolically reburied/reborn in the form of a masculine sign, the next part will demonstrate the danger inherent in such an exchange with liminality.

Since the termination of a phase of development or transition is conceived in terms of death, the notion of a 'social' death takes on more than one meaning. Along the lines of Hertz, Lacan distinguishes between a 'first' death of the biological body and a 'second' death, marked by rituals of mourning, which occur in the symbolic order.[47] The texts I will analyse, however, show how the change of identity attributed to biological death can be found in instances of a social position as well, so that the sequence of first and second death is reversed. A dissolution of the social person occurs before physical demise. An *unheimlich* feminine body emerges, dead in the social order, but not yet dead in its real biological aspect. To recast Hertz's terminology – 'first' burial is in the symbolic, second burial involves the biological and the social body, undoing the separation between the two. This liminal position is one of uncanny power because it is the site of danger and/or healing, of a disturbing double, which must ultimately be purified by being recuperated into a clear social status – as the biologically dead body is replaced by a tomb and socially reborn.

The liminal, the polluted, the unstructured disorder that will eventually be expelled to maintain the system is both destructive of existing patterns and also has potency. The person who enters into a marginal state, into a disordered realm beyond the confines or external boundaries of society acquires a power inaccessible to those remaining within the realm of order. However, the transitional state, because it is undefinable, because it is not in a fixed position, is considered dangerous. Those passing between fixed states endanger themselves along with emanating danger to others. This duplicitous function of power and danger finds its expression *par excellence* when the liminal involves the death process to indicate both the ultimate unity of life and death and the need to use forms of ritual to separate death from life.[48] Woman is killed or kills her substance to signifiy the unity of life and death and her interred corpse, replaced by the symbolic gravestone, serves as the boundary resurrected between the living and the dead.

Notes to Chapter 9

1 With the term 'value' I am introducing a new category into my discussion to illustrate the social issues at stake in representations of the death of a beautiful woman, as well as to show how these intersect with aesthetic issues raised so far. While I begin with the implicit definition of value as the moral and cultural principles, beliefs or accepted standards of a social group, my discussion of C. Lévi-Strauss will introduce the additional meaning of worth and desirability in respect to property and economic exchange.

2 S. de Beauvoir, 1974. I am refering back to my earlier discussion of myths of femininity. Though she is not concerned with the issue of gender, M. Douglas, 1966, argues that both the 'sacred' and the 'polluted' body is considered contagious, unstructured, out of place, and must be separated and demarcated from a system, be it a personal or a collective order, by erecting barriers against it.

3 S. Gilman, 1985.

4 R. Barthes, 1972.

5 M. Warner, 1985.

6 S. Freud, 1924.

7 Carmen functions along the lines of what M. Douglas has described as the 'polluted body' and what J. Kristeva, 1982, reformulating Douglas, has called the abject; as that type of being which 'disturbs identity, system, order. What does not respect borders, positions, rules. The in-between, the ambiguous, the composite . . . [it] is perverse because it neither gives up nor assumes a prohibition, a rule or a law; but turns them aside, misleads, corrupts, uses them, takes advantage of them, the better to deny them', pp. 4 and 15.

8 S. Felman, 1981, argues that Woman functions as a metaphor of man, so that the signifer femininity often has masculinity for its signified, and serves as a figurative substitute that refers to man. The ideal woman functions as a metaphor of the phallus, a repetition of the phallic mother; pp. 19–44. For José, Carmen is the signified of a sequence of signifiers, her lovers. Killing Carmen means to terminate this sequence and with it his position in it.

9 He tells her, 'I am tired of killing your lovers; it is you I will kill' (236).

10 G. Bataille's, 1957, discussion of eroticism as an experience of continuity within the discontinuity of human existence can be understood as a sexualisation of the non-sexualised experience of unity the child has in relation to the maternal body. The

dialectic of love for and aggression against this maternal body transforms, in adult experience, into the ambivalence between desire for dissolution of self-boundaries and an anxiety about such experiences of continuity.

11 In this sense her function can be seen as analogous to that of the birth-mark on Georgiana's face in Hawthorne's story.

12 In this sense the feminine corpse is an 'ideal body' and can be seen as a metaphor for the phallus, the body of wholeness, security, constancy.

13 S. Felman, 1981.

14 The maternal body as object of desire was, furthermore, the privileged object of both the erotic drive, as this aims at complicating life, by progressively combining living substances which have been dispersed as well as preserving life, and of the death drive, whose aim is to lead organic life back into the inanimate state. The notion that both drives are conservative in that they aim to re-establish a state of things disrupted by the emergence of life turns the maternal body into the privileged site for the basic contradiction underlying life. S. Freud, 1923, writes 'The emergence of life would thus be the cause of the continuation of life and also at the same time of the striving towards death; and life itself would be a conflict and compromise between these two trends', p. 43.

15 S. Freud, 1915. He repeatedly suggests that dreams of the death of others satisfy the ego's desire for survival. Otto Rank, 1945, elaborates on this notion, suggesting that fantasies of killing and of sacrifice are a major way of defending the ego against the fear of its own death.

16 J. Laplanche, 1976.

17 See H. Segal, 'De l'unité clinique du concept d'instinct de mort', in A. Green, 1986b.

18 This scenario fits the model of supplementarity discussed earlier, in the sense that the threat of death and femininity is excluded from the norm by virtue of the fact that they are exteriorised. The system defends itself by expelling values, always already inhabiting it, by naming them as Other, and this act of 'sacrifice' or 'rejection' can be seen as an economy of death employed to defend against death. J. Derrida, 1978, writes, 'Is it not already death at the origin of a life which can defend itself against death only through an economy of death', p. 202.

19 See M. Klein, 'The Importance of Symbol Formation in the Development of the Ego', 1975a.

20 S Freud, 1933, p. 111.

21 S. Freud, 1923, p. 52.

22 P. Ricoeur, 1970, p. 309.

23 It must be noted that Kristeva's use of the word 'semiotic' runs counter to the more general use of the term I also employ to designate the semantic value of a signifier. To prevent misunderstandings I will always refer to her particular concept as 'semiotic chora' or 'semiotiké,' and will continue to speak of a 'non-semiotic' body or a 'non-semiotic real' to refer to that which lies outside any form of signification.

24 J. Kristeva, 1984, p. 26f.

25 J. Kristeva, 1984, p. 75.

26 W. Burkert, 1983 explains that sacrifice allows a sense of community to arise from collective aggression; R. Huntington and P. Metcalf, 1979, speak of the sacrificed corpse as a symbol of community; C. Duverger, 1989, voices the central paradox inherent in rituals and representations of sacrifice: 'Putting death to the service of life, sacrifice appears at first glance to be a paradox . . . Death was thought always to release

surplus vital energy', p. 369.

27 In Lacan's terminology this social/linguistic sacrifice functions as a *point de capiton*, momentarily arresting the gliding of the signifieds under the bar of the signifier.

28 J. Kristeva, 1984.

29 See R. Girard, 1972.

30 E. Morin, 1970, p. 132.

31 R. Girard refers back to J. Derrida's discussion of the *pharmakon*, 1981.

32 J. Irwin, 1980, notes that in sacrifice, 'man attempts to transform death from something passively suffered into something actively controlled ... If the literal (the physical body) is death, then the slaying of death is rebirth, the reanimation of the corpse as an image', p. 147.

33 S. Humphreys, 'Death and Time', 1981, p. 267. In Christian iconography, predominantly women are associated with Christ's dying body and corpse. They stand beneath the cross, care for the dead body and find the empty grave, while men look away from death and are concerned with continuing their everyday existence.

34 J. Whaley, 1982, p. 21. The double projection of a fear of death and of nature on to the feminine body informs modern European mentality among other instances in the form of witch hunts. As C. von Braun, 1989, demonstrates, the *Hexenhammer* says of woman her 'name is death', from which the argument ensues that a triumph over mortality and nature occurs concommitant with a triumph over the feminine body on to which nature, fleshliness, unpredictability had been projected. The tragic dilemma is that feminine sacrifice came to transform myth into physical reality even as psychical reality continued to contain mythic elements.

35 W. Burkert, 1983.

36 For an overview of the anthropological concepts discussed here see P. Metcalf and R. Huntington, 1979.

37 V. Turner, 'Death and the Dead in the Pilgrimage Process', 1977. Turner writes, 'Liminality is frequently likened to death, to being in the womb, to invisibility, to darkness, to bisexuality, to the wilderness, and to an eclipse of the sun or the moon', p. 95. See also C. W. Bynum's critique of Turner, 'Women's Stories, Women's Symbols', 1984, pp. 105–125. She rightly points out that for industrialised western culture 'liminality' is only a metaphor, and it is precisely as a rhetorical figure that it functions so prominently in western representations. She further argues that the concept of liminality is applicable only to male stories, useful for understanding them, just as to see woman as fully liminal always presupposes the position of the dominant, masculine perspective.

38 V. Turner, 1977b.

39 M. Eliade, 'Mythologies of Death: An Introduction', Frank E. Reynolds and Earle H. Waugh, 1977, p. 15.

40 M. Eliade, in F. Reynolds and E. Waugh, 1977.

41 V. Turner, 'Death and the Dead', F. Reynolds and E. Waugh, 1977, points out that in Catholic theological thought, the dead were thought to fructify the living spiritually, and the 'death and resurrection paradigm' inspired 'early martyrs whose "imitation of Christ" lead to their death for the faith and future faithful at the hands of the pagan political authorities. Hence the well-known expression "the blood of the martyrs is the seed of the church," where blood = spiritual semen', p. 32. This unintentionally points, for my purposes, to another aspect of how the feminine body, once dead, can serve as a metaphor for the phallus. See also C. Bynum, 1987, for a discussion of

female martyrs and the feminine imitation of Christ.

42 M. Bloch and J. Parry, 1982.

43 In this double aspect of the funeral one side focuses on pollution and sorrow as that to be removed in the end, the other reasserts the continuity of an order by vanquishing the former and in so doing legitimises its own authority. Within this dialectic the normative order can only be reaffirmed as eternal by virtue of a negation of the processes of death, so that, even as a triumph over the 'bad' death is enacted, an inextricable dependancy on it is acknowledged.

44 M. Bloch and J. Parry, 1982, p. 18.

45 M. Bloch and J. Parry, 1982, p. 22. Much of their work is based on the funerary rituals observed by the Merina, where those women who are in contact with the corpse, are attacked and defeated by the men, who alone enter the tomb and speak from it on behalf of the community. Yet they insist that such social constructions of gendered death are implicit in western culture as well. They point out that incorruption of male corpses is attributed to exemplary social and economic behaviour, while in female corpses this was interpreted as a sign of the deceased woman's sexual purity, of which the Blessed Virgin's Assumption in corporeal form is a prime example. She, too, can be read as a metaphor of the 'phallus', in so far as complete circumvention of the state of decomposition suggests a triumph not only over death as process but equally over a feminine sexuality associated with this 'bad' death.

46 M. Bloch and J. Parry, 1982.

47 J. Lacan, 1986. A. Jaulin, 1984, suggests that silence, cleavage, usurpation, is a form of feminine death before real death, signifying that 'here' is not the right place for one who has 'no place'. See also G. Vernon, 1974, pp. 21–32, who distinguishes between a pre-inevitable 'social' death, and inevitable 'biological' death and memory and representation as an acceptance of biological but denial of socio-symbolic death.

48 M. Douglas, 1966, pp. 178. The dialectic in the notions of double violence, double burial or double aspects of death suggests the following analogy between the inter-related discourses I am invoking. While Kristeva speaks of a destabilising unstructured semiotic chora that must be translated into a structured, stable symbolic sign of death, she recalls the two aspects of Freud's notion of the death drive, where the first aims at a process of strife and division, the second at a static and constant inanimate body. Kristeva's concept of the semiotic chora can also apply to the decomposing, polluted body/corpse in Hertz's model, which is ritually translated into the stable figure of the fully decomposed bones. It can equally apply to Blanchot's discussion of the cadaver as disrupting all sense of position and reference which solicits a stabilising duplication in the form of a representation of the corpse. By implication, since the first position is often marked feminine, the last analogy would be that of woman as purturbation, as *unheimlich*, as real difference, soliciting a translation into the stereotype of Otherness, be it in relation to an encoding of eroticism or death, of the venerated or the glorified.

10

Femininity – missing in action

This, then, is the reason why woman has a double and deceptive visage: she is all that man desires and all that he does not attain . . . She is all, that is, on the plane of the inessential; she is all the Other. And, as the other, she is other than herself, other than what is expected of her.
Simone de Beauvoir

There is woman only as excluded by the nature of things which is the nature of words . . . Her being not all in the phallic function does not mean that she is not in it at all. She is in it *not* not at all. She is right in it. But there is something more.
Jacques Lacan

Every theory of culture is ordered around the hierarchical opposition between masculinity and femininity. As Hélène Cixous notes, death is always at work in the construction of this conflict-ridden opposition, 'for meaning only gets constituted in a movement in which one of the terms of the couple is destroyed in favour of the other'.[1] At the same time, the fear of death translates into a fear of Woman, who, for man, is death. She is constructed as the place of mystery, of not knowing, Freud's 'dark continent', as the site of silence but also of the horrifying void that 'castrates' the living man's sense of wholeness and stability. She is desirable because distant, absent or not quite there, a dream, a phantom, a mediatrix, a muse. Woman and death are considered to be the two 'unrepresentable' things and yet they are ubiquitously present 'allegorically' in western representations as precisely such a limit and excess. Woman not only stands for death in a multitude of ways, but death is also the agency on which a drawing of oppositions produces meaning even as it is also the value that such gendering helps destroy, at least conceptually. The conjunction of femininity and death is not just to be located on the thematic but also on the structural, rhetorical level of a text. An elimination of the feminine figure is a way of putting closure on aspects of mortality allegorically embodied through her.

In this chapter I will present the way Lacan positions masculinity and femininity in relation to cultural laws, to the unconscious, to imaginary objects of desire and to the non-semiotic real so as to elaborate the mythic association of femininity and death presented earlier on. By way of introduction into this topological conjunction of femininity and death, however, an anecdote. In the early part of the twentieth century a cult grew up on the European continent around the plaster cast of a young woman's death mask, whose title was significantly 'L'inconnue de la Seine'. A copy of this young girl's immobile head, seemingly pure and calm – with her straight hair tucked in at the back of her neck so as to frame her face, her eyes peacefully closed and her lips fixed into a sweetly serene, enigmatic smile, which could signify the relief but also the ecstasy of death – adorned the rooms of countless young women. It also served as the model for the novels of several French and German authors, from the surrealist Louis Aragon to the kitsch writer Reinhold Conrad Muschler.

The meaning of her smile was as enigmatic as the cause of her death. No one knew whether she had committed suicide owing to an illicit romance, out of despair or in order to shirk the responsibility of an illegitimate pregnancy; no one knew whether she was the victim of murder or her death an accident; whether her death should be condemned as a crime, praised as a form of redemption or whether it should horrify as an instance of necrophiliac desire. As Alvarez suggests, the cult may well have flourished because the girl was genuinely 'inconnue'.[2] The only known facts are that she was fished out of the Seine in the 1880s, exposed in the Paris Morgue but never claimed and that her face, smiling in death, impressed some spectator to such a degree that he took her death-mask. Other anecdotes suggest that even the fact of her death cannot be unambiguously confirmed, for a researcher is said to have followed her trail to the Hamburg factory producing the plaster casts only to encounter a living model in the shape of the daughter of the manufacturer, who had become prosperous by producing her death image.

One could add that the reason why her enigmatic deathly smile fascinated to the degree of collecting its plaster copy was as ambivalent and uncertain as an explanation for the cause of her death. This cast could be seen as a *memento mori*, a warning and threat of death's presence in life, just as the preservation of her beautiful intact face could signify the opposite, could assuage the fear of bodily dissolution in death and assure that death was not painful but easy, a promise of peace. It could also have fascinated to such a degree in that it represented death by drowning as a viable alternative to unbearable conflicts and constraints of life, functioning as a *pharmakon*, a sign for the possiblity of relief through suicide that makes the need to commit the act itself obsolete.

In a sense, the enigmatic smile is constructed only by virtue of the plaster cast of the death mask. While the taunt muscles of the corpse's face are indeterminate in their meaning, the plaster cast reproduction translates these into a signifier univocal in meaning: an unambiguous smile whose motivation (or referred to signified) is indeterminate. While the cast draws its legitimation by virtue of implying a mimetic concept of representation – the cast is awesome and moving

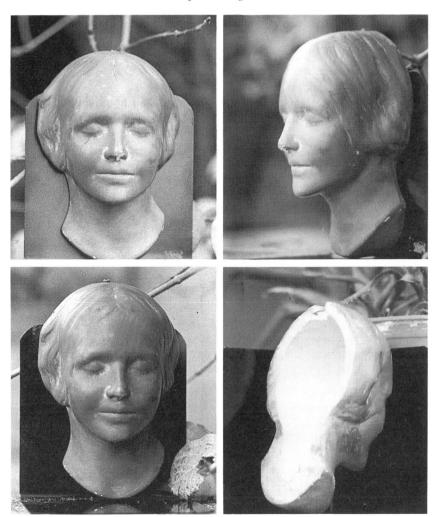

Fig 21 *L'inconnue de la Seine*

because it pretends to evoke a real dead body as model – it also perverts this notion of mimesis by introducing the surplus of serial production and commodification. Given that conventionally one corpse is given or figured by only one death mask, the pleonasm inherent in this particular representation of feminine death resides in the serial reproduction even as it invokes parodistic excess.

It is crucial, however, not only that this endlessly reproduced head of a beautiful dead woman is completely empty, signifying nothing concrete, and as such a cipher for all possible divergent explanations and desires which its spectators wanted to project on to it. It does so, furthermore, in a manner of complete disembodiment or rather by being exclusively textual. Not only is the head dissevered from the body but the absence of a physical body is duplicated by the absence of a social body. She has no name, no fixed position within a kinship structure, and no story. Finally, the uncertainty emerging from this cult object involves the possible absence of any model or real body corresponding to the artificial copy. The imaginative power of this plaster-cast lies precisely in the fact that, though it pretends to have an object of reference in historical reality, it works as a stereotype, which Barthes calls 'that emplacement of discourse *where the body is missing*, where one is sure that the body is not'.[3] Though one would have to add that the cast works as a stereotype of a stereotype, in so far as any clear semantic content or signified is missing as well.

One aspect, however, is certain and necessary for this kitsch object to work – the feminine gender of the corpse. The cult may well have flourished because it tacitly involved and implicitly invoked the paradoxical status of femininity in western representational discourse. Woman, Teresa de Lauretis argues, is the very foundation of representation: its object and support, its telos and origin. At the same time Woman 'is nowhere' as reference to her image. Western representations work as texts telling 'the story of male desire by performing the absence of woman and by producing woman as text, as pure representation'.[4] In this sense also, death is at work in the cultural construction of femininity.

One seminal contradiction raised by the 'Inconnue' is that the elimination of the feminine character does not mean the elimination of femininity. On the contrary it serves the production of stereotypes of femininity contingent on the absence of women's bodies. Though the semantic encoding of the effaced feminine characters I am concerned with is extremely diverse, they resemble each other in so far as each is in some way connected with aspects of death during her lifetime, so that the final dead feminine body repeats and doubles the feminine body of death present throughout the narrative. My emphasis will lie with the rhetorical similarity underlying these representations that gender death, for they all seem to rely on the principle that 'dead woman' is a pleonasm used to confirm the social structure of gender and efface the reality of death.

Another contradiction brilliantly staged in the dissevered head of the 'Inconnue' involves the feminist critique of the inadequacy of images of women to female reality, given the constant slippage between the allegorised Woman as the object and the very condition of representation and woman as a historical being, subject of real relations. Such a critique is concerned with the way in which a feminine character is not only used as a figure of silence, of erasure, as simulacrum but also functions as such an absence within a text. Arguing that literature speaks about the way in which what is not known is not *seen* as unknown, Barbara Johnson suggests that Woman may function as one of the things we do not know we do not know.[5] In the chiasmatic relation of woman figured as death/death figured as woman, the referent woman is absent from the text, but this absence is occulted by a plethora of myths of femininty, even as absence (or death) is equally 'missing' from the text, beyond representation, yet rendered at and over a plethora of representations of a woman's dead body.

Fig 22   Heinrich Mücke. *Übertragung des Leichnams der Heiligen Katharina zum Berge Sinai* (1836)

Femininity is culturally constructed as a figure of contradiction, and positioned as the symptom at which culture's repression of death re-emerges. Woman functions as a sign not only of the essence of femininity but also of the Other in whose mirror or image masculine identity and creativity finds its definition. Femininity is also installed in representations as the material through which (and as the barrier against and over which), the hero, society, culture and their representation are constituted. As the mythic construct Other-than-man, Woman functions as ground and limit, as the vanishing point of culture's representation of itself and the condition for these representations.[6]

The ambivalence of Woman's position is that she is supplement to man and point of an original unity. She is fluid, undifferentiated, yet her function is to define man and she serves as the limit or boundary at which difference is drawn and confirmed. She is not whole, a sign for human mortality, yet also the body over which man and culture can be defined as being whole. The wholeness she promises and disillusions is connected both with her proximity to nature and to the artistic image. These notions of integrity, used as confirming mirrors by the surviving spectator, are duplicitous because inhabited by real decay (in respect to nature) or by the uncanniness of the image, as it hovers between presence and absence, is a double of its model inscribed by misrecognition. The allegory of the female body is an ambivalently coded figure and the rhetorical figure of ambivalence *per se*; a figure thematising difference and a rhetoric enactment of difference, be it in relation to the definition of self or a mythic construction on which this definition is contingent. In the midst of this aporic rhetorical usage Woman's position is analogous to that of death.

Lacan's insistence that femininity can be understood only in terms of its construction must be seen in relation to his general theory that the human subject emerges from a radical split, both in relation to the void introduced at birth with the loss of the primordial mother and with the creation of the unconscious, as the child is grafted on to a system of laws and symbols. If in one sense identity emerges from imaginary relations to other love objects, as the subject forms a stable and integrate image of itself by virtue of identifying with or reflecting itself in others, in another sense sexual identity operates as a law, whose fictional nature is enjoined on the subject. Masculinity and femininity must be understood as signifiers, so that a discussion of gender construction in fact involves questions about the other signifiers in relation to or in the midst of which each gender position emerges, as well as what signifieds they serve to articulate. If 'man' and 'woman' are 'signifiers bound to the common usage of language', then all subjects must place themselves either in the masculine or in the feminine realm, but any one can 'cross over and inscribe themselves on the opposite side from that to

Fig 23   Anne-Louis Girodet de Roucy-Trioson. *Atala au tombeau* (1808)

Fig 24   Baron Pierre Guérin. *Le retour de Marcus-Sextus* (1808)

which they are anatomically destined'.[7] When one speaks of 'man's imaginary relation to other love objects', the designation equally includes anatomical females engaged in narcissistic self-construction, just as a discussion of woman's proximity to radical Otherness does not exclude anatomical males.

The usefulness of Lacan's typology resides precisely in the fact that it evades essentialism or mystification by talking of gender in terms of positions and relations. In contrast to Lotman's mythic model, the feminine in this model is also given a subject position, like the man constituted by virtue of crossing boundaries and relating to the Other. Though woman in this typology is also identified with Otherness, she is so by virtue of being construed in relation to signifiers that are different from the ones to which man relates. Lacan, however, never loses sight of the fact that these constructions, operating with notions of sexual lack, do so as a superimposition on to a ubiquitous, non-gendered split of death's presence in life. If I have argued in the previous part that death lacks a fixed signified in cultural representation, functions, that is, as a superlative trope, Lacan's discussion shows in what sense woman as 'not all' (*pas-tout*), as non-existing ('La femme n'existe pas') and as more than her reference to the phallic signifier (*encore*) marks, in an analogous manner, the lack of a fixed place, an uncanny shifting of position, a fading, an absence within representation as well as a superfluity.

Since in Lacan's terms the conscious subject is necessarily not coherent, always already divided against itself and persistently so (a 'split subject'), conscious mastery of the self belongs to the realm of a life-preserving fantasy and is supported by the imaginary relations to others as love objects. Within these fantasies of coherence and identity Woman functions as a promise that the void or split inscribed into human existence can be overcome by the sexually different Other or exteriorised on to her *and* as the disturbing proof that this lack is irrevocable and ubiquitous. In her cultural construction, however, Woman is not only linked to the split within the subject, but hers is also a split representation, in which she appears as purity *and* lust, as victim *and* destroyer and in which the feminine serves as a cipher conjoining the threat of sexuality with that of death. 'Femininity becomes the place in which man reads his destiny,' Lacan claims, 'just as the woman becomes a symptom for the man.'[8] Because any realisation of the self as whole within the love relation comes down to fantasy, Woman as object of desire is a symptom for man's yearning for full identity, for ego coherence and for narcissistic pleasure along with the failure necessarily built into this undertaking. She is man's symptom because he projects his lack on to her, and by virtue of this projection both articulates and disavows it.[9] If woman in her idealised form, absent, elevated and inaccessible, stands in for male lack – occults a knowledge of the split in the self and masks a knowledge that all sexual relations as self-realisations are lacking – her defamed or denigrated aspect articulates precisely this split, so that her exclusion is a precondition for man's sense of eternal existence, his soul, to come into being.

Like cultural constructions of death, like the tombstones and portraits that

Fig 25   George F. Watts. *Found drowned* (1848)

Fig 26   Paul Delaroche. *La jeune martyre* (1855)

simultaneously mark the deceased and their absence, Woman is man's symptom in the sense of that site of repression where the repressed returns, where the void of existence returns as sexual void. For Lacan to argue that 'Woman doesn't exist' is to say that the feminine is defined purely against the signifer man and to point to the fact that such a definition is always imaginary, in the same manner that her function is to support the fantasy of self-realisation and wholeness to be gained in relation to an Other. This 'not one' also means that woman has a negative because no fixed place in the symbolic order of culture because she points out the lack fundamental to human existence, and her fading and shifting is constructed as the site where *aphanisis* pervades discourses and representations. But the 'not all' which Lacan suggests Woman represents within culture also refers to the fact that any system of representation is 'not all', and as such refers to its vanishing points, to the limitations which it must acknowlege even as it attempts to deny them.

Femininity is paradoxically seen as occupying a borderline position, within the symbolic yet also beyond it, protecting and shielding the symbolic or social order from the imaginary, with its link to the soma and from the non-semiotic real before which both culture's laws and the imaginary repertoire falter. Woman is also the privileged object of imaginary activity as well as being part of the threatening non-semiotic real, of Kristeva's disruptive semiotic chora, both of which are connected to the unmitigated death drive. Woman 'does not exist' in the sense that she has an unstable place within the norm even as she is also positioned beyond it. Yet she must receive a fixed designation, so that this norm can define itself with and against her by virtue of this demarcation. She is 'not all' because, structured around the phallic reference 'man', she comes to represent potential loss, difference, the exterior, so that her mythic constructions serve to secure the cohesion of a system and to secure a reference point in precisely this Otherness. The mythic construction of Woman however also articulates the disturbance and trouble behind the cohesion, which once again enters by affirming her negative position.

For Lacan to argue 'woman is not all' implies that her body is site of a split or lack, that she is 'not all' there is of a social system, but also that she is 'not all' of one order, the site of conjunction between more than one order, that which is in excess of an order, an impossibility within the system, a vanishing point or

Fig 27 Roy Lichtenstein. *Drowning girl* (1863)

Fig 28   John Everett Millais. *Ophelia* (1851–52)

oscillation between absence and presence. Like an aesthetic order, a social order is constituted by virtue of what is seeks to evade, and Woman is set up as the guarantee of the system. In this function she comes to represent two things – 'what man is not, that is difference, and what he has given up, that is excess'. In this paraphrase of Lacan, Rose replaces 'sexual difference' with 'difference' and I would add difference as death's work; she replaces Lacan's 'jouissance' with 'excess', and I would add the excess of the rhetorical strategy of the superlative and the 'uncanny', again in its conjunction with death.[10] The deception posed by Woman is that she embodies two threats to the symbolic – she is the privileged object of the imaginary (outside the social) and she seems to recall the primary processes, the 'semiotic chora', and with these the non-semiotic real.

Woman, in her split representation, is construed as a symptom for the split in the self, a symptom of death's presence, precisely because she is the site where the repressed anxiety about death re-emerges in a displaced, disfigured form. Yet the point of Lacan's typology is to illustrate that if Woman is not whole because she lacks one fixed position, not being 'one' can also mean having more than one position. Up to now I have discussed ambivalence in respect to a duplicitous semantic encoding of Woman. Lacan's model shows how ambivalence can also be seen as the figure Woman traces within culture, making her not only a figure of death on the thematic level of a representation, but also the site at which, on the rhetorical level, the figure traced by death (*Unheimlichkeit par excellence*) is allowed to emerge within the representational process.

Within his typology Lacan argues that the adult or 'split subject' is a 'male' subject positioned within the 'masculine' field, whose privileged signifier is the 'phallus' – to be understood as a signifier referring only to other signifiers which 'has no signified' and as such functions as an arbitrary but conventionally accepted symbol for the social order, the paternal law, the 'name of the father'. The 'split subject's' relation to the other gender is the imaginary relation to objects of desire (*objet a*), positioned within the 'feminine' field, because they function as a repetition of the maternal body. Though these objects of desire are duplicitous, supporting a narcissistic desire for wholeness, integrity and security even as they articulate the illusion and misrecognition underlying this fantasy, their function is to reflect and support the subject and the masculine realm it metonymically represents, so that, in this relation to the other gender, what is barred is precisely sexual difference as radical Otherness. Here the feminine serves as a detour to an Otherness that leads back to the same, a canny trope for Otherness occluding and like the fetish also articulating uncanny difference within the self.

The position of Woman is located within the feminine realm but split between and in relation to both the 'phallus' (social, cultural law and language) and to that radical Otherness within the self whose direct knowledge is barred, which is present as a hole or loss that can only be signified, without an immediate access to its point of reference. Lacan uses the 'barred Other' to designate the unconscious, the non-semiotic real as well as death. While for Woman a relation to the phallic reference entails a boundary-crossing into the realm of masculine gender (in analogy to the child's renunciation of the maternal body and its identification with the father's interdiction), her relation to the radically Other is one that lets her remain within the feminine realm. Lacan implies an equation of the phallus (privileged in the masculine) and the signified though barred radically Other (privileged in the feminine), in so far as both are formulations of the Law – the phallus of patriarchal 'law' and the barred Other of the 'law of death.' Equally symmetrical are the split subject (again in the masculine) and the barred woman (in the feminine).[11]

However, these two forms of subjectivity assert themselves in very different relations. Though the masculine subject is split in its relation to feminine objects of desire, it has a fixed position in the realm reigned by the phallic reference as Law. Woman's subjectivity, in turn, asserts itself as a lack of a fixed position, and entails an oscillation between two points of reference or Laws. She is constituted in the symbolic relation to the privileged signifer for paternity, the 'phallus' and fulfills this position once she is mother. But she is also constituted in relation to the law of the radically Other, the non-semiotic real. Furthermore, in this relation to the barred Other, there is always something with her that eludes discourse.[12] While it is the line of sexual difference, the boundary between the masculine and the feminine realm that divides the 'split subject' from its desired 'feminine' object, what divides the 'barred' woman is her position between the 'masculine' phallus and the 'feminine' radically Other.[13] In this sense she is at once doubled and in excess of the normative system, because more than the object within a narcissistically informed imaginary relation and pointing beyond her relation to any symbolic law. In both cases her position in relation to death is diametrically opposed, though in a sense parallel to that of the split subject. Where the latter hovers uncannily between denial and acknowledgement of death by virtue of producing images and allegorising the Other, Woman's uncanniness resides in the fact that she shifts between two signifiers, both of which, however, mark moments of fading rather than any narcissistic protection against death's presence in life. These relations in fact enact precisely the wound to such a sense of wholeness, whether this involves the subjects's fading before language and submission to cultural laws or the dissolution of the subject in the face of death.

The following reading of narratives will illustrate that Woman, stabilised in relation to the 'phallus,' submits to cultural law, accepts her position as 'lacking,' supplements and supports masculine culture even if this requires, in extremity, a fading of the self before laws and language. Stabilised in relation to the radically Other, however, Woman gives up her narcissism and all bonds to symbolic laws and enacts a dissolution of the self in the face of the unconscious, the semiotic chora or real, material death, often bringing about a destruction of herself and/or of her lover. One trajectory of these narratives is to effect and implement closure against the disturbance the feminine causes by fixing her position in relation to one or the other signifier and translating her into an allegory of this reference point – the woman as 'phallus' or the woman as figure for the barred radically Other. Another trajectory involves the self-protection guaranteed by virtue of an allegorising gaze on the part of the subject that supports a narcissistic desire for unity and an oscillation between roles. While the masculine subject preserves itself based on an illusion of being all, the feminine subject preserves itself by maintaining its status of 'not one', of a double, divided and shifting subject position between references, a stable position being as fatal to her as it is healing to the man.

Relating woman to the radically Other means identifying her with the infinite, the unknown, with the unconscious as absence, as a gap or a negation.[14] While gender identification allows the masculine subject to repress his relation to the unconscious, positions him as whole, woman's gender identification positions her in relation to two overlapping lacks. Her 'not all', her 'other-than-man', her lack of the masculine signifier for wholeness (the phallus) is the stake on which a social construction of gender difference is based. At the same time her identification with sexuality points to the biological constitution of the human being, where all bodies are 'lacking' in respect to the law of mortality, in a real sense.

Woman is ambivalently placed in the position of culture's truth, more directly 'divided' or split by symbolic laws, interdictions, language and closer to the real lack traced by mortality, even as she is also the symptom by which masculine culture can repress or displace this truth. Positioned within the register of paternal law, the masculine subject protects itself against the threat of the double wound inflicted by social laws and that of death, by virtue of precisely the construction of gender oppositions and the allegorisation of the Other. As cultural construct, Woman is symptom for the hope of masculine wholeness and because her relation to death is seen as a relation to Otherness, she enacts precisely the fact that this relation is missing from the masculine; that masculinity is constructed as that which lacks death. The cultural construction of gender functions as a superlative example for the illusory hope that by culturally placing 'lack', 'doubleness' and 'division' on the side of the feminine, real lack is exteriorised as well.

Of course Lacan's equation of Woman and the unconscious, as the truth barred from culture, the Other, can either elucidate difference and lack at the centre of subjectivity or create a mystification of Woman as enigma, can serve either as the disruptive point of a system or as that which fully confirms and assures it.[15] One of the paradoxes Lacan's typology poses, Heath points out, is that 'what is designated as unrepresentable is what is finally the most strongly represented, an absence or lack named and figured as such, a real which comes back to the subject in its system, its suture of symbolic and imaginary'.[16] In so far as this 'unrepresentable' refers simultaneously to femininity and death, in its allegorisation of the place of the Other, of the truth of man, we return to the question of the pleonasm.

Three types of femininity presided over the literary imagination of the nineteenth century: firstly, the diabolic outcast, the destructive, fatal demon woman, secondly, the domestic 'angel of the house', the saintly, self-sacrificing frail vessel, and thirdly a particular version of Mary Magdalene, as the penitent and redeemed sexually vain and dangerous woman, the fallen woman. It is significant, however, that the feminine perfection, excess because it lies beyond the human, and its counterpart, the feminine monster, excess in that it falls short of the cultural code's limit, can be seen as medium for the death drive. The first type, demonstrating, in imitation of the Virgin Mary and Christian martyrs, how physical weakness, self-sacrifice and self-denial taken to the sheer materiality of the body fading into absence serve as proof of physical and spiritual purity, can be seen as embodying fantasies of a masochistic turning inward of the death drive that results in a self-negation and self-obliteration. Though these fading, ethereal women types, of which Little Nell and Little Eva would be examples, contradict the Virgin Mary's attribute of body wholeness beyond any physical inhabitation by death, they too serve as mediators and intercessors for men's souls. Their death purifies the sins of the living and, as angels, they help the living prepare for heaven by leading them to death. The suffering and diseased feminine invalid, dying of self-effacing inanition can, Dijkstra notes, be seen as 'the perfect representative of woman as Christ figure'.[17]

The second type can be understood, instead, in the sense of a fear of Woman as being an incarnation of a sadistic turning outward of the death drive, transferring aggressive violence from the self to the feminine lover, to which he reciprocates by destroying her. Positioned in between the innocent, ethereal feminine type, staging an excessive absence of artifice or a fading of body, and the witch, the demonic feminine type staging an excessive presence of the dangers of the body and the duplicity of artifice, the seduced, penitent and redeemed 'fallen woman' is also an agent or medium of the death drive. Not only because her 'fall' implies an introduction to Eve's sin, and thus physical as well as spiritual decay, but also because her cultural representation often presented death as the necessary climax to the fallen woman's trajectory. Whether the semantic coding of the feminine involves the purity of the fading loss of body, the danger of an excessive bodiliness or the conjunction of the two, the death drive which is given presence is secured into absence when death translates the typified woman into the perfect allegorical type, where body is completely missing.

Countless examples could be given to illustrate how the death of a woman helps to regenerate the order of society, to eliminate destructive forces or serves to reaggregate the protagonist into her or his community. A common pattern emerges even if the cultural values that are connected with the dead woman and debated in connection with her death vary. When the topos of martyrdom serves as model for the narrative, then the death of the innocent, virtuous woman, as in the case of Clarissa, appears inculpatory as well as edifying and soothing to the spectators, who undertake a pilgrimage to the dying body. The potential for change is shifted away from the self on to the signifier of the sacrificed body so as to be transferred into the existing order without fundamentally changing it.

Another kind of recuperation, in respect to threatening, because undomesticated or irrational aspects of nature, occurs when a figure like Carmen, unable or unwilling to comply with assigned role behaviour, is punished or sacrificed. A woman may also consciously break conventions or commit a crime punished with death, such as adultery, infanticide or murder, as an expression of liberating subjectivity, of assuming authorship and responsibility for her destiny. The following analysis of Charlotte Brontë's *Jane Eyre* (1847) is meant to be a paradigmatic illustration of the conjunction of femininity, semantically encoded as a metonymy for death, with the feminine character's ambivalent position – divided, shifting, contradictory – as the uncanny figure traced by death, in order to show how this conjunction culminates in the sacrifice of the feminine agent of disturbance.

In the course of her education from orphanage to marriage, Jane Eyre occupies various positions of social liminality that include encounters with death. I will focus only on the two equally liminal feminine figures who embody extremities of death's agency: the orphan Helen Burns, whose desire for death stages a 'masochistic' violence against the self, a total subjugation before cultural laws, and Bertha Rochester, the bodily living though socially dead wife, who embodies a defiance of cultural laws that translates into a 'sadistic' violence against others. In her own liminality as orphan and maiden, Jane is divided between these two figures of death, as her two 'Others', and, provoked by an identification, she can confront aspects of the death drive within herself. Yet she must also mitigate this Otherness to survive and to enter a fixed position in her social order. The logic of the text implies that in their extremity these two women are not only objects of punishment, but must ultimately also be destroyed. While Bertha reflects in extremity Jane's excessive passion, her destructive impulses of hatred and vengeance which must be corrected, Helen reflects her shy, frightened self-abnegation which must be transformed to boldness. Jane learns from each of her doubles that value which will mitigate the extremity of the other.

Jane's first impression of Helen is of an ignominiously punished girl who bears her degradation with gravity and composure, whose gaze is directed 'beyond her punishment', beyond 'what is really present' (84). Living the posture of a martyr she not only completely submits to the laws of Lowood School, endures her punishment patiently and forgives the cruelty of her teachers, but also fully acknowledges the legitimacy of their chastisement. This leads her to see herself as 'wretchedly defective', slatternly, careless, lacking method (88).

In two senses she lives more in reference to death than to life, is divided between and inhabited by two agencies of death. Her propensity to dream lets her privilege the past, lost and absent world of her childhood, the 'dead' memory images, over the present, so that she is metaphorically more with the dead, 'beyond' the living. At the same time, her total obedience to her punishers obliterates all narcissistic self-preservation and lets her identify so exclusively with the guilt they induce, that her superego, Freud's punishing conscience, has been entrenched with destructive components to such a degree that it becomes the site of 'a pure culture of the death drive'. Because the logical consequence of her stigmatisation as 'defective' would be a destruction of herself and because the objects of her desire are not among the living, what Helen in fact desires is death as an agency of radical Otherness, beyond or more than the paternal law, beyond Lacan's 'phallic' referent. This excessive and exclusive embrace of death lets narcissistic impulses like revenge and degradation appear inconsequential – 'I live in calm, looking to the end' (91). In this active not passive self-denial she strikes Jane as a 'martyr, a hero', against her own posture of 'slave or victim' (99), a warning against the indulgence of resentment and fury.

Her ultimate form of death, consumption, enacts, at the body, her belief in the supremacy of the spiritual, and her disinterest in her corruptible 'frame of flesh'. Her gradual etherealisation also serves as the symptom of a guilt-induced turning of the death drive against herself. Given that Helen dies in Jane's arms while the other sleeps, and that Jane wakes to find her body missing, may indicate that, though she has embraced the aspects of death which Helen incorporates, she must also renounce this in its extremity. Not only is her direct knowledge of death barred – she hears of her embrace of the corpse belatedly. She will also use her memory of Helen's dying to understand subsequent deaths, notably that of her foster mother Mrs Reed, to assert her own survivial, and will replace, at the end of her own liminality, the unmarked grassy mound with a 'grey marble tablet' bearing Helen's name and the word 'Resurgam'. This final mark is a social aggregation of a woman who remained marginalised during her life. It is the gift of a signifier that marks her existence but only as an absent body.[18]

In contrast to Helen's self-renunciation and excessive spirituality enacted in a self-destructive fading of the body, Bertha Rochester is an agent of the death drive as a sadistic impulse turned outward with an emphasis on the big, corpulent, virile body conjoined with extreme vengeance and passion. Where Helen obeys the law to such an excessive degree that she literally becomes its vanishing point, Bertha is that which disrupts the law and is abjected, an agency of Freud's murderous Id. Her form of self-articulation, her preternatural laugh, her eccentric murmurs, her threatening 'snarling, snatching sound', in fact recall Kristeva's concept of the 'semiotic chora'. For her husband she is all that lies below acceptable femininity, the feminine body as dangerous Other to man; a cunning and malignant lunatic, a maniac, a monster, a wild beast, a goblin, a fury. Because she 'castrated' him socially, 'sullied' his name, 'outraged' his honour, 'blighted' his youth and threatens his life, she is a superlative figure of death.

Like the perfect feminine body of Helen, excessive in that her spiritualisation places it beyond the human, this monstrous feminine body, polluted because Creole, because 'bad, mad and embruted' – equally excessive in that it falls short of the 'expected' code – can be maintained in the social order only as a dead body. In the first stage Bertha, like Helen, occupies the liminal position of a social death, not dead-in-life as the latter, but rather living though interred in an attic, termed 'dead and buried' by her husband in an effort to have her 'identity . . . buried in oblivion' (336). Her abode is perceived by Jane as a 'home of the past – a shrine of memory', as the 'haunt of Thornfield Hall's ghost', a vault, 'a corridor in some Bluebeard's castle' (138). Where Helen 'fed' off her dead ancestors, Bertha feeds off the living, bites and draws blood from her brother, repeatedly threatens the life of her husband, and embodies a return of what they would like to repress, yet what, in Jane's words 'could neither be expelled nor subdued by the owner' (239). In her perception, Bertha is a figure of ambivalence, appearing alternately as a foul, ghastly spectre or vampire, between living and dead, and as a figure of which she can't at first sight tell whether it is 'beast or human . . . it snatched and growled like some strange wild animal: but it was covered with clothing' (321). In this position of nominally dead woman, Bertha is also analogous to Jane, whose foster mother spread the news of her death of a typhus fever at Lowood in order to prohibit an inheritance.

Bertha can be seen as Jane's darkest double, as her ferocious secret self, who appears whenever an experience of anger or fear arises on Jane's part that must again be repressed. Acting for and like Jane, she enacts the violence Jane would like but can't express, especially in respect to marriage.[19] I would like to shift the focus away from Bertha's literal madness and sexual threat to the fact of her figural 'death', and suggest that she also articulates Jane's fears and desires about her own mortality. Significantly her presence at Jane's bed on the night before her marriage induces the 'second' loss of consciousness in Jane's life and points back to the scene in the red room, Mr Reed's death chamber, where she falls insensible because she fears the dead man's ghost; because she fears the uncanny presence of death as an intimation of her own physical demise. Bertha's existence introduces a fatal division into the harmonious unity between Jane and Rochester, turns Jane's cherished wishes of marriage into 'stark, chill, livid corpses that could never revive' (324) and prolongs her own social liminality.

Like Helen's, Bertha's death is also symptomatic of the aspect of death she incorporates; namely of the unstructured, diffuse aggressive drives that must be controlled and restrained for culture to exist. In an effort to totalise her destruction of her external world, Bertha sets fire to Thornfield Hall and standing on the roof, triumphing over her fatal creation, 'waving her arms above the battlements and shouting', she recedes from her husband's call to safety, synonymous with the social death of interment, to embrace real death instead; 'she yelled and gave a spring, and the next minute she lay smashed on the pavement' (453). While for Helen death is the liberation from potential suffering, procured by her sense of social defectiveness, and her body as 'corruptible and cumbrous', Bertha's death is a last exertion of that body equally termed by others as socially defective and physically corrupt. For both, the second, real death puts closure on their liminality and the disruption their presence caused. From the logic of the plot, they signify those aspects of femininity along with unmitigated death, that ground notions of 'normal' femininity as well as grounding the survivor's attitude to mortality, while, owing to their extremity, they must also be eliminated.

Precisely by virtue of their respective deaths, Jane can triumph over her inwardly and outwardly directed aggressive impulses. These 'sacrifices' allow her to externalise securely her own proclivity towards destruction by focusing her own violence on these two 'victims' or extreme versions of herself, and burying it along with each of the two feminine corpses. To signify the end of her own liminality, Jane emerges from her position of ambivalence by drawing a safe boundary between herself and the two women whose bodies figuratively and then literally marked the site of death's presence in life, so that their demise secures Jane's triumph over her own ambivalent position in her world as well as her anxiety about and her desire for death.

While Helen and Bertha remain positioned within social liminality and divided, in Lacan's sense, between the paternal, social law and the radical Otherness of death, Jane, survivor, heiress and wife, ultimately takes on a fixed position within the masculine symbolic order. She functions as a hero in Lotman's typlogical sense, in that she enters into death, in her encounter with two feminine figures of death, only to be socially 'reborn'. What is enacted as the novel's plot unfolds is that society requires a violent but recuperative regulation of the violence of death's presence as this is condensed, along with other aspects of difference such as 'non-white race', 'physical and mental illness' at the bodies of two 'defective,' not assimilable feminine members. What is implied is that Jane's psychic and social education requires not only an encounter with death, in the form of identificatory doubles, but also a destruction of death enacted successfully by virtue of their sacrifice.

The two feminine figures of death, once sacrificed, provoke regeneration, though not without leaving scars – in the form of the gravestone Jane erects for Helen, in the form of the burnt mansion that incites public gossip about Bertha Rochester. The social signifiers that result from a 'sacrificial' death (and one could include Jane Eyre's own narrative as confession), assign a fixed position within the newly established social order to the disruption each woman traced, but can do so only by translating the marginalised into figures of Otherness, of excessive purity or excessive pollution. They are uncanny scars because they can 'mark the spot' and acknowledge the presence of these two feminine bodies previously positioned ambivalently between life and death only once the bodies of both are definitely missing.

Jane Eyre illustrates the most conventional association of femininity with death – the innocent, passive, fading woman as signifier for the desired Otherness of the sublime and the powerful, self-assertive woman as signifier for the threatening Otherness of the body, of nature, of sexuality. Apart from standing for contradictory values Woman, however, also stands for ambivalence as value, and in that sense she is not just a figure of death but the rhetorical figuration of death in narrative. Her ambivalence is such that she merges various psychic registers, serving as the source of the imaginary, as the body that allegorically figures ideas of Otherness in the symbolic, yet whose Otherness also positions her in the non-semiotic real, as the limit of signification, the exteriorised factor which grounds the system. As a metonymy for that which has no fixture, the sacrificed woman translates the disruptive into the system, giving it a fixed position, regardless of whether the normative order is assured or critiqued. However, as aspects of the self or the community are expulsed in the condensation of death and femininity at the body of the Other, we are left with an uncanny sense of ambivalence. Does the recuperated homogeneity contain difference and/or its negation? Is the Other safely outside, or still uncannily present despite all efforts at closure. Is Woman conjoined with death as a way to articulate real difference or to exclude Otherness and difference? The pleonasm 'feminine death' also stands for the force which simultaneously supports and undercuts attempts to construct oppositions like uncanny interiority/canny exteriority.

Notes to Chapter 10

1 H. Cixous, 1981, pp. 44–45.
2 A. Alvarez, 1971, pp. 156–8.
3 R. Barthes, 1977, p. 90.
4 T. de Lauretis, 1984, p. 13. I use 'absence' and 'death' interchangeably, following the psychoanalytic model discussed in chapter 2.
5 B. Johnson, 1987.
6 T. de Lauretis, 1984.
7 J. Lacan, 1985, p. 49. In the following, my discussion is based above all on J. Lacan, 1975, but, as far as possible, my quotes will be from the translation by J. Rose, J. Lacan, 1985.

8 J. Lacan, 'Seminar of 21 Jan. 1975', 1985, p. 168. In 'A Love Letter', 1985, he writes, 'What was seen, but only from the side of the man, was that what he relates to is the *objet a*, and that the whole of his realisation in the sexual relation comes down to fantasy . . . when one is a man, one sees in one's partner what can serve, narcissistically, to act as one's own support.'

9 J. Rose, 'Introduction – II', J. Lacan, 1985.

10 J. Rose, 1986, p. 219.

11 S. Melville, 1987, pp. 355–7.

12 J. Lacan, 1975.

13 J. Lacan, 1985. These positions are, of course, 'constructions'. The anatomical female characters may well be in the narcissistic position of the split subject and a male character, subjected to the paternal law or the law of death may equally assume the position of the 'barred' woman.

14 E. Ragland-Sullivan, 1987.

15 Lacan's formulation, 1985, that woman is 'not all' is also meant in the sense that, though an absolute category, woman is short of any qualification. Rose suggests that Lacan's reference to woman as Other is in danger of collapsing two moments – 'that which assigns woman to the negative place of its own (phallic) system, and that which asks the question as to whether woman might, as a very effect of that assignation, break against and beyond that system itself', p. 52.

16 S. Heath, 1978, p. 82.

17 B. Dijkstra, 1986, p. 33.

18 For a different discussion of Helen's death see, R. Keefe, 1979.

19 S. Gilbert and S. Gubar, 1979.

11

Close encounters of a fatal kind

Allegory thereby declares itself to be beyond beauty. Allegories are, in the realm of thoughts, what ruins are in the realm of things.
Walter Benjamin

Though it has become almost a commonplace to invoke Lévi-Strauss when speaking of woman as a privileged commodity within culture, I do so in order to demonstrate the ambivalences inscribed into any acts of exchange, where a body is transformed into a sign. As Lévi-Strauss explains, 'there is no need to call upon the matrimonial vocabulary of Great Russia, where the groom was called the "merchant" and the bride, the "merchandise" for the likening of women to commodities, not only scarce but essential to the life of the group, to be acknowledged'.[1] His basic premise is that exogamy, acting permanently and continually, is 'the archetype of all other manifestations based on reciprocity, and that it provides the fundamental and immutable rule ensuring the existence of the group as a group'. Because marital exchange forms the basis of all other systems of exchange women are seen as valuables *par excellence* 'without which life is impossible, or, at best . . . reduced to the worst forms of abjection'.[2]

The exchange Lévi-Strauss is concerned with here is in fact a double one – both socio-economic and semiotic. The Woman is bartered in the first place so that a bond between father or brother and bridegroom may be established and the existence of the community ensured. This act of exchange is in turn symbolic, for the Woman is bartered not only as a physically real body but also as a sign referring to something more and something other than her corporality. Into the double status of Woman – because bearer of an economic and a semiotic value – Lévi-Strauss introduces a second collapse of categories by adding 'woman could never become just a sign and nothing more, since even in a man's world she is still a person, and since in so far as she is defined as a sign she must be recognized as a generator of signs'.[3] Woman contributes to culture as a sign, and functions as its protective stake, even as she serves as the generator of signs, and as the source of cultural exchange. Woman is valuable *par excellence* because of her double function as body and as trope, as semiotic source and economic stake, blurring any fixed boundaries between these two functions and making indetermination one of the signifieds of this sign.

Within this collapse of the economic and the semiotic orders, a crucial displacement occurs. While the signifier is the woman's body, the substance or meaning of the sign, its signified, is not the concept Woman.[4] The primary signified of 'Woman-as-sign' is instead the establishment or recuperation of kinship structures and culture. Yet the ambivalent status of this sign is such that it also marks a self-reflexive moment within the process of signification to become a signifer for exchange itself. If 'Woman as sign' evokes a self-reflexive turn because this trope articulates the economics of semiotics, the configuration 'dead woman as sign' – 'sign as death of the woman' unfolds yet another aspect of the pleonasm at the heart of this conjunction. A work about death not only modulates readily into a work about literature but also into one about exchange The more obvious signified themes – erotic, economic or semiotic exchange – transpire into a displaced trope for the exchange between life and death. The value of the exchanged feminine body resides precisely in the multi-levelled ambiguity that this kind of exchange implies.

Even though stability is the aim of this double exchange, the means for gaining order involves that which lacks a fixed place, for the body can be traded as a sign only on the basis of a continual slippage between any stable distinction between the two. This inability or unwillingness to secure a fundamental difference between concrete bodies and figural signs not only engenders their uncanny interchangeability but also allows one level of meaning to be substituted arbitrarily and sometimes incorrectly for another, a form of blindness endemic to allegory. As Hillis Miller points out, the duplicity involved in this particular tropic turn of 'speaking otherwise' is such that word becomes flesh in allegory, even as flesh becomes word, the word either preceding its incarnation or the embodiment generating a spiritual meaning.[5] This confusion of body and sign becomes the rule ensuring the production and dissemination of meaning that is the basis on which aesthetic and hermeneutic activities depend. Only due to this confusion can women's bodies be simultaneously the generators of signs and the signs themselves. But the theme of a necessary 'exchange' also exposes corollary violations and dangers. The exchange of female bodies and the forms of exchange occurring at their bodies prove how fatal it can be to confuse a body with a sign. As each heroine's body is gazed at, deciphered, imitated, and ultimately replaced by something else, as physical inscription passes into metaphorical inscription or vice versa, the troping involved either engenders the protagonist's death or results from it.

Although it is the two male parties giving or taking the valuable – Woman, as object received, is engaged in the exchange as well. Even if she is not the instigating agent she is nevertheless implicated in the pass or substitution. She is a form of payment, but she also pays, by turning herself into the agent disposing of her body. When Hardy uses the phrase 'the woman pays' as title for the fifth phase of *Tess of the D'Urbervilles*, he is referring to its figural meaning. The heroine is primarily held responsible for transgressions in which she has been involved and punished with the death sentence. In this exchange she is substituted for the other guilty person. Although the figural meaning points to her passive function as receiver, the literal meaning of the phrase suggests an active act of giving, implicitly in return for or in response to something. While the figural reading suggests she is paid to secure the serenity of her community, the literal reading indicates that a purchase is made, that on some level she too gains something.

Given that the woman is implicated not only as the pivotal though essentially passive object in an exchange, but that she may also turn into the subject and producer of this exchange yet another ambivalence emerges. The notion of a remuneratory exchange blurs the difference between active and passive, giving and receiving, responding and inflicting. While a root word for paying is *pacare* (to pacify) the fact that many instances of feminine payment in cultural representations revolve around and result in death, suggests that pacification always also implies violence and violation. Revenge, one could say, is a form of payment in which exchange, violence and appeasement most prominently intersect. It is significant that the form revenge most often takes is the transformation of a woman's body into a sign, by others and by herself. The point where violence enters into the exchange also forms the link between the institutionalising action of exogamy, which turns Woman into a commodity, and the cultural project of representation, which turns her into a trope. The aporia articulated is that, even as a turn to allegory is a way to give fixture and externalise the disruptive element, this stability is negotiated by virtue of an exchange based on the inability to draw a distinction between concrete and abstract. It demystifies any attempt to fix the boundary between the pure and the decaying, between life and death, even as it constructs a mythic text from which the body of the woman, in its historical reference, is missing.

In the previous chapters I have discussed the way culture employs sacrifice to externalise disruptive forces by turning a 'victim-body' into the trope for Otherness. I will turn to two novels by Hardy, *Far from the Madding Crowd* (1874) and *Tess of the D'Urbervilles* (1891), to illustrate another strategy of self-protection and self-generation. By virtue of an 'allegorising gaze' the Other, the woman's body, can be translated into a sign whose signified is the spectator's need for an eradication of difference and disturbance from a personal or collective sense of self. Both her living and her dead body is treated primarily as a text, and this depersonalising sight induces a blindness towards the body's physical materiality. On the one hand, the living female body is viewed allegorically by others as though it were a figure or representation that in part always reflects and sustains the narcissism of the viewer; by virtue, that is, of a tropic 'mortification' of the body. The feminine tissue is treated like a page on to which lovers, society's laws or the repressed past write themselves. On the other hand, feminine corpses are treated like sites of inscription that must be deciphered. As they pose a hermeneutic task, the reading that evolves also transpires into a self-portrait of the survivors. In the second instance the dead body functions as the necessary prerequisite for the aesthetic and hermeneutic process. The first instance implies that a process of perception that objectifies and depersonalises a body 'kills' substance to make it signify, 'mortifies' bodies into tropes. A somatisation of the idea allows an allegorical reading to emerge.

In both instances the uncanny doubling is such that the body is 'missing' from the signification, absent as signified even though it is physically present, and again the issues raised are not just socio-economic but also semiotic. In her discussion of language as a defensive construction against the death drive underlying it, Kristeva emphasises that signification protects against the death drive through 'narcissistic, specular, imaginary investment' by taking it out of the body and translating the body into a signifier. By virtue of this transition, the chaotic and inexpressible real experience can take on an ordered and intelligible form, inducing a release from the violence of the unstructured semiotic chora, of the real beyond semiosis.[6] While the death drive tends to disrupt narcissism, the gesture of narcissism in turn ensures life and acts as an antidote against the knowledge of one's own death, in the sense that it protects the self either against the unconscious drives or against death as the severity of the law. Significantly both aspects of narcissistic self-protection are sustained by an allegorisation of the feminine body – either by using an allegorising gaze to turn it into a reflection and completion of the self (eradicating any difference between self and Other, any difference within) or by turning it into an allegorical figure of Otherness, drawing a solid boundary between the self and difference, which is externalised in the process.

Barthes transforms this general problem of signification as an exchange between absence and presence, into a description of the semiotics of myth. Reversing his argument that myth turns meaning into a speaking corpse, I will suggest that speaking corpses produce mythic meaning not only in that, as he suggests, they sever meaning from the facticity of a historical context and provoke the artificial reprieve of language that won't die. These figurative and literal corpses speak in the same shift between signifier (body) and signified (secondary meaning) that Barthes proposes for myth. The presence of the body is put at a distance, recedes, its subjectivity is put into parenthesis, made almost transparent so that it can make room for the concept it is used to signify. In this exchange the body seems to die, yet 'it is a death with reprieve', it 'loses its value, but keeps its life, from which the form of the myth will draw its nourishment'.[7] The 'distortion' myth works with is that the deformation occurring in the tropic process is not an obliteration, the body/signifier remains (analogous to the living remains of the deceased). The body is 'deprived of history, changed into a gesture', remains present in the representation though devoid of its meaning. Both the 'feminine corpse-as-text' and myth are based on what Barthes calls a 'duplicity of the signifier' – the form (body) is empty but present, secondary meaning absent, unreal but full.

A central aporia, however, inhabits allegory as a rhetorical strategy given that this figure is also structured around a duplicity of the signifier. Speaking in other terms it reveals a secondary meaning even as it hides a primary one, so that one of its signifieds is difference itself[8] – either in reference to the literal meaning, the body that must 'disappear,' or in reference to the difference between the body and the figurative meaning it makes room for. By stressing its internal difference, as a disjunction between signified meaning and signifier, allegory points to the gap which is inscribed in all production of meaning. To interpret the literal body, in its alterity to the spectator, as 'meaningful', it must be translated into another mode, yet it always also articulates the 'fictitiousness' of interpretation. Not only because the historicity and subjectivity of the body in question are different from the way they spoken 'in figure', but also because they point to the fact that personification of the abstract, such as death, in a sense also fails to express univocally the truth beyond and ungraspable by language because it can never rid itself of the other body, the signifier. Both death and femininity are articulated as this alterity, present in the void or difference between these two levels. Not only in the sense that allegory only imperfectly articulates the abstract, eternal signifieds of alterity such as death, but more importantly in the sense that because this trope demystifies the blindness it induces, the effaced as effaced can emerge. The enigmatic face of the 'Inconnue' demonstrates both points – the need to turn a body into 'another mode' to satisfy one's interpretive needs and the failure inherent in this enterprise, in that the banality of the material signifier, the plaster cast, is never entirely effaced. Its excess lies in the fact that it could be seen as an allegory of the allegorising interpretive process. In that allegory has as one of its signifieds difference, it fragments that wholeness, for the illusory production of which it is invoked in the first place. Because it is a mode of figurative speaking that emphasises difference (other speaking) and a truth beyond language (radical Otherness), allegory emerges as one of the movements by which death is rhetorically articulated in language.

In my reading of the two novels by Hardy I will return to two aspects of allegory as they coalesce with the semiotics inherent in an exchange of feminine bodies. On the one hand a gaze which protects by producing a blindness to disturbing Otherness is seen as following one strategy of allegory – the blindness toward the body/signifier, a privileging of the second meaning, the suspension of the first, or a confusion between the two. On the other hand, allegorisation articulates precisely the difference and incompatibility between material base (body) and spiritual meaning (signified), the blindness it evokes yet also demystifies. Because of the doubleness of allegory, however, the blindness toward the material base also fails and this trope not only shows the effort of language to protect against the death drive located in non-semiotic matter by translating it into a signifier, but also the failure of this process, as materiality returns, reasserts itself against any alterior meaning, by materialising the signifier. It points to the fact that something is beyond the distance and 'mortification' that this speaking figure produces, that allegory is also 'not all' there is of a designation. Allegory can be understood, like the fetish, as an uncanny trope in that it too articulates ambivalence as the displaced sign for the death drive. Given that 'not all' emerges as the position one could ascribe to allegory, when the material base, hidden and returning in this figure, is the feminine/dead body, this process turns into one of rhetorical pleonastic excess.

In *Far from the Madding Crowd* Fanny Robin's passage from living body to corpse can ironically be seen as one from near-silent invisibility to speaking visibility. The first mention of her name is in connection with her disappearance (103). In a gesture prophetic of the way body and story come together to form a symbolic unity only at her death, Gabriel gives money to an 'unknown woman,' who wishes to remove all traces of her body – 'let your having seen me be a secret' (88) – and learns to attach a name to her only after her absence, that is only to her image stored in his memory. Throughout the rest of her corporeal existence Robin will never again be directly addressed by her name except clandestinely by Troy. To have her name publicly attached to her body will be the privilege of the corpse.

Instead what follows is a series of incidents that confirm her process of disembodiment. In the scene at Troy's barracks she is described as a 'small form' that seems human, a 'little shape', a 'blurred spot in the snow' (119f.). This is followed by her marked corporeal absence at the wedding ceremony and the equally marked absence in the text of a description of her first sexual experience.[9] When she reappears she continues to remain anonymous – a woman. Though Troy recognises her on the road and consents to meet her, he will not openly acknowledge knowing her name. Her last living hours are spent travelling unseen and unaided by all but a dog until at the door of the poor-house she becomes a 'prostrate figure', an impersonalised traveller, a 'small and supple one'. What can be read as an ultimate confirmation of the way her corporeal presence is disavowed, negated and exchanged for a belated acknowledgement is the second significant narrative ellipsis – her birth-giving and death. Once a corpse Fanny makes her first and only public statement. She 'speaks' the story she could not tell while alive and becomes present and visible.[10] Fanny, who is not skilful at using linguistic signs, can only signify through her body by establishing a perfect corollary between signifier (body) and signified (her story). But the price for this achieved signification is death.

The chapter in which Fanny's corpse is exposed bears the provocative title 'Fanny's Revenge' (319ff). This suggests that we are to understand her death both as a form of paying for the transgression committed by her and as a form of paying Troy back for the trespass he committed at her body. Her speaking corpse embodies the past Troy has tried to keep secret and on a very literal level inflicts an irreparable wound upon his marriage to Bathsheba in retribution for the wound inflicted on her by Troy (the abandonment) that resulted in such a violent form of death. As a corpse Fanny changes from a disembodied and depersonalised object of actions inflicted on her to the subject of an action – her revenge.

But the title can also be read ambiguously to suggest that the move that lets Fanny become an active subject in the story of her life is almost immediately subverted by a counter-move on the part of her survivors, which turns her again into a non-determined, depersonalised figure, functioning as a register of the others' responses. While it is made evident that as a corpse she poses 'a hermeneutic task', the question remains whether those reading her ever really look for her story, whether the signified is the historical subject Fanny or each spectator's projection. The workman Cogan's response is the first indicating that any meaning assigned to a corpse must ultimately be allegorical. By way of defending Joseph, who stopped for a drink rather than driving Fanny's corpse directly to the graveyard, he explains 'Nobody can hurt a dead woman . . . The woman's past us – time spent upon her is thrown away: why should we hurry to do what's not required? Drink, shepherd, and be friends, for to-morrow we may be like her' (315). He does not see the corpse as a concrete body but as a *memento mori*, a sign that speaks 'other' than itself – precisely as an allegory signifying the urgency to enjoy life.

While the responses Fanny's corpse elicits from the two characters most implicated in her death are complex, they ultimately take the same turn, and as such raise the metapoetical issues the analogy between text and corpse entails. In order to elucidate both the challenge Fanny's dead body poses to her survivors and the impossibility of looking at her with anything but an allegorising gaze, I will turn to the two stages Blanchot delineates for the surveyal of a corpse. The first is a fundamental destabilising of established categories of reference and position. The corpse is neither the living person nor someone else, is neither present nor absent, is 'nowhere'. At the site/sight of the corpse, the real destabilises and ruptures accepted cultural forms of symbolic codes. The strangeness of the corpse's presence, which promises to furnish an insight into that not yet known, however, quickly becomes a form of resemblance. The corpse is translated into a representation of the corpse, the 'choratic soma' into a signifier outside or Other than the body. The dead body resembles its former self.[11]

From the start Bathsheba feels 'a strange complication of impulses' toward Fanny's corpse. When she finally opens the coffin she does so in an effort to find the 'truth' of the story suggested by this death and asks 'speak and tell me your secret, Fanny!' Yet the 'conclusive proof of her husband's conduct' that this double-corpse offers does not as she thinks cast light 'beyond doubt' on the last chapter of Fanny's story. The moment of strangeness and insight experienced at the corpse quickly translates into one of self-recognition, as Fanny is allegorised into a figure of triumph – 'in Bathsheba's wild imagining (fate had turned) her companion's failure to success, her humiliation to triumph, her lucklessness to ascendency; it had thrown over herself a garish light of mockery, and set upon all things about her an ironical smile . . . In Bathsheba's heated fancy the innocent white countenance expressed a dim triumphant consciousness of the pain she was retaliating for her pain.' Light is only cast on Bathsheba's misconception about her marriage, so painful because it subverts her notion of being superior, unique and original and shows her to be but a repetition, a supplement of her rival. Both the vindictive hatred she feels towards the corpse and the gesture of atonement – she lays flowers around the dead girl's head – indicate that for her the corpse is a cipher on to which she can project a range of conflicting emotions. In that Fanny's historical body is missing, it works on the basis of the 'duplicity of the signifier' informing the mythic/allegoric sign – an empty present body-signifier expressing an absent, full meaning.

Troy, caught in a similarly allegorising mode of gazing, uses Fanny's corpse to demonstrate his remorse and reverence, by exchanging the previous public disavowal with an exaggerated and eccentric acknowledgement. In his confrontation with Bathsheba he not only confesses that Fanny was a previous lover but idealises her into the supreme and only love of his life – 'This woman is more to me, dead as she is, than ever you were, or are, or can be . . . You are nothing to me – nothing.' The bitter secret about Troy that is revealed ultimately deals less with his infidelity and deception than with his valorising the female trope at the expense of the female body. The exchange between figural and literal is such that Bathsheba becomes 'nothing' at the sight of Fanny's body decomposing into nothing, while Fanny becomes the valuable lover, not although but because she is 'dead as she is.' In what is a perfect final act in his exchange with Fanny, Troy engraves on to the tombstone marking her grave himself as subject and Fanny as reflecting object of the utterance – 'Erected by Francis Troy in Beloved Memory of Fanny Robin' (346). This kind of cliché public confession not only seems contingent on its object's death but ultimately serves the function of a romantic self-display. It is supremely allegorical – speaking of other things in public, 'keeping secret in the act of making public'.[12]

While Fanny's corpse ruptures the stability of Bathsheba and Troy's marriage, their allegorising gaze immediately translates it into a representation, which in turn serves as the site for self-recognition and self-presentation, and simultaneously effaces the reality of the corpse. The other 'secret' Fanny's corpse reveals is then concerned with how the articulation of violence in representation always also contains the moment of its own failure. The corpse's ability to signify goes hand in hand with the reader's ability to mistake it for a twofold sign – in part speaking literally, that is the story of her pregnancy and death, and in part speaking other, that is the version of death's meaning each viewer chooses to read into her. In both cases, however, signification requires that alterior meaning can only emerge uncannily at the cost of the material body, semiotically absent though visually present. While the fatal misdemeanor in Fanny's story is that Troy can acknowledge her only as an inanimate body, as a set of characters inscribed on a tombstone, forcing her literally to change her body into a sign before she can be recognised, his allegorising gaze also affords peace.

The discussion of *Far From the Madding Crowd* suggests that the analogy between corpse and trope exposes two allegorising processes, structurally distinct and yet having the same kind of effacement as their goal. In the first, the movement is from animate body to a deanimated corpse, which then functions as a sign and instrument of revenge: Fanny turning herself into a 'speaking corpse.' In the second process the movement is from the deanimated body of the corpse to a sign or narrative. When Bathsheba and Troy turn Fanny's corpse into a figure of triumph, the process of allegorisation becomes part of an act of resurrection that benefits the survivors by defusing and revising the old and affirming the new. In this act of disembodiment the figure of the corpse is refigured in a new vein, narrative. The corpse performs a double function – it is both an allegory and the real dead body that precedes language as its ground and vanishing point. Moreover, the act of resurrection when the corpse as sign is exchanged for a narrative, proves also to be a veiled instance of revenge, precisely because it robs the corpse of its initially invested semantic value which wreaked the first revenge. By detaching the dead woman from her self-inscribed corpse, and with it from her revenge, the second allegory works its revenge on her and her process of allegorisation; it undoes both the reality of the corpse and the first allegory of the corpse, induced by Fanny's detextualisation. One exchange is exchanged for another, at a moment when the implicated woman is once again passive and cannot pay back, but only be paid back. This second form of allegorisation displays the survivor's privilege of having the last word which, to reformulate Roland Barthes, liquidates and disorganises the adversary, inflicts upon her a 'narcissistically' moral wound, covers her in silence and rapes her speech.[13]

Though, in contrast to Fanny, Tess is never exposed as a corpse, she is from the start a woman sought out by and so forced into an exchange with the dead, who choose at her body to have their 'sport'. Through the parson's discovery that Durbeyfield derives from the signature D'Urberville, the 'ancient and knightly family' rise from their vault to claim kinship with their poor descendants. When Tess later says of these ancestors 'she almost hated them for the dance they had led her' (156), she points to another aspect of allegory informing this novel – the Dance of Death motif. As Tess becomes the privileged object of an economic, erotic and semiotic exchange, her story becomes an allegory of the process of dying, an interplay of wounding and retribution that occurs at her body. Because her death forms the logical fulfilment of an exchange that marks her from the start of the narrative as the privileged object of an allegorising gaze, her story offers both a critique of the violence engendered by such allegorisation and a representation of the stages one must move through in order to reach the 'right' moment of death. Like Fanny, her body functions as a 'duplicitous signifer' in that it is inscribed and translated into a trope that embodies the process of death, while simultaneously it inscribes and ultimately signs life.

The moment Tess is first introduced into the narrative prophetically marks her difference from her companions – though she is a mere 'vessel of emotion untinctured by experience', a pronounced red ribbon adorns her hair. The student Angel, who dances with the village girls, does not choose Tess because she remains unobserved until he falls out of the dance. Only when he looks back from afar does he notice her – 'a white shape stood apart by the hedge alone'. In contrast to Fanny, who was from the start vanishing from sight, Tess is initially presented as visually present but standing apart from her companions, both because her womanly appearance is more pronounced (though this contradicts her virginal body) and because she is noticeable in her superiority only when seen from a distance, as the 'pretty maiden with whom he had not danced' (54f.). The fact that her pronounced visibility is contingent on the disembodying focalisation of the protagonist Angel, and can emerge only from the distance, foreshadows not only her fatal dependency on her lover's gaze but also the fact that in some sense she is always already distanced from life into an allegorical figure of fatality. Precisely because Angel chooses not to dance with her, Tess's figure remains in his imaginative memory, though in its presence empty, making room for the other meanings he wishes to project on to it. The exchange Tess is implicated in from the start is one that requires her to be kept at a distance, transformed into a figure, so that the narcissistic needs of her lover can be satisfied to the utmost.

Her story begins with the recognition of one claim and the disavowal of another, for she is interrupted in her May Dance by her father's claim to 'a-gr't-family vault-at-Kingsbere'.[14] Angel's not choosing Tess, which she will later read as a metaphor for the fatal belatedness of their love, also signifies that she has already been chosen by the dead, who speak through the father's name; that she has been summoned away from the May dance of marriage, children and old age to enter the dance macabre.

In Freud's discussion of choice in his essay 'The Theme of the Three Caskets', the correct one is the most attractive but also represents death. Tess is faced with the choice of three possibilities – her ancestors, Angel and Alec – but is as yet too innocent to choose. The plot of her story enacts a detour with the goal of returning to this moment of choice in such a way that Tess is no longer its object but its subject, translating necessity and destiny into choice, acknowledging death by choosing it. The theme of body–sign exchange interacts with the more global representation of the death process precisely because the former is an enactment of incisions where death not only underlies life but breaks through, violently ruptures and makes itself visible in its signature or trace left on living bodies. Between the ancestors' first calling of Tess and her final reciprocation a chiasmic arrangement marked by such moments of violent incision informs the plot of this text. Tess moves from a first bodily inscription, Alec's rape, through a series of self-allegorisations reciprocated by the allegorising gaze of others. These acts, whereby others or she herself 'kill' her body into a trope, repeat the first incision of death's slow process toward disintegration. Her narration to Angel becomes the first attempt to avenge her rape. After his rejection of her she returns to bodily inscription and with it the embrace of death, which leads to the completion of her rape in the murder of Alec and her subsequent disembodiment under the auspices of the law. Within this scenario the two lovers Angel and Alec embody the two aspects of the death drive as discussed earlier. Alec, the false representative of her ancestors, is an agent of duplicity and division. His rape fragments wholeness and taints purity but in this destructive function he also creates tensions as a safeguard against a short-circuiting of the death process in the form of a pre-mature stasis. Angel's inscriptions in turn, are an attempt to deny division and regain the death-like state of transparent purity before the fall.[15]

Obeying the principle recommending a commodification of female bodies, her parents choose Tess to claim kin with what they think are their rich relatives. Well aware that Tess's value for this economic exchange resides in her feminine beauty, she is explicitly transformed into an object designed to arouse Alec's erotic desire. The duplicity her parents embark on is that on a literal level they send her beautiful body as an ostensible sign to testify to their blood kinship, but in fact rely on transforming her into a sign of seductive womanliness. Her mother deviously dresses Tess with a pink ribbon 'broader than usual', and a white frock 'supplementing her enlarged coiffure' to emphasise what is already a contradiction in her appearance – 'a fullness of growth, which made her appear more of a woman than she really was' (82). Again Tess is a valuable *par excellence*, standing apart from others, because her body and the meaning it signifies are forced apart. By sending Tess's body to signify 'other' than what it is, staking a claim with a false coin, her parents are prefiguring death's fracturing of her body in rape by already forcing her to efface her maidenly body. The mother's strategy succeeds in so far as Tess becomes supremely attractive to Alec precisely because she is a sign for womanliness, not a womanly body, and the defeat of his attempts at seduction engendered by this separation is also what keeps his desire alive. As he will later explain, 'Why I did not despise you was on account of your being unsmirched in spite of all' (402).

The Durbeyfield appeal ironically ricochets from hope of restored fortune, health and life to signs of death. By claiming kin with Alec on the authority of the family vault, Tess recognises her ancestors' claim on her. By acknowledging that her body is a site where these ancestors have left their generic traces, she acknowledges that she is not only fractured by this inscription but also a metonymy of the dead. The tragic irony is that while her signification as allegory of womanliness is based on a false claim but engenders real erotic desire, her signification as metonymy of the dead is based on a legitimate claim but has in Alec a false respondent since he is himself not a genuine representative but a false copy of the D'Urbervilles. Alec's role as a sham figure not only of her aristocratic ancestors but also of death is shown to Tess when upon entering a church containing the tombs of his family, she discovers Alec posing as an effigy only to wake and tempt her away from 'the dynasty of the real underneath' (449) to which she is drawn ever more strongly.

The description of the rape itself enacts the complex exchange of disembodiment it sets out to signify. Before her violation, Tess's body transforms into 'a pale nebulousness at his feet, which represented the white muslin figure he had left upon the dead leaves . . . she was sleeping,' and the ravishment that is then inflicted on this unconscious body already perceived as a deanimated figure turns into a metaphor for inscription: 'Why it was that upon this beautiful feminine tissue, sensitive as gossamer, and practically blank as snow as yet, there should have been traced such a coarse pattern as it was doomed to receive' (119).[16] By occulting a description of real physical violence and substituting for it a metaphorical speculation on metaphysics, the narrator repeats Alec's turning her body into a sign which must bear another's inscription. An undoing of this alterior signature in an act of auto-signing will define the ensuing trajectory of her life. But the destabilising of any distinction between body and sign that the narrative itself enacts when concrete rape can be presented 'only' as an elliptic trope points also to a disturbing duplicity fundamental to allegory in general – for in it the word precedes its incarnation and becomes flesh but simultaneously the embodiment generates meaning when the flesh becomes word. For Tess rape is a form of death in that it irrevocably wounds the intact wholeness of her body when the hymen is ruptured and forces her to exchange a 'previous self' for a new one (119), with the designation 'previous self' excluding its signified even as it is uttered. Beyond any speculation whether this rape is a moment of 'retribution visited' upon her body for 'sins of her fathers' (placing it in the Dance of Death Motif), concrete death in this moment speaks through her body, becomes, so to speak, flesh. The 'duplicity' inherent in this exchange engendered by rape is that her maidenly body dies, while simultaneously death is embodied. Mieke Bal argues that rape reduces the violated body to a sign, in the process of which the victim falls silent and becomes invisible because her subjectivity is destroyed. As the 'allegorical' nature of Hardy's prose suggests, 'rape is by definition imagined; it can only exist as experience and as memory, as image translated into signs, never adequately "objectifiable" '.[17]

Tess's ensuing melancholic desire for death (a response to this 'figurative murder') transforms into various attempts at self-figuration that enhance her disembodiment by concretising the separation between the bodily appearance and its natural meaning at the same time that she valorises the trope over the body. At first she looks upon herself as 'a figure of Guilt intruding into the haunts of Innocence', emphasising her death-like liminality not only by insisting on a separation between herself and nature's laws when in fact she is perfectly in accord with them, but also by 'killing herself' into a trope along with the child she baptises 'Sorrow the Undesired' shortly before its natural death. Looking into a mirror she does not see her own physical fairness but rather reads this image of her body as a *vanitas* picture, signifying the day of her death, and with it total disembodiment, 'when all these charms would have disappeared' (149).

The burial of her child becomes part of a recuperative act, an attempt to escape the past by annihilating 'all that appertained thereto' (150), which culminates in a second form of self-figuration, her resurrection, or second 'social birth' as 'dairymaid Tess, and nothing more', as an insubstantial imagined figure, revealing no traces of a past. The exchange she undertakes at her person is the substitution of a deanimated figure for a body incised by the first traces of death. By merely changing the allegorical value of her figure from womanliness to purity, she of course structurally repeats the fateful separation between what her appearance signifies and her body's true meaning. A fundamental inconsistency informs her attempt to banish 'all D'Urberville air-castles in the dreams and deeds of her new life', for the dairy she choses as site of her rebirth lies near the 'great family vaults of the ancestors' (151). She constructs a crypt within herself, ambivalently hiding and securing the corpse of her maiden self. She disavows her ancestors in an attempt to reconstruct herself outside the dance of facticity and fracture they have led her along, even as she enters her 'ancestral land' as though returning to the point of her origin, in the hope of healing all previous ruptures.

In this nostalgic desire for a return to a state prior to the fall into division, impurity and sexuality, Tess corresponds perfectly to Angel, who seeks purification from the evils of urban existence in the pastoral of dairy life. His allegorising gaze translates the already duplicitous figure 'dairymaid Tess' into a 'fresh and virginal daughter of Nature' and 'actualized poetry'. In a narcissistic effort to stabilise his fractured sense of self, Tess comes to stand for all those values he lacks – purity, innocence, genuineness, newness, uncultured and unconstrained naturalness – which, if he could posses them by possessing her, would give him the lacking sense of wholeness. In this exchange Angel seeks a deanimated figure of Nature, a phantom or corpse and not a natural feminine body, and this becomes prominent in a passage where Tess appears in the aspect when 'she impressed him most deeply'. In the 'non-human hours' of dawn she 'looked ghostly, as if she were merely a soul at large . . . She was no longer the milkmaid, but a visionary essence of woman – a whole sex condensed into one typical form' (187).[18] This privileging of purity contains two aspects. On the one hand, his desire for her spiritualised figure suggests that the more divested she is of bodily substance and specific meaning the more entirely is she available to his libidinal investment without threatening the construction of his self-image. She must become 'ghostly' to satisfy his narcissistic self-reflection to the utmost. On the other hand purity also implies freedom of all other 'imprints' (both sexual and cultural), so that once inscribed she will be a sign bearing exclusively his signature and as such testifying to its supremacy.

An obvious failure inherent in Angel's project lies in the fact that Tess, as trope for the spotlessness missing in his life, confirms this lack even as she functions to stabilise Angel's self-representation. Moreover the 'incrypting' Tess has enacted in the course of her resurrection is such that it leaves her in a state of hesitation between two forms of living death: a mere figure or a fractured body. Her attempt to defer the marriage is an expression of her desire to postpone a choice. The narrative she presents to Angel in exchange for his own confession, a narrative with which she pays for the trust and forgiveness she expects to receive and which she gives as a form of security that their marriage will, from the start, be one of honest reciprocity, marks the pivotal point in her story. Her narrative repeats Alec's rape in that she traces on the tissue of Angel's imagination a copy of the coarse pattern Alec traced on her body. If she previously tried to 'undo' her past by killing herself into a figure, speaking, for Tess, becomes a way of undoing this fated transformation. She is, when she gives her narrative, a 'speaking corpse' because at the acme of her tropic disembodiment, the result of which was a total disavowal of her natural body.

Given the fact that Tess is well aware that Angel loves not her real self 'but one in my image; the one I might have been' (281), her disclosure articulates the desire for another kind of substitution. If her rape was the result of a discrepancy between appearance (signifier) and natural body (signified), a marriage based on a similar contradiction can only become an equally fateful exchange. Since her conception of their marriage is 'two selves together, nothing to divide them' (271), its successful consummation presupposes that the division which grounds their mutual allegorisation of her body must also be reversed to nothing. Giving her narrative also means attempting to undo the separation between her body and what it signifies; it undoes the process that led to the split in herself and the split from her ideal lover. By narrating the death of her maidenhood and of her child she reciprocates her passive reception of a wound by actively inflicting another – namely a wound to Angel's narcissism – in the hope of healing her own. Her decision not to uphold the self-presentation which corresponds to Angel's allegorising gaze marks the beginning of her triumph over death by acknowledging and choosing it. For the self-representation of 'dairymaid and nothing else' was based on the fundamental division of signifying 'other', even though it semantically articulated a disavowal of division.

While she gives her narrative to bring the past she has incrypted within herself into the open, Angel responds by re-incryptment. In his eye she has become the Figure Purity, so that the supreme safeguard to his human existence, his sense of self and of his actions in the world as meaningful are fundamentally disrupted by the revelation of her bodily impurity. Finding her tissue already with traces means in part accepting that the only possible imprint he can make is a palimpsest, which is always in danger of being subverted by previous hidden inscriptions. The uniqueness, originality and supremacy that his inscription and creation of Tess were to ensure are ambiguously threatened. His accusation – 'You were one person; now you are another . . . how can forgiveness meet such a grotesque – prestidigitation as that' (298) – unintendedly turns into a a self-accusation. While Tess practiced deception by not telling her story earlier, the sleight of hand lay also in his allegorizing gaze which continues to function even as it discloses itself. By insisting he loved 'another woman in [Tess's] shape', by seeing her as 'a guilty woman in the guise of an innocent one' he re-enacts the 'duplicity' he faults her with – disaccord between appearance and body. Like Troy he valorises the female trope over the female body: 'With these natures, corporeal presence is sometimes less appealing than corporeal absence; the latter creating an ideal presence that conveniently drops the defects of the real' (315). Ultimately at stake, beyond any debate on the necessary valuable of female virginity, is the stability and truth of his allegorising gaze. Because her body is the subject of Tess' revelation, a blindness to it, to the material carrier of a message, becomes impossible. She forces Angel momentarily to acknowledge that body he has preferred to efface in his spiritualised image of her. The revelation also forces him to realise that Tess's body can incite more than one allegorisation – putting both the validity and the uniqueness of his reading into question. Since Tess is but a mirror image of himself, once he accepts the possibility that, while her gaze may not express any divergence, she may, even as she speaks, be seeing 'another world behind her ostensible one, discordant and contrasting' (305), he opens the possibility of duplicity in his own perception of the world.

The violent incursion of the past into the present results in a feminine corpse whose power to destabilise must be diffused. Sleepwalking, Angel enters her bedroom several nights after the non-consummation of their marriage and murmurs 'my dearest, darling Tess! So sweet, so good, so true . . . my wife – dead, dead' as he carries her outside and places her into an empty stone coffin next to the Abbey. In this state he can suspend the taboo of touching Tess imposed by his conscious mind. After kissing her the second time he breathes 'as if a greatly desired end were attained' and immediately falls into a slumber of exhaustion. In Tess leading him home he fancies 'a spirit . . . leading him to Heaven' (320f.). This corporeal enactment of a desire is once again based on a blurring of any distinction between bodies and signs. In burying a 'Tess deanimated' by virtue of his designation 'dead', Angel also incrypts Tess as the trope of Truthfulness and Goodness. Unconsciously, he secures intact, as a repressed presence, the figure of Tess he has created which her bodily presence contradicts. His ambivalent attitude toward the female body as sexual object emerges. Where before his marriage he desired Tess as an essence or typical form, after his marriage an erotic embrace seems possible only in a moment when he exhibits absolute possession, when the body to be embraced is totally at his disposal – not only because it is a corpse but because it is in his power to designate it as such. In this symbolic enactment of a burial Angel not only exchanges Tess's living body for her corpse, he does so to preserve the figure in his mind which will allow him, when he subsequently leaves England, to exchange her corporeal presence for an image, a 'vague figure afar off', that becomes untainted in her absence; distance making 'artistic virtues of . . . stains' (338).

Duplicitous as it may be, Angel's allegorising gaze reciprocates and stabilises Tess's own self-image, and with it a narcissistic desire for self-preservation. The loss of a gaze that had momentarily barred her from choosing death results in the return of a melancholic desire for death, as she retraces her steps back to her family vault. She realises that by some fateful logic the price she must pay to ensure Angel's gaze is that of establishing a one-to-one correspondence between her body and the corpse he buried in effigy. What bars her body from being in perfect correlation with the pure figure he desires and has incrypted in his unconscious is her living substantiality irrevocably marked by rape. That the realisation 'Bygones would never be complete bygones till she was a bygone herself' (385) is also a fatefully semiotic concern, is made evident in her inability to draw a distinction between body and sign the second time she repeats her rape – now paying back both Alec and Angel. Angel's desire for purity is such that he wants her not only to signify 'no trace of a division' in her self (semantic purity as chastity) but to do so in such away that there is no division between what the body's appearance signifies and what the signified body is (structural purity as obliteration of the difference between signifier and signified). While this desired transparency was possible semantically, when Angel's gaze allegorised Tess into the figure of feminine essence, structural transparency is possible only when she moves from allegory to a materialisation of the sign, that allows the body and its meaning to collapse into a perfect unity.

The paradox informing her story is that she is preserved as a living self by virtue of an allegorising gaze that acknowledges difference and tension in its speaking 'other' even as it kills the body into a trope, to make it signify. When she chooses to murder Alec she changes into a figure of death by embodying death. Through her hand death ruptures Alec's body, takes on his flesh. As an instrument of death, Tess gives up irrevocably her sense of self-preservation – and changes into a disembodied figure self-reflexively signifying its own dissolution, signifying 'nothing' by signifying nothing 'other' than itself. Tess's excess lets her exchange her reference to the law, moving beyond it in an embrace of radical Otherness as death. Seeing her shortly before she commits the murder, Angel has a 'vague consciousness of one thing', though significantly he will recognize it only belatedly: 'that his original Tess had spiritually ceased to recognise the body before him as her – allowing it to drift, like a corpse upon the current, in a direction dissociated from its living will' (467). Murder is Tess's way of paying Alec back in the same coin – one bodily trespass reciprocates another – but it is also a payment Tess makes to get Angel back (474). Yet the price to retrieve Angel is the impossible gift of a pure body, so that Tess pays by extinguishing both the agent of her division (Alec) and the site of its inscription (her body). In so doing she also repeats her first payment to Angel by undoing the two moments of division it contained – she substitutes for a narrative about her body the gift of her body, for the narrative about impurity one about purgation.

Hardy's narrative itself remains ambivalent as to whether true understanding between Angel and Tess ultimately occurs when they finally consummate their marriage in the abandoned country mansion. They repeat the conditions of the pastoral setting for their first love by choosing once again a realm markedly outside history and culture. It remains unclear whether the move Tess makes beyond both the narcissistic realm of self-imaging and the symbolic realm of culture's moral laws is one Angel truly follows, entering with her the current of the already dead, in which she will not think 'outside of now' (480). It also remains open whether the proximity of her death suspends for him also the economy of an allegorising gaze and with it his demand for purity, or whether his realisation of Tess's innocence and purity is yet another form of allegorising. Finally it remains ambiguous whether he can consume the erotic embrace impossible to him before because she is what he has desired all along – a disembodied woman – so that the immanence of death has indeed purified her for him, undone the barring taint not just traced on to her body but also represented by her body.

Regardless of whether this erotic exchange is an experience of real unity or not, the fact that it depends on one partner's embrace of death casts light on the inter-dependence of self-preservation and allegorising gazes. Angel, who survives, must re-enter both the rules of culture and marry Liza-Lu, 'a spiritualized image of Tess'. The violent rupture of the symbolic order of culture that Tess enacts through and at her body by giving and receiving death must be stabilised in the form of a re-allegorisation. Not only must her transgression of the law be punished by hanging, an exchange in which her dead body becomes a sign that the moral rules destabilised by her act have been reaffirmed. She is narratively re-inscribed into the language of allegory even before her hanging is described. When the 'law' catches up with her, she has again been transformed into an allegorical figure ambivalent in its reference – into a body sacrificed on the heathen stone altar at Stonehenge. This form, a 'lesser creature than a woman', simultaneously signifies Tess's sacrifice to nature, to culture's rules on rape and murder, to one man's inability to love a woman's body, to another's promiscuity or even to the 'sport' dead knights and dames play on their descendant. But in all these readings her fulfilment is such that the series of violent incisions based always on a treatment of her body as trope is now irrevocably complete.

Allegory is grounded on a quintessential ambivalence in respect to the exchange of body with sign. For the point at which to distinguish whether this is an instance of a word gaining body or a body objectified into a sign is not secure. By self-consciously admitting that it speaks 'other', allegory articulates discrepancy even as, in the act of gazing, it transforms the discrepant ambivalence of a concrete body so threatening to the self-image of the observer into the reassuring stability of a figure. What makes an allegory ultimately so pleasing is that by shifting the question of ambivalence from the literal to the rhetorical, it can be signified and effaced at the same time. To take the body of a woman, 'deceptive' to the narcissistic gaze because it will always exceed the image it is meant to reflect, and change it into a trope for deception, is a superlative 'prestidigitation'. It means visibly acknowledging the rhetorical discrepancy (where the signifer and the signified ostensibly don't compare) in order to occult the threat of ambi-valence in the realm of concrete bodies that initiated the turn to the tropic in the first place. At stake in the self-reflexive analogy of corpse and text is the fact that the move to the rhetorical is often in response to discrepancies posed by an exchange with concrete bodies that threaten to wound the narcissism of the Other.

While allegorising gazes in Hardy's narratives ultimately afford peace and the recuperation of order, the emphasis in my last example, Hawthorne's *Blithedale Romance* (1852), lies on the disquieting destability that remains once the grave has been filled, the failure to achieve closure, the scars and differences that stay on. My discussion will revolve around two questions – how does Zenobia construct herself, how does her community construct her as a figure tracing difference and

Otherness within, with her death engendering its stability? What is the relation between Zenobia and the narrator, the poet Miles Coverdale, with her death engendering his text? I end this third part with Zenobia because she is an 'excessive' example for all the issues raised. She is a superb embodiment of the doubleness of the feminine body exchanged in an economic and a semiotic manner. She is a figure at which the double aspect of allegory, its reassuring and its disfiguring mode, unfolds. Because her death must be seen in conjunction with the narrator's fantasies, with his ability/failure to imagine and represent, it points back to my earlier discussion about the deanimating gaze of the artist. Because her death constitutes an enigma and engenders her spectral reappearance, her story also opens to the central themes of the next section.[19]

Because I will read the novel in light of the grotesque spectacle of Zenobia's corpse and its burial pose, it is useful to introduce Benjamin's analogy between allegory and ruins. He chooses the analogy because ruins embody *par excellence* the fact that natural existence is meaningful only because it is marked by the irrevocability of decay.[20] He proposes that only the corpse (like a ruin, mere decomposing materiality without soul) can achieve a radical allegorisation of physical materiality. His emphasis on the 'disfiguring' that occurs in the allegorising process serves to clarify two of its aspects. For one, the insurmountable disjunction between inscribed meaning and its material embodiment makes allegory appear as the supreme interstice between eternity and decay.[21] At the same time, in that allegory also functions as the point where one extremity changes into another (*Umschlagen von Extremen*): it 'disfigures' any rendition of aesthetic harmony, of beauty as physical rendition of spiritual purity and integrity, not only by articulating fragmentation and difference. The beauty it presents, by being excessive, in its splendour overladen (*prunkvoll*, *überladen*), uncannily also subverts any false illusion of totality and immortality by changing into a signifier for the decay art is meant to hide. Its sumptuousness implies a plurality of meaning and a transgression of boundaries that contradicts any purity and unity of meaning. For ambiguity as duplicity in meaning (*Zweideutigkeit*) is the opulence or wealth (*Reichtum*) of wasteful extravagence (*Verschwendung*).

If ruins are beyond beauty because they demonstrate a 'process of unstoppable decay', their rhetorical corollary, allegory, is beyond beauty because marking the point of excess where one extreme – eternal wholeness – changes into irrevocable decay; where one meaning – immortal beauty – articulates its opposite, inexorable rotting decomposition. If beauty is meant to hide the fact that human life is from the start a ruin, its pleonasm – excess as redundancy – articulates precisely this vulnerability. In that allegory demonstrates the conjunction of 'overripeness and decay' (*Überreife und Verfall*), of excessive perfection and splendour as decay, it fragments the illusion of wholeness. Allegory introduces semantic difference as duplicity and break within one and the same image; it articulates real death and decay. The rotting body is not just what literature, according to Blanchot wants, but that which allegory, when concerned with excess – as the grotesque, the splendidly redundant, the sumptuously exaggerated – figures, as a disjunction that can't be overcome, as a failure of symbolic unity and univocality.[22]

The ground and vanishing point of *Blithedale Romance* is a corpse petrified into a grotesque posture. The 'duplicity' of Zenobia's dead body is such that it materialises two men's efforts at disembodying in the sense of distancing and refiguring her during her lifetime. Her corpse is not only a sign of her total defeat, given that prosperity had failed her as well as love. In that the materiality of her body returns in death to assert itself against its incision by their secondary meanings, her corpse can also be seen as a superlative sign of revenge against both her lover Hollingsworth's and her spectator Coverdale's allegorising gazes.

In respect to her lover, Zenobia's suicide is a fulfilment of her being 'put on trial for her life' by him, a literalisation of his rejection, of his flinging her aside, 'a broken tool', and, by implication, of his having instrumentalised her for his own ends from the start. After the trial she is already 'like marble', her hand 'cold as a veritable piece of snow . . . deathlike!' Zenobia alludes to this confusion between literal and figural when she explains, 'the extremities die first, they say . . . this poor, despised, rejected hand' (830). Her suicide also literalises the vindictive threat she asks Coverdale to transmit to her lover – 'Tell him he has murdered me! Tell him that I'll haunt him' (829). Enlisting the sheer materiality of the dead body as sign legitimizes her accusation and her claim.

In respect to her privileged spectator, Zenobia's death also repeats and fulfills a previous disembodiment, for he had turned her, along with her rival and her lover, into characters of his 'private theater' so as to position himself as the 'one calm observer aloof from . . . personal concernment', caring not for the realities of these people but the 'fancy-work' with which his imagination decked them out (720). Fully aware of his proclivity, Zenobia alludes to this 'mortifying gaze' when she suggests that he is already 'turning this whole affair into a ballad', making her absent though still bodily present. Here too Zenobia's death is duplicitous, repeating the difference she had all along traced on to the tissues of Coverdale's imagination. Revenge takes the form of haunting him after her death as she had during her life. While his allegorising gaze made her absent in her presence, her infecting his fancy preserves her presence in absence. If she threatens to haunt her lover in the guise of guilt, she will haunt her spectator by commissioning a tale that will displace all his other poetic powers – 'write this ballad, and put your soul's ache into it.'

Where the living Zenobia, by virtue of her excess and abundance, traces the figure of difference in her community, 'disfiguring' in Benjamin's sense any belief in wholeness, univocality or purity, her death equally evokes the figure of allegory. She suggests two morals as the allegorical reading of her life. For one, that woman's vulnerability in love is fatal, for another, that a woman transgressing norms will be punished. In so doing she fuses a romantic with a social message, producing, in Benjamin's sense, a surplus of signifieds and a confusion of two semantic paradigms. The theatricality of her corpse serves to enact her critique of their utopian enterprise, though it remains open whether this was intended or not. It justifies her claim that 'we have surely blundered into the very emptiest mockery, in our effort to establish the one true system' (830). The reason for her death remains unexplained, and her corpse poses an enigma whose signified is beyond reach, disturbs because it remains to haunt. Zenobia's grave can never be perfectly closed because her corpse remains positioned uncannily in the tension between a surplus of explanations and an absence of one fixed meaning.

When they pull her out of the water, the spectacle of her corpse is such a 'perfect horror' that it remains in Coverdale's memory for twelve years, as freshly as when he was faced with its presence. Horror is provoked by the rigidity of her body, a 'terrifble inflexibility' of her limbs, her arms 'grown rigid in the act of struggling . . . but before her, with clenched hands . . . her knees, too, were bent' (837). Coverdale understands this corpse as an allegory – 'she was the marble image of death-agony', yet the excess of her posture makes it difficult for him to determine its signified. Though he wishes to read her grotesquely contorted body as the fixture by death of Zenobia's kneeling in prayer, so that the meaning of her corpse is that of a deliverance and submission to God 'reconciled and penitent', her arms and hands provoke a second 'hideous thought'. For this grotesque body can also be read as a mockery of death as serene unity with the divine, 'as if she struggled against Providence in never-ending hostility . . . in immitigable defiance'.

In this confusion of the somatic with the semiotic, the survivors can not 'arrange the arms of the corpse decently by its side', because these extremities defy this effort of reharmonising the ugliness of death by always returning to their 'indecent', 'unseemly aspect'. Coverdale can find no one interpretation to cover up and beautify the horror of this spectacle of death. Confessing that Zenobia was 'not quite simple in her death', he tries to convince himself that, had she known how hideous a spectacle she would produce, she would not have 'committed the dreadful act', even as the text contradicts him in that it presents this disfigured body in its radical moment of unmitigated difference as her apotheosis. Coverdale tries further to allegorise this body in ways to recuperate his disrupted narcissistic stability, suggesting that her death be seen as an attempt to imitate pictures Zenobia had seen of village-maidens, wronged in their first love, drowned 'in lithe and graceful attitudes.' He chooses to read the parody of her ugly death, in its difference to such Ophelia-inspired models, as a sign of 'the Arcadian affectation' which had been visible in their community, analogous to his presentation of the living Zenobia in the preceding part of his tale as embodying the disjunction between real rural life and their playing of it. His final reading suggests that Zenobia's disfigurement be seen as an allegory of the 'awful sophistication' of their world, that forbids a putting oneself 'to death in whole-hearted simplicity'.

Even as he tries to find a way to recuperate a sense of univocality, harmony and identity disrupted by this corpse, any allegorisation leads him inevitably to notions of disjunction between signifier and intended signified, to notions of difference and failure as part of what is signified and to a plurality of readings that offer no peace. This is so because allegory maintains the disturbing semantic surplus (Benjamin's *Zweideutigkeit*), and because it so explicitly demonstrates that any reading is 'not all' of the grotesque body of death. In its materiality the corpse will not be contained in any one semantic fixture and explicitly embodies the deformation the tropic turn tries to hide in that no one meaning is really secure. Unlike Fanny's corpse, Zenobia's affords only an imperfect closure. Its rigidity alludes to the fact that the one idea it embodies with certainty is eternally fixed disruption. In death she is fixed into the figure she drew in life – the agent of strife that kept her lover and her sister apart, that induced disturbing fantasies in her poet friend. Yet her form of fixture remains disturbing because it is excessive and ambivalent. It continues to point to difference uncannily present within, to the ugliness always inherent to beauty, to the disfiguring any tropic figuration implies, and in a metapoetical sense to the decay always present in the allegorical 'duplicity of the signifer', its turning point from one extreme to another (*Umschlagen von Extremen*), its conjunction of 'overripeness and decay'.

If the corpse can be called the interstice in Zenobia's presentation within the narrative, it sheds light in two directions – forward to the description of her grave; backward to the way that her beauty and brilliance in life always also rendered difference as decay hidden though implied in the sumptuous. Her burial recalls Coverdale's conviction that a design of a funeral ceremony was necessary as a symbolic expression of their spiritual faith and eternal hopes in the community: 'I shall never feel as if this were a real, practical as well as poetical system of human life, until somebody has sanctified it by death' (746). Ironically Zenobia's corpse grounds the dissolution and collapse, not the unity and eternity, of this social system. It marks the disjunction between their utopic aspirations and their realisations. Even as Zenobia's absence puts an end to the tension she caused among the others, the experiment dies soon after.

In the personal realm, though her death sanctions the unity between Hollingsworth and Priscilla, her spectral presence is a more perfect dividing presence than her living body ever was. Her lover fails utterly at the philan-thropist project to reform criminals for which he had sacrified her, because her death forces him to focus his attention on 'a single murderer' – himself. Though her death literalises Coverdale's longing 'for a catastrophe' to put an end to his compulsion to watch her, to calm the irritation this obsessive watching causes to his nerves and to obliterate the uncanny presence in his dreams that the 'knot of characters' around Zenobia presented, the release he gains is one of 'self-mortification'. With her, his poetic gift dies, and he remains preoccupied with only one narrative, the story preceding her death, which itself encodes another 'duplicitous' failure. It represents his inability to find a univocal explanation for the course of events as sign for the fact that he was not master of his fantasies but mastered by them. It also represents his inability to acknowledge his romantic desires for the two feminine objects of his speculation, as a sign of his sexual 'castration', analogous to his artistic one. Both cases mark his incision by death.

Just as the corpse can be read as an allegory of the triumph of dissolution, of decay and difference within, its grotesqueness a mockery of the 'very emptiest mockery' of their game at philanthropy and progress, nature's response is again one that points to decay inmidst growth. Though nature is the one element in this tale that can regenerate after Zenobia's death, it does so in a significantly 'duplicitous' manner to show death's presence in life as that which can't be stabilised because it exceeds. Coverdale explains, 'the grass grew all the better, on that little parallelogram of pasture-land, for the decay of the beautiful woman who slept beneath . . . nature . . . adopts the calamity at once into her system, and is just as well pleased . . . with the tuft of ranker vegetation that grew out of Zenobia's heart, as with all the beauty which has bequeathed us no earthly representative, except in this crop of weeds' (845).

Given that the adjective 'rank' implies something haughty or proud, something vigorous and luxuriant in growth, excessively abundant and copious, standing out as something absolute, completely marked, but also an offensively strong smell, lustful, excessively loathsome and strongly marked in the sense of violent or virulent grossness and coarseness, the narrator's choice of word invokes not only a duplicitous exchange between beauty and decay but also that moment where the difference between a luxuriant and a foul body – in that both are excessive – cannot be determined. As was the case in Carmen's association with bile, Zenobia's association with rankness also articulates that the feminine dead body, by virtue of its redundant signification of difference, is dangerous precisely because it defies the clear drawing of distinctions which it simultaneously provokes. The two moments in Zenobia's death – the grotesqueness of the corpse and the rankness of her grave's vegetation – in that they both enact excess analogous to the disruptive redundancy Benjamin attributes to the allegory, imply that it is this tropic figure which Zenobia traces in her community and which she assumes for the narrator. She draws a collapse of extremities, where the splendid and brilliant woman articulates decay and decomposition as death's presence in life, and in so doing, its presence in representation as well.

In his narrative, Coverdale presents Zenobia as having an abundance of faults as well as noble traits; a haughty yet brilliant, talented woman, distinguished by a 'character of eccentricity and defiance' (722), by an uncomfortable surplus of vitality, by 'inequalities of temper'. She is 'on the hither verge of her *richest* maturity', '*remarkably* beautiful', marked by a '*bloom*, health and *vigor* which she possessed in such *overflow*' (645).[23] In this 'rankness' she induces various allegorisations in the poet's representation of her. He feels compelled by her free manner to disrobe her mentally and recreate in his mind her 'fine, perfectly developed figure, in Eve's earliest garment'. Disrobed of her historical setting, she emerges as the mythic figure of quintessential Woman, Eve emerging from her creator's hand. Ironically the attribute she emanates also links her to death. It is 'a certain warm and rich characteristic, which seems . . . to have been refined away out of the feminine system' (647). The peculiarity of this description is such that, even as Coverdale narrates, Zenobia has literally been refined out of the system, her body replaced by a crop of weeds. The complex interplay of absent/

present bodies in this allegorising process is such that he empties/disrobes her present body to make room for a secondary meaning and doubles this figural disembodiment after her death. In her bodily absence she is mentally present in that she has so much affected his imagination that he seeks constantly to figure out her secret, and this form of imaginative presence in absence is also repeated after her death in the form of her narrative.

Apart from the fact that her abundant feminine form disturbs in that it provokes sexual fantasies in the narrator which he wishes to suppress, Zenobia is also dangerous because she is not what she seems to be. The fact that her name is a *nom de plume* her friends have adopted because it fits the magnificent queenliness of her posture, means that she also constructs herself outside her historical context, presents herself allegorically, in figure. Disclosing her real name means disclosing her position within her kinship structure, including any reference to an earlier marriage. This opens up conjectures whether she is still to bloom as a woman or whether her flower 'has already been taken' – the riddle being whether potential bloom or decay is her privileged sexual signified (671f.). Coverdale's position of observer presents the undressing of her body as coterminous with discovering the 'mystery of her life', since both circulate around the enigma of woman's sexual difference. The ambivalence of feeling inscribed in the narrator is such that while in one gesture he mentally strips Zenobia of her social position along with her clothes, by turning her into a myth, in the other he wishes to lift the veil of her assumed figuration to present her historical past. Repeatedly he tries to discover the secret she seems to hide beneath her name, which he compares to 'the white drapery of the Veiled Lady'. The problematic indeterminacy Zenobia embodies, reduces to the following question. Is her self-construction to be understood, analogous to the invoked performer in the mesmeric line, a device that insulates her from the material world and endows her with the privileges of a disembodied spirit? Concomitant with this comparison, she is reduced by Coverdale to a disembodied idea – woman incarnate, the enigma of femininity – while she simultaneously figures as a disembodied ghost whom he can summon up in her absence, during her life and after her death.

The assumed name, however, also points to its own difference, declares a secret in public, says it names duplicitously. Like allegory, it refers to the impossibility of identity and univocal meaning; not only opens a gap but defies its closure. Even as Coverdale's two responses to Zenobia have the one aim of making her the site of discovered truth – disclosing her as figure of true womanhood, disclosing the truth beneath her artificial appearance – her excess defies such a reduction. For the analogy with the Veiled Lady also serves to suggest that both women's bodies are nothing but surface, signifers embodying arbitrarily a plurality of indeterminate signifieds.

That excessive adornment provokes a dangerous sense of difference more disturbing than quieting is exemplified by virtue of the artificial, outlandish flower Zenobia has in her hair. It is a hot-house flower, 'the very weeds of which would be fervid and spicy', each day different. In this difference it marks abundant artificiality, each flower perfectly 'assimilates its richness to the rich beauty of this woman'. The abundance of sumptuousness is, like the word *rank*, a mixture of beauty and decay, figuring death in two senses. Coverdale uses the flower to suggest Zenobia is an 'enchantress', the Veiled Lady's sister, who would vanish once the veil/flower has been snatched away. She is always already dead – mere appearance, illusion without soul or substance. The flower, thrown away and renewed each day by another artificial one is, however, also the detail Coverdale focuses on to explain how Zenobia traces difference within her community by pointing out the artificiality of their utopic enterprise, the disjunction between intent and realisation. The presence of Zenobia, he notes, 'caused our heroic enterprise to show like an illusion, a masquerade, a pastoral, a counterfeit Arcadia' (650).

Her danger for the community and his narcissistic imaginations is that, by virtue of her excess, she is more than any one reduction, the point that demarcates a system by demonstrating that it is 'not all' there is. She explicitly figures the difference between Coverdale's imagined Zenobia and her reality when she rejects him as a confidant and when she disrupts his observation by withdrawal. She enacts the 'duplicity of the signifier' by making her body absent in presence, hidden beneath an assumed name and beneath a plethora of roles and clothes, and then again by making it present in absence in that she threatens to haunt her lover and commissions a narrative from her poet. Her grotesque corpse is her apotheosis since it traces the same figure of disjunction by which her lived abundance dis-figured her presence in life. Both the living and the dead body elicit a hermeneutic desire in her spectators yet defy the possibility of a univocal meaning. Like her corpse, her life can not be figured out or figured into one stable narrative. Both her corpse and her living body have only one stable constant – decay as inextricably inscribed in beauty and life – and both present her, in a metapoetical sense, as a trope for the allegorising process.

Ultimately, however, tragedy resides more in Coverdale's than Zenobia's fate. Over her disembodied and then dead body she points to his own inscription by death – his death in life. Coverdale emerges from his narrative in the figure of the poet 'castrated' by the objects of his fantasy. This imaginary engrossment places him beyond the living, denies him sexual fulfilment and it places him beyond any aesthetic control, denying him artistic fulfilment. The duplicity of allegory resides superlatively in his own effort at representation. He disembodies his living friends into the figures of 'his private theater', vampiristically sucks their blood to revivify his own impoverished life. Yet this process is shown to disembody him as well. Not only, as I have suggested in my discussion of von Max's *Der Anatom*, because the imaginative and interpretive activity places the spectator–writer into a position closer to the dead than the living, requires an identification with the dead objects perused. But also because in the process, the poet and his life is absorbed into the 'dead text' of the absent/dead figures, into 'passions, errors, misfortunes' that are not his own, so that he becomes the empty body at which allegorically their absent meaning gains full presence (801ff.).

This 'fatal' absorption occurs without any clear explanation of the events emerging, without his final 'moral' controlling and distancing the events into a univocal meaning. He can neither disclose the 'secret hidden even from themselves', nor force them to fit his aesthetic design. Just as Zenobia's grotesque corpse is fixed into a figure of difference, Coverdale's death-in-life is a fatal fixture to this drama of his fantasy. One ambivalence remains in all readings of this case – an inability to determine who is the agent, who the object of the disembodiment. In this exchange, where the dead are present and the living absent, it can never be determined whether the narrator fades before the allegory of his text, as body at which it materialises, or whether he doesn't in fact use the complex narrative to signify his self-portrait, at the expense of the figures evoked. The displaced or hidden signified inevitably turns out to be the portrait of the artist as a living corpse.

The central move I have been describing in this third part is that real difference (in relation to death and to sexuality), ruptures the symbolic order, where stability is recuperated by virtue of a turn to tropes. To sustain itself, culture must repeatedly substitute these disruptive instances of the real for representations. Narratives discussed in this section articulate the belief in renewal and regeneration of corruption, i.e. a desire for closure. The texts to be discussed in Part IV will represent how the dead feminine body cannot only *not* be recuperated for cyclic renewal but actually infects this cycle with a deadly virus. Having focused on strategies of displacement and effacement meant to engender restability, I will now turn to examples where a desire for closure encounters an opposing desire that undermines this totalising ambition, and this subversive tendency emerges on the very site of presumed mastery and control, the feminine corpse.[24] While I focused on the stability of the image, the aesthetic reproduction in its reflection of the maternal body in Part II and on the stability of social order and its paternal law in Part III, I merge both concerns in Part IV – focusing once more on the desire to 'close' the grave's plate, to 'stabilise' images, but always in relation to the destability or dis-closure that remains, the difference between body and image that stays, the desires that continue to be deferred, unfixed, impossible: in short not the triumph over femininity *as* death, but the subversion of life by death *as* femininity.

Allegorical figuration proved to be a way to 'kill' the body in a complex strategy of exclusion. The living woman's body turns into a sign by virtue of a distancing focalisation. This prepares the reader for her death by already diminishing her *avant la lettre*. The woman as sign is literally eliminated or eliminates herself, in a highly ambivalent gesture that simultaneously materialises the sign by literalising the disembodiment that the foregoing semiotic exchange implied. The preserved sign as representation of the woman's body, now missing, signifies 'other' than the historical woman or Woman *per se*. Woman and death, tracing uncanny difference within, can, by virtue of allegorisation, become the canny difference of Otherness. But – the exclusion is never entirely perfect, the boundaries are never entirely clear. The disruptive element is banished beneath the bar of the grave's plate, beneath the signifier/signified break, though only imperfectly, never eternally, and certainly not without leaving scars.

An analogy between allegory and the fetish emerges given that both can be seen as strategies that hide even as they present the real – Blanchot's 'rotting Lazarus', Kristeva's 'semiotic chora', de Lauretis's woman as 'ground and vanishing point' – underlying the representation from which it is also excluded. These representations are, in Coverdale's terms, 'not quite simple' in their exchange with death and with femininity. They articulate *the* 'Other' repressed or hidden (real death and sexual difference); they articulate *that* it is a repressed, hidden signified; they articulate *what* is 'Other' to this repressed signified – the woman's body, beautiful, pure and whole in death. Ultimately the regulation of the semiotic chora in the symbolic, the confinement of the death drive in the act of ritualised murder runs alongside art. For the artist is constituted precisely as one who having interiorised death in order for artistic practice to function, and who, having exported death as semiotic mobility across the border on which the symbolic is established, undergoes a form of second birth.[25]

Sacrifice and art come to pose as diametric opposites, both feeding on death and femininity as semiotic mobility. The former assigns to the disruptive force its productive limit in the social and symbolic order, the latter, as 'semiotisation of the symbolic', as materialisation of the sign, marks the moment where the socio-symbolic order cracks open. While the former is a prohibition of death by language, the latter emerges as an introduction of death into and through language. Art's duplicitous function is that, through binding and through vital symbolic differentiation, it produces a seemingly acceptable representation as safeguard of society, even as it re-introduces the heterogeneous rupture and rejection, that is death's figure.

Notes to Chapter 11

1 C. Lévi-Strauss, 1969, p. 36.
2 C. Lévi-Strauss, 1969, p. 481.
3 C. Lévi-Struass, 1969, p. 496.
4 E. Cowie, 1978, pp. 49–63, and T. de Lauretis's discussion, 1984, of C. Lévi-Strauss.
5 J. H. Miller, 1981.
6 J. Kristeva, 1984.
7 R. Barthes, 1972, pp. 188–93, passim.
8 See J. H. Miller, 1981; T. Todorov; 1977, M. Warner, 1985; P. de Man, 1983.
9 The counter-episode is the one in which Troy seduces Bathsheba with his sword excercises, and it is not only significantly present in the text but in a suggestive way casts light on the repressed 'other' seduction scene. While in both seduction is linked to the threat of death, Bathsheba gets a kiss rather than death because Troy is dextrous enough with his sword not to cut into her body, while Fanny gets death as the result of a corporeal penetration and its reverse: insemination and birth-giving as ejection.
10 For a discussion of corpses as signs see M. Bal's analysis, 1988, of the raped and murdered wife in Judges 19.

11 M. Blanchot, 1981. See also E. Donato, 1984, pp. 30–45 for a discussion of Blanchot. Strictly speaking, the corpse as such has a neutral gender, and it is precisely the return to recognition and representation that lets the gender of the corpse re-emerge.

12 J. H. Miller, 1981, p. 357.

13 R. Barthes, 1978.

14 E. Ragland-Sullivan, 1987, points out that the father's name in Lacanian terminology refers to a symbolic effect of division, causing both loss of a previous wholeness, difference and individuation linking, that is, negation and naming/designating: 'Lacan refers . . . to the Law of the Name-of-the-Father, a play on the identical pronunciation of French non and nom', p. 55.

15 The stasis implied by Angel's narcissistic desire can be seen in conjunction with an aspect of the death drive, for as J. Kristeva, 1984, points out, though narcissism ensures life, it is only temporarily a position against the death drive: 'Narcissism and pleasure are therefore inveiglings and realizations of the death drive. The semiotic chora, converging drive discharges into stasis, can be thought of both as a delaying of the death drive and as a possible realization of this drive, which tends to return to a homeostatic state,' p. 241.

16 J. H. Miller, 'Tess of the D'Urbervilles. Repetition as Immanent Design', 1982, discusses the interplay between acts of sexual conjunction, of physical violence and writing, pp. 116–46.

17 M. Bal, 1991.

18 This recalls S. de Beauvoir's discussion of woman as an inessential figure, a disembodied sign without a referent, lacking reciprocity. Various other critics have discussed Angel's desire to spiritualise Tess, and thus deny her body. See P. Boumelha, 1982; T. Tanner, 1968; H. Michie, 1986.

19 Another link would be to the earlier section on feminine suicide, her corpse and the message attached to it, the last 'text' this woman of letters presents her audience with. The enactment of the poetess, dethroned by her lover, recalls another narrative: Madame de Staël's *Corinne ou L'Italie* (1807).

20 W. Benjamin, 1974. The relevant chapter is entitled 'Allegorie und Trauerspiel', pp. 336–65.

21 See J. H. Miller's discussion, 1981, of Benjamin.

22 M. Blanchot, 1981, uses the image of a rotting corpse to suggest that what literature articulates is the real that preceds language by which it has been blunted, yet which remains as a trace of an impossible fascination: 'Literature [wants] Lazarus in the tomb and not Lazarus brought back into the daylight, the one who already smells bad, who is Evil, Lazarus lost and not Lazarus saved and brought back to life', p. 42. The fascination for the female corpse within representation may lie in the fact that it operns up a space where the desire for that which ruptures the symbolic order can be articulated while simultaneously the impossibility of fulfilling such a desire is ensures, and with it the existence of the symbolic community.

23 My italics.

24 I am rephrasing C. Bernheimer slightly, in that he limits his discussion, 1989, to the display and dissection of the prostitute.

25 J. Kristeva, 1984.

PART IV

Stabilising the ambivalence of repetition

Love is not beautiful – only the dream of love enchants. Hear my prayer, serious youth! Do you see my beloved at my breast? Oh, break her off quickly, the rose, and cast the white veil over her blooming face. The white rose of death is more beautiful than her sister, for she recalls life and makes it more desirable and rare. Over the grave of the beloved her figure floats for ever young and decked in flowers and never will reality disfigure her appearance, nor will reality touch her so that she turn cold and the embrace find an end. Steal her away quickly, youth, for the fugitive will return in my dreams and my song. She makes a wreath out of my song and fades in my sounds towards heaven. Only the living beloved can die; the dead beloved remains with me and our love and our embrace is eternal!

The Nightwatch of Bonaventura

12

The speculated woman

We insisted on the excess of meaning that 'speculation' gives to the death instinct as compared with the deciphering of that instinct in its representations, of whatever level or order they may be.
Paul Ricoeur

Death and femininity are culturally positioned as the two central enigmas of western discourse. They are used to represent that which is inexpressible, inscrutable, unmanageable, horrible; that which cannot be faced directly but must be controlled by virtue of social laws and art. They serve as privileged tropes for the existence yet ineffability of truth and, as these two values are condensed at the site of the feminine corpse, this figure serves as a superlative instance of proof for the existence of truth as well as for a specific interpretation. Both pose as the privileged site for and legitimation of a hermeneutic quest. Both serve as the seminal question that grounds human existence, on the basis of which life can be defined even as no fixed answer, no stable truth can emerge. Death and femininity function as privileged enigmas to be solved yet also defying decipherment in another sense; they *must* not be solved, must be left open, undecided, indeterminate, marking the limit a system sets itself.

Significantly, Freud aligns a fear of death with the radical Otherness of Woman not only explicitly (in his notes on the Medusa figure and on the motif of the three caskets), but also implicitly in his late writings, given that writing on both subjects involves speculation and incompletion. Freud not only calls femininity a 'dark continent' but also brings forward his findings based on analytic research without waiting to obtain necessary proof because 'the time before me is limited'.[1] He speaks about the riddle of femininity 'uncertain . . . of the extent of my licence', and though he begins his famous lecture with the claim that he will present only observed facts, 'almost without any speculative additions', he closes by admitting the fragmentary nature of his theory. To find an end he is obliged to invoke the authority of experience in his listeners and turns to the poets for completion of what he must leave open.[2] In his formulations on the death drive, his inability to substantiate his claims with proof is, in turn, explicitly stated – 'what follows is speculation' – and here, too, an appeal to a poet is made to excuse the prematurity and uncertainty of his text.[3] To elaborate the double threat of death as femininity into an insoluble enigma is a form of distancing and boundary drawing that protects Freud from precisely the threat of an end, of incompletion, under the aegis of which he writes.

Up to this point I have illustrated how femininity and death mark the interstice of the supremely tropic, engendering a plethora of other signs with no fixed signified available, *and* of the non-tropic, the agency of the real which cannot be fixed into imaginary and symbolic signifiers. In this part I will focus on the latter aspect of the psychic process – the breaks that puncture the imaginary and the symbolic register, the crack that disrupts both orders so that, momentarily, the real emerges.[4] The central question is whether the crack of sexuality/death can be closed, with representation solving the enigma by virtue of disclosure. Whether such 'laying bare' implies the return to a univocal transparency of meaning that undoes all tensions resulting from ambivalence or whether disclosure sketches a trajectory towards renewed difference, with the resolution of the enigma of femininity/death only opening up to new ambivalences and uncertainties and in so doing enacting a radical failure to effect stable closure. At stake is the duplicity of the second term in Freud's 'fort--da' model, the undecidability and impropriety of the *fort* feminine body *da* in representation; of the way this *da* transports the feminine body *fort*, of the *da* as *fort*.

Jean Baudrillard argues that the phenomenon of survival must be seen in contingency with a prohibition of death and the establishment of a social surveillance of this prohibition. Social power and control is first and foremost grounded on manipulating and legislating death by breaking any unity between life and death, disrupting the exchange between the two, severing life from death and imposing a taboo on the dead. Power is installed precisely over this first boundary and all later, secondary aspects of division – between soul and body, masculinity and femininity, good and bad – feed off this initial and initiating separation that partitions life off from death. All forms of ensuing economy – be this monetary, libidinal or aesthetic – are based on this separation.[5]

Sacrifice and second burial transform a reversible exchange between life and death into an irreversible act. Culture's aim is to expel the ambivalence posed by death's presence in life, to rupture any reversibility of death so as to privilege a perpetration of life – whether this be in the form of religious notions of survival and eternity, of scientific truths or of economic reproduction. Once the boundary to Otherness is drawn by virtue of ritualised death, an endless sequence of symbolic exchanges among the survivors emerges – reduplicated death masks, images, narratives, kinship and gender relations. In the narratives now to be discussed, the effort at obliterating the exchange between life and death, highlighting the residue of this exchange with the dead finds expression in the hysteric bride and the melancholic mourner; in the creation of *unheimlich* doubles as an anticipation of death; in the experience of reading and writing as a dialogue with the dead.

For Baudrillard, death, however, also reappears in the shape of the inanimate symbols that serve as reference points once life is reduced to value under the aegis of accumulation. He criticises the depravity of modern life by virtue of a comparison to earlier periods or other cultures where the exchange between death and life has, supposedly, not yet been 'perverted'. I, however, will argue against this notion of supersession and illuminate instead how death's enmeshment with life and the expulsion of death from life are simultaneously present, with the feminine corpse serving as precisely the site at which the gains and losses of each attitude toward death can be debated.

Informing this fourth part is the issue of mourning and representation as psychic and aesthetic forms of repetition emerging from a position of liminality between life and death. Representation is inscribed by several aspects of repetition, as this rhetorical strategy involves doubling and restability. Repetition, engendering doubles, fragmentation or division functions as either a safeguard against or an omen of death. Repetition as the refinding of a love object engenders a libidinal identification with another over a sense of loss, so that love is inscribed by mourning. Repetition as the reanimation of a model, the return of a genuine first body in its artificial copy, articulates the duplicity that is inextricable from the production of art. The represented corpse effects a freezing of rupture, an erasure that transforms the threat of ambivalence posed by the living woman into the survivor's aesthetic gain.

Yet the question of an uncanny interplay between ambivalence and recuperated stability subtends my entire discussion. Either the dead feminine body – collapsing the two riddles, feminine sexuality and mortality, into one – will be shown to defy any clear explanations or the case will be such that precisely due to her death the woman can be read, can receive a stable meaning and, vice versa, by virtue of gendering, death can be endowed with a fixed signifier. Repetition and representation will be shown as either dangerous and/or healing, presenting a stable or an undecidable meaning. As the *unheimlich* liminality of the corpse translates into its own double in the form of representation, this repetition will either perform a safe fixture or preserve threatening oscillation. The texts will either encompass a *killing of repetition*, a killing of the feminine body to make repetition impossible. In this case the scenario serves as a trope for a triumph over repetition as that part of the death drive that traces discord, progression, and facticity on to life. Or these texts will represent *repetition as killing*. By making the second term, the supplement, the copy, repeat and confirm the first image, the uniqueness, autonomy and the alterity of the second term, i.e. its difference to the first, is obliterated. Finally, repetition also serves as an act that kills a body *avant la lettre* by replacing it with a symbol, which controls absence by virtue of such replacement. It enacts the satisfying illusion of a triumph over mortality by virtue of killing off that other aspect of the death drive whose aim is the static unity of the preanimate state.

Fig 29   Gustave Courbet. *La toilette de la morte (mariée)* (1850–55)

Fig 30   X-ray detail of the bride from illustration 29

To introduce my discussion of death and femininity as the two central enigmas of western discourse I will turn once more to a picture and the anecdote framing any possible reading of it. In 1919 one of Gustave Courbet's unfinished paintings (*c.*1850) that had never been exhibited during his lifetime, was posthumously put on the market under the title *La toilette de la mariée.* The dressing it depicts was considered to be that of a bride until 1977, when Helen Toussaint noted a strange disjunction between the assigned title and the subject of the painting.[6] For three reasons, she argued, the painting in fact represents the funeral toilette of a bride, the preparation of a corpse for its wake or its coffin. The title *La toilette de la morte* can be found in two inventory lists of Courbet's works, the iconography suggests mourning rather than nuptial rituals and, finally, the x-ray photograph of the central figure shows the young woman to be both nude and strangely lifeless; her head leaning on her left shoulder, a left arm, just like the right one, hanging limply along the left side of her body. The relation between the face of the 'bride' and the mirror is so unnatural that she could in fact not see herself at such an angle.

Even without the x-ray one could argue that the arm holding the mirror and the face of the 'bride' are so poorly executed to suggest that these details were added later. Toussaint concludes that we are faced with an uncanny toilette scenario. A painting depicting the dressing of a feminine corpse was made up *post facto* – the nude body covered with a corset and a skirt, the dead body given an additional animate, bent arm, opened eyes, taut mouth – and rebaptised. This resurrection of a dead woman, she conjectures, may have been the result of economic speculation, a ruse to make the painting more saleable by covering up a doubly macabre, threatening subject – death and feminine genitalia.

Linda Nochlin, however, points out that it is unclear whether others re-dressed the canvas or whether Courbet undertook the transformation himself.[7] It is equally undecidable whether the painting should, as Toussaint suggests, be read 'realistically', as the rendition of a rural custom that asks young women of the community to pay their last respects to the deceased friend of their childhood before the corpse is publicly laid in state. Or whether, as Nochlin argues, the canvas contains an allegorical dimension, equally based on French rural customs and, in that light, depicts the nuptial scenario as a melancholy leave-taking from youth and freedom before passing into the sad responsibilities of the married state. 'Such solemn song', Nochlin claims, was 'customarily sung to the bride by the young girls of the neighborhood on the morning of the wedding.'[8] In this painting, which involves the question of dressing thematically and structurally, the viewer must undress the canvas in an act of disclosure, if any form of closure is to be found for the riddle it manifests, even as she or he knows full well that owing to its unfinished palimpsest condition this case is undecidable. Two indeterminacies seem to cross in this canvas for, even as the truth (of the protagonist's feminine and dead body) eludes by virtue of the dressing, a second question emerges. How stable is the veil?

Courbet's canvas brings the interchangeability of bridal and death ritual into focus in a complex way. Because of its own toilette, because the posterior changes produce not a death but a life mask, the painting not only poses an undecidable question but poses as an uncanny representation in more than one sense. The original 'incorrect' assignment of a name has been transformed into a double title – 'Dressing the dead girl or Dressing the bride'. The former title is present though contradicted by the later revision, and the 'second'/'original' title, added/ returned to the painting, chiasmically undoes the second layer of paint on the canvas, the third arm and the face. In this palimpsest the bride is only uncannily animate, with the dead body shining through its beautified disguise to disclose not only once again that beauty hides death but also that inanimation is inherent to all representation. Either the deanimated corpse implicitly shines through the clothed body as its double, or, if one reads the figure indeed as a 'dead girl', then this cadaver poses as a double of the deceased, once living person. From the perspective of the representational process in general, where one image always phantomatically doubles a model or an implied referent in the material world, the process of duplication is raised to a still higher degree – making the canvas a revenant of a revenant. Precisely because of this doubledness of canvas surface and depth (the latter recognisable in the x-ray but spectrally visible even to the naked eye), the painting poses an enigma evoking speculation in three senses of the word – as an issue of visibility/occlusion; as an issue of economic risk and gain; and as the issue of a hermeneutic quest.

In more than one sense this canvas is a counterpart to von Max's anatomist for here also the centrality of the woman's death is so perfectly visible that art historians could only see it with some difficulty. Rather than arresting the moment just before a man unclothes a woman to open up her body and get to its centre, the artist or his imitator arrest the moment after the two aspects of the human body that most prominently figure lack and as such effect a castrative threat, have been covered – namely death and female genitalia. In both canvases the feminine body is in a liminal position, either about to be fully clothed, made up to procure the illusion of wholeness (as bride, as corpse laid out in state), or fully undressed and completely dismembered into a set of body fragments. Again one can draw a parallel with the painting process, where a model is revivified, made present in absence and the disjunction of the human body forced into the image of aesthetic unity but as an inanimate, aesthetic body.

Restability occurs in the Courbet painting both literally in the sense of dressing the corpse so it can be exposed as a beautiful whole body during the wake as well as figurally, in the sense of dressing the canvas to turn a cadaver into a bride. In one sense the protective veil procured by the additional layer of paint renders western culture's two central enigmas representable in the form of a resurrected, clothed bride. Just as it diffuses the superlative threat posed by the sight of the two privileged figures of lack, which are joined together at one and the same body. Closing the crack that death's encroachment on life induces by denying the body's deanimation, covering the gaping absence of female genitalia, seems at first glance to recuperate the woman's body in such a way that it supports the narcissistic desire on the part of the viewer to be reassured in his survivor's sense of unity as not castrated by death; i.e. as neither a decaying nor a sexually lacking body.

As in von Max's painting, however, death shines through beauty, disfiguration through the articulated illusion of wholeness. Furthermore, the sight of the dead sexual Other, though initially threatening, also empowers once the object of the gaze is clearly separated from the viewer as being different, so that a strange paradox can be formulated. The same gesture that reassures because it veils what is threatening to the eye also, by enforcing a mitigated vision, occludes the possibility of any clear boundary drawing between life and death and, furthermore, disturbs, since what emerges in this field of vision is an uncanny figure, the problematic of the double. Even as it conceals a double lack it produces a representational double and with it semantic instability. Erasing difference here also means highlighting this act of erasure and the production of difference. As Freud repeatedly shows, the double works by inducing a blindness towards, yet also an insight into, one's own mortality. Even as doubling is a compensation for death, the assurance of immortality, it can also figure as a harbinger of death. Courbet's canvas unwittingly poses questions about which aspect of difference to privilege. Should we focus on the difference death's presence causes in life, which preserves an uncanny exchange between the living and the dead? Or should we highlight the difference of the boundary, which fixes the living and the dead on opposite sides?

This transforms the question whether the central figure is alive or dead or both into one which asks whether the 'bride' doubles the 'dead girl', whether she is a trope for the impossibility of denying an exchange between the two or for death's inextricable inscription of life? But due to the *Unheimlichkeit* produced by the representational doubling, it can not be determined which signified to privilege: 'death' or 'bride', and if the latter, is the bride 'resurrected', a 'phantom', or 'socially dead'? What figure is the trope and for what idea – the bride for death, death for the bride; the bride for veiled genitals, veiled genitals for a a repression of death's castrative threat? At the same time that each figure can interchangeably serve as the trope for the other yet another possible signified for the image surfaces – the rhetorical strategy of hesitation between animate and inanimate, between absence and presence. The painting radically subverts any desire on the part of the spectator to establish any fixed points of reference – for the theme of the image, for its protagonist and for its tropes.

Furthermore the canvas-double, the palimpsest of the third arm holding the mirror over the effaced left arm, also marks a self-reflexive moment in the image, a comment on the way the representational process implies an exchange with the dead. Either in the sense of the artist reanimating a dead body to represent presence in absence, or in the sense that regardless of whether the implied subject of an image is a living body or not, the canvas's materiality implies the translation of life into inanimate visual or verbal characters. For this point it is worth noting the position of what probably is a mirror, but could also be a painting or a writing tablet. If we look at the gazes of all the women in the painting we note that no one is looking directly at the dead-bride. Only the woman standing behind her looks at her, but sees her as she is reflected in the mirror. This relay of gazes suggests an analogy to the position of the spectator, and in both instances viewing the corpse implies an indirect form of sight. Femininity and death can be conceived only as images even as they also refer to the real gap subtending all imaginary and symbolic relations, knowable only in bits and pieces.[9] The standing woman, who could equally be holding the mirror to the dead girl's face, sees the corpse as a reflection, as we see not a model but its painted copy reflected off the canvas.

By adding the implied double of the reflection in the mirror, the canvas contains yet another extension of the series of doubles, and introduces further questions. Does the painting, seen from this angle, tropically express that the standing woman sees her own death in the form of the reflected dead girl? Is this the axis we are to identify with – so that the dead girl functions as a tropic harbinger of our, the spectator's death? If we take the standing woman's gaze as our point of reference we must ask what do we see – is it death as feminine figure ricocheted back to the spectator in the refraction of the painting, reduplicating the way that the dead girl reflects back her companion in a mirror in which she can't see herself, not only because the open eyes are a faked addition but because the angle of the mirror precludes her seeing her self-reflection? The scenario we are then faced with is that the privileged object of our gaze, who is blind to her own image, can be seen only by a second woman, and our view intercepts the living woman's double sight – her gaze of the dead gaze of the bride.

To return to a comparison with von Max's *Der Anatom*, Courbet's painting enacts the ambivalent tension between a literal and a figurative reading, whereby to take the painting at face value, to see the woman as a living bride requires a form of blindness that I have called endemic to allegory, since it means overlooking the traces of death by turning them into metaphors of a bride's psychic state. To read literally in turn requires looking beneath the surface, requires an x-ray gaze that is equally inscribed by oversight. The uncanniness that ensues allows me to recall my earlier discussion of the fetish as an object which sets a permanent memorial to precisely that figure of lack it tries to deny and in so doing acknowledges it. As in the 'fort--da' scenario, where the player affirms the feminine absence which he also denies, the success of Courbet's painting also works on the multiple effacement of the woman. The 'deceased' is present again, repeated in the image, but it is her *Fortgehen* that is represented.[10] At the same time the represented woman is never present in her historical reality, but only as phantom, so that we have the representational revenant of a revenant.

This hinges on two further aspects of affirmative denial. Affirming the woman's spectral presence can be attained only by virtue of denying that the body is absent in its historical space because dead and absent in the pictorial space owing to the fact that it is covered. What remains undecided is whether this representational gesture reveals or effaces, preserves or obliterates, speaks or silences the woman's position; whether it subverts or confirms the lack she figures. Something repressed returns here, the *fort* as *da*, the dead feminine body not replaced by a spool or the spectator's own image, but present as absent in a duplicitous way. She is present yet absent because dead but unburied, and present but absent because her real condition, her death, is veiled. The analogy is also between dressing a dead girl to make her into the animate/inaimate fetish of the exposed body at the wake and dressing the canvas to make its subject the same type of uncanny fetish to be exposed in an art studio.

The made-up canvas destabilises precisely due to the fact that it entails duplicity, in the twofold sense of double and deception. The double crack is covered but not closed, the canvas now a permanent memorial to the dangerous exchange between life and death. The repainted representation constructs a unified, stable substitute for the first image of lack, and as such acknowledging it by virtue of covering the fragmented body, by placing a second layer on top. But the ensuing palimpsest works as a fetish to preserve the hesitation between denial and acknowledgement, to keep the boundary between lack and stable unity open. The uncanniness is such that in the disjunction between the first and second layer of paint, meant to hide death and feminine sexuality, a gap is produced in which the real instability of the human subject 'slips its mask'.[11] In the same vein one could say that the second coat of paint produces the imaginary unity over the knowledge of a fragmented body and of an irrevocable loss grounding life.

Lacan's typology assigns to Woman a position of division and oscillation between more than one point of reference, i.e. the lack of a stable, fixed place in opposition to the masculine position of mastery whose illusory stability masks a lack. In respect to Courbet's painting one could say that covering the double lack posed by the dead feminine body is a form of mastery, even as this gesture opens up a second lack – the lack of a fixed position. The same gesture that denies death as lack confirms it by denying a stability of position and it is not gratuitous that this real instability in all its duplicity should be figured as a body that is culturally constructed as having no stable position – Woman. If one takes Blanchot's analogy between images and cadavers/revenants, as one based on the fact that these bodies are nowhere and adds the feminine body to the sequence, the lack posed by death and the lack figured, in cultural constructions, by female genitalia can now be aligned with the lack which every image stages. Even as the body is covered to hide the fact that it is a corpse, the canvas structurally turns the body into a corpse, by presenting it without a fixed position or point of reference – dead/or alive, dead in life (bride), alive after death (revenant); the *aphanisis* of fading and re-emerging.

The fact that in respect to Courbet's painting it cannot be decided whether the enigma itself can be determined as such will be the theoretical leitmotif for this section. For one can read the positioning of 'woman as death as enigma' to be yet another rhetorical strategy which establishes canny difference, reducing the woman safely to the allegorical trope for a truth that remains eternally unknown, elusive. Or it establishes uncanny difference, in that the obliterated site shines through, the answer recedes and returns. It encompasses both an exchange between life and death and its prohibition. The riddle of feminine sexuality and death is both safely located in the beyond or beneath the grave plate, functioning as the inaccessible referent barred beneath the signifier-signified break and uncannily present within life as an unknown alterity. On two scores this undecidable enigma points back to the viewer, for one, in an eternal deferral of fixed meaning, in the proliferation of tropic readings that the painting engenders but also in the real that lies beyond and disrupts signification.

To say 'woman is nowhere' can mean two things. Woman serves allegorically as the site of a truth which is beyond man's reach. What he can't know, namely woman's lack (be it in respect to death or sexuality), translates into a lack in his knowledge. Or Woman is 'non-determinable', incessantly shifting, tracing a figure that defies the idea of a fixed, stable truth. She captivates precisely because her inaccessibility defers the unveiling of truth and keeps the promise of unveiled truth alive.[12] To pose Woman as an enigma, within such a conceptual frame, implies both that truth has no place and that Woman won't be pinned down by truth. The dissimulation ascribed to her lets Woman function as a trope for the veil that covers even as it articulates a gap or loss, and as such pointing to a truth in the real, inaccessible to language.

Woman's function is duplicitous. She is seen to figure as the site of truth and as embodying the proof that there is no truth; the enigma and its impossibility. Her body hides a truth that could potentially be disclosed or it hides the fact that there is nothing to hide. Reading the 'nowhere' or 'nothing' of Woman once again in relation to death evokes Blanchot's discussion of the strangeness of the corpse lacking a fixed point of reference. It also recalls Kofman's discussion of the image as revenant, in that Woman's dissimulation functions analogously to that of the artwork – she is and isn't what she seems to be. The *no-where* of the represented dead Woman may well be called an excessive enigma, or an enigma of excess.

Kofman's critique of Freud's theories on femininity focuses precisely on the way Woman as patient is transformed into the bearer of a secret which the analyst brings out into the open.[13] The implication is that Woman readily serves as metonymy for any other question not solved, such as death. The riddle of death can be solved by solving the riddle of Woman and vice versa, with the speculating man in the position of the analyst, trying to discover the concealed secret. In Freud's construction of femininity, the enigma that Woman is thought to pose readily transforms into dissimulation. Because Woman is silent about herself, she creates an excess of mystery and obscurity, turns herself into an indecipherable riddle, and her inability to disclose herself turns into a lack of sincerity. In his search for truth, the masculine speculator takes on the position of one who watches the other, tries to decipher the riddle she incorporates, tries to solve what she is silent about. The crux is whether Woman has a secret of which she is ignorant and which she is hiding from herself or whether she knows her secret and is wilfully hiding it. Will she, furthermore, collaborate with the speculating men in their attempt to solve the riddle that they choose to locate at her body or not?

As the initially silent body incorporating an enigma within a process of disclosure and resolution, Woman can, Kofman claims, assume three different attitudes. If she acknowledges that her silence about her 'secret' is the cause of her illness and is willing to collaborate with the speculator in a process where disclosure means cure, she belongs to the first type, the 'hysteric' woman. The speculating man needs woman's complicity in order to legitimise the value of his 'solution' even as he knows that a solution injected from the outside could only be inappropriate. As such, the truth disclosed at the body of the enigmatic woman is that of the investigating man. His success also marks his failure, in that the solution is predetermined and ricochets back the viewer's self-concepts, with his truth confirmed by her complicity. This leaves woman's alterity only the more inaccessible and unspoken as she now seems to be restored to speech. Dissimulation resides not only in the speculated Woman but equally in the speculating man. Woman's silence, however, invokes that other agency of silence in Freud's theory – the silent work of the death drive.

The second type of femininity is the 'narcissistic' Woman, characterised by an inaccessibility, and as such not unlike the criminal. She is enigmatic owing to her self-sufficiency and her indifference.[14] She fascinates because she has preserved an original narcissism, an unassailable libidinal position which man has irrevocably lost. The intactness he has lost is refound, by virtue of projection, at the site of this type of Woman. Once again the essence of femininity is associated with death for man's fascination with the eternal Woman as figure for preserved intact narcissism signifies a fascination with his own double or with a ghost. The narcissistic Woman is an *unheimlich* figure, the site at which what one thought had been overcome or lost for ever abruptly reappers. In the fascination for the narcissistically intact feminine body, a fascination for death returns under the double veil that feminine beauty as riddle draws. Woman's refusal to betray her secret, however, is also frightening in that it 'castrates' man's privileged speculator position on two scores. Her indifferent self-sufficiency denies any relation to the man and in so doing subverts the desire for re-confirmation for which he turns to her in the first place. Her inaccessibility and impenetrability again pose an insoluble enigma.

At issue in the representations to be discussed is both the violence with which the threat posed by death's inscription in life is countered, and the violence with which Woman is forced into the position of man's accomplice, supporting his search for an answer or solution. The fatality is that this solution not only figurally destroys the Woman by turning her into a site of an exterior meaning but also that she must literally die for the solution to emerge – either because she refuses to comply or because, even if she were a willing accomplice, the disjunction which her living body poses remains a threat. However, though the hysteric seems to be a more gratifying solution, because seemingly an accomplice, my discussion of Courbet's 'redressed' canvas suggests that this form of 'complicity' is threateningly destabilising on another, namely the rhetorical level. Unlike Kofman I will argue that the narcissistic position of 'self-sufficiency' of woman located beyond masculine culture may, in fact, ultimately be more reassuring.

Kofman's third type, fundamentally ambivalent like Freud's 'third casket', is the 'affirmative' Woman. Like the fetish, she is split between denial and affirmation of lack, leaving room for doubt as to her castration or noncastration.[15] Undecidable by nature, she oscillates between positions of incarnating truth and deception, affirming her femininity but denyings any notions of castration, and as such denying a fixed sexual alignment. Difference is seen as the affirmation of an undecidable compromise, the reconciliation of incompatible attitudes to lack and integrity, be this in respect to gender or to death's presence in life. This type of Woman oscillates between a complicity with man's attempt at deciphering her 'riddle' and a complete recession from his gaze, in order to avert any rigid fixture in the one or the other position.

The fetish is not a substitute but rather a concealment that points to the fact that the compromise is undecidable, that the incompatible is never reconciled. Woman sharing this position remains an 'enigma' yet discloses that she is such – fading and returning; lifting the veil even as she covers herself; oscillating between being immobilised as the disclosed woman, laid bare, and being relegated as the eternally enigmatic woman to the realm safely beyond, untouchable, forbidden, irrevocably veiled. If the hysteric type is no longer threatening because stabilised in her disclosure, because completely accessible to the speculator, and the narcissistic type is no longer dangerous because, though veiled, unreachable, clearly Other, the affirmative type disrupts this clarity of oppositions. She introduces veiling into disclosure, the receding into the graspable and returns as irreducible.

Of course all three types are cultural constructions that help conceive and stabilise the masculine speculator's world precisely in relation to the double enigma of feminine death. In Courbet's painting all three position of sight can be located. Acknowledging only the x-ray image discloses the riddle, only seeing the second coat of paint relegates the riddle to the beyond. A gaze shifting between the two denies and affirms the lack that the uncanny double of the dead-bride poses. The crucial position is, then, that of the affirmative 'fetish' as marking a gesture of possibilities left open. Yet one must make a distinction between two versions. On the one hand we have an undecidability that subverts the safety of the spectator's position, that makes living and dead, masculine and feminine, an ambivalent relation. On the other hand we have a plethora of possibilities of interpretation that ultimately results in a safely intact spectator position. The first form destabilises by virtue of inscribed difference, the latter confirms by virtue of plurality.

With my argument being that gender constructions are supplementary to the division between life and death and serve to draw a boundary between these two mutually implicated terms, I will work with a reformulation of Kofman's typology, locating the traits of the 'affirmative type' in the hysteric. In so doing I follow Stephen Heath's discussion of the hysteric position, as one vacillating between being a man and a woman, resisting and accepting the 'castration' culture assigns to her. Psychoanalysis, as Freud's fragmentary analysis of Dora documents, fails before the hysteric and must close its discussion of femininity by posing Woman as the great enigma, the 'dark continent'. It must do so precisely because the logic of a sexual identity, where the masculine phallus is the gauger and standard and difference an issue of having or not, is unable to envisage any other economy of identity. If one sees hysteria only as an issue of sexual identity, and as such a part of Woman's nature, one overlooks that hysteria is also the site of Woman's resistance in culture.[16] The other economy of identity, whose inscription the hysteric could be seen to trace, is that of our exchange with death. Her refusal to accept a clear gender postion may also be resistance to the way a fixed sexual identity implies an occultation of this other exchange.

The histrionic oscillation of the hysteric is an enactment of keeping boundaries (between life and death, self and Other, masculine and feminine) fluid. This puts into question whether her complicity is sincere or only yet another turn of dissimulation. She traces an affirmative as disruptive figure, miming the speculator's solution even as she knows it is not her own. In so doing she preserves a dangerous doubleness and while the narcissistic Woman (as demonised criminal or deified muse) is clearly in a position of canny Otherness, exterior and beyond, the hysteric marks the position of difference preserved, which is located neither clearly outside, nor only on the margin, but also unsettlingly within.

Notes to Chapter 12

1 S. Freud, 1925a, p. 249.
2 S. Freud, 1933, pp. 112–33.
3 S. Freud, 1920, p. 24.
4 Like the double coding of the word 'nothing' discussed in Part II, the meaning of the word 'crack' is significantly duplicitous. It can refer to both a fissure introducing a gap or void, and the vulva. In the same vein as the mythic figure of Medusa, crack readily transforms into a trope articulating the conjunction of feminine genitals and mortality.
5 J. Baudrillard, 1976, especially chapter five.
6 H. Toussaint, 1977.
7 L. Nochlin, 1988.
8 L. Nochlin, 1971b, pp. 37f.
9 For a discussion of the way blind eyes turn into a trope of death see M. Bal's discussion of blindness in Rembrandt's paintings, 1991. P. Barber, 1988, explains that in popular belief the mirror was thought to contain the soul of the deceased in the form of a reflection, so that by inversion the reflection of an image is potentially the receptacle of the soul of a deceased.
10 This works even if one reads the painting as depicting a bride, whose marriage is a form of *Fortgehen* from her paternal home.
11 E. Ragland-Sullivan's definition of the real, 1987.
12 J. Derrida, 1979.
13 S. Kofman, 1985a, p. 65.

14 S. Kofman is citing Freud's discussion, 1914, of the narcissistic woman as *selbstgenügsam* and *unzugänglich*.
15 See also Elizabeth L. Berg's review, 1982, pp. 11–20.
16 S. Heath, 1978.

13

Rigor has set in – the wasted bride

If a woman insists she can and does love and her living isn't loveless or dead, she dies. So either a woman is dead or she dies.
Kathy Acker

Freud ends his lecture 'On Femininity' (1933) with a discussion of the woman at thirty. As though the difficult development to femininity has exhausted her possibilities, she 'often frightens us [*erschreckt uns*],' he claims, 'by her psychical rigidity [*psychische Starrheit*] and unchangeability [*Unveränderlichkeit*]'.[1] Feminist critics have argued that by virtue of the 'cadaverous' connotation of the word *Starrheit*, Freud unwittingly exposes the mortifying tendencies western culture inflicts on its daughters. Assimilating the prescribed position of femininity is a 'death sentence' for women.[2] At thirty, Woman is characterised by fixture into a definite posture, by an impossibility of evolving further, a psychic death. Like the sight of Medusa, this 'rigidity' of the mature Woman, however, not only frightens the viewer but confirms his psychic survival, his changeability. Critiquing Freud, Kofman argues that the designation 'Woman's deathlike rigidity,' implies the desire to put an end to the enigmatic and ungraspable nature of Woman, to the perpetual shift between masculinity and femininity. This act of rhetorically making a dead body of Woman translates into a desire to fix instability and mobility into a definitive and immovable position.[3]

Freud implies that only at the price of death, as the triumph of one fixed position over an oscillation between various points of reference, can a woman at thirty reach maturity. That a feminine character will say no to such psychic rigidity by choosing real death instead, is the trajectory sketched in the two novels I will discuss – Edith Wharton's *The House of Mirth* (1905) and Arthur Schnitzler's *Fräulein. Else* (1923). In both the living protagonist, whom I will call a 'bride' in the sense that she is in transition between a father's and a husband's home, shifts between various points of definition (in respect to sexual, class and professional identity) with a multitude of possibilities open to her. She represents an enigma to herself and to those she lives with, for which her death serves as a solution. She is an object of spectulation – owing to her beauty she is the object of an erotic and an aesthetic gaze, owing to her bridal liminality she gives rise to epistemological conjectures or becomes the site for risky economic transactions.

The oscillation of her sexual desires and the instability of position within a social order is always coupled with a more general discussion of the ambivalence of meaning, i.e. the impossibility of reaching univocal, stable truth. Each text revolves around the way that sight solves an enigma, even as procuring a solution also entails violence inflicted on the resolved 'body', which had posed as the site of the question. What remains open to debate, however, is whether the bride's death is a moment of real subjectivity because it reflects the choice of her fate, or whether it is the acme of her social victimisation. The former case implies that death is a moment of subjectivity because it engenders a destruction of the gendered body, which, were the bride to accept it, would also mean accepting the constraints culture requires of the 'mature' feminine position. Destroying her body is coterminous with destroying the site at which culture locates the curtailment of her subjectivity. In other words, these representations of the 'dead bride' raise the question whether the position ascribed to fulfilled femininity is a form of psychic death or whether death is the only agency of real feminine power and self-articulation.

Following Lily Bart's spectacular performance in a tableau vivant at the Welling-ton Bry's evening entertainment which marks the *peripeteia* in her story, Wharton has a man, who was not present at the spectacle yet informed of the gossip it provoked, comment, 'when a girl's as good-looking as that she'd better marry; then no questions are asked' (166). Questions *are* asked, when superlative beauty is displayed by a feminine body that has no fixed position socially – the potential wife. Existing between the positions of daughter and wife, in a position of transition that is disturbingly ambiguous, the premarital bride belongs to no one, which means that she is nobody.[4] But if the danger of the transitional resides in the fact that this state is undefinable, the danger and fascination that the bride exerts can also be attributed to the fact that she could potentially belong to everybody, that she could be anything and everything. Posing as an enigma, in the sense of an endless potentiality of meaning and social possibilities, Lily's body consciously displayed in all its decorative rarity serves as the interstice for various forms of speculation and its ultimate decipherment directs the novel's trajectory.

Part of her 'rarity' resides in her double difference from the social group she inhabits – her extreme beauty which places her beyond and her impoverishment which places her beneath them. She signifies lack in a double sense – she lacks their wealth and a secure place in their society, yet embodies the refinement they in turn lack. Owing to her premarital liminality, she not only more readily gets involved in episodes that gossip terms 'queer' but is also readily cast into the position of scapegoat, sacrificed to the double standard of her culture. Repeatedly she is used by a wife to cover up an illicit romance or serves as the bait by which an estranged husband can be retrieved. She herself is undecided about settling in the fixed position of a prosperous marriage, fearing this might be a form of psychic death, a closing of precisely the plethora of possibilites as yet undefined. Though she stakes her entire existence to entice a rich suitor, she repeatedly hesitates in the decisive moment only to lose her catch. Even as she is the object of various social intrigues, she never fully enters this exchange, never uses discriminating evidence against one of her rivals. Ironically her success in the end encompasses her superlative failure to achieve the social position of rich wife. The central ambivalence, however, is that Lily, by speculating with her own beauty, turns herself into an object of sight and in so doing doubles herself. In the gap between the 'real' Lily, impenetrable even to herself, and the appearances she stages, which point to an ever receding subject, the living body seems to fade before its function as deanimated sign in an aesthetic, erotic and socio-economic exchange.

When Lily chooses to exhibit herself as Reynolds's 'Mrs Lloyd' because this guise allows her to 'embody the person represented without ceasing to be herself', presenting to the public eyes a picture in the flesh which 'was simply and undisguisedly the portrait of Miss Bart' (141), she merely stages to excess her position within this wealthy New York society and by virtue of this excess discloses its premises. The brilliance but also danger of this guise of undisguised self-presentation is that she has dressed to perfection by not dressing in splendid clothes and jewels. She has used the citation of a painting to veil the fact that she is standing before her audience with all her own 'flesh and blood loveliness' unveiled.

The disturbance the beautiful Lily Bart poses in general, since she is always on display, engenders contradictory and fatal semiotic-economic speculation precisely because, having no clear social position, she is from the start in a social boundary realm, nowhere. These speculations range from bartering for, violating and possessing her body, to passing a moral judgement that results in a social death. All are attempts at giving fixture to or obliterating that body which threatens because it is undefinable, incalculable, indeterminate. Lily is liminal in more than one sense. She is an orphan with no secure home, vacillating between her aunt's and her rich friends' houses. Addicted to luxury but impoverished, she lives parasitically off her friends and card gambling. Decorative but unskilled, she can find no position in the work force yet remains undecided whether she wants a mercantile marriage or a romance equivalent to poverty. Owing to this position of nowhere, Lily is *unheimlich*, representing death in a complex manner. Again it is no coincidence that the disruption of death into this society of wealth should be traced at an excessively beautiful feminine body.

The different interpretations Lily's tableau vivant elicits, crystallise the way that she, by being the site of endless possibilities, of desires potentially realised, not only provokes a plethora of fantasies in her audience but also, at her body, collapses the distinction between literal and figural meaning; between the art of play and the reality of life. In so doing, she disrupts the code of conventions by causing a confusion as to how to respond to, how to read her spectacle. Her tableau's success as well as its scandal resides in the fact that it is ambivalent in an undecidable way. Her costume is perfidious in that it dresses her in such a way that she could be perceived as being undressed, crossing an aesthetic with a pornographic self-display. In that the dressing serves to feign simplicity even as the body is completely stylised, it also crosses the tropic with the real. Consequently what her tableau leaves undecided is whether this is an indecent self-display or a rare aesthetic moment; whether it calls for a moral or an aesthetic reading. Owing to this uncanny shifting between stylisation and honest simplicity, it is further undecidable whether Lily hides her truth behind the veil of her costume; or whether the costume hides that there is nothing behind, that she is only appearance; or whether it sanctions the forbidden, the presentation of a disclosed/disclothed body.

As a tableau vivant, she is both image and body, leaving unclear whether she has displaced the doubly absent model (the deceased Mrs Lloyd replaced by an image) or vice versa. Is she tropically enacting her own death because identifying with a dead woman, because vanishing beneath an alterior image, or is this an act of self-creation at the cost of and over her body, which fades and is highlighted simultaneously in this gesture? This scene also serves to demonstrate most explicitly how the speculations which the spectacle of her beautiful body arouses intertwine an erotic, a hermeneutic and an aesthetic gaze. Lily's is the privileged body at which desire is invested even as it enacts the dialectic of appearance and true self and as it poses the question whether Lily fades into an imitation of a painting or fades the painting into a creation of herself as art. It couples the issue of the body as stake in a financial investment transaction and the social speculation called gossip on the basis of which communal dynamics and restability are assured.

The least involved spectators read her self-presentation as an example of excessively honest vanity – 'Deuced bold thing to show herself in that get-up; but, gad, there isn't a break in the lines anywhere, and I suppose she wanted us to know it!' (142). Or they read it literally, as a comment on her premarital status, 'a girl standing there as if she was up at auction' (166). The Jewish art connoisseur Rosedale's response merges the economic with the aesthetic, 'if I could get Paul Morpeth to paint her like that, the picture'd appreciate a hundred percent in ten years' (167). The sight of Lily's spectacle provokes him to propose marriage to her precisely because she seems reducible to a natural/material sign for wealth. She would be his perfect representation, wearing the crown he could give her 'as if it grew on her', and in the transformation dissimulating that his social superiority was natural rather than acquired. Gus Tenor (who deludes Lily into thinking he is speculating with her money when instead he is giving her money of his own), libidinally speculating that this gift will procure him her body, chooses to read Lily's pose as an invitation to call in his claim. In his case sexual and social desires cross. For the money he has been lending Lily he wants her to acknowledge him in public by privileging him with her look. Wounded in his pride because she keeps the exact nature of their relationship unclear, in fact distinctly avoids acknowledging any privileged position to him in public, he tricks her into a nocturnal visit whose 'deceptive appearance' will be read by others as a clear confirmation of the gossip already circulating about them.

Seldon, the suitor she acknowledges emotionally yet must deny for financial reasons, reads Lily's performance as the presentation of her truth or essence – 'for the first time he seemed to see before him the real Lily Bart, divested of the trivialities of her little world, and catching for a moment a note of that eternal harmony of which her beauty was a part' (142). Detached into the realm of aesthetic display, she seems to him no longer in complicity with and no longer 'cheapened and vulgarized' by the world of the rich. It is precisely this purity she is meant to represent to him. If untainted, eternally harmonious beauty can, by virtue of its materialisation at her body, be detached and preserved, then he is assured of its existence in the world. His response, not unlike the other two men who believe they have a claim to her, is to offer his love.

What he has read in the spectacle is that Lily, separated from her context, is the desired companion 'who should confirm, by deliberate observation, the truth to which his intuitions had leaped' (162). The performance seems to have closed the division Lily previously embodied, the disjunction between his sense of her true purity and the gossip about her immoral manner. If he were to take her 'beyond the ugliness, the pettiness, the attrition and corrosion of the soul' into which her context has forced her, her purity, and by extension his truth, would be assured. Concomitantly, the fear that her dissimulation and her 'ugly uncertainties' are in fact an inextricable difference within would be expelled.[5] Because Seldon, in search of truth, ironically believes it to be located on the surface, his deification readily changes to a univocal condemnation. Seeing Lily leave Gus Tenor's apartment at night he will not accept that appearances are deceptive, and without explanations disengages himself from her.

For Lily herself, the spectacle of her body takes on various interpretive aspects, typical of her psychic vacillation. At first she is motivated by an undirected, one could say polymorphous exhibitionism – the narcissistic 'exhilaration of display-ing her own beauty, the desire to show that her loveliness was no fixed quality' (138). In the presence of Seldon, the self-intoxication is suddenly directed and because his gaze confirms her triumph, it seems to her that 'for the moment . . . it was for him only she cared to be beautiful' (144). She is drawn into his romantic notions that his love would cleanse her from the taint of her social position, but diametrically opposed to him, her performance only serves to clarify the irrevocable split within herself.

After she has escaped Tenor's attempted violation, she is forced to realise the full import of the duplicity she has enacted; 'she seemed a stranger to herself, or rather there were two selves in her, the one she had always known, and a new abhorrent being to which it found itself chained' (156). Playing to the fantasies of the masculine gaze irrevocably means complicity; self-display can never be innocent and all readings, even the crudest, are somehow intended by her. While Seldon obliterates the division, sees Lily first as figure of truth and then of duplicity, Lily is forced to face her own doubleness, i.e. that ugliness and calculation are merely veiled by her decorative self-display. By extension, the splendour of her rarity, much like the rankness of Zenobia's beauty discussed earlier, is a trait that readily transforms into its seemingly opposite value, articulating not only the uncommonly fine but also that which is about to be extinguished. It is only logical that Seldon's love would appear to be her only hope and that its aim at purifying any difference within her, resolving the tensions of her psychic and social existence, would be figured in language evoking another kind of death – the thought of confiding in him became as seductive as the river's flow to the suicide" (183). It is also logical that she will reverse these two reference points and choose real suicide when her other suitor fails her.

It is worth noting several further aspects of uncanny doubleness raised by the tableau vivant scene, for not just the response it elicits but also its success is duplicitous. Even as the audience's approval is 'called forth by herself, and not by the picture she impersonated' (143) the completeness of Lily's triumph in this society, in which she is a stranger, can significantly also only happen when she positions herself in a 'boundary world between fact and imagination' (140). The ambivalent doubleness or division produced is multiply inscribed by the rhetoric of *Unheimlichkeit*: death's figure in life. In a complex manner the dress she assumes places her in a position of undecidability between the living and the dead and renders her as the site of their exchange. Imitating Reynolds's 'Mrs Lloyd', the bride not only dissimulates a wife but, in doing so, poses as the body double of a dead woman. Depending on the spectator's perspective either Lily repeats a dead wife, borrows her position, to give herself a false appearance while occulting her from the field of vision or Lily in some sense fades into the appearance of the dead woman, given that she appears to be like her and in so doing resurrects this dead woman over her own living body. Given that she is imitating not the model but her portrait, the question of doubles is itself doubled: 'It was as though she had stepped, not out of but into, Reynolds's canvas, banishing the phantom of his dead beauty by the beams of her living grace' (142). Even as she gives life to a portrait as revenant she fades into a portrait, becomes the dead beauty of the image she simultaneously revivifies.

In a sense Seldon's disillusionment with Lily, which causes the fatal break in their relation, can be located in his mistaken belief that an image of beauty signifies intact purity. My discussion of images has shown that though it articulates the lack grounding unity, excessive beauty can be seen as the summit of the perfect image turning back on itself. Beauty is an escape from ephemerality even as it is itself elusive, just as Lily states her rarity by constantly receding from a fixed position. Three signifiers are thus contained in her beautiful self-display – the illusion of eternity and stability beyond any taint of facticity (her historical context), an awareness of the elusiveness of this gesture which confirms her facticity, and a denied affirmation of the disjunction between the two. The image she installs with her body is inscribed by uncannines and engenders a sense of insolubility.[6]

In a similar manner the issue of power invoked is complex. Though as an object of sight Lily seems to confirm the act of appropriation, domination and possession by her spectators, she is also the creator of this body-image. Because she eludes each individual spectator's grasp, she works as a fetish breaking the illusion of control even as she inspires it. At the same time that others speculate with her body, use her as stake in marital feuds only to expel her in the end, she speculates with her self and subverts the opposition between victim of an act of objectification and its agent. She 'kills' herself before her time by turning herself into an artwork, and in so doing emerges as an accomplice to the culture that requires such reification of its feminine members. Yet this gesture is also her form of individual, creative self-expression. Given that in staking herself as 'speculated woman' she is inconsistent and uncalculable, never clearly directed at one intended spectator and shifting between an affirmation of this position and its refusal, she demystifies such a reduction to the status of image. In doing so, she seems to disclose the mortifying tendencies of the very conventions she complies with, turning her feigned complicity as dissimulation into the hysteric's form of resistance.[7]

I have presented such a detailed reading of Lily's tableau vivant firstly because it summarises the way Lily is not clearly placed and instead occupies the position of nowhere. As in the Courbet painting the question is whether the real Lily is 'dead', buried beneath the social requirement to be a decorative object reflecting its spectators, whether like an image she is a cadaver without an individual personality.[8] Or whether her self-display, presenting undecidable aspects of doubleness, evolving from her own sense of being divided and undecided, doesn't give figure to the rhetoric of death's presence in life. Secondly, this self-creation has a corollary and resolution in her other attempt at speculating with her body, when she takes a fatal dose of the 'incalculable' chloral. Her corpse, an uncanny double of the tableau vivant, in a sense its chiasm, poses one final time as an object of speculation for Seldon and as the site of his truth. In order to illuminate the import of these final scenes of the novel it is necessary to sketch the other ways in which Lily traces the figure of death throughout her twenty-ninth year before its actual event.

Freud argues that the death drive is that force which strives for a state of tensionless constancy within the psychic apparatus. It is that force which translates freely flowing, unstable energies or any unbound state of excitation, into a bound stability, with its aim the complete absence of tension. A second aspect of the death drive, however, resides in any process that produces divisions and disjunctions, and in so doing protects against the stagnative fixture that is inscribed into any illusion of wholeness or univocal stability (the *unheimlich* double). This latter notion conceives of death not as the tensionless origin and aim of life but rather as the mark of difference and lack always inhabiting life.

By virtue of her self-speculation, Lily Bart incorporates and enacts both aspects of death. By turning herself into an object of display, she uncannily doubles herself, and the undefined subject position of nowhere she inhabits lets her repeatedly trace the second aspect of the death drive – the disruption of the notion of a secure, eternal and stable position or meaning. However, she not only marks lack by virtue of her impoverishment and unsure social position, but also embodies a lack in conviction that a fixed position in society is all she wants. Her inability to decide on one husband, her hesitation in crucial moments that lets her fail at binding the man of her choice, makes her actions incalculable. Her 'difficulty of deciding' can be seen as a disguised form of social critique. By striving for a stable position within this society even as she repeatedly engineers her failure, she puts into question the desirability of this life of wealth. She is an uncanny accomplice, tracing a disruptive crack on the self-assurance of this group because she seems to confirm its values even as she questions them.

Her psychic indecision can also be seen at the heart of her love for taking risks, with gambling emerging as another form of that aspect of death which disrupts certainty and stabilities. Because of her card playing for money, her financial speculation with Trenor as well as the chances she takes with the husbands of her friends, gossip represents her as an agent of strife, as a dangerous threat to the preservation of moral standards, at the same time that her body comes to serve as the site at which these couples resolve their conflicts by expelling her from their group.

She marks the enigma of difference within this society and subverts its conventions either by virtue of a disjunction between her intentions and her actions, so that she remains unfathomable – as one friend says, 'I can't make you out' (78). Or she figures as an enigma because she will not clear herself after she has become entangled in queer situations because she believes that there is no place for her story precisely because she is liminal: 'What is truth? Where a woman is concerned, it's the story that's easiest to believe' (236). Lily is also matchless and rare, owing to the beauty of her 'unexplained scruples and resistances' (315) against fully becoming an accomplice in the network of intrigue, and in that sense, too, she serves to figure a marked distinction from the vulgarity of her aspired society.

Lily's vacillation could be read as her source of strength. It enacts that a firm position may not only not be desirable but also questionable in a social and a semiotic sense: a form of resistance against the urge to totalise, to produce a penetrable story.[9] Her 'passion for gambling' expresses itself in part in the fact that she will never tell the truth behind any of the scandals she is involved in. She will keep the solution to herself, yet she justifies this reticence by explaining that any one story is merely one of many possible versions (236). In that she always slips the grasp of her spectators, she traces death's figure in life by provoking the emergence of the real instability beneath any effort to transform the other into a representation of a stable truth. Precisely because she will neither let herself be solved (semiotically bound to one position), nor be fixed as unfathomable (bound to the position beyond the system), she causes disjunctions to become visible and disrupts notions of transparent univocal truth. Her social death can also be read as a trope for the way such an appearance of death in life must be occulted. Her elusive oscillation, her nowhere on the social and semiotic level also suggests a 'castrative no' to the position of femininity culture offers. It suggests a resistance against this safe but rigid definition to the point of annihilation. The tragic paradox is that in its extreme consequence, she needs to destroy her body to maintain her resistance against psychic rigidity, even as society must, at least figurally, destroy her to preserve its rigid definition against the threat of difference, ambivalence and disjunctions she embodies.

Yet even as her incalculability encompasses an embrace of the unbound, the undefined, the ambivalent, Lily also desires a release from tensions, longs for the shelter of the bound: 'Any definite situation would be more tolerable than this buffeting of chances, which kept her in an attitude of uneasy alertness toward every possibility of life' (101). In this last year of her life, a definite situation takes on three guises – the rigidity of a rich marriage with all the ugliness of calculation its splendour hides; the escape from this life of dissimulation that Seldon's love promises and the obliteration of all tension in real bodily demise. Significantly the choice she finally makes – the third option – is immanently connected to her privileged spectator Seldon.

Throughout the novel these two characters are perfectly matched in that they mark the other's lack. Seldon repeatedly provokes Lily's awareness of her difference within: 'there were in her at the moment two beings, one drawing deep breaths of freedom and exhilaration, the other gasping for air in a little black prison-house of fears' (67). His presence makes difference appear; it 'always had the effect of cheapening her aspirations, of throwing her whole world out of focus' (92). The thought of him turns what she wished to gain into what she will give up and he is repeatedly the reason why she lets her marriage plots fail. Indeed, he understands himself as 'the unforeseen element in a career so accurately planned' (72). The cruel irony is that even as Seldon transpires into Lily's superlative risk, she is that which he desires as long as it means no risk; an exquisite, vigorous, and expensive object he enjoys 'as spectator'.

Their romantic choices are informed by their attitude toward death, with the latter (as in the conflict between Carmen and José), highlighting their core difference. While Lily will embrace the disruption to stable unities that death causes, indeed sees Seldon as an encouragement to do so, he denies the presence of difference within, seeks as a collector of rare objects the eternally static form of death rather than death as unbound and oscillating energy. He admires the fluctuation of Lily's beauty, the difference her rarity makes to her common surroundings because he can read it as a sign for her soul, a sign for ideal truth. But he scorns her fluctuation when it appears as dissimulation only to signify an enticement to 'dangerous accident' (195).[10] She also represents difference for him – the way 'matchless beauty' stands in difference to the vulgarity of social wealth, her 'special poignancy, her grace' cheapening the world she aspires to. Yet he can not accept that *this* difference, a mark of superiority, is inextricably linked to that *other* difference – the vacillation between positions that causes 'ugly uncertainties' (345) to appear.

At no point is the issue of risk more critical than in the case of the letters between Seldon and Bertha Dorset, which Lily having bought by chance could use as the final stake in her gamble to return to the society from which gossip and disinheritance has barred her. Torn between the desire for luxury that blackmail would ensure and an abstract notion of honour, she interrupts her walk to Bertha's home and visits Seldon. In this final meeting, the value each had for each other is confirmed one last time. For Seldon she continues to embody difference, to represent what is rare, the ideal lacking in his world but also beyond his reach. He, in turn, preserves her sense of integrity, but over an awareness of irrevocable loss – his offer of love marks the life 'I had missed', showing integrity and wholeness to be both desirable and impossible.

The realisation of this impossibility means acknowledging the lack inhabiting her life and she formulates it as the need to sever forever from herself and leave with him his idealised version of her, the 'Lily he has known', i.e. the Lily of his loving gaze (325). This separation is explicitly a form of suicide – 'they stood in the presence of death. Something in truth lay dead between them' (326). Having decided against her second choice – love as healing her difference within – she also decides against the first choice – social success. With a gesture Seldon 'hardly noticed at the time' she drops the letters into the fire. This 'last great effort' leaves her willpower completely 'spent', 'lost in the blank reaction which follows an unwonted expenditure of energy' (328).

This gesture, I want to argue, is an empty gesture in the sense used by Lacan to formulate that becoming subject means freely assuming what is imposed on us, the real of the death drive. Reformulating Lacan, Slavoj Zizek writes, 'sub-jectivization is a name for the gaze by means of which we confront the utter nullity of our narcissistic pretensions.' Woman, who is nowhere, constitutes herself as subject, 'at the moment at which, through the hysterical breakdown, she *assumes* her non-existence . . . beyond hysterization is the death drive at its purest'.[11] This empty gesture marks the moment that Lily moves beyond the two aspects of beauty perfected in her tableau vivant – beyond the histrionics and discrepancies contained in her hysterical complicity with culture's demands that Woman pose as a decorative display in which she is other than herself *and* beyond the ideal enigmatic perfection completely removed from any common context, the pose of eternal truth. Instead she embraces death in its pure form, hidden yet in some sense also affirmed by her desire for luxury, by virtue of the vacillation, con-tradiction and incalculability she figured in her gamble for it. She now literally moves beyond, rarifies herself out of existence. In death she is disengaged from her culturally constructed gendered body, from the narcissistic protection her self-stylisation as 'specialised product' had offered, but also freed from the constraints and contradictions it posed to her subjectivisation.

Lily's death bifurcates and must be viewed in respect to the meaning it has for her and the meaning Seldon gleans from it. Death is the logical extension of Lily's attempt to turn herself into an art object during her lifetime. She trans-forms into a text from which Seldon can glean edification and her dead body doubles the letters and cheques she wrote to vindicate her life just before ending it.[12] Indeed her death scene epitomises the proximity between self-representation and self-obliteration. Lily, 'seized with a sudden fever of activity', examines her possessions, unfolds 'the atmosphere of her old life' with every dress she unpacks until she resurrects the Reynolds dress, only to 'lay away' with each dress she puts back a part of her past. If the various roles she assumed were based on an unacknowledged void, burying these dresses through which she emerged leaves her facing her own 'rootless' existence, her solitude, her inner destitution. Writing the cheque to Trenor is an alternative form of self-representation that counters the 'baser possibilities' that her dresses, with the fetish position they made possible, signified.

This new position, which will result in the complete depletion of her funds, fixes, in an 'embrace of the emptiness of renunciation', the tragic yet sweet vision of 'lost possibilities' signified by giving up Seldon's faith. And she can write the cheque, create this new Lily in the same gesture that she desires death – 'If only life could end now' (338). In this 'mysterious nocturnal' silence and emptiness, in a state that borders on the 'dizzy brink of the unreal' which prematurely stages social death before physical demise, Lily sorts her papers and writes. Though we are never told what she writes, what we find enacted is the move from self-materialisation, a writing with the body in the form of dressing, to a de-materialisation, a writing with letters that moves beyond the body and engenders or is the prerequisite of the body's literal obliteration.[13]

This last act of writing stages a transition from the fugitive quality of any material aspect of language (iconic or indexic) to the written (the symbolic) word as an attempt to fix the fluidity of language. Indeed Lily takes the 'slight risk', the 'one chance in a hundred' with the incalculable drug in order to 'shut out' the unbearable fluidity of her memories: 'her whole past was reenacting itself at a hundred different points of consciousness' (339). Seen in that vein, this second gesture closes the earlier one that left her confronted consciously with the solitude of pure death. The uneasy sense of excitement turns into a happy, indistinct sense of drowsy peace. The sense of having irrevocably lost Seldon is recuperated into the assurance that she has found the word 'that should make life clear between them' (341). The dressed-up bride, whose position was undefined, fluid and fugitive, transforms herself into a corpse that can assume a fixed position. For her there are two deaths – the realisation of her fate, on the basis of which she writes her cheques and the longing for a release from tensions. Until the end, the uncanniness of difference remains – through her drowsy sleep 'a sudden, a dark flash of loneliness and terror tore its way'. This disjunction so inextricably a part of Lily can be solved only with the last breath, and with it the truth she has found, the word that will explain her to herself, recedes as well. She remains uncannily between being laid bare completely and relegated completely beyond, and so preserves the enigma's veil.

Duplicity remains to the end, since Lily's death is a sign for her radical refusal to assume a fixed position of psychic rigidity even as her death fixes the oscillation she traced in life. She remains unfathomable to the end, for like the drug itself, the motivation for taking the fatal doses is incalculable. Reminiscent of her attitude toward marriage, it is unclear whether her failure to wake the next morning should be attributed to flightiness or to a conscious rejection of the life her future held. The fatal logic within which the feminine body is placed is that, as site at which culturation occurs, it must be destroyed to let subjectivity emerge. Yet Lily's narrative implies a discrepancy – for her body is both the site of her alienation and of her power. The shifting she stages is as much a resistance as a complicity, so that a destruction of the body means a destruction of her material for self-articulation as well. Her death hovers undecidably between being a moment of perfect culturation as a complete effacement of her subjectivity and an irrevocable transformation into an image *and* being a moment of subjectivisation by obliterating that body over which she could be turned into an image which in part effaced, in part articulated her difference.

Seldon is faced with precisely this question in the presence of her corpse, so that where death for Lily is an issue of writing, it becomes for him one of reading. Having himself 'found the word' he was not able to speak the evening before, he finds 'with motionless hands and calm unrecognisable face, the semblance of Lily Bart' (343). What follows is a series of readings tantamount to restabilising the image of Lily he had preserved in his mind and which her last uncanny representation, her corpse, threatens in that it is a semblance, unrecognisable. This deanimated body indeed marks the apotheosis of her enchanting tableau vivant, yet not only by recapturing and fixing for ever Seldon's esteem for her,[14] but also in that it poses as a hermeneutic task. It promises to be the site of truth recognised but only when its duplicity is fixed.

Seldon at first denies that the corpse could be 'her real self' since it 'neither paled nor brightened at his coming.' Her real self is still close to him, 'yet invisible and inaccessible'. This realisation leads him to read the division between corpse and 'real Lily' as a trope for their relationship, with 'a little impalpable barrier between them' to keep them apart (344). As he goes through her letters, Seldon discovers another reading of her life under the sign of death, at the site of her corpse. Seeing an envelope addressed to Trenor reactivates all the 'ugly uncertainties' surrounding her, 'mocks' and 'defiles' any sense of reconciliation, forces him to acknowledge the limit of his knowlege of her, of his supreme right to her confidence 'which death had left unbarred'. As he, in the gesture of an anatomist, continues the perusal of her desk, admittedly a displaced sign for her body, he finds his own letters and he turns her death into a trope for his own 'cowardice', for the way 'he had always feared his fate' (346). Seeing that the letter to Trenor in fact contains a cheque, he can finally stabilise uncanny uncertainties into a canny enigma, the mystery now 'explained and deepened', the surface appearance of her transaction 'unraveled' while 'the mute lips on the pillow' refused any deeper insight.

Having acknowledged that she will not respond, he sees her corpse as the sanction to read into their last meeting 'all that his heart craves to find there'.

What results is a transformation of the hysteric into the narcissistic woman who keeps her knowledge to herself while her silence mirrors her spectator as he wishes to see himself. In the end, her corpse turns into a sign that mitigates his lack of courage even as it articulates this lack; that turns his failure into a sign of fate 'conspired to keep them apart'; that turns into the sign of loss over which a self-representation as whole can emerge. His solution to the question she posed is that he 'had loved her', and though the moment of love passed from them, it 'had been saved whole out of the ruin of their lives', had kept them from 'atrophy and extinction.' As in the tableau vivant, her body confirms 'his faith' in a wholeness beyond the ruin of life, so powerful precisely because it can never be seized, because it was always already beyond.

In the course of his attempt to solve the meaning of Lily's dead body, and with it of the life preceding it, Seldon turns the uncanny corpse, posing insoluble questions, into a canny enigma; gives to Lily's difference the stable position of 'mute lips' which refuse any further solution than her written statements. Because in death all inconsistencies, for Seldon at least, are obliterated, the 'word which made all clear' can pass between them in silence. Seldon's solution is a distancing and reduction, which performs the absence of this woman by producing her as his representation, while her self-performance had staged an ambivalent dialectic of absence and presence, of text and body. His disclosure is a triple arrestation of death – it fixes the destability posed by the nowhere of Woman, of the image and of the cadaver. What Wharton leaves open is whether her narrative supports his reaffirmation or turns upon its own hysterical resistance to such a complicity with closure.

In Schnitzler's text undressing a bride (to return once more to my discussion of Courbet) is fatally at stake, in that, once exhibited, the undressed body of superlative feminine beauty literally transforms into a corpse. *Fräulein Else* is a stark and explicit rendition of the undefined premarital woman posed as the site of an enigma, displayed as a supreme object of an erotic, an aesthetic and an economic speculation, even as she is herself undecided about the position she wants to assume in her society. Schnitzler textually articulates the interstice of speculation and death by employing a doubled narrative stance – Else's conversations with others and the mental conjectures and questions accompanying her public gestures. In that the latter often contradict the former only to disclose the dissimulation Else's self-display entails, Schnitzler's text returns to a theme already discussed in *The House of Mirth* – that the 'speculated' woman has a double vision of her 'self', that she must divide herself as she anticipates her spectator's gaze.

In John Berger's terms, Woman's self-being is split in two, because, having been taught to survey herself continually, she is almost always 'accompanied by her own image of herself'. In that Woman appears so that men can look at her, her power to control the way she is perceived rests on her manipulation of her appearance and her ability to identify with the masculine gaze. For 'the surveyor of woman in herself is male: the surveyed female. Thus she turns herself into . . . an object of vision: a sight.'[15] Though Berger's aim is to denounce such cultural reification of the feminine body, two further aspects unfold in light of the psychoanalytic model I have been unfolding. If Woman is always accompanied by her image, she enacts to herself at least, a form of uncanny self-doubling that introduces death's figure before any physical demise. To say Woman encompasses both the male surveyor and the female surveyed also recalls the hysteric's uncertainty as to being feminine or masculine. Woman must know the masculine desire if she is to simulate its object with her appearance. In her complicity with her cultural gender position, she must vacillate between masculinity and femininity. She can never be narcissistically whole because she always also includes the masculine gaze that makes her other than herself.

The question in Schnitzler's as in Wharton's text is then, whether woman, by staging herself *other* than she is, in order to comply with the internalised masculine gaze, confirms or discloses her objectivisation; whether she stages an appearance that has nothing to do with her, that reduces her to the medium of another's fantasies, or whether she uses this histrionic self-display as her source of self-authorship, as the materialisation of her own fantasies? Is the unveiling of her body a disclosure of her sexuality or merely an appeal to her masculine viewer's sexual fantasies? Does she potentially exert power over her viewer because he desires her sight or does she, as Berger argues, merely stabilise the viewer's power to possess her? Since in this text at least, the unveiling of her body functions like the choice of the third casket, disclosing death beneath beauty, does this gesture mark Else's absolute acknowledgement of her reduction to a single definition, namely her sexuality, or is this precisely a refusal of such a semantic fixture, an empty gesture that points to the nullity not only of narcissistic but also gender pretensions?

The hysteric's is a superlatively uncanny position, and as such another aspect of death's figure in life. Precisely because of the hysteric's doubleness between self and image and her oscillation between sexual signifiers, she uses her body to collapse the difference between opposite terms like masculinity/femininity, object/agent of spectatorship, confirmation/disclosure of cultural values, only to pose undecidable questions. This uncanny doubleness of Woman is articulated in Schnitzler's text on two scores: by virtue of Else's hysteric dissimulations, which let her appear *other* than she really is[16] and by virtue of the bifurcated, *unheimlich* narratorial stance, which reduplicates the protagonist's *unheimlich*, split body. For if the process by which Else doubles herself with a self-image aimed at a masculine spectator is one aspect of the figure that death traces in life, the fact that Else's speech is doubled by her unspoken thoughts transposes her uncanny doubleness between appearance and being on to the narrative level. Else, by commenting on the calculation underlying her appearance, by in fact presenting a plethora of versions of herself, undertakes yet another form of splitting herself in two – into actress and commentator; into medium and author. She splits herself into the surveyed sight and the surveyor at the same time that she splits herself between enacting and disclosing this scenario of gendered dissimulation.

Given that a semiotic designation causes the absence or 'annihilation' of the signified body, so that a designation like 'that woman' takes her flesh and blood reality away, Else's self-commentary can be seen as a form of rhetorically 'killing' herself into her own object of conjectures. It serves as the textual double of the imaginary 'killing' which is thematically articulated in her transformation into an object of the masculine gaze. Schnitzler's choice of narrative technique limits the text to Else's position. Her voice is precisely what never falls silent. What instead remain a mute blank in this text, as inaccessible to her as to the reader, are the actual responses she elicits in others and with the absence of this perspective any interpretive closure is also lacking. The reader is faced with an uncanny spectacle in yet another sense. While we are shown that Else withholds her truth from her speculators, and once dying, completely recedes from any exchange with them, we also hear the solutions she conceals, see the recession from the position of the one receding, so that her hysteric dissimulation irrevocably covers the narcissistic type she seems to enact for her spectators.

Schnitzler's narrative significantly begins with Else's 'no' to her cousin Paul's offer to continue her game of tennis. As she turns away she enters into a sequence of self-speculations that articulate her transitional state. During her fatal residence at the spa, the nineteen-year-old Else anticipates leaving her position as virginal daughter yet remains undecided as to what position to assume instead: 'where will I go? I want to travel and do as I please' (223). Given that Else's father simulates a life of prosperity to hide his impending bankruptcy, Else's lack of a fixed position and her vacillation between various possible choices encompasses two questions. On the one hand she is unsure about her sexual desires, sees herself simultaneously as an exhibitionist in love with her own body, as sensual, as repulsed by heterosexuality. On the other hand she is unsure of her social position. Like Lily, she realises that her superlative beauty is coupled with a lack of wealth, that she must either marry for money or learn a profession (and she hesitates between actress, governess and accountant). The image she has of herself is plural, 'I the arogant, the aristocrat, the marchesa, the beggar, the daughter of an embezzler' (219), just as she imagines different versions of marriage; to an American with a villa on the Riviera, or to the owner of a country estate.

Once she has received her mother's letter, asking her to borrow money from the art dealer Dorsday on her father's behalf, these two issues merge, so that even as she speculates about her future position in her society she does so by speculating with her beautiful body. Always aware of her striking appearance, she acts as her own surveyor each time she comments on her own beauty – 'today I am truly beautiful' (220). Her self-division is also such that she continually feels herself to be an object of sight, in fact perceives sight as a form of being touched. She anticipates that her power lies in holding this alterior gaze; 'I must look enchanting when I speak with Dorsday . . . his eyes will probe my décolletée'

(218). She assumes what Laura Mulvey calls the traditional exhibitionist role that lets Woman connote a to-be-looked-at-ness and lets her hold the look of a male viewer, play to it so as to signify male desire.[17]

That this highly conscious self-display is in fact a form of self-division is shown most clearly, however, in Else's relation to her mirror image. Reflecting her own beauty to herself Else sees herself double – 'beautiful Fräulein in the mirror, keep me in good memory' (222),[18] and she will address this uncanny double just before and just after her public self-disclosure. To counter her sense of extreme solitude, Else seeks to transform the liminiality which makes her look available to anyone, into a relation with a defined, fixed addressee. She asks herself 'for whom am I beautiful', 'whom should I greet . . . my lover . . . my bridegroom . . . my friend' (220f.) Yet she can directly greet only her reflected body double, and as in *Madame Bovary*, the refracted self-image readily transforms into the image of death as the final bridegroom, as the sole real addressee.

Her response to Dorsday's demand to see her naked in return for the money he is to lend her father, merges her two points of indecision because it implies that acknowledging her sexuality, accepting her feminine position, is coterminous with becoming the object of her privileged spectator's or suitor's erotic–aesthetic voyeurism as well as the object of her father's economic exchange. Else consciously realises that her beauty is the stake in a transaction where erotics and finance merge, and one of the forms of self-fashioning is in the image of the 'noble daughter selling herself for the beloved father', of the beautiful body up for auction (218). Dorsday merely makes explicit the duplicity with which she finds her feminine position irrevocably inscribed. Given that in accordance with the gender position society assigns to her, feminine beauty is never used without calculation, his demand discloses that an erotic encoding necessarily underlies all her social relations even as it may not be openly acknowledged.

Because Else is in complicity with the fantasies and desires of her culture, this demand is perplexing in more than one way. It enforces an awareness of the disjunction between being and appearance that her beautiful self-display engenders. As she appeals to Dorsday for money she wonders 'how strange my voice sounds. Is that myself who is speaking? . . . I am sure to have a completely different face than usual' (226). The narrative doubling of appearance and commentary opens up yet another disjunction enacted by Else's gestures, namely that she both desires and despises the appeal to the male gaze she signifies; that she wishes to affirm her seductive powers while hoping to deny that this implies a lack of innocence. On the one hand she complies, 'you want to see me naked? Many do. I am beautiful, when I'm naked' (231). On the other hand she experiences shame, 'how I debase myself . . . how common I am' (228). For she perceives that the sight of her naked body is already a form of possession, that unveiling herself before Dorsday is coterminous with acknowledging him figuratively as bridegroom. Indeed he diminishes his original demand 'je vous désire', (*sic*) into 'this time I want nothing else, Else, than – to see you' (231).[19]

The dilemma is that she cannot decide whether she is in complicity with

Dorsday's desire, with its cultural prohibition or with neither – she would like to reject him, 'but I can't. Or don't I want to?' His demand also troubles her because it articulates the contradiction between her desire to show herself in all her beauty and the shame such a desire provokes: 'I am sitting here like a poor sinner.' In so doing she enacts the double standard of a culture which asks a woman to turn herself into a sign of masculine desire even as it denounces the impropriety of such behaviour. Else's sudden public nudity before all the other hotel guests is called 'an attack of hysteria'. Because she is confused about the aim of her own sexual desire, she can neither reject nor accept Dorsday, and her solution of public display hovers fetishistically between both options. While Dorsday's demand to see her clandestinely secures their exchange by virtue of ambivalence ('it is to remain a secret betwen you and me'), her public appearance clarifies this relation by virtue of nullifying it, and lets her recede from this symbolic exchange into a real one with death.

As Dorsday explains, Else provokes an unveiling of her body because her beauty poses as the sight of an enigma, 'magic emanates from you'. In that her body is Else's medium of language, somatic undressing translates into semiotic disclosure, a transparency between signifier and signified, the obliteration of difference. Undressing the bride, however, reveals the dead woman in more than one sense. By taking her social objectification literally, by materialising the projected masculine fantasies she is meant to signify indirectly with her appearance, Else causes her hysterical dissimulation to collapse, assumes her culturally prescribed non-existence by enacting, in Zizek's terms, the death drive at its purest as it lies beyond hysterisation. A reduction to the status of an image is possible only over a dying body. The full materialisation of her status as object of vision, power and possession requires her deanimation. This discloses that fatality is inscribed into the choice of the feminine position, by making the implied non-existence of Woman real.

Any speculation with the exhibition of her beauty is, however, inscribed by death even before she has read about the gravity of her father's financial situation. Because she has no clear position, she repeatedly invokes death as one of the possible aims of her life. Holding her mother's unread letter she sits on the window sill and imagines the responses her fall might call forth: 'Reports have it that a deplorable accident has occurred in San Martino . . . of course they will claim I killed myself owing to an unhappy romance or because I was expecting a child. Unhappy romance, ah no'. (213) This raises the question whether the bridal plot isn't used to cover a death plot, whether the conjectures about her social/sexual choices don't veil that by choosing her superlative beauty Else has from the start already chosen the third casket, death.

As one follows the ways in which death figures in her image repertoire and her conjectures about her future, another question emerges. Is death chosen as a superlative form of self-display or as a release from the tensions of her perplexing situation? Repeatedly Else evokes death as the solution to her dilemma, as what will foreclose any further worries, as what will prevent or what will follow the shameful deed required of her. Before she approaches Dorsday she exclaims 'I wish I were dead' (218); while she listens to his proposal she believes 'the best thing for me to do, would be to throw myself off those cliffs and it would be over' (229); after his offer she feels 'I am half dead'. She can entertain the possibility of exhibiting her nudity in public only if death is engendered, 'If I die immediately afterwards' (234). In a sense her fatality results from the fact that she transforms what Baudrillard calls the supplementary oppositions, her as yet undefined sexual/social relations, into an issue of the originary division of life and death. Repeatedly she simultaneously wishes her father's death as a solution to his financial difficulties ('Kill yourself, papa'), is spurred on by the notion of impending death ('At stake is a human life') and fears that he will die and she be guilty ('He will hang at the window cross . . . and I will be responsible' (332ff).).

Death is imagined as a superlative moment of self-display just as the naked spectacle of extreme beauty is a figuration of death. After her conversation with Dorsday she has a dream in which she stages her own death – 'Oh, how beautiful it would be to be dead. Lying in state in the salon' (237). Upon awakening she consciously reduplicates her dream by imagining a macabre testament. In an exact inversion of Clarissa's last will, she plans to grant Dorsday the right to see her 'beautiful naked virginal corpse . . . I bequeath the sight of my corpse to the art dealer Dorsday' (244). Her explicit argument is that their contract does not stipulate that she must be a living sight, yet by inversion she implies that to be an object of aesthetic/erotic voyeurism, to have her nude body perceived as an artwork, is itself a form of death. In her dream she had already represented Dorsday watching her corpse and comparing it to an artwork – 'I have never seen such a beautiful body. It only cost me three million. A Rubens would cost three times as much.'

In the same manner that her future remains enigmatic, her dream represents her death as engendering a patchwork of clichés with no fixed answer: 'suicide? Owing to an unhappy romance . . . she was to have a child. No . . . an accident . . . she only wanted to have beautiful visions, but she took too much hashish and didn't wake up again.' In her conscious imaginations she explicitly claims that no one is to know why she killed herself. Her dream represents a division between the dead person's perceptions and the survivors' responses. In so doing it allows a fantasy to emerge which is as impossible as that of knowing death from experience. Her dream fulfills the desire to know how people will respond to her death, though once she is conscious again she recognises this as an unrealisable desire. In a sense Else dreams what she will later enact, her liminal position between life and death, her splittage into an inanimate fainted body and an animate commenting mind. In her dream her corpse remains mobile, leaves the bier, and walks to the graveyard only to find that it has been defrauded of its vault. This image of the uncanny revenant, lacking the fixture of a burial place, present in absence, sheds light on Else's social positioning as premarital daughter or as mature woman, so that by implication both states are figured as a suspended animation. It also foreshadows the uncanny fixture on which Schnitzler's text ends, namely Else's truncated words, 'I drea [. . .] drea [. . .] drea – I fly [. . .]' (266).

Dorsday's demand forces her to exchange her undefined position with its plethora of possiblities in favour of a fixture. While one possible result is the life of prostitution the one she is more inclined towards is death – 'I have known for a long time that I will end up this way' (243). Dorsday's demand merely serves as a pretext, not as the cause for her choice. Indeed death appears as the best possible option against any psychic rigidity that she can imagine for herself in a bourgeois existence; the work as a servant, the wife of an older man, the mistress, 'all is equally repulsive'. Conceding to his desire is also perceived as a form of death which engenders liberation, 'now life will really begin'. (247).

In all cases the choice she makes is understood as an irrevocable incision. She addresses her mirrored-self for the second time, conscious that she is about to undertake a form of death as rebirth not unlike the bridal ceremony: 'There will be no return, no turning home . . . I will no longer be Fräulein Else . . . I will be born a second time.' By undressing she casts off the ambivalence, the indecision, the duplicity inscribed in the designation 'Fräulein'. She puts closure on the questions about her future, the difficulty of her father's financial problems, the perplexity of being culturally positioned as object of sight. She rids herself of the deceptive clothes that inspire even as they forbid the desire for a total view of her beauty. Covered with only a cape, she is 'nothing . . . but I, I myself' (252). She takes the 'figural' defloration that Dorsday's clandestine eye threatens to under-take to an excess and images the loss of her maidenhood amongst a public visual penetration.

Undressing could then be read as her first attempt to reach a narcissistic unity, a wholeness beyond disjunction and dissimulation, an effacement of the lack or division her feminine position is inscribed with. As she presses her red lips and her breast to the mirror, she invokes an obliteration of the difference between self-being and image: 'How sad that the mirror separates us . . . We need no one else' (250). This gesture is understood as assuming her non-existence, a move beyond the self-protection of hysterisation. In the uncanny merging of first and third person she declares her death, 'For the earlier Else has already died. Yes certainly I am dead.' Not unlike Elaine of Astolat or Lily Bart, she writes in the face of death, doubles her naked as dead body with a letter to Dorsday which contains the acknowledgement of their transactions. As in the other narratives, the sheer facticity of her body is meant to legitimate her claim, in this case that he must pay for the sight he has had. This letter has the quality of testamentary writing, to be received when the writer is absent. That this is also another aspect of Else's departure from the symbolic into a somatic materialization of the sign that is coterminous with death is rendered by virtue of the fact that she omits her signature. Naked, having undertaken her own social death, she has no name, can sign her writing only with her body.

Having placed the letter at Dorsday's door, she descends into the music room to fulfill the 'representation', the scandalous tableau vivant so long imaginatively invoked. Yet even as she descends, she continues to devise versions of her death: dying of pneumonia after exposing herself to Dorsday in the woods; climbing the Cimone della Pala to be found frozen the next day, or much later 'decayed. As a skeleton.' Like her earlier fantasies, these also end on the note of excess, where the beautiful breaks into the macabre. At the moment of her performance, she not only collapses the extreme beauty of her body with death, but also translates the imaginary into the real; the imaginary desires her spectators have projected on to her and her own. She says, 'I am dead' and faints into a hysteric somatisation of a death-like state, unable to open her eyes, unable to speak though she remains conscious. Like Lily's self-display, this is a moment of ultimate complicity and ultimate resistance because it not only disclothes the feminine body but also discloses the fatality such complicity incurs. The liminality of the uncanny revenant, represented in her dream, becomes real as she hears but is forced into silence, as she asks 'Was I not dead already? Must I die once more' (259).

The figure of excess inscribed into Schnitzler's text is not only such that the bride's situation is so hopeless that her only viable choice is death, but that she psychically lives through or anticipates many versions of death before its reality sets in. As Else drinks the fatal dose of veronal she combines her different death fantasies for the last time – the suicide induced by shame ('let me not wake up again'), the collective accusation of murder ('they all killed me'), a desire for death ('how good death tastes'), and a wish to be saved ('I don't want to die . . . don't let me die' (264f.)). While her death implicitly resolves tensions, Schnitzler's narrative ends on indecision and contradiction. It preserves uncanny hesitation through the last psychic representation of Else dreaming, not falling but flying.

Though her public display stages that the solution to her bridal conjectures are irrevocably enmeshed with fantasies of death, it leaves other questions unsolved. Does this act signify a complete submission to or a subversion of her value as object of exchange? Does she disclose her own exhibitionist desires, or the voyeuristic desires of her culture? Does she lay bare the social transactions undertaken at her body, or offer merely another dissimulation to induce a blindness toward her subject position and toward these transactions? Moving from private to public display, does she cross the hysteric's dissimulation with the narcissist's withholding of truth? In these last moments she enacts the analogy between Woman as image and as corpse – hearing, knowing she is being seen but not seeing, falling silent. This can be read as a trope for the feminine position, for her division between self-being and image, for her non-existence as an uncanny position because it is grounded on an awareness of this split.

That the only language Else finds to express herself should be her nude as dead body raises the perplexing case that her power necessarily also entails her self-obliteration; that her active choice of fate (subjectivisation), is also a form of sacrifice and of murder; that she can design her self-representation only from within her cultural image repertoire. The impasse Schnitzler traces sheds light not only on the divided position of Woman in culture but also on the way femininity, writing and death conflate. Else uses her split to turn her body into the medium of her text in a fatal confusion of the semiotic and the somatic. In that writing is a distancing from and disembodiment of the writer's body, it engenders the 'death' of the author. Though Else stopped writing in her diary two years before her death and though she herself says, 'why speculate on my condition, I am not writing my memoirs' (210), she spends the last day of her life designing a plethora of death plots for herself. In this activity she hovers between an awareness that she is merely repeating novels she has read and trying to find an adequate form of self-represenation. Her dying body, in a sense, serves in lieu of her memoires and fuctions like the materialised text of an imagined biography of 'death' plots. The enmeshment of this plethora of 'death' plots, and the macabre turn each seems to take, with the real end with which she concludes this imaginary activity, suggests that the writing of/with death marks the point of excess of the superlatively beautiful feminine body on display; its ground and vanishing point.

For Lacan, the hysteric's discourse is inhabited by a particular relation to death in response to the position of femininity culture proposes. What her body, her simulations and discrepancies, her silence, communicate is lack. By identifying with culture's dictates and showing fidelity to the paternal law, the hysteric allows herself to be appropriated by the Other and fashions herself as an alternate ego (a double). Because her unconscious desire motivates her to remain lacking, because it tells her that she is no-body, her life emerges as an impossible desire to be by not being, always spent in proximity to loss, symptomatisation and annihilation.[20] Life becomes a dangerous game when circumstances force the hysteric to recognise that her position in the symbolic order is contingent on supplementary supports. Since she is alive only when spurred on by the gaze of male recognition, of the Other, which she in turn rejects or manipulates, to cease being desired may cause her to fall out of what is from the start a tenuous and duplicitous connection with the laws of the symbolic and fall into the void of the real. Confronted in such moments of transition as marriage and motherhood with the knowledge that what she signifies is a lack of being, the fragility of her position emerges from beneath the appearance of mastery she simulates. Death is the only viable choice because what is at stake all along for the feminine body socially constructed as being nowhere, is the originary division of life and death before and amongst any supplementary divisions.

Notes to Chapter 13

1 S. Freud,1933, p. 126.
2 S. Kofman, 1985a.
3 S. Kofman, 1985a.
4 M. Bal, 1988. See also Mary Douglas, 1966.
5 This logic invokes a reference to Aylmer's aspirations in Hawthorne's 'Birthmark' as well as to José's desires in Mérimée's 'Carmen'.

6 D. Lublin, 1985.
7 Contrary to the texts discussed in Part II, those to be discussed here will often work with an opposition between men turning women into images and women transforming themselves, to suggest where moments of feminine subjectivity may be sought.
8 This is the standard reading of Lily's fate, argued by, among others, C. Wolff, 1977.
9 F. Restuccia, 1987.
10 For a discussion of the complex of risk, chance and accident involved in speculation see W. Michaels, 1987.
11 S. Zizek, 1989, pp. 53f.
12. S. Gubar, 1982.
13 F. Restuccia, 1987, argues for an analogy between protagonist and author, 'as if Wharton momentarily slips into Lily's body here and takes up her pen', p. 235.
14 C. Wolff, 1977.
15 J. Berger, 1972, pp. 46f.
16 See S. Mentzos, 1986, whose clinical definition of hysteria is 'the tendency to excperience oneself and show oneself different from the way one is, a quasi-altered self-representation', p. 92. Though my concern is with 'hysteria' as a strategy of feminine self-expression and not with a psychic illness, the notion of self-fashioning as staging oneself by virtue of a disjunction between true being and appearance to oneself and to others is the seminal trait of the characters I discuss, even if what they in fact 'are' beyond their hysterical self-representation is not necessarily clarified by the text.
17 L. Mulvey, 1975.
18 Addressing herself as Fräulein means addressing herself as a virginal, as yet unmarried woman.
19 In a sense this recalls the demand of Snow White's prince, just as Else's relation with her mirrored image recalls the superlatively beautiful queen.
20 For a discussion of Lacan's discourse of hysteria see E. Ragland-Sullivan, 1988.

14

Necromancy, or closing the crack on the gravestone

> If we could be sure of the difference between the determinable and the undeterminable, the undeterminable would be comprehended within the determinable. What is undecidable is whether a thing is decidable or not.
> *Barbara Johnson*

Certainly one of the more perturbing Victorian examples of the interstice between feminine speech and death is Robert Browning's poetic rendition of the Roman trial and execution in 1698 of Guido Franchescini, *The Ring and the Book* (1869). The accused nobleman had stabbed his wife's adoptive mother and father and then inflicted twenty-two dagger wounds on his wife Pompilia herself, five of them deadly. He claimed she had committed adultery with the priest Caponsacchi, who had assisted her in her unsuccessful flight from his house eight months earlier. The Roman court had allowed Pompilia to return to her parents' house, where she gave birth to a son two weeks prior to the event of her husband's assault, though it had left the verdict dangerously unclear, with neither party guilty nor a divorce granted. On her dying bed Pompilia, about to fall completely silent, articulates her lack of a public voice by accusing the court as it documents her testimony, 'Oh yes, patient this long while / Listening and Understanding, I am sure! / Four days ago, when I was sound and well / And like to live, no one would understand' (VII, 906–9). If Guido's fatal assault on his wife's body signifies an effort to put an end to a case the court left undecided, death also produces a moment of transition in which everything is called into question. The sheer materiality of Pompilia's body liminally suspended between life and death, the threat of its irrevocable absence, lets her pose as a hermeneutic task and serve as the site of its truth.[1]

Browning's text records the way this dying body provokes discrepant explanatory narratives before its actual death for although the facts of the case are clear, closure can be put on the disruption death causes only when the right interpretation engenders the establishment of a new order; when the somatic closure, the body safely interred beneath the earth, corresponds to a semiotic closure, the case's 'truth ... grasped and gained' (I, 471). Browning records narratives that defend Guido for having saved his honour, fought for his property and executed his husband's rights along with those that defend Pompilia's purity, invoking her despair due to her husband's cruelty and due to her own motherhood. These recounts hover between reading the husband's murder as 'vindictive jealousy' or 'justified revenge' and the wife's flight as the gesture of 'a saint, a martyr' or 'an adulteress'. They also use her murder to debate the status of marriage, the deficiency of the Roman legal system and the crisis in belief into which Christianity had fallen.

Leaving aside issues I have already discussed – Pompilia as the object of a financial exchange between parents and husband, her marriage as a form of death with real death her desired apotheosis, her sacrificial death as the sign of her purity with her blood 'washing the parchment white' (VII, 1781), her union with her forbidden beloved Caponsacchi in heaven – I point to the representation of the dying Pompilia as a structural paragon of the themes to be discussed in this chapter. For the 'one beauty more' of her story is that on the fatal night she 'simulated death ... obtained herself a respite, four days' grace / Whereby she told her story to the world' (IX, 1421–2), embodied 'the miracle of continued life'. Not only does the public listen to her precisely because she is dying, not only does her impending death imbue the search for the correct representation of her death with urgency, but death restrained authorises the truthfulness of her speech and the idea that truth can be found even if only over a dying feminine body. The public claims, 'Confession of the moribund is true' (IV, 1478). Pompilia seeks time not simply 'to confess and get her own soul saved – / But time to make the truth apparent ... lest men should believe a lie' (IV, 1428–30). She uses the knowledge of impending death to fashion her story into its final version and in so doing she can control her public representation after her death, even if she could not design her existence as a living woman.

Pompilia's dying body and its generation of solutions to the 'mystery of the murder' is paradigmatic in two ways. The disruption that death incites must be resolved in a semiotic as well as a physical sense; the deceased and her story must receive a stable meaning even as the grave is closed to assure that the process of mourning is complete. But narratives aimed at solving the ambivalence death poses also emerge from the site of liminality, emerge precisely because Pompilia is a kind of revenant, so that representations seem inextricable from the resurrection of the dead. Guido in fact emphasises that Pompilia speaks as her own uncanny double: 'she too must shimmer through the gloom o' the grave ... o' the death-bed ... Tell her own story her own way, and turn / My plausibility to nothingness! ... Four whole extravagant impossible days ... Had she been found dead as I left her dead / I should have told a tale brooked no reply' (XI, 1680–703).

Resurrection is also a stake on the narrative level of Browning's poem. Though Pope Innocent XII closes the case by affixing to Guido the signifier 'guilty,' and to Pompilia the signifiers 'perfect in whiteness', he admits that 'truth, nowhere, lies yet everywhere . . . evolvable from the whole' (X 228–30). A fixed representation, though grounded on disjunctions, emerges from their elimination. Browning's narrator supports the Pope's verdict that while each individual testimony contains falsehood the synthesis art presents 'may tell a truth obliquely' (XII, 856), yet his text is also explicitly uncanny. For at the start of the narration Browning describes his poetic gesture as a reopening of the exchange between the living and the dead, 'the life in me abolished the death of things . . . as then and there acted itself over again once more / The tragic piece' (I, 520–3). Not only does this imply an analogy between Pompilia's desire to speak as a means of abolishing her death for four days. It also suggests that with the resurrected dead, the narrative discrepancies, which the Pope's final reading buried along with the bodies of the husband and wife, return as well. This raises the question whether symbolic replacement of the dead body in the form of gravestone inscriptions and narrative documentation truly produces a canny representation or whether the representational process doesn't irrevocably return to uncanny difference, by returning the dead back to the living.

Pompilia is the crux of a mystery story precisely because she is a revenant and as such figures as a nodal point in two distinct though enmeshed plots – that of detection and that of mourning. If the living woman is unstable because ambivalent in her meaning, seemingly dissimulating (adulteress, saint, both, neither), her death affords somatic fixture, resolves the lies and intrigues with which her existence was inscribed. It figures as an enigma whose solution implies a second semiotic fixture, the binding of a univocal signifer to the signified body. If the living woman threatens that truth is nowhere, a reading of her death allows truth obliquely to emerge at the hands of the survivors. Dressed in the solution imposed from outside (the Pope's, the poet's), the dead Pompilia confirms that in a world of disjunctions and lies, truth can be found. Her dying body is in fact transmitted as its incarnated emblem, the martyred saint whose death speaks her truth and thus truth *per se*.

Yet the explanation of her murder not only solves the meaning of her story retrospectively by translating the disjunction her femininity traced into a stable figure, 'perfect in whiteness'. Rather, in that the detective story traces the uncovering of hidden facts about an event of death, hidden truths about characters' motivations in relation to death, what it in fact must solve is death itself.[2] The dead woman who remains and in so doing engenders narratives, functions as a body at which death is once again coupled to the other central enigma of western cultural representation – femininity. The solution of her death is a form of documenting both of these unknowns. The dead woman, embodying a secret, harbours a truth others want and since the dead body is feminine, with death and femininity metonymies of each other, the condensation of the two allows one and the same gesture to uncover a stable, determinate answer for this double enigma.

As Todorov notes, detective fiction tells two stories, the story of the crime and the story of the investigation. As such it depicts two murders, the first committed by the actual murderer, the second by the pure and unpunishable murderer, the detective.[3] In the texts to be discussed – Wilkie Collins' *The Woman in White* (1859–60), Emily Brontë's *Wuthering Heights* (1847) and Bram Stoker's *Dracula* (1897) – the duality of these two plots is such that two events collapse. Unearthing the answer posed by a woman's death becomes coterminous with placing the dead feminine body into the earth. A corpse spurs on the urge to detect missing facts with death explained by virtue of a reconstruction of the events – the doubled narrative imitating the uncanny position of the dead / remaining woman. Once her death has been explained the corpse can lie peacefully, the end of the narrative double plot equal to the end of her revenant position. The divided woman poses questions which are resolved as her division is undone, as the uncanny double is transformed into the canny division between buried corpse and transmitted emblem. By solving the murder, the detecting survivors can re-establish the illusory belief that they have expelled the uncanny difference that woman's duplicity and death's disjunction traced in their lives. If in the last chapter I discussed the feminine position as one posed between bride and dead girl, I will now turn to the masculine position as that of the mourner as detective.

In that each of these women, in the guise of the double, preserves a corpse (literally as vampire woman or phantom, figurally by virtue of resemblance), each stages the uncanny. As harbingers of death the double incarnates the end of bodily existence, figures ephemerality and contradicts notions of wholeness and uniqueness due to the division of the self it traces, even as the double also incarnates the notion of endless preservation of the body, the beginning of immaterial existence. The revenant, occupying the interstice between two forms of existence – a celebration and a triumph over death – calls forth two forms of anxiety, i.e. the anxiety that death is finitude and the anxiety that death may not be the end. Because the heroines are revenants of sorts, because their appearance deceives, they function as living tropes for the notion that a secret, a truth, lies hidden beneath the surface of the body. They embody the site of two disjunctions – a dead body remaining in the guise of a living one, a feminine body dis-simulating an identity which hides her true being – and both ambivalences are brought to rest when, in the instance of their second death, ambivalent doubleness is brought into a transparent relation of signifier and signified (the dead body no longer remains, the woman's appearance no longer dissimulates a false identity). The logic these narratives unfold is that to attribute a fixed meaning to a woman, to solve the mystery of her duplicity is coterminous with killing her, so that her death can be read in part as a trope for the fatality with which any hermeneutic enterprise is inscribed. The achievement of a stable semiotic meaning, which excludes semantic difference and ambivalence, is debated over the establishment of another stable division – that between the living and the dead.

Precisely because it involves two deaths, however, the detective plot can be seen analogous to another plot beginning in death – the trajectory of the mourning process. For the purpose of mourning is to kill the dead by ceasing to reanimate psychically a body physically absent; by withdrawing one's libidinal investment in a lost love object, forgetting or preserving it as dead.[4] While the solution of the detective plot is to kill the 'dead' woman twice by virtue of deciphering and affixing a truth to her duplicitous body, the solution of a successful mourning plot is to kill the lost woman psychically preserved as a phantom, by virtue of decathexis. The solution of death that both detection and mourning provide in part serves to avert the idea that the death of another in fact threateningly signifies the presence of death in oneself. Mourning is a way to repress the threatening realisation that death can never be solved except in the form of one's own demise. Mourning allows one to retrieve those parts of the investment made in the lost object.[5]

Before the detection plot has found its end, however, those related to the murdered body are like mourners, the corpse not yet safely beneath the graveplate, the survivors not yet severed from the dead, the detecting survivors like the revenant in liminality. Only the psychic solution (successful disinvestment of the dead beloved) and the hermeneutic solution (successful deciphering of the enigma) arrests an uncanny body into a recuperated stable division between living and dead, between fluidity of appearance and fixed answer. Mourning requires a participation of the living in the mortuary state of the deceased. A process of mental disintegration precipitates the closure of the case which occurs when society triumphs over death and recovers its peace by assuring itself that the dead are univocally beyond or beneath the worldly realm.[6]

The newly dead are conceived of as double, simultaneously present in the tomb and in some spiritual realms.[7] In this liminal position they are regarded as dangerous and polluted because they appear between all pure classifications and unambiguous concepts.[8] The social group has a vested interest in hastening along the liberation of the soul from the corpse in order to eliminate the impurity and duplicity of the decomposing body. Mourning and funeral rites were originally determined by decomposition and by the desire to protect the living and assure the double's liberation. They aimed at preserving of the corpse only the bones or replacing it by a symbolic substitute – in the form of an effigy or a gravestone.

Vampires in turn were understood as doubles that were not successfully delivered from the corpse, as animated corpses preserved in the dangerous liminal realm, as moments of failed decomposition that consequently also meant an arrestation of decathexis on the part of the mourners.[9] The intact corpse of the revenant, artificially reanimated, has a correlative in the Christian saint, immune to decay. A rational explanation for the image of the vampire in folklore is that it was merely an exhumed dead body, monstrously threatening because still undergoing a process of decomposition. The killing of the revenant, a second killing of a corpse, a second burial, indicates the end of mourning and marks an attempt to bind the corpse in place, so as to protect the living from the dead. Revenant tales feed off the notion that after death the body has a second destructive life, that while it is decomposing, it is still changing, and still involved in the world. If they remain, the dead are a potential source of danger because death is thought to come from the dead body. The second killing puts an end to this double's life by holding the dead body in one place and rendering it inert, incapable of undergoing further changes.

Paul Barber reads the revenant as a trope for the fear of contagion transmitted by the corpse and the destabilisation of notions of the intact body that decomposition figures.[10] He distinguishes between two versions of the corpse – the monster or bad corpse (the body in the early stages of decomposition), and the good corpse (the body successfully decayed into harmless bones). In that the first body is in the liminal position, it corresponds to that of the premarital bride, dangerous due to her indefinite state, while the good corpse implies the canny rigidity of mature femininity. The fear of the somatically contagious and semiotically indeterminate revenant provokes a desire to neutralise the corpse; to 'kill' it a second time; to solve its death and preserve not the body but its appearance; to replace the dead body double (the revenant that in decomposing keeps changing, the phantom that inhabits the mourner's mental realm), with a fixed, unchanging form of double, a grave inscription, unambiguous, marking a clear distinction between living and dead. A protection of the living from the dead requires repetition not on the indexic / somatic but on the arbitrary / symbolic level. It prescribes a translation from body to skeleton, from unconscious memory representations to culturally controlled ones.

The deceased is no longer dangerous when its body stops undergoing change, stabilised into its last ossified state and when its image has receded and stops entering the survivor's dreams and memories, stabilised into a commemorative representation. To delineate how the feminine revenant serves as a trope for the conceptual enmeshment of mourning, detection and representation, I will problematise the notion that a stable closure of the crack the revenant opens is achieved through the second killing. Though the dangerously fluid revenant's body which dissimulates death may find some stability in the written documentation and gravestone ornaments meant to replace it, the rhetoric of any pictorial or textual representation is also based on difference and semantic indeterminacy or duplicity and transforms into a disturbing double in its own right. Finally, one can define the vampire as 'a dead body that appears to be dead except that it doesn't decay' so as to conjoin it to my definition of the hysteric as being someone whose appearance or self-representation is other than she in fact truly is. In these texts the heroine's chosen or induced duplicity is such that she appears as dead, but without a body to prove her death, so that the revenant emerges as yet another aspect of the hysteric's rhetoric of dissimulation.

The exposition of *The Woman in White* presents a woman bearing a secret, socially dead because buried alive in an insane asylum to procure her silence, literally dying of a heart disease, as she escapes her confinement and returns to the world of the living. As Walter Hartright walks home along the lonely road to

London at the 'dead of the night', about to embark for Cumberland to begin work as a drawing master for the daughters of Mr Fairlie, the 'touch of a hand laid lightly and suddenly' on his shoulder from behind petrifies him 'from head to foot' (47). What he sees as he turns instantly, 'with my fingers tightening round the handle of my stick', is an apparition which 'seriously startled' him because of the suddenness of its appearance, 'as if it had sprung out of the earth or dropped from the heaven' and because of its extraordinary guise – 'a solitary Woman, dressed from head to foot in white garments'. Like Medusa, she fascinates and terrifies, because her femininity is not only doubly encoded but also resonates death. She is thought to emerge from the beyond (angel) or beneath (demon), while the whiteness of her clothes refers simultaneously to a bridal gown or a shroud. The touch of her hand laid with 'a sudden gentle stealthiness' elicits a sexual response. He notes it was a 'cold hand' when he 'removed it with mine', and excuses himself by claiming 'I was young . . . the hand which touched me was a woman's' (50). The woman's touch, however, also effects a death-like experience in the touched masculine body – 'in one moment every drop of blood in my body was brought to a stop'.[11]

The feminine figure appears at precisely the moment when Walter wonders 'what the Cumberland young ladies would look like.' Her uncanny touch initiates a first enigma, which in turn generates a plethora of secrets and detections that propel this tale of sensation and mystery but which itself remains undecided even after the diverse plots and conspiracies have been resolved. This nocturnal walk towards London with a woman 'whose name, whose character, whose story, whose objects in life, whose very presence by my side, at that moment, were fathomless mysteries to me', arouses a sensation in Walter which is so perturbing because strangely undefined. An erotic desire is displaced on to a curiosity to penetrate her social identity, 'to lift the veil that hung between this woman and me' (52). Yet the eroticised form of detective desire further displaces the fact that the initial sensation was one of death. What is left open is whether the plot of detection arising from this uncanny encounter is erotically encoded merely to displace the anxiety of death her touch produced or precisely to occlude a forbidden desire for the death this woman seemingly incarnates.

A second indeterminacy is maintained throughout Collins's text, namely the fact that along with Walter's motivation, the feminine object of his desire is not entirely clear. The entire narrative is constructed around the seeming coincidence that one of the Cumberland ladies, Laura Fairlie, looks like the mysterious woman in white, who withholds her identity, who preserves her secret – Anne Catherick. Even before Walter has seen the woman he will eventually marry and for whose sake he undertakes the dangerous and cumbersome task of detection, the other woman has inscribed herself in his imaginary register. She disturbs his drawing and his reading and is the object of his first conversation with Laura's companion Marion. Given the extraordinary physical and psychic similarity between Anne and Laura (who herself is 'rather nervous and sensitive' (63)), the question Collins raises is whether Walter doesn't in fact love Anne in Laura.

Within such a scenario, his wife serves as the repetition and displacement of the startling woman, and the domestic happiness repeatedly invoked as the context from which he writes veils the fact that his initial object of desire was the death-like Anne not the bride Laura. Walter desires Laura precisely because she recalls the other woman who, insane and dying, is an impossible choice, with his choice of Laura denying even as it affirms that what initiated desire in him was this impossible woman on the edge of death. That the ambivalent desire for Laura veils the desire for Anne as she represents the trauma of a death sensation, finds implicit articulation in the first description Walter gives of Laura. He argues that the 'mystery which underlies the beauty of women', of which Laura's is the paragon, is such that it touches sympathies other than the charm the senses feel, that it is the 'visionary nurseling' of the viewer's 'fancy'. Yet his first sight of Laura is mingled with a sensation that 'troubled and perplexed' him, with the impression of 'something wanting'. Significantly the source of this lack is undetermined – 'At one time it seemed like something wanting in *her*: at another, like something wanting in myself.' Like Georgiana's birth-mark it articulates itself in a contradictory manner, a sense of incompleteness troubling the harmony and charm of her face, eluding his discovery (77).

Only when Marion reads the part of Mrs Fairlie's letter pertaining to the accidental resemblance between Anne and her daughter can Walter affix a signifier to the 'something wanting', namely that of 'ominous likeness'. More importantly, only when looking down at Laura from a window, while she, dressed in white, walks in the moonlight, when he sees her *as* 'the living image . . . of the woman in white', (the word living implying he fancied the original as a dead image), is Walter chilled again by a 'thrill of the same feeling which ran through me when the touch was laid upon my shoulder on the lonely high-road' (86). While Laura's type of beauty can claim kin with the 'deeper mystery in our souls' (76), in her function as Anne's double she induces those other charms which Walter feels with the senses.

Solving the uncanny relation of ominous likeness between these two women by cleanly severing the one from the other may as much involve a foreclosure of the necrophilic thrill of the senses that the one feminine figure of death evokes, as it involves the social restitution of the other. While Walter can allow himself to want woman as the visionary nurseling of his fancy, he must repress his desire for woman as an uncanny apparition, who thrills him even as she must be forbidden precisely because she evokes the presence of death in life, because she represents what lies beneath the veil of Laura's bright, innocent beauty, because she enacts the decaying body not the beautiful body masking its mortality. As Walter calls out 'let me lose the impression again as soon as possible. Call her in', he refers to the twofold threat this instance of uncanny doubling poses. He literally sees that Laura is divided, is more and other than her fair, sweet and simple appearance, and he figurally sees her as a double of Anne. If to see one's double is a harbinger of death, the twist Collins gives to this folklore motif is that Laura does indeed herald Anne's death. She will herself experience a form of death due to this duplicity, even as she will also be the living image that death has not taken place. From the moment of her escape from the asylum Anne traces the figure of death in more than one sense. Given that she appears only to disappear and reappear again elsewhere, as the material bearer of a secret, as elusive in body as the truth she can not tell, incessantly receding from the grasp of those who seek her until death fixes her in place, she enacts the figure of *aphanisis*; a paragon of the rhetoric of death. She is also the image Walter compulsively returns to in his fantasies, whereby compulsive repetition functions as another sign of the death drive. She causes difference to emerge in Walter's imaginary relation with Laura because speaking of Miss Fairlie repeatedly raises the memory of Anne Catherick, 'setting her between us like a fatality that it was hopeless to avoid' (97). When Marion trusts Walter she does so because of his conduct towards 'that unhappy woman'; when she asks him to leave because Laura is engaged she appeals to the same honest, manly consideration for his pupil which he had once showed to 'the stranger and the outcast'. The mention of Sir Percival Glyde as Laura's betrothed reinvokes 'again, and yet again, the woman in white. There *was* fatality in it' (100). His farewell from his mother and sister are irrevocably connected with 'that other memory of the moonlight walk', and even as he leaves England with the image of Laura Fairlie 'a memory of the past', the name of Anne Catherick remains present, 'pronounced behind him as he got into the boat' (205).

In a less rhetorical and a more literal sense, Anne appears and fades in Laura's proximity as an overdetermined figure of death. She is literally dying and shows Laura what she will look like when death sets in. Her letter warning her of Sir Percival's fiendish nature beneath his fair appearance implies that Laura's 'beautiful white silk dress' and bridal veil could by virtue of marriage turn into a shroud, and in so doing confirms the bride's own nervous premonitions. Her proclivity toward Mrs Fairlie's grave and her choice to wear only white lets her appearance be interpreted by spectators such as the schoolboy Jacob Postlewaite as that not merely of a ghost but 't'ghaist of Mistress Fairlie'. The brilliant turn on which the other villain Count Fosco's masterful death plot hinges is that by turning the bride Laura into the dead girl Anne, the former will become her own ghost, will literally repeat at her own body what the schoolboy saw. As Laura's double, then, Anne is a figure of death in life on several scores – she literally signifies a dying body, her repeated appearance is a trope for fatality and, though she means to warn against danger, she will be the concrete instrument by which Laura's figural burial succeeds, by which the trope becomes materialised reality.

Significantly this image of the 'ghost of Miss Fairlie' standing beside the marble cross over Mrs Fairlie's grave repeatedly draws Walter to the graveyard, first to meet Anne a second and last time and then, upon his return to England, to see her double, the 'dead' Laura. At the grave Walter himself consciously reverses the relation beween the two half-sisters, sees not Anne in Laura, but 'Miss Fairlie's likeness in Anne Catherick'. Even more startling, analogous to the thrill he felt standing at the window, is the dissimilarity this likeness articulates, because it imposes the hateful thought that if 'ever sorrow and suffering set their profaning mark on the youth and beauty' of Laura, the two would be 'the living reflections of one another' (120). Given that he never fancies what Anne would look like in health, his interest is clearly in the common denominator he finds in the process of dying. What startles him is not merely the issue of likeness but the way likeness points to the figure of death. The effect of this body double is contrary to that of the gravestone. Rather than indicating the presence of the dead in the beyond she represents uncanny difference, as a figure of death, in the realm of the living.[12]

Anne's own desire for death articulates itself in her longing to clean Mrs Fairlie's grave, to whose memory she clings as the one kind person in her youth. Kissing the gravestone, she expresses the wish to die so as to 'be hidden and at rest with *you*' (127), with death understood as a closure of the gap, as the release from tension. It is precisely this desire which Fosco, having overheard Anne repeat it to Laura, will fulfil as he exchanges the identities of the two women, so that his plot merely materialises what the mentally unbalanced Anne enacts and fancies. Walter's and later Laura's attraction to Anne, nominally because she harbours the secret of Glyde's past which could destroy him, draws both towards the realm of the dead. Walter meets this woman a second time at an equally lonely, noctural site, 'a grave between us, the dead about us' (119). When Laura is faced with her double, with the 'sight of her own face in the glass after a long illness', she too experiences a death-like shock, incapable of speaking for the moment. What she elicits from Anne is, however, not the secret that would empower her against Glyde but rather the madwoman's fantasies about being buried with her mother, to 'wake at her side, when the angel's trumpet sounds, and the graves give up their dead at the resurrection' (302). Like Walter, Laura is startled not only at the likeness between herself and a dying woman but also because this sight is duplicated by a spoken representation of death and its encroachment on life – 'I trembled from head to foot – it was so horrible to hear her.'

As Walter's later investigation shows, Anne serves as the embodiment of two enigmas – of dying and of Sir Percival's secret. Yet while she has a true knowledge of dying, the truth of Glyde's illegitimacy is only in her mother's possession and inaccessible to her. In a manner fatal to her, she mimicks possessing the truth of his past, has the signifier (her mother's threat to expose Sir Percival's secret) but not the signified. Given that the answers Walter and Laura receive from her only pertain to her fantasies of death and resurrection, Collins's narrative implies that the search for a truth to the mystery of a man's past as it relates to a woman's future materialises another desire – the search for a contact with those on the edge of death, with the fantasy of Christian resurrection as a counter-image to that of the socially-dead returned, the revenant. Under the influence of Walter and Laura's contact with Anne even the reasonable Marion, supposedly beyond superstition, repeatedly dreams of death in the form of the representation of Walter 'kneeling by a tomb of white marble', and the shadow of a veiled woman, or 'the veiled woman rising out of the grave and waiting by his side' (296, 310). This dream representation connects the schoolboy's fanciful vision with Anne's fantasies of resurrection and will, owing to Fosco's brilliant creation of death and resurrection, find a materialised representative in Laura's body. In the figure of the woman in white, haunting the fantasies of all those involved with her, death is given a representation before its occurrence and preserved even after the event, because the revenant remains in a double guise – in the body of the living-dead Laura and in the survivors' memory of Anne.

Though the narrative privileges Walter's relation to this revenant, Anne continues to appear and disappear even after he has left England. By dissimulating that she could disclose a powerful secret she poses as a threat to Glyde and Fosco while figuring the sign of hope for the two sisters. By simulating a form of living death, she serves as a source of inspiration for the villains and a source of anxiety for Laura and Marion. For the two sisters, catching Anne's incessantly eluding body means disclosing the secret it bears, while for the two villains tracing Anne means preserving the secret. While she haunts in the double guise of a harbinger of death and a bearer of a secret, her detection offers Fosco the possiblity of yet another form of double plot, in which mourning hides an economic speculation. Because Laura's sole heir is her husband, the conspiracy he devises is such that Glyde can pay his bills with his wife's fictional death.

For the three detectives in the narrative, Marion, Walter and Fosco, disclosure is meant either to ward off death, to distance death from life or to create it in life. Marion writes in her diary, spurred on by 'a fear beyond all other fears', the fear of impending death. Walter collects written narratives from all those involved owing to the desire to put closure on the event of death that has occurred. Fosco traces Anne in order to create a death artificially, to give a fatal fixture to the doubleness her body staged. Having been tricked into entering his London home, Anne dies of a heart attack under the false name Laura Glyde and is buried ironically where she wished, in the grave with Mrs Fairlie, while Laura, passed off as Anne Catterick, is returned to the asylum. Although the enigma she falsely signified, Glyde's past, seems to be buried with her body, the other, death, is precisely what does not remain under ground, for in the body of Laura, Anne continues to haunt until the headstone inscription has been undone, fixing the ghost of Anne in place and separating a living from a dead woman.

There are, then, two sets of doubles. Firstly, the somatic double of one woman by another resulting in a fatal exchange which leaves Laura socially dead, psychically numb and without a will of her own. Secondly, two semiotic doubles, the gravestone inscribed 'Sacred to the memory of Laura, Lady Glyde', which restitutes her in the beyond as well as Walter's collection of narratives meant to undo the false inscription and give Laura a second symbolic birth. While the first leaves death present in life, the second marks an effort to sever death from life cleanly.

Upon his hearing of Laura's death Walter is drawn to her grave, yet as he approaches he recalls not only his lost beloved but also that this was the site where he watched 'for the coming of the woman in white', so that once again the one woman covers the other, the knowledge of the disappearance of the former recalling the uncanny apparition of the latter. The headstone inscription is the sema replacing the absent soma, a form of biography 'which told the story of her life and death', meant to preserve the individual in the collective memory. Michel Serres notes that the designation of the gravestone *ci-gît*, 'here lies', generalises and combines two other designations of place – 'subject' (*subjacere*) as something lying or thrown beneath and 'object' (*objacere*) as something thrown before. While the designation 'here lies' is self-reflexive, designs and stabilises the sense of place in that the tombstone has death define the concept of 'here', the other two designations demand a missing reference. They raise questions such as, placed before or beneath whom, beneath what, in relation to whom, to what, to where? The object before and the subject beneath are non-referential, insisting on, requiring spacial fixture. In the form of the revenant this triadic issue of placement in reference to the site death marks is given a curious figuration, for the resuscitated dead body lies here, beneath the ground and is thrown before the founding mark of death, the tombstone; the subject (beneath) becomes the object (before). In relation to their reference to death, object and subject can be substituted for one another. The object (the double as image) becomes equivalent with the body returned, the subject resuscitated (the double as apparition or revenant).[13]

It is this triadic relation – an inscription of death marking the *here*, with a body split *beneath* and *before* this reference to death – which Collins represents in the *peripeteia* of his narrative. As Walter kneels by the tomb, wearily recalling his lost love – 'I . . . closed my weary eyes on the earth around, on the light above. I let her come back to me' – a veiled woman approaches him. Analogously to the apparition at the crossroads , she takes possession of him 'body and soul'. Standing 'close to the inscription on the side of the pedestal . . . the black letters' she lifts her veil. Walter is faced with a superlatively uncanny moment, a multiplied love object collapsing all points of reference into one site – Laura recalled in his memory, a headstone inscription 'Sacred to the memory of Laura, Lady Glyde' assuring her doubled restitution in the beyond; i.e. the same body beneath and thrown before him (subject collapsing with object), for 'Laura, Lady Glyde . . . was standing by the inscription, and was looking at me over the grave' (430f.). Like the apparition that initiated the plot, 'sprung out of the earth or dropped from the heaven', this Laura as figure of death in life marks the site where the two half-sisters can stand in for each other perfectly; where in an uncanny sense their difference collapses; where Laura as social subject/heiress and Anne as desired object/madwoman merge; where Walter can have both, just as, in reference to death, object/revenant (before) and subject/corpse (beneath) merge.

While Anne as Laura's double served as a harbinger of death, signified what Laura would look like dying, Laura as Anne's double signifies that death has only taken place in an uncanny sense, with a body beneath connected to its double before rather than beyond. By virtue of death exchangeable with Anne, Laura is forced to retrace the social and psychic death of her double, must duplicate the socially hidden, mad and dying Anne in the guise of the symbolically dead Laura, with a confused and weakened memory, without strength, without any will of her own, her mental faculties shaken and weakened. The fatal resemblance that had thrilled Walter earlier, as an idea only, is now by virtue of death realised – now 'a real and living resemblance which asserted itself before my own eyes' (454) – the subject become object.

Because Laura is symbolically designated as dead, none of her community will recognise her. Because she wears Anne's clothes, the director of the asylum accepts her back. Once she has, like her double, escaped, she strikes all others as a mad impostress who is dissimulating 'the living personality of the dead Lady Glyde' (434); an excessive figure of duplicity in that she dissimulates herself as dead and living alike. Though Walter claims that, unlike all the others who refuse to recognise Laura, no suspicion crossed his mind from the moment she lifed her veil, the scene of recognition can be interpreted in a more complex manner. If to lift the veil is understood as a cultural sign for the disclosure of truth, the truth Walter sees is not only that Laura is alive, in contradiction to the headstone, but that the beloved he invoked, with his head on the grave, and that means in relation to death, is precisely the uncanny merger of the two – the figure of fatality that had initially thrilled him; the feminine body which merges object (thrown before) and subject (thrown beneath) in its relation to death; the revenant. For significantly he affixes his claim of possession 'mine at last' to the description of a woman more like Anne than Miss Fairlie, 'Forlorn and disowned, sorely tried and sadly changed – her beauty faded, her mind clouded – robbed of her station in the world, of her place among living creatures' (435).

The mourning and the detection plot merge in such a way that the object of mourning must be exchanged, Anne's death acknowledged and Laura's life reconfirmed. Death is in this case literally solved when it is proved that it did not occur. The trajectory of the investigation is twofold. Firstly, there is the investigation of the conspiracy, discovering and convicting the guilty. Secondly, there is the denial that death has occurred by healing Laura's psychic/physical feebleness and by symbolically healing her social loss of place produced by the false headstone inscription. The veil Laura lifts to expose an uncanny figure, the 'dead-alive', the Laura–Anne now united at one and the same body, must fall again. The dead girl once again becomes a bride, Mrs Hartright socially reaggregated. In the course of a dual social ritual, a second burial/birth and second marriage, the revenant is undone, the doubled body cleanly split into two separate beings. Until this solution has been found, however, the twofold revenant remains in the form of Laura impersonating Anne, and Anne mentally reanimated as the woman in white through whose mystery the way to the secret lies (475). The urgency to restore the one to the living is coterminous with restoring the other to death and both acts hinge on solving the secret that her first appearance in their midst heralded. The doubled bride/dead girl engenders two plots. The one an economic speculation of a husband fulfilled by virtue of dissimulating death, the other the spectacle of an uncanny resemblance transformed into a living trope for fatality. Both plots, however, use the likeness achieved by the double to articulate death in a manner where the literal and the rhetorical merge. The literal death of Anne evokes a conspiracy of dissimulation, where the dead body serves as instrument to victimise a second body into living death, while the rhetoric of the double as harbinger of death finds a 'living resemblance' when Laura equals the dead Anne.

In that sense Fosco's conspiracy is the acme of the chain of uncanny double events, a masterful creation of death in life, with the gravestone precisely not dividing the two. Indeed his plot uncannily blurs another opposition, that between life and art, when he compares his grand scheme to 'the modern Rembrandt' and suggests in his narrative testimony that the situation he created in life – the resurrection of the woman who was dead in the person of the woman who was living – might serve as model for the 'rising romance writers of England' (630). He takes particular pride in his function as the resurrectionist of the dead Anne in Laura and privileges this part of the conspiracy over the production, even if accidental, of Anne's real death. Solving Laura's fictional death also means resolving what was intertwined with her by Fosco's plot and by Walter's eroticised fancy, the ghostly figure of Anne, which, in Walter's words, 'has haunted these pages, as it haunted by life' (576). If Fosco turns death into an artwork, Anne even before her entanglement with Laura's story, served as a living emblem of death, so that her second burial implicitly buries the body that thrills as a figure of death in life.

The final opposition, then, is between two forms of creating signs out of death, between Fosco's creation of death in life and life out of death, with women's bodies his instruments, and Walter's retracing of events in the form of collecting and combining documents that are meant to double the absent like the headstone, and to restitute the absent not here but beyond. Both men represent themselves in relation to death with women's bodies as the site of this exchange. Fosco, the creator of a fatal conspiracy plot, employs the indexic/iconic mode of semiosis when he uses two women's bodies as his material, and turns his written confession of the crime into a remarkable creation meant to represent 'my own ingenuity, my own humanity' (632). Walter represents himself in the collection of testimonies as the one who resuscitated Laura, as the one who repeats and surpasses the maternal by giving a symbolic rebirth to his wife.

Installing the ritual of second burial, Walter calls together Laura's community before which he leads her back into the home from which she had left as bride and was later expelled as a madwoman. Before the collected audience he presents a public disclosure of the funereal conspiracy, outlines its course and the motives behind it, only to close the proceeding by informing those present of Sir Percival's death and his own marriage. Once the symbolic recognition has occurred, Laura is socially reaggregated. Raised by her husband's arm 'so that she was plainly visible to everyone in the room' the community responds by declaring her regained identity – 'there she is, alive and hearty'. Though the grave is not reopened, the disjunction it signified is obliterated, the false inscription erased and replaced with Anne Catherick's name and date of death. This socially sanctioned burial of Anne resolves the uncanny likeness between the two half-sisters, and with it one aspect of death's rhetoric in life. It also fixes the ghost which had haunted Walter independently of Fosco's conspiracy plot, and resolves the uncanny desire for/anxiety about death, puts closure on his compulsive return to Anne as the figure whose sudden appearance had initially brought every drop of blood in his body to a stop. In the end he has successfully decathected Anne, by symbolically severing the woman whose appearance thrills from the innocent beauty of his restored wife. Second burial puts an end to the bad corpse of Anne's ghostly haunting figure and Laura's simulation of a revenant, by disjoining the bride's name from the tombstone and inscribing it so that it truly doubles a woman restituted in the beyond. In an analogous manner, Fosco's bad art, using women's bodies to materialise death and resurrection, to produce uncanny representations is exchanged for the stable art of narrative documentation that results in a recuperation of canny division.

Emily Brontë's *Wuthering Heights* also revolves around an imperfectly closed grave, owing to which the buried woman remains among the living. Though Catherine Earnshaw-Linton's body lies beneath the headstone bearing her name, she is repeatedly resurrected imaginarily by two survivors – by her lover Heathcliff and by her servant Nelly Dean. The former preserves her as a libidinal revenant, as part of his process of mourning, in fact literally loosens one side of her coffin to keep the borders of her burial site open. The latter preserves her as a representational revenant, with her narrative of the past events meant as a strategy by which to find a husband for her mistress's daughter Cathy Heathcliff. Because he is both the spectator of Heathcliff's mourning and the chosen addressee of Nelly's tale, Lockwood, the tenant at Thrushcross Grange, not only offers the narrative frame of the text but is also the interstice between these two processes of resuscitation.

Visiting his landlord at Wuthering Heights he encounters two women liminally positioned and doubles of each other in so far as the daughter Cathy has exactly the same eyes and the same appearance of haughtiness as her mother Catherine. This daughter, left a disinherited widow by her husband's death, strikes Lockwood as 'being buried alive' (55) and herself remarks that she is locked in, forbidden to go beyond the garden wall. The mother, in turn, appears to him first in the form of a triple signature scratched repeatedly onto the ledge of a couch window where he is to spend the night, so that as he closes his eyes, 'white letters . . . as vivid as spectres' haunt him – 'the air swarmed with Catherines' (61). Finding her writing covering the white blanks of nearly all the books stored in this bed-couch, an interest for the 'unknown Catherine' is kindled in Lockwood, and he reads bits of her autobiographical sketches until he falls asleep and is befallen by the intense horror of nightmare. The touch of a child's 'little, ice-cold hand' as it tries to get in through the window, wailing to be let in, complaining of its twenty-year waifdom, so maddens him with fear that he yells out in 'a frenzy of fright' (67). He had rubbed the ghost's wrist on the broken glass pane to keep it out, for the fancied touch is implicitly understood as a threat of death.

To Heathcliff, who responds to his cry, he describes her as a spectre 'who probably would have strangled me' (69). Yet not only the true nature of this ancestor but also Heathcliff's agony – he tears open the lattice, calls the absent Catherine to come in – leaves Lockwood faced with an enigma. While the daughter appears to him locked in and buried alive in her widowhood, the mother appears as an unburied ghost, locked out yet resuscitable over her signature and her diary. She further returns as the object of anxiety in Lockwood's nightmare visions and as the object of desire in Heathcliff's anguished mourning. While Lockwood tries to partition off the ghost and with it the presence of death, Heathcliff desires precisely to undo this division; with a desire for the return of his lost beloved and for death interchangeable.

Though it does not bring him death, Catherine's spectral appearance is one of the causes for Lockwood's five weeks of 'torture, tossing and sickness' (130). During this period of confinement she returns yet again, in Nelly's relation of the past, in which the plot of the spectral bride is used uncannily by the narrator to foster her listener's interest in 'that pretty girl-widow', accompanied by hanging her picture over his fireplace, hoping her story will induce him to 'win Mrs Heathcliff's heart' (346). Yet the opposite occurs, for in the same manner that he locked out the ghost of Catherine Linton, Lockwood shields himself from the 'fascination that lurks in Catherine Heathcliff's brilliant eyes', fearing an uncanny repetition, 'the daughter . . . a second edition of the mother' (191).

The frame Brontë's text sets up revolves around two instabilities – Heathcliff's mourning which preserves Catherine's ghost on earth and the daughter Cathy's widowhood, which has her liminally positioned between two marriages. The mourning and the detective plot are enmeshed in such a way that Heathcliff seeks to retain Catherine's ghost, seeks to view her corpse, to preserve the dead woman and with it death's presence in life. Lockwood seeks Nelly's narrative to decipher the fascination that the girl–widow, and the horror that the spectral-mother provoked. By not choosing the beautiful Cathy he also rejects the notion of death's presence in life. At the end of the plot, Heathcliff's death and Cathy's betrothal to her cousin affords fixture to these diametrically opposed responses to death. Heathcliff, who has "a strong faith in ghosts", designs his funeral in such a way that his partly opened coffin will face the opening he made on Catherine's, so that he can walk the earth after death united with his spectral bride. Lockwood's solution is to exclude all belief in ghosts, to divide death from life. He not only rejects the daughter but also denies, in the presence of the graves, that 'anyone could ever imagine unquiet slumbers for the sleepers in that quiet earth' (367).

Before the resolution of these two plots – of mourning and of marriage – the dead Catherine Linton remains present, however, in the shape of two doubles. On the one hand, she returns as the ghost her forbidden lover clings to, since he conceives of the dead woman as holding his soul. Their relation is that of a symbiotic imaginary duality, where the beloved other is the same as the self, present as long as the survivor exists, absent or lost only over his absence. Their love embodies a notion of oneness that allows for difference only in the sense of annihilation. On the other hand, the mother returns in the shape of her daughter who repeats her, but with a life-sustaining difference.[14] The fatality of repetition traced by the plot occurs not at the site of the body double but rather of the mourner. Heathcliff's death puts closure on the disruption or gap engendered by the mother's death. He severs the maternal revenant from the daughter by reuniting him with her instead. In that death is repeated at Heathcliff's body, Cathy is prevented from repeating her mother's self-destructive fate. Not unlike Laura, Cathy's possible identity with a dead girl is foreclosed by virtue of a second burial, which lets her in turn re-emerge as a bride. In contrast to Nelly's uncanny narration – in which both the ghost of the dead mother and the daughter as its double are invoked – the bride of Hareton Earnshaw can dispel any fear that fatality may be inscribed in her life because an arrestation of repetition has occured. With her second social birth (her second marriage) occurring over the mourning lover and the maternal spectres' expulsion, her new life will be undisturbed by revenants. Like Lockwood she can reject the uncanny double and with it the rhetoric death traces in life.[15]

The story Brontë frames with Lockwood's detective and Cathy's marriage plots, and which like these finds its resolution in Heathcliff's death, traces the diametrically opposed articulation of death's rhetoric in life: a symbiotic love which cannot be sustained within the 'castrative' subjugation and prohibitions that the social order requires but rather must annihilate itself. While Catherine enacts the hysteric's choice of self-destruction against the fear of being divided from her lover, shows the bride becoming a dead girl rather than dividing herself in childbirth, Heathcliff desires death as an undoing of the divisions and differences that sustain life and invokes the dead girl as his revenant bride. The teller of this uncanny tale, Nelly, hesitates between both attitudes – the expulsion of death from life and the embrace of death against life. Though her common sense assures her that the 'dead are at peace' she fears to be out at night. Though her aim is the closure marriage puts on death, her tale uncannily raises the dead to contradict the 'three headstones on the slope next the moor', whose sight so reassures Lockwood.

From the start she depicts Catherine's relation to Heathcliff as one placing them beyond the social law – implicitly forbidden because incestuous, explicitly because a misalliance between a landowner's daughter and a servant. The fact that they resist any separation implies a narcissistic bond which tries to obliterate difference by insisting on an absolute oneness or an absolute non-existence. Catherine explains to Nelly, she loves Heathcliff 'because he's more myself than I am', because whatever 'souls are made of, his and mine are the same,' because he is 'always in my mind . . . as my own being' (121f.). Though set against death as a force causing separations and divisions, Catherine sees her love in light of two other aspects of death – a notion of eternal fixture against temporality ('my love . . . resembles the eternal rocks beneath') and the uncanny lack of position belonging to the revenant. Equating a marriage to Edgar with being in heaven, she recounts a dream in which she wept to come back to earth and was flung back on to the heath by the angels.

Against the wound to her narcissism which a division from Heathcliff implies, she retaliates in the form of self-destruction, much as Heathcliff responds to loss by directing his aggressive energies against others. During the period Edgar woos Catherine, she threatens to go with her illict lover, should her brother send him away. Her immediate response to Heathcliff's departure is a psychosomatic enactment of the unconscious knowledge of her non-existence. She falls into a delirium that turns into a fever, abstains from eating and becomes suicidal. Because the presence of her lover, who gives her the sense that she is whole, sustains her life, his absence makes death the object of her desire.

The hysteric knows that she is inscribed by a lack and seeks an alternate ego or double as representative of herself. Catherine, however, designs this double not as a version of herself but precisely in the shape of another. The hysteric's knowledge that she is no-body means that she spends her life in proximity to symptomatisation and annihilation – histrionic when she tries to capture the masculine gaze, suicidal when she loses it. In moments of transition, where a position of security is disrupted and transformed, she is confronted with the knowledge that she signifies a lack of being, with the real void of death located beneath all gestures of dissimulation that keep her within the symbolic order. Transitional moments such as marriage and motherhood are dangerous, and it is precisely these that bring on Catherine's fevers and suicidal desires.

Her very first separation from Heathcliff had occurred when a wounded ankle forced her to stay with the Lintons, only to learn at Thrushcross Grange the prohibitions and restrictions of the cultured social world. Her first exposure to social prohibitions was concomitant with not only a somatic wound but also a wound to her narcissism, embodied in the absence of her companion. Their second separation brings her into a proximity of real death (her fever), turns her into an agent of death (she fatally infects the Linton parents), and encourages her marriage, which is later described as a form of living death, her body a 'corpse' because its soul (Heathcliff) has been severed from her. Heathcliff's response to the loss of his beloved is also 'violent exertions', but turned outward, a carefully designed strategy of getting 'levers and mattocks to demolish the two houses' (352). Whenever the two lovers reunite, this violence is abated.

In that the force of their love seeks a complete imaginary unity of total sameness or complete annihilation it disrupts social codes, transgresses taboos, disrupts family structures even as it destroys the lovers' bodies and as such can be seen as a trace of the semiotic chora. In that their love aims to attain the static union before and beyond social divisions and compromises, it transforms into a love for death. Because it resists the mitigated death drive embodied in the agency of the superego, of cultural laws, it transforms into an articulation of the

unrestrained pure death drive, located in the primary processes, in the unconscious. Whenever the threat of division re-emerges, that of the real void of death
reappears as well. Fearing a repeated disappearance of Heathcliff after a fight
with Edgar, Cathy once again falls ill and this brain fever, which now cannot be
deflected on to others, is the main cause of her subsequent death in childbirth.
Her hysterical symptomatisation signifies the recognition of her non-existence,
given that it is induced by the fear that she will lose her alternate ego. Her 'fit of
frenzy', her rage, 'dashing her head against the arm of the sofa, and grinding her
teeth' (156), her three-day confinement behind a barred door, her refusal of
food, are in part consciously designed to direct aggressive passions against
others. She wishes to frighten her husband and her lover by using her own
destruction as punishment – 'I'll try to break their hearts by breaking my own'
(155). Forced by her husband to make a choice between him and her illicit lover,
the former implying the irrevocable acknowledgment of a split within herself,
Catherine chooses death, as a movement beyond divisions.

The scene describing the acme of her fit of frenzy, which Nelly and her doctor
understand as a repetition of her 'former illness', is a return to consciousness
after a near-death experience of 'utter blackness'. In a manner that will prove
fatal, Nelly decides that Catherine 'acted a part of her disorder'. Because she
does not comprehend that a hysterical simulation always also signifies real pain
she remains blind to the 'true condition', which her mistress's 'ghastly countenance, and strange exaggerated manner', bespeaks (159). Catherine splits into
various persons, vacillating between violent, feverish bewilderment and an
absent-minded return to childhood memories. She notes a division between
herself and her mirrored image, asking 'Is that Catherine Linton'. Later she is
unable to recognise her mirrored face and associates this image instead with a
ghost haunting her, until she finally gasps at the realisation that what she sees is
'myself'. This forced recognition of herself as being other than the image of the
beautiful, loved and undivided self she has fashioned for herself articulates on
several scores that the mirrored double signifies death. Rhetorically in the
manner Blanchot describes, this distinction between self and self-designation
evokes the absence of the speaker. Figurally the fact that she can't recognise
herself can be seen as a trope for the alienation her married life entails, for the
absence of her true self in the role of wife and mother. It can also be read as a
trope for her desire to return to a symbiotic unity before the mirror stage, given
that the latter always implies the division of the dyad by a third agency (father,
language, absence). Literally the image she sees in the mirror is that of a dying
woman, much as Laura saw an image of her dying self reflected in her double
Anne's face.

The fact that she will not accept the split in herself, which every division form
Heathcliff as her 'all in all' gives figure to, that she will prefer a real non-existence
over being no whole body in her social world, entertains an aspect of duplicity.
Her madness is such that she hovers between her present condition of illness and
memories of her youth; between being 'the wife of a stranger; an exile and

outcast' and the recollection of the first time she 'laid alone', separated from Heathcliff by her brother's interdiction. Her hysterical simulation of death is brilliantly doubled, for not only does she alternate between raving and half-dreaming, but she is also simultaneously in two places, 'knows those about her' even as her mind is filled 'with all sorts of strange ideas and illusions' (167). Against these images of repeated experiences of the loss of the positive double and of her married self as an embodiment of a negative division, she posits an image of death as a return to the sense of total unity, as a return home. Its completion involves another aspect of the double in that a release from the psychic death becomes coterminous with the state of the revenant.

Opening the window, implicitly a call for death, she recalls her childhood games when she and her companion stood 'among the graves' and asked the ghosts to come. Calling Heathcliff, so as to undo the 'abyss' their separation draws, becomes a double call – she calls herself to death so as to call him to follow her – 'I'll keep you . . . they may bury me twelve feet deep, and throw the church down over me; but I won't rest till you are with me' (164). This image of the restless deceased is a chiasmic reversal of her married existence, conceived by her as a separation of her body (belonging to her husband) and her soul (belonging to her lover). Threatening Edgar that she will 'spring from the window! What you touch at present, you may have; but my soul will be on that hill top before you lay hands on me again' (165) retrospectively implies that what he had all along was merely the 'corpse' of her body. Her death is merely the exchange of one form of revenant existence for another. The division her marriage signified not only finds an apotheosis in her hysterical fit, where with her body as medium she writes her sense of social non-existence and her proximity to death. Rather it is also chiasmically repeated in the division she imagines to embody after death. At the origin and the end of this divided or doubled existence stands the union with her alternate ego, the release of all tension possible only, in Freud's terminology, in the inanimation of the pre-organic state.

Even her actual death is divided in the sense that it has a dual cause – the brain fever, with the 'permanent alienation of intellect' it induces and the pregnancy from which a 'puny, seven month's child' is born over her dying body.[16] The former responds to the fear that by losing Heathcliff a division of the self and a loss of her soul will be repeated yet again, and her madness duplicates this split in that her body is present while her mind wanders; her eyes with 'dreamy and melancholy softness,' vague, distant, always gazing beyond. The latter instead responds to the fear of literally splitting her body in two by giving birth, a somatic repetition and reinforcement of her psychic division. Her death also articulates that the perfect identity of two bodies is a form of love which transgresses social laws, outside marriage, even outside the realm of the living. Against the notions previously discussed that death reunites the lovers in heaven, this love can also not be restituted in the beyond, but must remain located in between, in the transgressive and liminal position of the ghost.

The scene initiating her death repeats and condenses these themes of duplicty and division into one final image. As the two lovers fall into their embrace, from which Catherine emerges 'a lifeless-looking form,' (199), she accuses him of murder ('You have killed me'), desires his death ('I wish I could hold you . . . till we were both dead'), invokes her postmortal unrest ('I shall not be at peace'), curses him to feel the same distress she will feel 'underground', even as she invokes death one last time as a form of liberation from the 'shattered prison' of her married existence. Death will fulfil her supreme desire, 'never to be parted', because once dead she can call him as she can't in life: 'my Heathcliff. I shall love mine yet, and take him with me – he's in my soul' (196). Her death is a doubly directed act of aggression. Though it destroys her, it also inflicts on her lover a renewal of the 'hell' of division, so that he conceives of his mourning as a slow form of being murdered by the ghost of the deceased, a 'strange way of killing' (321). Catherine's death-like loss of consciousness during her last embrace, from which she emerges bewildered – 'she sighed, and moaned, and knew nobody' – significantly occurs as Edgar's approach threatens to break the symbiotic dyad and finalises her hysteric desire to repress all signs of division. She dies without recovering 'sufficient consciousness to miss Heathcliff and to know Edgar', without being forced to acknowledge that she is divided in the two senses discussed – lacking her lover and delivered of a daughter.

Nelly sees her corpse as the semblance of 'perfect peace' and tranquillity, her body an 'untroubled image of Divine rest.' Implicitly she misreads her mistress's belief that in death she would be 'incomparably beyond and above' her survivors, much as she misread her earlier fit of frenzy. In support of the double attitude toward death that the novel's frame exhibits, Brontë leaves the question undecided whether Nelly's view that 'her spirit is at home with God' is adequate, whether she fully condones Nelly's allegorisation of the corpse into a figure legitimising a belief in 'the endless and shadowless hereafter – the Eternity . . . when life is boundless in its duration and love in its sympathy, and joy in its fullness' (201). Or whether she also recognises Heathcliff's contrary assurance that the dead woman is not beyond, 'not *there* – not in heaven'.

While for Nelly a narcissistically informed desire for wholeness requires that the dead be fully restituted in the beyond, Heathcliff's same desire requires an obliteration of the division between the living and the dead. He calls to the absent to haunt him, to wander on earth, not to leave him alive alone. While Nelly sees the corpse as a figure whose peace assures the division of death from life and supports a canny notion of a peaceful existence after wordly strife, – Heathcliff wishes to see her corpse as a sign that death can uncannily be preserved in life, that the absence death causes is incomplete. While for Catherine death signifies the liberation from an enclosure, for Heathcliff the corpse remains a signifer of a gap. The ghost of his beloved tempts and recedes from his grasp, just as the forbidden wife of Edgar Linton had, and her death is not a release of tensions but merely a shift in its manner of articulation.

The first of several instances of tampering with her corpse so as to assure an exchange is that he places a lock of his hair into a locket around her neck to be buried with her. On the day of her burial he tries to undo the division that the grave affords by literally uncovering the coffin, wishing to have her in 'his arms again'. Yet his necrophilic desire turns into mourning because his 'strong faith in ghosts' lets him sense the spectral presence of Catherine 'there, not under me, but on the earth'. Relinquishing his initial desire to embrace the corpse initiates 'that strange feeling' which shapes the next eighteen years of mourning until he does indeed open the coffin. This uncanniness, spurred on by a refusal to see the corpse, lets her remain as an immaterial body, present though absent in body. In his psychic reanimation, she traces the figure of *aphanisis*, an 'intolerable torture', because constantly oscillating between fading from his view and returning in his sensation and imagination. At Wuthering Heights, Heathcliff 'felt her by me – I could *almost* see her, and yet I *could* not!' When he closes his eyes she is there – outside the window, entering the room, resting her head next to his, yet once he opens his eyes she is again gone. This uncanny preservation, the woman simultaneously *da* and *fort*, remaining yet receding from any concrete vision and grasp, keeping him alive yet in constant relation to death, is what Heathcliff ultimately calls 'a strange way of killing . . . to beguile me with the spectre of hope'. While he defines his mourning as a form of murder, with the revenant bringing him death by 'fractions of hair-breadths', what remains undecided is whether the hope he refers to is her complete resurrection in body or his complete physical annihilation. His mourning represents the lost beloved in the image of the female vampire, who returns to bring death to her bridegroom. The indeterminacies this motive is inscribed with are such that the relation of signifer to signified is opaque. Does death desire him because she desires him? Does he, by desiring her, desire death? Or does he desire her as a displaced desire for death?

The liminal phase of mourning – in which he retains her on earth as the revenant who haunts him – finds closure when Heathcliff does indeed open the coffin, for the sight of the dead body affords 'some ease'. Concomitant with the invoked revenant theme, her body has not decomposed. Implicitly, because he has preserved her mentally, her body will begin to dissolve only when he too shares this process. The vampirisation is such that her uncanny presence strangely kills him, sucks his life even as his psychic clinging to her sustains her body, with his mental anguish serving as the blood that arrests her bodily dissolution and precludes any form of dissolution. The sight of the corpse, 'the distinct impression of her passionless features,' removes that 'strange feeling' of her intangible presence, assures him that she is indeed dead. The tranquillity he gains from this sight closes the uncertainty that the thwarted first disinterment provoked, because it discloses a repressed knowledge – the truth of her death. Had he initially aimed at literally lying with the corpse, disregarding whether she be cold or motionless, as an act of defying the gap death produced, he now imagines such a necrophilic embrace as a trope for his own demise – 'I dreamt I was sleeping the last sleep, by the sleeper, with my heart stopped, and my cheek frozen against hers' (320).

Though Catherine's second burial does not put closure on her revenant status, but on the contrary fixes it (Heathcliff has used the opening of the grave to loosen one side of her coffin), it does terminate the spectrality that fed his mourning and introduces his dying. The second burial terminates his fetishistic position of mourning, his hesitation between a denial of her disappearance and the fact that the intangibility of her ghost forced him to acknowledge her bodily absence. Before he saw the corpse he could still conceive of his beloved in terms of the living, could sustain his life uncannily over her psychic reanimation. Once he has seen her corpse, her death is certain, and in his invocations he now does not ask her to return but rather to help him be gone as well. Because he can no longer focus his attention on the one image of her spectral body, he sees her everywhere, 'in every object . . . the entire world a dreadful collection of memoranda that she did exist and that I have lost her' (353). His form of death is a repetition of Catherine's – abstaining from food, he stares beyond into 'a vacant space'. All absorbed by the dead woman, he bars himself from the living, withdraws into the panelled bed of their childhood unity. Where she died so as not to 'miss Heathcliff', he hopes death will assuage this lived lack.

Though Heathcliff understands this death as an irrevocable obliteration of the division between himself and his other, Brontë's text ends on a note which embellishes the crack of duplicity – thematically and structurally. For the heaven Heathcliff has 'nearly attained' is their spectral reunion, their wandering between earth and heaven, not a fixture in a grave and in the beyond (the heaven of Christianity 'altogether unvalued, and uncoveted'). Rhetorically the doubled narrative, the frame and its embedded tale, remains split between a notion that the dead are cleanly severed from the living and one that locates the dead on their margins – in the room at Wuthering Heights closed to signify their absence but just as plausibly shut up 'for the use of such ghosts as choose to inhabit it' (366) and in the tome of their textual representation serving either as a repetition of the gravestone, assuring the quiet slumbers of the dead or as the correlative of the panel oak bed, to whose inhabitant Catherine's ghost so tauntingly will reappear.

Much has been written about the theme of sexuality in *Dracula*, about masculine homoeroticism, the exchange of women's bodies among men, perverse sexual practices connected with sucking and the fear of female sexuality.[17] Yet vampire lore also serves as a central trope for western attitudes toward death, so that Stoker's text represents not only an ambivalent desire for/fear of sexuality but also the same ambivalence toward mortality with the theme of sexuality put forward to veil that of death. His narrative presents the mourning for a woman, whose death poses as an enigma – what took out the blood of four strong men put into her veins? (151) – equivalent to detecting and obliterating the source of death. Decathexis is here completed once a preserved corpse has been transformed into a decomposing one, replaced with a secondary double, a funeral symbol.

Stoker illustrates that after death the body can return in a fascinatingly dangerous or a soothingly safe form: the former a material somatic return, the vampire as body double, the latter an immaterial semiotic return, with documents, headstone inscriptions and memory images standing in for the absent body, doubling it not in an iconic/indexic but rather a symbolic mode. While the vampire penetrates the body, sucks blood to preserve itself as a death-bringer, the vampire-hunters also incite the body with their staking and decapitation, yet this act of penetration preserves the social body against death. As an undead body, disseminating an uncanny state of living-death with each body he bites, Dracula embodies a form of death which threatens two aspects of the paternal symbolic order. In a cultural sense the vampire's false death is a serious falsification of Christian notions of death as the sleep before Judgement Day. The empty grave of the vampire, with its permeable plate, suggests that these bodies are not waiting for any teleologically oriented resurrection but, based on a cyclic notion of return, reappear prematurely in the world of the living, with their bodies preserved whole. In a semiotic sense the vampire traces the return to inscriptions on the body and counteracts the process of culturation, where language, as the cornerstone of paternal law, is a 'murder of the soma', where the body's contingent form of signification is replaced by arbitrary symbolisation. The language of the vampire keeps the originary exchange between life and death open to undermine the hegemony of secondary symbolic exchanges.

Vampire plots serve as narratives about the trauma that death poses once it is returned to the living, inscribed within the community, on the bodies of its members, and that the response that death – traced by Count Dracula's presence – elicits can be divided into a hysteric and an obsessional discourse.[18]

The hysteric recognises a lack or void in the symbolic order of laws and knows her non-existence. She exists within her cultural system by evoking the presence of a double; a rhetorical articulation of death. In this relation the hysteric is protean, able to appear in more than one guise, hiding the knowledge of her non-existence even as the fluidity of her position, because of which she is not fixed by any one cultural master signifier, is such that one of her relations is to radical Otherness outside the symbolic, as the site of her truth. Responding to the vampire can be read as the trope for the hysteric's relation to that radical Otherness beyond the social, the acknowledgement of the real void of death as one of her points of reference.[19].

While the hysteric accepts her division, feeds off her lack of a fixed identity, and preserves a fluid boundary to the unconscious, the obsessional tries to repress the real void of death by erecting clear divisions. He uses language and knowledge in an effort to exclude radical Otherness, lest it allow the lacks and gaps, which make him anxious, to appear. Against the hysteric's celebration of duplicity and her fluid relation to the unconscious, he fears duplicity, seeks to control the indeterminate and identifies with dead objects to close out death as the truth in his unconscious. The aim is to keep the ego impenetrable, the fantasies intact, even if this means killing off all living desire and difference within oneself, for any fixity is preferable to acknowledging death's presence in life. To block out fluidity, multiplicity and instability as remnants of the impossible burden emanating from Otherness as real death, the obsessional clings to the death-like fixity of mastery and certain knowledge. Desire, in being illicit, bringing surprises and subverting control is his enemy, and Woman as the instigator and object of desire, especially the hysteric's fluidity of appearances, must be petrified and purified of any taints. She can be a safe object for identification when she is no longer an uncanny figure representing death but rather cannily dead. The obsessional masters death as an uncanny difference within by fixing an ambivalent, fluid, oscillating body to a stable signifier, and precisely for this process, the vampire hunt with its staking is a trope.

In Stoker's text the hysterical discourse is embodied by the two brides, Lucy Westenra and Mina Murray, who respond to the trace of death the vampire evokes and, once bitten, hover uncannily between wakeful conscious and death-like unconscious states. Their psychosomatic symptoms signify that death's Otherness speaks through the medium of their bodies. Apart from histrionics, emotional lability and simulation, early psychoanalysis also saw as descriptive traits of the hysteric character 'demanding dependency', 'excessive excitability', and a proclivity toward semi-conscious states, towards 'suggestibility' as an acceptance and acting out of the desires others have induced in hypnosis.[20]. Freud and Breuer's discussion of the hysteric's double conscience as a split in consciousness (between a daytime lucidity, favouring a cure and a nocturnal irrationality, resisting the analyst's efforts at healing), as well as hypnoid conditions, somnambulism, hallucinations and amnesia, evokes both Lucy's and Mina's behaviour as they oscillate between responding to Dracula's call and to that of their men.[21]. The position of the obsessional is in turn assumed by the suitors and doctors, who hunt and destroy vampires to redraw the separation between bodies beneath the graveplate and funerary signs, between unconscious desires and conscious deeds. They precisely do not respond to death's call except to expel its living presence and identify instead with dead objects – mutilated corpses, memory images, the documents reduplicating their investigation.

These two responses to death are debated over the bodies of the two brides. Lucy and Mina respond hysterically in the form of a double conscience to death's incision (Dracula's bite) even as their bodies are the sites at which the men attempt symbolic restitution in the form of blood transfusions and second burials. Detecting Dracula is coterminous with obliterating the difference death traces in the community, even as his destruction along with that of the vampire Lucy serves to fix the disruption of the symbolic by the semiotic chora that the dying and dead feminine body enacts. The two brides are positioned between the paternal law and radical Otherness as their two points of reference, with the death of Dracula putting closure on this oscillation by placing Mina securely in relation to the phallus (as wife and mother) and Lucy in relation to canny death (as decomposing corpse). What returns with the vampire's bite are the two repressed enigmas – femininity and death – while a solution of the uncanniness of both is here, too, coterminous.

At the outset of Stoker's novel, both Mina and Lucy are in the premarital state, waiting for their future husbands. Mina remains rationally controlled in the absence of Jonathan Harker, in fact writes in her diary to exercise her conscious memory, practises stenography and typewriting. Lucy is psychosomatically disturbed by this 'waiting' (72) and gives her liminality as bride the figure of the somnambulist. Even before Dracula has appeared she walks in her sleep, has an 'anaemic look', is 'excitable', 'supersensitive' to influences, and has chosen as her favourite seat, which she 'cannot leave', the grave of a boy suicide (67). To a degree this restlessness can be seen as the banal symptomatisation of her uncertainty about her upcoming marriage to Arthur Holmwood. The fact that her symptoms – heavy, lethargic sleep, frightening dreams which she forgets – do not correspond to any bodily illness lets Dr Seward conclude 'it must be something mental' (111). Though Mina started the habit of visiting the churchyard, she initially resists the call of death. Sleepwalking Lucy, in turn, immediately responds to the desire or call of the Other, like the sexton Swales, who says 'if (Death) should come this very night I'd not refuse to answer his call' (74) and who is Dracula's first victim. She enacts that a desire for death is located in her unconscious, even if her conscious self cheerfully anticipates the return of her future husband. This conjunction is made explicit by the fact that Lucy is waiting for Arthur to take him to her seat on the churchyard cliff, while it is at precisely this 'favourite seat' that she is bitten by her other suitor, Dracula. The duplicity Lucy's self-division initially entails is that though her restlessness and her nocturnal yielding to an unconscious desire suggest a fluidity between various states of the self, this knowledge is foreclosed or rejected by her conscious self. She does not, in Mina's words, understand her restlessness nor will she admit to any cause. Once bitten she implores Mina 'not to say a word to any one . . . about her sleep-walking adventure' (92), and as her friend notes, exposure could cause not only her health but also her reputation to suffer.

The text gives Lucy two doubles: her own split-self which will eventually return as a vampire, and her friend Mina. The latter shares her oscillation between semi-conscious states that articulate a desire for death and a conscious desire for marriage, yet unlike Lucy, who withholds her secret from the vampire-hunters, Mina is more clearly an accomplice of the paternal law. She writes down her unconscious dreams, transcribes the other documents. As secretary she helps undo Lucy's somatic resurrection as revenant and is instrumental in replacing it with a textual resurrection. This semiotic restitution helps Mina redraw a boundary between herself and her dead friend as well as between her actions and her own unconscious response to death.

Throughout her illness, as she grows more languid and weak, as she fades away, the enigma Lucy poses is located in this enactment of a split self; on the one hand her unconscious attempts to get out of her room to the spot in the graveyard, her 'half-dreamy state', her hallucinations, and on the other her suddenly becoming 'her old self again', in 'gay spirits' and 'full of life and cheerfulness' (97). Her own description of her illness repeatedly invokes images of Otherness that contradict her conscious sense of self – 'a great press of water', noises, distant voices, coming from 'I know not where and commanding me to do I know not what' (135). Her description of her first encounter with Dracula emphasises that a near-death experience is one of division. While she is drawn inexplicably to the churchyard, she seems to be asleep though the experience seems to be real. The bite of the vampire is 'very sweet and very bitter', accompanied by a sense of sinking and of singing in her ears, her soul leaving her body and floating in the air, only to return finally to her body (98).

The four blood transfusions meant to undo the vampire's death work, as it manifests itself in her corpse-like, ghastly waxen pallor, in her wan-like motionless body, do not only raise the issue of an implicit sexual exchange. Arthur feels that giving his blood to Lucy is a form of marriage, 'she was his wife in the sight of God' (174), just as the other donors never speak of their gift, afraid to 'enjealous' him (128). The operation also reveals that Lucy's body serves as a medium between the men and death, Dracula sucking their blood by virtue of this detour, as he will later speak to them through Mina's hypnotised body. This substitution allows for the displaced articulation of a repressed desire for death. Lucy's body is uncanny not only as the site of a dual exchange – she feeds Dracula even as she receives the gift of vampirism – but also as that of a double signature, his red marks on her neck countersigned by the men's mark on her arms. At stake in the repeated depletion and rejuvenation of her dying body, and later the mutilation of her corpse, is the question of which signature – Dracula's somatic or the men's symbolic form of signification – will be privileged. This artificial reanimation is also a representation of paternal birthgiving ('a feeling of personal pride' (128)), pitched against natural decay, and implicitly against the maternal function. Lucy's mother unwittingly counteracts their intentions by removing the garlic and she dies in Lucy's bed having torn the protective wreath from her daughter's neck, exposing her once more to the vampire's bite.

Once vampirism sets in, the duplicity of Lucy's split self becomes bodily more manifest – sleeping she looks stronger, though more haggard, her breathing stertorous, her teeth longer and sharper; awakening, the softness of her eyes changes her expression back into the earlier Lucy, 'her own self'. In the end, because death gives her 'back part of her beauty' Lucy makes a 'very beautiful corpse' (162). Once death has set in, the earlier self-division now articulates itself in an uncanny restoration of her previous beauty against the natural process of 'decay's effacing fingers' (164). Every hour in fact 'seemed to be enhancing her loveliness' (168). Seward's duplicitous response to this sight – 'It frightened and amazed me' – voices the survivors' ambivalence of feeling. Even as her lovers want to preserve her in life they also need her decomposition to complete their mourning.

Though in one sense she is a figure for sexualised death – Arthur repeatedly kisses the corpse – the trajectory of Van Helsing's detection is to put closure on any necrophilic desire. Unlike Heathcliff, who wished to open the coffin of his beloved so as to embrace both her and death, to preserve her death in life, Van

Helsing opens her coffin to mutilate her body – to stake her heart and decapitate her – so as to begin the process of decomposition. He wishes to arrest the uncanniness which began with her oscillation between conscious and unconscious self, to resolve the duplicity of a body's beauty hiding that it is in fact decaying, to undo the split between angel and demon, to obliterate the perversion of the maternal that her biting of children entails. If the ill Lucy was safely pure during the day while dangerously semi-conscious at night, once undead her dual life is such that she is doubly threatening, 'more radiantly beautiful' while lying in her coffin and violently sexualized at night, her sweetness an 'adamantine heartless cruelty', her purity 'voluptuous wantonness' (211).

The second killing or paternal resurrection Van Helsing instigates – Arthur staking the vampire Lucy in the presence of the other men – is a counterpart to the blood-transfusions and this operation again appears like a covert sexual act. As they confront the vampire, she is likened to Medusa, a figuration of death – 'If ever a face meant death – if looks could kill – we saw it at that moment' (212). The effort of staking is meant to separate into two canny opposites what is so threateningly intertwined – death's and a beautiful woman's face – and this operation will work if the death-beauty can be proved to be false rather than inextricably intertwined with femininity. The vampire is designated as a 'nightmare of Lucy . . . the whole carnal and unspiritual appearance, seeming like a devilish mockery of Lucy's sweet purity' (214). At stake in the mutilation of this mock Lucy is the effort to counteract the false death of the undead ('working wickedness by night', 'growing more debased by day') and to arrest any further dissemination of death by her bite. By restituting the 'true Lucy', with her soul released, her dead body doubled as an angel in heaven because her earthly double, her corpse is safely decomposed, they have material proof for their Christian notion of true death. Here, too, the turn to the sheer materiality of the body serves to antidote a crisis in belief.

The staking will also restore that image of Lucy which they require as a safeguard of their own sense of stability. They aim 'to restore Lucy . . . as a holy, and not an unholy, memory' (215). This operation expels the image of the 'foul Thing' and leaves a Lucy, 'as we had seen her in her life, with her face of unequalled sweetness and purity'. The traces of death her face now draws, 'pain and waste', are no longer a mockery of death. Her long phase of oscillation is fixed in the aspect of the 'holy calm' that lies over what is now no longer a grinning devil but 'God's true dead,' (308).[22] This staking fixes semantic instability which the vampire Lucy enacted in two ways – as a dead body mocking a living woman, and as a woman who is superlatively beautiful while sleeping yet who mocks this beauty by exhibiting violent feminine wantonness while awake. Her semantic duplicity is arrested as she is resurrected as an angel and a holy image. The secondary form of representational double, used to obliterate the primary body-double, however, affords a second form of arrestation in that it covers up the traces of death's material work with inanimate signs. If Lucy, lying so radiantly beautiful in her coffin, resonates with the image of Snow White, her body may not awaken to become once again the bride. Rather it is replaced with a safe, purified memory image, over which a separation of the living and the dead, the exchange of the difference of death and femininity within, for a canny image of difference located outside can be fulfilled.

The last part of the narrative seeks to conclude what this second burial begins. The detection plot, the tracing and destruction of the vampire, completes the mourning plot. Having solved the duplicity and oscillation of the feminine body, the hunters must now solve death. Repeatedly they justify their mission by claiming to undertake it 'For dear Lucy's sake'. Implicitly she continues to haunt their imagination and will be completely decathected only when the agent of death is also seemingly destroyed. Lucy's other double, Mina, undergoes the same near-death experiences as her deceased friend before the two can be fully separated. She too is bitten in her sleep, polluted with his blood; she has the same visions as Lucy, the same symptoms of fatigue, pallor and disquietude. Yet unlike Lucy, who withheld her knowledge, 'who did not speak, even when she wrote that which she wished to be known later' (323), Mina is more clearly on the side of the paternal law. She relates her near-death experiences to the vampire hunters and is a seminal accomplice in their search. Unlike Lucy, whose desire for death is coterminous with an insecurity about her status as bride, she accepts her fixture within the symbolic order and resists the call of death, despite her initial response to it.

The transparency and purity of women's bodies serves in both cases as the proof that the abject, toward which they are shown to incline more than men, has been expelled. The touch of the paternal sign – the holy wafer – leaves a 'red scar' on Mina's forehead to indicate that her body is tainted though her soul is pure. Killing the vampire will be coterminous with purifying her forehead, 'all white as ivory and with no stain'. Before this restitution, however, Mina doubles Lucy's somnambulism in her hypnotic trances during which Dracula, as death, speaks through the medium of her body. While initially she transcribed events in shorthand and typed them in order to help the men in their documentation, she later also translates that Otherness to which they have no access, because her hysteric proclivity toward semi-conscious states endows her with the 'power of reading the Count's sensations'. In her trances, Van Helsing notes, she is 'as though she were interpreting something. I have heard her use the same tone when reading her notes' (312). Under hypnosis Otherness speaks through her and this Other is death's trace. Identifying with Dracula's sleep, she speaks the state of death – 'I am still – oh, so still. It is like death' (313). She is, however, also the muse who leads the men to the vampire, as 'scribe . . . writing him all down', so that they 'shall know' that which they bar from their conscious (343). Though in the course of the journey she becomes ever more like Lucy, split between being the familiar 'old self,' 'alert and wakeful' and falling silent, enveloped in lethargy and pallor, she nevertheless remains in complicity with the symbolic order of the living. In a 'strange scene', impressive for 'its solemnity, its gloom, its sadness, its horror and withal its sweetness', she has them read the Burial Service for her to assure the purity of her soul.

The moment of solution, the final staking of Count Dracula, is quite literally a moment of final dissolution as his 'whole body crumbled into dust and passed from our sight' (377) and Mina's forehead is once again 'stainless', the 'curse . . . passed away'. With the source of death that provoked uncanny duplicity and oscillation in the women gone, their memory of the dead Lucy becomes perfectly purified. She is completely severed from Mina, who can now give birth to a boy on this day's anniversary. Stoker presents three positions in relation to the figure of death Dracula traces. Firstly, Lucy's hysteria, her silence and her inability to resist death embodies a completely fluid boundary between the conscious sense of self-preservation and an unconscious desire for death. Secondly, Mina and Jonathan's responses to the call of death which, over the second killing of Lucy and Dracula, can be repressed. While Mina cedes to the vampire's call, the three women vampires at Castle Dracula excite Jonathan's imagination, evoke a 'burning desire that they would kiss me' (37). The thought of being kissed by an undead feminine body which is 'both thrilling and repulsive' evokes an anticipation of 'languorous ecstasy'. To obliterate the source of death's call in life serves as a trope for the successful repression of that part of the self that responds, the unconscious, the imagination, for the foreclosure of the split in/of oneself, for an obsessive shutting out of death as one's truth. Finally, Van Helsing's unambiguous, obsessional identification with death is signified in his belief that he has a mastery over death. With the assistance of his instruments – his needles, his stakes, his wafers – he can revive dying brides and destroy the undead. This drawing of separations expels uncanny body doubles and uncanny semantic duplicity, as two signs of the difference death traces within and marks a complete lack of response to death's call.

Yet, even as, in Van Helsing's words 'the stake we play for is life and death' (365), their detection was also meant to assure the supersession of documentation, of secondary transcriptions believed to be semantically stable over primary sensations, over unconscious desires and dreams. For the 'horrible imaginings', as Jonathan notes at Castle Dracula, will be his destruction unless he can shield himself by taking down 'prosaic notes' (25). Throughout the novel, the danger of an unhinged mind, of the unconscious desires triumphing is apotropaically soothed by accurate documentation. Mina significantly starts typing Jonathan's journal once she realises Dracula is in England so as to set this typescript against the figure of death that takes hold of the imagination and 'tinges everything with something of its own colour' (180). Stoker's text ends on an image of fathers, a son Quincy and a text, the papers documenting their detection. The intention behind this collection is that by translating a primary exchange with death into a secondary one, the resulting interpretation lets death cease to have a grip on the body; transforms conscious death anxiety into repressed unconsious desire even as the violence used to bring about this transformation is also repressed.

Stoker, however, brilliantly undermines the obsessional discourse of his protagonists not only in the banal sense that his entire text works by exciting the reader's imagination, drawing her or him into the dangerous realm of uncanniness, duplicity and longing for Otherness. He also explicitly states that the semiotic double replacing the somatic double is not stable, that the truth the men seek can not be fixed. While the true dead are such only when buried beneath a graveplate, turned to dust and irrevocably eliding the grip of the surivivors, the documents representing them are equally elusive. As Jonathan notes, 'in all the mass of material of which the record is composed, there is hardly one authentic document! nothing but a mass of type-writing . . . We could hardly ask anyone . . . to accept these as proofs of so wild a story' (378). Though these documents are meant to afford stability, the sema can not transparently repro- duce the soma, making the papers a secondary form of signification, with difference and distance inscribed between the sign and the real events, while the real, the authentic eludes this signification. These papers ironically enact pre- cisely the duplicity and impurity between signifier (appearance) and signified (truth), for whose effacement the men resorted to the process of documentation in the first place.

Though their aim is to close the crack on the gravestone, to obliterate all doubling and all uncanny otherness by killing the agent of difference, they end up with fragments of transcripts and ruins – decaying bodies, ashes, gravestones. In that there is nothing to assure their desire for purity and wholeness except Mina's cleared forehead and her boy, Stoker's text ends on the note of disjunction which I have argued is figured by allegory. Indeed, Swales's earlier discussion of the duplicity of gravestones suggests how the replacement of the bad double, the dead soma returned as vampire, with the good double, its semiotic repre- sentation, is in fact equally a mockery. He describes the tombstones as 'steans "simply tumblin" down with the weight o' the lies wrote on them, "Here lies the body" or "Sacred to the memory" wrote on all of them, an' yet in nigh half of them there bean't no bodies at all; an the memories of them bean't cared a pinch of snuff about, much less sacred. Lies all of them, nothin' but lies of one kind or another' (65). He evokes an image of the Day of Judgement not as a moment of clarity but as a 'quare scowderment' with the dead dragging their tombstones to prove 'how good they was'. His disclosure focuses on two aspects of duplicity and deception. In those instances where no body has been placed beneath the ground so that the headstone marks an empty grave, its inscription 'here lies' indeed lies about the question of the dead body's place, conceivably to ward off the fear of wandering ghosts. For another, because the signifier 'in the memory of' may falsify the actual relation between deceased and mourner, it uses the site of death to produce a fictional version of the deceased. As Swales relates about Lucy's favourite grave, its headstone asserts that a sorrowing mother commemorates a beloved son to hide the fact that a man committed suicide to anger a mother who hated him. By implication the textual representation duplicitously reveals what Lucy's headstone hides – that her sacred memory could emerge only from a violent mutilation of her corpse and the desecration of her grave.

The feminine bodies in liminality – premarital brides, somnambulists, vampires and hypnotised mediums – are the very image of death's work in life, driving men to distance themselves obsessively from any erotically encoded experience of disintegration even as these images drive the text, the compilation of their papers tracing and reduplicating their obsessional discourse, toward a self-reflexivity by revealing its figurative hysteria.[23] Given that textual self-reflexivity is also achieved because the text serves as a trope for the allegorical process, this figurative hysteria resides in the fact that the text duplicitously enacts a real void which it cannot consciously acknowledge. The allegorical disjunction produced by the textuality of the compiled papers, analogous with the headstone inscriptions, traces Otherness so that paradoxically the real, which on the thematic level returns with the vampires and is effaced in the course of the second killings, remains rhetorically. That documentation and transcription occurs while the vampirised women and the detecting men are in a position of liminality, of near death or in mourning, articulates the possibility that writing, meant to assure a division of death from life, originates in precisely the marginal realm in between.

Notes to Chapter 14

1 See N. Auerbach, 1982, who emphasises that Pompilia is perfect in whiteness and exemplifies truth because her death enables her to speak with purity.
2 M. Holquist, 1983.
3 T. Todorov, 1977.
4 J.B. Pontalis, 1978.
5 H. Cixous, 1981.
6 R. Hertz, 1960.
7 M. Eliade, 1977.
8 V. Turner, 1977.
9 E. Morin, 1970.
10 See P. Barber, 1988.
11 D. A. Miller, 1988, argues that this scene is the novel's 'primal scene which it obsessively repeats and remembers . . . as though this were the trauma it needed to work through,' p. 152. He emphasizes that the protagonist is nervous about the possibility of being contaminated by virtue of the unknown woman's touch, whereas I will argue that this touch elicits an uncanny desire for and anxiety about death.
12 J.-P. Vernant, 1988, argues that the gravestone holds the place of the deceased as a double, incarnating its life in the beyond. It marks a clear opposition between the world of the living and the world of the dead. As sign of an absence, it signifies that death reveals itself precisely as something which is not of this world. Though this double marks the site where the dead are present in the world of the living or the living project themselves on to the universe of the dead, it makes the invisible visible even as it reveals that death belongs to an inaccesible mysterious realm beyond, fundamentally Other.
13 M. Serres, 1987.
14 S. Gilbert and S. Gubar, 1979, argue that Heathcliff is Catherine's almost identical

double, while Cathy is her mother's non-identical double, because a more genteel version, of her.

15 For a similar plot resolution see Daphne Du Maurier's modern gothic romance *Rebecca* (1938), where a second wife must 'kill' the revenant of a first wife, lest she be completely absorbed by the image of her predecessor. In my next chapter, the solution of the mourning process will be shown to resort to the opoposite choice – the double sacrificed so as to preserve the mourner from death.

16 See also M. Homans, 1986, who discusses Brontë's novel as an example of how the mother's death is a prerequisite for the daughter's entrance into the social order. S. Gilbert and S. Gubar, 1979, read the novel as delineating the movement from nature to culture. J. Boone, 1987, discusses her death as the only liberation from a fragmented existence, found especially in mariage. See also E. Lemoine-Luccione's, 1976, psychoanalytic discussion of pregnancy as one of the crucial moments of self-division in the feminine life cycle.

17 See M. Carter's, 1988, excellent collection of recent criticism. For an overview of vampires in literature see J. Twitchell, 1981.

18 Explicating Lacan, E. Ragland-Sullivan, 1988, argues that the hysteric's discourse is usually encoded as a feminine, the obsessional's as a masculine one. Where the hysteric's desire is related to her Otherness, and she accepts death's presence in life, the obsessional uses language and knowledge in an effort to avoid desire, a rejection coterminous with excluding Otherness as this also signifies death.

19 As an aside it is interesting to note that physicians in the nineteenth century themselves used the analogy between hysteria and vampirism, though in a different sense. Oliver Wendell Holmes, for example, judged that 'a hysterical girl is a vampire who sucks the blood of the healthy people about her', quoted in C. Smith-Rosenberg, 1985, p. 207.

20 See S. Mentzos, 1980. I use this term not as a description of illness but rather to discuss discursive positions in Lacan's sense, as well as to point out correspondences between aesthetic and psychoanalytic imagery.

21 N. Auerbach, 1982, explicitly draws an analogy between Lucy mesmerized by Dracula and the hysteric women hypnotised by Freud, suggesting that Stoker could conceivably have known the work of the Viennese doctor through reports at the Society for Psychical Research in London in 1893.

22 C. Craft, 1984, discussing the connection between sexuality and textuality calls this a post-penetrative peace meant to stabilise both woman's body and her semantic fluidity.

23 C. Bernheimer, 1989, makes a similar point for the death of Zola's prostitute Nana.

15

Risky resemblances

There are thus good reasons why a child sucking at its mother's breast has become the prototype of every relation of love. The finding of an object is in fact a refinding of it.
Sigmund Freud

To love an image means finding without knowing it, a new metaphor for an old love, the love for a mother. As soon as one loves with all ones soul that reality is a memory.
Gaston Bachelard

If Freud is right to claim that all love objects are refound, then love is based not only on repetition but also on loss. The lover not only chooses a desired object because he has discovered the resemblance to an earlier one, but also mourns the old in the new. A paradox seems to be inextricably embedded in an economy of love based on repetition. To recover a lost love object in the embodiment of another means acknowledging precisely that loss for the denial of which the process of reinvesting libidinal energy was undertaken in the first place.

Yet repetition does not only imply a return to a previous point, in the sense of retrieving something lost, undertaking once again an earlier activity, recapitulating the past. Repetition also implies a plurality of events, a sequence of actions that relate to each other on the basis of similarity and resemblance. It implies that difference, deferral, belatedness finds itself inscribed in the relation of the second to the first term.[1] The resemblance repetition effects is a rhetorical category, in which the bringing of one term close to another meets the resistance of being distant, of being other.[2] The repeated event, action or term always contradicts its predecessor because, though similar, it is never identical, and though recalling the unique, singular and original quality of the former event, it emphasises that it is 'more than one', a multiple duplicate, occurring at more than one site. Repetition describes a longing for an identity between two terms, even as it stages the impossibility of literal identity.

To repeat also implies that the second term doubles by copying the first. It can be a citation that renews or a reproduction that mocks. The relation between the two terms is inscribed not only by a dialectic of similarity and difference, but also by reciprocity. Although the value of the latter term is dependent on, because derived from, the former, the former exists, as 'recollection', only by virtue of the latter. The appearance of the latter allows the former to reappear out of and over its initial disappearance. Repetition does not merely imitate but also reproduces something new out of an earlier body.

Rimmon-Kenan distinguishes between constructive repetition, as a strategy emphasising difference, and destructive repetition, as one emphasising sameness. The former serves the pleasure principle, for it allows repetition to be used to transform a passive into an active position which results in a mastery over a disturbing, wounding event. While this form of repetition is constructive precisely because it works on a principle of difference, another form of repetition, based on undifferentiated oversameness without variation, comes close to being an occlusion of approximation and distance, a complete repetition, which is death, beyond life and narrative.[3] A repetition which succeeds perfectly may become fatal because the space of difference between model and copy has been eliminated, collapsing both terms into one entity, abolishing the singularity of each separate term.

Freud's discussion of the death drive in *Beyond the Pleasure Principle* suggests a similar distinction. On the one hand, the death drive operates as a fundamental process of unbinding and of breaking up.[4] Repetition here articulates itself as a sequence that fragments and reformulates entities into new versions, as life's detour toward death in an effort at avoiding a fatal short circuit. On the other hand, Freud's discussion of the compulsion to repeat also argues that 'all repetition repeats an original identity that it seeks to restore: the lovers, their original unity; life, its original death'.[5] Repetition traced by the death drive is either the source of division and/or that which reduces tension and reproduces an earlier situation or unity. Paradoxically, even as the death drive (or desire for death) articulates a triumph over temporality by returning to and repeating the preorganic inanimate state of stasis beyond division, it also supports a narcissistic desire for constancy, for a binding of energies and a reduction of psychic tension. Though this latter desire sustains life, it also strives for a suppression of alterity and the subordination of difference to identity. In that repetition, by producing perceptual identities or representations of resemblance, affords a rediscovery of the same, it supports both this narcissistic desire and a desire for death. Lacan, moreover, gives the interrelation of repetition, return and sameness another dimension when he argues that 'that which always comes back to the same place' is the real.[6] What repeatedly returns in ever the same guise, or what the subject seeks to return to, is the facticity beneath and beyond images and symbols – death, as originary loss of the maternal body, of a full unity.

The distinction between an originary *fort*, a lost origin impervious to an exteriority and its repetition in life, the *da* as a return of what is always already *fort*, cannot, however, be made by the conscious subject. For life to originate, the origin from which it departs must in some way be inscribed by difference, so that repetition can not be conceptualised only as a movement of identity, a return to a moment before and beyond life but rather also as a form of departure.[7] Repetition is a double movement, a return to something primary and the production of something new. Refinding love objects as a trope for refinding the origin of unity and death is also an act of constructing representations that occlude the real origin, just as any surrogate love object never fully satisfied because, though similar, it cannot be identical. Any primordial point of origin as the teleological aim of repetition can only be thought from the position of belatedness, as a return to a point never known, or rather known for the first time in an act of repetition which is based on difference.

Repetition articulates loss not only by virtue of enacting a lost object in the midst of difference, but also in the sense that the first repeated term refers to something that is not only a presence but also an absence. What the child in the 'fort-da' game repeats is not the mother but rather her absence, and it allows him to repress this experience of absence from his consciousness. Repetition is a duplicitous rhetorical strategy, for what it enacts lies in the past, yet because it is also different from, in fact quite possibly the first representation of, the original lost term, repetition is also informed with novelty, becomes in Rimmon-Kenan's terms 'the first presence, the first performance of the absence'.[8]

This theme is inaugurated by Poe with his story 'Ligeia' (1838) and repeated in Gustave Rodenbach's *Bruges-la-Morte* (1892) as well as Alfred Hitchcock's *Vertigo* (1958). Each text revolves around the protagonist's loss of a 'first' beloved and her refinding in the body of a second woman whose death ends this plot of mourning and detection.[9] Comparing these narratives I will illuminate how love, because it involves the repetition of loss, is intimately bound to the production of images; how a love for images implies an exchange with revenants that places the lover in the position of the mourner; and explore which position the beloved occupies in this process.

The man's initial response to the loss of his beloved is a form of melancholy – he withdraws from the world, his desire is invested in the dead.[10] The world of the living regains his interest only when he sees that he can retrieve his 'lost' love object by falling in love with a second woman who resembles the first. Because she is used as the object at which the lost woman is refound or resurrected, the second woman's body also functions as the site for a dialogue with the dead, for a preservation and calling forth of the first woman's ghost, and for the articulation of necrophiliac desire. The reciprocity of original and copy is such that while the copy may be the first presence of her model, she can disappear within the process of repetition, subsumed under the representation of the first wife, who in turn may be just a copy of an original absent feminine body.

The mourning process involves an identification between living mourners and the newly deceased in that both are located between the world of the living and the world of the dead.[11] The interest of the mourners is either to 'kill' the dead a second time as quickly as possible, so as to leave their shared position of liminality, or, as in the case of Heathcliff, to preserve the dead and prolong one's stay in the realm in between. Mourning inspires an ambivalence of feeling toward the deceased, a merging of love and hatred, which, owing to the identification between the dead and the living, can also be turned against the surviving self. What results is a merging of manic joy with depressive sadness. The accusation against the other may turn into melancholic self-accusation; the desire for the dead other may transform into a desire for one's own death; the vengeance felt towards the other may result in an exaggerated sense of triumph. My discussion of Lucy Westenra's second burial suggested that mourning restitutes the image of the good beloved against that of the bad beloved. It confirms a gesture of love that has resigned itself to loss against the hatred or vengeance felt because a woman chooses death as her suitor. Mourning is successfully completed when the wound death inflicted on a lover's narcissism is healed because the mourner feels secure in his possession of an internal 'good' image of the lost beloved.

In psychoanalytic terms the healthy trajectory from mourning to remembrance or commemoration is marked by a freeing of libidinal energies from the first lost object that must be reinvested in a second surrogate object, who may be perceived in the image of the deceased, yet notwithstanding the introduction of difference. Successful mourning is repetition as forgetting a lost object sufficiently to reinvest one's love in another, accepting the other as Other, even if the new beloved in part suggests the refinding of the former. John Bowlby distinguishes several phases of mourning – a period of numbing, distress and anger, followed by one of yearning and searching for the lost object, of thinking intensely about the lost person, of calling for her or him, scanning the environment to find her or him again, concerned only with stimuli that suggest her or his presence. After a phase of disorganisation and despair, based on the recognition that the lost love object cannot be retrieved nor repeated to perfection, a last stage of greater or less reorganisation concludes mourning.[12] This closure is a healthy failure, on the part of the survivor, to preserve a continuing sense of the dead person's presence, a detaching of memories and hopes from the dead.

In the texts to be discussed, however, the repetition is such that a libidinal reinvestment tries to coalesce the refound with the lost object. The memories of and hopes in the dead body are preserved precisely by virtue of a detour over another woman's body. For the other woman is chosen either because she uncannily resembles the first, seemingly recalls her, or because she is completely different and owing to this difference clarifying the meaning of the first. If the difference between model and repetition is foregrounded, the double affirms the first woman's death, while she serves to deny death if what is privileged by the mourner's eye is an undifferentiated sameness. The second beloved is ultimately to become an identical substitute for her predecessor, yet such an achievement of oversameness requires a blindness toward the singularity of both women. Regaining a lost amorous unity, denying the narcissistic wound induced by death, occurs in the repetition of a beloved as an image, but an image materialised at and over another body. Typical of the rhetoric of the uncanny, a fatal blurring of the distinction between the imagined and the real occurs, in that a sublation of signifier into signified disaffects the difference between real materiality and semiosis.

For the second woman to repeat or double a predecessor means that she functions as a revenant in more than one sense. She represents a dead woman, her body lodges and rematerialises a deceased whom a mourner seeks to retain among the living. 'Dead woman' is the semantic value which she signifies for her lover. She is denied her own body, and is only a figure for a meaning alterior to herself, prematurely turned into a ghost, into a body without the soul or personality unique to her, into a living cipher for her lover's desired lost object. This other woman also employs the discourse of the hysteric. She simulates a dead woman and in so doing signifies both her own division and her social non-existence. Functioning as a double, the second woman's uncanny resemblance to a dead woman signifies fatality, for the teleology of all the texts is that the exchange between mourner and second beloved ends in a second killing.

Is this motif a trope for the desire for death or the denial of death? Does the mourner desire the woman because she is a corpse/revenant, or does he force the second beloved to re-enact the dead woman in an attempt to deny the irrevocability of death, by denying its inscription on the body of the first beloved? As a double, the second woman dissimulates the presence of death even as she is also a sign of immortality beyond physical demise. These doubles embody both aspects of the death drive, depending on whether similarity or difference is privileged. They either enact the death-like stasis of a return to an original unity, or they enact the principle of dissimulation, division and non-identity which splits any sense of wholeness. What remains undecidable is whether this repetition of the event of death is an excessive representation of the mourner's own death by virtue of a detour over two women's bodies, or an excessive exclusion of death. The second woman's death also raises the question whether we can distinguish between desire and denial, for by forcing a living woman to become the exact copy of a dead one, the mourner indicates a desire to transcend the limits of natural mortality. Yet he also reproduces another uncanny return of the same, not only in respect to a lost woman but also in respect to her death, for the repression of which the mourner had turned to repetition in the first place.

Indeed, Cixous argues, the uncanniness repetition provokes suggests that 'death is never anything more than the disturbance of the limits'. The double enacts that if what has been lost returns, nothing is ever lost, 'nothing has even disappeared and nothing is ever sufficiently dead.'[13] Even as a return of the dead at the body of a second woman apotropaically enacts that death is not irrevocable because the lost returns, what also returns is death itself. The gesture of repressing death betrays death everywhere. It not only surmounts but also effects death. The compulsion to repeat the familiar in the unfamiliar, the known woman in the stranger, allows that other familiar value, mortality, which was to be repressed, to return as well. In general, Freud notes, at the figure of the double death returns as something known but defamiliarised by virtue of a substitution. In these texts, repetition is an apotropaic gesture because it displaces death from the self, from the masculine position by letting it return as the double of a feminine body.

The mourner's fascination, however, clearly resides not with the first woman's bodily presence, since her value becomes clear to him only after she has entered the liminal zone of revenant. These mourners desire the beloved as ghost, placed in an uncanny position that subverts clear distinctions between living and dead. This position of revenant implies either the preserved ghost image in the mourner's memory, and/or the ghost body-double of the second wife, with both renditions hovering between an absence and a presence of the first dead woman. The repetition of a dead beloved turns the second woman into the site for an uncanny blurring of distinctions between animate and inanimate body, between real love object (the maternal body, the actual beloved) and the lover's image. Her body induces an intellectual hesitation whether she is a sign for life's triumph over death or death's inhabitation of life; whether her presence signifies that a corpse has been resurrected or a living body turned into a corpse; whether the first beloved is alive or the living woman dead by virtue of repetition.

Her duplicitous presence induces an uncertainty as to whether she is indeed the same as the deceased or different, a marvellous instance of the dead returned or merely a perfect imitation. While the former instance of oversameness through repetition implies a canny identity which soothes the lover's desire for narcissistic wholeness, the latter similarity crossed with difference emerges as a disturbingly uncanny figure which must be expulsed. The aporia is such that the two women can be identical, with all difference eradicated, only when the second is dead. But once dead, she too is completely lost, completely Other, defying any belief in the recuperation of a lost unity, just as her uncanny presence thwarted such desires in that her dissimulation of death always also implied a division or split. The second killing eliminates precisely the gesture of hesitation which left the spectating mourner suspended between bliss and mockery.

The second beloved is killed because she proves autonomous to the image of her lover's self, which she is meant to assure; because she enacts that mis-recognition and difference is always inscribed in the illusion of finding a 'lost' wholeness in and through another. The killing is meant to serve a denial of death's 'castrative' threat to life as this threat shows itself whenever narcissism's stability and wholeness is wounded. Yet ironically the reproduced dead body of the second beloved confirms death in its total identity to the first dead wife, confirms the irrevocable loss of a prenatal unity. Though her death places the second woman outside the surviving lover's control, it also affirms his omnipotence of thought since he can mentally reanimate her, continue the sequence of refinding and killing her in further surrogate bodies.

These mourning plots also implicitly invoke the issue of representation and mimesis, given that their protagonists literally carve their image of the lost beloved with the material body of another woman. Kofman suggests that mimesis is necessary because life always already implies death and requires a mortal supplement so as to be fixed and take on shape.[14] Feminine bodies doubling a deceased are living representations of death, affording the mourner with a fixture to death, in the double sense of a realised form and a displacement on to another feminine body. The linkage between the artist and the mourner, between representation and revenants, also implies that mimesis does not fix death in a canny sense alone. The duplicity of representation is such that it shows that life necessarily passes by death, lets death emerge and be repelled at one and the same time. While images, repeating a lost object, serve the mourner to assuage loss, Kofman argues for yet another conjunction between image and mourning, namely that the resemblance any mimetic representation is grounded on is the work of melancholy. Because the image is created on the basis of the same elusiveness it tries to obliterate, what art in fact does is mourn such beauty, and in so doing it mourns itself.

In this ambivalent contingency on loss, art exemplifies the uncanny. Replacing or doubling an absent object, it represents something which it both is and is not, while at the same time the beautiful form both is and isn't eternal. The resemblance which representation is based on involves similarity and difference, the second body stands in for but is not identical with its model and it is precisely in this doubling that Kofman locates the analogy between representation and revenant. Both hover uncannily in a liminal zone, neither living nor dead, neither absent nor present, both stage a duplicitous presence, at once sign of an absence and of an inaccessible other scene, of a beyond. Resemblance topples all categories of oppositions that distinguish model from copy, the animate from the inanimate. It makes signs semantically indeterminate and meaning undecidable. Yet the anxiety that an experience of resemblance provokes in the viewer, because this resemblance points not only to the possibility of refinding a dead object but also to death, can successfully be masked only by re-establishing fixed boundaries. These assure that the living body resembling a dead body is truly dead, assure that the portrait resembling an absent body is a figural, not a material representation; assure canny Otherness. Not only, then, does a dead woman become a revenant because her image is preserved in and over the body of a second woman, but the image, owing to the uncanny resemblance it evokes, is itself another form of the revenant. The second killing of a woman serves as a trope for the reveiling of this fascinating and threatening resemblance that emerges when a deceased beloved returns at the site of a living representative of the dead.

Poe's tale 'Ligeia' is told in retrospect: the narrator writes after and in response to the death of his second wife, Lady Rowena of Tremaine and the concomitant experience of a resurrection of the first wife over her corpse. The narrative frame functions as the written repetition of the recent uncanny events in his life ('and now, while I write' (262)). His act of textual representation as recollection is clearly marked as an attempt to deny the absence of his beloved, as this gesture emerges precisely from an acknowledgement of his loss.[15] Invoking her name in order to bring 'before his eyes in fancy the image of her who is no more' repeats, on the narrative level, a resurrection that will also be the topic of the narrative.

The narrator, himself unnamed, recalls that the body of his first wife came, even while she was alive, to pose as an enigma to such a degree that it turned into the measure for his heuristic and imaginative abilities. The description he offers of her presents her in proximity to death, yet does so in two very different ways. She lacks a fixed position in her social order, and her etherealised body signifies that she is no longer fixed in the realm of the living. He implies that for him she was always present as a name and an image, completely severed from any historical context. He cannot remember any external facts about her, how, when or even where they first met. Cut off from any but his imaginary world, she is merely an image invoked by dint of a signifier, 'Ligeia', without a proper name that would place her within a specific kinship structure, 'I have never known the *paternal name* of her' (262). Such a privileging of the name and image of the beloved over the woman's real body is found in all three phases of the tale, for the image takes the place of the model while she is alive, while she is psychically resuscitated during mourning and while she is textually resurrected in his written narrative.

Her invocation as a non-given name, 'Ligeia' (referring back to other literary women posed between the human and the divine – a dryad in Viergil's *Georgics*, a siren in Milton's *Comus*), invokes the idea that for the lover she is from the start always already a representation, her presence arising out of an originary absence. This reduction of a woman to a signifier is another artistic rendition of woman's non-existence in the symbolic order. For the narrating lover she is no body because devoid of alterity, because a body-image and a name, reproduced by and dependent on his spectatorial gaze.

In contrast to the narrator's inability to present any external facts about his first wife, his memory never fails him in respect to 'the *person* Ligeia.' This description of her appearance also presents her in conjunction with death by emphasising her ethereal being, her more than human, enigmatic perfection. She seems to be positioned between life and death. She enters his closed study 'as a shadow', her hands of marble, the beauty of her face superlative, like 'the radiance of an opium dream' (263). Precisely because she seems to embody an uncanny blurring of real and image, Ligeia serves as the object of his obsessive gaze. By analytically exploring her body, imaginatively fragmenting it bit by bit, he hopes to gain access to the answer her strangeness poses. Yet the fascination for this enigma seems to be contingent upon its always eliding his grasp, making the living Ligeia ultimately not accessible. From the start Ligeia exists primarily in the imaginary register of the narrator. Here she traces the figure of death because she is conceived as an inanimate signifier (not a contextualised body) and because her body is treated like an inanimate substance which his gaze fragments.[16]

Above all her other body parts, the narrator privileges Ligeia's eyes as the source but also the failure for his analytic abilities.[17] His 'intense scrutiny of Ligeia's eyes' becomes tantamount to speculating on metaphysical truths, for in the way that 'Ligeia's beauty passed into my spirit, there dwelling as in a shrine, I derived, from many existences in the material world, a sentiment such as I felt always aroused within me by her large and luminous orbs' (265). Yet full knowledge remains beyond his reach, approaching and then departing again. Though he explains that he has incorporated Ligeia's beauty into himself, in a formulation that significantly presents her as a sacred dead body, because 'enshrined' in his spirit, he stresses his dependence on her. In respect to knowledge, the narrator assigns to Ligeia the position of the maternal body: 'I was sufficiently aware of her infinite supremacy to resign myself, with a child-like confidence, to her guidance through the chaotic world of metaphysical investigation' (266). She offers the promise of satisfying his desire for knowledge while simultaneously defying its fulfilment on two scores. He believes her learning to be so superior to his own that only her readings can render the mysteries of the world transparent to him even as her body literally functions as the site at which a fundamental enigma could be solved.

To lose Ligeia to death means the loss of that figure through which a promise of gaining absolute knowledge seems to be secured. In his depiction of her death, he interprets her last living moments as a 'wild longing . . . an eager vehemence of desire for life', and the poem she writes, 'The Conqueror Worm', is a call to defy death by virtue of one's will. The irony inherent in this explanation involves for one the fact that it seems as though Ligeia's death were the result of her husband's fatal appropriation. His usurping gaze reduces her not only to one meaning, namely that of being a figure signifying absolute truth. Rather, he reduces her to a meaning from which she is alienated, for she is merely the body at which his truth, but not necessarily hers, is reflected and secured. For another, her death not only liberates him from his dependency on her but proves to become the successful test for the omnipotence of his thoughts. Once he recollects the absent Ligeia in memory by virtue of the power of *his* will he is no longer 'a child groping benighted' when deprived of her intellectual tutelage. Rather he now fully possesses the knowledge she had – 'I revelled in recollections of her purity, of her wisdom . . . Now, then, did my spirit fully and freely burn with more than all the fires of her own' (272). By implication her absent body resurrected in spirit satisfies his will to knowledge more fully than her living body could.

The knowledge at stake is one surrounding death, for it involves a revelling in the recollections of the deceased, a calling aloud upon her name, as if 'I could restore her to the pathway she had abandoned – could it be forever? – upon the earth' (272). It involves a defiance of death's irrevocability, and the impossibility of mastering death through knowledge. It isn't incidental that Ligeia's strangeness is from the start connected with her liminal position between life and death. Alive she has a truth that is beyond worldly knowledge, but she will not yield it. She not only marks the limit of mortal knowledge but also metonymically represents that truth which is beyond. Once dead, she becomes the site at which the mourning narrator can prove his imaginative will. Denying that she is now inanimate and absent brings about a second kind of liminality. If as a living woman she always already belonged to the Other world because of the knowledge she represents and the insubstantiation of her body, as a dead woman she again hovers between the two realms because he will not let her die. Although she is bodily absent his imagination repeats her presence as a remembered image. As representation, Ligeia is the complete possession of her lover since he can revive her at his will, precisely because he is possesed by her ghost. Though in the process of his recollection he fragments her into many body parts, he does so to reconstruct a satisfying image of wholeness, now fully reliable because solely dependent on his ability to imagine. Given that it was the image, as signifier for his wholeness, which he loved all along, the absence of her material body logically affords pleasure. Yet the story he tells is that mourning this image requires its rematerialisation first as another body and then as a text.

That the possession of truth, the solving of an enigma and a triumph over death are interconnected is metaphorically enacted in the repetition of Ligeia at the body of his second wife. The narrator omits all descriptions of Ligeia's corpse, and turns immediately to the second phase of his story – the unhappy marriage to Lady Rowena, Ligeia's physical opposite. Just as the fervour of Ligeia's love became clear only under the auspices of the threat of life's opposite ('But in death only, was I fully impressed with the strength of her affection' (267)), so too it is the difference of Rowena that allows the narrator to delineate and realise the meaning Ligeia has for him. Only in the presence of his utterly different second wife can he reassemble the memory image of his first wife. Because the trajectory of this undertaking is to reach a perfect repetition, the fatal over-sameness of identity, and to foreclose difference between the two, its result is a move beyond life.

Giving way to a 'child-like perversity' and a hope of alleviating the sorrow of lost wholeness, he furnishes rooms in a way that suggests a fantastic destabilisation of any difference between the real and the imagined, the animate and the inanimate by virtue of phantasmagoric effects induced through lighting and artificial wind currents behind draperies. In these bridal chambers, that are also the shrine of his first wife, he doubles his corporeally present bride with the recollected dead girl. Making the dead Ligeia present by virtue of a continual invocation of her name seems to drain the living Rowena, until an exchange occurs in which the latter becomes ever more like the invoked first wife, herself losing bodily substance. In this attitude of melancholic mourning, the narrator uses the name Ligeia to repeat a form of usurpation in respect to Rowena which he had already enacted in his epistemological appropriation of his first wife. The reciprocity contained in this repetition of one wife by her opposite is such that the mourning husband desires the first dead body as a way to deny death yet in the same gesture causes death to re-emerge in the form of the second wife's corpse. Though in the process the second wife is effaced, both as a living body and as a remembered image, the first wife can be preserved at the expense of but also only by virtue of the body of her predecessor.

The culmination of this exchange is Rowena's actual death. If he needed

Rowena's difference to define and secure those qualities that make Ligeia perfect for him, he now literally uses her body to recall his dead wife, undoing her death by giving her a second birth. While Ligeia's process of dying but not her corpse were described, Rowena's moment of death is eclipsed while her corpse is excessively described in the famous scene of transfusion. Not unlike the repeated blood-transfusions that Van Helsing undertakes to artificially reanimate Lucy's dying body, the dead woman's body repeatedly gains life only to lose it again, though in this operation the infusion consists exclusively in the survivor's psychic energy. Each time he remembers Ligeia as he sits next to Rowena's corpse the figure of the dead Rowena seems to come alive; each time he physically re-animates the body, it falls back into stillness, until he is so fatigued by these efforts that he gives in to his fantasy completely and the image of Ligeia rises out of the body of Rowena.

This end, of course, poses several questions for the reader. Are we to see this resurrection of a dead woman as a trope for the fact that the protagonist can love Rowena only as a perfect repetition of Ligeia (that is, a belated statement of his love, induced by an opium dream, and to be articulated only through the displacement of one body for another)? Or is this a trope for his inability to love a corporeal woman, desiring exclusively an intellectual relationship, and one, to boot, which privileges the image over any concrete presence? Or is this an opium-induced, wish-fulfilling dream representation, concerning the triumph of his will to knowledge and his creative imagination which defies the limits of natural mortality?

The doubling of one wife by another, by virtue of metempsychosis, is meant to prove a continued existence of the 'soul' after bodily decay and serves to soothe the mourner about his own fear of mortality. The resurrection assures the repossession of a lost love object, implicitly a repetition of the maternal body, which promised infinite knowledge and at which the child first experienced a sense of unity and wholeness. This doubled corpse – the dead Rowena/the resurrected Ligeia – also functions as a conglomerate of real and figural death, in that Rowena's actual demise also signifies the death of her two predecessors, the maternal body and the 'first' wife. In that a representation always points to the absence on which it is grounded and always articulates its difference from the original term, even if semantically it signifies the identity between copy and model, its rhetorical value is duplicitous. The resurrected corpse signifies death as the fracturing of and separation from the sought after unity with another even as she is used to signify the recuperation of a lost unity. By implication, she signifies the split within the self, the primary castration by death that grounds life even as she is used to re-present the narcissistic wholeness of the mother–infant dyad.

In the act of repeating a first dead woman in the figure of a second one the surviving lover desires death even as he attempts to deny it. The repetition enacted at the body of the second wife, aimed at making her identical to the first, both succeeds and fails. To be the same means eradicating structurally all difference and division between the two women, a move from double to oneness. This is only possible when the body-double is exactly what it signifies, when the space between copy and model is unambivalently obliterated, when it is dead like the model it repeats. But as such a figure of death she becomes completely Other and defies any unity with the survivor. Ultimately eliminated is the disturbing and threatening factor of hesitation, the hovering between anxiety and desire. Poe's narrative articulates the fascination with the revenant materialised at a living representative of the dead and stages an imaginative triumph over the intellectual hesitation it induces.

What the narrator reproduces in the bridal/death chamber is an uncanny representation, a scenario that enacts an analogy between portrait and revenant. The emergence of the image of the first dead wife within the narrator's psychic reality involves the denial of loss engendered by an acknowledgement of loss. The production of this image signifies an escape from the mutability of the material world into the illusion of an eternal image repertoire, even as the resurrected body signifies an elusive, intangible, receding entity. This representation obliterates and articulates mutability in one and the same gesture. The uncanniness of this representation resides in the fact that it both is and is not the living body of Ligeia, neither image nor body, neither living nor dead, neither absent nor present, neither the model nor the copy. It enacts a moment of ambivalent undecidability *par excellence* as it points simultaneously to the refinding of a lost object with its ensuing erasure of death, and a perfect repetition as the presence of death.

Yet this second death also marks a closure of the protagonist's uncanny exchange with the dead, ushers in a new phase in his mourning. Realising that the lost object can be retrieved in the form of a mental image confirms his belief in the omnipotence of his thoughts. The story's frame implies that from this experience of the uncanny, he gains the canny satisfaction that he is in possession of a reassuring image, endlessly composable, completely reliable – that of Ligeia's person as the 'one dear topic . . . on which my memory fails me not' (263). She is now at his disposal, severed from the danger of mutability that had threatened both Ligeia's and her double's body. If she was initially the cipher and key to an inaccessible knowledge of the Beyond, the security of this image reassures him that he now has power over and knowledge of death.

Repetition is both inscribed by death and is its apotropaic charm. Repetition of the first wife at the body of the second enacts a fatal stasis of oversameness, while the repeated invocation of the name Ligeia throughout the story stages absence. Both the body double and the free floating signifier 'Ligeia' are used to show that death is not irrevocable because a first lost object can be returned to the living. The response to the uncanniness of the collapsing of a model and her repetition, of the imagined resurrection of the former and the real death of the latter, is one of putting closure on liminality. The narrator needs the second wife to prove the strength of an imaginative mastery over death, to enact the triumph over death occasioned at a literal translation of a dead body into a resurrected image. After this experience, he seems to have found the answer to the enigma that Ligeia's ambivalent presence between the Here and the Beyond posed, and can bury both wives' bodies underneath the image and name of Ligeia, of whose possession he is now assured. The new fixing of semantic boundaries is such that resemblance shifts to the purely figural level and needs no further literal enactment. The frame of the story presents the successful exchange of uncanny ambivalence or intellectual hesitation, for canny uncertainty. The latter term implies a reassuring distinction between what is certain and what is not, while the former engenders a disturbing obliteration of the security of distinct meanings, even if it also entails the magic of a dead wife's literal return.

Poe repeats the scenario enacted in his tale in a description of his own response to his wife's dying. In a letter to his friend George Eveleth, dated, 1848, he offers a detailed narrative of his own desire for an obliteration of the psychic tension which the uncanny oscillation between his wife's fading and returning body caused.

> 'Six years ago, a wife, whom I loved as no man ever loved before, ruptured a blood-vessel in singing. Her life was despaired of. I took leave of her forever & underwent all the agonies of her death. She recovered partially and I again hoped. At the end of a year the vessel broke again – I went through precisely the same scene. Again in about a year afterward. Then again – gain – again & even once again at varying intervals. Each time I felt all the agonies of her death – and at each accession of the disorder I loved her more dearly & clung to her life with more desperate pertinacity . . . I became insane, with long intervals of horrible sanity . . . I had indeed, nearly abandoned all hope of a permanent cure when I found one in the *death* of my wife. This I can and do endure as becomes a man – it was the horrible never-ending oscillation between hope and despair which I could no longer have endured without the total loss of reason.'[18]

The resemblance between his tale and his epistolary narrative raises undecidable speculations that haunt any posterior reading of his texts. Is the textual repetition to be understood as the gesture of a poet, who, when faced with the real of death beyond signification, mechanically takes recourse in imagery and rhetorics developed earlier on in his narrative representations of feminine death, when this was merely an imaginative operation? Or does Virginia Clemm's death uncannily materialise what her husband had previously imaginarily designed in his art, so that he can retextualise an originary absence in his posterior letter?

In Rodenbach's *Bruges-la-morte* a resurrection of the dead beloved requires the presence of a second, palpable body which the mourner can reinvest with desire, making the second woman into his image of the first. Unlike Poe's tale, the similarity not the difference between the two women is forced into a relation of identity, fatal for the second one. Hugues Viane has lost his first wife and in a phase of psychic numbness secures the image of his wife by collecting portraits of her at different ages. Most importantly, he places the braid of her hair, the only part of her body which will not fade, into a crystal box in which it lies (not unlike

Snow White's non-decaying body) so as to be seen and honoured 'ceaselessly'; an icon of 'the immortality of his love' (12). In his first phase of mourning he sees a correspondence between his environment and the deceased, indeed chooses to live in Bruges because it is a 'dead city', just as he contemplates his own suicide. After five years, however, at precisely the moment when he fears that his failing memory will obliterate the beloved a second time, he meets the dancer Jane Scott, whose uncanny resemblance to his dead wife evokes 'an almost terrifying miracle . . . the illusion of the dead beloved refound' (34).

She comes to signify his 'living memory', a figure of 'fate's pity', a 'connivance against oblivion', because she 'refreshes' the image of the beloved in danger of fading. At the body of the double, the dead woman seems to have been 'resuscitated', descended from her stone sepulchre and possessing her means 'repossesing the other', the dead woman. In the protagonist's descriptions of this miracle, the repeated usage of the prefix 're' does not merely imply return but also the illusion that the difference inscribed in repetition can be obliterated when the distinction between original and copy is blurred. At stake in this collapsing of distinct bodies is above all the effacement of the irrevocability of death. Jane's body signifies that death was merely a form of absence, because that which seemed finished forever can now 'recommence' (35). Hugues begins to convince himself that the years of mourning the loss of his first wife were an illusion.

The mourner's attitude is duplicitous – even as he uses a living resemblance to deny his wife's death, it is the dead woman, and traces of her, which he seeks in the living. He desires not the second woman as resemblance, but her body as the site where he can 'eternalise the illusion of this mirage' (37). He must not only obliterate any space of difference between the copy and the model but also assure that nothing in the copy changes, so as to foreclose the possibility that his 'first' love refound may transpire into parody; the mirage be disclosed as mockery. Hugues wishes exclusively to honour the original dead woman in the 'simulacrum of this resemblance'. He wishes to use Jane as merely another icon, analogous to the dead bride's exposed braid; as the living portrait of the dead woman. In his love for her 'he never thought for one moment that he had become faithless to his cult or his memory' (49). Jane is meant to give fixture to a lost body so that fetishistically he can simultaneously acknowledge and disavow his loss.

Yet the more Hugues tries to rematerialise the dead woman at the living body of Jane Scott, forcing her to wear the clothes of the deceased, the more Jane insists on demonstrating that difference is at the heart of resemblance. Mocking his desire to see his dead wife returned, she transforms this macabre fashion show into the travesty of 'sad mascarade' and offers him the atrocious experience of his virginal wife degraded even as her appearance is repeated. Forced to recognise the distinction between the two women, he sees his relation to Jane as a sinful infidelity to his wife and a blasphemy against the divine law that posits death as eternal absence and separation. The difference Jane enacts also threatens to eclipse the deceased in the sense that it is she, not her resurrection of the dead woman, who arouses his sexual desire; that her difference makes her the object of his blissful embrace.

Difference, duplicity, mimicry is, then, what must be sacrificed in the reproduction of a stable image of the dead. Though he wishes to assure himself of the reliability of his internal image of his dead wife over the body of the copy, the repetition fundamentally calls into question the reliability of any representation. As long as he preserves the distance between model and copy, death is suspended in the uncanniness of resemblance, put under erasure, but not overcome. In the same move that the gap between the two terms closes, death emerges ever more radically; in the same measure that distance is given up, the discrepancy between the first and the second wife becomes ever more distinct. Only the general outline is the same, while the details that make Jane an individual, differ. As long as distance is preserved, with 'the mist of death' dividing the repetition from the model, the illusion of identity is possible. In the same gesture that the intellectual hesitation induced by such an uncanny resemblance is to be clarified by reducing all distance, what appears is difference. Hugues needs to preserve the resemblance without the uncanniness, without the distance, the doubt, the oscillation, and this is possible only once the copy literally dies. If he at first uses the special artifice of resemblance to 'triumph over and deride death' (75), he can be fully satisfied that he possesses death by embracing death as the dead beloved.

The final scene emphasises the grotesqueness and violence inherent in Hugues's necrophiliac desire. Visiting his rooms for the first time, Jane desecrates the relics that pertain to his cult of mourning by touching the portraits of the deceased, the bibelots belonging to her, and making jests about the funereal museum. The sanctity of the dead woman is excessively profaned, however, when she stops in front of the holiest relic, the braid of hair Hugues's has preserved in the crystal case and with a 'sonorous laugh' dances around the room, brandishing this fetish object, placing it about her neck. Unwilling to return the braid, taunting with the difference between herself and her predecessor as she adorns herself with the one preserved body part of the latter, she irrevocably puts fixture on the lack of authenticity inscribed in Hugues's preservation of the dead woman at the body of her living representative. Unable to tolerate the double wound Jane inflicts on his narcissistically informed cult of mourning, he strangles her with the braid.

Having violently eliminated all instances of difference, he has achieved perfect identity as a fatal repetion of oversameness. While the living Jane was a medium through which he could prevent the image of his first wife from fading in his memory, even as she posed as a threat to this image by virtue of her discrepancies, her corpse assures the resurrection of the dead woman. In this moment, 'the dead woman was more dead, the two women were identical. Resembling each other in life, they resembled each other even more in death, which gave them the same pallor, he could no longer distinguish the one from the other . . . Jane's corpse was the phantom of his old love, visibly there only for him' (113f.). In his retrograde posture, Hugues recommences his mourning. The uncanniness of resemblance must become a fatal tautology, if it is to qualify as a truly satisfactory repetition. Only as a corpse can the body double assure the stability of the image it repeats and represents in a reliable way. Yet the aporia contained in sustained mourning is such that the perfect repetition of one dead woman by another, even as it attempts to elude and triumph over mortality, asserts the presence of death. Far from ending the presence of death in life, this moment marks the first in a potential series of murders repeated.

In Alfred Hitchcock's film *Vertigo* (and the novel *Sueurs Froides* by Boileau-Narcejac on which it was based), the theme of a lover, whose inability to give up the dead lets her return at another body is altered so as to disclose its own premises. A crucial difference introduced is that the beloved who is lost and refound is the wife of a friend and as such a forbidden lover. Furthermore, Madeleine is from the start a revenant because possessed by a dead ancestor, her greatgrandmother Carlotta Valdes, so that her body is the medium through which this dead woman returns. The story begins when Madeleine's husband Gavin Elster asks his ex-detective friend Scottie Ferguson to follow and watch his wife for fear she might kill herself, because Carlotta had done so when she was Madeleine's age. The latter accepts the job, fascinated not only by Madeleine's beauty but also by her suicidal attraction to death. Much like Lucy Westenra, she periodically falls into a trance, enters an Other world, splits herself in two and suffers from amnesia when she regains consciousness. As Gavin Elster explains, 'when she is in this state, she is no longer my wife'.

One of the implications this reversion discloses is that Madeleine's proximity to death sanctions a forbidden romance. Since when called by death she is no longer her husband's wife, she may be the protagonist's lover. Scottie desires Madeleine precisely because from the start she is not only an image of feminine beauty but more importantly a living representative of a dead woman. This morbid desire is duplicated when, having stopped Madeleine once from committing suicide the detective fails to do so a second time and she fatally falls from a church tower. In the second part of the film, the mourner refinds his dead beloved in a second woman Judy and she serves as the body double of someone dead (Madeleine), who herself was conceived from the start as the double of the dead Carlotta Valdes. She is a double revenant. In the first half of the film Scottie not only falls in love with an image of perfect feminine beauty as it is enmeshed with the enigma death but also confronts her with questions, probing her to disclose her secret. In the second half he redresses a second woman in the image of the first, and again seeks to obtain the truth she, as an embodiment of death, seems to harbour.

Hitchcock's film discloses that the desire which resuscitation hides is the desire for a dead feminine body. To love a woman haunted by a ghost, and then a revenant of this 'first' revenant, is to love a corpse with impunity, to embrace death by proxy in the figure of a woman returned and to do so without a threat to one's survival. Hitchcock explained, 'I was intrigued by the hero's attempt to re-create the image of a dead woman through another one who's alive . . . To put it plainly, the man wants to go to bed with a woman who's dead; he is indulging in a form of necrophilia.'[19] The desired woman oscillates between a husband (representative of the symbolic order) and a dead maternal body (the radically Other, the real of death whose access is barred to conscious knowledge). The protagonist, because he identifies with the divided, oscillating woman, is himself positioned between two points of reference. On the one hand he tries to cure Madeleine, so as to draw her away from the dead ancestor, and in this sense his desire for the haunted woman rivals not only the husband's but also the dead mother's. To cure here means to kill her fascination with death but since this is also his fascination, the solution he seeks is a form of curing himself of death and assuring his position as a survivor. On the other hand courting Madeleine is a form of courting death, of identifying precisely with the position of non-existence she embodies.[20]

Yet this story does not only fall into two halves but also into two plots, for here a romance plot is again fatally intertwined with an economic speculation. The brilliant twist introduced by Hitchcock is that the desired beloved is not merely an image and a revenant but in fact a masquerade, a false image, the dissimulation of a revenant. As the plot resolution shows, the Madeleine that Scottie loves was always an impersonation by Gavin's lover, designed to cover the murder of the real Madeleine Elster so that the husband could inherit her wealth, with Scottie serving as the witness who would attest it was suicide. The woman he finds and forces to re-enact the dead Madeleine is the same one who did the first impersonation, so that in making Judy into Madeleine he merely repeats the husband's gestures. The woman he refinds is indeed absolutely identical to the one he lost, yet both have been redressed so as to function as a living representative of a dead woman, a materialised representation. What this reversion deconstructs is that an economy of love based on the refinding of a dead love object is a death-bearing illusion. As Spoto puts it, the relationship between Scottie and Madeleine must 'involve a fraud and a deadly game, for the major theme of *Vertigo* is that a romantic fantasy is a dangerous hoax, potentially fatal'.[21]

Given this second plot, Judy, unlike the Madeleine she represents, is not divided between her husband and her dead ancestor's desire, this being a scenario designed for Scottie's gaze. Rather, she oscillates between responding to two lovers' (Gavin's and Scottie's) desire, between being an accomplice to a murder and concealing this crime, and an accomplice to a necrophiliac love which in both parts of the tale reduces her to a materialised image of a dead woman returned. Faced with these two versions of love, real death emerges as a viable alternative. Where the first half of the story ends with a double death, the literal death of the real Madeleine and the figural 'death' of the false 'Madeleine' (the woman created by the husband for the detective), the second half ends with the death of the real Judy as this also implies the death of the false 'Madeleine' (now recreated by the detective for himself). The second death involves killing the double of the double, eliminating Judy masquerading as a 'false' Madeleine who had been designed to dissimulate a real Madeleine while this real wife remains unseen throughout except as the 'first' feminine corpse.

Hitchcock's version also deconstructs the notion that the image of the desired beloved can be a true image only once the death of the represented woman is confirmed. As de Lauretis argues, Madeleine's desire for (and identification with) the dead mother fascinates Scottie because it mirrors his own desire. Once Scottie discovers the hoax and Judy ('Madeleine') turns out to be alive and real, the image she embodies is 'untrue'. His search for the true image is not for the 'simple *image* of woman' but rather for the image of the dead mother represented and mediated for him by the revenant, as the constructed Madeleine.[22] That Judy embodies the true image again only once she is literally dead implies that Scottie's desire is an impossible one – a true image of a dead woman, from which all uncanny difference (death's rhetoric in life) is eliminated must necessarily be inscribed by real death instead, placing the body once again beyond his grasp.

Two important points distinguish the film from the novel. While the disclosure of the hoax marks the end of the latter, Hitchcock places it at the beginning of the second part, shifting his viewer's interest from the economic/murder plot to the romance plot. While *Sueurs Froides* ends, like the texts discussed so far, in murder, the last death in *Vertigo* is the result of a second jump, whose motive is complex and ambivalent. For what aim does the protagonist desire a dead woman returned and how does he respond to the discovery that she is a double of a double? How does he resolve the uncanny hesitation the revenant enacts? While in the novel murder occurs because the body double will not confirm that she is a revenant, the second death in *Vertigo* occurs precisely because such duplicity is to be resolved. The revenant of the revenant, once disclosed as a machination, must be destroyed so as to repress the sexual perversion this discovery also discloses. Scottie provokes the fatal jump after Judy's confession because this shows him the void out of which his desire arose – not only the absence of any real woman but also of any real dead ancestor – bringing him face to face with his own death, which to repress he has resorted to this romance in the first place. If he must punish her for not being the living representative of the dead he also punishes her for demasking both his necrophiliac desire and his desire to conceal his own mortality, of which his vertigo is the symptom of an unsuccessful repression.

Hitchcock's film demonstrate how repetition radically calls the notion of origins into question. For he emphasises that there is no original beloved, only a woman repeating in an act of dissimulation, a woman haunted by a ghost, who, furthermore, uses no original living woman but rather the representation of a dead one, the portrait in a museum, as her model. The Madeleine whom Scottie desires and chooses to refind is not only from the start a corpse but in fact the deanimated copy of a deanimated body, existing only in oral narratives of the past and in paint. The obsessional and the hysterical discourse fatally collide in a divergent identification that the woman and the man have with death. The irony that emerges, as the disclosure of the hysteric's duplicity produces her corpse is that the replica was always the real body, the object of desire precisely the body double.

While a portrait of Carlotta serves as the model for a series of surrogate love objects for the protagonist, a masculine body stands at the beginning of the sequence of revenants and deaths – a dead policeman. As the plot unfolds the reader learns that the reason why Gavin chose Scottie as his exonerating witness is that the latter left the police force because he has vertigo. While he and another another policeman were chasing a criminal over roof tops he was unable to follow and the other man, going for him, fell fatally. Gavin can be sure that Scottie will not follow Madeleine up the church steeple and discover the hoax.

Scottie falls in love with a woman who identifies with her dead greatgrandmother while he is in the state of guilt-ridden mourning for this dead friend and has been forced to recognise his own potential vulnerability before death. In Madeleine he believes he has found someone like himself, who knows that all the gestures of the survivor merely cover the underlying void of death. As he follows her on her visit to the cemetery where she leans, in an incomprehensible gesture, over the forgotten grave of Carlotta Valdes, to the rooms the dead woman used to inhabit, to the bridge where she jumps into the water, Madeleine is increasingly perceived as a mystery which he must solve if he is to find peace – the unrest of the mourner turned into that of the detective.

In her impersonation of Madeleine, Judy dissimulates an ignorance about her mysterious trances and incognisant behaviour and feigns a need for Scottie to interpret her dream of places she has never seen but where Carlotta probably lived. Her first 'death' (she seems to jump from a bell tower while Scottie's vertigo prohibits him from following while Gavin throws down the corpse of the already murdered wife) is seen in light of the fatality repetition gives figure to. For him death returns over her corpse. If his ability to resuscitate her after her jump into the water served, in a displaced manner, his wish for a return of his dead friend and an assurance of his own survival, the same mixture of melancholic mourning and guilt which his love for her had displaced returns in her absence. The nightmare of his falling friend's cry and stretched out body is now replaced by representations of her death. For the next years she remains as an image that incessantly torments him, as a dead woman preserved in his fantasy and her death suspends the solution to the enigma of death's exchange with life which her uncanny appearance installed.

The second half of the film begins as Scottie, who is suffering from 'acute melancholia together with a guilt complex' after Madeleine's suicide (a repetition and displacement of the guilt induced by the policeman's fall), sees Judy and recognises her resemblance to the lost beloved he has been searching for everywhere. Hitchcock inserts a flashback, with Judy as focalisor, disclosing the murder plot before the uncanny process of redressing her into a perfect replica of the internal image Scottie has preserved of Madeleine sets in. Giving the audience the truth about the hoax lets suspense 'hinge around the question of how (Scottie) is going to react when he discovers that Judy and Madeleine are actually the same person'.[23] The crucial difference between the film and the novel resides in the way that Scottie's response to his lover's confession implies an attitude toward death that lets him awake with sudden sobriety from the fantasy of fulfilled necrophiliac desire.

The romance plot in *Vertigo* allows Scottie fetishistically to invoke and avoid his own fall and articulates the ambivalent desire for and fear of falling as dying. Madeleine's fallen body lies on the church roof in the same posture as the policemen's, and if her death in a sense displaces that of his friend, he identifies with both in his nightmare vision after her inquest, which engenders his brief hospitalisation for melancholia. His dream represents his body falling as the other two did, and in so doing also imitates the dream of falling into the darkness of an empty grave which Judy as Madeleine recounted. In fancy he repeats real and invented images of bodies falling to death until these two realms come together again when the fancied image is given reality in the last death.

Once he has rediscoverd Madeleine in Judy, his courtship takes on the guise of redressing her in the clothes, hairstyle and make-up of the first Madeleine; teaching her the accent and gait of her predecessor. Judy doesn't resist Scottie's efforts to 'make her over' into his fancied image. Indeed she consents to her complete remodelling because she hopes, like the hysteric, to gain his love by virtue of his confirming gaze. She explains 'I'll do it, I don't care anymore about me.'[24] Already in the first half of the film, the impersonation she offers of a haunted woman was not independent. Judy's 'Madeleine' feigns not to know she is possessed, not to know about the strange visits to the graveyard, the hotel, the art gallery. This lack of knowledge places Scottie not merely in the position of the protecting spy but also in that of the master analyser who will scrutinise her gestures, her words, the dream material she offers him so as to 'find the key', the 'missing pieces' that will explain her symptoms. Preventing her from repeating her suicide transforms into a search for the truth she seems to harbour, a truth unknown to herself. The cure he comes up with is that of remembering and repeating those gestures and scenes her dreams evoke, until he gets her to return to the Spanish settlement Carlotta must have known. Here the murder hoax literally repeats the nightmare visions of falling, with which Madeleine has been feeding Scottie's imagination.

This scene is a successful representation of a successful suicide in which, for the spectator Scottie, the repetition of dreamed events transpires into their first actualisation. Though the audience soon finds out that Judy never died, that the real Madeleine Elster never committed suicide, what Hitchcock's version implies is that Scottie's obsessional desire for truth drives the impersonated Madeleine to her 'death' – this perfect repetition of dream material enacting the dis-simulation of a fatal undifferentiated oversameness. While in both parts of the novel the protagonist interrogates Madeleine so as to confirm his belief that she is a revenant, and even murders to preserve the illusion that the dead return to life, Scottie seeks to cure by dispossessing the haunted woman. He wishes to kill the ghost of the dead mother and the power she seems to have over a living woman by uncovering a canny explanation for uncanny events. This desire for knowledge, for the 'truth' about an event of death and a dead woman returned, as much informs the latter half of the film as does Scottie's necrophiliac desire.

Hitchcock's film structurally exploits repetitions in a way Boileau-Narcejac's novel does not. Scottie (albeit unknowingly) repeats Gavin's scenario and is disconcerted about his lack of originality when he discovers this – 'He made you over just like I made you over. Only better.'[25] Remodelling Judy into Madeleine haunted by a dead woman is meant to help him discover why she 'ditched him for another guy' (as Judy puts it), namely death. In this second recreation, Judy once again becomes a tool, the body double at which he can kill his own possession by the dead woman. Because she realises that he loves her not for her singularity but as the materialisation of an image, she will dissimulate what was from the start a dissimulation. But this remodelling is also a form of psychic and social deanimation. In the transformation scene, staged as one long sequence culminating in the perfect repetition, her change in appearance is shown to be a kind of death. Once the costume, hair, face and gait is perfect, the space between model and copy obliterated, Judy, like the dead Rowena over whose corpse Ligeia rises, is the image of the dead returned in the body of another. She signifies a dead woman, yet in the process her own personality is 'killed off', since she is reduced to the substance with which this resuscitation can be modelled.

What in *Sueurs Froides* is merely a detail turns into the *peripeteia* of Judy's story. Once the transformation has been completed and Scottie can, for the first time, truly embrace her, an unconscious slip of hand lets her don precisely the necklace that belonged to Madeleine and which Scottie duly recognises from the painting of Carlotta. This move can be understood as an empty gesture, as the beginning of a sequence of actions by which Judy signifies the recognition of her non-existence, the void underlying her dissimulations. It signifies the beginning of her acceptance of her facticity. With the return of the piece of jewellery (functioning as an *objet a*), Scottie begins to realise that a sleight of hand has been at play and his second round of interrogation, which ends (again unlike the novel) in a repetition of the fatal events at the Spanish settlement, is aimed at finding out the truth behind the woman's appearance. The confession he extorts from her is meant to clarify whether she is indeed a medium for a dead woman or a hysteric whose dissimulation can be solved. Hitchcock's solution reveals that her masquerade is twofold. It is the cover for a crime which can be solved to show that the woman is an imposter, her appearance false, and this solution leaves Judy intact as a person in her own right, even if guilty of murder. But it also proves to be part of the hysteric's discourse, by which she plays the role of an object of speculation (in all three senses of the word), impersonates an image for the male gaze to cover her lack in being, and this second disclosure leaves her faced with her non-existence.

Sensing that the identity between the two women is the sign of a superlative hoax, Scottie wants to establish clarity by undertaking yet another repetition of the uncanny events, so as to put an end to all liminality and the intellectual hesitation it engenders. He explains to Judy that he needs her 'to be Madeleine for a while. And when it's done we'll both be free.' He wants to stop being haunted, wants to kill the ghost and explains 'One doesn't often get a second chance. You're my second chance, Judy.'[26] The solution he believes her confession and the recreation of past events will offer is freedom from the guilt he felt about Madeleine's death as well as the guilt he feels for desiring to sleep with a dead woman. The repetition is meant to make him 'free of the past', of the inscription of death, of the fatality and his own facticity which this implies, just as repetition was meant to cure Madeleine of her ghost. Yet where the latter brought about Judy's mock suicide, this brings about a real fatal jump.

The last shots of Hitchock's film pose questions even as the detective and mourning plot find closure. The oversameness in repetition indeed seems to free Scottie from one uncanny experience, that of death's presence in life. Judy's real death puts closure on liminality and duplicity. She is now identical with what she staged earlier on, and Madeleine, who has been cannily proved to be both a fraud and dead, can no longer haunt him. In one sense he overcomes his 'castration' symptomised as vertigo (in this second attempt he does get to the top of the church tower), by 'castrating' Judy, forcing her to be the tool and medium of his discovery of truth. He overcomes the death haunting him, the fallen policemen repeated in the fallen Madeleine Elster, by making Judy the *pharmakos* and letting her take death on to herself.

As in Poe's narrative, the aim of this last death is to eliminate uncanny hesitation, and the oversameness of repetition secures an identity between model and copy. Judy's corpse, lying on the roof redressed by Scottie's hand, makes the first, figural death literal, even as it confirms that, in Madeleine, Scottie loved the representation of a dead woman. What the film leaves open is whether this last repetition is a triumph over or a final subjection to death, whether Scottie is left in the posture of a madman, about to jump himself or cured of his fascination and anxiety about death. The film viewer never sees Judy's dead body, only its reflection in Scottie's gaze, in the imitation of her fallen body which he, standing on the brink of the church steeple, slowly enacts by spreading his arms and legs as though he too were falling. If Stephen Heath's claim is correct, that representations assert sameness by virtue of fixing difference so as to ground and mask a masculine domination, at the expense of woman,[27] difference here is fixed in two senses. The difference of representation as the disturbing and uncanny articulation/concealment of death in life is effaced along with the difference that the living feminine body always poses to the masculine survivor's psychic representation of that body.

Maybe the most significant divergence introduced by Hitchcock involves the question why Judy, as she sees the black outline of the nun approach, jumps to her death calling 'Oh, no'. In his reading, Zizek suggests that *Vertigo* can be read as a film about the way that sublimation is concerned as much with death as it excludes sexualisation. Scottie loves Judy when she is idealised as Madeleine who is dead and yet in this sublimation Judy is also already dead. The second part of the film enacts a desublimation of the beloved object and her jump from the tower transforms into the realisation of her diminuation as sublime object in Scottie's eyes.[28] Since her ability to fascinate masks the void of her non-existence, when she is finally rejected, her whole ontological consistency is dissolved. Her jump, following her declaration of love ('I walked into danger and let you change me because I loved you') and Scottie's rebuttal ('It's too late. There's no bringing her back') can, however, also be read as the ethical attitude Lacan connects with 'subjectivisation'; with Judy accepting without reserve the immanence of her own death, accepting that she is a victim of fate.[29] Having fallen from being Scottie's idealised object of desire, she experiences the breakdown of her hysterical discourse, assumes her non-existence and constitutes herself as subject. As the fascination Scottie feels turns into aversion, because her appearance transforms into mere dissimulation, the mask he has loved and recreated proves tautologically to be indeed a mask, and he can distance himself from her and reject her. Judy recognises that she has not only manipulated her lover, even as she seemingly lets herself be manipulated by him, but that she is also the object of fate's manipulation. Her jump signifies an active act, a moment of subjectivity where she accepts the facticity of death she has so precariously been dis-simulating throughout. In Zizek's terms, what is menacing about the femme fatale is not that she could be fatal for men but that she presents a 'subject fully assuming her fate.'[30] I would add that it is the denial and repression of precisely this ethic stance which underwrites Scottie's behaviour throughout this film. This form of feminine subjectivisation always harbours a disquieting aporia. Even as it lets Judy fall out of the illusion that any narcissistically informed images of wholeness procures, she always also repeats and fulfills the image of her model. Even as she insists on her difference to any image Scottie may have formed of her and confirms her subject position by embracing her own fatality, she gives up her difference to the dead woman she was incessantly asked to repeat.

While in Part II the death of a woman was shown to be the result of her exchange for an image, the narratives discussed here articulate the mourning lover's desire for excessive sameness as an image is given body. My readings have emphasized that such repetitions deny the alterity of the copy, and if they are successful also mean her mortification. These mourners resort to the force of death to cover the castrative wound to narcissism which an earlier instance of death had provoked. They re-enact the real loss of their love object to repress the incision of the real, and return by way of a second death to an illusion of their eternal stability, the revocability of death, the occlusion of facticity. The position of the mourner is also the one in which images are born and materialised. As such it serves as a recuperation of the mirror-stage where, supported by the security of a wholeness with the maternal body, the child experienced its first jubilation at recognising its own integrity over the images it psychically formed. In the next chapter I will illuminate this interstice between the production of imaginations and the dead feminine body preserved.

Notes to Chapter 15

1 P. P. de Man, 1983, notes that repetition asserts the impossibility of rigorous identity because it is a temporal process.
2 P. Ricoeur, 1975, especially chapter six.
3 S. Rimmon-Kenan, 1980.
4 J.-L. Pontalis, 1978.
5 S. Weber, 1982, p. 150.
6 J. Lacan, 1978, p. 49. The gesture of the fetish denies a wound even as it affirms it by substituting a body that signifies the threat of castration (be it of mortality or sexuality) with a seemingly stable body occluding such a threat. In this sense all fetishism is a form of uncanny repetition. But since a completed repetition, namely that which exchanges uncanny resemblance for the tautology of oversameness, undoes all hesitation between denial and affirmation, not all repetition is fetishistic.
7 S. Weber, 1982.
8 S. Rimmon-Kenan, 1980, p. 156.
9 One could add Villiers de L'Isle-Adam's 'Véra' (1874), Guy de Maupassant's 'La Chevelure' (1884) and Arthur Schnitzler's 'Die Nächste' (1923) to the list.
10 See S. Freud, 1917, pp. 237–60.
11 A. Van Gennep, 1960.
12 J. Bowlby, 1980, pp. 81–111.
13 H. Cixous, 1976, p. 543.
14 S. Kofman, 1973. See my discussion of beauty and melancholy in chapter 4.
15 For another kind of discussion of representations of death in Poe see J.G. Kennedy, 1987.
16 See also D.H. Lawrence, 1923, who reads Ligeia's death as a form of being murdered by the husband's scientific observation, arguing that 'to know a living thing is to kill it', p. 70.
17 It should be remembered that in Freud's discussion of the uncanny, eyes are the displaced trope for castration anxiety, so that a discussion of Ligeia's eyes could be seen as a displaced discussion of her sexuality. But if one understands castration in the more global sense I am implying, they are also the body parts privileged as shield against and as threshold to death.
18 See E. A. Poe, 1948, p. 356.
19 F. Truffaut, 1984, p. 243f. D. Spoto, 1976, tells the anecdote that Samuel Taylor suggests that a suitable subtitle for the film would be 'To Lay a Ghost', for 'the British idiom, signifying the exorcism of a spirit puns amusingly in American English', p. 294.
20 T. Modleski, 1988, 'if woman, who is posited as she whom man must know and possess in order to guarantee his truth and his identity, does not exist, then in some important sense he does not exist either' p. 91. She reads Scottie's interrogation of Madeleine as a way to force her to turn her gaze away from the mother and acknowledge his supremacy.
21 D. Spoto, 1976, p. 335.
22 T. de Lauretis, 1984, p. 154. See also V. Burgin, 1986, pp. 96–109.
23 F. Truffaut, 1983, p. 244.
24 All quotes are taken from D. Spoto, 1976, p. 329.
25 Quoted in D. Spoto, 1976, p. 332.
26 Quoted in D. Spoto, 1976, p. 332.

27 S. Heath, 1978.
28 S. Zizek, 1988.
29 Quoted in D. Spoto, 1976, p. 332.
30 S. Zizek, 1989, p. 54.

16

Spectral stories

Storytellers are Death's secretaries. It is Death who hands them the file. The
file is full of sheets of uniformly black paper but they have eyes for reading
them and from this file they construct a story for the living.
John Berger

Set against mortality and oblivion, narrators also consume death. Absent from
the world and therefore 'dead' as a social person, feeding off previous 'inanimate'
texts, producing fictions that in turn are alive in the realm of the imaginary but
immaterial in respect to social reality, storytellers are positioned in an intermediary site between life and death. Their power of imagination is like a vampire,
feeding off this exchange, for they rely on a preservation and production of 'dead'
figures – the teller's and the listener's temporary social death and the uncanny
presence as absence that fictions embody. Or, to reverse the analogy, storytellers
are like revenants in that the liminal realm between life and death inspires and
produces fictions. Blanchot suggests that when we tell stories we are resting on an
unclosed grave and the emptiness of the grave is what makes language true even
as this void is also a reality which lets death come into being.[1]
  Dickens's *Great Expectations* (1861) can be read as a novel about the way the art
of storytelling conjoins representation with the revenant and with the intermediary. In so doing it reveals that the rhetoric of death is like a sword that cuts
both ways. Fictions are shown to feed off the teller's and the listener's proximity
to death even as real death breaks into the realm where fancies and fictions are
born and nourished to disrupt the illusions that these macabre representations
produced. Linking femininity, death and the emergence of fiction over the body
of a revenant bride, this novel centres on Miss Havisham, a woman who remains
beyond her social death to provoke a mystery and inspire a tale. From within her
self-made tomb, she moulds a surrogate daughter Estella (as the instrument of
revenge) and mothers the fanciful expectations of a surrogate son Pip (as the
privileged object of destruction). Disempowered in life, she gains demonic power
by speaking from the position of an empty grave. In this transitional site, fiction is

more 'real' than social or natural reality, precisely owing to its proximity to death. As a world without substance, it stands in double opposition to the reality of the living. Furthermore, commenting self-reflexively on the scenario it enacts, Dickens's novel also shows that the act of storytelling involves listeners and speakers that are absent from the world, doubles of their social selves, at the same time that, located in such a liminal realm, fiction also produces tales about doubles, about figures and plots emerging out of absence.

André Green argues that the work of reading and writing occurs in a private space. Though the writer and the reader are absent to each other they are mutually positioned in the site of a transnarcissistic communication, where the writer's and the reader's doubles communicate through the fictional text. Since the figure of the double signifies death and since absence implies potential death, the pleasures fictions offer, he concludes, draw their power from death.[2] Dickens's novel represents precisely such a scene of death-inspired trans-narcissistic communication, where the absence as doubling of speaker and addressee in a liminal realm occurs. Strictly speaking, of course, no written but rather oral texts are produced and fictions are heard and acted out. Reformulating Green's scenario one can say that the speaker Miss Havisham and the listeners Estella and Pip are present to each other and their fictions are materialised at their bodies. These narratives mark a turn back to a literal form of signification even as the actors are also caught in a figural absence and self-doubling.

Imaginary activity, symbolisation and the creation of fictions serve to negate reality, to repair or mitigate one's own destructive impulses and patch up wounds to one's narcissism. In that it presupposes loss, storytelling involves the work of mourning, with the engendered text transforming a narcissistic wound into a fictitious positivity. The site of fiction is transitional because it is posed between the inner and the outer, with the speaker, the addressee and the unfolding plot uncannily present-in-absence, absent-in-presence. In that it suspends rules of reality and plausibility, it is the realm of endless potentiality and in that it comprises both an aspect of doubling and of absence, it shows the fascination for and the power of the split even as it articulates this power over a void, a lack. In Green's terms, the storyteller or producer of fictions is, therefore, significantly 'caught between the double and the absent',[3] and it is precisely this dual figure I wish to trace in my discussion of *Great Expectations*. Here the tellers and listeners of fictional stories are doubles because each produces or receives another image of her or himself and exists in another world. And each is absent, because they emerge from an absence of social reality and return to a void; the nullification of romantic illusions in the case of the two children and the silence death induces in the spectral bride.

Miss Havisham, an 'immensely rich and grim lady', leads a 'life of seclusion' in a dismal barricaded house (81). Though she is not the only character in the novel who makes art out of life, the duplicitous plot she enacts by paying Pip to 'go and play' in her presence for her 'diversion' interlaces the great romantic with the great economic expectations of Dickens's protagonist in such a monstrous fashion that its disclosure deconstructs the folly underlying both. Significantly, the realm where Pip's self-fashioning (by which he creates an image of himself that transcends his social position) is born and thrives, is her artificial crypt. And the woman who authors these fanciful expectations, these 'poor dreams', who awakens Pip's creative even if deluded poetic faculties, is repeatedly described as a revenant.

When Pip sees her for the first time, he recalls a 'ghastly waxwork' of a personage lying in state, which he had seen at a fair, as well as 'a skeleton in the ashes of a rich dress' that had been dug out of a vault. This first sight is supremely uncanny, because at Miss Havisham's body the inanimate comes to life again – 'Now, waxwork and skeleton seemed to have dark eyes that moved and looked at me' (87). She is not only the material embodiment of a living dead, but more importantly, a living sign of the bride as a dead woman. She is dressed in the rich white materials, the satin laces, silks and jewels of her bridal gown, a long white veil and bridal flowers in her hair. She is 'not quite finished dressing', the room in which she receives Pip is scattered with half-packed trunks. Furthermore both bride and dresses are withered, her hair white, her eyes sunken, her body shrunk to skin and bone, and all the objects that were once white are now yellow; unused or ragged, paled, decayed objects. In this strange, melancholy, candlelit realm she has buried herself alive.

All clocks have stopped at twenty minutes to nine, all objects have remained unchanged, while her own gestures and appearance endlessly repeat that fatal moment. After more than a decade, her bridal dress looks 'like grave-clothes', her long veil 'like a shroud', and inmidst 'this arrest of everything', she herself sits 'corpse-like'. Yet this is a double arrestation of death – the representation of a sudden cessation of life and a seizure that puts death under erasure. Even as time, change, and that is to say the facticity of natural mortal existence, have artificially been put to a stop 'a long time ago', Miss Havisham and her surroundings have become a superlative sign for mutability and decay, the enactment of death inmidst life. When the narrating Pip recalls this scene long after it has occurred, he evokes 'bodies buried in ancient times, which fall to powder in the moment of being distinctly seen'. He further implicitly refers to the vampire myth by suggesting that she looked as if 'the admission of the natural light of day would have struck her to dust' (90).

As Pip learns later on from one of her relatives, she was a rich, proud and spoilt heiress, who fell passionately in love with an impostor. A conspiracy between the groom and the bride's disinherited half-brother turned the wedding day into an event of 'cruel mortification'. Instead of the groom, a letter breaking off the engagement arrived, and Miss Havisham, once she had recovered from the 'bad illness' that this announcement engendered, took the hysteric's dissimulation of her non-existence to a superlative degree, simultaneously affirming and denying her wounded narcissism. Refusing ever again to look 'upon the light of day', she lays her entire house to waste so as to turn it into a museum that preserves and exhibits precisely the moment of this 'cruel mortification'. The unaltered wedding clothes, trousseau and wedding banquet table mark for ever the moment of excessive expectation and excessive loss (205). In this case the masculine gaze which ironically preserves her against any breakdown of her self-sustaining hysteric discourse is that of the absent groom Compeyson.

In her dissimulation of the waiting bride, Miss Havisham is indeed caught between the double and the absent. She is absent, because socially dead, addressing the outside world with missives written from within the silence of her barricaded, wasted mansion. People who wish for any exchange with her must enter this intermediary realm between life and death. In part her hysterical discourse discloses that the jilted bride is socially dead in any case. At the same time she explicitly uses this self-fashioning to demonstrate that with the loss of her loved object, with her heart broken, any further existence is merely a mechanical continuation of the body. Indeed she takes the metaphor literally. Since the organ that sustains life by pumping blood and inspiring love has been broken, she becomes bloodless and withers away, even as her transactions with others become heartless.

Against real suicide she opts for what could almost be seen as a parody of the dead bride theme – the staging of her process of waiting for a bridegroom as waiting for death. She is not merely absent but also double, in part because she remains, in the figure of a double of her former self, beyond her social death. The lawyer Jaggers also compares her to the nocturnal vampire when he says that she will not eat in the presence of others, but rather 'wanders about in the night, and then lays hands on such food as she takes' (263). Pip himself observers her one night wandering through her empty, mildewed realm, 'in a ghostly manner, making a low cry' and carrying a 'bare candle in her hand' (325). In addition, Pip articulates the notion that she, as a figure of death, expresses death's desire not only for herself but for him as well, when in 'fancy' he sees a body with Miss Havisham's face hang by the neck from the wooden beam on the side of her house, all in yellow white, her movement as though 'she were trying to call me' (94). Significantly this 'childish association' is revived many years later just before her actual death. Finally, her half-brother Arthur also evokes this image of the dead bride calling her survivors to death in the nightmare vision preceeding his own demise. In this dream representation he sees the sister whom he helped destroy 'awful mad', dressed like Ophelia, all in white, with white flowers in her hair and 'where her heart's broke . . . there's drops of blood'. In his fancy this harbinger of death shakes the shroud over her arm at him (363).

Above all, however, Miss Havisham is a double in the sense that she incessantly re-enacts the moment of supreme loss, using a materialised form of fiction, namely her body dressed in the guise of the eternal bride, to transform a narcissistic wound into positivity. In the hysteric repetition as representation of her bridal preparations, staged for her own benefit and for her relatives who visit her annually on her birthday, she not only inextricably conflates dead girl and bride. Rather she also doubles herself by staging a self-representation which preserves the moment of loss, ensures perpetual mourning even as, by virtue of the re-enactment, she also stages a triumph over loss and 'castration'. Yet Miss Havisham does not only use this potential transitional realm to represent her process of dying, to make the effect of her broken heart a continual spectacle for others. She also uses this liminality to mould her peers into two plots – one economic, one romantic – of which Pip serves as the interstice.

The first plot involves those who patiently observe her dying because they are speculating on an inheritance. Once again she takes a metaphor literally when, with Pip's help, she evokes a macabre rendition of such cannibalism for the eyes of these 'self-seeking relatives'. In the room where the table, now covered with dust and mould, had been set for her wedding feast, her rotten bride-cake hidden by cobwebs and the habitat of mice and beetles, she dictates the procedure of her wake. 'When the ruin is complete,' she explains, she wishes that 'they lay me dead, in my bride's dress on the bride's table' (117). In this sketch, her body thus placed serves as a fully materialised sign, signifies superlatively her tragic romance and is meant to be 'the finished curse upon him' who transformed her from bride to living corpse. In the same testamentary gesture she also designates the place where, in respect to her dead, laid out body, each relative is meant to sit during the wake, so as visually to invoke their wish to feast on this wealthy relative. Once again the rhetoric of the double inhabiting such a premature rehearsal of one's death is observed by Pip. He has some 'vague misgivings that she might get upon the table then and there and die at once, the complete realization of the ghastly waxwork at the Fair' (113); and he shudders at the uncanny possibility that this fiction may become real. He also has the impression that, as Miss Havisham describes her wake, she is 'looking at the table as if she stood looking at her own figure lying there' (117).

From the moment Pip is introduced into her mansion, she encourages his fancy that she 'would do something' for him. Once he has acquired 'a handsome property' from a secret unnamed source, she can, however, use this 'coincidence' to add another dimension to her inheritance plot. She leads Pip on in his mistaken conviction that she is his benefactress, his 'fairy godmother', and in so doing fosters both her relatives and his delusion that he has superseded them as heir in her will. While for the relatives this plot is merely a sign of her proud nature, Pip connects his economic speculation – that he has mysteriously been given money so as to be removed from his present sphere of life and raised as a gentleman in London – to the second plot Miss Havisham concocts from within her crypt. This second fiction, originally implanted by her in his imagination, concerns his love for her adoptive daughter Estella. From the begining he realises that the 'diversion' Miss Havisham sought by calling him was not the vicarious pleasure of watching children play but rather the tie she wished to establish between these two adoptive children. Only later does he learn, however, that far from being the privileged heir, he has been chosen as the first victim to test the effectivness of the monster which Miss Havisham, not unlike Frankenstein, has moulded inmidst her mansion of decay. Though it is not his death she seeks, her aim is to inflict a similar mortal wound to his narcissism, to break his heart in repetition of her own castration. For she has raised Estella into a beautiful but hard, haughty and capricious girl, 'stole her heart away and put ice in its place' (412) so as 'to wreak revenge on the male sex' (200).

From the start, the girl's condescending attitude toward him inspires a sense of humiliation at the same time that it turns her into an idealised love object to be desired from afar. The disruption her acquaintance causes to his previous existence significantly produces fictions in more than one sense. Because he, as a child, can neither adequately describe the strangeness he encounters in the Havisham crypt, nor is willing to confess the humiliation he experiences there, he invents 'marvels', and relates 'pretended experiences' to his sister (97). The events in this transitional space – the card game with a beautiful girl, played 'by candle light in the room with the stopped clocks' (157) before the eyes of a living wax figure – spur on Pip's imagination and let him produce wild fictions. The lies he tells are, however, also experiments in fashioning himself in images more appealing than reality and it is precisely such acts of artificial self-fashioning which Miss Havisham fosters, though in another sense, when she repeatedly asks Pip whether Estella grows 'prettier and prettier'. By soliciting his comment on her beauty she implies that her beauty is in some sense contingent on his gaze, something developed for him. Owing to the double of himself she fosters, the image of him as a potential suitor for Estella, Pip becomes dissatisfied with his social position and wants to fashion himself so as 'to be a gentleman on her account' (156). In retrospect he recalls that the influence of the mysterious 'dull old house', where daylight never entered, where time had stopped, 'bewildered' him and each time after his annual visit, he hated his trade and was ashamed of his home (152). When he suddenly discovers his great economic and educational expectations, he believes Miss Havisham not only means to 'make my fortune when my time is out' (160) but that she will do so because 'she intended me for Estella' (174).

In this potential space between social life and death, Miss Havisham is a vampire in another sense. She uses the lives of others to feed her desire for revenge on the man who misused her, by recreating her adoptive daughter into her artificial double who embodies what she lacks. In this beautiful and brilliant woman, in whose looks and gestures Pip finds 'that tinge of resemblance to Miss Havisham which may often be noticed to have been acquired by children' (259), her surrogate mother has produced a monstrous woman without a heart, without memory, to assuage her broken heart, her incurable 'steady memory', which can't forget her wounded pride. At the same time that she seems to keep her dying body alive by sucking the energy from this daughter by adoption, invigorating herself at the thought that Estella will do to Pip and other men after him what was done to her, she also inspires or feeds the imagination of this first victim. Like Dracula, who transforms the women he bites into revenants, she gives Pip some of her spectral blood in the sense that she engenders in his mind other, potential images of the self. For Pip also turns into a double of himself in this transitional realm, when he imagines himself as the rich young lover of Estella whom he could not and will not become in social reality. Pip serves in part as the audience for Miss Havisham's own staging of death, in part as the privileged victim of her lethal creation. Yet in the process, he also emerges as her other double, as a living image of her own broken heart and thus diametrically opposed to the perfect image of a non-woundable self which she has materialised at Estella's body.

As the author of this romance plot, by coincidence so beautifully enmeshed with the economic one, Miss Havisham is, then, caught between two doubles. Using Estella, returned from France, as bait, she calls Pip to her house to finalise the scene she has been planning throughout. Responding to her call, Pip imagines himself as 'the hero' and Estella as the 'inspiration, the heart' of 'a rich attractive mystery' and believes that the role Miss Havisham has designed for him is that of the one 'to restore the desolate house, admit the sunshine into the dark rooms, set the clocks a going . . . destroy the vermin – in short, do all the shining deeds of the young Kight of romance, and marry the Princess' (253). Once the two meet after the long separation, she commands Pip to love Estella, in a manner imitating her own tragic passion; commands him to give up 'your whole heart and soul to the smiter – as I did' (261). She decks Estella with her own jewels so that, while Pip is to repeat her romantic emotions, Estella's appearance will correspond to the way she looked as a young bride. She hangs upon Estella's beauty, words, and gestures as though, in Pip's words 'she were devouring the beautiful creature she had reared' (320). Positioned in between these two doubles, she splits her former self in two, repeats the beautiful bride in the body of Estella and the blind, unquestioning, submissive lover in the figure of Pip. If she devours Estella with looks and embraces because she is to be her instrument of revenge and torment, she has also already consumed him by transmitting those notions of love, which were so fatal to her, into his imagination.

Once his real benefactor, the convict Magwitch appears, Pip discovers that Miss Havisham's economic intentions towards him 'were all a dream' (341). He is also forced to recognise that the repetition Miss Havisham seeks is neither aimed at restoring lost happiness nor such that Estella is the prize reserved for him after she has tormented men 'for a term.' Rather, the repetition Miss Havisham has designed is one that re-enacts loss and wounded narcissism – the breaking of a second heart. Pip's declaration of love marks the self-reflexive moment in Dickens's text, where the narrative superlatively repeats, as a *mise en abyme*, how the act of fiction is caught between doubling and absence. In this spectacle, which the two young people unwittingly began to rehearse the day Pip first played cards with Estella, Miss Havisham is the director and the only audience. She glances from Pip to Estella, from her to him (375), to see how her refashioned woman will respond to Pip's narrative of romantic infatuation.

The re-enactment of her psychic trauma – a lover's marital expectations unremittingly destroyed – is doubly successful as though, to venture a pun, she were finally enabled to have and eat the long hidden bridal cake. In Estella, Miss

Havisham sees her destructive desires realised because this remoulded daughter enacts to perfection the scene which, with her mind 'mortally hurt and diseased' she has, for so many years, longed to watch. She offers her the sight of a woman saved from 'misery like my own' (411), because under her hand the feminine position transforms from a castrated into a castrating one. Owing to the nature Miss Havisham formed within Estella, she remains untouched by Pip's words of love, doesn't care for what he says and cruelly discloses how his images of love lack substance. Yet, watching for Pip's response, Miss Havisham puts her hand to her own heart and holds it there for cover throughout the scene. As she later explains, caught between Pip's 'ecstasy of unhappiness' and Estella's 'incredulous wonder' (378) at such outburst of emotion, she sees in Pip 'a looking-glass that showed me what I once felt myself' (411). This repetition of her own pain by proxy engenders the realisation of another long nourished desire, lets her undertake a second killing which is diametrically opposed to the desire to inflict a mortal wound on a lover. Seeing her own sorrow reflected in another 'kills' her hysterical self-representation as vindictive, spectral bride; puts an end to her wild resentment, to her wounded pride, to the fetishisation of her sorrow and her desire for vengeance. Marking the breakdown of her hysterical dissimulation, this identification with the pain of another allows her to accept her fate, and that means to assume real non-existence, which her representation of the fatally wounded bride had sought to occlude. When the scene is over she seems like 'a spectral figure . . . all resolved into a ghastly stare of pity and remorse' (378).

Dickens's interest in this staged declaration of love seems to be itself duplicitous. Even as Miss Havisham falls out of the mania of her self-mourning by virtue of the language of love that 'welled up' within Pip, this 'rhapsody' can touch her precisely because Pip's love for Estella is as narcissistically fanciful as hers was for Compeyson. This scene, in which Pip for the first and only time speaks the language of a poet, also discloses that his love for Estella is not only without substance because the outgrowth of what was suggested by Miss Havisham. It is also a fiction because it transpires into the infatuated folly of worshipping an idealised woman, of fashioning himself in the image of a prince who will awaken the dormant heart of a princess. Even as this scene supports a conventional notion of Christian love and forgiveness, in the figure of Miss Havisham's awakened remorse, it also discloses that romance is grounded on delusions, with the emotions it signifies not original but rather assumed, originating from an alterior imprint. Pip's declaration of love implicitly discloses the design of a fictitious relation between two beings: 'you are part of my existence, part of myself. You have been in every line I have read, since I first came here . . . The stones of which the strongest London buildings are made, are not more real . . . than your presence and influence have been to me'. Even though the emotions may be felt as true, his declaration articulates that the language of love has no referent in reality but rather serves to support the stability of the self he has designed for himself.

For Pip, the intermediary realm transpires not only into the site where his fancies about romantic expectations arise, but also where they can finally be declared, in the double that language always represents. This representation of romantic feeling proves not only to be primarily inscribed by the poetic function which, in Jakobson's terms, least emphasises a reference to a non-semiotic reality. Rather it is also spoken when the speaker is beside himself, though his speech supports his narcissistically informed desires; when he is absent and double in an 'ecstasy of unhappiness'. In this pose Pip is, to a degree, desubstantiated, speaking a rhapsody that 'welled up within me, like blood from an inward wound, and gushed out'. For all three characters, this *peripeteia* is an excessive moment of absence and doubling. Pip speaks to a woman who is a double of herself, because her nature has been remoulded in the image of another's wild resentment, and whose absence is that of human affection. At the same time he is observed by another woman, who, in a blasphemous gesture, absent from social reality, has created a double, thus reversing 'the appointed order of their Maker' (411). Faced with this living monument to her own ruin, meant simultaneously to affirm and deny the castrative wound to her narcissism, the author of this scene in turn is confronted not only with her monstrous creation but also, in the living image of a second double, with the sin of such idolatrous representation.

What becomes clear in the last interview Pip has with her is the cathartic value of the dual story – Pip's romantic infatuation and her own romantic vengeance – staged by her two doubles in the liminal realm of her constructed crypt. Recognising that she has not only created a monster but also killed a woman, she asks for a different kind of representation, symbolic rather than iconic, to commemorate her. She wants Pip to write on a leaf of paper bearing her name another declaration – 'I forgive her' – as though the signature of her wounded double would authenticate her redemption for posterity. She wants his written forgiveness to supersede the dual monument of her vengeance – the mansion laid to waste and Estella. Where seeing her wound doubled in him breaks her hysteric dissimulation, receiving his forgiveness finalises her spectral existence and allows for the introduction of real death. The restaging of her psychic trauma in this intermediary space is then doubly successful because it offers her both the triumph of seeing her vindictive plot completed and a triumph over this narcissistically informed plot by virtue of Pip's pardon.

Already outside the house, Pip has the second hallucination of Miss Havisham hanging from a beam and returns to her rooms just in time to see her body, seated in a ragged chair close to the hearth, catch fire. The hysterical break down becomes complete as her 'faded bridal dress' turns to tinder, no longer 'alight but falling in a black shower'. Pulling off the great cloth from the banquet table to smother the flames, Pip also drags down 'the heap of rottenness in the midst', with all the ugly parasites sheltered there. In an uncanny manner her real dying repeats the dying scene she had prematurely invoked. Her hurt body, endangered primarily by nervous shock, is indeed 'laid upon the great table', now bare of the ghastly rotting bridal paraphernalia, so as to dress her injuries.

Though all her own clothes are burnt, she still has, to Pip's eye 'something of her old ghastly bridal appearance', because they have covered her with white cotton-wool. Lying thus, the phantom air still upon her, she speaks, at first collectedly and then, once her mind begins to wander (as her body used to at night), she utters over and over again the three sentences that declare her recognition of guilt, her excuse and her desire to be forgiven ('What have I done', 'When she first came, I meant to save her from misery like mine', 'Take the pencil and write under my name, "I forgive her" '). As though to complete her last wish, Pip leans over and kisses the dying bride just as the lips 'not stopping for being touched' once again form the third sentence (415). Miss Havisham's displayed dying body, incessantly repeating these three sentences, is possibly one of the most ghastly images for the way the triadic desire – for death, for a lover and for self-representation – inscribes itself at a feminine body. In a sense analogous to Pip's language of love, her utterances of remorse emerge from a deanimated body, and like his, they too are comparable to blood welling up from an inward wound and gushing out. Her body is merely the medium for a language that issues from Otherness, in her case the superego as the locus of guilt.

Her unconscious body, incessantly speaking even as she dies, serves as the most powerful trope in this text for the way self-representation and storytelling are an act caught between double and absence. In the absence of her conscious self, deployed of all her bridal/burial dresses, her last death representation fulfills all the fatal images and lethal enactments she had previously designed for herself – the transformation of her mansion into an open grave from which she, as revenant, authored the lives of her self-seeking relatives, moulded the nature of Estella and fed Pip's fancies even as she excessively exhibited her own dying process. At the same time it supersedes these fictions precisely because the figural becomes literal, because the potential is fulfilled, the transitional space finalised, as real death confirms and concludes, in a last moment of doubling now irreversibly arrested in absence, all previous representations and expectations of dying. Though Dickens's second ending of the novel undoes the unremitting cruelty of Miss Havisham's materialized fictions, uniting Estella and Pip after years of suffering, even this mitigated version preserves the uncanniness that is rendered in that last image of the dying spectral bride. This image offers no closed grave and restituting tomb, no peaceful body serenely smiling in death but rather the burnt, unconscious body of a woman repeating over and over again her three final sentences – the figure of death speaking.

The production of fiction requires an absence from worldly reality and a duplication of the teller in a site of potentiality positioned between life and death. The fictions produced are contingent on a beloved woman, who is herself marked by a bodily absence of sorts – the socially absent spectral bride Miss Havisham, whose heart was broken by a fickle lover and Estella, who, lacking a heart, resists Pip's romantic infatuation only to disclose the illusion of the lover's discourse. In the sense of Foucault's mirror, erected against death, Miss Havisham's final act of self-representation – the last three sentences her unconscious body utters –

articulates the endless resourcefulness of language, which headed toward death and emerging from death turns back upon itself and gives birth to its own image in a process of seemingly limitless self-reflections.[4] The next chapter is set against such endless free play of a death-inspired poetic language by moving once again to the historical anecdote. In my last group of dead brides, real deaths in history engender their reformulation in poetic or epistolary narratives.

Notes to Chapter 16

1 M. Blanchot, 1949. I am also referring to M. Foucault's discussion of the proximity between authorship and death, 1977.
2 A. Green, 1978.
3 A. Green, 1978, p. 288.
4 M. Foucault, 1977.

17

The dead beloved as muse

Woman is not a poet: She is either muse or she is nothing.
Robert Graves

Of course, a woman is the muse. If she were the maker instead of the muse
and opened her mouth, she would blast the notion of poetic creativity apart.
Kathy Acker

In Berlin, on the night of 29 December, 1834, Charlotte Stieglitz (aged twenty-
eight) sent her husband Heinrich to a concert in order to be alone while
committing an incredible act. After having washed, dressed in a clean white
nightgown and placed a white cap on her head, she went to bed and there stabbed
herself directly in the heart with a dagger she had bought as a bride.[1] In her
farewell note, strategically placed so that her husband would find it immediately
upon his return, Charlotte suggested that her suicide be understood as an act of
self-sacrifice meant to inflict such pain and sense of loss on her manic-depressive
husband that he would break free from his psychic lethargy. In this way she hoped
to liberate his petrified poetic powers. His wife's violent death would enable him
to regain what he had lost – his self and his poetic genius. Indeed, Heinrich
Stieglitz justified his wife's suicide by writing in his diary two days after her death,
'Her great sacrificial death, the sense of redemption, which she strove for, must
not be a lost action. To comemorate her in public, grandly and freely, will be my
aim in the future. I will thereby gather strength.'[2]

Although Charlotte's death failed to inspire a new phase of poetic creativity in
her husband, it did make her into a public muse. Triggering a vicarious pain, her
suicide provoked a plethora of interpretations from her contemporaries. Some
saw her sacrifice as an act of true feminine genius, bridging the gap between flesh
and spirit, others as an attempt to renew not only her husband's stifled energies
but in fact the suppressed or thwarted energies of an entire generation of
Germans suffering under the constraints of Biedermeier society. Opponents of
the writings of the *Jungdeutsche*, who idealised her death, in turn saw her suicide
as an emblem of the dangers of free morals. Far more striking than the ideological

intentions inherent in the texts written about her, however, is the fact that Charlotte, who had never had any public role during her lifetime, came by her suicide to leave such an impressive mark in the public realm. One has the impression that in its freshly washed Biedermeier garments, with the red blood flowing from her pale skin to the white bed linen, her dead body became the site for the interpretive inscriptions of her survivors – inscriptions that say more about those interpreting than about the object being interpreted.

Susanne Ledanff suggests that what makes Charlotte's story so compelling is that she took the bombastic metaphors of self-obliterating love, heroism, self-sacrifice, and liberation of the soul from the body seriously, rather than treating them as quotations from previous cultural texts. She seems to have made the fatal mistake of applying literary conventions to her own personal history. Yet even more disquieting, and, perhaps, more fascinating, is the strange mixture of seduction by a false pathos of romantic and pietistic delusions and the calculation of effect inherent in her act, the doubling of deluded victim and consciously responsible actress. For she exposes the conventions of feminine self-sacrifice at exactly the same moment that she fatally enacts them. Far from being innocent or naive, her suicide is pregnant with literary citations. It is, in fact a cliché – suggestive of both Werther's and Caroline von Günderode's suicides[3] after failed romances, of the iconography of sacrificial brides and martyrs dressed in white, for whom death is a mystic marriage and an erotic unity with God, as well as that of women dying in childbirth. Her act perverts the image of the selflessly devoted housewife by introducing violence into the idyllic bedroom, by adding self-assertion to self-submission. Her self-sacrifice is so disquieting because it is both an imitation of cultural clichés, hovering between irony and kitsch, and a self-conscious effort to make herself into an object of discourse. Though she wrote only a handful of poems and letters, she assured herself a distinctive place in literary history by becoming the author of her own death, with her staged dead body serving as her superlative art work.

Owing to the exaggerated manner in which she performed her suicide, how-ever, this act also lays bare several implications of the traditional notion of creative power as an external gift bestowed upon a chosen artist by his muse. Because Woman is positioned in western cultural discourse as the very substance of man's poetic work, de Beauvoir argues, 'it is understandable that she should appear as his inspiration'. As a muse she 'mediates between the creator and the natural springs whence he must draw. Woman's spirit is profoundly sunk in nature, and it is through her that man will sound the depths of silence and of the fecund night.'[4] Yet at the same time that woman inspires in the poet a knowledge of nature he lacks, the poetic act, producing an autonomous text, serves to efface the materiality Woman stands for. As the poet repeats the depths of silence and the fecund night in his artistic representations – images which one could say are drawn from the enmeshed paradigms of femininity and death – he seemingly triumphs over and defies his own mortality, his material facticity.

What Charlotte Stieglitz's fatal exaggeration so uncannily discloses is that death transforms the body of a woman into the source of poetic inspiration precisely because it creates and gives corporality to a loss or absence. Since her gift to the poet is the removal of her body, what occurs is the exchange of one loss for another, the implication being that her presence has displaced his poetic genius. This equation reveals the central dichotomy of the muse–artist relation. The poet must choose between a corporally present woman and the muse, a choice of the former precluding the latter. What must occur is the transformation of a direct erotic investment of the beloved woman into a mitigated one (of the same woman who is now absent, or of another woman who never was present). The distance created by loss, the shift from presence to absence, opens up the space for poetic creation. In this respect the relation between muse and artist is, of course, only another example for the way any form of symbolisation requires the disappearance of natural presence.[5] However, although any form of absence would suffice, the death of the beloved is its perfect embodiment, not only because it seems to secure the distance and the loss for ever but also because, in the gesture of the fetish, it creates a monument to precisely that unencompassable body of the maternal, factual, materiality as death which it also tries to deny. In an uncanny manner Charlotte Stieglitz seems to collapse Graves's definition of woman's relation to art. By making her self nothing she makes herself into the ultimate incorporation of the muse.

Charlotte's suicide, and the rhetoric surrounding it, point to the inter-connection between artistic renewal as a form of giving birth and death. Heinrich's diary entry for 19 January describes her act in the terms of a Caesarean – 'to save the child, the mother lovingly sacrificed herself.'[6] Charlotte herself repeatedly wrote to her friends that through her death she hoped to mother the genius of her husband while at the same time endowing him with the faculty of giving birth. For his poetry, written 'in memory of' the deceased, by invoking and making present her who is absent, will be a rhetorical animation of the dead beloved.[7] The disturbing twist Charlotte's suicide gives to the rela-tionship between artist and muse is the suggestion that poetic renewal – the birth of the poet – necessarily entails someone else's death. Artistic symbolisation entails the 'murder of the soma', a fading and returning of the maternal body. In this case the maternal body is refound at the site of the beloved in that the bride dies not only like but indeed as the mother of the poet. Extreme as Charlotte Stieglitz's form of self-textualisation might be, it is nevertheless only an exagger-ation of the changed conception of the muse that informs nineteenth-century imagination. In order to discuss the inversion that occurs here it is necessary, therefore, to recall the original function ascribed to the muse.

While it is not clear whether in classical Greek culture the muse had an objective divine reality or was merely a projection, a familiar and convenient metaphor for the creative process, her invocation points to a conception of the poet's gift as being dependent on an appeal to a higher power other than itself. Divine inspiration was the designation given to that element in poetry which exceeded craftsmanship and the exchange between poet and muse implied a moment of loss of self and possession by an Other. The muse was thought to speak through the poet, making him the medium of her speech. She was mother to the poet in the sense that she literally inspired by singing her material to him – she animated his poetic ability by breathing her song into him. As Plato in the famous passage in *Phaedrus* explains, the muse was the source of divine possession or madness, stimulating the lyric poet's untrodden soul to rapt passionate expression: 'glorifying the countless mighty deeds of ancient times for the instruction of posterity'.[8] For a poet not to acknowledge the holy breath of the muses as quintessential to poetic creation and to depend on his skill alone was to result in poetic failure and public oblivion. The self-sufficient poet and his work would, in Plato's word's be 'brought to nought by the poetry of madness . . . their place . . . nowhere to be found'. For a mythic version of the muse's intolerance for rivalry one could cite the story of Thamyris, as found in Homer. Because he boasted that he could surpass them in a competition, the muses maimed him, took away his 'voice of wonder' and made him a 'singer without memory'.[9] Ecstatically devoted to the muse, the poet's utterances were also meant to glorify her, which suggests the occurrence of a two-way exchange. For the muse's gift to the poet allows him to give birth to a text celebrating her. She inspires or animates his poetic power so that he may, by virtue of his invocation, in turn reanimate the muse. As a figure of inspiration, she is directly addressed, and serves a threefold function in this poetic dialogue. She is simultaneously maieutic producer, object of reference and privileged addressee of the poet's speech. In addition she is always incompletely accessible, always beyond reach. For the rhetoric of invocation, always one of apostrophe, requires her absence while at the same time making the lack of presence, the distance of the addressee, its privileged theme and causing her, as the object reanimated by the poet's speech, to take on the status of presence-in-absence (life-in-death), a kind of double presence.

Significantly, the muses were the daughters of Zeus and Mnemosyne – goddess of memory. As mother of the muses, Mnemosyne is also the mother of the source of poetic authority itself and as such the point of origination to be invoked in the poetic act. She is the powerful agent whereby the gap is closed between any poetic endevour and a timeless source of memory, even though her voice can exist only in absence, as the point of origination, simultaneously put under erasure and articulated in the daughters who repeat and indirectly represent her. The poet's apostrophe not only served to render the bodily absent addressee present, but also through her to make present an absent past knowledge or alterior truth. The muses not only initiated the poet into passionate expression, as Hesiod's archetypal relation of his poetic experience at the foot of Mount Helican suggests, but also served as the source of knowledge outside the poet's realm of experience. Poets invoked the muses to make present what they were not present to see, needed them to remember, including that which was never part of their own personal history. By addressing the absent muse, the poet attempted to overcome his absence at previous historical events, his lack of complete knowledge. Among the knowledge the poet lacks, the event of personal history from which he is absent, is of course that of death, with the muses making present that facticity which is irrevocably beyond the knowledge of the living.

In the course of the centuries, the vitality the muse was said to possess paled, as Steele Commager puts it, into an abstraction, so that one could characterise her 'biography as the history of a fading metaphor'. What in Classical Greece was a conviction became in Augustan Rome a conceit. By assigning to the muses a merely decorative status or seeing them reincarnated in specific human beings, as Propertius does when he declares his mistress Cynthia's folly to serve as source and subject of his poetry, the poet 'no longer feels himself the creature of some higher power, but assumes that his own creative potency is sufficient.'[10] In the same rhetorical move that gives a concrete body to the muse, secularises her so to speak, she is denied that divine power which would be other and more encompassing than the poet's. As such she becomes a figure for the poet's peculiarly own poetic powers, mothering genius that is innate rather than inspired. She transforms into a metaphor for the poet as 'possessing a special ability rather than as possessed by it', with the apostrophe addressing 'his own peculiar genius.'[11] As the muse is supplanted by the poet's *usus*, the notion that poetic inspiration implies a fluctuating relation between poet and radical Otherness turns into one where the boundary between the self and the other is clearly drawn, with the poet self-sufficient, relying not on alterity but on his own experience to justify the truth of his song. The paradox inherent to this changed poet–muse relation is such that while the poet is portrayed as being possessed, it is he who possesses; while the poet seems dependent on the inspiration by another, he is the lover and begetter with the muse as the beloved, the begotten. The poet 'asserts his power over his creative inspirer even as he invokes her (in) an act of appropriation and control,' DeShazer argues, 'absorbing her creative energy into himself.'[12]

What became occluded as the vitality of the muse paled into abstraction was the notion that the source of poetic inspiration as possession points to difference and alterity within, which radically disrupts notions of ego-stability and which gives figure to a lack or gap, a real void grounding artistic representation. Originally, Bloom notes, the function of the muse was to make the poet remember what he has forgotten, 'that he is bound to origins and not to ends, that his autonomy is (at best) a saving fiction'.[13] In the Romantic and modern inversion, a muse is invoked in the poetic act of such remembering, yet the apostrophe is aimed at ambivalently preserving a blindness toward the castrative threat of death that is accrued by birth. These historical events and the texts they engendered illustrate the move from the body (with its inscription by maternal–materiality–mortality) to representations, as the sign of a symbolic, autonomous self-reliancy beyond the facticity which a position in personal history implies. Ironically, the fading metaphor, used to put real alterity under erasure, used to remember only impartially the forgotten origin and lack of autonomy, is revitalised by turning to real death.

Remarkable about the inversion of the poet–muse relation that once again becomes prominent at the turn of the eighteenth century is the fact that the status of muse is transferred again on to a corporally existent beloved, only now she is dying or already dead. Signification on the boundary between life and art is once again sanctioned by death, but the thematic interplay between poetic creation and loss, distance, or absence of the beloved is given a new twist. The rhetorical invocation refers quite literally to a female body, as though not only the poet's gift but also the fading metaphor were to be reanimated. In the course of this reconception several important changes occur. It is no longer the poet, daring to disacknowledge the muse, who is punished for his audacity but instead the woman chosen to be muse. What she gives is not her song but rather her body and her life. And though it is her death which inspires the poet and takes possession of him, whether it provokes the experience of ecstasy or the production of narratives, the concept of possession has also taken on a duplicitous character. While the original act of taking possession and giving birth to the poet is mimicked, the Romantic inversion is in fact an example of the poet's taking ultimate control over the departed woman.

Inspirational power is first drawn from a dead beloved and then rendered in poetic narratives commenting on this exchange. Far from wishing to preserve a beloved on earth beyond her death, these mourning poets need absence to create, at the same time that they need the fructifying power of the dead as mediators with that Otherness which lies beyond the knowledge of any survivor. Here the poet, positioned between life and death, is a mourner and his act of remembering serves as a dialogue with a dead historical woman as well as with previous cultural texts. With the dead beloved acting as source for poetic inspiration, what is at stake is the preference for distance, for the textual copy of the beloved, for a vicarious and mitigated Romantic experience. Though it is clear that reanimated, the beloved muse is under the poet's control and that with her body obliterated in the course of such a translation into a trope she serves as emblem for his projections, what remains undecided is whether the reanimation is a triumph over death or an obsessive attachment to the dead.

To write about someone who is gone – the gesture of the 'fort–da' game – manipulates absence and delays as long as possible the moment when conceptually absence turns into death.[14] But when the object of this invocation is already dead, whose death is being deferred? Is the invocation of the dead beloved an attempt to preserve her artificially against death, or an attempt to eternalise the poet's skill? Whose triumph is it, when the poet reanimates and resurrects a dead beloved, and what desire is enacted when the artist defies the irrevocability of death? Above all, what is ultimately being signified by this dialogue? While the addressee of this invocation is a beloved woman quite literally dead, she simultaneously serves a figurative function, namely as metonymy for death. Although she is being reanimated, she is likewise being effaced again when used as an emblem for something else, to which she is (in the end) incidental. Indeed, the original seems to be effaced more than once, literally by virtue of her death, and rhetorically not only because she is replaced by a text, but also because she serves an allegorical function amid this replacement.

Precisely in her proximity to death Virginia Clemm unwittingly served as the muse who gave birth to Edgar Allan Poe's creative powers. The pale and fragile cousin whom he married in 1835, when she was thirteen years old, ruptured a blood vessel in singing seven years later and, never fully recovering from the accident, lived until her death on 30 January, 1847 in precarious health. During her protracted period of dying she incessantly oscillated between a seeming restoration of health and relapses into pain, engendering, as Poe's letter quoted in chapter 17 illustrates, the same shifting between serious illness and health in her husband, as he also moved between hope for recovery and despair. As the beloved, dying from a consumption which was from the start hopeless yet which kept her alive for five years, Virginia repeatedly served as model for his half-dead, prematurely buried, or (through metempsychosis) resurrected heroines Madeline, Morella, Berenice and Ligeia. Her illness, which forbade any direct consummation of erotic desire, inspired those texts in which the fascination for a woman is dependent precisely on her unattainability – that is, her being physically absent while present when remembered or artistically recreated. Poe's narrators hold on to an intermediary position, balanced between an embrace of death and a successful denial or repression of it. The continued bond with a departed lover marks death not as the sought-for goal but rather allows the speaker to acknowledge both the mysterious way in which death penetrates the world of the living, while using his poetic inscriptions to fill the gap created by loss. Virginia Poe, whether as model or as implicit addressee, serves as a signifier for the poet's own psychic states, with the focus on where she leads. Her invocation has as reference her husband's ambivalent states of psychic petrification caused by an obsessional clinging to the dead and the hopeful defiance of or triumph over death by virtue of poetic inscription.

A comparison of the poems 'Ulalume' (1847) and 'Annabel Lee' (1849) will serve to illustrate these two variations. In the first poem, the speaker describes his involuntary return to the vault of his beloved Ulalume. While he has repressed all memory of her death, signalled by his not recognising the path he is moving along, she is preserved in the form of an incorporation in his unconscious, poetically rendered as a name 'on the door of this legended tomb'. The speaker depicts himself as unwittingly possessed by the dead, his return as an unconscious obsession. Ulalume's vampiristic hold stands in direct rivalry to Psyche, representing the soul's search for a new erotic attachment, so that her warning 'let us fly' remains unheeded. Poe describes a psychic impasse, for while the dead beloved draws the speaker to her tomb, binding him so that he is not free to find an alternative object of desire among the living, she does not lead him to death. While Poe leaves unexplained the kind of erotic satisfaction such an arrest of libidinal drives entails, he makes explicit that the speaker is in a duplicitous position, neither directed toward the living nor willing to give up life. His speaker experiences death by proxy, in the sense that his incorporation of the dead beloved turns his emotional state into a death-in-life.

'Annabel Lee', implicitly addressed to Virginia, can be read as the jubilant counterpart to the obsessive-compulsive form of memory. Although the speaker invokes his lost bride in order to idealise their love, this recollection ultimately serves to illustrate his imaginative and poetic powers, by virtue of which he places himself beyond the natural law of death. The rarity of their love – 'more than love' – consists for one thing in its exclusivity: 'she lived with no other thought than to love and be loved by me'. The measure of its value lies in the fact that it both attracted the coveting envy of the Seraphs and surpassed the result of their usurping desire. For while Annabel's 'high kinsmen' bear her away and 'shut her up in a sepulchre' (a metaphor used to indicate her affinity to angels), his imaginative powers guarantee that nothing 'can ever dissever' their souls. For his response to the physical loss of his beloved is to endow his surroundings imaginatively with her ubiquitous presence and resurrect her in his poetic utterance ('the moon never beams without bringing me dreams ... the stars never rise but I see the bright eyes / Of the beautiful Annabel Lee'). While he is drawn to the tomb of his beloved ('all the night-tide'), this attraction to the site of death ultimately leads to its poetic rendition, a sepulchre surpassing her tomb, because it not only preserves her bones but makes her image present-in-absence.

While on a literal level the invocatory reanimation of Annabel serves to prove the inseparability of their souls ('I lie down by the side / Of . . . my bride / In her sepulchre'), the displaced signified of this figure is the power of his poetic triumph over death. The focus in these depictions of the presence-in-absence of a dead beloved shifts to the question of what it means to maintain a fixed distance, regardless of whether this leads to compulsive repetition or to compensation and substitution of loss through poetic resurrection, to an expression of the unfulfillability of desire.

A plethora of other examples can be cited to illustrate how the death of a beloved turns her into the muse for her mourning lover's poetic inspiration. Novalis, Friedrich von Hardenberg, minutely records his response to the death of Sophie von Kuehn (on 19 March 1797) over a period of three months in his journal and reanimates the dead beloved precisely because he wants to be made the object of death's desire.[15] Waldo Emerson used journal entries and poetic fragments to communicate with his wife Ellen after her premature death from tuberculosis on 8 February , 1831, until opening her coffin on 29th March puts an end to his invocation of the idealised dead woman. Nerval offers a poetic rendition of his relation to the actress Jenny Colon in *Aurélia ou la rve de la vie* (1855), with her death and burial serving as the precondition for mystic visions and an imagined union beyond worldly existence.

Dante Gabriel Rossetti's poem 'The Blessed Damozel' (1873), composed ten years after the death of Elizabeth Siddall, stages the poet's dialogue with a dead beloved, who like his own wife is ten years dead.[17] He reanimates his lost beloved so as to fashion an image of himself after death, for the speech she delivers in his vision anticipates his entrance into heaven and describes how she will initiate him into celestial mysteries. Though inspired by the dead beloved, his invocation in fact endows her with speech, and the object of her discourse is a representation of his resurrection after death and a legitimation of his earthly love by virtue of its perfect celestial repetition.

One could further cite James Thomson who, in explicit imitation of Novalis (whose poetry he translated), chose the death of his fourteen year-old beloved, Matilda Weller (1853) as his poetic inspiration and, like his literary predecessor, made an icon of his relation to the dead bride.[18] Repeatedly throughout his life he returned to a rendition of this tragic event in poems and prose fantasies. Or one could cite the seven poems by W. B. Yeats entitled 'Upon a Dying Lady', written while Mabel Beardsley was dying of cancer in 1913, but published only after her death in 1917 and documenting his fascination for the 'strange charm – the pathetic gaiety' his friend exhibits in the face of an imminent approach of death.[19] Or Thomas Hardy's *Poems of 1912–13*, the sequence of elegies which he wrote for his first wife Emma Gifford shortly after her death, on the eve of his second marriage to Florence Dugdale.

In all cases – in the absence of the beloved, the poet can best picture her, namely as his creation, with a reference not so much to any historical reality as to his poetic gift. The poet faces the void of death in order to defy mortality and represents himself as survivor, even if the survival at stake is a reanimation in the celestial beyond. Hélène Cixous distinguishes between two forms of libidinal economy – one a masculine economy of preservation, the other a feminine one of excessive exhaustion – which, she adds are, nevertheless, both ruled by the relation each subject has to death.[20] The former desire to preserve implies a stasis and repetition which inevitably touches what it seeks to avoid – death. The latter, the transgressive delight in risk and expenditure, inevitably appears as a form of animate mobility, despite its embrace of fatal risk. In his relation to the death of a beloved, and in his representation of her in the medium of inanimate images and texts that inspire and conserve both his romantic and his artistic desires, the poet assumes the masculine position of preservation, while the beloved lives out the feminine position of excess by virtue of her real embrace of death.

That the poet not only gains his artistic powers at the loss of a beloved but that he prefers his reanimated version of her to the real woman is explicitly thematised with astonishing candidness by Henry James. Like Novalis, he recorded his reactions to the death of a woman – his New York cousin Minny Temple, who died of tuberculosis while he was visiting England. In several letters, James explains wherein the charm and satisfaction of privileging a supplement lies.[21] The most striking feature of his response is its ambivalence. He confesses to 'feeling a singular mixture of pleasure and pain', asks both his mother and his brother for details about her last hours, finding 'something so appealing in the pathos of her final weakness and decline' while expressing gratitude that he did not himself see her suffer and materially change. While he repeatedly asserts that 'it is too soon to talk of Minny's death or pretend to feel it', he expresses a certain satisfaction at having written more than twelve pages about her to his brother. This preference for the 'soft idea' over the 'hard fact' in respect to Minny's death signals the more global tendency to prefer a fixed distance, to privilege the mitigated and vicarious over the immediate. It seems that this distance allows the departed beloved to become an object entirely at his interpretative disposal and as such the central stake in his self-definition as an artist.

For Minny's death is not only the key to the past, inspiring a host of memories, but also the means by which he can take possession of this past and structure it as a meaningful whole. He reiterates that her death is a definite gain – 'the happiest, fact, [*sic*] almost in her whole career'. While there may be a certain validity in this appraisal when one considers her illness, it seems that the gain is more his than hers. For as a dead body she becomes an 'unfaltering luminary in the mind', an image. As a living body she was a 'divinely restless spirit – essentially one of the "irreconcilables" ' – 'flickering' in the sense that, like any living being, she was ambivalent and fickle enough to elude any attempt at fixing her meaning. As a dead body, however, she is translated from 'this changing realm of fact to the steady realm of thought'. As an image preserved in his mind she becomes a figure of whose stable meaning he cannot only be sure, but which he can also semantically designate at his will. She can stand for 'serenity and purity' as a 'sort of measure and standard of brightness and repose' or she can take on the function of representing aspects of his life. He sees their relation as an exchange of energies – she 'sinking out of brightness and youth into decline and death', while he 'crawls from weakness and inaction and suffering into strength and health and hope'.

By reducing her purpose in his life to 'the bright intensity of her example', the emphasis yet again is on where she leads. Her inspiration has a double goal, for she not only reanimates him by serving as the guiding example toward an embrace of life while herself yielding this intensity, standing as an emblem of his youth and the end of an episode in his development. As a dead beloved she also becomes a privileged object for memory – a 'pregnant reference in future years'. Embalmed in his mind, like Snow White 'locked away, incorruptibly, within the crystal walls of the past' and waiting to be reanimated, she becomes above all the measure for his skills at recollecting and creating. While her life was a 'question', disquieting because he could not offer 'the elements of an answer', her absence could be met with such satisfaction because it both fixes her into a stable figure 'incorruptible' and opens the space for poetic interpretations within which he could design, shape, and recreate her (and their relationship) in infinite variations.

In his work, James repeatedly used the memory of Minny as model for his heroines, notably Isabel Archer and Milly Theale (as well as in his autobiography, *Notes of a Son and Brother*). Yet he also wrote narratives which, doubling his own biography, can be read as a critical reflection on his relation to a dead muse and the aesthetics inherent in this relation, above all from the point of view of mourning and erotic desire. In 'The Altar of the Dead', (1895) the protagonist Stransom creates a shrine of remembrance for his 'religion of the Dead', as a means by which to stay 'in regular communion with these alternative associates', of whom Mary Antrim, who died after their wedding day was fixed, is the central voice. He understands this dialogue as a 'connection more charming' than any possible in life (87) and designates the effort of keeping the dead alive by force of his memory to be the central purpose of his life. What might on one level be seen as an attempt to possess the past, animating a departed lover in order to appropriate the shared experience she metonymically stands for, turns into Stransom's possession of the dead. As the central measure used to evaluate and interpret his world, his dead also eclipse other emotional bonds. Because this form of 'communion' allows the absent woman to prove more powerful than her corporally present rival (signalled by the fact that the latter remains 'nameless'), it becomes for Stransom a way to shield himself from any direct erotic investment and he becomes emotionally deathlike. The exchange places both in an intermediary position. Her presence-in-absence is reciprocated by his absence-in-presence, his inability to invest the living, immediate world with any form of desire. Ultimately she inspires the wish to share her position, to become the last candle on the altar, and as such fill the existent gap with his own body.

However, while the nameless woman is rejected as a direct object of desire, it is for her benefit that he wishes to translate himself into the one last candle to fill and complete the altar, asking 'Isn't that what you wanted?' (118). Their dispute had centred on the fact that she used his altar to worship the memory of the one friend he had rejected among his dead – Acton Hague. The knowledge he gains in the church when Mary's 'far-off face' smiles at him from the 'glory of heaven' is an insight not only into the rapture that his communion with Mary affords him, but also that this is marred by the fact that he refuses bliss to the other woman. Death suggests itself as the resolution of his ambivalent position between the two women and of his jealousy for the unnamed woman's communion with Acton because it allows him to appropriate Acton's position and cast himself as the absent addressee of her worship. In what seems to be both paradoxical and repetitious, his conception of his own death entails both a unity with Mary and the opening of a new gap in respect to the unnamed woman and leads to the preservation of the intermediary position, which is informed by a tension between the living and dead. It translates into a glorification of loss and distance, not its effacement. His loss is also seen as his gain, because the distance of death is understood as the way to have a communion with the nameless woman that would not be possible in life.

While Stransom recalls Charlotte Stieglitz's act, he inverts the Romantic version by imagining for himself the position of the muse, who will inflict loss on a survivor as a way to procure his reanimation. What is striking is both the reversal of gender roles, making the man muse to the woman, and the fact that this conception takes *ad absurdum* the traditional privileging of a fixed distance over immediacy, the reanimation over direct presence. In so doing, the text brings into play an element of ironic distance between protagonist and implied reader, who, cast into the role of outside observer, is led to question and destabilise the primacy of mitigation and approximation. The narrative stance of James is in itself duplicitous, in that, without condemning or offering an alternative, it simply leaves the question of gain and loss open. Graves suggests that when a muse turns into a domestic woman she fades in her ability to inspire, and engenders the poet's demise. This leads one to speculate whether the Romantic fascination with the death of a young bride is not connected with a desire to prevent the muse from turning domestic and thus ceasing to function as inspirational source.[22]

I began this chapter with an anecdote where a woman's suicide uncannily transcribed literary clichés into real death in such a way as to position her staged corpse ambivalently between victimisation and self-assertion. It is, therefore, only fitting to end with another revitalisation of transmitted clichés involving femininity and death, where it is precisely the hyperbolic mode which also reintroduces ambivalence. Much has been written about the allusions and parodies in *Lolita*; about Lolita as trope for artistic imagination; about the way Nabokov's muse is as often language as Mnemosyne, following his own assertion that this novel was the record of his love affair with the English language more than with the romantic novel.[23] Since its publication Nabokov's novel has incited debates about whether his protagonist Humbert Humbert is a madman, a criminal, a victim, a lover or a poet; whether his narrative should be condemned on ethical grounds or praised for its aesthetic merits.

I will limit myself to a discussion of the plethora of allusions to the conjunction of femininity and death – dead mothers, Dante's idealised Beatrice, Bürger's vampire-beloved Lenore, Mérimée's fickle Carmen and Poe's dead wife Virginia Clemm, recreated as Annabel Lee.[24] This excessive citation, as well as the enmeshment of seemingly disparate topoi, paradoxically uses the strategy of ironic distance to disclose the implied effacement of any reference to a world outside the image repertoire of the narrator. In this narrative an excessively figural rendition of the beloved 'killed' into the trope of muse (with this gesture supported by references to other texts undertaking the same figure), inevitably also articulates the real subject position of the effaced child-bride Dolores Haze, though only uncannily, as a presence in absence. As Appel suggests, the novel is 'a parody of death with real suffering in it'.[25]

The fictional forward by John Ray, Jr., Ph.D. situates the ensuing confession within the frame of a dual death – H.H. dies of coronary thrombosis in legal captivity after having completed his writing of 'Lolita' in 'tombal seclusion', thirty-eight days before Mrs Richard F. Schiller does the same in childbed on Christmas Day 1952, after having given birth to a stillborn girl. In the most literal sense, then, the public birth of the text is grounded on the death of its author and its privileged object of representation. Indeed H.H. ends his confession with the wish that 'this memoir . . . be published only when Lolita is no longer alive. Thus neither of us is alive when the reader opens this book' (307). Yet the death of the actual girl who inspires the poet H.H. is significant in more than one way. In his postscript Nabokov himself isolates the image of the 'pale, pregnant, beloved, irretrievable Dolly Schiller dying in gray Star' as one of 'the nerves of the novel' (314).

More crucially, perhaps, by having his infatuated poet explicitly designate her death as the condition for a reading of his text, her actual death completes his figural killing. Their final scene of meeting in fact works on the basis of a transposition of the actual into the imaginary. When H.H., invoking Carmen one last time, asks Dolores to come with him and she replies 'No', he writes 'Then I pulled out my automatic – I mean, this is the kind of fool thing a reader might suppose I did. It never even occurred to me to do it.' Yet in the next sentence, the parody of a murder fantasy is undone, for the girl waving goodbye is described as 'my American sweet immortal dead love; for she is dead and immortal if you are reading this' (278).

The movement of signifiers is from a literary death (Carmen's) to its parodic disruption, to a metaphor where the girl stands for his dead love, to its literalisation by virtue of a reference to an anticipated real death. This movement from death fantasy, through banalisation, to literalisation of the trope also occurs in respect to her maternity. Upon seeing Dolores again, H.H. admits, 'the death I had kept conjuring up for three years was as simple as a bit of dried wood. She was frankly and hugely pregnant' (267). Yet reality catches up and confirms this fantasy in the sense that, if figurally a nymphet dies once she turns mother, Lolita literally dies giving birth. What the narrative frame states on the surface, then, is that while for H.H. Lolita merely dies figurally into irretrievable absence (her smiling 'no') and into a trope ('immortal dead love'), she actually dies as Dolly Schiller for Nabokov; her corpse feeds the text not the narrator. Yet by implication, H.H. invokes her actual death even as he also invokes her eternal survival as a signifier. He can accept her rebuttal, the loss of this desired object, because in his narrative representation he immediately exchanges the actual girl chanting 'Good by-aye' with a premonition of the text he will have written about her. As in the 'fort–da' game, he translates her forced absence into his symbolic representation where he has seeming control over her death and her immortality; the one being the condition, the other the result of his poetic activity.

In the last sentence of his memoirs, anticipating his own death and invoking that of his lost beloved, H.H. in a sense places himself and his Lolita between the absent and the double, when he claims that his finished fiction is 'the only immortality you and I may share, my Lolita' (307). From the perspective of the poet, this is a gesture defying death, for he eternalises not only his image of her, 'my Lolita', and concomitant the fiction of their love (their shared immortality), but above all his signature. In respect to the represented woman, however, this gesture commemorates the absence of Dolores in the text. Invisible beneath the tropes and allusions to feminine figures of death, she marks the site where absence inscribes itself rhetorically into the text only to be recuperated on one side by real death and on the other by the poet's recourse to symbolic immortality

– to 'prophetic sonnets, the refuge of art'.

Framed within the context of the event leading up to its writing – namely Dolores Schiller's refusal to leave her husband – the first paragraph of H.H.'s memoirs can be read as an apostrophe in a dual sense. He not only addresses a beloved who is by implication dead but also one who is decontextualised: 'Lolita, light of my life, fire of my loins . . . She was Lo . . . She was Lola . . . She was Dolly . . . She was Dolores . . . But in my arms she was always Lolita' (9). This list of names in part serves to show the various roles she could be associated with as well as the chain of supplementary signifiers attached to her body. Above all, however, by addressing her without a patronymic, the narrator weakens her representation as a historical person and emphasises her function as a freely floating signifier, an empty sign he possesses and on to which he can impose alterior meanings to produce a supplementary textual matrix. By privileging language over the body, restructuring Dolores Haze into the sign Lolita ('My sin, my soul'), H.H. undertakes a figural 'murder of the soma', a blindness toward this girl's irreducible alterity, so as to make her signify his desire. He can master her material absence (the *fort* of the mother-to-be), by virtue of a symbolic control over her presence.

Because the real beloved is absent she must be represented and because the woman's body is missing, stereotypes of femininity that seem to assure the narrator are possible. Yet, in this recreation, the perturbing difference she marked throughout in a somatic and a semiotic sense – because she eventually succeeded in running away from him even as his designations repeatedly missed their mark – is only imperfectly elided. Like a fetishist, H.H. commemorates with this narrative the castrative wound to his narcissism it is meant to negate, namely that Dolores successfully eludes his grasp because his love is a non-reciprocated fiction.

Furthermore, to heighten the paradox, the language he uses to effect a translation from the ungraspable soma to the controllable sema, so as to occlude uncanny difference within (femininity and death's encroachment on life), repeatedly articulates precisely this 'castrative' paradigm because his imagery compulsively returns to feminine figures of death. Nabokov effects a brilliant critique of the dangers and necessities of the imaginary, in that he shows Dolores Haze fading beneath H.H.'s tropes and allusions even as she eludes his physical and mental grasp. H.H.'s success in translating her into the completely textualised Lolita neither solves her enigma nor represents her. Even as the signifier 'Lolita' condenses a plethora of feminine stereotypes (including the dead mother, the fickle murdered bride, the death-bringer, the bride threatened to die), it posits her as an enigma, a blank, the narrative's failure before alterity.

In the relation between Humbert and Dolores, three interrelated issues emerge. In Humbert's imaginative transformation of this girl into 'my Lolita' she recalls and repeats various earlier dead women in his life – his mother who died 'in a freak accident (picnic, lightning)' when he was three (10), his first beloved Annabel Leigh ('there might have been no Lolita at all had I not loved . . . a certain initial girl-child' (9)) and her own mother, his actual bride Charlotte Haze. At the same time various literary figures are repeated in Lolita, lead to her, indeed make her up into a literary patchwork; notably the feminine death figures of Dante, Mérimée and Poe. What is refound, then, is not only the maternal body but also the literature that nurtured his imagination.

Finally, Dolores Haze's body functions not only as the site of a libidinal repetition of earlier love objects and an imaginative repetition of previous cultural texts. As she translates into 'my Lolita' – a designation only H.H. gives her while her mother calls her Lo and she herself signs the final letter asking for money as Dolly (Mrs Richard F. Schiller) – the exchange of body for sign is such that the difference between the two is part of the semiotic articulation. In the course of the narrative, the composite image of a lost beloved is materialised over a girl's body, effacing the latter prematurely in the process, until the girl rejects the poet. Her irretrievable physical absence in turn engenders her respiritualisation as textualisation in the form of a written narrative. Death is here not just a parody but real, for the deconstruction Nabokov's text traces discloses that the latter is present in the text only under erasure. The text's uncanny representational strategy is such that Dolores Haze is redressed, like Courbet's bride, by H.H.'s language, present beneath his parody, though imperfectly visible to anyone without an x-ray eye.

In the narrative H.H. offers of 'my life and my bride', Annabel Leigh is shown to recuperate his motherlessness by serving as the ideal beloved where 'the spiritual and the physical had been blended in . . . a perfection' (14). This girl, with whom a sexual union was not possible owing to the ribald intervention by 'the old man of the sea and his brother' and then her death of typhus four months later, haunts him for twenty-four years until 'I broke her spell by incarnating her in another' (15). Dolores, the superlative nymphet, not merely repeats his first beloved, but at the site of her body he is able to create what he was never allowed to possess owing to the 'castrative no' of the older men and of death. Fitting the thematic topos of the second dead beloved discussed earlier, the ghost of a dead girl comes to inhabit the body of a second, implicitly 'killing' the individuality of the latter.

H.H. attributes his nympholepsy to the fact that the first refinding of the phallic mother was so cruelly thwarted. Yet paradoxically the 'girl-children nymphets' that come henceforth to attract his desire are characterised as little deadly demons, possessing a 'fey grace', and an 'elusive, shifty, soul-shattering, insidious charm', (17), at the same time that they must never grow up. The word 'fey' itself points out the paradox – they are supernatural creatures, both fated to die and presagers of death. If in a literal sense the precariousness of their existence refers to their death at the onset of puberty, in a figural sense it invokes the fact that they are from the start figments of the viewer's fancy – inhabitants of 'an enchanted island . . . surrounded by a vast, misty, sea' (17); perceptable only to H.H., the artist, madman and melancholic. They are also immaterial creatures because from the start 'living incarnations of Queen Nefertiti's prenubile Nile daughters . . . intact after three thousand years'. As nympholept, H.H. 'involves the image' of a living girl in his 'voluptas' without her knowledge (21), and possesses previous historical and literary girls that fall outside his realm of experience and creation. For he repeatedly excuses his own behaviour by referring to the child-brides of Dante, Petrarch and above all Edgar Allan Poe – 'Lolita, you are my girl, as Vee was Poe's and Bea Dante's' (107).

When he sees Dolores for the first time, temporality and the loss it implies are suspended, for in a moment of 'passionate recognition' the intervening years vanish and he sees in her 'the same child . . . I had fondled one immortal day' (39). Yet this repetition not only perfectly reproduces every detail of the 'bright beauty' of his 'dead bride', but, with the emphasis on his creation and possession, comes to supersede the former – 'this *nouvelle*, this Lolita, *my* Lolita, was to eclipse completely her prototype' (40). Even if his 'discovery of her' is seen as the 'fatal consequence' of his 'incomplete childhood romance' (164), it also serves to efface the historical event, and with it the wound to his narcissism, by translating it into the realm of pure immortal textuality. Even as the dead bride becomes alive again at the body of Dolores, she is now irretrievably eclipsed.

As in 'Ligeia', over the created signifier 'Lolita' the real Dolores Haze also fades. While all previous nymphets remained objects of sight alone, this is the first one he can reach, a materialisation of the image that makes it specific. H.H. explains that '*this* Lolita, *my* Lolita, has individualized the writer's ancient lust' (45). By implication, however, though she is singular and tangible, she is so as figure for his desire. If the absence of Annabel can be doubly recuperated in that she is recreated and then fully effaced over the body of Dolores, the absence of the latter, which grounds the entire memoirs, in turn is overcome by recreating this beloved as 'my Lolita'. Though H.H. complains, 'Oh, my Lolita, I have only words to play with' (32), his narrative in fact aims at turning the elusive body of a beloved into a seemingly stable sign. By privileging as his eternal beloved the dead Muse, H.H.'s narrative lets the translated woman come to signify the poet's creative power, to serve as trope for his ability to possess intangible feminine beauty, 'to fix once for all the perilous magic of nymphets' (133).

His narrative is meant to preserve 'the eternal Lolita' against her physical absence and then demise. For H.H. explains that although he has fallen in love 'with Lolita forever', he knows that Dolores 'would not be forever Lolita', with only two years of remaining nymphage. Even as her body concretises his 'ancient lust' it is itself precarious, inscribed with the threat that in this materialised form he eventually 'would lose forever . . . *that* Lolita, *my* Lolita' (65).

The repeated allusion to Virigina Clemm draws an analogy not only to Poe's love for a fourteen-year-old, but also for a 'fey girl' doomed to die of tuberculosis. At the same time his childhood love Annabel is so explicitly herself a repetition of Poe's 'Annabel Lee' that H.H.'s 'real liberation' from the trauma of loss merges a refound beloved with a refound text. Annabel Leigh is called the 'initial little Miss Lee' and the feminine body that appears to him so blissfully on Charlotte Haze's porch is 'Annabel Haze, alias Dolores Lee, alias Loleeta' (165). As is true for Scottie in *Vertigo*, what H.H. refinds in 'my Lolita' is from the start not only a repetition of his childhood love and of the lost maternal body. More importantly, because Annabel in his memory herself repeats a literary figure, what he refinds is a representation, split between two textual signifiers, the historical Virginia Clemm and the poetic Annabel Lee; a repetition of previous libidinal and representational revenants, a repetition of a repetition.

His text, moreover, uses the recreated beloved not only to confirm the supremacy of spiritual over physical love but also to show that the birth of the poet and his symbolic creation occurs over the effacement of the complex I have been calling 'materiality-maternity-mortality.' For Dolores not only herself dies in childbirth but H.H.'s consummation of his love requires another dead maternal body – that of his newly wed Charlotte. In an inversion of the normal sequence of events, H.H. is attracted to Charlotte because he hopes to 'evoke the child while caressing the mother'. He gets his bride-to-be to unearth an old album of photographs so that in these images of Lotte as child he is 'able to make out a dim first version of Lolita's outline . . . Lottelita, Lolitchen' (76). This premature eclipsing of the mother, in that she merely functions as a repetition of her daughter, foreshadows both H.H.'s fantasies about murdering Charlotte and the subsequent fatal accident.

Her death removes the last obstacle to a seduction of Dolores, at the same time that it also lets him sever his beloved from historicity and recreate her beyond the maternal function. Having grown to regard Lolita 'as my child', he now insinuates to Charlotte's closest friends that he is in fact her illegitimate father. Curiously, however, the only description of Charlotte's dead body occurs belatedly, as an apostrophe to his beloved, uncannily linking the absent daughter to the dead mother: 'when they lifted the laprobe for me [Charlotte] had been revealed, curled up, her eyes intact, their black lashes still wet, matted, like yours, Lolita' (104).

With the mother irretrievably gone, H.H. has eliminated 'all the superfluous blur', and in the hotel he has chosen to fulfil his long awaited desire, Lolita's anaesthetised body appears to him as the apotheosis of the nymphet, the 'final picture' that has evolved from the 'stacking level upon level of translucent vision' (124). In that the seduction of Dolores's body is, according to H.H., not 'so-called sex at all' but rather seen as fixing 'the perilous magic of nymphets' (133), its gesture can be interpreted as that of the *point de capiton* – an arrestation of floating signifiers on to one point. The materialisation of his desire is meant to put the ghost of Annabel to rest; to turn deferral into completion; to translate his ambivalent desire for the fey girls possessed only as images into the stability of a concrete physical ravishment. In that Dolores is perceived as incarnating a 'final picture' she clearly serves as a figure for H.H.'s allegorising gaze, not as a unique personality, and the trope she renders in flesh is meant to be canny not uncanny.

In imitation of Poe's narrator, H.H. fashions himself in the attitude of the mourner, when he repeats these past events in his narrative. He speaks about writing inmidst 'present boundless misery', which, however, is due not only to the fact that the beloved is irretrievably lost, but more importantly, to his failure to achieve a stable definition of her. His concern is that in nymphet love the 'beastly and beautiful merged at one point and it is that borderline I would like to fix, and I feel I fail to do so utterly' (134). His is a double failure in so far as neither the Lolita he creates in Dolores's presence, nor the narrative 'Lolita' he writes in her absence achieves the effect of semantic stability. The *point de capiton*, the arrestation of all his fancied girls, be they real or imagined, at the body of Dolores transpires into a *punctum*, showing the difference between her actual body and his image as well as engendering new semantic ambivalences and uncertainties about his love object. Once he has materialized his image of the beloved, a new fear arises, that he cannot possess her. The 'realisation of a life long dream', he explains, has 'overshot its mark – and plunged into a nightmare' (140).

Such overshooting or excess takes two forms in the second half of the book. It points for one to the real that breaks into his fictitious world to mark precisely its limit; namely the sobbing, the resistance and the flight of Dolores not only from her seducer but from the fictions under which he seeks to subsume her. For another, the seduction materialises and completes only one fiction, that of the thwarted first romance. Far from reaching any quiescence in his imagination, this fulfilment produces a plethora of new fancies. At one moment, sitting next to Lo in a car, H.H. feels as though she were the 'small ghost of somebody I had just killed' (139), while shortly before he had wondered whether she was 'some immortal daemon disguised as a female child' (138).

As he is forced to realize that Dolores is not only 'quite different from innocent Annabel', but different also from his final picture of Lolita, his effort at recuperating an image of the beloved against the real disruption she poses shifts his literary focus. Though in moods of relief he still at times sees her as a repetition of 'gay, innocent, elegant Annabel' (160) and invokes 'Charlotte's face in death' when he is jealous, he moves from the Poe topoi of the fey girl whom death will snatch away to Merimée's Carmen – the infidel who must be imprisoned or killed. Concomitantly he casts himself in the role of the victim of feminine daemonic lust, the jealous lover of a deceitful and duplicitous girl and her monstrous ravisher and murderer. Far from using Dolores's body to fix the desires that haunt him and the ambivalence of meaning they evoke, he turns her into the figure of elusive femininity *par excellence*, who desires volatility, who will not be possessed, of whom her lover can only be sure once she is dead. At the same time that she serves to give figure to his rendition of Carmen, Dolores literally eludes his grip, so that her flight crosses his epistemological desire for a possession of secure knowledge with that of possessing the feminine body.

If before the threat to his object of desire was that he might not be allowed to possess Dolores and then that she would grow up, the threat, now, is that he might not be her sole and eternal possessor, that every move she makes threatens his image of her and as such his own self-representation. He describes his jealousy at the way Lolita seems to reciprocate other men's gazes, 'putting on a show of gambol and glee' (235), because this infidelity implies that she is more than and other than the image he has of her as his sole possessed object. It also implies that she has control over her spectator while his nymphet love, before its consummation at least, worked on the principle of the surveyed girl being oblivious to his gaze and fully at his disposal. Within the economy of his fancies and desires, it will again be possible to animate her exclusively as a body that signifies him, his love and his life, only once she is actually absent. Indeed she now is invoked as being 'so tantalisingly, so miserably unattainable and beloved', because, being on 'the very eve of a new era' when she will stop being a nymphet, her loss is inevitable (237).

As 'my Lolita' transforms into 'my Carmen', he begins to produce fantasies that link the beloved with two forms of loss; her infidelity and flight stand for a figural death feared, and the natural facticity of aging stand for death's literal inscription on the body which he anticipates. To explain the strength of his anxiety, passion and pain, for example he chooses the metaphor, 'it would have been instrumental in wrenching open the zipper of her nylon shroud had she been dead' (234). Again his tropes connecting the desired feminine body with death and literal bodily illness cross. Once Dolores has asked to be brought to the hospital, so as to use the separation this affords to undertake her escape, he accelerates the references to Carmen until he believes to notice that 'her illness was somehow the development of a theme' (240).

Significantly the recognition that he has lost his beloved – in the double sense that she has actually run away and that semiotically she only imperfectly signifies 'his love' – intertwines two textual allusions to men who kill their brides so as to possess them. Sensing that Dolores is about to flee from the hospital he ruminates, 'Poor Bluebeard. Those brutal brothers. *Est-ce que tu ne m'aimes plus, ma Carmen?* She never had. At that moment I knew my love was as hopeless as ever' (241). The excess of this citation is one of those moments where hyperbole moves into the comic and the mad in such a way as to reveal H.H. not only not in control of the body of his beloved but also not in control of his text. This is part of the confusion that lets Dolores return, in his narrative representation, as a motley cross between, in part, contradictory stereotypes of women from his past life and his previous readings. Late in his memoirs H.H. explains that the attraction of nymphets resides in the fact that 'infinite perfections fill the gap between the little given and the great promised' (262). If a concretisation of the promised ends in the nightmare of overshooting the mark, only another dematerialisation allows the 'great rose-grey never-to-be-had' to emerge in the uncanny gesture of nonfulfillable possiblity.

One of the paradoxes Nabokov reveals is that H.H.'s act of fixing is from the start undermined by virtue of the fact that the created beloved he repeatedly calls 'my Lolita' is indeed only a parody of earlier texts, neither his authentic creation nor truly under his control, in that the assumed plots become increasingly entangled and in a sense subsume him. More cruelly, however, and as such perhaps most befitting as my concluding example, Nabokov demonstrates to excess that the violence done to a feminine body as precondition to its artistic representation is located above all on the rhetoric level – the sublation and effacement of the feminine subject position engendered by the allegorising gaze of the poet and lover. This is the counterpart to the refiguration of Dolly Schiller into the apostrophe 'my Lolita, my love' once she seems irretrievably gone to the imprisoned H.H.

At certain moments in the narrative, H.H. unwittingly articulates the difference between the beloved he possesses and the actual girl. In the very first sexualised encounter between them, the dual figure I am concerned with underlines the scene. With both listening to a popular song about Carmen and her lover's wish to kill her with a gun, H.H. experiences masturbatory ecstasy in the seeming ignorance of the girl who inspires it: 'What I had madly possessed was not she, but my own creation, another, fanciful Lolita – perhaps, more real than Lolita . . . floating between me and her, and having no will, no consciousness – indeed, no life of her own' (62). The ideal beloved is not only created in reference to literary predecessors, as a cliché or dead metaphor of representations of feminine figures of death, nor is she herself merely understood as a mental corpse. Rather in the process, the actual Dolores Haze is also 'safely solipsized,' equally lacking a life of her own, because superseded and effaced by his 'creation . . . more real'.

His ecstasy shows him caught between the actual Dolores, absent because beyond the solipsism of his image-repertoire and the double, the fanciful Lolita. What Nabokov discloses is that possessing her body as an image he has created means being blind to the fact that her actual body is there, that her subjectivity contradicts his allegorising reduction. Seeing only the image of his own creation he can oversee that his contact is indeed with the material body of a girl. He can delude himself into believing that his incursion involves only an image. Pushing her outside the frame of his vision, he denies her presence in that she is outside the parameters of the world he creates in the same way that the imagined body supplanting her also has no life of her own, because totally his creation. The duplicity of his behaviour, a form of violent gazing, is that by denying her actual presence and her subject position, he deludes himself into believing that he has touched an image not a body. In so doing he not only violates the body but also denies that any violation has occurred. What this leaves undecided for the reader is whether s/he chooses to read only the surface H.H offers, or whether s/he chooses also to focus on that beneath the confession and his own self-parody.

The resistance of the real body of the girl to H.H.'s imaginary appropriation again comes to the fore in the scene where he picks her up at the summer camp after her mother's death. For a second she seems to him 'less pretty than the mental imprint' he had cherished, but as his glance turns into a longer gaze he adds 'I overtook my prey . . . and she was my Lolita again – in fact, more of my Lolita than ever' (111). In such moments H.H. unwittingly, or consciously, reflects on the way the real, the alterity of the girl, must be silenced or transformed to fit his image. Narrative moments where the real disrupts the unity of his narcissistically informed memory text are also found in his reference to the sobs he hears every night, once he feigns sleep, and which he leaves uncommented (173), or in the description of her innocence, frankness and kindness when she plays tennis, which contradicts the cruel and crafty deceitfulness he wishes to attribute to her. Or when a 'chance combination of mirror aslant and door ajar' gives him a a view of Dolores's disappointed face because he will not let her go out alone, he briefly realises that 'an outside world . . . was real to her'. In these moments he acknowledges the existence of her desires in a world beyond his fancy.

Of course these moments, where he acknowledges that he does not know a thing about her, that he has in fact been ignoring her states of mind, are repeatedly recuperated by such statements that describe their life as a 'parody of incest' (286). Here the real facticity and materiality disrupt the parody of freely floating signifiers in the same narrative gesture that articulates the occlusion of the feminine subject position, precisely because this is coterminous with an attempt to use the trope of the beloved to efface real death. Unlike Proffer, who suggests that Humbert invokes 'Carmen' or 'Bluebeard' to signal premonitions of Lolita's death as red herrings meant to play with the literate reader, I argue that these allusions duplicitously point to the real effacement of the feminine subject that grounds this representation and are used to veil the figural murder of Dolores Haze that does occur in the text.

These false leads are not only part of the process that turns the actual girl into a trope, 'my Lolita', but because they result in a frustration of the reader's expectation, where an expected murder is shown not to occur, they shift the focus away from the figural murder that underwrites the entire system of representation. I follow Shute's cue that Nabokov's parody 'appeals to something other than itself', a disengenuous strategy whereby it simultaneously invokes and negates the psychoanalytic economies of desire.[26] I would merely add not only that the act of citation and parody, like the fetish, simultaneously effaces and leaves intact the theme of love as repetition, but that what is equally effaced and left wholly visible is the feminine subject position in its alignment with death as that which grounds and disrupts the illusory portrait of the artist as an autonomous man.

Significantly, H.H. can only narrate that part of his final conversation with Dolly in which she irrevocably shatters his romantic fiction in the indirect speech of the third person – 'And *I* had never counted, of course? . . . In her washed-out grey eyes . . . our poor romance was for a moment reflected, pondered upon, and dismissed . . . like a humdrum exercise, like a bit of dry mud caking her childhood' (270). As the reality of her Other desire imposes an irrevocable wound on his narcissism, the maternal reasserts itself against his paternity. Over the body of Dolly Schiller smoking, 'Gracefully, in a blue mist, Charlotte Haze rose from her grave' (273). If before the mother had been seen in the light of reincarnating her daughter, Dolly now serves to resurrect her mother. With gestures of pointing her cigarette and removing its paper from her underlip that are 'like her mother', the mother-to-be asserts herself against his fancies.

Hopelessly worn out at seventeen she appears as the 'dead echo of the nymphet' (276), but also as the return of the disappeared maternal body. Against the real sight of Dolly, 'pale and polluted and big with another's child', H.H. does try to realign the image of 'my Lolita . . . still grey-eyed, still sooty-lashed, still auburn and almond, still Carmencita, still mine' (276) until she unambiguouly rejects him.

Unlike that of her literary predecessor's, Dolly's 'no' to his offer – 'come to live with me, and die with me' – does not arise from an acknowledgement of her own facticity, though the narrative frame implies that the choice for motherhood proved to have been a choice for death. Yet as the one assertion of her subjective desire which he cannot ignore, it irrevocably discloses the illusion of H.H.'s romantic text. It is true that, like Carmen's 'no', Dolly's engenders that irrevocable natural, real absence out of which the declined lover can construct an intact, canny image of the beloved – 'my Lolita'. In the self-accusation that follows he turns her into an enigma – the girl whose mind he never knew and stylises himself into the ravisher of an innocent body. In this recreation, which translates the deceitful daemon child into the glorified innocent and helpless waif, the real Dolores Haze is as absent as she was from all earlier textual reformulations, and it smoothly leads the narrator back to the fey beloved, the angelic girl bride with whom he began. Like all others, this idealisation places her in the beyond before maternity does. In the end, as the first paragraph of his memory text declares, the imagined nymphet once again reasserts itself against the real maternal body of Dolores Haze. Yet for the reader willing to listen to this text's uncanniness, her 'no' resonates against H.H.'s apostrophe, 'my Lolita'.

What has emerged as a central aporia inherent to the conflation of the enigma of femininity and mortality is that this culminating point of victimisation can also be read as the emergence of feminine subjectivity, power and self-articulation. I have used the notion of an empty gesture to define that moment where thematically the feminine protagonist recognises her real non-existence beyond any fictions of identity and have traced a similar gesture in those moments where fictions were disrupted by moments of real death, with the point of conjunction again a dying or dead feminine body. Representation, as a form of presence of what is absent, involves, Barthes suggests, not a synthesis but a translation: 'everything comes back, but it comes back as Fiction, i.e., at another turn of the spiral'.[27] I have discussed how the unencompassable body of maternity– materiality–mortality returns, as the repressed real, at the site of the dead bride coming back as a revenant. Such spectral presence involves the hysteric's dis- simulation of her non-existence and the obsessional mourner's appropriation of a second woman as body double of a no longer existing beloved. The translation, the return of the absent woman as fiction, works on the basis of rematerialising an image or a literary convention. Even if portraits and texts stood at the end of each narrative, replacing the materialised sign once again with pure textuality, I have sketched precisely the movement from textuality to the real which representation falls short of.

In the past four parts I have repeatedly returned to the image Benjamin offers of the poet, born as an autonomous self beyond the materiality-maternity-mortality matrix by killing the feminine function in himself. At the same time I have shown that woman's subject position emerged as a radical blank, silence and negation or as a return to the body, with her writing/speaking authenticated by death. In my final chapter I will ask what such a concept of art and writing raises for a self-definition and self-representation of the writing woman. I will address the way that notions of death, self-effacement and resurrection also inscribe women's self-fashioning as authors. Cixous, seeking to define an *écriture féminine*, suggests that one must have been loved by death to be born and pass into writing.[28] If in the course of this book I have moved from texts where male and female writers speak of dead women (and in so doing either critique or confirm the mortification of the feminine body within culture), to texts where the male poet uses the apostrophe to speak to a dead beloved as muse, I will now shift my focus away from the issue of speaking of and for her, in the sense of the painted image, the commemorative text, the tombstone inscription that stands in for her body and her history. Nor will I further address the issue of speaking to her, in the rhetoric strategy of invocation where the absent body serves as inspiration and source of the apostrophe, is given voice, but only through the poet and with her body signifying him. In all these forms, feminine death is in some sense Other, outside, beyond the representational system. By way of conclusion, I will look instead at texts that, rather than speaking of, for, or to a dead feminine body, explore the event of *speaking her*. In these texts, feminine death is not used as a double-edged trope that lets real death or feminine subjectivity shine uncannily through the dress of the bride, not the ground and limit of the text, but rather its explicit centre.

Notes to Chapter 17

1 See S. Ledanff, 1986, for a detailed discussion and documentation of this incident.
2 Quoted in S. Ledanff, 1976, p. 129.
3 S. Ledanff points out that the confusion was shared by her contemporaries as well. Gutzkow calls her Caroline Stieglitz.
4 S. de Beauvoir, 1952, p. 205.
5 See J. Derrida, 1976.
6 Quoted in S. Ledanff, 1976, p. 130.
7 For a discussion of reanimation and its rhetorical function see B. Johnson, 1987, pp. 184–99.
8 Plato, 1961, p. 492.
9 Homer, 1951, pp. 91–92 (lines 594–600).
10 S. Commager, 1967, p. 8.
11 S. Commager, 1967, p. 20ff.
12 2. M. DeShazer, 1986, p. 2.
13 H. Bloom, 1976, p. 264.

14 R. Barthes, 1978.
15 Novalis 1790–1800. See also E. Bronfen, 1990 and C. von Braun, 1989.
16 See G. Allen, 1981, for a detailed account of her marriage and death. He calls this act 'so unnatural as to seem almost insane', a satisfaction of a morbid compulsion, p. 182; See also J. Porte, 1982.
17 D. G. Rossetti, 1870.
18 See A. Ridler's introduction, 1963, and L. Hönnighausen, 1971.
19 See M. Easten, 1972.
20 H. Cixous, 1979, here adds the issue of gender to George Bataille's discussion of expenditure and death, 1967. One could also draw an analogy between the 'feminine' discourse of the hysteric and this notion of excess on the one hand, and the 'masculine' discourse of the obsessional and this notion of preservation on the other.
21 See H. James, 1974, especially the letters to Mrs Henry James Sr, William James, and Grace Norton, pp. 218–29.
22 R. Graves, 1966.
23 See C. Proffer, 1968, and A. Appel, Jr, 1970, for a discussion of the allusions; R. Hof, 1984 on irony and unreliability of the narrator; C. Ross, 1979, on the muse metaphor.
24 C. Proffer, 1968, notes that Humbert alludes to 'Annabel Lee' and to 'Carmen' more often than to any other texts.
25 A. Appel, 1970.
26 J. Shute, 1984, p. 648.
27 R. Barthes, 1977, p. 69.
28 H. Cixous, 1989, p. 48.

Henry's Sister – Alice James (1848–92)

Dying
Is an art, like everything else
I do it exceptionally well.
I do it so it feels like hell
I do it so it feels real.
I guess you could say I've a call.
Sylvia Plath

This case study once again illustrates how cultural representations, in this case those of the premarital woman oscillating between marriage, profession and death, found a 'parody with real suffering in it' in the case of Alice James. Shortly before dying of breast cancer on 6 March, 1892, having spent the past two decades as an invalid, she wrote to her brother William, 'I always rejoiced that my temperament had set for my task the attainment of the simplest rudimentary ideal, which I would . . . work away upon . . . in complete security from the grotesque obstructions supposed to be life . . . so when I am gone, pray don't think of me simply as a creature who might have been something else had neurotic science been born; notwithstanding the poverty of my outside experience I have always had a significance for myself'.[1] The 'imperfect accomplishment' she sought, the vocation she chose, was to 'get myself dead',[2] and the significance she attained both for herself and others entailed the ceremony of dying she conducted in the midst of her family and friends between her nineteenth and her forty-fourth birthday, along with its textualisation in letters and diary entries.

The sister of William and Henry James was initially a playful and clever girl, physically and intellectually energetic. Though she took part in all the family activities that made the James children distinct from their peers, she found herself set apart from her brothers as the only girl in the family. Her father was exclusively concerned with the education of the boys and her feminine sex often made her the object of family teasing and mockery. In retrospect Alice called herself 'one more amid a million of the superfluous' (36), a creature 'born with no chance, as if made of the scraps left over in the great human factory' (76). Realising that she could 'only take a passive part in life', she responded by developing a nervous condition which would be diagnosed, at different periods in her life, as neurasthenia, hysteria, rheumatic gout, suppressed gout, cardiac complication, spinal neurosis, nervous hyperaesthesia and spiritual crisis.

As her biographer Jean Strouse notes, girls of the middle- and upper-middle class in mid-nineteenth-century America were often socially peripheral. Because their education had raised expectations that could then not be realised, their increasing sense of isolation and irrelevance made them prone to dangerous extremes of excitement and lassitude.[3] In her own lucid self-analysis, Alice describes her nervous illness as emerging from a courtship with death, which she claims to have developed early on against living in 'this deadness called life' (38). Writing from the position of middle age serenity, she represents her youthful self as one 'crushed and bewildered before the perpetual postponements of its hopes . . . Owing to muscular circumstances my youth was not of the most ardent, but I had to peg away pretty hard between 12 and 24, "killing myself," as someone calls it – absorbing into the bone that the better part is to . . . possess one's soul in silence.' If she could not fulfil 'things promised' by life, she seems to have reasoned, then 'the only thing which survives is the resistance we bring to life and not the strain life brings to us' (98).

While both William and Henry also suffered from nervous disorders, their renunciation of a physically active existence in a sense merely confirmed their intellectual and artistic vocation. In Alice's case, however, nervous ailment was intimately connected both with the feminine role her culture ascribed to her and with her resistance to the lethal boredom of enforced uselessness, the stifling of her active nature, the frustration of her youthful hopes that went along with being a young woman in mid-nineteenth-century New England. Alice's hysteria can be seen as an effort to arbitrate the claims of traditional femininity with those of an independent self. Nervousness, like consumption, was seen as a sign of complexity and sensitivity – a mark of intelligence, subtlety and a finely tuned nature. Taken to extremity, however, nervousness surpassed fashionable high-strung refinement.[4] Neither fulfilling nor rejecting the norm, the hysteric's slight but crucial exaggeration of ideal nineteenth-century femininity undermined these norms in that her fits violated any sense of refinement while her incapacitating physical symptoms made her so helpless as to parody the delicacy and softness she was meant to incorporate. They left her an accomplice with her culture's dictate that she should renounce any active part in public life.

At the age of nineteen, Alice had her first acute breakdown, which took the form of fainting spells, pains, attacks and nervous prostrations. In her diary entry for 26th October, 1890, she belatedly describes these 'violent turns of hysteria' as a 'never-ending fight' between 'my body and my will, a battle in which the former was to be triumphant in the end'. As her 'physical weakness' and 'excess of nervous susceptibility' engendered an 'infinite succession of conscious abandonments' and 'pauses in moral power', her body would become immovable, with 'waves of violent inclination suddenly invading my muscles'. The 'myriad forms' these unconscious desires took wavered from self-directed aggression ('throwing myself out of the window') to outward directed aggression ('knocking off the head of the benignant pater'). The split she experienced was not, however, simply between immobile or uncontrolled body and violent unconscious desires. Rather she also felt herself divided between 'all the horrors and suffering of insanity' and an inability to abandon her consciousness, so that she had 'the duties of doctor, nurse, and straight-jacket [*sic*] imposed upon me, too' (149).

In her hysteric symptoms she offered a representation of her social liminality – her active mind but inactive life – by preserving her conscious mind against the body which refused to keep sane. Choosing the paternal library as scene for the description of one of her hysteric fits, she represents herself as one unable to continue reading. One 'moral impression after another' gleaned from the books she reads implicitly confirms the social suffocation she is bound by and produces a somatic despair, terror and anxiety felt in the 'pit of your stomach', the 'palms of your hands', the 'soles of your feet'. The fits her body inflicts on her not only signify her desire to destroy a stifling external world but also serve as the very medium of 'castration', interrupting any sustained intellectual or physical work. In this battle between social constraints, somatic illness and a will to abate insanity, the compromise she was forced to choose, she explains, was to abandon 'conscious and continuous cerebration' beyond any knowledge that 'sticks of itself'.

Realising unconsciously that an intellectual profession was not possible, her hysterical symptoms used bodily illness to thwart any such hopes, repeating the peripheral existence in this 'deadness called life' which her social position dictated. Within a society that assigned to her the role of passive onlooker, she turned all her attention to the body, and existence became 'one long flight from remote suggestions and complicated eluding of the multifold traps set for your undoing' (150). She found herself positioned between two lethal points of identification – a social existence that is 'deadness' and an equally fatal aban-donment to the violent inclinations of the body 'abjectly impotent before the immutable laws' – with her will alone preventing her 'mechanism [from] falling to pie'.

As Strouse argues, choosing nervous illness 'justified her failure to achieve while allowing her to preserve a sense of potent capacity'.[5] In one and the same gesture she could cede her body to the feminine edict of frailty and submission and cultivate a masculine strength of will. The intellectual activity she could partake of consisted in representing to herself, and later registering on paper in diary and letter form, precisely this fight between body and will, which was to occupy her attention henceforth. For she could return to conscious cerebration, in so far as it served to reflect and represent her condition: 'after the storm' she lies prostrate 'with my mind luminous and active and susceptible of the clearest, strongest impressions'.

Endorsing her father's wishes, she gave up any thought of preparing for a career, divided her efforts between tending her illness, social visits, a tour of Europe and leisure reading. Yet by the time she was about to turn thirty, she had no prospect of marriage, and in her own words 'nought else of importance to do'.[6] She was also about to be ousted from the life of her brother William by his newly married wife Alice, her opposite in strength of health and domestic competence. During her second acute breakdown in the summer of 1878, she found herself wishing to choose suicide over a marriage that in her case seemed most unlikely. She appealed to her father, and in a letter to her brother Robertson he describes the conversation that was to prevent her from killing herself, only to embark instead on what she came to call her 'mortal career'.

He writes, 'I told her that so far as I was concerned she had my full permission to end her life whenever she pleased; only I hoped that if ever she felt like doing that sort of justice to her circumstances, she would do it in a perfectly gentle way in order not to distress her friends.' Her response, he adds, was that she 'was very thankful to me, but she felt that now she could perceive it to be her right to dispose of her own body when life had become intolerable, she could never do it: that when she had felt tempted to it, it was with a view to break bonds, or assert her freedom, but that now I had given her freedom to do in the premises what she pleased, she was more than content to stay by my side'. Her father was right not to fear 'suicide much since this conversation, though she often tells me that she is strongly tempted still'.[7] Because it removed all bonds which her choice of suicide could be seen as breaking, such lack of paternal resistance made any concrete realisation of her 'mortuary inclinations' (250) obsolete. Abandoning the idea of suicide as the one decisive step, the one unique act open to her, she fell back on a liminal existence she was later to define as the state of being 'neither dead nor recovered' (142); too ill to live a normal life but too healthy to die. Yeazell suggests that in rejecting suicide, Alice literally made the difference between death and life, with death remaining an intensely desired goal as well as a conclusion.[8]

But in point of fact, unable to choose either actual death or a life of health, she chooses instead an uncanny hybrid, the simulation of dying, and through this hysterical discourse she could simultaneously hide and reveal her real non-existence. Her health briefly flourished once her mother died and she could take care of her father, only to collapse once more after his death in December 1882. After residing in a sanatorium and then an unsuccessful attempt to live alone, she finally left for England to stay with her brother Henry, accompanied by Katherine Peabody Loring. These two were to remain her devoted companions until her death. Her final London years were spent succumbing to the invalidism her body dictated and asserting her will against these incursions of pain, paralysis and uncontrollable fits. She stayed alive, but only to serve as a living representation of death in the midst of life. By the early 1890s she began hypnosis therapy and sensing, four years before the publication of Freud and Breuer's *Studies on Hysteria*, that psychoanalysis might have offered her an alternative to invalidism, she wrote on 4 December, 1891, 'I have come to the knowledge within the last week or so that I was simply born a few years too soon' (222).

Henry James suggested that Alice's tragic health was, in a manner, the only solution for her of the practical problem of life.[9] Yet as her own rendition of her life after the breakdown in her thirtieth year has it, the solution she found was that of a revenant existence, a remaining beyond death, a career in mortality that left her positioned on the limen between real death (natural absence) and real health (social presence). With her mind always thinking 'that I wanted to die', but her body deferring the desired moment, she turned her earthly existence into an explicit enactment that life is a form of dying. She not only incessantly found herself in death-like moments of incapacitation, but also ceaselessly thought, talked and wrote about her death. One month before her death she wrote in her diary, 'The fact is, I have been dead so long and it has been simply such a grim shoving of the hours behind me as I faced a ceaseless possible horror, since that hideous summer of '78 . . . that now it's only the shrivelling of an empty pea pod that has to be completed' (230).

If her adolescent fits and nervousness were a slight exaggeration of the feminine ideal of frailty and passivity, the career of invalidism she embarked on after her renunciation of suicide was a kind of fatal self-artifice, in which she prematurely staged her coming death. Yet because she did so for more than thirteen years, this self-representation as a dying woman encompasses an exaggeration of several topoi discussed – of Clarissa's self-contemplation in the face of death and her minute preparations for her death ceremony, of the precarious authority ascribed in general to the deathbed scene as well as, by virtue of an ironic inversion, of the psychic rigidity of the woman over thirty. Smith-Rosenberg suggests that a large number of Victorian women chose hysteria so as to express dissatisfaction with a life situation that deprived them of their promised social role. By virtue of invalidism, they could opt out of the traditional role of caretaker to enjoy instead the special power, prerogatives, indulgences and sympathy to which the sick are entitled. At the same time, the hysteric's hostility and aggression was also self-directed and often resulted in self-punishing psychosomatic illnesses.[10] Indeed, Alice repeatedly describes her body as the stage for a paradoxical fight between spiritual potency and somatic impotence 'What a grotesque I am to be sure! Lying in this room, with the resistance of a thistle-down, having illusory moments of the throbbing with the pulse of the Race . . . the sense of vitality, in short, simply proportionate to the excess of weakness!' (49).

In the course of my discussion two strategies have emerged by which women were shown to articulate their non-existence in western culture. Firstly, I have discussed the way that the cultural construction of femininity over the woman's body makes it the privileged site at which her social subjugation hooks into the world. The reduction of woman to her anatomy produces a curtailment to any definition of a feminine subject position. The urge to destroy the medium through which the destruction of such subjectivity occurs, to undo the site where it is effected and guaranteed, transpires into an urge to obliterate the body itself. Decorporalisation is privileged over an expropriation of her language and her being.[11] In an *empty gesture*, illness culminating in implicit or explicit suicide serves as a means of self-articulation out of silence, where the dying and dead body turns into the one self-portrait, the one means by which women leave a public mark.

Secondly, I have spoken of the way the hysteric's simulation of different roles is the duplictous way in which a woman remains in complicity with her culture, even as she rejects the simple equation of femininity with death. The hysteric figurally simulates the role of the dead woman by turning her social existence into an act of histrionics. In order to evade a destiny which dictates that *to be a woman* is coterminous with *to be dead*, she transforms her cultural construction into a dramatic role and treats her public appearance like a theatre performance.[12] Pretending to be dead in the sense that her real self is hidden beneath the roles she plays, the hysteric survives social mortification.

In the case of Alice James these two strategies merge. Though her psychosomatic illness attacks her body precisely because its femininity is the source of her frustrated hopes, hers is not an effacement but an excessive staging of the body as a death-inscribed entity. She writes that, though her long slow dying is no doubt instructive, it is 'disappointingly free from excitements: naturalness being carried to its supreme expression' (229). The parody resides in the fact that, rather than destroying the body as source and site of her social castration, she enacts her incapacitation to excess, focusing on her desubstantiation even as what precisely doesn't occur for so many years is actual death. Like Sylvia Plath's Lady Lazarus, she comes back from a death she can not realise, and gains social presence and voice by sustaining over thirteen years what is usually the question of a moment – the gesture of destroying the body so as not to destroy the self. She writes on 1 June 1891, 'Having it to look forward to for a while seems to double the value of the event, for one becomes suddenly picturesque to oneself, and one's wavering little individuality stands out with a cameo effect' (208).

The particular twist Alice James gives to the discourse of the hysteric is that she makes literal what the histrionic self-display figurally signifies. For she not only chooses to turn her life into a theatrical scene, enacting her absence or lack of social place by taking on other roles. Rather what she simulates is the scene of perpetual dying. Repeatedly she speaks of death as her one dramatic moment, her one significant gesture, for which she must prepare and which she must contemplate in advance. Always adding self-irony to the imaginative staging of this somber moment, she suggests, 'I might pose to myself before the footlights of my last obscure little scene, as a delectably pathetic figure' (222), and worries that the sudden presence of the curate rather than her brother at her deathbed 'would curdle my soul in its transit & at any rate entirely spoil my post mortem expression of contenance'.[13] She complains that the 'difficulty with all this dying is that you can't tell a fellow anything about it, so where does the fun come in?' (223). Or she worries about her absence at the one moment where she will fulfil her vocation: 'I may fizzle out . . . the only drawback being that it will probably be in my sleep so that I shall not be one of the audience, dreadful fraud! a creature who has been denied all dramatic episodes might be allowed, I think, to assist at her extinction' (135).

By virtue of her invalidism she literally enacts that she, as woman, does not exist, that she can only be 'dead', that dying is the one vocation she as a woman can excel in. In this she moves beyond any passive acknowledgement of her limits and turns these into her strength. Early on she discovered that rather than struggling to be 'not as other ones are', her 'talents lay in being more so' (75). By a slight exaggeration of her peripheral position she managed to carve for herself a position of centrality. As 'devotee to common-sense' (125), she, however, also judges any Romantic self-absorption in the face of death, such as Marie Bashkirtseff's Journal, to be 'the perverse of the perverse'. In the midst of her real suffering, she is herself never oblivious to the parody her invalidism traces and can call one of her prostrations 'rather excessive and comic in its combination . . . of rheumatic gout . . . ulcerated tooth, and a very bad crick in my neck' (129).

The paradox emerging from her invalidism is that on the one hand it makes her fully dependent on her body, forcing her to subject herself to its immutable laws. On the other hand, focusing her existence exclusively on the 'obscure scene' her soma dictates lets her retextualise her peripheral existence. She uses her body to produce her self-representation in its dual contingency on death, as the source of social non-existence and the site where real facticity inscribes itself in life. She also turns dying into her 'first and last ceremony' (216) and into her mode of fiction writing. For it allows her to split her contemplating self imaginatively from her body and record her own courtship with death from an ironic distance.

Positioned as an invalid between complete somatic rest and complete turmoil, she is between two forms of death: 'I never expect to be deader than I am now, nay, not even after the worms have gorged themselves.'[14] In what Yeazell calls a characteristic inversion, death takes on the value of vitality, the sense of oncoming death makes 'the sounds of life reverberate' (185). Death, Alice argues, gives definitive contours to the indeterminacies of life, 'making them so complete and clear-cut, all the vague & wobbly lines lost in the revelation of what they were meant to stand for'.[15] As she writes to William in July 1891, death indeed translates into the superlative moment of vitality: 'It is the most supremely interesting moment in life, the only one, in fact, when living seems life and I count it as the greatest good fortune to have these few months so full of interest and instruction in the knowledge of my approaching death.'[16]

Once she begins, in 1889, to record her death in her diary, one can even speak of two forms of writing. In this liminality she, like the storyteller I discussed earlier on, is also caught between the absent and the double. Focused excessively on the mortality of her body she is absent from the social world at the same time that both her written comments and her self-conscious staging once again fictionalise, and in so doing double, this body with its traces of real death. Indeed she repeatedly presents her dying in par with the writing activity of her brothers. To William's wife she writes in November 1890, 'I am working away as hard as I can to get dead as soon as possible . . . but this play of Harry's makes a sad complication, as I don't want to immerse him in a deathbed scene on his "first night," too much of an aesthetic incongruity.'[17] In her diary, listing the books her two brothers published in 1891, she adds 'not a bad show for one family! especially if I get myself dead, the hardest job of all' (211).

Reminiscent of Poe's despair at the prolongation of his wife's illness, Alice James admits that what is so difficult about her invalidism is that 'the long ceaseless strain and tension have worn out all aspiration save the one for Rest' (131). When her doctor finally diagnoses a tumour in her breast, she receives this 'uncompromising verdict' as an 'enormous relief'. Having throughout her protracted illness 'longed for some palpable disease', only repeatedly to be 'driven back to stagger alone under the monstrous mass of subjective sensations', this death sentence figures as the long-awaited apotheosis: 'My aspirations may have been eccentric, but I can not complain now, that they have not been brilliantly fulfilled' (206). Since December 1890 she had been too weak to write and Katherine Loring had not only served as hypnotiser and administrator of drugs to relieve her pain, but also as her secretary, transcribing her self-reflections.

Not unlike Miss Havisham, fashioning herself in the image of a bride waiting for death as the suitor who will release her from her uncanny presence in absence, Alice also keeps making sentences even at the onset of actual death. In the final entry to Alice's diary, Katherine describes the completion of her friend's first and final ceremony. One of the last things Alice asked of her companion was to make a correction in a sentence in the dictation of 4 March. Katherine notes, the worry of authorship 'was rushing about in her brain all day, and although she was very weak and it tired her much to dictate, she could not get her head quiet until she had had it written: then she was relieved' (232). On the afternoon of 6 March Alice died, having whispered the message to Henry, which was to announce to her other brother her final triumph over life – 'Tenderest love to all farewell am going soon.'[18]

William's reply to his brother's cable, confirming that Alice had passed away painlessly, is, in Yeazell's words, 'a telegram whose gothic speculations offered a fitting climax to the whole strange performance that had been his sister's dying'.[19] He seems to have warned Henry that Alice's death might prove to be an illusion, with her body merely mimicking the appearance of the longed-for death. For in a letter written to follow the cable he apologises 'I telegraphed you this A.M. to make sure the death was not merely apparent, because her neurotic temperament & chronically reduced vitality are just the field for trance-tricks to play themselves upon.' Yet before Henry could have received the letter, he sent his own description of her death across the Atlantic: 'I have sat many hours in the still little room in which so many months of her final suffering were compressed, and in which she lies as the very perfection of the image of what she had longed for years, and at the last with pathetic intensity, to be. She looks most beautiful and noble – with all of the august expression that you can imagine – and with less, than before, of the almost ghastly emaciation of those last days.'[19]

One month before her final end, Alice wrote that the 'success or failure of a life, as far as posterity goes, seems to lie in the more or less luck of seizing the right moment of eclipse' (229). The fascination her life has for posterity, however, lies in the way her long slow dying so grotesquely misses its *kairos* by expanding a moment into a lifetime, for the exaggeration turns failure into success. The diary Katherine insisted on publishing, against Henry's desire for 'a few eliminations of text and dissimulations of names' (20), brilliantly translates Alice. It lets her 'come back, as Fiction', to cite Barthes, lets her voice return not only beyond the grave but as the feminine subject speaking precisely in the attitude of a legislator of the exchange between death and life.

Notes to Case Study

1 A. James, 1981, p. 187.
2 A. James, 1934, p. 211. Since I will be quoting extensively from these diaries, I will mark the page references in my text.
3 J. Strouse, 1980.
4 J. Strouse, 1980.
5 J. Strouse, 1980, p. 125.
6 Quoted in J. Strouse, 1980, p. 179.
7 A. James 1981, p. 16.
8 R. Yeazell, 1981.
9 Quoted by L. Edel in his introduction to A. James, 1982, p. 8.
10 C. Smith-Rosenberg, 1986, p. 197–216.
11 V. Exports, 1987.
12 C. von Braun, 1985.
13 A. James, 1981, p. 131.
14 A. James, 1981, pp. 180 and 129.
15 A. James, 1981, p. 145.
16 A. James, 1981, p. 186.
17 A. James, 1981, p. 185.
18 A. James, 1981, p. 192.
19 R. Yeazell, 1981, p. 45.
20 Quoted in H. James, 1980, p. 378.

CONCLUSION

Aporias of resistance

We went through a door at the back and reached a room where there was a bed in which lay a woman, motionless and probably dead. It seemed to me that she must have been there a long time, for the bed was overgrown with grass.

'I water her every day,' the greengrocer said thoughtfully. 'For forty years I've been quite unable to tell whether she is alive or dead. She hasn't moved or spoken or eaten during that time. But, and this is the strange thing, she remains warm. If you don't believe me, look.'

Whereupon he lifted a corner of the bed cover and I saw a large number of eggs and some newly hatched chicks.

Leonora Carrington

18

From muse to creatrix – Snow White unbound

These were two of the adventures of my professional life. The first – killing the Angel in the House – I think I solved. She died. But the second, telling the truth about my own experiences as a body, I do not think I solved.
Virginia Woolf

When (to me) death takes you and puts you thru the wringer, it's a man. But when you kill yourself it's a woman.
Anne Sexton

In order to define herself as an active creator rather than as a passive inspirer, DeShazer argues, 'the woman poet must invent her own metaphor for poetic inspiration; she must name a muse of her own'.[1] She continues by sketching a lengthy tradition of women poets who redefine the muse as a potent force. What interests me in the three examples with which I begin this last chapter, however, is that at least one variant of such redefinition continues to present a dead woman as the source and address of poetic inspiration. I choose to frame my discussion in this way to emphasise that although the narratives to be analysed revise the canon, represent the topos and trope of feminine death differently, they remain uncannily between a disavowal and an affirmation of the dominant image repertoire; hovering between cultural complicity and critique. As women writers reflect upon the relationship between authorship and feminine death (as this often translates into issues of feminine authorship and death), the crucial point is that femininity, which in its linkage with death marks uncanny difference within, has not been translated into canny Otherness. With the feminine position coalescing with that of the writing self, death in these narratives is also connected with femininity. Yet the death these authors write can only be defined *ex negativo*. It is not the death of the other, or death as Other. Rather it remains somehow within this representational system. The feminine subject position writing out of death is still a position of oscillation with no defined or fixed place, but here somehow within.

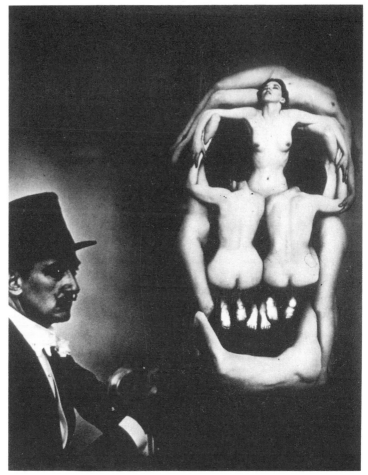

Fig 31   Phillippe Halsman. *Salvador Dali – In voluptate Mors* (1944)

One of the most frequently cited anecdotes for the thwarted, hindered, suppressed and lost poetic gift of women is Virginia Woolf's tale of Judith Shakespeare. Concurring with the commonplace that it would have been impossible for
a woman to have written 'the plays of Shakespeare in the age of Shakespeare', she
speculatively imagines 'what would have happened had Shakespeare had a
wonderfully gifted sister'.[2] In contrast to her brother, she was not sent to school,
forced to scribble her verses on the sly and carefully hide them. She was
betrothed against her will before the age of seventeen and her only option was to
flee to London clandestinely. Here she found it impossible to get employment as
an actress until the actor manager took pity on her. 'She found herself with child
by that gentleman, and so', Woolf concludes, 'killed herself one winter's night
and lies buried at some cross-roads.'[3]

It is often overseen that Woolf imagines Judith Shakespeare as her muse, invents her precisely as a metaphor for feminine poetic inspiration. In her function as trope for the suffocation of the woman's poetic gift, for the anonymity or lack of signature of her work had she survived, she inspires the writing of a woman three hundred years after her demise. In the final paragraph of *A Room of One's Own* Woolf returns to her story about this dead woman poet to suggest that her silence and her effacement opens a space for the poetic endeavors of her predecessors. Though she died young and never wrote a word, Woolf contends, she still lives 'in you and in me' as a continuing presence which merely needs 'the opportunity to walk among us in the flesh'.[4] This opportunity, she adds, 'is now coming within your power to give her'. With the preparation, effort and determination of contemporary women to prepare the environment for such female creativity as she lacked, 'the dead poet who was Shakespeare's sister will put on the body which she has so often laid down . . . she will be born'.

Woolf legitimises her own work by reversing Benjamin's model, where the birth of the poet means the death or effacement of femininity. Any women's writing is worthwhile, she claims, even when written in poverty and obscurity, for 'I maintain that she would come if we worked for her'. The birth of the originary, effaced woman poet here requires that feminine subjectivity has already attained a space within the symbolic order of culture. Given that Judith Shakespeare is from the start dead and imagined, Woolf's writing seeks to resurrect a potential feminine poetic gift into an actual poetic presence, to turn fiction into fact, indeed to invent a historical person after the event. In a sense this model also reverses the

Fig 32   Susanne Hermanski. *Die Erpresste Frau* (1985)

Fig 33   Diana Blok. *That's Life* (1984)

one analysed in the last chapters. While the poets discussed used the death of a historical woman so as to turn her into the rhetorical figure of the muse, the death of this imagined figure is seen to engender actual women's poetic gift. Woolf's apostrophe is not a rhetorical strategy aimed at disempowering her muse. On the contrary, the invocation serves to endow her with a power and with a historic subject position she never had. Woolf's is a double dialogue, for the apostrophe to a dead, absent woman is simultaneously addressed to a community of women listeners who are implicitly present and whose function is precisely to actualise the absent but potential feminine voice. Woolf's model also grounds writing in the death of a woman, yet the paradox that emerges in her anecdote is that, having inspired the writing of other women, the dead woman poet as muse will come into being again, for the first time.

In her poem 'Letter from Chicago' (1953), a love letter 'For Virginia Woolf', May Sarton similarly uses the death of her literary precursor to enact her own death and rebirth as a poet, at the same time that her poetic gift resurrects the dead beloved writer she has chosen as her muse.[5] She begins with an elegiac address, 'Four years ago I met your death here.' The scene for this experience of loss is 'a city of departures,' an unfamiliar site, both to her ('where I had never been before') and to her addressee ('where you never were'). The declaration 'Virginia Woolf is dead' mortifies both the scene and the receiver of the message – 'The city died. I died in the city.' Above all, she identifies with the death of

Woolf because she sees it as an interruption of her poetic work. In that she compares herself to a child 'Who cannot give his present after all', she implies that her writing is from the start conceived as a gift to her literary precursor. Here too, death, as I have repeatedly argued, is a moment of radical destability. Finding 'the world arrested at the instant of death', Sarton describes herself as having 'met your death and did not recognize you'.

After a four-year period of mourning, Chicago transforms into a 'city of arrival.' Wherever she goes, she recuperates the beloved dead writer – 'I found

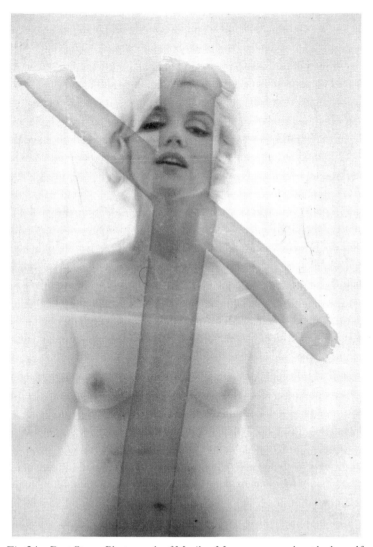

Fig 34 Bert Stern. Photograph of Marilyn Monroe, crossed out by herself (1962)

Fig 35   Cindy Sherman. *Untitled #153* (1985)

you', 'I recognized you' – even as she restitutes her own poetic gift – 'Wherever I went I had presents in my hands.' In a paradoxical argument, lament turns into rejoicing. A recognition of Woolf's death, of her irrevocable absence, translates into an affirmation of her presence, turns loss into repossession – 'You are not, never to be again / Never, never to be dead.' Implicitly comparing Woolf to Persephone, Sarton acknowledges her factual demise so as to allow for her repeated return – 'Never to be mourned again, / But to come back yearly . . . with the spring . . . / Freshly as agony or resurrection; / . . . Remaking itself, never still, / Never static, never lost.' Because she needs the inspirer and addressee of her speech to survive the event of death, she has split her muse from the event of facticity. While she could not recognise Woolf when she was confronted with her death, she can do so once the instant of death has been transcended by virtue of her poetic gift; once the irrevocability of death is successfully severed from her muse, yet also contained in her. The recuperative representation she finally achieves shows Woolf remaking herself, reappearing in a gesture of incessant mobility and revitalisation out of the earlier moment of disappearance. Here, too, death grounds both the imagined eternity of a literary precursor's presence and the writer's own creative power. With the dead poetess as muse come into being again, Sarton can establish another form of identity between herself and Woolf – 'I speak to you and meet my own life.' Her poetic gift to Woolf is a conflation of past, present and future: 'I send you love forward into the past.'

Sylvia Plath and Anne Sexton probably come most readily to mind when one thinks of twentieth-century woman poets who resort to the topos of the dead woman as muse. They repeatedly invoke their own suicide attempts, their fascination and desire for death, yet the apostrophe to the dead muse is addressed to themselves. The imagined own death makes up the inspirational source and the thematic content of this poetry. Given that the death they invoke carries their own gender, they themselves take on the dual function of referential object and addressee of the poetic utterance. In this act of autopoesis muse and creator coalesce such that the woman writer is liberated from her reduction to the merely inspirational function, which assigns to her the task of being mediatrix, material or mirror for another's creation. Plath and Sexton cite conventional conceptions of feminine death so as to recode these radically in such a way that death emerges as an act of autonomous self-fashioning. The theme in their poetry is neither the role of the muse nor a repression of death but rather feminine death as the creative resurrection of the represented woman.

In her poem 'Lady Lazarus' (1962), Plath proclaims 'Dying / Is an art, like everything else. / I do it exceptionally well / . . . I guess you could say I've a call.'[6] She reverses common notions of life and death, suggesting that her three suicide attempts and her repeated return from the realm of the dead should be seen as an expression of autonomous authorship. In that she herself legislates the boundary between life and death, she comes into a power of her own. Her return is a 'sort of walking miracle', a 'big striptease', a 'theatrical / Comeback in broad day / To the same face.' Only in relation to the doctor, who seeks to restitute her, does she take on the function of a reified body, which serves not her own but someone else's act of creation: 'I am your opus, / I am your valuable.' Yet the power inherent in the art of dying encompasses self-revivification as well. Not the doctor but rather she herself possesses the body in which she returns 'Out of the ash / I rise with my red hair / And I eat men like air.'

Sexton picks up the notion that the poetic representation of the art of dying may serve to preserve, indeed to constitute, a woman's subjectivity in her poem 'Sylvia's Death', dedicated, like Sarton's, to a dead woman poet. For the issue of *Triquarterly* commemorating Sylvia Plath, Sexton precedes this poem with a narrative, in which she explains that she wrote it for her at the news of her death, and that she added a second poem, written a year later, because it was 'written directly for both of us and for that place where we met . . . "balanced there, suicides sometimes meet" '.[7] In this narrative she describes how they 'talked death' at length and with burned-up intensity. Death served as a way to talk 'opposites'. Plath, for example, spoke of her suicide in sweet and loving detail. Indeed, this shared discourse on death is seen by Sexton as a form of stimulation, as though they were 'Sucking on it!' Though Sexton maintains that 'suicide is . . . the opposite of the poem', speaking about it was 'as if death made each of us a little more real at the moment'. She adds oxymoronically 'We talked death and this was life for us, lasting in spite of us, or better, because of us.' Yet, though she feels that they shared and reflected each other in death, giving each other the same answers, she denies any mutual influence between the two poets, 'Except for death – yes, we have that in common.' Death also makes for impersonality, for a type of speech beyond the personal. In a letter to Ted Hughes, dated 1967, she explains, 'That poem of mine makes everyone think I knew her well, when I only knew her death well.'[8]

Sexton's poem presents itself as the site for a dialogue about, for and to the dead woman poet as muse, even as she uses the apostrophe 'O Sylvia . . . Thief!' to imagine her own longed-for death. She invokes a woman who has realised what is for her as yet or rather again, merely potential, to voice her jealousy – 'how did you . . . / crawl down alone into the death I wanted so badly and for so long.' She represents death as what they share ('the one we talked about so often'); as what connects them, what 'we said we both outgrew', what they 'drank to' and what talked to them 'like brides with plots'.

This invocation of Plath's death serves to revivify her own fascination for suicide, even as it reflects her outgrowing. She, too, uses the body of a deceased woman to endow death with a signifier, yet her aim is to recognise death as perpetually present within life. Here the death of another woman does not serve as stabilising sign for death's absence, does not signify the speaker's own preservation of life against death, does not place death cannily outside. Rather Plath's suicide makes Sexton realise 'we store [death] up / year after year / . . . And me, / me too.' The news of Plath's act returns death as an irremovable presence within Sexton's own life.

Sexton adds 'what is your death, / but an old belonging, / a mole that fell out of one of your poems?' She suggests that this death was not only always present in both their lives but, more importantly, always already inhabiting Plath's poetic work. She merges the signifiers death and poetry in a way that does not use the latter to erase the former but rather presents them as being simultaneously present though opposites. In that Sexton uses suicide as a metonymy for Plath's poetry, what triumphs in her version of the dead woman as muse is the artistic potential of the invoked woman poet. For in Sexton's rendition, Plath's poetic expression always preceded death (the latter 'fell out of' the former), even as it was nourished by death.

The final address 'O tiny mother, / you too' is, then, significantly lacking in univocal reference. For the 'you too' not only refers to the fact that Plath also / again has responded to death's call, to 'our boy', the drummer who would beat on their eyes with an old story asking to let him come. It also refers to the bar fly, which 'ought to sing' when the world is in havoc (the king's gone, the queen's at her wit's end). This final apostrophe makes both Plath's death and her poetic voice present in a figure where the 'you too' implies 'me too', only to establish an identity with Sexton's own juggling of the opposites 'suicide' and 'the poem'. Havoc is invoked as a trope for the disruption Plath's death meant for her, with her poem imitating the voice of Plath, assuming the position of the bar fly which ought to sing, and as such in a sense speaking with and as Plath, representing the dead woman speaking through her. In this oxymoronic identification with the other poet's death – which serves to return the dead woman poet in the enmeshed image of Sexton's jealousy for her achieved death and the call for her poetic voice which ought to sing – in this aporia we have a representation where beyond speaking of, for or to a dead woman, Sexton explores the event of speaking her.

Turning to narratives by women writers I do not wish merely to offer a summary for the triangulation of femininity, death and textuality I have been tracing, but also to raise issues about feminine authorship, whose complexity can be formulated in the following way. The cultural topos or image, whose ubiquitous prevalence in western representation I have been concerned with, presupposes and confirms that Woman is constructed as Other than man; as that which is not the centre of a social or representational system. Hers is a position of non-coherence, of the void or an empty space between signifiers precisely because she is constructed as the vanishing point and the condition of western culture's fictions of itself; as the object and foundation of representation; as the telos and origin of man's desire to represent his culture; as the object and sign of his exchange with life and death, of his socio-economic exchanges and of his creativity.

The dilemma, as Teresa de Lauretis notes, is that women, meaning the real historical beings, cannot as yet be defined outside these discursive formations, even though their material existence is certain. Given that speaking as a woman implies a contradiction in terms, she suggests that a critical feminist reading of all the texts of culture 'instates the awareness of that contradiction and the knowledge of its terms.' In that it enacts the contradiction, such reading demonstrates the non-coincidence of Woman and women, and changes the representation into a performance which exceeds the text. This critical act of reading (which I have sought to undertake in the narrative analyses of the previous chapters), is also what the women writers I have chosen to end with do in their narratives. De Lauretis concludes that 'to perform the terms of the production of woman as text, as image, is to resist identification with that image'.[9] The particular cultural text I have been critically tracing and disclosing is that of authorship – with the masculine poet coming to birth over the effacement of the matrix materiality–

maternity–morality, and woman's authorship coterminous with a turn to a process of detextualisation, where the body functions as a sign, speaking out of death
and silence, or in the midst of a simultaneous enactment of incompatible roles.

How do women constitute and establish themselves as authors within a culture
which has not drafted this role, except as a blank, an aporia, a presence under
erasure? How can they substantiate their authorship as women, even though this
concept is culturally predetermined in such a way as to contradict their claim, and
even though they can not offer a definition outside these discursive formulations?
Because the historically real woman writer can not articulate herself entirely
devoid of cultural fictions of femininity, writing as a woman transpires into an act
of reading cultural texts (in this case the conjunction femininity, death and
textuality) critically, so as to enact the implied contradiction.

In a sense the impasse is a triple one. Firstly, the performance women's writing
enacts, so as to exceed the text it reads, involves the fact that the position of the
real historical woman writer is one of non-existence, in the sense that it has not
been established as a fixed occurrence in western culture's definition of
authorship. That is not to deny, of course, that at different historical moments
writing women were sanctioned, indeed praised. Secondly, the form of speech
conceded to women is in some sense always connected with death, in that either
woman speaks in silence, absence, anonymity, behind a pseudonym, as medium
secretary or muse or, in that it is precisely her death which for the first time
endows her with a publicly acknowledged voice. Thirdly, authorship, as the
production of symbolic textuality, requires the death of the feminine, and all the
values belonging to this cultural paradigm. This may explain why death in
childbirth is such a poetic theme. For here the explicitly sanctioned feminine
form of authorship, the creation of a child, falls together with the actual death of
the feminine body.

I argue against Barthes's notion of the death of the author, even though some
of the narratives I will present show that in the act of writing a process of
desubstantiation takes place. For the impulse of writing always also presupposes
the life of the author, a signature and a position in culture. It is, however, also true
that writing, as the act of translating a cultural representation into a performance
which exceeds the given text, does for women often mean a writing out of social
death, a writing inhabited at its centre by the uncanny resonance of the rhetoric of
'death' as silence, effacement, self-denial. This writing can never entirely deposit
the topos that links feminine self-articulation with death beyond its system of
representation; it can never securely turn feminine death into a canny trope
outside, so as to disavow this cultural heritage and be done with its curtailment.
This impasse is the crux of Woolf's anecdote. Reformulating Poe, she argues that
the most poetic theme for a woman, the one most likely to engender a community
of women writers, is after all the death not so much of a beautiful as of a poetically
gifted woman. Seeking to substantiate the feminine self as author, the woman
writer also embraces death. The gesture of her writing repeats *and* resists the
discursive formation from which it emerges and against which it performs.

Juliet Mitchell suggests that the woman writer might well be a hysteric. Hysteria, understood as the simultaneous acceptance and refusal of the fictions of femininity culture offers, is 'what a woman can do both to be feminine and to refuse femininity, within patriarchal discourse'. Rejecting the notion of female writing, of an authentic woman's voice, she argues for 'the hysteric's voice, which is *the woman's masculine language* . . . talking about feminine experience. It's both simultaneously the woman novelist's refusal of the woman's world – she is after all a novelist – and her construction from within a masculine world of that woman's world.'[10] Or, to align the gesture with an attitude toward death, it is the woman writer's refusal of the 'death' or non-existence culture ascribes to her – for, after all, she writes and signs her text – and her performance from within the masculine discursive formations of that death which is woman's terrain. Though my reading of all the cultural texts has sought to uncover moments of uncanny duplicity, what I will now add to my considerations is the altered position of the speaker, since explicitly and self-consciously writer and written dead feminine body occupy the same site.

Admittedly, to ask how women writers substantiate their authorship is a contemporary question, just as my choice to end with texts by women written since 1945 emerges from a desire to show the contemporariness of the issue I have been tracing. I have, of course, been interested throughout in not only the way that the enmeshment of femininity and death was culturally constituted but, more interestingly, how at times the same texts that served to sustain, also undermined this cultural project. In this discussion I did not distinguish women from men writers, because both wrote within the cultural context that uses femininity (as image, enigma, aporia) to represent alterity. Inevitably women write, in Mitchell's terms, from a masculine position, even if they do so to point out and denounce the way women's position arises from, through and with death. As the succession of my texts showed, some of the most radical critiques and disruptions of cultural conventions were, in fact, written by men and indeed my discussion privileged the question of deconstructive narrative strategy over that of gendered writing.

One of the arguments for a gender-specific difference in writing involves the question whether a cultural topos is reproduced in such a way as to allow for various readings, simultaneously confirming and disrupting the norm, so that the text's feminist critique is an effect of our reading; or whether a topos is repre- sented in the form of a critical scenario which can never be read in the con- firmative. The former would be the masculine, the latter the feminine variant. Though even this distinction may be an effect of our reading, one could argue that while women writers of earlier periods developed strategies, such as the pseudonym, to circumvent the aporia between their non-existence and their authorhsip, writing in the postmodern period they do not merely draft a feminine poetics or a feminine plot, but rather turn the theme of their authorship into a metatextual concern. To write explicitly out of indignation, in the language of the culture that produced it and resisting its logic (as Charlotte Brontë perhaps could not), may require the theoretical and social awareness contemporary culture offers to women writers. If earlier texts (by men and women) go so far as to disclose Woman as absence, ground and vanishing point of representatior women today write out of this aporia, out of this negation of their own voice.

Linda Hutcheon suggests that postmodern parodic strategies are often used by women writers 'to point to the history and historical power of those cultural representations, while ironically contextualizing both in such a way as to deconstruct them'.[11] She adds that such a strategy may make for an ambivalent political stance, since its double encoding means the simultaneous complicity with and contestation of the cultural dominants within which it operates. Yet I argue that though parodic strategy, understood as a rereading against the grain, may be complicitous with the values it inscribes even as it subverts them, the subversion does remain. In what I prefer to call a hysteric strategy, so as to link parody explicitly with the feminine position, there is no dialectic resolution or recuperative evasion of contradiction even as there is also complicity. The problem is that if the mastering gaze which separates subject from object of gaze is inherently masculine, can there be a feminine gaze? In response to this impasse hysterical writing installs conventions such as the masculinity of the gaze, the deadness of the feminine body, only to subvert and disturb the security of these stakes in cultural self-representation. Though such a critique is inscribed by complicity, such complicity may also be the most effective critique. As Hutcheon notes, complicity inevitably conditions the radicality of the critique and the possibility of suggesting change, but it may also be one of the only ways for feminist art to exist.

Remaining in a position of double encoding, articulating the dominant and the contestatory, as opposed to embracing change, implies an acceptance of castration which could refer not only to symbolic laws but also to the law of death. This conjunction is superlatively at stake in women writers' configuration of text and femininity. For a woman, complicity means a dual form of 'castration' – a subjection before language and before a social law that dictates her lack of position. Both bring her closer to an unveiled acknowledgement of mortality. One could speculate whether feminist writing, aimed at denying complicity with culture by drafting a feminine subject position outside its alienation, does not merely miss the point that all human beings are irrevocably subjected by cultural language. More crucially this may be a strategy by which death once again, as the other mark of castration, is repressed. Theirs would be as illusory a position of wholeness as the one I have been critiquing for masculine culture. My concern is to highlight not only the woman writer's complicity with culture, in her rereading of gender constructions, but also her complicity with death. For to speak – and therein lies the true fascination that these narratives pose – she must not only assume a masculine position but she must also perform the position of absence, of the double, which is the rhetoric of death. If masculinity, in the terms of Cixous, is the position of preservation, the aporic inclusion of its diametric opposite, namely excess and expenditure, may be what women's resistance addresses.

There are a multitude of examples for the way women writers today turn back to their heritage of cultural image repertoire, to repeat, invert and re-invent in the duplicitous gesture of miming and disclosing, of complying and resisting. The narratives I have chosen are of an exemplary nature, in so far as they can be read as a radical re-reading of the texts discussed in part PIV. Sylvia Plath's *The Bell Jar* (1963) offers the story of a premarital bride, faced with the choice of marriage, career and death. With *The Life and Loves of a She-Devil* (1983) Fay Weldon offers another version of the second beloved doubling a mourner's first wife. Margaret Atwood shows, in *Lady Oracle* (1976), how writing occurs on the threshold between life and death, with the writer caught between the double and the absent. Finally, Angela Carter's *The Infernal Desire Machines of Doctor Hoffman* (1972) can be read as a reworking of the theme of the dead beloved as muse.

These texts demonstrates the hysteric's voice, oscillating as they do between complicity and resistance. They accept the validity of masculine narrative formations and tropes only to show that these may be a necessary but not the only truth there is. They play with these narratives, take them seriously by representing what it looks like if conventions are taken to their extreme, or purposely misunderstood so as to be taken literally. By using distance and comedy they take conventions to excess only to transform them into the macabre or the grotesque. Whether this excess, this hyperbolic overturning of the trope, engenders a comic or a tragic mode, it makes the resulting clichés true, and in this tautology unbearable because obvious, unavoidable, irrevocable. Whether the narrative strategy is one of reliteralising tropes, of making explicit the meaning of ambivalent gestures or of disclosing the presuppositions hidden beneath cultural commonplaces, in all cases the parody or excess of the hysteric voice makes the impasse women find themselves in unambivalently clear, on the thematic and the rhetoric level of the text. In a sense these texts compulsively repeat so as to disclose the point of non-existence beyond which a woman writing as yet can't move.

In these texts the social construction of the feminine self, fixed by a masculine gaze, is both confirmed and ironised, because the body, as site for this social inscription, is self-consciously present. The woman writing shows herself as subject and object of her representation of woman as sign; of woman positioned by gender and by death. Rather than moving towards a recuperation of stable order, these texts emphasise the precariousness and illusion of any regained stability and preserve the difference of sexuality and of death within. The dance on the boundary between life and art is once again shown to be coterminous with a game between life and death. Their parodic play with images is always disrupted by a sense of the real, of the fact that they write explicitly out of the concern of historic women, just as any utterance emerging from real outrage and urgency invariably moves back to language, resorts to and perpetuates predetermined images, tropes, narratives.

One could see Sylvia Plath's protagonist Esther Greenwood as a modern Fräulein Else, living in suburban New England in the 1950s, for she too is a premarital bride in a transitional state. For her, also, the vacillation between possible choices encompasses both an insecurity about her sexual desires and an inability to decide between marriage and a career as a writer. With sexual pureness 'the great issue', she longs for the day she can cross 'the boundary line' (85). Although this desire for defloration divides her from those friends who remain pure until marriage, she can also not carry through the promiscuity of her sexually daring friends.

Her internship with a New York fashion magazine confronts her with a situation where, after nineteen years of good marks, prises and grants, she is forced to recognise that she is not perfect. Rather than acknowledging her limits, she translates the fear that she may not always be successful into a radical questioning of all her earlier plans about her future as professor and writer. In her world of stark contrasts she is either a complete success or a complete failure. The prospect of marriage, in turn, seems equally perplexing. Because she wants 'change and excitement and to shoot off in all directions' (87), because she conceives of herself as 'flying back and forth between one mutually exclusive thing and another for the rest of my days' (98), she fears psychic rigidity. To be married and have children, if it means not writing poems any more, strikes her 'like being brainwashed . . . numb as a slave in some private, totalitarian state' (89).

As her internship comes to an end she finds it more and more difficult to decide to do anything, and once she has returned to her home, the weight of her undefined position and of the seemingly incompatible possibilities open to her induces an overwhelming sense of impasse. Her existence seems like a 'black, airless sack with no way out' (136) to which she can respond only with mental and physical inertia, lack of interest in her world and insomnia. One escape she imagines for herself is that of changing her name, moving to another city, so as to abandon all the conflicts that confront her – the pressure to excel at her prestigious women's college, her shortcomings in the New York publishing world, marriage to the promising medical student and the threat of psychic numbness. In her conjectures she would be 'simple Elly Higginbottom, the orphan' (140).

To counterbalance the private dissolution of her heroine, Plath introduces the public electrocution of the Rosenbergs. As this piece of news repeatedly inscribes itself in Esther's thoughts ('I couldn't get them out of my mind' (1)), death increasingly emerges as the solution to her dilemmas. Suicide, she believes, will foreclose the need to make a decision and appears as the sought for release from conflicts. She transfoms supplementary social exchanges, notably her as yet undefined sexual and professional relations, into an issue of the originary division of life and death. Death is, on the one hand seen conventionally as a form of purification, of throwing off stifling materials. During her last night in New York, she throws her fashionable wardrobe out of the hotel window, signifying her desire to shed burdensome roles only to leave her with no sense of self. In this transitional phase, to lose the complete acknowledgement of the masculine gaze – be it literally that of her boyfriend, or that of her culture as it is represented by the magazine editor and her teachers – makes her aware of her non-existence beneath her hysterical pose as the successful prize-winning student and poet.

On the other hand, the plethora of death plots she designs for herself before she finally takes an overdose of sleeping pills occur significantly after she realises her limitations as a novel writer. Having been rejected for a poetry course at Harvard, she decides to spend the summer months instead writing a novel about a heroine called Elaine, 'myself, only in disguise' (126). She realises that her lack of experience impedes the project – 'How can I write about life when I'd never had a love affair or a baby or seen anybody die . . . I decided I would put off the novel until I had gone to Europe and had a lover' (128). This recourse to experience implies that she has to write the narrative of her life with her body as medium before she can write it as a novel in disguise. Yet the narrative she must enact is precisely not the marriage (lover and baby), but rather the death plot.

In this confusion of the semiotic with the somatic, she, like Else, precedes her suicide attempt by fashioning herself in the image of diverse death plots. If her idea of changing her identity to the orphan Elly Higginbottom is a fancied social death, she tries to imagine Japanese disembowelment as another alternative 'when everything went wrong' (145). She ends her detailed description of this ritual with the ironic comment, 'It must take a lot of courage to die like that. My trouble was I hated the sight of blood' (146). In the same vein she compares a snapshot of herself with the newspaper photo of a starlet who died after a 68-hour coma, only to find that mouth and nose matched, and that if the dead girl's eyes were opened, they would have 'the same dead, black, vacant expression as the eyes in the snapshot' (154).

Such mental images of her deadness and fascination with death are counterbalanced with the first experiment in suicide, and here too the reference to other cultural images and the staging of the act is crucial. For enacted on the narrative level is a distance between the narrator and herself as the protagonist, so that Plath supplements Esther's death speculations with a comic, self-ironic commentary which seems possible only upon hindsight. Her narrative strategy is to acknowledge a complicity with cultural images by presenting her protagonist's fantasies as clichés, yet turning these to excess so as to undermine them. The effect produced is that the impasse of her death plot catches Esther between clichés of death and a real desire for it. To give authority to her narrative beyond these conventional images she must simultaneously present them and disclose them as clichés.

Imagining 'some old Roman philosopher or other,' Esther decides to lie in a tub of water and open her veins. Finding herself unable to cut the white and defenceless wrists, however, she tries looking in the mirror of the medicine cabinet, so 'it would be like watching somebody else, in a book or a play'. Yet these lengthy conjectures and experiments in pose waste the morning. Fearing that her mother will find her before she is done, she is forced to interrupt the entire attempt. Later, lying on the beach she continues to play through her suicide fantasies, only to find herself each time at an impasse that moves the seriousness of her undertaking to the grotesque. She decides that she can't slit her wrists on the beach, because she 'had the razors, but no bath'; to use the bath in a boarding house wouldn't work because 'I'ld hardly have time to do it and step into the tub when somebody would be pounding on the door'; the thought of sharks' teeth and whales' earbones littered at the bottom of the ocean like gravestones leaves her too coward to attempt drowning.

As though death, too, were defying her desire for a clear definition, her attempt to hang herself fails because the ceilings in her home are too low, so that she likens the silk cord dangling from her neck to a 'yellow cat's tail' finding no place to fasten it. Her attempt to strangle herself while sitting on her mother's bed in turn fails because her body has all 'sorts of little tricks' to protect itself, like making her hands go limp in the crucial second (168). In the same vein, her second attempt at drowning herself in mid-ocean fails, because each time she dives down she pops up again, her will to die beaten by the laws of gravity (170). Even her description of the attempt to take an overdose of sleeping tablets in the basement of her home is not entirely devoid of such a grotesque tone. The narrator emphasises the discrepancy between Esther's desire to 'do things in a calm, orderly way', and her imperfect realisation of this death plot. Only after many tries does she manage to fit her body into a gap in the wall, and in the voice commenting this scene retrospectively, she depicts herself in the posture she has chosen to wait for death as one 'crouched at the mouth of the darkness, like a troll' (179). Like the rehearsals she describes in such fond and yet comic detail, this attempt also fails, and her desire to embrace death only ends by returning her to the world.

The description of Esther's mental and social process of recuperation, of course, makes this narrative different from texts discussed so far. Having chosen death, she finds herself forced to conclude her liminality as premarital bride by directly confronting a sexual and a professional choice. This significant sexual encounter with a man, her return to college, as well as the textual repetition of the entire period of mental breakdown and recovery in the form of an auto-biographical novel, contradict the choice of death, yet are possible only once she has chosen suicide and returned. As she recovers, her fantasy of killing herself and its frustration remain with her. The narrator spends the same loving detail describing Esther's failure to jump out of the car of her sponsor as it passes over a river. Because she is wedged in between her mother and her brother in the back seat, when she moves forward, each lays a hand on the door handle (196). With the same self-ironic humour that she used for the earlier episodes she comments 'I missed a perfectly good chance'. Along the same lines her defloration, resulting in a haemorrhage, is also connected with images of fatality she remembers from Victorian novels 'where woman after woman died, palely and nobly, in torrents of blood, after a difficult childbirth' (244), only to be told by the doctor that her trouble can be cured.

Even after her shock treatment is completed and the bell jar suspended above her head she admits that the images of death remain with her as 'my landscape' (250). Though she has learned to make decisions about romantic and professional questions, her mental restability is precarious, the sense of being 'blank and stopped as a dead baby' only indefinately forestalled, and with it the desire for suicide only deferred as a future potential – 'I wasn't sure at all. How did I know that someday . . . the bell jar, with its stifling distortions, wouldn't descend again?' (254).

The ritual of being born twice – 'patched, retreaded and approved for the road' – with which the novel ends requires the death of a woman like her. As in *The Woman in White*, Esther's social restitution follows upon the funeral of her double Joan, the girl her boyfriend dated before her, and who, like Esther, was hospitalised after a failed suicide attempt. Though both girls initially progess, Joan ends up hanging herself, and the news of Esther's leaving the hospital is presented between an account that she feels responsible for Joan's death and her presence at the funeral. The final scene, where she enters the doctors' weekly board meeting so as to get the approval for her departure immediately follows upon a rendition of the vitality she feels standing at Joan's grave – I am, I am, I am" (250).

The latter had read about Esther's disappearance and the police search in the newspaper, saved all the clippings and, inspired by Esther's story, ran way to New York to imitate her death. Meeting her in the mental hospital, Joan shows these photographs to her model, and Esther is faced with the printed narrative of her suicide attempt, the version of the headlines and copy accompanying each image. For the first time she perceives her suicide as a story severed from her and she has difficulty remembering where each shot was taken. This outside story, representing her worried mother calling the police once she finds her daughter gone and bloodhounds searching for the missing body, is, chronologically speaking, the first moment that creates distance between Esther and the event of her attempted death. When Joan suggests 'keep them . . . you ought to stick them in a scrap book', she recommends a translation of suicide into narrative, the textualisation of an actual near death experience, which the narrator will indeed undertake, though in a different tone, with her narrative of The *Bell Jar*. The fact that this first suicide narrative available to Esther should be that of the cliché images of news reporting is yet another example for the duplicitous way in which Plath's heroine is positioned within her cultural image repertoire. Implicitly Esther's suicide fantasies feed off such conventional images even as her novel about her suicide attempt also tries to convey the realness of this desire.

While in Schnitzler's text Else's dying body stands in for the memoirs she does not write, with death encoded as a form of rebirth, Plath resorts to a chiasmic structure. At first Esther uses her body as medium, fantasising and then realising death *in lieu* of the novel about Elaine she can't write. Yet The *Bell Jar* is implicitly the novel that Sylvia Plath, disguised as Esther Greenwood, couldn't have her fictional self write until she had experienced death. It is written out of death, in contradistinction to the external rendition of her suicide attempt in the newspaper as well as to the fantasy of spectators like Joan. In this novel she offers a reading of her death-like self, not only by repeating the death and rebirth she designs for herself but also by supplementing it with the double of the self-ironic commentator. Even as she tells the story of how her body and her text turn death back into life, death remains potentially a revenant in this sublation.

Regina Barreca suggests that one variant of women writers' cultural critique as complicity could be called 'metaphor-into-narrative,' to indicate that 'by attaching a buried literal meaning to what is intended to be inert and meaningless, women subvert the paradigmatic gesture of relief that is seen to characterize comedy'.[12] Reliteralising what has become merely symbolic, this strategy serves to uncover some of the presuppositions tacitly accepted in an act of 'feminine transsubstantiation that makes a word the thing itself as well as the representation of the thing'. Where the joke depends on the mistake of taking something figuratively when it turns out to have been meant literally comedy is more apocalyptic than reassuring. Giving somatic materiality to what seems safely symbolic can involve fatality not only in the sense of turning a living body into a dead sign but also as an 'ability to bring the dead back to life'. The duplicity this narrative strategy unfolds is that, even as it reduplicates cultural conventions of femininity, to 'kill' a real woman into a cliché, it also revives the 'dead' metaphor in a twofold manner. The cliché as dead metaphor is shown to be alive after all, even as this resubstantiation also serves to articulate another meaning, namely feminine power, buried beneath woman's social deformation by cultural representations.

In Fay Weldon's *Life and Loves of a She-Devil* the rhetoric of reliteralising is doubled by the theme of revivification. A safe, figurative meaning loses its reassuring quality by turning literal when the protagonist kills her body so as to return as the living embodiment of a cliché of feminine beauty. As a dead woman is literally unburied and revived, two forms of rhetorical unburying occur. The socially dead feminine body has its analogy in the supposedly inert and meaningless figurative phrase used to characterise it. Ruth realises that the world wants women to 'look up to men'. However, this 'dead' trope or cultural convention can be materialised only in the advent of death. Ruth literally cuts her body up so as to comply with the dimensions culturally conceived as beautiful in a woman and she gains power by confirming to excess the cultural formations that were shown to turn her prematurely into an inert and meaningless being. Deconstructing clichés of femininity, Weldon uncovers tacitly accepted presuppositions and shows that curtailing language can conceivably produce real suffering, only by having her protagonist perform these cultural formations to excess in a representation with her body that reliteralises the contradiction – Ruth has power but she is bodily transformed. The enactment of a non-coincidence of Woman and women is such that she self-consciously turns her historical self into a figure, resisting an identification with these curtailing images precisely by complying with them, but to excess 'a comic turn, turned serious' (278). In an aporia of resistance Ruth enacts what it looks like if the language that performs tropes of femininity becomes reality, so that the figuratively dead feminine body is literally killed, only to become alive and socially powerful for the first time.

The big, clumsy and sulky Ruth enacts her social death as the first step in an intricate plan of revenge against her husband Bobbo, who has deserted her to live with the graceful, delicate and elegant romance writer Mary Fisher. She burns down her house, sends her children to their father, and disappears, taking on the duplicitous position between presence and absence. As a result Bobbo can't marry Mary Fisher, because he cannot get divorced from a woman he can't produce in court, and though she might very well be dead, the law will not declare her so without specular proof of her corpse. In the liminality between a social and a biological death, with no distinct identity, Ruth assumes different names to perform a variety of professions as part of a brilliant design meant to destroy her rival and get her husband back, 'but on my own terms' (85).

She works as a nurse in an insane asylum, learns accounting and bookkeeping, opens an agency that places secretaries with firms and finds a position as housekeeper to a judge, and then a priest. In the course of her monstrous plan, she breaks into Bobbo's office, alters his files to assure that he will be put on trial for embezzlement, convinces the judge to give him a seven-year-sentence with no bail and transfers two million dollars from his personal account to their joint account in Switzerland. Mary Fisher, in turn, loses all her money in the law case, is forced to watch the slow deterioration of her beautiful home in a tower by the sea, and loses her gift for writing successful romance novels. Tired, impoverished, with Bobbo in prison and refusing to see her, she wants to be dead in the romantic image of being 'at one with the stars and the foaming sea' (243). Yet she dies in a hospital, forlorn and deserted by all, deprived even of her beauty as a result of medical treatment.

The text's rhetorical turn of excess engenders a sublation of the comic into the serious, a disturbingly uncanny enmeshment of the figural with the literal. The brilliant twist Weldon gives to the resolution of Ruth's vengeance against her husband and her rival is a critical rereading of the theme of the dead first wife returned at the body of her double, for which I used Poe's 'Ligeia' as model. The exchange between social death and rebirth Ruth enacts with each new profession becomes concrete, is enacted at her body when, in the course of surgery, it is literally killed and reborn. And this desubstantiation and return, is, furthermore, mirrored by the trajectory of her double, Mary Fisher's life. The more Mary Fisher's beautiful body deteriorates physically, the more Ruth changes her ugly body into a beautiful one; she gets new teeth and loses weight. The body she convinces her surgeons to change her into, with the money she has transferred to Switzerland, is precisely the pretty, delicate body of Mary Fisher, as Ruth finds it on the dust jacket of one of her novels. Recreating herself in the image of the woman her husband preferred to her, she recreates herself as a repetition of the publicity image of that image.

The trope Weldon installs so as to critique it is the cliché that woman needs to kill herself into a beautiful ideal to have power over her husband. She also deconstructs a definition of love, which poses Woman as man's phantom, as the symptom of his fantasies. Her story of a woman of six foot two, 'who had tucks taken in her legs', literalises the cliché of the perfect beloved serving as the site where an earlier love object or mental image is refound by the masculine lover, yet she does so to such an excess that the result is 'a comic turn, turned serious'. Owing to her exaggeration, Ruth exceeds, even as she performs the cultural dictate that if woman needs man's gaze to assure her being alive, she is as good as dead once she has lost this eye, so she can just as well literally kill her body. She fulfills the social death her husband performed by leaving her, and which she embellished by literally disappearing when, about to enter surgery she says goodbye to her body 'that had so little to do with her nature, and knew she'd be glad to be rid of it' (242). Her social resurrection can only occur when she takes on the body of the woman who displaced her in her husband's gaze, when she returns as a copy of the body of the second beloved.

Her recreation is seen in analogy to conventions of fairy tale and gothic imagery, as though her reshaped body were not only resurrecting her dead predecessor but also revitalising these clichés. Of one surgeon she says 'he was her Pygmalion', only to add 'but she would not depend upon him, or admire him, or be grateful' (249). When she finally leaves the hospital she evokes the Little Mermaid, for the final dance with her doctor is such that 'with every step it was as if she trod on knives' (275). Another surgeon refers to her 'as Frankenstein's monster, something that needed lightning to animate it and get it moving' (271), and indeed, what is being reanimated are doubly dead body parts – her killed body and the imitation of the dead Mary Fisher. Rhetorically, Ruth seems to resubstantiate these cultural texts in the same gesture that she revitalizes Mary Fisher's conventional beauty. Yet this feminine transsubstastiation is duplicitous. In the monstrous act of totally refashioning her body, she both is and isn't the first Mary Fisher; she confirms and critiques the textual models of Pygmalion's and Frankenstein's creations.

In that she re-emerges in the guise of the second beloved, who herself has died for loss of Bobbo's supporting gaze, Weldon's narrative ends with the first wife returned at the site of the second beloved's body, but as the ghost of the second woman. At Mary Fisher's funeral Ruth makes her first appearance, and is duly recognised by her rival's mother as the deceased sending 'her own ghost to her funeral!' Bobbo, to whom she says she is his wife, answers 'My wife died . . . long ago . . . But there was someone called Mary Fisher. Aren't you her?' (272f.). With the resubstantiation of a trope over the resurrected body of a dead woman, Weldon suggests that when the beloved is literally a refound mental image, she proves to be monstrous and duplicitous – the angel and the she-devil in one, both alive and dead. Ruth's self-creation out of death permanently installs a double – she is Mary Fisher in body and the vindictive Ruth in spirit, the dead body of her rival returned and her own body destroyed. She says of Bobbo, 'he has us both in the one flesh: the one he discarded, the one he never needed at all. Two Mary Fishers' (277).

In this pose of the double, Ruth is so monstrous because external bodily perfection shelters the aggressive desire to wreak destruction. As she explains 'I cause Bobbo as much misery as he ever caused me, and more.' Yet, realising this desire for destruction is a sword that cuts both ways. Ruth has gained power by having resubstantiated an image. But this acquisition of power required that she should deform herself into the image of perfect feminine beauty. Taking the desire of her husband too seriously, Ruth exaggerates her attempt to comply to such a degree that she discloses the underlying cruelty. The impasse her excessive performance enacts is that in order to castrate her husband, and with him the cultural formations he represents, she has to castrate herself, to die socially and then somatically.

In Lady Oracle, Atwood explicitly thematises the proximity of death to the production of fictions of the self and to issues of feminine authorship. Her protagonist Joan Foster exemplifies to excess that the writer feeds off an exchange between life and death. Caught between an elimination and a constitution of the self, because present to others only in the guise of various doubles of herself, and living various degrees of figural absence, Joan's spectral and multiple existence as writer encompasses a slippage between materiality and textuality. Atwood also uses the strategy of hyperbolic parody, yet she installs cultural conventions that link women, writing and death only to have these go awry. They do so significantly at those moments where the real inadvertently breaks in and discloses the protagonist's imaginary confusion between art and life.

At the onset of her narrative, Joan explains 'I planned my death carefully, unlike my life . . . I wanted my death, by contrast, to be neat and simple . . . to disappear without a trace, leaving behind me the shadow of a corpse, a shadow everyone would mistake for solid reality' (7). The narrative frame sets in after Joan has staged a boat accident in Canada, attempting to destroy a self which has outgrown manageable contours. Moving from writing texts to performing suicide this writer of Costume Gothics and female occult poetry hopes to regain control over her life. By turning art into life, she seeks to discarded her historical biography and design herself anew.

Significantly this enactment of her social death is based on a story she read in the newspaper about a woman who drowned in Lake Ontario and was officially pronounced dead though her body was never recovered. Having fled to Italy, she crops her head and burns her long red hair, fearing it is her one traceable trait and she buries her old clothes in effigy of her 'former self'. She feels as though she were 'getting rid of a body, the corpse of someone I'd killed,' so as to 'start being another person, a different person entirely' (20). Through death Joan seeks to give birth to a new personality once an inquest has been held and a death certificate issued though the corpse is missing. Her stay in Italy is explicitly perceived as being on the 'Other Side', in limbo, and she sees herself in analogy to 'the dead come back to watch over the living' (309).

In this liminality she waits to hear whether the death plot she constructed in life has indeed succeeded; at the same time that she undertakes two forms of writing. She literally writes a new Costume Gothic and she figurally writes her past life in the form of mental reminiscences. These three narratives become more and more enmeshed in that Joan perpetuates the cliché images of gothic stereotypes in her fiction but also fashions herself in life in complicity with these clichés. In the course of her stay in Italy, Joan discovers that, far from materialising into a new identity, her old self returns. Her landlord returns the buried clothes 'neatly pressed and ironed' (324), assuring her that the villagers were never deceived into thinking her other than Joan Foster who had been there last year with her husband. She discovers that her staged death resulted in anything but a neat solution. Extra witnesses, who watched the accident from the beach, contradict the testimony of her two friends, and Sam and Marlene are arrested for murder. Once a reporter has discovered her, her only option is to return to the world, and Atwood ends her novel by implying that Joan will now acknowledge the contradictions her life has imposed on her rather than seek to efface multiplicity within her self.

The self-portrait which Joan embeds within this narrative frame represents her repeated attempt to vanish and re-emerge as someone else, only to be forced to acknowledge the eternal return of the same. Her confusion between the literal and the figural enacts a process of feminine transsubstantiation, in the course of which 'I fabricated my life, time after time' (150), even as she produces written texts. In so doing she traces a threefold gesture of doubling and absenting the self. For one, she tries to kill her actual historical identity to fashion herself a new one, each time she seeks to gain control over her life. Secondly, the texts she produces alongside her fabricated life imply an oscillation between the double and the absent in so far as she signs her Gothic fiction with a pseudonym. Though her poetry appears under her own name, it, in turn, implies absence in so far as the inspiration arose from a trance at the same time that it doubles her other writing, only as 'a Gothic gone wrong' (232). Finally, the texts she writes and the plot she fabricates with her life increasingly involve feminine death figures, citing the cultural conventions of vanishing and reduplicated ladies.

Early on she uses her body as the medium by which to actualise an image of herself. The war between her mother and herself is waged with her body as the 'disputed territory' and she turns herself into a two-hundred pound woman precisely because she won't let her mother 'make me over in her image, thin and beautiful' (88). Once she has lost a hundred pounds, so as to fulfil the condition her Aunt Lou set when she made Joan her sole heiress, she feels she has become someone different, 'like being born fully grown at the age of nineteen: I was the right shape, but I had the wrong past. I'd have to get rid of it entirely and construct a different one for myself, a more agreeable one' (141). Staging her first social death, she disappears from Canada after her mother tried to stab her with a knife, and endows this second, thin self, with a new name – Louise K. Delacourt. In this guise she has her first sexual encounter with a Polish Count and begins her career as a writer of Gothic romances.

When she meets her future husband Arthur, a radical Marxist who believes in true paths, she feels she must fashion yet another double, fearing that the actual historical facts would displease him. She assumes her old name, though she invents 'a mother for his benefit, a kind, placid woman who died of a rare disease . . . shortly before I met him' (41) just as she fashions herself in the image of the popular high school cheerleader. Part of this reduplication of her self means denying past selves, so that when she shows him a photograph she cannot admit that the fat woman in the picture is herself and instead devises an 'entire spurious past for this shadow on a piece of paper' which is in fact 'my own shucked-off body' (91). She keeps her other identity as writer of Costume Gothics hidden from him. Like Tess she feels she can only marry Arthur if he knows the 'truth about me and accepted me as I was, past and present' (197) yet unlike her literary predecessor she decides to postpone her revelations to some later date.

Indeed throughout she tries to keep her 'two names and identities as separate as possible' (33) because she thrives on being two people at once, 'with two sets of identification papers, two bank accounts, two different groups of people who believed I existed' (213). Once she adds yet another double to the existing list of fat and thin self, of Joan Foster and Louise Delacourt, namely her clandestine relation with the performance artist Royal Porcupine, she realises that her self-duplication involves excess – 'I was more than double, I was triple, multiple' (246). Accordingly her public figure, the Joan Foster her Canadian publishers send on tour to promote *her poetry* is seen as yet another impersonation, 'my dark twin, my funhouse-mirror reflections. She was taller than I was, more beautiful, more threatening. She wanted to kill me and take my place' (251).

In this dialectic of disappearance and return, the repressed is everything but successfully effaced. As it returns and catches up with her, the multiple selves, rather than superseding each other in sequence are all simultaneously present and produce a monstrous hybrid of contradictions: 'a sorry assemblage of lies and alibis, each complete in itself but rendering the others worthless' (211). Repeatedly, people disappear only to reappear in her life, such as the ingenious inquisitor of her childhood, Marlene, or the spiritualist Leda Sprott, who performs her wedding ceremony as a minister called E. P. Revele. Most crucially, the astral body of her mother appears to Joan during a spiritualist meeting even before her death, only to repeat this uncanny presence at the moment of her death, during Joan's marriage ceremony, and in her daughter's dreams. The dead mother she figurally killed when she left her, and again when she invented a different one for her husband, functions as a lost body which remains even after death, just like her other, fat self which she sees whenever she looks in the mirror.

After the mortician Fraser Buchanan tries to blackmail her with his discovery of her two secret identities, anonymous death threats should follow. The disclosure of her multiple fictions would, indeed, be a kind of death. The cliché, whose hidden meaning Atwood unburies without denying its validity, is that romance/death fantasies offer an escape from reality. Joan must literalise a fantasied escape to undo the impasse her recourse to fantasy has created. If the *peripeteia* of her duplicitous married life in Canada is marked by the recognition that it was Arthur who was sending the death messages, escape means realising the fiction of this desire. She believes he wants her to go and she decides 'I would have to die' (293).

Yet the form of complicity as critique Atwood lets her protagonist trace is such that she is fascinated with the cultural image repertoire that links women to death even as she knows these clichés are unhealthy. The excuse Joan gives for not letting her husband know she writes Gothics is that he would consider them worse 'than trash, for didn't they . . . perpetuate degrading stereotypes of women as helpless and persecuted.' To which she adds, they 'did and I knew it, but I couldn't stop' (34). Indeed, she invokes Andersen's little mermaid and Moira Shearer in *The Red Shoes*, to distinguish herself from these two literary predecessors even as she compares herself with them. They had not been able to 'please the handsome prince; both of them had died' while she will survive not because she doesn't dance, but because she does her dancing 'behind closed doors' (216). Later, she dances on broken glass, so that the pain in her cut feet, like those of the little mermaid, impinge any escape from her Italian rooms.

More central is her repeated citation of the Lady of Shalott, who is initially invoked to demonstrate that Joan is romantic despite herself. Imagining her floating down a winding river in a boat as the supreme icon of romantic desire, she explains, 'I really wanted to have someone . . . say I had a lovely face, even if I had to turn into a corpse in a barge-bottom first' (143). The woman who emerges from her trance-induced writing, enormously but unhappily powerful, resonates the Lady of Shalott – 'in the death boat, why does she sing' (222). She is cited again at precisely the moment where actuality disrupts Joan's fictions by making them literally true. Once the newspapers suggest her death was a suicide, she turns into a public 'death cult'. With the press speaking about her morbid intensity, her doomed eyes and her fits of depression, her collection of poems becomes a necrophiliac success – 'I'd been shoved into the ranks of those other unhappy ladies . . . who'd been killed by a surfeit of words. There I was, on the bottom of the death barge where I'd once longed to be, my name on the prow, winding my way down the river' (313).

Joan finds herself confronted with a narrative of her supposed suicide that is other than her intention. At first she thinks that she could now imitate the news version because it seems plausible ('I began to feel that even though I hadn't committed suicide, perhaps I should have'). Then she comes to realise that her public can express regret and remember her ethereal beauty only if she is dead, while a rematerialisation in the flesh would be extremely upsetting. At stake in her fatal self-authorship is an inversion of the notions of death and life. Joan ends by disagreeing with this interpretation, 'I pretended to die so I could live, so I could have another life. They were being perverse and it made me angry' (315).

In the same manner, the Bluebeard theme is initially introduced as a comic point of reference. Describing her own lack of self-control, Joan suggests that in a fairy tale 'I would be one of the two stupid sisters who open the forbidden door and are shocked by the murdered wives, not the third, clever one who keeps to the essentials' (152). This citation, however, takes on a life of its own in the same gesture that she collapses the distinction between her life and the Gothic novel she is writing. In her tale about Charlotte's love for Lord Redmond, Joan has the housekeeper explain that the current Lady Felicia is the third wife, the other two having disappeared into a maze. Even though Joan's plot plays with Charlotte's premonition that 'someone was trying to kill her' (194), the conventions of Gothic fiction demand that 'Felicia, of course, would have to die; such was the fate of wives' (316).

Joan's trouble with getting her Gothic plot right transpires into the symptom for the way her three distinct forms of doubling and absenting the self – her fabrications in life, her writing while absent from life, and her rereading of previous texts – increasingly coalesce only to go awry. Finding herself in sympathy with Felicia, unable to sacrifice her for a Charlotte whose purity was begining to bore her, she realises that this Gothic is turning into an autobiography at the same time that her life seems to become a Gothic gone wrong. As her Gothic narrative and her stay in Italy reach their apex she finds herself in a new impasse. Having discovered that she in fact identifies herself with Felicia, she finds herself in the position of the wife to be killed. Her staged suicide ricochets back in the fanstasy of murder.

Typical of Atwood's strategy of excessive doubling, Joan comes to believe that Bluebeard is ubiquitously present in a plethora of figures that return from death. The sequence begins with her imagining that her buried clothes are growing themselves a body, namely that of the Fat Lady, 'my ghost, my angel'. She imagines being absorbed within her former body, 'Disguised, concealed ... obliterated' (321). Next, she lets Felicia drown in an unfortunate accident, only to find her character returning in her own guise, 'an enormously fat woman ... Damp strands of red hair straggled down her bloated face', and fading again when, having addressed Redmond as Arthur, Joan's fictional character resists such absorption into his writer's personal history (322). In what seems the excess of a 'hysterical' (328) woman, Joan adds to her conjecture that her Italian landlord is trying to kill her, the spectral presence of her mother, stretching her arms, wanting her to join her on the Other Side. Significantly she uses this spectral presence to decode her dead mother as the Muse for her poetry – 'It had been she standing behind me in the mirror ... her voice whispered the words. She had been the lady in ... the death barge' (330).

If she comes to recognise her mother as the inspirational 'reflection' of her poetry, and as such, one of the sources for her fascination with/anxiety about death, her husband emerges as the pivotal source for death anxiety in her Gothic texts. Art and life completely collapse, when Joan rewrites the maze scene, taking the perspective of Felicia, to discover the other wives in the central plot, and Redmond as the killer in disguise: 'he wanted to murder her as he had murdered his other wives . . . to replace her with the other one'. In Atwood's deconstruction, if every love object is a refound object, then the found object also always replaces by killing the predecessor it resembles. As the fictional Redmond turns into Joan's fiction of Arthur, a knock on the door lets her reach for the Cinzano bottle so as to be ready to face the man 'who was waiting for me, for my life'.

With all her fictions condensed into one death-threatening vortex – her fat self, her mother, her characters, her husband – the entrance of a representative of reality into her transitional space completely disrupts her liminal existence between self-absence and self-double, by disclosing that the death plot was a complete fiction. The man she hits is a total stranger, a reporter looking for a story, and his appearance forces her to return to the world, to undo the fatal artwork that had been the apex of her fabrication with life and engendered the messy resolution in her mind and in her social world. Though the tacit assumptions underlying the image of feminine death have been unburied (like her discarded clothes and the multiple selves they represent), this cultural convention, with the confusion of art and life it engendered, has also not been entirely dispersed. Though Joan renounces writing Costume Gothics she ends on the note 'I don't think I'll ever be a very tidy person' (345).

Angela Carter's *The Infernal Desire Machines of Doctor Hoffman* is also a feminist re-reading of the cultural cliché that Woman is man's symptom, the phantom of his desires. Her text performs the theme of the dead beloved as muse, with the heroine functioning as a free floating signifier, absent in any actual sense from the text she inspires. As the narrator Desiderio explicitly states in his introduction, he dedicates this memory-text to the daughter of the magician he destroyed, the 'inexpressible woman . . . the miraculous Albertina' (13f.). Writing as he does at the onset of his own death, his text recalls Albertina because it is his desire to see her, whom he has killed, 'again before I die' so as to delude himself that he will 'rejoin my lover' in the transcendental realm after death. Because he murdered her, his 'desire can never be objectified' and without her, he has been condemned to live 'in a drab, colourless world . . . a faded daguerreotype'.

The act of dedicating 'all my memories' to Albertina Hoffman is, however, an ambivalent gesture. Even as he admits that his memory is to a great degree 'dissolved in the medium of Albertina', who has a power over him from beyond the grave, she has this power precisely because she is dead and absent from the text. The completion of Desiderio's autobiography will first and foremost elevate and eternalise *his* deeds: 'I will stand . . . like a commemorative statue of myself in a public place, serene, equestrian, upon a pediment.' The Albertina he possesses and represents is merely imaginary or textual, 'a woman as only memory and imagination could devise, well, such is always at least partially the case with the beloved. I see her as a series of marvellous shapes formed at random in the kaleidoscope of desire'.

The narrative strategy Carter uses to exceed the conventional representation she rereads in her own novel is less the literalisation of a joke, the excessive turn of a trope, which makes a cliché serious and true. Rather, she discloses the convention by attaching an explicit commentary, embued with the technical vocabulary of psychology, to the description of her character's behaviour. In a tale about a man who finds his desires made explicit at the body of a beautiful woman, she renders the cliché explicit, attaches univocal explanatory meanings to gestures otherwise read as ambivalent. This elimination of ambivalence by virtue of explanatory commentary not only assures that we interpret the events in the book as the critique she means her narrative to be. By stating as obvious what would otherwise require interpretation (the beloved is such as only memory and imagination could devise), her rhetoric imposes an impasse on the reader. The duplication of event with explicit commentary is, in fact, a reduction of semantic freedom and mirrors rhetorically the impasse which is the novel's theme: woman can only exist as and in the meaning her lover, as author of her, intends. A move on her part into articulating alterity, into signifying a meaning beyond the one he narcissistically constructs, is fatal.

The story Desiderio tells, retraces his quest for Dr Hoffman, who has instigated the Great War by disrupting social order and replacing it with a 'time of actualized desire'. In these chaotic, tumultuous and kinetic times, a socially codified reality has been superseded by 'lawless images', materialised because they existed in the minds of the population. In a sense, Hoffman's order is a literalization, a calling into existence of the buried image repertoire of the world Desiderio inhabits. As such, it produces a complete suspension of the division between life and death; between the animate and the inanimate; between an image referring to non-semiotic reality and a freely floating signifier. Because he has extended the limits of the dimension conventionally called the world of the living, his shades, whether 'the apparitions ... of the dead, synthetic reconstructions of the living or in no way replicas of anything we knew' now all inhabit the same dimension as the living.

As Desiderio sets out to destroy the man who has transformed a system of semiotic relations that privileged arbitrary but socially codified meanings for one wherein the process of a ubiquitous omnipotence of thought, everything that can be imagined, can also exist, he discovers that his quest is for his ideal beloved as she is materialised at the body of the magician's daughter. Albertina, a cross between Dr Hoffman's somatic progeny and Desiderio's semiotic creation, is the object of exchange between the two rivals; the bait with which the father seeks to enlist the son in his campaign and the stake over whose destruction the son re-establishes the conventional law of culturally regulated images. She initially appears to him every night in his sleep as a 'young woman in a negligé [which] ... did not conceal her quite transparent flesh, so that the exquisite filigree of her skeleton was revealed quite clearly' (25). This visitor 'with flesh of glass', this 'visible skeleton', has the function of an ambassador. Hinting at the mysteries encompassing them, she seems comparable to 'angels' and 'miraculous revenants' and seems sent to herald the immanent arrival of the 'Emperor of the Marvellous'. That she should do so in the guise of a body signifying the conjunction of femininity and death in an explicit manner – as a 'visible skeleton, this miraculous bouquet of bone' – is an example for the rhetoric of the explicit I am attributing to Carter's prose.

In a second dream the feminine death figure is translated into a second obvious sign, a black swan singing, and her meaning is also transparent to him – 'I knew it was about to die and I knew, too, she was a swan and also a woman.' On her collar he finds engraved the single word 'Albertina'. This name duly becomes the clue to lead his quest, for when he finds it stitched in the silk handkerchief of the transvestite emissary Hoffman has sent, he desires that the glass woman, the black swan and the ambassador be three magic entities beneath which he will find 'a living being', 'an authentic woman' before whom he can fall on his knees in worship (41). As the explicit symptomatisation of his libidinal desires, Albertina's image keeps reappearing throughout his travels. He refinds 'the beautiful face of Dr Hoffman's ambassador' (47) in the set of samples that serve as the core image repertoire from which the many lawless images incessantly configure. This particular exhibition piece, modelled in wax, represents the 'perpetual motion' of orgasm. With the head of the man invisible while the woman's oscillates in the socket of her neck and roles from side to side in the 'tormented snarl of orgasm', it represents the woman's face as sign for masculine sexual passion (46).

Albertina's face displaces for 'a single, fleeting second' that of a gypsy girl at a market, which serves as a contrast to the bride that the river people offer him, and she is again invoked when he describes the scene of leavetaking from this bride. She reappears only to vanish again at the body of the Madame of a house of prostitution, and again materialises as the Count's manservant Lafleur. Desiderio explains this conjuring trick in yet another explicit comment – 'she travelled with me for she was inextricably mingled with my idea of her' (142). Her repeated disappearance and return, together with the flexibility of her substance, materialises in an obvious manner the cliché that, because woman is man's idea, existing because he imagines her, she is always and only a part of him, even as she appears in a myriad of realisations. Indeed, Carter lets Albertina offer an explanatory comment to obliterate the possiblity of any ambivalence in interpretation, and to turn the seemingly uncanny moment of a transmigration of souls into a cannily explained instance of the marvellous – 'I projected myself upon the available flesh of the Madame . . . Under the influence of intense longing, the spirit . . . can create a double which joins the absent beloved while the original template goes about its everyday business' (167).

What Desiderio comes to realise in the course of their journey, however, is that if the original image he desired linked the feminine body with death, what he indeed longs for is woman as signifier for his desires, not the authentic woman. He remains a little in awe, for example, of those moments when Albertina signifies that she is more or in fact other than his creation. At such moments 'a sense of her difference almost withered me for she was the sole heir to her father's kingdom' (187). Indeed, when she takes on a shape that does not arise from his personal image repertoire, namely that of a crisp, antiseptic soldier, she is the absolute 'antithesis of my black swan and my bouquet of burning bone', and he feels an 'inexplicable indifference towards her' (193).

Once Desiderio has reached the castle, the 'powerhouse of the marvellous', he has fulfilled his double quest and must confront the adversary father and the beloved daughter. On the one hand he thinks he has completely transformed himself into the image of the beloved – 'Now I was entirely Albertina in the male aspect' (199). On the other, he fears that the fleshly possession of Albertina may be 'the greatest disillusionment of all' (201). Carter has her narrator explicitly comment, 'Even if it is the dream made flesh, the real, once it becomes real, can be no more than real.' Desiderio makes obvious what is tacitly implied in the theme of the dead beloved as Muse. While the woman is unknown she is 'sublime', once she has materialized into a specific desired object she is 'loved,' but as a possessed body she is a superlative disillusionment. It is not, however, merely the actualisation of the desired beloved Desiderio fears, but rather Albertina's alterity. As she explains to him, 'You have never yet made love to me because, all the time you have known me, I've been maintained in my various appearances only by the power of your desire' (204).

Desiderio has given a name to his erotic desire, 'Albertina', and this act of naming, owing to the Doctor's powers, has brought her into being. The impasse he now finds himself in when asked to comply with Hoffman's designs is seen by him as the choice between 'a barren yet harmonious calm and a fertile yet cacophonous tempest'. Indeed, from the onset of his narrative, Desiderio claims that in the tumultuous time of actualised desire 'I myself had only the one desire. And that was, for everything to stop' (11). Furthermore, Albertina is more than a creature brought into being by Desiderio. She is also the magician's daughter. The only solution for Desiderio, who wants calm not chaos, who prefers the woman fashioned as an image of his desire to any actuality which may cause the strife of disappointment or contradiction, is then to actualise her imaginary existence by making her irrevocably absent. The fact that Carter has her narrator offer such obvious explanations for the murder that is about to follow is yet another example of her strategy of adding reductive commentary to the events of the narrative. These make the inevitable explicit so as to mirror rhetorically the impasse of Desiderio's libidinal economy, whose laws make the destruction of the feminine body, as site of difference within, unavoidable. The hidden meaning Carter unburies by naming it so obviously as the message of her text, is that the desired beloved is superlative when she is a memory image.

In an inversion of the Carmen motif, it is the lover who cries a repeated 'No', when faced with the real nude body of Albertina, baring itself beyond the allegorical designations he gives her, such as 'my Platonic other, my necessary extinction, my dream made flesh' (215). In a 'grotesque dénouement' of his great passion, Albertina responds to his cry by pulling out a knife from under her dress, while the Doctor shoots at him only to break his neck by falling out of his wheelchair. Over the 'father's flaccid corpse', Albertina and Desiderio have the first and only real bodily encounter devoid of mirages of materialised desires. The meaning of this event is, once again, made obvious by the commentary: 'we wrestled . . . for the possession of the knife as passionately as if for the possession of each other' (216). Only after a long, long time does Albertina lose her strength and he kills her by stabbing her below the left nipple. As though her dying body were already transforming into another materialised desire, her last words articulate one of the clichés of feminine death I have been tracing – 'I always knew one only died of love' (217).

To a degree Hoffman's power triumphs over Desiderio's double murder, for the latter acknowledges that the 'father has gained a tactical victory over me' (14). Having reached the desired calm, Desiderio remains susceptible to the Doctor's powers. He preserves the name Albertina to designate his desire, and is consequently haunted by images of her. He can resuscitate her with ease, but significantly he can no longer 'tell the difference between memory and dream", since she is beyond any historical reality. Upon completing the manuscript, which he calls a 'coffin' for his younger self, able to embrace death, he closes his eyes and 'Unbidden, she comes' (221). Yet she reappears to the writer Desiderio, as well as in the narrative he writes, only as the canny image his desire creates, not at all as an alterity. In contrast to Lolita's representation in H.H.'s narrative, the real subject position of the effaced Albertina is never articulated as an uncanny presence in absence. She does not mark an invisible presence buried beneath tropes and images of desire. Her subject position is hermetically excluded from Desiderio's world and from his text so that any actualisation of her alterity, even as a blank, a silence or an aporia is foreclosed. For she cannot be thought other than the material of the son's or the father's desire.

Disquieting, then, about Carter's marvellous world is precisely the lack of uncanny disruption, such as Nabokov's use of ironic distance produced. Unlike her literary model Lolita, Albertina cannot elude because she is indeed nothing other than a fiction. Indeed, what is never disclosed as an illusion is Desiderio's romantic text. Rather, Carter's deconstruction is such that she exceeds the cultural representations her novel rereads by performing in a rhetoric of explicitness which leaves nothing to implication, that the only way the feminine body can have a position is as a canny illusion, as a desire come into being because it could be named. Neither of her two paternal worlds leave space for the uncanny difference of femininity, not even that of oscillation, whether it be Hoffman's order of actualised desire and lawless images that emerge from a set of samples he controls, or Desiderio's order of arbitrary but conventionally accepted symbols. In the same manner, the narrator's commentary leaves no space for any semiotic difference, for the slippage of meaning, for semantic ambivalences and indeterminacies.

Moving beyond hyperbolic parody, Maggie Gee rhetorically enacts the impasse of woman's authorship and death by making possible, in the space of an aesthetic construction, what is impossible in life. Like an Escher drawing, *Dying, in Other Words* (1981) traces a plot that works on the page but not in human space. Maggie Gee represents Moira Penny, who writes her autobiography by writing her own death. The resulting narrative proves to be an act of legislating the boundary between life and death, with Moira 'writing' her own death to resist mortification in and by culture. Gee traces a chiasmic figure – because Moira lives in an attitude of self-expenditure, she consciously acknowledges death, but in that she chooses death, she lives. This vitalising embrace of life's excess stands in opposition to an attitude of self-preservation, implicitly coded as a blindness towards death and a lethal stasis in life.

Writing a death of her own also means imposing an aesthetic pattern on the chaos of real existence. It refers to the freedom not given by real life to transform an arbitrary into a personally significant moment of closure. The complex aporia Gee's narrative explores is that while death is always fortuitous and necessary, we want a narrative of death – a story of murder or of suicide – that shows death in some way to be the logical and meaningful consequence of life. We want to be able to read the corpse as a text which reflects the life of the deceased in such a way that it fits patterns sustaining our desire for a sense of wholeness. By virtue of a triple narrative frame, Gee presents a heroine who writes the biography of her life by writing her own death, yet does so in such a way as both to confirm and to frustrate this desire for an ending that makes sense.

Gee begins her text with an author's note, in which she explains that her critical reading diverges from conventional representations of sexual violence against women and narratives written in the aftermath of a 'suspicious death'. She warns that this is not 'a realistic novel', because in life characters behave differently, because in 'Life, we spend more time living than dying away from our fictions', because in 'Life, moist Moira was not permitted *entirely unaided* to write this novel' (5). Gee doubles her own text. Her protagonist writes her own death by writing her own life, in a gesture which is possible only in a non-realistic narrative world. Yet Gee introduces realism by referring to herself as the concrete author who comes to the aid of her fictional character. Gee adds, though the subject matter is serious, 'moribund characters' and 'ritual death of the whole sad world', the narrative structure is such that 'on the face of things' it is not 'a serious novel', indeed it is 'not quite a novel'. The impasse within which she inserts her narrative is that although both life and fictions end in death – 'the end result is the same (dying, in other words, gone)' – so too, each demise opens up to narratives – 'at the other end of destruction, the will to stories goes on' (6).

Gee's 'dying, in other words', the title and leitmotif of her text, is a multiple trope. For one, it signifies an effacement – life is, in fact, a form of dying, only in other words. The term 'living' hides, by standing in for, the term 'dying', such that the latter irrevocably inhabits the former. Secondly, it signifies that the representation of death is always in other words. These words are other than real death. To endow a woman's suspicious death with other words marks the translation of an unnameable event into a sustained narrative sequence, with the other words articulating the event of death by circumventing it.

The frame narrative, following the author's note, begins with the statement of death – 'The naked body of the girl was found on the pavement by the milkman, reaching the Crescent just after 7 a.m. on a frosty brilliant morning.' After a brief description of her fallen body, the narrator adds, 'The papers were found on her desk in the third-floor attic room' (7). Seeking facts, the two policemen read this manuscript only to conclude that 'it was suicide', hoping with such a designation that 'the case . . . would be closed'. The trope they settle upon to resolve this mystery aims at restituting their world view – 'the kinks and the mutters would always be found smashed to bits on the sensible pavement'. Yet in point of fact, their conclusion is a violent reduction, for the papers 'didn't make sense'. The more they read, the more they note that what they call 'to know Life' is missing, in a rhetoric of excessive expenditure of life – 'there was violence and horror in everything, everything ended in death. There was nothing but death and no logic.' However, although the represented events are seemingly illogical, the manuscript itself is far from unorderly. Badly typed but carefully corrected, it is complete in itself, 'no passionate last minute scrawl of ink at the end'. It stands to contradict their hope that it might bear the clue to her death.

While the dead woman they find is not named, the writer of the papers they find calls herself 'Moira, your author'. The prologue to these papers shows her standing on her balcony, commenting that the balustrade is 'not deep enough, as they found, to prevent someone falling' (9). Though in a sense she anticipates the fall with which her own narrative, succeeding her prologue, will begin, she is resurrected in this self-representation as 'Moira, your author.' Standing 'high above' the normal everyday world, her 'death' is that of the writer, caught between the absent and the double. She fashions herself as absent from those 'pilgrims (who) troop meekly and doggedly . . . to their regular work', and sees them as being in a state of living death: 'They are earning their living, dying, in other words, dying. Saving it up for the future . . . Saving up life, which is dying, in other words, dying' (12). She is doubled, because also present both as 'your author' and as the twenty-five-year-old Moira who dies after having completed her papers. But she also reduplicates the unnamed woman found dead by the two policemen with a finished manuscript in her room.

In this prologue Moira, in analogy to the author's note, prefaces her narrative by undermining its mimetic value – 'in some non-narrative world there is somebody splitting and bleeding, storyless, blood-splattered, splayed on the cold stone, dead – the stories, while memory lasts, will always go on.' Her narrative, in turn, duplicates the frame narrative, beginning with the sentence 'The naked body of the girl was found on the pavement' and 'The papers were found on her desk'. In this embedded narrative the policemen's response to the papers is not included. The content of the papers written by the protagonist Moira are also an autobiography of sorts, in a prose that freely associates on the theme of death and destruction, but not a reduplication of Moira the author's narrative of the events leading up to her protagonist's death and the responses its suspicious circumstance elicits. In the first set of papers, an explanation of Moira's death is given but in such a way as both to confirm and to frustrate any desire for a meaningful end. The unexpected presence of a fellow tenant in her room, after she has completed her manuscript, evokes anxiety and as Moira attempts to escape, she simply falls. Death happens, though she doesn't want to die and though C. Hans doesn't want to kill her.

Gee's text is a circular novel, the nominal plot beginning with an unnamed woman's death, only to resurrect her as author of a set of papers in the prologue to this manuscript. This set of papers, in turn, begins with the death of the protagonist sharing the name of the author, and ends with a description of the moment of her death, and the papers found on her desk. Though Gee's narrative, written with and out of a woman's death, traces the figure of an impossible puzzle, she represents a dialectic where life and fictions contradict and supersede each other in an endless succession. While it is true that stories 'go on' to replace death, the second Moira (your author) replacing the first (the unnamed dead woman) and the third (her protagonist), it is equally the case that the frame enacts that real death catches up with a narrative representation of death. This literalisation of the narrative end the author Moira writes for her story is also disclosed as being 'not realistic' by the author Gee's note.

The reader is faced with at least two ways of making sense of this interstice of death's actuality and the fictions that go on; of the naked body of a dead woman on the pavement and her papers on her desk. One can either reconstruct the chronology of events such that Moira writes her biography as an extended obituary only to re-enact in reality, and to undermine uncannily, the fall she fictionally fashioned for herself. Or one can reconstruct the chronology such that Moira falls, only to return in the image of an author, for the embedded narrative sustains the theme of the woman writer as revenant, who has a dual power. For one, even as her peers want to turn the unsemantic event of death into a meaningful story, she draws them into death. For another, the entire narrative can be seen as an effort to write a second death for herself, which will fit a pattern, even if the last sequence shows that the catalyst for Moira's death is arbitrary. In this reading, the first death, or rather the image of the girl's fallen body on the pavement which we find in both frames, is 'wrong' and in an 'unrealistic' turn, must be repeated, so as to become 'real' only after Moira has written her own death plot.

In either case, the last sequence folds in on the first sentence of both embedded narratives, which work by using the pattern of a first death, a liminal existence and a second death as the overriding trope for the position of the writer, socially dead because absent fom the world of the work force and doubled by her fiction. Both suggest that the structure fictions offer works against but also under the auspices of death. The act of plotting is shown to be coterminous with the arbitration of life and death, feeding off the living, influencing the lives of the survivors. More explicitly than any of the other novels discussed, the frustration Gee enacts is above all a rhetorical issue. This compilation of plots emerging from a desire to make the event of death meaningful, is unsatisfying in the end precisely because the overriding structure does not make sense. Owing to this lack of logic on the metapoetical level of her text, Gee's text exceeds any representation of death (in other words), by performing a rhetoric articulation of real death.

Within the embedded narrative two aspects of writing as arbitrating the exchange between life and death emerge. In that Moira, your author, chooses the obituary as her narrative model, she can represent how her protagonist's naked body on the pavement poses a hermeneutic task. A direct account of her life is replaced by the way her survivors construct plots to explain this suspicious event, and how, with her death in mind, they represent her life to themselves. The journalist Les Hawtrey creates his news version of her death by trying to reconstruct her life on the basis of several interviews. He is confronted with contradictory images of her, made concrete in the two photographs that circulate among the various men that knew her: one 'a simpering portrait' in a pose of 'painful artificiality' (18) with Moira leaning coyly against a tree, the other showing her stark naked sitting on a bare wood floor, leaning back on her hands; a mischievous smile on her face. He finds himself rewriting his dramatic recon-struction, unable to find the right tone with which to describe her 'fatal plunge', and unable to decide whether it was suicide, murder or an accident. He is left to choose arbitrarily between a Moira who 'danced the night away at wild clubs' and one who was studious and dedicated to her work, writing for weeks on end alone in her attic (46). While the milkman, a disguised sexual murderer, and the thug Macbeth use Moira's corpse to project their fantasies of violence against women, the writer Clothilde uses this dead body to voice her jealousy of the younger woman, and the tenant Frank his unrequited romantic longing.

The clearest representation of Moira, however, evolves from her reflection in the eyes of her two closest male friends. They represent the notion of saving up life and setting it against death, standing diametrically opposed to her attitude of expenditure, her anxiety that also acknowledges the presence of death as difference in the midst of life. Implicitly referring to the circularity of the novel, John retrospectively sees her obsession with writing and with dying intertwined, and her death the result of her 'obsessive fear of the freaks she invented to people the house' (61). He recalls her as one who loved 'all extreme sensation' even as she couldn't bear it; as one who recognized death as that which is real, beyond stories – 'she saw death, undeserved and unchosen, might fall on them all from the skies' (65). While to John, Moira's last act of climbing through the bars of her balcony with no clothes on, signifies the apotheosis of her death anxieties and her embrace of 'extreme sensation', Jean-Claude sees her death as a wound to his narcissism. To him, her sudden death means '*his* memories, *his* sympathy, *his* concentration, splayed on the cold stone, dead' (94). His first response is to read her death as a sign that 'she had failed to protect him, failed to inform him, failed to involve him' (108).

Significantly in connection with John, the spokesman for a clear distinction between life and death another aspect of 'writing death' is first explicitly introduced. Throughout the text someone is typing away, 'hard metal feet are still tapping, the typing goes doggedly on' (82). The author Moira does not simply represent her protagonist as a dead girl resurrected in a kaleidoscope of images produced by those who survive her, out of and against death. Rather, she constructs two axes of identification. The one between herself and her protagonist results in a superfluity of indeterminacies. For the other characters evolve as parts of the author Moira's fantasies, even as they fantasise about her destruction, and it remains open whether they are part of herself or different, real or imagined. Like the corpse, the narrative corpus which the two policemen find begs to be made sense of but resists any definitive closing of the case. The second axis of identification, equally fraught with indeterminacy, is that between the author Moira and the body typing in the attic. This someone repeatedly corrects, comments on or agrees with the characters' thoughts and, as the policemen note in response to the plethora of bodies flying and falling, 'It had to be *her* . . . and yet she was supposed to be dead and these other deaths just to come tumbling illegally after' (161).

The indeterminacy is that in a narrative about the way survivors try to fit death into a plot that satisfies their needs, the prologue makes explicit that this is Moira your author writing a narrative in which she imagines how others respond to her death. But as she pieces these narratives together to give a meaningful structure to her life, if only to say her life was ended by chance, she also writes death plots for all those involved with her. She legislates the exchange between life and death in two ways. In life she served to articulate the presence of death by virtue of her oscillation between anxiety about and embrace of extreme sensation. After death, in the pose of the revenant author ('up in a dark room some kind of justice is typing' (174)), she forces her peers to acknowledge the presence of death in life which they choose to be blind to.

While they try to put closure on her death by reconstructing the meaning of her death so it will confirm their notion of survival, Moira the ghost suggests to them what will also be the final meaning of her narrative, namely that the threat of death is ubiquitous and arbitrary. Whenever they tell themselves that life wasn't so bad, she reminds them that 'it was dying, in other words, someone said' (157). If alive she was a figure warning of death's inhabitation of life, her corpse is a *memento mori* that transpires into an angel of death. She has power over her survivors not only because they must restructure their lives and their sense of self in reponse to this loss. Even as she describes the plots each person constructs around her death, she plots for each a death that corresponds to the meaning they have chosen to read into hers.

The text anticipates Mrs Evans's fatal fall on the pavement, the milkman's indictment for six sexual murders, the journalist's death in a plane crash, with his body cut in half in analogy to the way he tore the second photo of Moira. While

John would never have left his wife for a living Moira, her death fills the sober man with such sentimentality that he follows his image of 'beautiful snow-white Mo' into a snow storm. He dies in the figure of a wonderful snowy-white angel while the ghost of Moira 'is gaily and acidly typing, quite happy at least that those dull marble lips had stopped talking' (69). In a similar vein John's wife Felicity imitates Moira's embrace of extreme sensation by burning down her flat in a drunken state. To her best friend Clara, living an equally rootless and vacillating existence, Moira's death seems like an arrival, 'Mo had become a resident forever'. It serves to highlight her own agonised yearning for 'warmth and safety and home' (169), and she dies choking on fudge in her bathtub.

Gee's text is a radical rereading of the model I have been presenting, where a poet or a community require the death of a woman to produce an aesthetic work or establish a social order. For here a woman can fashion herself in and out of death by killing to excess those who represent the attitude of saving up life, against death. This is most clearly shown in the sequences involving Jean-Claude's mourning. Once he has assured himself that although 'she thought a lot about dying, not distant or general' (142) she nevertheless expected to survive, in a gesture of fearing and nimbly eluding death, he can restitute his image of her, and reassure himself of his own desire to go on. Translating the fear that she had committed suicide into the more comforting thought that 'just mad chance . . . had sent her sprawling to horror' he is assured that he wasn't abandoned, wasn't unloved. In parentheses, however, the narrator explicitly discloses Jean-Claude's narcissistic 'bright new version', by adding '(yet the cold feet said the opposite, equally clearly: she hadn't expected that life or that peace would go on)' (144). Though Jean-Claude tries to ignore 'the clumsy intrusion of death and of dizzy blank falling' by recuperating the non-semiotic real into an explanatory order which fits his emotional needs, the typing revenant Moira literalises her disagreement with his image of her by drawing him into death. As the narrator Moira, your author, explains, he 'could not be aware of how coldly and carefully Moira was shaping her own alternative image, up in her dark attic room: and had sent John walking out numbly through the white park . . . to meet . . . with her cold white dream . . . Moira wrote on' (145). After her death, in the impossible world of 'unrealistic' fiction where she can refashion her life to fit the meaning she wants, she fixes the odds to prove that not the logic of preservation but rather her 'cosmic forces of violence' rule the world.

Where John imitated Moira's love for extreme sensation by throwing himself into a blizzard, Jean-Claude literalises in his own way Moira's 'vast fears, of how death would come from the sky' (149) by embracing the risk of violent sexuality and meeting his murderer, the thug Macbeth, in the park at night. The dreams and nightmares which the various characters fulfil, are indeed produced up above the world, namely in an attic by a girl who dreams on, who writes on, having herself realised the ubiquitous threat she was so uncannily aware of. As the narrator explains, 'There was Moira's death, which changed everything . . . leaving a warning, an aching gap: that she meant what she said when she talked of a permanent sense of threat, of trapdoors to violent death in the regular surface of the pavement.' Her attitude stands against any notion that death is just an anomaly, 'ink falling random and black on the smooth bright patterns of life which were pledged to go on. And then after it happened, the patterns reformed and every day comforting habit blotted it quietly up' (155). What the typing revenant performs is a narrative that supplements the 'dying in *no* words' (156), which Moira's solitary death enacts. Yet paradoxically, though the actuality of death lies beyond language, the recourse to the facticity of the body in fact convinces her peers, legitimates her world view that living is dying and engenders narratives. The companion narrative she creates from within her spectral existence also carries them into her world of death's immanent and arbitrary presence, because 'all the characters kept dying off' (155).

The revenant Moira produces a meaningful alternative image of herself even as what her plot enacts and proves is precisely the arbitrariness and ubiquity of death. In the same gesture that she uses death (her own and that of the other characters) to construct a representational unity, death asserts itself as that moment of the real beyond language – a dying in no words, located in non-narrative space. The power of Moira's spectral authorship resides not only in the way she fixes the odds to perform an excessive death plot, but, more crucially, in the fact that the irritation her sudden death caused in the narrative world is reduplicated rhetorically by the text's structure. Not entirely unaided, Moira constructs circular novel that ultimately defies recuperative closure.

Her narrative ends where it began, on the day of her twenty-fifth birthday, by depicting the event that immediately preceded death: Moira, having finished writing the night before her birthday, having reached 'the end of her strenuous plan' (193), with 'each of her little constructed inhabitants dwindled according to system', with 'each chapter in order, each orderly chapter numbered, only one final stanza remained' (194). This final stanza is, however, enacted literally at her body. Naked because about to take a bath, and turning her music on to celebrate a new beginning, Moira finds herself confronted with her nemesis, the noseless, mysterious tenant C. Hans, whom her noise has disturbed. Where her ghost embodies 'someone typing', he embodies 'something disturbing the system', yet something she herself built into her representations 'which threatened to . . . do *all of us* harm as the hard metal feet in the attic insisted . . . which toppled them out of their towers' (187). If she warns of death, he undertakes death. As the living embodiment of death's threat, as an embodiment of 'the horror', he frightens Moria, who tries to edge away from his terrible hands by climbing over her balustrade. The completion of her text is fulfilled somatically – 'she clutched for a long stanza of pain at the stone, and she screamed at the end to nothing and no-one, and then Moira Penny was gone' (195).

C. Hans disturbs the representational system in several ways. While the message of Moira's complete narrative is that 'the proper order of all things human was death', his sudden appearance confirms the notion of death but frustrates that of order: 'yet her corpse in the end was a mess, the straight spine shattered, the face in a bloody confusion of stone and ice' (193). His presence at the same time prohibits a neat closure for the embedded narrative, and engenders instead the circularity by virtue of which this fateful Wednesday morning can move back to the the prologue, with Moira your author standing on the balcony on an unnamed morning. Or it can move to the Wednesday morning and the dead girl's body on the pavement, with which her narrative began, and which is repeated before the inclusion of 'The Papers', though only as sentence fragments. Included after this third and final representation of the dead girl's body on the pavement is now an explicit comment on the interstice of authorship and death – '(she was ended, the book could begin) . . . for the hands which have sculpted a world must be first and last self-destroying' (196).

With the papers and the naked dead body signifying the two poles of what 'stayed real', the narrative can move either back into itself or outside to the double frame, Moira your author and to the author Gee's notes. Death – in the dual sense of the body's facticity and the inanimate words and images outside which reality is inconceivable – catches up with Moira's process of uncanny writing, her return to life so as to plot death. On the page at least the author Moira and her self-representation Moira collapse to become the nameless dead woman of the frame narrative and the one invoked in the prologue, dying in a 'non-narrative world, splitting and bleeding storyless'.

Gee ends her narrative by placing her reader into the impasse of an interminable narrative. Like the policemen seeking facts so as to close the case, we as readers are caught between the 'sound of the typewriter' reverberating throughout Moira's house of fiction and the wordless, non-narrative presence of death which threatens to disturb the unity of any representational system. For any critical reading produces our own story that goes on in response and in contradiction to this non-narrative moment. Gee's complicitous critique of western culture's representational fantasies of violence against the feminine body, and its violent blindness towards death's real presence in life, is then a text which undermines its own parameters by calling itself a fiction, though not a realistic novel, not a serious novel, not quite a novel. Even as the beginning of the book requires the end of Moira, she returns in her duplicitous function as subject and object of this representation of a naked dead girl serving as sign for her spectator's desire for an end that makes sense. Oscillating interminably between Moira's actual death and the death plots she produces on paper and in life, Gee's text pleads her protagonist's case for a way of seeing that does not end by blotting up quietly the disturbance traced by femininity and death. As Moira's impossible revenant voice insists that living is dying, in other words, it performs the uncanny difference located within any system.

These narratives by women writers self-consciously install the cultural paradigm that links femininity with death in the same gesture that they critique it. They simultaneously perform the terms of the production of both woman and death as text so as to duplicitously comply with this convention even as they also resist an identification with this Janus-faced image. Owing to this self-awareness, they serve as a fitting conclusion for the multifarious pattern I have sought to trace – a pattern which I unfolded by spanning two centuries, by comparing narrative texts with visual images and by illuminating analogies between the figures and strategies that poetic and theoretic discourses have developed to describe femininity and death. For these texts by women writers themselves instate, within the parameters of their representational system, the knowledge of the dual contradiction my critical reading has sought to uncover: the dilemma that Woman cannot be defined outside discursive formations that assign to femininity the position of the void, of silence, of a lack of fixed place, *and* the aporia that death is at once the real before and beyond language, as well as a hyperbolic trope.

My readings have sought to illustrate that the interstice of femininity and death often signals a moment of non-reading in the narrative in which it is contained, albeit at times unconsciously so on the part of the author. Indeed, my claim has been that femininity and death do not only (when each term is taken on its own), stand as the absence, the ground and the vanishing point of our cultural system of representation. It is precisely the ambivalent and indeterminate conjunction of the two terms that takes on a seminal position in our cultural image repertoire even as it is elided by the authors and more often than not ignored in the critical discussion of the narrative or the image as well.

My own critical readings were meant to enact the following complex aporia. The historical reality of death and of women does not coincide with their representation by and in culture, even though these texts not only absent by doubling death/femininity by virtue of their respective or often enmeshed pictorial or narrative rendition, but also employ the duplicitous articulation as effacement in a chain of double-coded signifiers – beauty covering decay, the bride veiling the dead girl or the dead maternal body, presence standing in for absence. This multi-layered strategy of doubling goes yet one step further, in the sense that the uncanny convergence of femininity and death can also serve as a displaced signifier for masculinity, survival, preservation and continuation.

By enacting this complex aporia, I, like the women writers with whom I ended, hoped to resist the gesture of mere identification with the referred-to cultural image repertoire, though admittedly my own readings were never entirely devoid of a certain fond complicity with the representational corpus I sought to critique. By using my critical reading to re-tell these texts – in other words, in a different light, with a different focus and privileging different aspects – I sought, in de Lauretis's sense, not merely to translate a given theoretical or poetic text into a critical meta-representation but rather to change representation into a performance which exceeds the text it represents. Though this is in part always the aim of a critical reading, the particular form of excess I sought was that of exposing by exceeding the contradictions tacitly assumed in respect to femininity and death in their function as ground and vanishing point of western culture's self-representation. I sought not only to lay bare unconscious structures, making visible an effaced feminine subject position and the repressed presence of death in life, but also making visible that we are often culturally so blind to this doubly disturbing presence, to this uncanny difference within, that we don't even see that we don't see the conjunction of femininity and death. My claim throughout has been that this double figure of femininity as death is not only prevalent in a disguised or effaced way but can often also be found on the very surface of an image or a text, as the literal, the banal reading we immediately dismiss or disregard in our search for a more tropic interpretation.

I have therefore tried rhetorically to preserve the uncanniness of the interstice of femininity and death, neither resolving it into a canny trope for Otherness nor expelling it entirely from issues of representation and aesthetics by claiming it is exclusively part of that realm of the real which has nothing to do with, indeed stands in diametric opposition to, the products of art. I have sought to preserve the aporia that death is both superlatively real and superlatively tropic, as well as the often murky exchange between cultural representations of passed-on images or conventions and lived historical reality. I resisted deciding the case as to what definite way the real deaths of historical women were implicated in, indeed the influence for, the construction of certain theoretic formulations and aesthetic productions.

My own duplicitous resistance transpired into a perpetual movement; at times seeking to explore what by dint of being so self-evident seemed to fall short of previous critical readings and what, emerging in the respective text as a moment of repressed unconscious cultural material, could be decoded only when read under the auspices of the complex theoretical frame I had constructed. Having installed a theoretical and textual corpus to deconstruct a particularly salient aspect of our culture's self-representation – the articulation as effacement of the unencompassable body of materiality–maternity–mortality – my own reading, in turn, emerged from and repeatedly returned to a close analysis of texts. In so doing, however, it always self-consciously oscillated between the obvious and the speculative, from which we can never strip our relation to first and last things – to Woman and death – and outside of which this uncanny figure is inconceivable.

Notes to Chapter 18

1 M. DeShazer, 1986, p. 3.
2 V. Woolf, 1929, p. 48.
3 V. Woolf, 1929, p. 50.
4 V. Woolf, 1929, p. 117.
5 May Sarton, 1978, pp. 141–2. S. Gilbert and S. Gubar, 1988, discuss this poems as an example of the dynamics of maternal literary inheritance.
6 S. Plath, 1981, pp. 244–7.
7 A. Sexon 1966, p. 89–94. In a letter to Robert Lowell she writes about this poem 'I tried to make it sound like her but, as usual, this attempt was not fruitful; the spirit of imitation did not last and now it sounds, as usual, like Sexton', 1979, p. 170.
8 A. Sexton, 1979, p. 308.
9 T. de Lauretis, 1984, p. 36.

10 J. Mitchell, 1984, p. 290. I am referring back to my discussion of the discourse of the
     hysteric developed in PIV, to use the word hysteria once again in a sense that moves
     beyond its designation of a neurotic illness. Needless to say, 'clinical hysteria' involves
     illness as a somatisation, a writing with the body and in this strict sense Alice James is
     the perfect example of a hysterical author. To postulate a hysterical voice, in turn,
     implies that the woman writer has once again moved away from writing exclusively
     with her body, with the narratives produced merely commenting on her body-text; that
     she has moved back to language, to the production of symbolic texts. I hold on to the
     term 'hysteria', however, so as to highlight the issue of duplicity, i.e. of a simultaneous
     denial and affirmation, of complicity and resistance.
11 L. Hutcheon, 1989.
12 R. Barreca, 1988.

Bibliography

Primary literature

Atwood, Margaret (1976). *Lady Oracle*. London: Virago (1982).

Boileau-Narcejac (1958). *Sueurs froides*. Paris: Folio.

Braddon, Mary Elizabeth (1861). *Lady Audley's Secret*. Oxford: Oxford University Press (1987).

Brontë, Charlotte (1847). *Jane Eyre*. Harmondsworth: Penguin (1966).

Brontë, Emily (1847). *Wuthering Heights*. Harmondsworth: Penguin (1965).

Browning, Robert (1842). *Dramatic Lyrics*. *Poems* ed. Donald Smalley. Boston: Houghton Mifflin (1956).

— (1869). *The Ring and the Book*. Harmondsworth: Penguin (1971).

Carter, Angela (1972). *The Infernal Desire Machines of Doctor Hoffman*. Harmondsworth: Penguin (1982).

Collins, Wilkie (1859–60). *The Woman in White*. Harmondsworth: Penguin (1974).

Dickens, Charles (1841). *The Old Curiosity Shop*. Harmondsworth: Penguin (1972).

— (1861). *Great Expectations*. Harmondsworth: Penguin (1965).

Flaubert, Gustave (1857). *Madame Bovary. Moeurs de province*. Paris: Gallimard (1972).

Gee, Maggie (1981). *Dying, in Other Words*. London: Paladin (1987).

Grimm, Jacob and Wilhelm (1819). 'Schneewittchen'. *Kinder und Hausmärchen*, 2nd edition. München: Winkler (1973).

Hardy, Thomas (1874). *Far From the Madding Crowd*. New Wessex Edition. London: Macmillan (1974).

— (1891). *Tess of the D'Urbervilles*. Harmondsworth: Penguin (1978).

— (1976). *The Complete Poems* ed. James Gibson. New York: MacMillan.

Nawthorne, Nathaniel (1837). 'The Prophetic Pictures'. *Tales and Sketches*. New York: Literary Classics of the United States (1982).

— (1843). 'The Birth-mark'. *Tales and Sketches*. New York: Literary Classics of the United States (1982).

— (1852). *The Blithedale Romance*. New York: Library of America (1983).

James, Alice (1934). *The Diary of Alice James* ed. Leon Edel. Harmondsworth: Penguin (1982).

— (1981). *The Death and Letters of Alice James* ed. Ruth Bernard Yeazell. Berkeley: University of California Press.

James, Henry (1895). 'The Altar of the Dead'. *Selected Tales*. London: Dent (1982).

— (1934). The Art of the Novel. *Critical Prefaces*. New York: Scribner's Sons (1962).

— (1974). *Henry James Letters* ed. Leon Edel. *Vol. 1: 1843–1875*. London: Macmillan.

— (1980). *Henry James Letters* ed. Leon Edel. *Vol. 3: 1883–1895*. London: Macmillan.

Mérimée, Prosper (1845). 'Carmen'. *Nouvelles II*. Paris: Livre de Poche (1983).

Nabokov, Vladimir (1955). *Lolita*. Harmondsworth: Penguin (1980).

Novalis (1790–1800). 'Tagebücher'. *Werke, Tagebücher und Briefe Friedrich von Hardenbergs Band 1* ed. Richard Samuel. München: Hanser (1978).

Plath, Sylvia (1963). *The Bell Jar*. London: Faber (1966).

— (1981). *The Collected Poems* ed. Ted Hughes. New York: Harper and Row.

Poe, Edgar Allan (1838). 'Ligeia'. *Poetry and Tales*. New York: Literary Classics of the United States (1984).

— (1842). 'The Oval Portrait'. *Poetry and Tales*. New York: Literary Classics of the United States (1984).

— (1846). 'The Philosophy of Composition'. *Essays and Reviews*. New York: Literary Classics of the United States (1984).

— (1847). 'Ulalume'. *Poetry and Tales*. New York: Literary Classics of the United States (1984).

— (1849). 'Annabel Lee'. *Poetry and Tales*. New York: Literary Classics of the United States (1984).

— (1948). *The Letters of Edgar Allan Poe* ed. John Ward Ostrom. Cambridge: Harvard University Press.

Richardson, Samuel (1748). *Clarissa or, the History of a Young Lady*. Everyman's Library. London: Dent (1962).

Rodenbach, George (1892). *Bruges-La-Morte*. Paris: Flammarion (1978).

Rossetti, Dante Gabriel (1870). *Poems*. Everyman's Library. London: Dent (1961).

Rousseau, Jean-Jacques (1761). *Julie ou la Nouvelle Héloïse*. Paris: Flammarion (1967).

— (1781–8). *Les Confessions*. Paris: Gallimard (1959).

Sarton, May (1978). *Selected Poems* ed. Serena Sue Hilsinger and Lois Brynes. New York: Norton.

Schnitzler, Arthur (1899) (1923). 'Frülein Else.' *Das Erzählerische Werk* 5. Frankfurt am Main: Fischer (1978).

Sexton, Anne (1966). 'The Barfly ought to sing'. *Triquarterly* 7 (Fall), pp. 89–94.

— (1979). *A Self-Portrait in Letters* ed. Linda Gray Sexton and Lois Ames. Boston: Houghton Mifflin.

Shelley, Mary (1818). *Frankenstein or, The Modern Prometheus*. Harmondsworth: Penguin (1985).

Stoker, Bram (1897). *Dracula*. Oxford: Oxford University Press (1983).

Stowe, Harriet Beecher (1852). *Uncle Tom's Cabin or Life Among the Lowly*. Harmondsworth: Penguin (1981).

Tennyson, Alfred Lord (1859). 'Idylls of the King'. *Poems and Plays* ed. T. Herbert Warren. Oxford: Oxford University Press (1971).

Weldon, Fay (1983) *The Life and Loves of a She-Devil*. New York: Random House.

Wharton, Edith (1905) *The House of Mirth*. *Novels*. New York: Library of America (1985).

Wilde, Oscar (1891). 'The Truth of Masks'. *Complete Works*. London: Collins (1948).

Woolf, Virginia (1929). *A Room of One's Own*. New York: Harcourt Brace Jovanovich (1957).

Wordsworth, William (1984). *William Wordsworth. The Oxford Authors* ed. Stephen Gill. Oxford: Oxford University Press.

Bibliography

Secondary Literature

Abel, Elizabeth ed. (1982). *Writing and Sexual Difference.* Chicago: University of Chicago Press.

Abraham, Karl (1982). 'Versuch einer Entwicklungsgeschichte der Libido auf Grund der Psychoanalyse seelischer Störungen'. *Gesammelte Schriften II.* Frankfurt am Main: Fischer, pp. 32–102.

Abraham, Nicolas and Maria Torok (1976). *Cryptonomie. Le verbier de l'homme aux loups.* Paris: Flammarion.

— (1978). *L'écorce et le noyau.* Paris: Flammarion.

Allen, Gay Wilson (1981). *Waldo Emerson. A Biography.* New York: Viking.

Altick, Richard (1970). *Victorian Studies in Scarlet.* New York: Norton.

Altner, Günter (1981). *Tod, Ewigkeit und Überleben.* Heidelberg: Quelle und Meyer.

Alvarez, A. (1975). *The Savage God. A Study of Suicide.* Harmondsworth: Penguin.

Anz, Thomas (1983). 'Der schöne und der häßliche Tod'. *Klassik und Moderne* ed. Karl Richter and Jörg Schönert. Stuttgart: Metzler, pp. 409–32.

Appel, Alfred Jr. ed. (1970). *The Annotated Lolita.* New York: McGraw-Hill.

Ariès, Philippe (1977). *L'homme devant la mort.* Paris: Seuil.

— (1977a). *Essais sur l'histoire de la mort en Occident du Moyen Age ǹos jours.* Paris: Seuil.

— (1983) *Images de l'homme devant la mort.* Paris: Seuil.

Asche, Susanne (1985). *Die Liebe, der Tod und das Ich im Spiegel der Kunst. Die Funktion des Weiblichen in Schriften der Frühromantik und im erzählerischen Werk E.T.A. Hoffmanns. Königstein: Hain Verlag.*

Assmann, Jan (1983). 'Schrift, Tod und Identität. Das Grab als Vorschule der Literatur im alten Ägypten'. Schrift und Gedächtnis. Archäologie der literarischen Kommunikation I ed. Aleida Assmann, Jan Assmann and Christof Hardmeier. München: Fink, pp. 64–80.

Auerbach, Nina (1982). *Woman and the Demon. The Life of a Victorian Myth.* Cambridge, Harvard University Press.

— (1985). *Romantic Imprisonment. Women and Other Glorified Outcasts.* New York: Columbia University Press.

Bachelard, Gaston (1942). *L'eau et les rêves.* Paris, José Corti.

Bächtold-Stäubli, Hanns (1987). *Handwörterbuch des deutschen Aberglaubens.* Berlin: de Gruyter.

Bal, Mieke (1982). 'Mimesis and Genre Theory in Aristotle's *Poetics.' Poetics Today 3*, p. 171–80.

— (1985). *Introduction to the Theory of Narrative.* Toronto: University of Toronto Press.

— (1987). 'Force and Meaning: The interdisciplinary struggle of psychoanalysis, semiotics, and aesthetics'. *Semiotica 63*, pp. 317–44.

— (1988). *Death & Dissymmetry. The Politics of Coherence in the Book of Judges.* Chicago: University of Chicago Press.

— (1991). *Reading 'Rembrandt': Beyond the Word-Image Opposition.* Cambridge: Cambridge University Press.

Barber, Paul (1988). *Vampires, Burial, and Death. Folklore and Reality.* New Haven: Yale University Press.

Barkan, Leonard (1975). *Nature's Work of Art: The Human Body as Image of the World.* New Haven: Yale University Press.

Barker, Francis (1984). *The Tremulous Private Body. Essays on Subjection.* London: Methuen.

Barreca, Regina (1988). 'Metaphor-into-narrative: being very careful with words'. *Last Laughs. Perspectives on Women and Comedy* ed. R. Barreca. New York: Gordon and Breach, pp. 243–56.

— ed. (1990). *Sex and Death in Victorian Literature*. London: Macmillan

Barthes, Roland (1972). *Mythologies*. New York: Hill and Wang.

— (1974). *S/Z*. New York: Hill and Wang.

— (1975). *The Pleasure of the Text*. New York: Hill and Wang.

— (1977). *Roland Barthes*. New York: Hill and Wang.

— (1978). *A Lover's Discourse. Fragments*. New York: Hill and Wang.

— (1981b). *Camera Lucida*. New York: Hill and Wang.

— (1981b). 'Textual Analysis of Poe's "Valdemar".' *Untying the Text* ed. Robert Young. London: Routledge and Kegan Paul, pp. 133–61.

— (1985). *The Responsibility of Forms*. New York: Hill and Wang.

— (1986). *The Rustle of Language*. New York: Hill and Wang.

Bassein, Beth Ann (1984). *Women and Death: Linkages in Western Thought and Literature*. Westport, Conn.: Greenwood Press.

Bataille, Georges (1957). *L'Érotisme*. Paris: Minuit.

— (1961). *Les Larmes d'Éros*. Paris: Pauvert.

— (1967). *La Part Maudite*. Paris: Minuit.

Baudrillard, Jean (1976). *L'Échange symbolique et la mort*. Paris: Gallimard.

Becker, Ernest (1975). *The Denial of Death*. New York: The Free Press.

Benjamin, Walter (1972) 'Denkbilder'. *Gesammelte Schriften IV.1*. Frankfurt: Suhrkamp, pp. 305–438.

— (1974). 'Ursprung des deutschen Trauerspiels', *Gesammelte Schriften I.1*. Frankfurt: Suhrkamp, pp. 203–430.

— (1977) 'Der Erzähler.' *Gesammelte Schriften II.2*. Frankfurt: Suhrkamp, pp. 438–65.

Berg, Elizabeth L. (1982). 'The Third Woman'. *Diacritics 12*, pp. 11–20.

Berger, Harry Jr (1987). 'Bodies and Texts'. *Representations 17*, pp. 144–66.

Berger, John (1972). *Ways of Seeing*. Harmondsworth: Penguin.

— (1986) *The Sense of Sight*. New York: Pantheon.

Berger, Renate und Inge Stephan eds. (1987). *Weiblichkeit und Tod in der Literatur*. Köln: Böhlau.

Bernheimer, Charles (1989). *Figures of Ill Repute. Representing Prostitution in Nineteenth-Century France*. Cambridge: Harvard University Press.

Blanchot, Maurice (1949). *La part du feu*. Paris: Gallimard.

— (1981). *The Gaze of Orpheus and other literary essays*. Barrytown: Station Hill Press.

Bloch, Maurice and Jonathan Parry (1982). *Death & the Regeneration of Life*. Cambridge: Cambridge University Press.

Bloch, R. Howard (1987). 'Medieval Misogyny'. *Representations 20* pp. 1–24.

Bloom, Harold (1973). *The Anxiety of Influence. A Theory of Poetry*. Oxford: Oxford University Press.

— (1976). *Figure of Capable Imagination*. New York: Seabury Press.

Bloomfield, Morton W. (1981). *Allegory, Myth and Symbol*. Cambridge: Harvard University Press.

Bonaparte, Marie (1949). *The Life and Works of Edgar Allan Poe. A Psycho-Analytic Interpretation*. London: Imago.

Boone, Joseph Allen (1987). *Tradition Counter Tradition. Love and the Form of Fiction*. Chicago: Chicago University Press.

Boumelha, Penny (1982). *Thomas Hardy and Women. Sexual Ideology and Narrative Form.* Madison: University of Wisconsin Press.

Bowlby, John (1980). *Loss. Sadness and Depression.* New York: Basic Books.

Braun, Christina von (1985). *Nicht-Ich: Logik, Lüge, Libido.* Frankfurt: Neue Kritik.

— (1989). 'Männliche Hysterie – Weibliche Askese. Zum Paradigmenwechsel der Geschlechterrollen'. *Die Schamlose Schönheit des Vergangenen.* Frankfurt am Main: Neue Kritik, pp. 51–79.

Brenkman, John (1982). 'The Other and the One: Psychoanalysis, Reading, The Symposium'. *Literature and Psychoanalysis* ed. Shoshana Felman. Baltimore: Johns Hopkins University Press, pp. 396–456.

Briand-Le Bot, Huguette ed. (1975). *Lieux et objets de la mort.* Traverses 1. Paris: de Minuit.

Bronfen, Elisabeth (1987). 'Die Weibliche Leiche. Eine Motivische Konstante vom 18. bis in die Moderne'. *Weiblichkeit und Tod in der Literatur* ed. Inge Stephan and Renate Berger. Köln: Böhlau Verlag, pp. 87–115.

— (1990). 'Dialogue with the Dead. The Deceased Beloved as Muse'. *Sex and Death in Victorian Literature* ed. Regina Barreca. London: Macmillan, pp. 241–59.

Brooks, Peter (1984). *Reading for the Plot. Design and Intention in Narrative.* New York: Knopf.

Brown, Norman O. (1959). *Life Against Death. The Psychoanalytic Meaning of History.* Middletown: Wesleyan University Press.

Brown, Peter (1981). *The Cult of the Saints. Its Rise and Function in Latin Christianity.* Chicago: University of Chicago Press.

Brüschweiler, Jura ed. (1976). *Ein Maler vor Liebe und Tod. Ferdinand Hodler und Valentine Godé-Darel. Ein Werkzyklus. 1908–1915.* Exhibition Catalogue Kunsthaus Zürich, Kunstverein St Gallen, München Museum Villa Stuck, Kunstmuseum Bern.

Brüschweiler, Jura et. al. (1983). *Ferdinand Hodler.* Exhibition Catalogue Kunsthaus Zürich, Nationalgalerie Berlin, Musée du Petit Palais Paris.

Bryson, Norman (1983). *Vision and Painting. The Logic of the Gaze.* New Haven: Yale University Press.

Buci-Glucksmann, Christine (1984). *La Raison baroque de Baudelaire à Benjamin.* Paris: Galilée.

Burgin, Victor (1986). *The End of Art Theory. Criticism and Postmodernity.* London: Macmillan.

Burke, Kenneth (1952). 'Thanatopsis for Critics: A Brief Thesaurus of Deaths and Dyings'. *Essays in Criticism 2*, pp. 370–75.

Burkert, Walter (1983). *Homo Necans.* Berkeley: University of California Press.

Bynum, Caroline Walker (1984). 'Women's Stories, Women's Symbols.' Anthropology and the Study of Religion eds Robert L. Moore and Frank E. Reynolds. Chicago: CSSR, pp. 105–25.

Cameron, Deborah and Elizabeth Frazer (1987). *The Lust to Kill. A Feminist Investigation of Sexual Murder.* New York: New York University Press.

Canetti, Elias (1980). *Macht und Masse.* Frankfurt: Fischer.

Carter, Margaret L. ed. (1988). *Dracula. The Vampire and the Critics.* Ann Arbor: U.M.I.

Caruso, Igos A. (1974). *Die Trennung der Liebenden. Eine Phänomenologie des Todes.* Frankfurt: Fischer.

Castle, Terry (1982). *Clarissa's Ciphers. Meaning and Disruption in Richardson's Clarissa.* Ithaca: Cornell University Press.

— (1987). 'The Spectralization of the Other'. *The Eighteenth Century: Theory, Politics, English Literature* ed. Felicity Nussbaum and Laura Brown. London: Methuen.

Chasseguet-Smirgel, Janine (1988). *Zwei Bäume im Garten. Zur psychischen Bedeutung der Vater- und Mutterbilder.* München: Verlag Internationale Psychoanalyse.

Choron, Jacques (1963). *Death and Western Thought.* New York: Collier Books.

— (1964) *Modern Man and Mortality.* New York: Macmillan.

Christ, Carol (forthcoming a). 'The Dead Body in Pre-Raphaelite Poetry and Painting'. Unpublished manuscript.

— (forthcoming b). 'Painting the dead'. Unpublished manuscript.

Cixous, Hélène (1976). 'Fiction and Its Phantoms: A Reading of Freud's *Das Unheimliche*'. *New Literary History 7.3*, pp. 525–48.

— (1976a). 'The Laugh of the Medusa'. *Signs 1*, pp. 875–93.

— (1979). 'Qui chant? Qui fait chanter? Qui est chanté? Qui (s')appelle (Orphée)?' Seminar Paper held at the Université Paris, Vincennes.

— (1981). 'Castration or Decapitation'. *Signs 7*, pp. 41–55.

— (1986). 'La venue à l'écriture.' *Entre L'Écriture.* Paris: des femmes.

Clément, Catherine (1979). *L'opéra ou la défaite des femmes.* Paris: Grasset.

Clément, Catherine and Hélène Cixous (1975). *La jeune née.* Paris: Union Génerale d'Éditions.

Cohan, Steven (1978). 'Narrative Form and Death: The Mill on the Floss and Mrs. Dalloway.' *Genre 11*, pp. 109–29.

Cole, Susan Letzler (1985). *The Absent One: Mourning, Ritual, Tragedy and the Performance of Ambivalence.* University Park: Pennsylvania State University Press.

Colman, E.A.M. (1974). *The Dramatic Use of Bawdy in Shakespeare.* London: Longman.

Commager, Steele (1967). *The Odes of Horace. A Critical Study.* Bloomington: Indiana University Press.

Condrau, Gion (1984). *Der Mensch und sein Tod. Certa moriendi condicio.* Zürich: Benzinger.

Cowie, Elizabeth (1978). 'Woman as Sign'. *M/F 1*, pp. 49–63.

Craft, Christopher (1984). ' "Kiss Me with Those Red Lips": Gender and Inversion in Bram Stoker's Dracula'. *Representations 8*, pp. 107–33.

Culler, Jonathan (1975). *Structuralist Poetics.* Ithaca: Cornell University Press.

Curl, James Stevens (1980). *A Celebration of Death: An introduction to some of the buildings, monuments, and settings of funerary architecture in the Western European Tradition.* London: Constable.

Daly, Gay (1989). *Pre-Raphaelites in Love.* London: Collins.

de Beauvoir, Simone (1974). *The Second Sex.* New York: Random House.

de Certeau, Michel (1984). *The Practice of Everyday Life.* Berkeley: University of California Press.

Deguy, Michel (1969). *Figurations.* Paris: Gallimard.

Delacroix, Maurice ed. (1982). *Thanatos classique. 5 étude sur la mort écrite.* Tübingen: Gunter Narr.

de Lauretis, Teresa (1984). Alice Doesn't. Feminism, Semiotics, Cinema. Bloomington: Indiana University Press.

— (1987). *Technologies of Gender. Essays on Theory, Film and Fiction.* Bloomington: Indiana University Press.

de Man, Paul (1979). *Allegories of Reading. Figural Language in Rousseau, Nietzsche, Rilke, and Proust.* New Haven, Yale University Press.

— (1983). *Blindness and Insight. Essays in the Rhetoric of Contemporary Criticism.* Minneapolis, University of Minnesota Press.

Derrida, Jacques (1976). *Of Grammatology.* Baltimore: Johns Hopkins University Press.

— (1977). 'Fors'. *Georgia Review 31*, pp. 64–116.

— (1978). 'Coming into One's Own'. *Psychoanalysis & the Question of the Text* ed. Geoffrey H. Hartman. Baltimore: Johns Hopkins University Press, pp. 114–48.

— (1979) 'Living On'. *Deconstruction and Criticism* ed. Harold Bloom et al. New York: Seabury Press, pp. 75–176.

— (1981). *Dissemination.* Chicago: University of Chicago Press.

— (1986). *Memoires for Paul de Man.* New York: Columbia University Press.

— (1987). *The Post Card. From Socrates to Freud and Beyond.* Chicago: University of Chicago Press.

DeShazer, Mary K. (1986). *Inspiring Women. Reimagining the Muse.* New York: Pergamon Press.

Detweiler, Robert (1972). 'The Moment of Death in Modern Fiction'. *Contemporary Literature 13*, pp. 269–94.

Dijkstra, Bram (1986). *Idols of Perversity. Fantasies of Feminine Evil in Fin-de Siècle Culture.* Oxford: Oxford University Press.

Donato, Eugenio (1984). 'The Crypt of Flaubert'. *Flaubert and Postmodernism* ed. Naomi Schor and Henry F. Majewski. Lincoln: University of Nebraska Press, pp. 30–45.

Donnelly, John ed. (1978) *Language, Metaphysics and Death.* New York: Fordham University Press.

Doody, Margaret (1974). *A Natural Passion. A Study of the Novels of Samuel Richardson.* Oxford: Oxford University Press.

Douglas, Ann (1977). *The Feminization of American Culture.* New York: Avon.

Douglas, Mary (1966). *Purity and Danger. An Analysis of the Concepts of Pollution and Taboo.* London: Routledge and Kegan Paul.

Dubus, Pascale and Jean-David Jumeau-Lafond ed. (1986). *Figures de la mort. L'Écrit-Voir: Revue d'histoire des Arts 8.*

Durkheim, Emile (1951). *Suicide. A Study in Sociology.* New York: The Free Press.

Duverger, Christian (1989). 'The Meaning of Sacrifice'. *Zone 5*, pp. 366–85.

Eagleton, Terry (1982). *The Rape of Clarissa.* Minneapolis, University of Minnesota Press.

Ebling, Hans ed. (1979). *Der Tod in der Moderne.* Frankfurt: Syndikat.

Easton, Malcolm (1972). *Aubrey and the Dying Lady. A Beardsley Riddle.* London: Secker and Warburg.

Edel, Leon (1972). *Henry James. The Master: 1901–1916.* New York: Avon.

Eissler, Kurt (1980). *Todestrieb, Ambivalenz, Narzißmus.* München: Kindler.

Eliade, Mircea (1952). *Images et symboles.* Paris: Gallimard.

— (1977). 'Mythologies of Death: An Introduction'. *Religious Encounters with Death* ed. Frank E. Reynolds and Earle H. Waugh. University Park: Pennsylvania State University Press, pp. 13–23.

Enright, D. J. ed. (1983). *The Oxford Book of Death.* Oxford: Oxford University Press.

Export, Valie (1987). *Das Reale und Sein Double: der Körper.* Bern: Benteli Verlag.

Favre, Robert (1978). *La mort dans la littérature et la pensée francaise au siècle des lumiéres.* Lyon: Presses Universitaires de Lyon.

Feifel, Herman (1965). *The Meaning of Death.* New York: McGraw Hill.

Felman, Shoshana (1975). 'Women and Madness: The Critical Phallacy'. *Diacritics 5*, pp. 1–10.

— (1981). 'Rereading femininity'. *Yale French Studies 62*, pp. 19–44.

Fiedler, Leslie A. (1966). *Love and Death in the American Novel*. New York: Stein and Day.

Fineman, Joel (1981). 'The Structure of Allegorical Desire'. *Allegory and Representation.* ed. Stephen J. Greenblatt Baltimore: Johns Hopkins University Press, pp. 26–60.

Fisher, Phil (1985). *Hard Facts. Setting and Form in the American Novel*. Oxford: Oxford University Press.

Fletcher, Angus (1964). *Allegory. The Theory of a Symbolic Mode*. Ithaca: Cornell University Press.

Foucault, Michel (1970). *The Order of Things*. New York: Vintage.

— (1973). *The Birth of the Clinic*. New York: Vintage.

— (1977). *Language, counter-memory, practice. Selected Essays and Interviews*. ed. Donald F. Bouchard Ithaca: Cornell University Press.

Freeman, Lucy and Dr Herbert S. Strean (1987). *Freud and Women*. New York: Continuum.

Freud, Sigmund (1895–1938). *Standard Edition*. London: The Hogarth Press.

— (1895). *Studies on Hysteria. SE 2*.

— (1900). *Interpretation of Dreams. SE 4–5*.

— (1905). *Three Essays on the Theory of Sexuality. SE 7*, pp. 123–245.

— (1910). 'A Special Type of Object Choice Made by Men'. *SE 11*, pp. 163–75.

— (1912–13). *Totem and Taboo. SE 13*.

— (1913). 'The Theme of the Three Caskets'. *SE 12*, pp. 289–301.

— (1914). 'On Narcissism: An Introduction'. *SE 14*, pp. 67–102.

— (1915). Thoughts for the Times on War and Death". *SE 14*, pp. 273–302.

— (1916). 'On Transcience'. *SE 14*, pp. 303–07.

— (1917). 'Mourning and Melancholia'. *SE 14*, pp. 237–60.

— (1919). 'The "Uncanny" '. *SE 17*, pp. 217–56.

— (1920). *Beyond the Pleasure Principle. SE 18*, pp. 1–64.

— (1923). *The Ego and the Id. SE 19*, pp. 1–66.

— (1924). *The Economic Problem of Masochism. SE 19*, pp. 155–70.

— (1925a). 'Negation'. *SE 19*, pp. 233–9.

— (1925b). 'Some psychological Consequences of the Anatomical Distinction Between the Sexes'. *SE 19*, pp. 241–58.

— (1926). *Inhibitions, Symptoms and Anxiety. SE 20*, pp. 75–175.

— (1927). 'Fetishism'. *SE 21*, pp. 149–57.

— (1930). *Civilization and its Discontents. SE 21*, pp. 57–146.

— (1933). *New Introductory Lectures on Psychoanalysis. SE 22*, pp. 1–183.

— (1933a) 'Why War?' *SE 22*, pp. 195–215.

— (1937). 'Analysis Terminable and Interminable'. *SE 23*, pp. 209–53.

— (1940). 'Medusa's Head'. *SE 18*, pp. 273–4.

— (1960). *Briefe 1973–1939*. Frankfurt am Main: Fischer.

— (1985). *The Complete Letters of Sigmund Freud to Wilhelm Fliess 1887–1904* ed. Jeffrey Moussaieff Masson. Cambridge: Harvard University Press.

— (1986). *Briefe an Wilhelm Fließ 1887–1904* ed. Jeffrey Moussaieff Masson. Frankfurt am Main: Fischer.

Fried, Debra (1986). 'Repetition, Refrain and Epitaph'. *English Literary History 53*, pp. 615–32.

Fuchs, Werner (1969). *Todesbilder in der modernen Gesellschaft*. Frankfurt: Suhrkamp.

Gallagher, Catherine and Thomas Laqueur eds. (1987). *The Making of the Modern Body:*

Sexuality and Society in the Nineteenth Century. Berkeley: University of California Press.

Gallop, Jane (1982). *The Daughter's Seduction. Feminism and psychoanalysis*. Ithaca: Cornell University Press.

Gallwitz, Klaus and Günter Metken (1973). *Präraffaeliten*. Exhibition Catalogue Staatliche Kunsthalle Baden-Baden.

Garland, Robert (1985). *The Greek Way of Death*. Ithaca: Cornell University Press.

Gatch, Milton (1969). *Death: Meaning and Mortality in Christian Thought and Contemporary Culture*. New York: The Seabury Press.

Gates, Barbara T. (1988). *Victorian Suicide. Mad Crimes and Sad Heroines*. Princeton: Princeton University Press.

Gay, Peter (1984). *The Bourgois Experience. Victoria to Freud. Education of the Senses*. Oxford: Oxford University Press.

— (1988). *Freud. A Life for Our Time*. New York: Norton.

Gennep, Arnold van (1960). *The Rites of Passage*. Chicago: University of Chicago Press.

Gervais, Karen Grandstrand (1986). *Redefining Death*. New Haven: Yale University Press.

Gilbert, Sandra M. and Susan Gubar (1979). *The Madwoman in the Attic. The Woman Writer and the Nineteenth-Century Literary Imagination*. New Haven: Yale University Press.

— (1988). *No Man's Land. The Place of the Woman Writer in the Twentieth Century. Vol 1. The War of the Words*. New Haven: Yale University Press.

Gilman, Sander L. (1985). *Difference and Pathology. Stereotypes of Sexuality, Race and Madness*. Ithaca: Cornell University Press.

— (1989). *Sexuality. An Illustrated History*. New York: Wiley.

Girard, René (1972). *La violence et le sacré*. Paris: Grasset.

Goodwin, Sarah Webster (1988). *Kitsch and Culture. The Dance of Death in Nineteenth-Century Literature and Graphic Arts*. New York: Garland.

Graves, Robert (1966). *The White Goddess. A historical grammar of poetic myth*. Amended and enlarged edition. New York: Farrar, Straus and Giroux.

Green, André (1978). 'The Double and the Absent'. *Psychoanalysis, Creativity and Literature* ed. Alan Roland. New York: Columbia University Press, pp. 271–92.

— (1986a). *On Private Madness*. London: Hogarth Press.

— ed. (1986b). *La Pulsion de Mort*. Paris: Presses Universitaires de France.

Greenberg, Jay R. and Stephen A.Mitchell (1983). *Object Relations in Psychoanalytic Theory*. Cambridge: Harvard University Press.

Greenblatt, Stephen J. ed. (1981). *Allegory and Representation*. Baltimore: Johns Hopkins University Press.

Gubar, Susan (1982). ' "The Blank Page" and the Issue of Female Creativity'. *Writing and Sexual Difference* ed. Elizabeth Abel. Brighton: Harvester Press, pp. 73–93.

Guiomar, Michel (1967). *Principes d'une esthétique de la mort*. Paris: Librairie José Corti.

Hall, James (1974). *Dictionary of Subjects and Symbols in Art*. London: John Murray.

Harris, Ann Sutherland and Linda Nochlin (1974). *Women Artists 1550–1950*. New York: Knopf.

Hartman, Geoffrey H. ed. (1979). *Psychoanalysis and the Question of the Text*. Baltimore: Johns Hopkins University Press.

Heath, Stephen (1978). 'Difference'. *Screen 19*, pp. 51–112.

Heimann, Paula (1970). 'Notes on the theory of the Life and Death Instinct'. *Developments in psycho-analysis* ed Melanie Klein, Paula Heimann, Joan Rivière. London: Hogarth Press, pp. 321–37.

Hertz, Neil (1985). *The End of the Line. Essays on Psychoanalysis and the Sublime*. New York: Columbia University Press.

Hertz, Robert (1960). *Death and The Right Hand*. Glencoe: The Free Press.

Higonnet, Margaret (1985). 'Writing from the feminine: Lucinde and Adolphe'. *Annales Benjamin Constant 5*, pp. 17–35.

— (1986). 'Speaking Silences: Women's Suicide'. *The Female Body in Western Culture* ed. Susan Suleiman Cambridge: Harvard University Press, pp. 68–83.

Hof, Renate (1984). *Das Spiel des unreliable narrator. Aspekte unglaubwürdigen Erzählens im Werk von Vladimir Nabokov*. München: Fink.

Hoffman, Frederick J (1964). *The Mortal No: Death and the Modern Imagination*. Princeton: Princeton University Press.

Holquist, Michael (1983). 'Whodunit and Other Questions: Metaphysical Detective Stories in Postwar Fiction'. *The Poetics of Murder. Detective Fiction and Literary Theory* ed. Gleen W. Most and William W. Stowe. New York: Harcourt Brace Jovanovich, pp. 149–74.

Holubetz, Margarete (1986). 'Death-Bed Scenes in Victorian Fiction'. *English Studies 67*, pp. 14–34.

Holy Bible (1974). *King James Version*. New York: New American Library.

Homans, Margaret (1986). *Bearing the World. Language and Female Experience in Nineteenth-Century Women's Writing*. Chicago: University of Chicago Press.

Homer (1951). *The Iliad* trans. Richard Lattimore. Chicago: University of Chicago Press.

Hönnighausen, Lothar (1971). *Präraphaeliten und fin de Siècle. Symbolische Tendenzen in der Englischen Spätromantik*. München: Fink.

Hough, Graham (1949). *The Last Romantics*. London: Duckworth.

Houghton, Walter E. (1957). *The Victorian Frame of Mind. 1830–1870*. New Haven: Yale University Press.

Huet, Marie-Helene (1983). 'Living Images: Monstrosity and Representation'. *Representations 4*, pp. 73–87.

Hughes, Peter (1987). 'Playing with grief: Hamlet and the act of mourning'. *Comparative Criticism 9*, pp. 111–33.

Huizinga, J. (1954). *The Waning of the Middle Ages*. New York: Doubleday.

Humphreys, Sally and Helen King ed. (1981). *Mortality and Immortality: the Anthropology and Archaeology of Death*. London: Academic Press.

Hunt, Violet (1932). *The Wife of Rossetti. Her Life and Death*. New York: Dutton.

Huntington, Richard and Peter Metcalf (1979). *Celebrations of Death. The Anthropology of Mortuary Ritual*. Cambridge, Cambridge University Press.

Hutcheon, Linda (1989). *The Politics of Postmodernism*. London: Routledge.

Hutter, Albert D. (1983). 'The Novelist as Resurrectionist: Dickens and the Dilemma of Death'. *Dickens Studies Annual 12*, pp. 1–39.

Irigaray, Luce (1981). *Le corps-à-corps avec la mère*. Paris: Les Éditions de la pleine lune. Montréal.

Irwin, John T. (1980). *American Hieroglyphics*. New Haven: Yale University Press.

Jacobus, Mary (1986). *Reading Woman. Essays in Feminist Criticism*. New York: Columbia University Press.

Jakobson, Roman and Morris Halle (1956). *Fundamentals of Language*. The Hague: Mouton.

— (1960). 'Closing Statement: Linguistics and Poetics'. *Style in Language* ed. Thomas A. Sebeok Cambridge: Technology Press of Massachussets Institute of Technology, pp.

350–77.
— (1971). *Selected Writings Vol. I.* The Hague: Mouton.
Jameson, Fredric (1981). *The Political Unconscious. Narrative as a Socially Symbolic Act.* London: Methuen.
Jankelevitch, Vladimir (1977). *La Mort.* Paris: Flammarion.
Jansen, Hans Helmut ed. (1978). *Der Tod in Dichtung, Philosophie und Kunst.* Darmstadt: Dr Dietrich Steinkopff Verlag.
Jaulin, Annick ed. (1984). *La femme et la mort.* Toulouse-Le Mirail: G.R.I.E.F.
Johnson, Barbara (1980). *The Critical Difference.* Baltimore: Johns Hopkins University Press.
— (1987). *A World of Difference.* Baltimore: Johns Hopkins University Press.
— (1989). 'Is Female to Male as Ground Is to Figure?' *Feminism and Psychoanalysis* ed. Richard Feldstein and Judith Roof. Ithaca: Cornell University Press, pp. 255–58.
Jones, Ernest (1953–7). *The Life and Work of Sigmund Freud.* New York: Basic Books.
Jordanova, Ludmilla (1989). *Sexual Visions. Images of Gender in Science and Medicine between the Eighteenth and Twentieth Centuries.* New York/London: Harvester.
Jullian, Philippe (1971). *Dreamers of Decadence. Symbolist Painters of the 1890s.* New York: Praeger.
Kalikoff, Beth (1986). *Murder and Moral. Decay in Victorian Popular Literature.* Ann Arbor: U.M.I.Research Press.
Kappeler, Susanne (1980). *Writing and Reading in Henry James.* New York: Columbia Books.
Kauffman, Linda (1986). *Discourses of Desire. Gender, Genre, and Epistolary Fictions.* Ithaca: Cornell University Press.
Keefe, Robert (1979). *Charlotte Brontë's World of Death.* Austin: University of Texas Press.
Keller, Evelyn Fox (1985). *Reflections on Gender and Science.* New Haven: Yale University Press.
Kennedy, Gerald J. (1987). *Poe, Death, and the Life of Writing.* New Haven: Yale University Press.
Kermode, Frank (1966). *The Sense of an Ending. Studies in the Theory of Fiction.* Oxford: Oxford University Press.
Klein, Melanie (1970). 'On the Theory of Anxiety and Guilt'. *Developments in Psycho-Analysis.* ed. Joan Riviere. London: Hogarth Press, pp. 271–91.
— (1975a). *Love, Guilt and Reparation and other Works 1921–1945.* New York: The Free Press.
— (1975b). *Envy and Gratitude and other Works 1946–1963.* New York: The Free Press.
Knoepflmacher, Ulrich (1979). 'Thoughts on the Aggression of Daughters'. *The Endurance of Frankenstein* ed. George Levine and U. C. Knoepflmacher. Berkeley: University of California Press, pp. 88–119.
Koerner, Joseph Leo (1985). 'The Mortification of the Image: Death as a Hermeneutic in Hals Baldung Grien'. *Representations 10,* pp.52–101.
Kofman, Sarah (1973). *Quatre romans analytiques.* Paris: Galilée.
— (1985a). *The Enigma of Woman. Woman in Freud's Writings.* Ithaca: Cornell University Press.
— (1985b). *Mélanchcolie de l'art.* Paris: Galilée.
— (1987). *Conversions. Le Marchand de Venise sous le signe de Saturne.* Paris: Galilée.
Kristeva, Julia (1980). *Desire in Language. A Semiotic Approach to Literature and Art.* New York: Columbia University Press.

— (1981). 'Women's Time'. *Signs 7.1*, pp. 13–35.

— (1982). *Powers of Horror. An Essay on Abjection*. New York: Columbia University Press.

— (1984). *Revolution in Poetic Language*. New York: Columbia University Press.

— (1987a). *Tales of Love*. New York: Columbia University Press.

— (1987b). *In the Beginning was Love. Psychoanalysis and Faith*. New York: Columbia University Press.

— (1989). *Black Sun. Depression and Melancholia*. New York: Columbia University Press.

Kübler-Ross, Elisabeth (1969). *On Death and Dying*. New York, Macmillan.

Lacan, Jacques (1968). *Speech and Language in Psychoanalysis* ed. Anthony Wilden. Baltimore: Johns Hopkins University Press.

— (1975). *Le Seminaire XX. Encore*. Paris: Seuil.

— (1977). *Écrits. A Selection*. New York: Norton.

— (1978). *Le Séminaire II. Le moi dans la théorie de Freud et dans la technique de la psychanalyse*. Paris: Seuil.

— (1981). *The Four Fundamental Concepts of Psycho-Analysis*. New York: Norton.

— (1985). *Feminine Sexuality* ed. Juliet Mitchell and Jacqueline Rose. New York: Norton.

— (1986). *Le Séminaire VII. L'éthique de la psychanalyse*. Paris: Seuil.

Laplanche, Jean (1976). *Life and Death in Psychoanalysis*. Baltimore: Johns Hopkins University Press.

Laplanche, Jean and Serge Leclaire (1975). 'The Unconscious: A Psychoanalytic Study'. *Yale French Studies 48*, pp. 118–75.

Laqueur, Thomas (1983). 'Bodies, Death, and Pauper Funerals'. *Representations 1*, pp. 109–31.

— (1990). *Making Sex. Body and Gender from the Greeks to Freud*. Cambridge: Harvard University Press.

Lawrence, D. H. (1923). *Studies in Classic American Literature*. New York: Random House.

Leclaire, Serge (1971). *Démasquer le réel*. Paris: Seuil.

— (1975). *On tue un enfant*. Paris: Seuil.

Ledanff, Susanne (1986). *Charlotte Stieglitz. Geschichte eines Denkmals*. Frankfurt am Main: Ullstein.

Lejeune, Claire ed. (1979). *La Mort à vivre et à mourir. Cahiers internationaux de symbolisme 37–38–39*. Mons: le Ciephum.

Lemoine-Luccioni, Eugénie (1976). *Partages des femmes*. Paris: Seuil.

Lévi-Strauss, Claude (1969). *The Elementary Structures of Kinship*. Boston: Beacon Press.

Llewelyn, Nigel (1991). *The Art of Death*. London: Reaktion Books.

Loraux, Nicole (1985). *Façon tragiques de tuer une femme*. Paris: Hachette.

Lotman, Jurij (1979). 'The origin of plot in the light of topology'. *Poetics Today 1*, pp. 161–84.

Lublin, David M. (1985). *Act of Portrayal. Eakins, Sargent, James*. New Haven: Yale University Press.

Luyten, N. A. ed. (1980). *Tod – Ende oder Vollendung?* München: Verlag Karl Alber.

McDannell, Colleen and Bernhard Lang (1988). *Heaven: A History*. New Haven: Yale University Press.

Macho, Thomas H. (1987). *Todesmetaphern. Zur Logik der Grenzerfahrung*. Frankfurt: Suhrkamp.

Macksey, Richard (1983). 'Last Words: The Artes Moriendi and a Transtextual Genre'. *Genre 16*, pp. 493–516.

McManners, John (1985). *Death and the Enlightenment. Changing attitudes to death in eighteenth-century France*. Oxford: Oxford University Press.

Marsh, Jan (1987). *Pre-Raphaelite Women. Images of Femininity*. New York: Harmony Books.

— (1989). *The Legend of Elizabeth Siddal*. London: Quartet Books.

Meltzer, Françoise (1987). *Salome and the Dance of Writing*. Chicago: Chicago University Press.

Melville, Stephen (1987). 'The Place of Jouissance'. *Critical Inquiry 13*, pp. 349–70.

Mentzos, Stavros (1980). *Hysterie. Zur Psychodynamik unbewußter Inszenierungen*. München: Kindler.

Merchant, Carolyn (1980). *The Death of Nature. Women, Ecology and the Scientific Revolution*. New York: Harper and Row.

Metzger, Arnold (1955). *Freiheit und Tod*. Tübingen: Niemeyer.

Meyer-Kalkus, Reinhart (1977). 'Werthers Krankheit zum Tode. Pathologie und Familie in der Empfindsamkeit'. *Urszenen. Literaturwissenschaft als Diskursanalyse und Diskurskritik*. Frankfurt: Suhrkamp.

Michaels, Walter Benn (1987). *The Gold Standard and the Logic of Naturalism American Literature at the Turn of the Century*. Berkeley: University of California Press.

Michie, Helena (1986). *The Flesh Made Word. Female Figures and Women's Bodies*. Oxford: Oxford University Press.

Miller, D. A. (1988). *The Novel and the Police*. Berkeley: University of California Press.

Miller, J. Hillis (1970). *Distance and Desire*. Cambridge: Harvard University Press.

— (1981). 'The Two Allegories'. *Allegory, Myth and Symbol* ed. Morton Bloomfield. Cambridge: Harvard University Press, pp. 355–70.

— (1982). *Fiction and Repetition. Seven English Novels*. Cambridge: Harvard University Press.

Miller, Nancy K. (1975). 'The Exquisite Cadavers: Women in Eighteenth-Century Fiction'. *Diacritics 5*, pp. 37–43.

— (1980). *The Heroine's Text. Readings in the French and English Novel, 1722–1782*. New York: Columbia University Press.

Mitchell, Juliet (1974). *Psychoanalysis and Feminism. Freud, Reich, Laing and Women*. New York: Random House.

— (1984). *Women: The Longest Revolution. Essays in Feminism, Literature and Psychoanalysis*. London: Virago.

Modleski, Tania (1988). *The Women Who Knew too Much. Hitchcock and Feminist Theory*. London: Methuen.

Moers, Ellen (1977). *Literary Women*. New York: Doubleday.

Morin, Edgar (1970). *L'Homme et la Mort*. Paris: Seuil.

Morley, John (1971). *Death, Heaven and the Victorians*. London: Studio Vista.

Muggenthaler, Johannes (1988). *Der Geister Bahnen. Eine Ausstellung zu Ehren von Gabriel von Max 1840–1915*. München: Mosel und Tscheckow.

Mulvey, Laura (1975). 'Visual Pleasure and Narrative Cinema'. *Screen 16*, pp. 6–18.

Nead, Lynda (1988). *Myths of Sexuality. Representations of Women in Victorian Britain*. Oxford: Basil Blackwell.

Nochlin, Linda (1971a). *Realism. Style and Civilization*. Harmondsworth: Penguin, 1971.

— (1971b). 'Gustave Courbet's Toilette de la Mariée,' *Art Quarterly 34*, pp. 31–54.

— and Sarah Faunce (1988). *Courbet Reconsidered*. New Haven: Yale University Press, pp. 126–8.

Ong, Walter J. (1977). *Interfaces of the Word: Studies in the Evolution of Consciousness and*

Culture. Ithaca: Cornell University Press.

Peirce, Charles S. (1955). *Philosophical Writings of Peirce* ed. Justus Buchler. New York: Dover, pp. 98–119.

Plato (1961). *The Collected Dialogues* ed. Edith Hamilton and Huntington Cairns. Princeton: Princeton University Press.

Pollock, Griselda (1988). *Vision and Difference*. London: Routledge.

Pontalis, J.-B. (1978). 'On Death-Work in Freud, in the Self, in Culture'. *Psychoanalysis, Creativity and Literature* ed. Alan Roland. New York: Columbia University Press, pp. 85–95.

Poovey, Mary (1980). 'My Hideous Progeny: Mary Shelley and the Feminization of Romanticism'. *PMLA 95*, pp. 332–47.

Porte, Joel ed. (1982). *Emerson in His Journals*. Cambridge: Harvard University Press.

Praz, Mario (1951). *The Romantic Agony*. Oxford: Oxford University Press.

Proffer, Carl R. (1968). *Keys to Lolita*. Bloomington: Indiana University Press.

Punter, David (1980). *The Literature of Terror. A History of Gothic Fictions from 1765 to the Present Day*. London: Longman.

Racek, Milan (1986). *Die nicht zu Erde wurden. Kulturgeschichte der Konservierenden Bestattungsformen*. Köln: Böhlau.

Ragland-Sullivan, Ellie (1987). *Jacques Lacan and the Philosophy of Psychoanalysis*. Urbana: University of Illinois Press.

— (1988). 'The Limits of Discourse Structure: Obsession and Hysteria'. *Papers of the Freudian School of Melbourne* ed. Oscak Zentner. Victoria: Monash University Press, pp. 69–80.

Rank, Otto (1945). *Will Therapy*. New York: Knopf.

Raphael, Max (1983). *Die Farbe Schwarz*. Frankfurt am Main: Qumran.

Reed, John R. (1975). *Victorian Conventions*. Athens, Ohio: Ohio University Press.

Restuccia, Frances L. (1987): 'The name of the Lily: Edith Wharton's Feminism(s)'. *Contemporary Literature 28.2*, pp. 223–38.

Reynolds, Frank E. and Earle H. Waugh (1977). *Religious Encounters with Death. Insights from the History and Anthropology of Religions*. University Park: Pennsylvania State University Press.

Rickels, Laurence A. (1988). *Aberrations of Mourning. Writing on German Crypts*. Detroit: Wayne State University Press.

Richardson, Ruth (1989). *Death, Dissection and the Destitute*. Harmondsworth: Penguin.

Ricoeur, Paul (1970). *Freud and Philosophy: An Essay in Interpretation*. New Haven: Yale University Press.

— (1975). *La métaphor vive*. Paris: Seuil.

Ridler, Anne ed. (1963). *Poems and Some Letters of James Thomson*. London: Centaur Press.

Rimmon-Kenan, Schlomith (1980). 'The Paradoxical Status of Repetition'. *Poetics Today 1*, pp. 151–9.

Roland, Alan (1978). *Psychoanalysis, Creativity and Literature. A French-American Inquiry*. New York: Columbia University Press.

Rose, Jacqueline (1986). *Sexuality in the Field of Vision*. London: Verso.

— (1989). 'Where Does the Misery Come From? Pschoanalysis, Feminism, and the Event'. *Feminism and Psychoanalysis* ed. Richard Feldstein and Judith Roof. Ithaca: Cornell University Press, pp. 25–39.

Ryan, Michael (1976). 'Narcissus Autobiographer'. *English Literary History 43*, pp. 184–208.

Sacks, Peter (1985). *The English Elegy*. Baltimore: Johns Hopkins University Press.

Safouan, Moustafa (1983). *Pleasure and Being. Hedonism from a Psychoanalytic Point of View.* London: Macmillan.

Sarraute, Nathalie (1968). *Entre la vie et la mort*. Paris: Gallimard.

Scarry, Elaine (1985). *The Body in Pain. The Making and Unmaking of the World.* Oxford: Oxford University Press.

— ed. (1988). *Literature and the Body. Essays on Populations and Persons.* Baltimore: Johns Hopkins University Press.

Scherer, Georg (1979). *Das Problem des Todes in der Philosophie.* Darmstadt: Wissenschaftliche Buchgesellschaft.

Scholl, Sharon (1984). *Death and the Humanities*. Lewisburg: Bucknell University Press.

Schor, Naomi (1985). 'For a Restricted Thematics: Writing, Speech, and Difference in Madame Bovary'. *Breaking the Chain. Women, Theory and French Realist Fiction.* New York: Columbia University Press, pp. 3–28.

Schur, Max (1972). *Freud: Living and Dying*. New York: International Universities Press.

Serres, Michel (1987). *Statues. Le second livre des fondations*. Paris: Éditions François Bourin.

Shell, Marc (1978). *The Economy of Literature*. Baltimore: Johns Hopkins University Press.

Showalter, Elaine (1985a). *The Female Malady. Women, Madness and English Culture, 1830–1980.* New York: Pantheon.

— (1985ba). 'The Death of the Lady (Novelist): Wharton's House of Mirth'. *Representations 9*, pp. 133–49.

— (1985c). 'Representing Ophelia: women, madness and the responsibilities of feminist criticism'. *Shakespeare and the Question of Theory* ed. Patricia Parker and Geoffrey Hartman. London: Methuen, pp. 77–94.

Shute, J. P. (1984). 'Nabokov and Freud: The Play of Power'. *Modern Fiction Studies 30.4*, pp. 637–50.

Smith-Rosenberg, Carroll (1986). *Disorderly Conduct: Visions of Gender in Victorian America.* New York: Oxford University Press.

Sontag, Susan (1977). *Illness as Metaphor*. New York: Farrar, Straus and Giroux.

Spivak, Gayatri Chakravorti (1984). 'Love Me, Love My Ombre, Elle'. *Diacritics 14*, pp. 19–36.

— (1987). 'Finding Feminist Readings: Dante – Yeats'. *In Other Worlds. Essays in Cultural Politics.* New York: Methuen, pp. 15–29.

Spoto, Donald (1976). *The Art of Alfred Hitchcock*. New York: Doubleday.

Stannard, David (1977). *The Puritan Way of Death. A Study in Religion, Culture and Social Change.* Oxford: Oxford University Press.

Sternberger, Dolf (1974). *Panorama oder Ansichten vom 19. Jahrhundert.* Frankfurt: Suhrkamp.

Stewart, Garrett (1984). *Death Sentences. Styles of Dying in British Fiction.* Cambridge: Harvard University Press.

Stone, Lawrence (1977). *The Family, Sex and Marriage. In England 1500–1800.* New York: Harper and Row.

Stratton, Jon (1987). *The Virgin Text. Fiction, Sexuality, and Ideology.* Norman: University of Oklahoma Press.

Strouse, Jean (1980). *Alice James. A Biography*. Boston: Houghton Mifflin.

Suleiman, Susan Rubin ed. (1986). *The Female Body in Western Culture.* Cambridge, Harvard University Press.

Taeger, Annemarie (1987). *Die Kunst, Medusa zu töten*. Bielefeld: Aisthesis Verlag.

Tanner, Tony (1968). 'Colour and Movement in Hardy's Tess of the D'Urbervilles'. *Critical Quarterly 10*, pp. 219–39.

— (1979). *Adultery and the Novel*. Baltimore: Johns Hopkins University Press.

Theweleit, Klaus (1988). *Das Buch der Könige. I. Orpheus und Eurydike*. Frankfurt am Main: Stroemfeld/Roter Stern.

Thom, Martin (1981). 'Verneinung, Verwerfung, Ausstossung: A Problem in the Interpretation of Freud'. *The Talking Cure. Essays in Psychoanlysis and Language* ed. Colin MacCabe. London: Macmillan, pp. 162–87.

Thomas, Louis Vincent (1979). 'La mort, objet anthropologique'. *Les Cahiers Internationaux de Symbolisme 37–38–39*, pp. 33–44.

— (1980). *Le cadavre – De la biologie à l'anthropologie*. Bruxelles: Édition complexe.

Todorov, Tzvetan (1977). *The Poetics of Prose*. Ithaca: Cornell University Press.

Tolchin, Neal L. (1988). *Mourning, Gender and Creativity in the Art of Herman Melville*. New Haven: Yale University Press.

Tompkins, Jane (1985). *Sensational Designs. The Cultural Work of American Fiction*. Oxford: Oxford University Press.

Toussaint, Hélène (1977). *Gustave Courbet (1819–1877)*. Grand Palais. Paris: Editions des Musées Nationaux, pp. 107–9.

Truffaut, Francois (1983). *Hitchcock*. New York: Simon and Schuster.

Turner, Victor (1977a). 'Death and the Dead in the Pilgrimage Process'. *Religious Encounters with Death* ed. Frank E. Reynolds and Earle H. Waugh. University Park: Pennsylvania State University Press, pp. 24–39.

— (1977b). *The Ritual Process. Structure and Anti-Structure*. Ithaca: Cornell University Press.

Twitchell, James B. (1981). *The Living Dead. A Study of the Vampire in Romantic Literature*. Durham: Duke University Press.

Vermeule, Emily (1979). *Aspects of Death in Early Greek Art and Poetry*. Berkeley: University of California Press.

Vernant, Jean-Louis (1985). *La mort dans les yeux*. Paris: Hachette.

— (1988). 'Figuration de l'invisible et catégoire psychologique du double: le colossos'. *Mythes & pensée chez les Grecs*. Paris: La Découverte, pp. 325–38.

Vernon, Glenn M. (1974). 'Dying as a Social-Symbolic Process'. *Humanitas 10*, pp. 21–32.

Vovelle, Michel (1983). *La mort et l'occident, de 1300 à nos jours*. Paris: Gallimard.

Walker, Barbara G. (1983). *The Woman's Encyclopedia of Myths and Secrets*. New York: Harper and Row.

Ward, Geoffrey (1986). 'Dying to Write: Maurice Blanchot and Tennyson's "Tithonus" '. *Critical Inquiry 12*, pp. 672–87.

Warner, Marina (1983). *Alone of all her Sex. The Myth and the Cult of the Virgin Mary*. New York: Random House.

— (1985). *Monuments and Maidens. The Allegory of the Female Form*. London: Weidenfeld & Nicolson.

Warner, William (1979). *Reading Clarissa. The Struggles of Interpretation*. New Haven: Yale University Press.

Watt, Ian (1975). *The Rise of the Novel. Studies in Defoe, Richardson and Fielding*. Berkeley: University of California Press.

Weber, Samuel (1982). *The Legend of Freud*. Minneapolis: University of Minnesota Press.

Welsh, Alexander (1971). The City of Dickens. Oxford: Clarendon Press.

Whaley, Joachim ed. (1982). *Mirrors of mortality: Studies in the social history of death*. New York: St Martin's Press.

Widmer, Peter (1984). 'Zum Problem des Todestriebs'. *Psyche 38*, pp. 1060–82.

Winnicott, D. W. (1971) *Playing and Reality*. London: Tavistock.

— (1975). 'The Observation of Infants in a Set Situation'. *Through Paediatrics to Psycho-Analysis*. London: Hogarth Press, pp. 52–69.

Wolff, Cynthia Griffin (1977). *A Feast of Words: The Triumph of Edith Wharton*. New York: Oxford University Press.

Wright, Elizabeth (1984). *Psychoanalytic Criticism. Theory in Practice*. London: Methuen.

Wulf, Christoph (1982). 'Körper und Tod'. *Die Wiederkehr des Körpers* ed. Christoph Wulf and Dietmar Kamper. Frankfurt: Suhrkamp, pp. 259–73.

Yeazell, Ruth Bernard ed. (1981). *The Death and Letters of Alice James*. Berkeley: University of California Press.

Zaleski, Carol G. (1987). *Otherworld Journeys. Accounts of Near-Death Experience in Medieval and Modern Times*. Oxford: Oxford University Press.

Ziegler, Jean (1975). *Les vivants et la mort*. Paris: Seuil.

Ziolkowski, Theodore (1977). *Disenchanted Images. A Literary Iconology*. Princeton: Princeton University Press.

Zizek, Slavoj (1988). *Tout ce que vous avez toujours voulu savoir sur Lacan sans jamais oser le demander à Hitchcock*. Paris: Navarin.

— (1989). 'Looking Awry'. *October 50*, Cambridge: MIT Press, pp. 30–55.

Sources of epigraphs

In order of appearance

Thomas de Quincey (1897). 'Joan of Arc'. *The Collected Writings V.* ed. David Masson. London: A. & C. Black, p. 406.

Sigmund Freud (1926). *Inhibitions, Symptoms and Anxiety. Standard Edition XXI,* London: The Hogarth Press, p. 125.

Sylvia Plath (1981). 'Edge'. *The Collected Poems.* New York: Harper & Row, p. 272.

Jacques Derrida (1979). *Spurs: Nietzsche's Styles.* Chicago: University of Chicago Press, p. 89.

Walter Benjamin (1974). *Ursprung des deutschen Trauerspiels. Gesammelte Schriften I.1.* Frankfurt am Main: Suhrkamp, p. 284.

Sigmund Freud (1930). *Civilization and its Discontents. Standard Edition XX.* London: The Hogarth Press, p. 90.

Aristotle (1954). *Poetics.* New York: Modern Library, p. 227.

J.-P. Vernant (1989). 'Dim Body, Dazzling Body'. *Fragments for a History of the Human Body. Part One.* ed. Michel Feher. New York: Zone, p. 21.

Michel Serres (1987). *Statues. Le second livre des fondations.* Paris: François Bourin, p. 43.

Nancy Huston (1990). *Journal de la création.* Paris: Seuil, p. 27.

Michel Deguy (1969). *Figurations.* Paris: Gallimard, p. 122.

Christina Rossetti (1974). 'In an Artist's Studio'. *The World Split Open. Four Centuries of Women Poets in England and America, 1552–1950* ed. Louise Bernikow. New York: Vintage, p. 125.

Richard Huntington and Peter Metcalf (1979). *Celebrations of Death. The Anthropology of Mortuary Ritual.* Cambridge: Cambridge University Press, p. 2.

Jacques Lacan (1978). *The Four Fundamental Concepts of Psychoanalysis.* New York: Norton, p. 263.

Simone de Beauvoir (1974). *The Second Sex.* New York: Vintage, p. 223.

Jacques Lacan (1985). '*God and the Jouissance of The Woman. A Love Letter*'. *Feminine Sexuality.* ed. Juliet Mitchell and Jacqueline Rose. New York: Norton, p. 145.

Walter Benjamin (1974). *Ursprung des deutschen Trauerspiels I.1.* Frankfurt am Main: Fischer, p. 354.

Bonaventura (1984). 'Der Traum der Liebe'. *Nachtwachen.* Stuttgart: Reclam, p. 88.

Paul Ricoeur (1970). *Freud & Philosophy. An Essay on Interpretation.* New Haven, Yale University Press, p. 293.

Kathy Acker (1986). *Don Quixote*. London: Paladin, p. 33.

Barbara Johnson (1980). *The Critical Difference*. Baltimore: Johns Hopkins University Press, p. 146.

Sigmund Freud (1905). *Three Essays on the Theory of Sexuality. Standard Edition VII*. London: The Hogarth Press, p. 222.

Gaston Bachelard (1942). *L'eau et les rêves*. Paris: José Corti, p. 157.

John Berger (1986). *The Sense of Sight*. New York: Pantheon, p. 240.

Robert Graves (1983). *The White Goddess. An Historical Grammer of Poetic Myth*. New York: Farrar, Straus and Giroux, p. 446.

Kathy Acker (1989). 'A Few Notes on Two of My Books'. *The Review of Contemporary Fiction 9.3*, p. 34.

Sylvia Plath (1981) 'Lady Lazarus'. *The Collected Poems*. New York: Harper & Row, p. 245.

Leonora Carrington (1988). *The House of Fear. Notes from Down Below*. London, Virago Press, pp. 55–6.

Virginia Woolf (1966). 'Professions for Women'. *Collected Essays II*. London, Chatto & Windus, p. 288.

Anne Sexton (1979). *A Self-Portrait in Letters*. Ed. Linda Gray Sexton and Lois Ames. Boston: Houghton Mifflin, p. 231.

Index

Notes: 1. Most references are to women and death, which have therefore been omitted as main entries. 2. Titles of works of art and literature are entered under their authors and under general headings, e.g. stories, paintings, poetry, etc.

Acker, Kathy 269, 360
Alvarez, A. 206
anatomy *see* von Max
Appel, Alfred Jr. 371
Aragon, Louis 206
Ariès, Philippe 85, 86–7, 88, 94, 100, 103, 112
Aristotle 59, 104
art *see* painting and drawing
Atwood, Margaret: *Lady Oracle* 407, 415–20
Auerbach, N. 323
autopsy *see* von Max

Bachelard, Gaston 324
Bal, Mieke 111, 236
Barber, Paul 267, 296
Barker, Francis 143
Barreca, Regina 412
Barthes, Roland 392, 404
  on last word 233
  on metaphysical into literal 156
  on myth 182, 228
  on perfection 130, 136
  on 'punctum' 46
  on representation 381
  on stereotype 208
Bashkirtseff, Marie 390
Bassein, Beth Ann 59
Bataille, Georges 147, 166, 186, 201–2, 383
Baudrillard, Jean 256–7
Beardsley, Mabel 368
beautiful woman: death as poetical topic 59–75
Becker, E. 37
Benjamin, Walter 382
  on allegory 225, 242, 243, 245
  on creativity 124–5, 134
  on death and birth 164, 397
  on deathbed scenes 80–1
  on morality 39
  on self-authorship 150
Bentham, Jeremy 88
Berger, Harry 151
Berger, John 121, 281–2, 349
Blanchot, Maurice 157
  on strangeness 85, 104, 145
  on unclosed grave 349
Bloch, Maurice 198–200, 204
Bloch, R. Howard 68–9
Blok, Diana 398
Bloom, Harold 364
bodies on display 95–109
Boileau-Narcejac: *Sueurs Froides see Vertigo*
Bowlby, John 327
Braun, C. von 203
brides 408
  dead 258–66

Kofman, Sarah 64, 116, 264–6, 269,
    329–30
Kristeva, Julia
    on double violence 193–5
    on 'fort-da' game 21
    on jouissance 98
    on language as defence 228
    on loss of mother 135
    on narcissim 251
    on pre-language sadness 37
    on semiotic chora 201, 204, 214, 221,
        250
    on 'semiotiké' 53

Lacan, Jacques xiii
    on *aphanisis* 26, 139, 150
    on beauty 62
    on captation 46
    on desire 96
    on fantasy and sexual relations 63
    on femininity 133, 205–6, 210–18, 220,
        224, 263
    on fetishism 347
    on 'first' and 'second' deaths 200
    on 'fort-da' agme 25–7
    on identity 105
    on Other and object 51, 118, 181, 289
    on real 52–3
    on subjectivisation 346
    on symbol 195
Lévi-Strauss, Claude 225
Ledanff, Susanne 361
Lemoine-Luccioni, Eugénie 64, 102
Lichtenstein, Roy 214
literature *see* poetry; stories and novels
Loring, Katherine Peabody 387, 391
Lotman, Jurij 50, 65–6, 211, 222

McManners, John 88, 93
Mary Magdalene 218
Mary, Virgin 67–8, 218
Mentzos, S. 290, 323
Mérimée, Prosper: *Carmen* 183–93, 219,
    246, 277, 371, 374, 377–81
Metcalf, Peter 179
Millais, John Everett 169, 215
Miller, D. A. 322
Miller, Hillis 226

Milton, John 331
Mitchell, Juliet 405, 435
Mnemosyne 363
Modleski, T. 347
Moers, Ellen 130–1
Monet, Claude 112, 139
Monroe, Marilyn 399
Morgan, J. Pierpoint 177
Morin, Edgar 92
Mücke, Heinrich 209
Mulvey, Laura 123, 284
murder 291–3
    detective fiction 293–322
    see also Carmen under Mérimée
Muschler, Reinhold Conrad 206
muse
    dead beloved as 168–78, 360–83
    women as own *see* women writers

Nabokov, Vladimir: *Lolita* 371–81, 424
necromancy 291–323
Nerval 367
Nochlin, Linda 139, 259
Novalis 367
novels *see* stories and novels

Ong, W. 75, 140, 166
Orbe, Claire d' 93
Other, stereotypes of 181–204 *see also*
    women

paintings and drawings 112, 396–400
    of autopsy 3–14
    of Elizabeth Siddall 168–78
    femininity 209–15
    'Oval portrait' (Poe) 111–17
    'Portrait' (Rossetti) 117–20
    Toilette de la mariée (morte) xiii, 258–66,
        275
    of woman dying 39–56
Parry, Jonathan 198–200, 204
Persephone 197
Petrarch 375
Pfister, Oscar 16
Plath, Sylvia 3, 384
    The Bell Jar 407, 408–12
    'Lady Lazarus' 389, 401
    Sexton's poem on 401–3